International
Financial
Management

INTERNATIONAL FINANCIAL MANAGEMENT

Rita M. Rodriguez

Harvard University

E. Eugene Carter

Massachusetts Institute of Technology

Prentice-Hall, Inc., Englewood Cliffs, New Jersey

Library of Congress Cataloging in Publication Data

Rodriguez, Rita M   (date)
    International financial management.

    Includes bibliographies and index.
    1. International finance. I. Carter, E. Eugene,
joint author. II. Title.
HG3881.R584   658.1'5   75-40208
ISBN 0-13-473009-7

Printed in the United States of America

10 9 8 7 6 5 4 3 2 1

The copyright on all cases in this book unless otherwise noted is held by the President and Fellows of Harvard College, and they are published herein by express permission.

With the exception of the cases on Citibank's Foreign Exchange Problems and Sola Chemical, all cases were authored or co-authored by Rita M. Rodriguez.

Case material of the Harvard Graduate School of Business Administration is made possible by the cooperation of business firms who may wish to remain anonymous by having names, quantities, and other identifying details disguised while maintaining basic relationships. Cases are prepared as the basis for class discussion rather than to illustrate either effective or ineffective handling of administrative situations.

Prentice-Hall International, Inc., *London*
Prentice-Hall of Australia Pty. Limited, *Sydney*
Prentice-Hall of Canada, Ltd., *Toronto*
Prentice-Hall of India Private Limited, *New Delhi*
Prentice-Hall of Japan, Inc., *Tokyo*
Prentice-Hall of Southeast Asia Pte. Ltd., *Singapore*

To Our Spouses

Contents

3 What Makes the Balance of Payments Accounts Tick?   28

4 How Do You Repair the Balance of Payments?   66

5 An Introduction to the Foreign Exchange Market   95

PART TWO

Financing International Trade 149

Exchange Risk and the Multinational Enterprise 188

8 A Framework for Analyzing the Finance Function in the Multinational Enterprise 244

PART THREE

9 Cash Flows in Capital Budgeting— The International Elements 299

10 The Appropriate Acceptance Criteria for Capital Expenditures   324

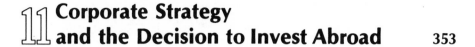

11 Corporate Strategy and the Decision to Invest Abroad 353

12 Portfolio Capital Budgeting for the Multinational Corporation 425

PART FOUR

13 The Euro-Currency Markets   461

14 The International Bond Market   501

15 Comparative Capital Markets   517

Appendix One: International Taxation   581

Appendix Two:
Glossary and Present Value Tables   598

Index   613

Preface

The tool kit of a financial officer operating in the international area is formed by contributions from several traditional disciplines. International monetary economics, usually referred to as international finance, provides the framework for understanding the environment where international business takes place. Corporate finance contributes the analytical concepts to manage the funds of an enterprise. Financial market theory furnishes the basis to appraise the institutions where funds are traded. The objective of this book is to scan these fields, to select those tools which individuals working in the area of applied international finance will find useful, and to illustrate their application in practice.

In Part One we focus on the assessment of the external position of countries. In this endeavor we center the analysis around the accounts presented in the balance of payments for the given country. Part Two deals with the problems that firms encounter as a result of dealing in a diversity of currencies. The financial problems associated with international trade are discussed in some detail. Also studied are the financial opportunities and risks involved in foreign operations other than trade.

Part Three approaches the issue of international capital budgeting, with the first two chapters in the section dealing with the problems attendant to the determination of the relevant cash flows and discount rate. The last two chapters of Part Three consider other theories of the motivation for foreign direct investment and the analysis of portfolio capital budgeting in the international setting. Finally, Part Four deals with financial markets on two levels. The international capital markets that operate independently of national boundary lines, the so-called Eurodollar markets, are analyzed first. Then, a framework for studying specific capital markets is presented while showing some of the major characteristics of the most important capital markets in Europe. Appendices dealing with comparative accounting practices, discounting, project risk evaluation, and the Euro-dollar multiplier follow the appropriate chapters. We also include appendices at the end of the book containing a glossary, present value tables, and material on international taxation. Bibliographies accompany each chapter to aid those who are particularly interested in specific subject areas.

The text is ideally designed for upper-level undergraduates or MBA/MS students who have completed introductory courses in finance and economics. There are exercises, questions, and cases at the end of most chapters, which can be used by the instructor to emphasize different points. Some instructors will want to include all the cases in their courses, perhaps using the chapters only for casual or background reading. Given the detail with which some of these cases may be handled (computer output and other materials are included in the Instructor's Manual), these cases and exercises can require at least 20 class sessions. Additional cases which are available through the authors could be used in the remaining classes in a typical 30-class, one-semester course. Other instructors will prefer to emphasize the text and exercises supplemented by articles. The detail of these chapters and exercises easily can support 20 or more classes. The supplementary articles and notes on various capital markets and other items (which again are available through us) could complete the one-semester course.

Instructors with a one-quarter course also could use this text, assuming they have only 20 or 25 classes. If all the topics are to be covered, we suggest having students read Chapters 2 and 3 and the summary to Chapter 4, with the instructor lecturing on various proposals for "fixing" the balance of payments once the students understand the background materials. Chapters 5, 6 and 7 could be read in total, and the more involved framework offered for handling exposure to exchange risk presented in Chapter 8 deleted or left for optional reading. Chapters 9 and 10 outline the basics of international capital budgeting. The additional material from other disciplines and the security/portfolio models in Chapters 11 and 12 could be deleted or reviewed in a lecture. Finally, selected readings from the two chapters on the Euro-markets could complete the text material. Four or five of the simpler cases and the exercises could round up the one-quarter course.

Our approach is to use a simple lecture or case to highlight a problem, then have a chapter and a lecture to suggest various ways of looking at the problem (the theory), and conclude with the application of the theory to the complex real situation presented by another case. Accordingly, the materials in this book can more than fill a one-semester course of 30 or 35 classes. The selection of materials will be at the judgment of the instructor, consistent with the instructor's background and interests, the previous exposure of the students, and their particular needs in the course.

Where students have a strong background in international economics, Chapters 2 through 4 can be skipped. For instructors who particularly want to emphasize this topic, additional readings and texts may be assigned with this material used only as background. Likewise, instructors who are not interested in the particular elements of trade credit financing will have their students skip the latter part of Chapter 6, whereas other instructors will want to supplement this material with one of the booklets from the major banks on international financial instruments. Students who have been exposed to international business courses will not need to read the first half of Chapter 11, which brings in various economic and behavioral theories of foreign investment; other instructors will supplement this chapter with readings from the international business area. In some classes, more time can be spent on the various international security portfolio studies and the capital asset pricing model, with the implications of these topics for corporate diversification. With other groups, Chapter 12 can be skipped if this topic is not of interest or if the small amount of algebra included here is beyond the level of the students. Finally, some instructors will not find the institutional material on the Euro-markets contained in Chapters 13 through 15 (Part Four) of relevance or interest to their students.

Thus, the segmentation of the text in various parts and the inclusion of cases, questions, and exercises are designed to give teachers and students a wide range of basic materials. In most classes, this material will provide sufficient coverage for a semester. For those instructors who wish further supplemental materials, the four parts of the text are somewhat self-contained, permitting use of the text as a basic book supplemented by other readings. Our desire has been to present a text which has a sufficient amount of basic material from which many instructors can select topics for their international corporate finance course.

This textbook reflects our biases and prejudices toward the blending of various disciplines under the umbrella of an international corporate finance framework, and toward the mix of theory, practice, and institutional description. We have benefited from the suggestions on portions of the text from many individuals. Gunter Dufey (University of Michigan) and Warren Law (Harvard Business School) both commented on the entire manuscript in detail with many useful and insightful suggestions. We thank them on behalf of the readers.

Our appreciation also to Michael McIntyre (School of Law, Wayne State University); David A. Ricks (The Ohio State University); Tamir Agmon (Tel Aviv University); Robert Stobaugh, Raymond Vernon, and William White (Harvard Business School); Jon Ingersoll (University of Chicago); and Charles Kindleberger, Donald Lessard, Franco Modigliani, and Richard Robinson (Massachusetts Institute of Technology) for reacting to various ideas and chapters. Our appreciation is offered to Professors Raymond Vernon and Robert Stobaugh for permission to use the *Sola Chemical* case. With the exception of *Citibank's Foreign Exchange Problems* (a collection of news articles), all of the other cases were authored by Rita M. Rodriguez, and we gratefully acknowledge the assistance or co-authorship of Marc Buxton, Henri de Bodinat, Cesar Duque, Joel Glasky, Kenneth Morse, Jules Pogrow, L. E. Simmons, and Endre Toth. We are also grateful for the outstanding contribution of our editor, Paul McKenney, who endured the convoluted prose emerging from an immigrant's and a technocrat's collaboration. His efforts have sharply improved the text. Any deficiencies in style or substance are the responsibility of the authors.

The typing of the final manuscript was in the patient and professional care of Brigid Haragan, who possessed amazing competence and good cheer in the face of our endless revisions as well as the paperwork imposed by copyright holders and various university administrators. We thank her for all these qualities.

Rita M. Rodriguez
E. Eugene Carter

CHAPTER 1

Introduction

During recent years, the corporate financial manager has become increasingly concerned with the changing international scene. Fluctuating foreign exchange rates, the power of multinational corporations, balance of payments deficits, and the growth of "petrodollars," have come to be important issues for all U. S. and foreign corporations with international operations. To confront these problems with some hope for resolution requires a knowledge of both the macro-economic environment in which the firm operates (balance of payments, government policies, credit availability) and the micro-economic environment which relates to the specific decisions that the manager will face (how the firm manages its exposure to foreign exchange risk, how it analyzes its capital budgeting problem, how it accommodates the demands for funds from subsidiaries in different countries). Before we embark on the discussion of specific financial problems, however, it may be useful to briefly introduce the business institution that houses the international decision makers: the multinational company.

THE MULTINATIONAL FIRM

For many critics, the multinational firm is a global octopus, which at best is spreading knowledge and technological pollution around the world while swallowing assets everywhere and evading all national attempts to control it. Multinationals have been charged with subverting governments (with or without another government's help), adding to the instability of the international money markets by switching funds between currencies, avoiding taxes everywhere by the use of tax havens,

and encouraging apartheid in South Africa and the continuation of low-wage unskilled labor forces in Colombia, among other sins.

In their own defense, the multinationals, emphasize their rationalization of
resources and the spread of technology. Deemphasizing the impact of their economic
power, they also argue that in seeking profits they are doing good in the societies in
which they operate by contributing much-needed capital and other resources of the
industrialized world to less developed areas.

While there are many definitions of the multinational firm, for the purposes of
this text the term will mean a company with substantial operations (usually 30% or
more of its total activity) carried on outside its own national borders. These activities
may be trading or manufacturing. There may be many separate corporations outside
the national borders, with the parent functioning as an operating/holding company.
Whatever the particular corporate form, the important fact is that the firm must
make decisions about project returns which have a sizable impact on the company
and are in more than one currency. A $500,000,000 business which occasionally
sells a few million dollars worth of goods to a Dutch manufacturer will probably
not care much about currency rates. The sale is infrequent; its size is relatively small;
and the guilder is a known, freely traded currency. On the other hand, a $10,000,000
firm which has three plants in three different nations and whose business represents
sales from all over the globe (such as a small specialty goods manufacturer) will be
very interested in currency rates and barriers to trade and fund repatriation.

The philosophy of business of international firms is a separate study, often
called international business policy, and is not the purpose of this text. Likewise, the
reform of the international monetary system and the analysis of why nations trade
belong in a course in international economics. However, the impact of judgments
in these two areas will affect the field of international corporate finance. Multinationals are often entangled as any domestic firm can be, in the web of doing nothing
(which supports the status quo) and acting for good or ill (which supports charges
of interference in the domestic affairs of one or more nations). Multinationals
usually have legal and financial talent beyond the level of the department of inland
revenue in a small nation of limited resources. On the other hand, the small nation
often has what the multinational wants (a market or a natural resource) and is in a
position to demand a suitable price for access to that desired feature. Some of these
relationships, and the behavior of various parties involved in these international
financial decisions, are explored in this text.

In making public pronouncements, many economists forget that the firm operates within society and not just within an industrial sector. Societies set the ground
rules for firm behavior. An important issue is whether the markets in which a firm
operates are sufficiently competitive for the benefits of firm rivalry to create an
efficient allocation of resources, the key benefit of the market economy. A second
issue is whether the resulting allocation of resources is desired. The firm may allocate assets efficiently, but is the final distribution equitable? There is nothing sac-
rosanct about free enterprise per se, nor is it enshrined in the U. S. Constitution, as
some social critics frequently remind business executives.

However, one should also bear in mind that the various proposals to reform
corporations on the international scene often come from social critics who ignore
the benefits of resource allocation. The evils of pollution and materialism may seem
less threatening when a booming economy slides into recession; unlimited personal
freedom can appear less important if one is out of a job.

An even narrower view than that of the economists and the social critics comes in the self-serving nonsense sometimes presented by the multinationals themselves. Anxious to assuage public opinion in a particular nation so as to move ahead with the task of making XYZ International more powerful and more profitable, rhetoric is put forth which frequently is based on little knowledge of the actions of various subsidiaries. Limits on information from the field and the whole problem of decentralization mean that headquarters officials rarely know details of activities in other lands and often are only vaguely aware of their lack of knowledge. Further, this ignorance may be deliberate, thus creating the possibility of "deniability," which has counterparts in political and military leadership. By design, the top managers can deny they knew anything about the nasty activities of underlings, while they continue to make subordinates aware that it is their job to see that "things are taken care of." This supervisory problem is merely an international extension of the common issues of accounting and managerial control, with the difficulties compounded by distance, culture, and language-related complexities.

This text is primarily concerned with international corporate finance, so many of the above issues will be left to the reader's appraisal of contemporary socioeconomic and political trends, and to his or her particular value system. Although most of our examples deal with the position of the U. S. multinational, the issues and problems that we address apply to all multinationals.

AN OVERVIEW OF THE TEXT

The following chapters are divided into four major parts. Part One provides a basic understanding of the forces that affect the relative values of currencies in international markets. This section of the text largely corresponds to the information traditionally related in a course on international monetary economics. We will approach this important material from the point of view of the participants in the international markets who have to take the world system as given. Chapter 2 begins with the mechanics of the foremost reporting tool used to assess the international situation of a country: the balance of payments. Chapter 3 confronts the economic forces that lie behind the figures reported in the balance of payments and that affect the international purchasing power of a currency. In Chapter 4, the situation of a given country and the insights derived from the previous two chapters are placed within the context of the international monetary system and domestic economic priorities. The objective of these three chapters is not to demonstrate how to forecast foreign exchange rates, but to build a framework for analyzing the forces which affect changes in foreign exchange rates. Chapter 5 focuses directly on the foreign exchange market. It analyzes how price relationships are established in this market and discusses in detail the behavior of the major actors in the foreign exchange market—the speculator and the banker.

Part Two discusses the major problems encountered by the firm in financing large international operations. The money market and the forward exchange market, as well as their mutual relationships, are emphasized in studying the financing alternatives open to the merchandise trader and the manager with business operations in foreign countries. Chapter 6 looks at the problems of financing international trade. How does an importer obtain credit? How does a merchandise trader approach exchange risk? Chapter 7 studies the management of the foreign exchange position of the company. Should the manager of a British firm hold an account receivable in liras? If not, what can be done about it? An appendix discusses differing accounting practices. Chapter 8 combines the elements developed in the previous two chapters with traditional financial theory on cost of funds and presents an integrated approach to the decision of how to finance the operations of a firm that functions across several national boundaries. This chapter also notes the impact of other factors of an institutional nature, such as taxation and organization theory.

Part Three covers the issues associated with capital budgeting. Chapter 9 discusses the analysis of a single project and discusses the types of international project risk. Chapter 10 introduces the problems of selecting the relevant acceptance criteria for projects. Appendices to these chapters, respectively, review discounting procedures and some of the approaches to project risk evaluation. Chapter 11 highlights the various economic and behavioral reasons for international investment. It provides an extended computer simulation model of a mining project in Australia. Chapter 12 reviews some of the evidence from international security portfolio studies, outlining how a corporation can employ these concepts in selecting its portfolio of capital budgeting projects.

Part Four returns the discussion to the macroeconomic area. Throughout the previous chapters, the business firm was presented as a rate taker, which make decisions on the basis of prices given to it. Part Four aims to create an understanding of the forces that shape rates in the international markets as well as in some specific national markets. Chapters 13 and 14 discuss the international capital markets, with Chapter 13 emphasizing the Euro-currency market and Chapter 14 concentrating on international bonds. The appendix to Chapter 13 analyzes the Euro-dollar multiplier and problems raised by the use of Euro-dollars. Chapter 15 completes the tour of international finance with a study of comparative capital markets. In this chapter, the problems of raising funds in domestic markets other than the United States, and the issues associated with understanding their functioning, are presented. An appendix to the text outlines the basic characteristics of international corporate taxation.

Bibliography

Aharoni, Yair, "On the Definition of a Multinational Corporation." *Quarterly Review of Economics and Business,* Autumn 1971, pp. 27-37.

Behrman, Jack N., *National Interests and the Multinational Enterprise.* Englewood Cliffs, N. J.: Prentice-Hall, Inc., 1970.

Eiteman, David K. and Arthur I. Stonehill, *Multinational Business Finance.* Reading, Mass.: Addison-Wesley Publishing Co., 1973, Ch. 1.

Ewigg, David W., "MNC's on Trial." *Harvard Business Review,* May-June 1972, pp. 130-143.

Phatak, Arvind V., *Managing Multinational Corporations.* New York: Praeger Publishers, 1974, Ch. 5.

Robinson, Richard D., *International Business Policy.* New York: Holt, Rinehart and Winston, 1964.

Stobaugh, Robert B., "The Multinational Corporation: Measuring the Consequences." *Columbia Journal of World Business,* Jan.-Feb. 1971, pp. 59-64.

Vernon, Raymond, "Economic Sovereignty at Bay." *Foreign Affairs,* Oct. 1968, pp. 110-122.

———, and Louis T. Wells, Jr., *Manager in the International Economy,* 3rd ed. Englewood Cliffs, N.J.: Prentice-Hall, Inc., 1976.

Weston, J. Fred and Bart W. Sorge, *International Managerial Finance.* Homewood, Ill.: Richard D. Irwin, Inc., 1972, Ch. 1.

PART ONE

One of the major problems that the financial officer encounters in the international markets is the fact that different nations have different currencies and that the relative value of these currencies is not always maintained constant through time. Accordingly, this section attempts to provide an introduction to the major macroeconomic considerations that shape the foreign exchange markets.

Chapter 2 covers the mechanics of the balance of payments. This is the piece of information most often used in evaluating the changes in the external position of a given country, and therefore the possible changes in the value of its currency. Once the technicalities of the balance of payments are understood, Chapter 3 proceeds to explain the major economic forces that contribute to the performance of the accounts in the balance of payments. The objective in this chapter is to develop an understanding of economic relationships that can be used not only to explain the past, but also to forecast the future behavior of the various accounts and the exchange rate. This understanding cannot be complete unless one also includes an analysis of the alternatives available to settle imbalances in the external position of a country. This is done in Chapter 4, which presents some of the automatic mechanisms that tend to solve a situation of imbalances in the external accounts, and also discusses the policy alternatives open to a country wishing to act upon a particular balance of payments problem. The methods used to adjust the external accounts together with the economic analysis discussed in Chapter 3 will provide a complete framework for analyzing and forecasting the future of exchange rates. However, this framework does not include the vagaries introduced in the market by political considerations or simple random (erratic) behavior.

Chapter 5 examines the characteristics of the market where currencies are actually traded and their foreign exchange rates determined. Besides introducing some of the technical aspects of these markets, this chapter concentrates on the behavior of the financial institutions that "make" the foreign exchange market. The behavior of nonfinancial businesses in the foreign exchange market is discussed in Part Two.

Financial Accounting Among Countries

One of the central problems in international finance is the need to deal in a multiplicity of currencies that do not keep their relative values constant. When a financial officer based in the United States contracts to pay £2,000 every year for the following twenty years, (s)he is bound by that obligation independent of changes in the exchange rate between the U. S. dollar and the pound sterling. Therefore, one of the most important pieces of information in international finance is an assessment of the future foreign exchange value of a country's currency. Such an assessment is not an easy task. However, it can be aided enormously by an understanding of the international economic transactions of the given country. These transactions for historic periods are summarized in financial statements that each country prepares in relation to the rest of the world. The statement most used to accomplish the financial reporting among countries is the so-called "balance of payments."

Like any system of record keeping, the reporting of the balance of payments figures is subject to preestablished rules. These include definitions of terminology as well as rules of procedure. Some of the most important rules used in the construction of balance of payments figures are contained in this chapter.

THE CONCEPT OF BALANCE OF PAYMENTS

The balance of payments summarizes the *flow* of economic transactions between the *residents* of a given country and the residents of other countries during a certain *period of time.*

The balance of payments measures flows, rather than stocks.[1] These flows represent payments and receipts. That is, only *changes* in asset holdings and liabilities are presented in this statement, not the *levels* of these items. In this sense, the balance of payments for a country is very similar to a statement of sources and uses of funds for a firm. For a country as a whole, sources of funds represent an acquisition of external purchasing power, the right a country has to claim goods and services or to invest in another country. Uses of funds for a country mean a decrease in its external purchasing power. When a country sells its goods and services to foreigners (a decrease in its asset holdings) or when it borrows from foreigners (an increase in liabilities), the country acquires external purchasing power. Conversely, when the country buys goods and services from foreigners (an increase in asset holdings) or redeems its obligations (a decrease in liabilities), the country uses some of its external purchasing power. These changes are measured in terms of a monetary unit, e.g., U. S. dollars or French francs.

In the context of the balance of payments, a resident is any individual business firm, government agency, or other institution legally domiciled (not necessarily a citizen) in the given country. Therefore, the subsidiary (but not a branch) of a German company legally established in the United States would be treated like any other U. S. enterprise for balance of payments purposes.

The balance of payments measures transactions among countries. Transactions that only affect the local residents and that only involve the national currency—in contrast to foreign exchange—are not recorded in the balance of payments. However, these domestic transactions can lead to conditions that are reflected in the balance of payments. For example, if the monetary authorities of the United States decide to sell part of their portfolio of securities to U. S. residents, this transaction will not enter the U. S. balance of payments accounts. However, as a result of the selling of the securities, an increase in U. S. interest rates is likely to occur which could induce the British, for example, to purchase U. S. securities. This latter transaction, in contrast to the first one, will be between the residents of two different countries, the United States and England, and it will be registered in the balance of payments accounts.

Finally, the balance of payments can be prepared for any specific period of time. Typically, it is prepared quarterly and annually. To facilitate comparisons, the quarterly figures are often multiplied by four and presented on an "annual rate" basis. When analyzing quarterly figures one must be careful to consider whether these figures have been adjusted for seasonal fluctuations. The presence of such fluctuations, if not identified, might lead one to confuse a recurrent seasonal pattern with a change in trends in the balance of payments accounts.

THE BALANCE OF PAYMENTS ACCOUNTS

The balance of payments may be divided into three major types of accounts: (1) the current account, (2) the capital account, and (3) the official reserves. Exhibit 2.1 presents a simplified balance of payments where these accounts are illustrated for a country called Lilliput in the year 1900.

---

[1] The statement measuring the levels of foreign assets and liabilities among countries is the *balance of indebtedness.* This statement will be discussed at the end of Chapter 3.

EXHIBIT 2.1   Balance of Payments for Lilliput for the Year 1900

(Sources of funds +; Uses of funds—)			
Current Account:			
Trade Account:			
Exports	$5,000		
Imports	−4,000		
Balance of trade			$ 1,000
Service Account:			
Receipts for interest and dividends,			
travel and financial charges	2,500		
Payments for interest and dividends,			
travel and financial charges	−1,200		
Balance in invisibles			1,300
Unilateral transfers:			
Gifts received from abroad	500		
Grants to foreign countries	−1,000		
			−500
Current account balance			$1,800
Capital Account:			
Direct Investment			
Sale of financial assets	2,000		
Purchase of financial assets	−4,000	$−2,000	
Portfolio Investment			
Sale of financial assets	5,000		
Purchase of financial assets	−3,000	2,000	
Short-term capital movements			
Sale of financial assets	8,000		
Purchase of financial assets	−2,000	6,000	
Capital account balance			6,000
Balance of current accounts and capital accounts			$7,800
Official Reserves Account:			
Gold exports less imports (−)			−5,000
Decrease or increase (−) in foreign exchange			−2,800
			$−7,800

Current Account. The current account records the *trade in goods and services and the exchange of gifts among countries.*

The trade in *goods* is composed of exports and imports. A country increases its exports when it sells merchandise to foreigners. This is a source of funds, a decrease in real assets. It increases its imports when it buys merchandise from foreigners. This is a use of funds, an acquisition of real assets. The balance between exports and imports is called the *trade balance.* Exhibit 2.1 shows that for the year 1900 Lilliput had a positive trade balance of $1,000. The *sources* of external purchasing power exceeded the *uses* on the trade balance by $1,000.

The balance on service accounts is called the *balance in invisibles.* Service accounts include interest and dividends, travel expenses, and financial and shipping charges. Interest and dividends received measure the services that the country's capital has rendered abroad. Payments received from tourists measure the services that the country's hotels and shops provided to visitors from other countries. Financial and shipping charges to foreigners measure the fees that the financial community and shipowners charged to foreigners because of the special services they rendered. In these cases the nation gave the service of assets it possessed (e.g., hotel) to foreigners. Thus, these transactions are a source of external purchasing power. When, in contrast to the above cases, the country's residents are the recipients of the services from foreign-owned assets, then the given country loses purchasing power to the rest of the world. Lilliput provided more services to foreigners (a source of funds) than it received from them (a use of funds). Therefore, Lilliput had a positive balance in invisibles of $1,300. That is, its sources of external purchasing power exceeded its uses on the invisibles account by $1,300.

Finally, gifts are recorded in the *unilateral transfers account*. A typical entry in this account is the money that emigrants send home. Another example is a gift that one country makes to another. In these cases when the country makes a gift it can be said that it is acquiring an asset which we may call goodwill. Like any other asset acquisition, the gift represents a use of external purchasing power. Lilliput had a negative balance in unilateral transfers of $500; uses of funds exceeded sources by this amount.

The total current account of Lilliput shows a positive balance of $1,800, composed of the positive balances in trade and invisibles and the negative balance in unilateral transfers.

Capital Account. The capital account records the international movement of funds reflected in changes in financial assets and liabilities. The various classifications within the capital account are based on the maturity of the assets and on the nature of the involvement of the owner of the financial asset in the activities of the security's issuer. Accordingly, the capital account is subdivided into direct investment, portfolio investment, and short-term capital flows. *Direct investment* and *portfolio investment* involve financial assets with a maturity of more than a year. *Short-term capital movements* consist of financial paper with a maturity of less than one year. The distinction between direct investment and portfolio investment is made on the basis of the degree of management involvement. Considerable management involvement is presumed to exist in the care of *direct investment* (usually a minimum of 10% ownership in a firm), but not on *portfolio investment*.

Lilliput had a deficit in direct investments. While foreigners invested $2,000 in Lilliput (Lilliput increased its liabilities to foreigners—a source of funds for Lilliput), Lilliput made direct investments in foreign countries in the amount of $4,000 (Lilliput acquired foreign financial assets—a use of funds for Lilliput). Many of these investments involved acquiring whole ventures in other countries. Although in some cases the ownership had to be shared with others, the direct investor retained a substantial share (at least 10%) of the total ownership (and therefore of the management). The deficit in direct investment accounts of Lilliput was more than compensated for by the surplus in the other two capital accounts. In the portfolio account, foreigners bought $2,000 more of long-term financial assets in Lilliput than Lilliput bought in other countries. The same was true in the short-term capital account where foreigners bought $8,000 worth of short-term securities issued by Lilliput, while Lilliput invested only $2,000 in short-term foreign securities. The result of these three accounts is a surplus in the capital account of Lilliput in the amount of $6,000, since a foreign purchase of Lilliput's securities is a source of external purchasing power and a Lilliput resident's purchase of foreign securities is a use.

Official Reserve Accounts. This account is composed of the immediate means of international payment that the monetary authorities and some private sectors in the country acquired or lost during the given period. These are composed of gold and convertible foreign exchange (i.e., foreign exchange freely convertible into currencies like Swiss francs or U. S. dollars, but not currencies like the Indian rupee where the Indian government does not guarantee the conversion of its currency into others). An increase in any of these financial assets, like an increase in any other asset, constitutes a use of funds. A decrease in reserve assets, like a decrease in any other asset, implies a source of funds. At times this fact seems to run against intuitive interpretations. This is the case when we say that an increase in gold holdings is a use of funds (signified by a minus sign in Lilliput's balance of payments). Well, it is! An increase in gold holdings is a use of funds in the sense that Lilliput might have chosen to purchase an alternative asset, for example, a bond issued by a foreign government.

   An increase in any of these accounts will occur as a result of a surplus in the current accounts and the capital accounts. The increase in reserves measures the excess of sales of goods, services, and financial assets of the given country over the purchases of such items by the given country from foreigners. Lilliput had a surplus in the current and capital accounts of $7,800, so the official reserves increased by this amount. The minus sign in front of the figures representing increases in reserves will be explained in the following section.

THE ACCOUNTING SYSTEM

   In the preceding section we discussed separately each major account in the balance of payments. However, the balance of payments accounting is a double-entry system in which the part of a transaction that gives rise to an *increase in the external purchasing power* of the country is called a source of funds and the part of a transaction that gives rise to a *decrease in the external purchasing power* of the country is called a use of funds. It is impossible to talk about any transaction in the balance of payments accounts without discussing both sources and uses of funds. Like any other double-entry accounting system, the balance of payments is kept in terms of debits and credits. In this accounting terminology uses of funds are debits (dr.) and sources of funds are credits (cr.).

   A country *increases* its external purchasing power whenever it *decreases* (sells) its tangible or intangible assets (exports goods and services), when it *decreases* its foreign financial assets (through their sale), or when it *increases* its liabilities to foreigners (by, for example, a corporation of the country taking out a loan from a foreign source or a bank of the country setting up a deposit account with foreign funds, both of which would cause a net capital inflow). All of these transactions represent *sources* of external purchasing power—credit entries.

   A country *decreases* its external purchasing power whenever it *increases* (buys) tangible or intangible assets (imports goods or services), when it *increases* (buys) holdings of foreign financial assets, or when it *decreases* its previous liabilities to foreigners (capital outflow). All of these transactions represent *uses* of external purchasing power—debit entries.

   Let us try to use these definitions in a series of examples for the United States:

Example 1. The United States exports $1,000 in goods to a customer in Greece. According to the sales terms, this account will be paid in 90 days. In this case two things happen: the merchandise exports, a reduction in real assets, provide the United States with an increase in claims on external purchasing power—a credit entry; but the exporter has simultaneously bought a financial document. He has made a short-term investment abroad (i.e., the exporter's accounts receivable have increased by $1,000). This acquisition represents a use of the country's external purchasing power—a debit entry. Therefore, in the U. S. balance of payments accounts this transaction will appear as follows:

	Debit	Credit
Increase in short-term claims on foreigners (the account receivable)	$1,000	
Exports		$1,000

Example 2. A Japanese resident visits the United States. Upon his arrival he converts his $2,000 worth of yen into dollars. By the time the visitor departs he has no dollars left. In this case the United States provided services to foreigners in the amount of $2,000. In exchange for these services U. S. banks now have $2,000 worth of yen. The services that the United States provided to the Japanese are clearly a source of purchasing power, and therefore a credit entry. However, the accumulation of yen in our banks is an increase in the U. S. holdings of foreign financial obligations, a use of purchasing power, and therefore a debit entry. In the U. S. balance of payments this transaction will appear as follows:

	Debit	Credit
Increase in short-term claims on foreigners (the yen)	$2,000	
Travel services to foreigners		$2,000

Example 3. A U. S. resident who left his family in Hungary sends a $1,000 check to his wife in Hungary. The gift that the U. S. resident sent is a unilateral transfer, a purchase of goodwill, and it reduces the U. S. purchasing power, a debit entry. However, this gift was made possible by the credit that the Hungarians extended to the United States when they accepted a financial obligation, a check, in U. S. dollars from a U. S. resident. This latter part of the transaction, an increase in U. S. liabilities to foreigners, is a source of external purchasing power, and therefore a credit entry. The entry of this transaction in the U. S. balance of payments would be as follows:

	Debit	Credit
Remittances	$1,000	
Increase in short-term liabilities to foreigners (the check)		$1,000

Example 4. A Swiss bank buys $3,000 worth of U. S. treasury bills. It pays by drawing on its dollar account with a U. S. bank. The sale of treasury bills to a foreigner is equivalent to the United States borrowing external purchasing power from foreigners, an increase in liabilities to foreigners, a credit entry. However, the purchase is paid by reducing another debt that the United States had to foreigners, U. S. dollars in the hands of foreigners. This reduction in U. S. liabilities is a use of funds, a debit entry. In the U. S. balance of payments the transactions would be entered as follows:

	Debit	Credit
Decrease in short-term liabilities to foreigners (the dollar account)	$3,000	
Increase in short-term liabilities to foreigners (the treasury bill)		$3,000

Example 5. A U. S. resident buys a $1,000 German bond which is paid with a check drawn on a New York account. As a result, the U. S. resident now owns a German bond, and the German owns U. S. dollar deposits. The acquisition of the German bond, a financial asset, implies a decrease in U. S. external purchasing power; therefore, the bond account (investment in foreign securities) must be debited. However, at the same time the dollar balances that the German now owns represent an increase in U. S. liabilities to foreigners, they increase the U. S. foreign purchasing power. Thus, the U. S. short-term liabilities (foreigners' short-term investment) must be credited. In the U. S. balance of payments this transaction will appear as follows:

	Debit	Credit
Increase in long-term claims on foreigners (the German bond)	$1,000	
Increase in short-term liabilities to foreigners (the U. S. dollar deposits)		$1,000

An alternative explanation for this set of entries would be the following: a German businessman wishes to maintain dollar balances in the United States for transaction purposes, or as part of his investment portfolio strategy. In return for these balances he is willing to issue a long-term claim on his company. The accounting facts of this transaction are the same as in the previous one. From the point of view of the U. S. balance of payments, long-term claims on foreigners (Dr.), and foreigners' short-term claim on the United States (Cr.), have increased. However, the motivations behind this transaction are different from the previous one. In this case the acquisition of a short-claim on the United States by the German is the primary active force leading to the transaction. In the previous explanation this short-term claim is only accepted passively as a means of payment which can be exchanged later. It is in this attempt to separate accounts in the balance of payments according to motivation that the concepts of balance of payments surplus and deficit emerge.

THE CONCEPTS OF SURPLUS AND DEFICIT
IN THE BALANCE OF PAYMENTS

The double-entry system of accounting of the balance of payments means that, by definition, *debits equal credits*. In this sense the balance of payments always balances. It is only when one tries to answer the question of what has been the change in the country's account of international cash and near cash (official reserves and liquid claims and liabilities) that the concept of a "balance" in the balance of payments emerges. To answer this question it is necessary to separate the accounts in the balance of payments into two groups: (1) those whose changes are induced by the existing economic relationships, e.g., relative prices and incomes and (2) those that change mainly as a result of the necessary financing that accompanies the first group.

In the economic literature the first group of accounts, that which is affected as a result of purely economic reasons regardless of other items in the balance of payments, is called *autonomous*. The second group of accounts, that which changes only in order to finance other items in the balance of payments, is called *compensating* or *accommodating*. Economists often refer to an imaginary line that separates the two groups of accounts. The accounts "above the line" comprise the *autonomous* accounts whose balance determines whether the balance of payments is in surplus or deficit. The accounts "below the line" present the *compensating* accounts that show how the balance of payments surplus or deficit was financed.

The balance of payments is in *surplus*, i.e., the international purchasing power of the country has increased during the period in question, if *autonomous receipts exceed autonomous payments*. In the same way, the balance of payments is in *deficit*, i.e., the international purchasing power of the country has decreased during the period in question, if *autonomous payments exceed autonomous receipts*. A surplus in the autonomous accounts is accompanied by an increase in foreign reserves in the compensating accounts (a net use of funds). A deficit in the autonomous accounts is associated with a decrease in foreign reserves or an increase in liabilities to foreigners (a net source of funds). These facts are of great importance in trying to forecast the future external value of a currency. A country cannot endure continuous deficits in its balance of payments without eventually having to devalue its currency.[2]

Examples of *autonomous* receipts would be all normal commercial exports, gifts, and capital movements which take place because of private enterprise's search for higher profitability. Examples of *accommodating* receipts are the sale of gold or foreign exchange by the central bank in order to finance imports into the country at the current exchange rate; or a loan to the government by an international agency for the explicit purpose of bridging the gap between payments and receipts of the country.

---

[2]Throughout this book, *devalue* and *upvalue* refer to changes in the parity of a currency vis-à-vis other currencies or gold. *Revalue* is often used interchangeably with upvalue to mean an increase in parity, but technically it means a change in either direction. Accordingly, revalue will be used in this text for any change and upvalue will be used to denote a positive parity change.

In our previous examples we could separate the entries in the following fashion. In the case of the exporter, the exports are an autonomous receipt, the short-term investment abroad is a compensating payment. In the case of the Japanese visitor, the travel services are an autonomous transaction; the yen received in payment are an accommodating transaction. In Example 3 the gift is clearly an autonomous payment; the way in which it was financed is an accommodating receipt. In the case of the Swiss bank buying U. S. treasury bills, the purchase of the security is an autonomous transaction while the reduction in the dollar account is an accommodating payment according to the motivations stated in the example. In the case of Example 5, the bond purchase under the first interpretation is an autonomous payment; the foreigner's short-term investment in the United States is a compensating receipt. However, under the alternative interpretation, when the German businessman wishes to acquire dollar balances for transaction purposes, both the payment and the receipt are autonomous.

The International Monetary Fund compiles balance of payments statistics for each of its member countries. These figures are presented in a standard format in its *Balance of Payments Yearbook*. For each country a number of tables analyzing the balance of payments situation are presented in addition to the standard format. These additional tables (especially the "analytic table") are a serious attempt to disaggregate the items in the balance of payments according to their true motivation. However, the problems encountered in this task in the area of capital flows are often insurmountable. Given that in practice balance of payments statistics are compiled by measuring only one side of physical transactions, and by taking the net of the changes in assets and liabilities, it becomes extremely difficult to establish the motivation behind a given change in assets or liabilities. The example presented above of a U. S. resident purchasing a German bond in exchange for deposits in New York is an example of the difficulty in determining the true nature of capital flows. The degree of inaccuracy in the compilation of the balance of payments data is partially reflected in the need to include an account called "errors and omissions" which is nothing more than a "plug" figure to make it possible for the balance of payments to balance arithmetically.

THE U. S. BALANCE OF PAYMENTS ACCOUNTING

The principles presented above apply equally to the United States and to the other countries in the world. However, in the case of the United States an additional complication must be taken into account: the U. S. dollar is an international reserve currency under the present international payments mechanism.[3] Until August 15, 1971, all the dollars in the hands of foreigners could potentially be presented to the United States for exchange into gold. However, it is also true that the reserve role of the dollar guarantees that not all the dollars in the hands of foreigners will be returned to the United States to be exchanged for other international

---

[3] The holdings of U. S. dollars by governments other than the United States are considered part of these governments' international reserves.

EXHIBIT 2.2   U.S. Balance of Payments, 1962-1974 (millions of dollars)

Line	(Credits+; debits—)	1962	1963	1964	1965	1966	1967	1968	1969	1970	1971	1972	1973	1974[p]
1	Merchandise trade balance[a]	4,521	5,224	6,801	4,951	3,817	3,800	635	607	2,159	-2,722	-6,986	471	-5,881
2	Exports	20,781	22,272	25,501	26,461	29,310	30,666	33,626	36,414	41,947	42,754	48,768	70,277	97,081
3	Imports	-16,260	-17,048	-18,700	-21,510	-25,403	-26,866	-32,991	-35,807	-39,788	-45,476	-55,754	-69,806	-102,962
4	Military transactions, net	-2,448	-2,304	-2,133	-2,122	-2,935	-3,228	-3,143	-3,344	-3,377	-2,908	-3,604	-2,266	-2,099
5	Travel and transportation, net	-1,155	-1,312	-1,149	-1,284	-1,332	-1,751	-1,548	-1,763	-2,023	-2,341	-3,055	-2,710	-2,435
6	Investment income, net[b]	3,311	3,326	3,936	4,169	3,782	4,127	4,270	3,811	3,785	5,021	4,526	5,291	9,679
7	U.S. direct investments abroad[b]	3,044	3,129	3,674	3,963	3,707	4,133	4,480	5,074	5,330	6,385	6,925	9,415	18,240
8	Other U.S. investments abroad	1,377	1,521	1,718	1,936	2,218	2,356	2,714	3,200	3,509	3,444	3,494	4,569	7,703
9	Foreign investments in the United States[b]	-1,110	-1,324	-1,456	-1,730	-2,142	-2,361	-2,933	-4,463	-5,055	-4,809	-5,893	-8,693	-16,263
10	Other services, net[b]	860	1,007	1,088	1,426	1,536	1,710	1,766	2,034	2,388	2,781	3,110	3,540	3,926
11	Balance on goods and services[c]	5,088	5,941	8,542	7,140	4,868	4,657	1,980	1,344	2,932	-170	-6,009	4,327	3,191
12	Remittances, pensions and other transfers	-712	-825	-867	-1,045	-1,015	-1,309	-1,234	-1,329	-1,522	-1,604	-1,624	-1,943	-1,775
13	Balance on goods, services and remittances	4,377	5,116	7,676	6,095	3,853	3,349	746	16	1,410	-1,774	-7,634	2,383	1,416
14	U.S. Government grants (excluding military grants of goods and services)	-1,916	-1,917	-1,888	-1,808	-1,910	-1,805	-1,709	-1,649	-1,734	-2,043	-2,173	-1,933	-5,441
15	Balance on current account[d]	2,460	3,199	5,788	4,287	1,943	1,544	-962	-1,633	-324	-3,817	-9,807	450	-4,025
16	U.S. Government capital flows excluding nonscheduled repayments, net[e]	-1,766	-1,988	-1,804	-1,826	-1,972	-2,430	-2,543	-2,113	-1,836	-2,111	-1,705	-2,938	408
17	Nonscheduled repayments of U.S. Government assets	681	326	123	221	428	6	269	-87	244	227	137	289	1
18	U.S. Government nonliquid liabilities to other than foreign official reserve agencies	203	511	328	66	65	88	110	267	-483	-478	238	1,111	634
19	Long-term private capital flows, net	-2,606	-3,376	-4,511	-4,577	-2,575	-2,932	1,191	-70	-1,429	-4,381	-98	62	-7,598
20	U.S. direct investments abroad	-1,654	-1,976	-2,328	-3,468	-3,661	-3,137	-3,209	-3,271	-4,410	-4,943	-3,517	-4,872	-6,801
21	Foreign direct investments in the United States	132	-5	-5	57	86	258	319	832	1,030	-115	383	2,537	2,308
22	Foreign securities	-969	-1,105	-677	-759	-482	-1,266	-1,239	-1,494	-942	-966	-654	-807	-1,951
23	U.S. securities other than Treasury issues	134	282	-84	-357	909	1,016	4,414	3,130	2,190	2,289	4,507	4,051	1,199
24	Other, reported by U.S. banks	-121	-722	-893	9	505	393	410	457	118	-862	-1,158	-647	-1,186
25	Other, reported by U.S. nonbanking concerns	-129	149	-523	-60	68	-196	495	277	526	216	341	-200	-1,167
26	Balance on current account and long-term capital[e]	-1,028	-1,328	-75	-1,829	-2,110	-3,723	-1,935	-3,637	-3,778	-10,559	-11,235	-1,026	-10,580
27	Nonliquid short-term private capital flows, net	f-657	f-968	-1,643	-154	-104	-522	231	-640	-482	-2,347	-1,541	-4,276	-12,955
28	Claims reported by U.S. banks	f-358	f-747	-1,333	-200	-220	-645	-44	-658	-1,023	-1,802	-1,457	-3,940	-12,223
29	Claims reported by U.S. nonbanking concerns	f-187	-198	-422	-103	-180	-376	-485	-73	-361	-530	-305	-1,240	-2,453
30	Liabilities reported by U.S. nonbanking concerns	-112	-23	113	149	296	499	759	91	902	-15	221	904	1,721
31	Allocations of special drawing rights (SDR)[d]									867	717	710		
32	Errors and omissions, net	-1,179	-418	-978	-494	64	-439	94	-1,805	-458	-9,776	-1,790	-2,303	5,197

33	Net liquidity balance	f−2,864	f−2,713	−2,696	−2,478	−2,151	−4,683	−1,611	−6,081	−3,851	−21,965	−13,856	−7,606	−18,338
34	Liquid private capital flows, net	f214	f779	1,162	1,188	2,370	1,265	3,252	8,820	−5,988	−7,788	3,502	2,302	10,268
35	Liquid claims	f−1	f159	−392	1,057	−14	−207	−558	162	282	−1,097	−1,247	−1,944	−5,464
36	Reported by U.S. banks	f34	f−34	−191	525	136	−85	−61	−209	−99	−566	−742	−1,103	−5,445
37	Reported by U.S. nonbanking concerns	f−35	193	−201	532	−150	−122	−497	371	351	−531	−505	−841	−19
38	Liquid liabilities	215	620	1,554	131	2,384	1,472	3,810	8,658	−6,240	−6,691	4,749	4,246	15,732
39	To foreign commercial banks	−138	470	1,454	116	2,697	1,272	3,387	9,166	−6,508	−6,908	3,716	2,982	12,655
40	To international and regional organizations	212	−235	−243	−291	−525	−214	48	−63	181	682	104	377	151
41	To other foreigners	141	385	343	306	212	414	375	−445	87	−465	929	887	2,926
42	Official reserve transactions balance	−2,650	−1,934	−1,534	−1,290	219	−3,418	1,641	2,739	−9,839	−29,753	−10,354	−5,304	−8,070
	Financed by changes in:													
43	Liquid liabilities to foreign official agencies	918	1,673	1,075	−18	−1,595	2,020	−3,101	−554	7,637	27,615	9,734	4,452	8,253
44	Other readily marketable liabilities to foreign official agencies[g]		9	149	−38	793	894	534	−836	−810	−551	399	1,113	596
45	Nonliquid liabilities to foreign official reserve agencies reported by U.S. Government	199	−125	139	123	15	452	1,806	−162	535	341	189	−475	655
46	U.S. official reserve assets, net	1,533	377	171	1,222	568	52	−880	−1,187	2,477	2,348	32	209	−1,434
	Memoranda:													
47	Transfers under military grant programs (excluded from lines 2, 4, and 14)	1,537	1,562	1,340	1,636	2,066	2,443	2,868	2,922	2,513	3,204	4,189	2,772	1,790
48	Reinvested earnings of foreign incorporated affiliates of U.S. firms (excluded from lines 7 and 20)	1,198	1,507	1,431	1,542	1,739	1,598	2,175	2,604	2,948	3,157	4,521	8,124	n.a.
49	Reinvested earnings of U.S. incorporated affiliates of foreign firms (excluded from lines 9 and 21)	214	236	327	358	339	440	488	431	484	498	548	945	n.a.
50	Gross liquidity balance, excluding allocation of SDR	−2,865	−2,554	−3,088	−1,421	−2,165	−4,890	−2,169	−5,919	−4,466	−23,779	−15,813	−9,550	−23,802

a Adjusted to balance of payments basis; excludes exports under U.S. military agency sales contracts, and imports of U.S. military agencies.

b Fees and royalties from U.S. direct investments abroad or from foreign direct investments in the United States are excluded from investment income and included in "other services."

c Equal to net exports of goods and services in national income and product accounts of the United States.

d The sum of lines 15 and 31 is equal to "net foreign investment" in the national income and product accounts of the United States.

e Includes some short-term U.S. government assets.

f Coverage of liquid banking claims for 1962-63 and of liquid nonbanking claims for 1962 is limited to foreign currency deposits only; other liquid items are not available separately and are included with nonliquid claims.

g Includes changes in nonliquid liabilities reported by U.S. banks and in investments by foreign official agencies in debt securities of U.S. government corporations and agencies, private corporations, and State and local governments.

p Preliminary

Note: Details may not add to totals because of rounding.

Source: U.S. Department of Commerce, Bureau of Economic Analysis, *Survey of Current Business.* June 1974, p. 30; March 1975, p. 33.

means of payments. It is when alternative assumptions are made on whether dollar liabilities are of an autonomous or compensating nature that various definitions of U. S. balance of payments surpluses of deficits arise. As noted before, the size of the balance of payments surplus or deficit is a direct function of the balance in autonomous transactions. Therefore, if the definition of an autonomous transaction changes, then the size of the balance of payments deficit or surplus changes. The problems presented by the availability of alternative definitions are reinforced by the difficulties in obtaining empirical support for any of the definitions. This difficulty is due to the nature of capital flows and the way they are measured, as explained in the previous section.

The issues involved in the various definitions are:

1. Whether short-term capital movements regardless of liquidity or nature of owner are autonomous transactions at all.

2. Whether short-term capital movements can be classified according to their liquidity.

3. Whether short-term capital movements can be classified according to the nature of the owner of the financial asset.

The *basic balance* addresses itself to the first issue, and it answers it in the negative: short-term capital flows are excluded from this definition. The balance is computed on the basis of the current account and the long-term capital account. "Errors and omissions" are considered disguised short-term capital movement and therefore are excluded from the basic balance. The rationale for this approach is that only transactions that reflect basic, long-term trends in the economy should be taken into account. Volatile, short-term capital flows, often associated with the financing of current transactions which might have large but only temporary impact on the balance of payments, are eliminated from the active balance.

The *net liquidity balance* is concerned with the second issue. Under this definition, only the *nonliquid* short-term claims and liabilities not in the hands of official agencies are of an autonomous nature. All liquid short-term claims and liabilities, regardless of who holds them, are considered of a compensating nature. The rationale behind this definition is that any short-term claim on the U. S. held by any foreigner can be converted into an immediate claim for redemption into gold (when convertibility exists) or into other foreign exchange.

Finally, the *official reserve balance* addresses itself to the third issue. It establishes that the relevant criterion to discriminate among short-term capital movements is whether the assets end up in the hands of official institutions or in the hands of private residents. If the transaction is made by private residents this definition considers any capital flow as autonomous, whether liquid or non-liquid. If the transaction changes the balances in the hands of official institutions, it is considered to be accommodating.[4]

---

[4] As this book goes to press the U. S. Department of Commerce is developing a new format for the presentation of the U. S. balance of payments and the definition of surpluses and deficits. With the movement of the international monetary system from a system of fixed rates to a system of managed floating rates, the interpretation of movements in the capital accounts and the reserve accounts is changing.

In both the net liquidity and the official settlements balances, errors and omissions are considered as autonomous transactions.

Exhibit 2.2 presents the U. S. balance of payments as prepared by the Department of Commerce and published in the *Survey of Current Business*. In this statement Line 26 presents the *basic balance*, i.e., balance on current account and long-term capital. Line 33 shows the *net liquidity balance* which does not include any liquid asset or liability in the definition of autonomous transaction. The latter are considered compensating items. Line 42 shows the *official reserve balance* which includes the flows of all liquid assets and liabilities which ended up in private hands, but not those in official hands. Changes in assets and liabilities in official institutions, whether liquid or illiquid are considered as compensating items. Lines 43 through 46 list the transactions that originated changes in assets and liabilities in official agencies.

The deficit in the U. S. basic balance of $10,580 million for 1974 is composed of a deficit in the current account of $4,025 million, a large deterioration over the preceding year, and a deficit in the long-term capital account of $6,555 million, mostly due to private capital outflows which have grown steadily over the postwar period. The current account, in turn, is made up of a deficit of $5,881 million in the trade account, a surplus of $9,072 million in the service account, and a deficit of $7,216 million in the unilateral transfer account (including government grants). The service and unilateral transfer accounts have shown a persistent pattern of surplus in the former and deficit in the latter. It is the trade account that has shown large gyrations in the last few years from sizable deficits in 1971 and particularly 1972 to a moderate surplus in 1973 and back to a substantial deficit in 1974, the latter deficit being largely due to the increase in oil prices.

In 1974, the large capital outflow in non-liquid, short-term capital flows (largely loans of U. S. banks to foreigners) and a positive errors and omissions combined with the deficit in the basic balance to produce the net liquidity deficit balance of $18,338 million, a deficit surpassed only during 1971, a year when the U. S. dollar was officially devalued. By adding to the net liquidity balance the changes in foreign assets and liabilities in private hands, we come to the official reserve deficit balance of $8,070 million in 1974.[5]

The economic forces behind the performance of the various accounts in the balance of payments are discussed in the following chapter.

Exercises On Balance of Payments Accounting

Below there is a series of transactions between country A and country B (the rest of the world). Assume the point of view of country A and that A's currency is dollars($). Do the following:

---

[5] Figures for 1974 are only preliminary as this book goes to press.

1. Indicate the accounts to be debited and credited in each transaction.

2. Enter these transactions in the appropriate "T-accounts" provided for that purpose in Exhibit 2.3.

3. Prepare the balance of payments for country A. Assume that all the short-term capital movements are of a compensating nature.

TRANSACTIONS

1. a. A exports goods to B for $1,000. B's importers sign a bill of exchange for the goods they imported from A.

   b. A's exporters discount the bill of exchange with their bank which in turn keeps the bill until maturity. (Assume 10% discount.)

   c. On the bill's maturity A's bank receives payment for the bill in B's currency (as it was originally drawn). A's bank deposits B's currency in B's bank. The interest accrued on the bill is $50.

2. A imports goods from B for $800. A's importers pay B's exporters for the $800 with a loan in B's currency which they get from A's bank.

3. A resident of country A, Mr. X, goes on vacation to country B. He spends all the money he had with him, $5,000, for services received while on his vacation in country B.

4. Mr. X is lucky, however, because on the last day of his vacation he finds in the street a purse with $100 in B's currency. He brings the money home and declares his finding to custom authorities.

5. Another resident of A who has migrated from B a few years ago decides to send $100 to his family. His father uses this money to buy a bond from another citizen of A.

6. A businessman of A, Mr. Y, decides to build a subsidiary plant in B. Therefore, he ships to B all necessary materials for this purpose, which cost $50,000.

7. Mr. Y very soon finds out that he needs another $20,000 for the completion of the plant. Thus, he issues bonds on the parent company for this amount and sells them to the citizens of B.

8. Mr. Y makes $10,000 profit during the first year of operation, which Mr. Y uses to enlarge his business in B. A's citizens are very impressed by the successful operation of Mr. Y's plant in B. Therefore, A's citizens buy from B's citizens half of the bonds issued by Mr. Y.

9. A resident of B, Mr. Z, migrates to A. His only property is $1,000 in B's currency which he carried with him to A, and his house in B which he rented to a friend of his for $100 a month. The house is worth $8,000. No rent payment, however, has been received.

10. Mr. Z decides to sell his house to his friend for $8,000. Payment is arranged as follows: $4,000 in cash and $4,000 in 5 years. Mr. Z deposits this money with his old bank in B. (Everything here is in terms of B's currency.)

EXHIBIT 2.3 Supporting "T Accounts"

Exports	Imports	Services	Unilateral Transfers

Direct Investment	Long-Term Foreign Financial Assets	Short-Term Foreign Financial Assets	Gold

Long-Term Liabilities	Short-Term Liabilities

11. Mr. Z, however, thinks he should give back to the church of his village $1,000. Therefore $1,000 is transferred from Mr. Z's account in B's bank to the account of the church.

12. B is a producer of gold. During the period of time for which the balance of payments is compiled, B produced $1 million. Half of this is consumed at home. However 20% is sold to B's central bank, 20% is sold to A's central bank, and 10% is exported to A for industrial use. For the amount of gold exported to A, B accepts a deposit with the central bank of country A.

13. A citizen of A, Mr. M, who migrated there from B a long time ago, finds out that he inherited the property of his uncle which consists of a farm worth $2,000 and a deposit of $1,000 in B's bank.

14. Mr. M keeps the money with B's bank but he buys a designer's dress for $200 which he sends to his sister in B as a gift. The dress is purchased in A with A's currency.

15. Finally, Mr. M sells the farm for $2,000. He uses the proceeds along with his deposit in B's bank to buy bonds issued by B's government.

16. Mr. M makes a gift to his brother in B. This gift consists of a watch which costs $500 and a check for $100. The watch is purchased in country A with A's currency.

Bibliography

The Balance of Payments Statistics of the United States. Report of the Review Committee for Balance of Payments Statistics to the Bureau of the Budget, April 1965, Edward M. Bernstein, Chairman, U. S. Government Printing Office: 1965.

Meade, J. E., *The Balance of Payments,* London: Oxford University Press, 1952.

Appendix: Important Dates in the World Monetary System

1944:   Bretton Woods conference creates fixed exchange rate monetary system based on the U. S. dollar.

1949:   British pound devalued.
U. S. gold stock peaks at $24.6 billion.

1950: U. S. balance of payments swings into deficit and stays in deficit for a protracted period, with only a few exceptions.

1960: Run on gold pushes price to $40 an ounce, and it forces central banks to intervene in London market to hold down price.

1961: German mark upvalued.

1962: French begin turning in dollars for U. S. gold. Policy continues through 1966 and costs United States $3 billion gold.

1963: United States levies interest equalization tax on foreign borrowing in this country.

1965: United States imposes "voluntary" controls on the export of dollars.

1967: British pound devalued touching off world money crisis that lasts into 1968.

1968: United States adopts mandatory controls on direct investment.
Run on gold in March brings central banks to Washington and leads to two-price gold market.

1969: French franc devalued in August.
German mark upvalued in October after floating in exchange markets for a very brief period.

1970: Special Drawing Rights (SDRs) go into use as supplement to gold and dollars in reserves of nations.
U. S. balance of payments deficit reaches record $10 billion.

1971: Massive inflows of money in early May enforce Germany to float the mark and Switzerland to upvalue the franc.
U. S. gold stock falls below $10 billion for first time since World War II.
United States runs international trade deficit in first half for first time in twentieth century.
U. S. payments deficit in first half is at a $23 billion annual rate.
On Aug. 15, the U. S. dollar is floated, convertibility of the U. S. dollar into gold is eliminated, and an import surcharge is imposed in the United States.
On Dec. 17, in the Smithsonian Agreement, "central rates" are fixed and the U. S. dollar is devalued. Also, a wider margin of 2.25% on either side of the "central rate" is established. The United States agrees to eliminate the import surcharge but the convertibility of U. S. dollar into gold is not reinstated.

1972: In May the original Common Market countries, the United Kingdom, and Denmark jointly agree to a narrow range of exchange rate flexibility of 1 1/8% among themselves while maintaining the currencies within the 2¼% band on either side of the par value vis-à-vis the U. S. dollar.
On June 23, the pound is floated after a brief speculative period, when British international reserves are at record highs. The United Kingdom is

joined by Denmark in withdrawing from the monetary agreement with the European countries.

1973:   In order to protect the domestic economy from international monetary problems, the Swiss franc is floated on January 23.

On Feb. 12, renewed speculation on the dollar leads the United States to devalue the U. S. dollar again.

On Feb. 13, the lira and the yen are floated.

In March renewed attacks on the U. S. dollar lead governments to close their exchange markets for two weeks. Finally it is decided to keep the major European currencies within 2¼% fluctuation from one another, but to float against the U. S. dollar.

During the summer, attacks on the dollar are renewed. Prices of major currencies move upward relative to the U. S. dollar. However, no official parity changes are made and during the last quarter of the year the pressures on the dollar recede. When the oil-producing nations establish an embargo on oil exports to developed countries, the United States is perceived to be in a more self-reliant position than the other developed countries. After the embargo is suspended, oil prices more than quadruple within a short period of time.

1974:   In January the three programs controlling capital outflows from the United States are eliminated for all intents and purposes. This leads to massive lending to foreigners.

In the first half of the year several bank failures with large losses in foreign exchange bring fears to international financial markets. Credit worthiness of institutions is questioned.

On June 28 the IMF redefines the value of SDRs. The new value is based on the weighted value of 16 major currencies, instead of reflecting only the value of the U. S. dollar.

Throughout the year funds accumulated by oil-producing countries are successfully recycled to importing countries.

1975:   Negotiations toward an agreement on a new international monetary system continue unsuccessfully. In practice, major currencies operate on a managed-float basis and the IMF votes to abolish the "official price" of gold.

SDRs gain in popularity. An increasing number of transactions are denominated in SDRs. The first Euro-bond denominated in SDRs is issued successfully on June 11.

The balance of payments surpluses of the oil-producing countries are reduced to almost half of the surplus amount of the preceding year as these countries step up imports from developed countries. The current accounts of developed countries improve considerably as a result.

The balance of trade of the United States becomes a large surplus; in late 1975, the balance on current account is forecast to be $10 billion for the year.

Appendix: Some International Associations

European Economic Community (EEC or Common Market)—The Original Six.
France, Germany, Italy, Netherlands, Belgium, Luxembourg.

Enlarged Common Market—The Nine. The original six plus the United Kingdom, Ireland, and Denmark.

Group of Ten. The ten major industrial countries (the six less Luxembourg plus the United Kingdom, the United States, Sweden, Canada, and Japan) which agreed in October 1962, to stand ready to lend their currencies to the International Monetary Fund (IMF) under the General Arrangements to Borrow. Meetings of the Group of Ten finance ministers and central governors (and those of their deputies) effected the main changes in the world's money system in the 1960s. Central bank governors of these countries hold regular monthly meetings in Basel. Switzerland attends these Group of Ten meetings; so may representatives of the IMF, the Organization for Economic Cooperation and Development (OECD), the Bank for International Settlements (BIS), and the EEC commission.

Group of Twenty. Group created to draft a proposal for the reform of the international monetary system after the Smithsonian Agreement in 1971. Membership based on the pattern of the IMF executive board. Six countries—the United States, the United Kingdom, Germany, France, Japan, and India—had their own national representatives; the other fourteen representatives each spoke for a group of countries so that all 120 members of the IMF were represented. Switzerland, a non-member of the IMF, attended sessions only as a visitor. This group dissolved itself and turned its responsibilities over to the IMF in June 1974, after unsuccessful attempts to carry out its mandate.

OECD. Organization for Economic Cooperation and Development. Established in 1961 as successor to the Organization for European Economic Cooperation. Group of twenty-three developed nations: the Group of Ten plus Austria, Denmark, Luxembourg, Norway, Switzerland, Finland, Greece, Iceland, Ireland, Portugal, Spain, Turkey, and Australia. (Yugoslavia is an associate.)

Group of Seventy-seven. The club of the developing countries, originally with a membership of seventy-seven. Formed by Mr. Paul Prebisch of the United Nations Commission on Trade and Development (UNCTAD).

Group of Twenty-four. Eight countries each of Latin America, Africa, and Asia, deputed by the Group of Seventy-seven to consider monetary matters.

OPEC. Organization of Petroleum Exporting Countries. Group formed by major oil producing countries. Its major function has been to provide a forum where a common oil pricing policy can be established and enforced through a cartel.

CHAPTER 3

What Makes
the Balance of Payments
Accounts Tick?

Because the multinational firm conducts business operations in many currencies, management needs to forecast the performance of various countries and their currencies. Balance of payments forecasting requires an understanding of the forces that trigger changes in the component accounts and, therefore, the country's economy at large, so the exercise of forecasting a country's balance of payments provides one with an excellent analytical framework to predict this performance. A simple listing of historical records of the balance of payments is not sufficient; historical figures may show trends, but they provide neither insight into the past nor an analytical foundation to predict the future.

In this chapter we shall present an introduction to the major factors that affect each balance of payments account. In this presentation, we look only at the *immediate* factors that affect the accounts. The whole cycle of events that a change in a given account engenders is not considered at this time. For example, we study the effect on exports of a change in the level of prices, but not the effects of the resulting trade balance on future exports.

The case of the United States will be used to illustrate the principles of analysis presented in the chapter. (The balance of payments of the United States for the period 1962-74 was presented in Exhibit 2.2.) The appendix to the preceding chapter, "Important Dates in the World Monetary System," provides a frame of reference for the international events that took place during the period analyzed. The checklists in the appendices to this chapter offer a listing of major items studied in the preparation of a country analysis and a forecast of the future value of its currency.

TRADE FLOWS

Two issues require major consideration when analyzing the trade accounts of a given country. The more general and basic issue is: Why do countries trade? What are the underlying long-term forces that induce countries to trade? The second issue is: Given the basic forces, why do changes in the trade account take place? What are the short-term factors that make trade behavior depart from the expected long-term behavior?

The Long-Term Factors

The questions of why countries trade and what items they trade have been the source of a number of theories beginning with David Ricardo in the early 1800s. In a nutshell, all these theories boil down to a relatively simple proposition: countries export those goods which they know relatively best how to make, or, in other words, for which they have a *comparative advantage*. The source of this competitive edge has been attributed to a number of variables, including labor productivity, the proportion of factors of production available in the country, and the technological lead of the country.

Labor productivity has often been considered one of the major factors determining whether a country will be an exporter or an importer of a given good. Especially in the case of goods that are capable of being produced in several parts of the world, it is easy to see that the countries most efficient in their production will tend to be the producers for the world. This relatively higher efficiency has often been measured in terms of labor productivity (output per man-hour). However, it is clear that labor productivity is affected by the amount of capital with which labor works.

In addition to labor productivity, the relative endowment of resources is also thought to play an important role in the determination of goods traded. Thus, the high capital endowment of the United States was considered to be at the core of the balance of trade surplus the United States enjoyed throughout most of the postwar period. The abundance of capital relative to the amount of labor in the United States was unparalleled by any other country. This factor was thought to explain the large amount of manufactured exports of this country.

However, research presented by Professor Leontief in 1954 suggested that U. S. exports were *less* capital-intensive than its imports.[1] The empirical evidence indicated that the exports of the United States had a higher labor-capital ratio in their manufacture than its imports. In view of the general belief that the United States was richer in capital than in labor, the country was exporting the products that required the most of what it had the least. Initially these surprising findings were explained by referring to the capital "imbedded" in American labor. If the U. S. labor force were adjusted for its efficiency, it was argued, the United States would appear as a relatively labor-rich country. What made U. S. labor more efficient than

[1] W. W. Leontief, "Domestic Production and Foreign Trade: The American Capital Position Re-examined," *Economia Internazionale,* Vol. 7, Feb. 1954, pp. 3-22; reprinted in American Economic Association, *Readings in International Economics* (Homewood, Ill.: Richard D. Irwin, 1968) Chapter 30.

the rest of the world's was thought to be the human capital (skills) that this labor possessed. Another factor related to the nature of the U. S. trade was the level of research and development activity in different industries.

Some economists still speak of factor proportions that include human capital. However, a newer trend is to consider labor skills and technology as factors fostering new products and new processes that in turn generate temporary trade advantages.[2] One of the main characteristics of this approach is its dynamism. It considers trade advantages derived from technological gaps to be temporary. This gap narrows continuously as knowledge of the innovation spreads abroad and foreign producers adopt it. Therefore, the entire structure of trade advantages is continually being modified by the simultaneous generation and destruction of technology gaps. Proponents of this theory note that the rate of technology transfer is accelerating. A decrease in the technological lead of the United States has been considered one of the important factors explaining the decline in this country's balance of trade surplus since 1964, and the deficit in the 1970s. The compounded annual rates of increase from 1963 to 1974 were 14.3% for exports and 17.8% for imports. This is in contrast to the rates of increase from 1955 to 1963 of 5.6% for exports and 5.0% for imports.[3] Further, the multinational corporation has been thought to be an important element in this transfer process.

Summing up, three major factors have been suggested to explain trade patterns: labor productivity, the relative availability of factors of production, and technological gaps. When analyzing the balance of payments of countries other than the United States, these principles must be accommodated to the specific circumstances. Thus, in a case where exports of a country do not contain any large degree of technological sophistication, the future of its exports would depend on its continued ability to provide raw material at competitive prices and labor at an efficient rate (e.g., keep wage rates low or increase output per man-hour). To the extent that this country can acquire new technologies, its chances to remain competitive in the international market will be enhanced.

Cyclical Factors

Given an understanding of the major forces that induce nations to trade, the next question is: what are the relevant variables that determine the volume of trade at a given point in time? These are mainly two: relative prices and relative national incomes.

Relative Prices. This variable affects trade in two fashions: its impact on production and its effects on demand. Assuming a free trade situation, relative prices will determine whether the country will be an importer or an exporter of a given commodity. As the world prices of a good increase, the chances increase for profitable produc-

---

[2] Raymond Vernon, "International Investment and International Trade in the Product Cycle," *Quarterly Journal of Economics,* Vol. 80, May 1966, pp. 190-207. Also see Louis T. Wells, Jr., "A Product Life Cycle for International Trade?" *Journal of Marketing,* Vol. 32, July 1968, pp. 1-6.

[3] Federal Reserve Bank of St. Louis, *U. S. Balance of Payments Trends, Period Ending: 4th Quarter 1974,* April 24, 1975, pp. 10-11.

tion of that good in a given country. For example, Australian gold production, once the world's highest, halved in the past decade to 615,000 ounces as a result of its high production costs. However, 1973 production was up 10%. The increase in the price of gold to $90 an ounce from $35 in 1970 made the old Australian gold mines economic again. As gold prices continued to soar in 1974, additional gold mines were brought back into production.

The impact of prices on demand depends on the nature of the goods involved. By and large, when prices go down, quantity demanded tends to increase. However, some commodities are indispensable and the quantity demanded of them is relatively independent of the prevalent price. In other cases, a decline in price produces a large response in the quantity demanded, which may be proportionally more or less than the decrease in prices. The difference in responsiveness of quantity purchased to changes in the price is called *price elasticity*.

An understanding of the price elasticity of the goods traded by a country is essential in determining the impact of forecasted prices. This is particularly so in predicting the effects on trade of a devaluation (or upvaluation) of the country's currency. A change in exchange parity is nothing else than a change in prices. The impact of a change in prices should be analyzed in terms of both local currency and foreign exchange or international purchasing power.

Take the case of the impact of a devaluation on exports. In this example, assume that B's currency is used as money internationally, i.e., it is a reserve currency.

Initial Conditions:

Exchange rate:	$1A = 1B$
Quantity exported:	100 units
Price per unit:	$5As$
Export revenues:	$500As = 500Bs$

Impact of Devaluation:

New exchange rate: $1A = .8B$ (A devalues by 20% relative to B)

	Case 1	Case 2	Case 3
Quantity exported:	130	125	120
Export revenues:	$650As = 520Bs$	$625As = 500Bs$	$600As = 480Bs$

In the three cases described above, the quantity demanded increases in response to the decline in prices, and so do the export revenues measured in A's currency. Measured in A's currency, A's devaluation has had an unmistakable beneficial effect on export revenues. However, the export revenues in terms of foreign exchange (B's currency) increases in only one case, Case 1. In terms of B's currency, the decline in price produced by the devaluation of A's currency depresses the revenues received for each unit. In order to compensate for this decline, the number of units sold must increase. If it increases proportionally more than the decrease in prices, there will be an increase in revenues. This is Case 1. However, if the increase in quantity sold is proportionally less than the decrease in prices, there will be a decrease in revenues. This is Case 3. In Case 2, quantity sold increases by a percentage equal to the percentage decline in prices. Therefore, for Case 2, export revenues remain constant and the product has *unitary price elasticity.* The product in Case 1 is considered to be *price elastic;* the product in Case 3, *price inelastic.* Notice that the quantity proportion is measured against the percentage price decline using the new price as a base. Thus, in the example, the price decline in terms of B currency is (5B – 4B/4B, or 25%. Hence, unitary price elasticity occurs when demand expands by 25% to 125, as in Case 2. A typical example of a price-inelastic product is a raw material. An example of a price-elastic good is machinery.[4]

Thus, the study of the impact of relative prices on trade must be done along two major dimensions: the magnitude of changes in relative prices, and the responsiveness of quantities traded to a given change in prices. Relative prices may change either because of outright changes in the exchange rate among currencies, or because the economic forces that shape domestic prices are altered. When the cost of factors of production such as labor and its productivity change, the prices of products in the local market change, and with constant exchange rates, the foreign price will also be affected. The second dimension, the responsiveness of quantity traded to a given change in price, is largely determined by the nature of the goods.

Let us look at the behavior of the trade accounts of the United States. Exhibit 3.1 presents annual total imports and exports of the United States classified by major types of goods for the period 1962-74. (Further disaggregation by product is available from the same source used in the preparation of the exhibit.)[5] Total net trade shows a continuous deterioration during the 1960s and an erratic behavior during the early 1970s. As to the component goods, the exhibit shows clearly the strong net export position which the United States holds in the area of equipment (capital goods except automotive) and the large net import position in the field of industrial supplies. The latter position was aggravated during the 1970s by the large increase in oil prices. Food products have oscillated from a net export to a net import, and back to a substantial net export position in 1973 and 1974 when the increased volume of U.S. exports of grain accompanied by higher prices of these products made a large positive contribution to the U. S. trade accounts.

The goods for which the United States has a strong export position, capital goods except automotive, are also the goods which one would expect to be price elastic; other developed countries, such as Germany, compete for supplying these

---

[4]More specifically, import price elasticity is measured by the percentage change in imports associated with a given percentage change in prices.

$$\eta_P = \frac{\Delta Q}{Q} \div \frac{\Delta P}{P} = \frac{\Delta Q}{\Delta P} \times \frac{P}{Q}$$

η_P = price elasticity $\eta_P < 1$ inelastic demand

Q = quantity $\eta_P = 1$ unitary elasticity of demand

P = price $\eta_P > 1$ elastic demand

[5]Note that these trade figures have been computed on the Census Bureau basis in contrast to the balance of payments basis used in Exhibit 2.2. This explains the small discrepancy between the total trade figures in the two exhibits.

EXHIBIT 3.1 United States Merchandise Trade by End-Use, 1960-1974 (millions of dollars)[a]

	1962	1963	1964	1965	1966	1967	1968	1969	1970	1971	1972	1973	1974[b]
Foods, feeds, and beverages													
Exports	3,829	4,282	4,849	4,928	5,489	4,998	4,813	4,688	5,839	6,054	7,489	15,075	18,459
Imports	3,573	3,753	3,915	3,946	4,499	4,586	5,271	5,238	6,154	6,366	7,265	9,113	10,562
	256	529	934	982	990	412	−458	−550	−315	−312	224	5,962	7,897
Industrial supplies and materials													
Exports	7,132	7,822	9,185	8,917	9,613	9,971	11,004	11,776	13,782	12,691	13,980	19,766	30,395
Imports	8,573	8,874	9,563	11,024	12,162	11,856	14,159	14,160	15,106	16,965	20,322	26,713	51,343
	−1,441	−1,052	−378	−2,107	−2,549	−1,885	−3,155	−2,384	−1,324	−4,274	−6,342	−6,947	−20,948
Capital goods, except automotive													
Exports	6,443	6,604	7,463	8,039	8,892	9,913	11,072	12,346	14,371	15,119	16,690	21,512	29,921
Imports	758	823	1,039	1,490	2,163	2,412	2,819	3,244	3,814	4,127	5,572	7,584	9,551
	5,685	5,781	6,424	6,549	6,729	7,501	8,253	9,102	10,557	10,992	11,118	13,928	20,370
Automotive vehicles, parts and engines													
Exports	1,301	1,468	1,729	1,929	2,354	2,784	3,453	3,888	3,652	4,396	5,119	6,343	8,162
Imports	521	586	767	907	1,883	2,604	4,256	5,288	5,894	7,917	9,327	10,886	12,352
	780	882	962	1,022	471	180	−803	−1,400	−2,242	−3,521	−4,208	−4,543	−4,190
Consumer goods (nonfood) except automotive													
Exports	1,455	1,558	1,751	1,799	2,035	2,111	2,334	2,576	2,719	2,847	3,492	4,705	6,267
Imports	2,276	2,389	2,694	3,305	3,912	4,213	5,375	6,616	7,553	8,561	11,355	13,185	14,805
	−821	−831	−943	−1,506	−1,877	−2,102	−3,041	−4,040	−4,834	−5,714	−7,863	−8,480	−8,538
Other Exports (include military-type goods)	1,554	1,654	1,674	1,909	2,047	1,846	1,961	2,731	2,862	3,023	3,007	3,937	5,302
Imports	500	591	660	791	959	1,212	1,346	1,471	1,400	1,627	1,742	1,993	2,359
	1,054	1,063	1,014	1,118	1,088	634	615	1,260	1,462	1,396	1,265	1,944	2,943
Total													
Exports	21,713	23,387	26,649	27,521	30,430	31,622	34,636	38,006	43,224	44,130	49,778	71,339	98,506
Imports	16,201	17,015	18,749	22,461	25,577	26,882	33,225	36,043	39,952	45,563	55,583	69,476	100,972
	5,512	6,372	7,900	5,060	4,853	4,740	1,411	1,963	3,272	−1,433	−5,805	1,863	−2,466

[a]Census basis, including military grant shipments.
[b]Preliminary
Source: U. S. Department of Commerce, Bureau of Economic Analysis, *Survey of Current Business*, March 1975.

goods to the rest of the world. In contrast, the largest net dependency of the United States on foreign trade is in goods that one may consider to be price inelastic, industrial supplies. However, the case of oil illustrates a point one must keep in mind when assessing the price elasticity of a commodity. Price elasticities are usually estimated for a known range of prices. Yet the prices for oil that prevailed in the mid-1970s had not been experienced before. Oil consumption in the United States traditionally has been considered to be price inelastic, for American society is based on a high level of industrialization, big cars, and other energy-dependent amenities. Thus, oil consumption was insensitive to price changes within the range of oil prices common before 1973. However, during 1974 the volume of oil imports in the United States increased much less than predicted. For the high oil price levels prevailing in 1974, oil consumption appears to be more price elastic. Oil may be relatively price inelastic in the short run, but elastic in the long run if prices remain high. As a counterpoint to the reaction of oil imports to large changes in prices, the large U. S. payments surplus in food reflect both record high prices and large quantities exported. Here we have a type of good traditionally held to be price inelastic which continued to be so at a different range of prices. However, in the case of food, one must also consider extraordinary temporary conditions affecting demand, such as crop failures in other parts of the world.

What role did relative prices play in explaining the historical behavior of the U. S. trade account? In terms of outright changes in exchange parity, the United States devalued its currency twice in the early 1970s: December 1971 and February 1973. The impact of these devaluations was not rapidly felt, as the trade deficits of 1971 and 1972 show. However, by 1973 the devaluations appeared to have had some impact as the trade account turned into a surplus. (See Exhibit 3.1.) However, the oil crisis was to make this surplus short-lived and in 1974 trade deficits appeared again. (See the appendix to Chapter 2 for changes in the values of other currencies.)

Exhibit 3.2 shows annual growth rates of relative prices for selected developed countries, including the United States, for the periods 1967-71 and 1971-74. Annual growth rates are also shown for the volume of trade and for some domestic variables thought to affect international prices.

The first panel in Exhibit 3.2 shows the growth rates for export prices expressed in both U. S. dollars and local currency and the growth rates for export volume. The dollar export prices allow one to put all export prices under a common denominator after accounting for changes in exchange rate parities. Export prices expressed in local currency reflect the rate of inflation in the country before adjustments for changes in exchange rates. Whatever measure of price one chooses to look at, the most striking fact is that export prices grew much faster during the 1971-74 period than during the preceding period, 1967-71. The well-publicized high inflation rate that has plagued developed countries during the early 1970s was reflected in the prices of exported goods.

For the 1967-71 period, the two countries with the highest growth rates in export prices in terms of local currency, France and the United Kingdom, had their increases in domestic prices more than compensated for by the devaluation of their currencies. So in terms of dollars, the export prices of goods from France and the United Kingdom were the lowest rates for 1967-71. France apparently succeeded in encouraging the growth of exports, for it achieved one of the fastest growth rates

EXHIBIT 3.2   Trade, Prices, and Costs for Selected Industrialized Countries
(Compounded Annual Growth Rates, 1967-1974, in percentages)

| | Export Prices | | | | | |
| | In U. S. dollars | | In local currency | | Export Volume | |
	1967-71	1971-74	1967-71	1971-74	1967-71	1971-74
France	2.5	17.1[a]	5.6	12.4[a]	12.7	11.4[a]
Germany	4.4	17.6	1.1	6.2	10.6	12.2
Italy	3.6	15.5[a]	3.4	18.2[a]	10.7	8.6[a]
Japan	2.8	19.2	2.5	13.7	19.3	9.5
United Kingdom	2.5	14.0	5.8	15.3	8.7	6.8
United States	3.4	15.6	3.4	15.4	5.2	13.6

| | Import Prices | | | | | |
| | In U. S. dollars | | In local currency | | Import Volume | |
	1967-71	1971-74	1967-71	1971-74	1967-71	1971-74
France	1.5	23.3[a]	4.3	18.4[a]	12.5	11.7[a]
Germany	2.8	20.5	−.8	9.2	15.2	4.8
Italy	3.5	29.7[a]	3.5	31.7[a]	9.1	6.3[a]
Japan	2.3	32.2	1.5	22.8	11.6	12.2
United Kingdom	2.5	24.6	6.0	26.2	5.4	8.4
United States	3.9	23.8	4.1	23.6	9.6	5.4

| | Wholesale Prices | | Wages | | Industrial Production | |
	1967-71	1971-74	1967-71	1971-74	1967-71	1971-74
France	4.6	15.7	10.9	15.6[a]	7.0	5.1
Germany	2.5	7.5	9.6	10.9[a]	8.1	2.9
Italy	3.7	19.7	9.5	17.8	4.1	6.0
Japan	1.4	15.3	14.3	19.6	11.8	7.2
United Kingdom	5.8	11.7	9.6	14.6	2.4	1.9
United States	3.3	12.0	6.0	7.2	1.6	5.2

[a]Figures for 1974 have been estimated on the basis of the first three quarters for that year.
     Source: International Monetary Fund, *International Financial Statistics,* January and May 1975.

in export volume for the period, 12.7%. However, the United Kingdom was not as successful and its export volume was among the lowest for the countries in the exhibit. This points to a higher price elasticity for exports from France than for those of the United Kingdom. In contrast, a low price elasticity appears to characterize German exports, for while the upvaluation of the deutsche mark in 1969 caused a substantial increase in export prices expressed in U. S. dollars, Germany's export volume growth remained above 10%. The United States and Japan, on the other hand, appear to have goods that are responsive to price changes. The growth rate in export prices of the United States was among the highest for the period and the volume of its exports grew the least among the countries studied. Japan had one of the lowest growth rates in export prices and the highest growth in export volume.

The apparently higher price elasticity for the exports of the United States and Japan in 1967-71 appears also to be supported by the data for 1971-74. In this latter period the United States had one of the lowest growth rates in export prices expressed in dollars and it had the fastest growth rate in export volume among the countries in the exhibit. Japan, with the highest growth rates in export prices, experienced a considerable reduction in the growth rate of its export volume from 19.3% in the preceding period to 9.5% in 1971-74. The price inelasticity found for United Kingdom exports in 1967-71 also appears to be supported by the data in the latter period. Although the United Kingdom had the lowest growth rate in export prices expressed in dollars, it also had the lowest growth rate in export volume. During 1971-74 the volume of exports from the United Kingdom was 6.8%, even less than the 8.7% for the 1961-71 period. Germany also continued its fast growth in export volume, 12.2% during the 1971-74 period, in spite of having one of the highest growth rates in export prices expressed in dollars.

The second panel of Exhibit 3.2 presents import prices and volume. The much higher growth rate in prices during the 1971-74 period compared to 1967-71 is also evident here. During the 1967-71 period countries with extreme growth rates in import prices expressed in local currency were also the ones with the smallest growth rates in import volume. Germany had a negative growth rate in the cost of its imports and it had the highest growth rate in import volume. The United Kingdom had the highest growth rate in import prices and it was also the country with the lowest growth rate in import volume. The other countries tended to follow the inverse relationship between growth in import prices and growth in import volume. This indicates that imports are fairly price elastic for all these countries. However, when one looks at the more recent period, 1971-74, a confusing picture emerges. The United States and Germany curtailed their growth rate in import volume drastically. To a lesser extent this is also true for Italy. The import prices for the United States increased substantially, 23.6%. However, the growth rate for German imports in terms of local currency increased by only 9.2%. The comparison of the two periods indicates a very high price elasticity in German imports and, to a lesser extent, in the United States. The United Kingdom, in spite of a 26.2% rate of increase in import prices, still increased the volume of its imports by 8.4%, a rate higher than for the preceding period. We must note that imports in 1974 in the developed countries shown in the exhibit were heavily affected by the price increases in oil during that year. The growth rates in import volume for 1971-74 measure to a large extent the success of each of the countries in reducing the growth in energy consumption and oil imports.

An analysis of relative prices and trade performance is not complete without looking into the domestic forces that forge local prices. In the third panel of Exhibit 3.2 three measures of the growth rate in domestic variables are presented: wholesale prices, wages, and industrial production. The ranking of countries by growth rates in wholesale prices produces an ordering similar to the one obtained when the ranking is made according to growth rates in export prices expressed in local currency. For the earlier period Germany and Japan had the lowest growth rates in both wholesale and export prices; France and the United Kingdom had the highest growth rates for both (the currencies of the latter two countries were devalued within the period). In the 1971-74 period, Germany had the lowest growth rates in both wholesale prices and export prices expressed in local currencies. Italy had the highest growth rate for both prices. However, the United Kingdom and the United States, which held the domestic inflation in wholesale prices within the lower boundaries in the exhibit, failed to achieve the same position in export prices. A detailed look into the composition of exports would reveal that food carries a much higher weight in U. S. exports than in domestic prices. A detailed analysis of the exports of the United Kingdom might also show the difference between the composition of exports and that of domestic production.

The next two statistics—wages and industrial production—attempt to look into the forces behind changes in prices. We may consider wages a proxy for the cost of labor, and industrial production one of the elements in the computation of productivity. In both periods the growth in wages was the lowest for the United States and the highest for Japan. Italy experienced much faster growth rates in wages during the recent period and this may be behind its high growth rate in domestic and export prices. In spite of the charges made against labor in the United States and the United Kingdom, these two countries have experienced relatively lower increases in wages. However, these two countries also fare the worst in their growth in industrial production during the period 1967-71. For 1971-74 the United States improved its performance in industrial production considerably, but the United Kingdom deteriorated in growth of industrial production even more, for growth in industrial production fell from 2.4% in the earlier period to 1.9% for 1971-74. Japan, on the other hand, although it had the largest increases in wages also had the largest increases in industrial production in both periods. For the 1967-71 period, when export prices in Japan increased only slightly, one may say that the increases in wages were more than compensated for by the increases in production. However, the relatively large increases in Japan's export prices for 1971-74 may indicate that production increases have not kept in step with wage increases.

Summarizing the previous analysis from the point of view of the United States, one can say that the deterioration of its trade account during 1967-71 is fully compatible with the fast growth in the prices of U. S. exports relative to other developed countries. This deterioration in the international competitiveness of U. S. goods was reflected both in a relatively slow growth in export volume and a relatively fast growth in import volume. The factors behind this deterioration in price competitiveness cannot be traced back definitely to the domestic inflation rate relative to other countries or to increases in wages. Rather, it seems that while the costs of production were not increasing very much relative to other countries, the slow growth in production was not sufficient to hold down export prices. In contrast, 1971-74 shows the United States in a much brighter light. The price competitiveness of the country's goods had improved as its export prices grew relatively less than those in other countries. As a result, the volume of goods exported increased considerably and the growth in volume of goods imported has been relatively less than that in other developed countries, in spite of the oil crisis. U. S. exports and imports both appear to have a relatively high price elasticity that makes the trade accounts improve when the competitiveness of the country's prices is favorable.

So far we have been using the relationships between changing prices and trade to explain the historical behavior of the U. S. trade accounts. What about forecasting the behavior of the trade account? Such a forecast is beyond the scope of this book. However, the variables and relationships one would want to forecast are the same ones that we have used to study the historical behavior. The complicating element in forecasting future behavior of international prices and their impact on the trade accounts, in contrast to studying historical relationships, is that an additional policy element must be taken into account in forecasting. In the preceding discussion we looked at changes in exchange rates and domestic prices separately. This separation can be accomplished for the past simply by looking at the historical data. But when the objective of the analysis is a forecast, it becomes much harder to anticipate the interaction between the two variables. Increases in domestic prices tend to lead to a devaluation of the currency in question. However, the timing of such a devaluation often becomes a political decision where domestic and balance of payments objectives are weighed one against the other.[6]

The forecasting problem is complicated further by the fact that one must analyze price behavior for each of the major trading partners and compare each with the country in question. Although a price increase in a given country may be unavoidable because of wage increases and the lack of increases in productivity, the trade account and the exchange rate may remain unchanged. This would be the case if the trading partners of the country experience comparable price increases— relative purchasing power remains constant—and the products traded have similar price elasticities in all the trading countries. The model that links exchange rates or trade performance to the changes in relative prices is the *purchasing power parity theory*. This theory proposes that, after a base period of relative equilibrium in two exchange markets and their domestic economies is established, the exchange rate in any given period should reflect the changes in relative prices since the base period. That is, the exchange rate between A and B should be halved if the price level in B is now twice as high relative to the base period as that in A.[7] If exchange rates are not modified accordingly, then imbalances will prevail in the trade account. However, as the evidence for the United States in the previous paragraphs suggests, this theory has not found great empirical support. Problems arise because, for the theory to work properly, all goods should be internationally traded, be without transport costs, and behave according to the law of one price. In fact, only a small proportion

---

[6] The relationships between changes in exchange rate and domestic economic variables are explored in detail in the following chapter.

[7] The purchasing power theory was developed by the Swedish economist Gustav Cassel to solve the problem of establishing new exchange rates after World War I. This theory is discussed in Cassel's *Money and Foreign Exchange after 1914* (New York: Macmillan Co., 1923). The best criticism of it appears in L. A. Metzler, "Exchange Rates and the International Monetary Fund" in *International Monetary Policies* (Washington, D.C.: Federal Reserve System, Oct. 1947).

A statement of "relative" and "absolute" purchasing parity theses and some empirical tests when adjusted for comparative service costs is contained in Balassa (1964). An absolute purchasing parity doctrine argues that equilibrium exchange rates occur based on price ratios of consumer goods taking account of comparative productivity and assuming mobility of resources (labor, capital, and free trade). The relative purchasing power hypothesis tolerates positions which would be considered in disequilibrium from the absolute purchasing power view. However, the relative purchasing power hypothesis would then say that *changes* in the exchange rates in the countries from that starting point would depend on changing comparative price ratios.

of goods and services are traded internationally, transport costs are a reality, and there is no reason for purely domestic goods, e.g., housing, to command the same price in different countries. In addition, trade patterns change in such a way that price comparisons between a given period and a base period may be meaningless.

Relative National Incomes. The impact of national income on trade derives from the impact of this variable on national consumption and investment. When national income goes up, both consumption and investment increase. Some of this consumption and investment is channeled to foreign markets via imports. Therefore, if we want to know the impact of relative national incomes on trade, we must first find out who are the major trading partners and what goods are traded with each partner.

Exhibit 3.3 classifies the major accounts of the U.S. balance of payments by geographic areas. The merchandise trade balances show the United States continually on a large net import position against Japan and Canada and as a net exporter to most of the rest of the world. Within the European Economic Community (EEC) one must keep in mind that net export positions contain sizable imports from Germany. Latin America and "Other Countries in Asia and Africa" were net importers of goods from the United States until recently. Venezuela in Latin America and the multiple oil-producing countries in Asia and Africa have made the United States a net importer in the trade account with these areas. We saw in Exhibit 3.1 the large increase in the trade deficit of industrial supplies (including oil) that the United States has experienced through the 1962-74 period, particularly during the 1970s.

EXHIBIT 3.3   Summary of Known Current and Long-Term Capital Transactions, by Area 1969-1974 (millions of dollars)[a]

Line	[Receipts by foreign areas (−)]	1969	1970	1971	1972	1973	1974p
	All areas, balances on:						
1	Merchandise trade[b]	593	2,176	−2,698	−6,912	471	−5,881
2	Goods and services	1,891	3,630	807	−4,609	4,327	3,191
3	Goods, services, and remittances	594	2,150	−745	−6,179	2,383	1,416
4	Current account	−1,050	416	−2,790	−8,353	450	−4,025
5	Current account and long-term capital[c]	−3,046	−3,037	−9,550	−9,842	−1,026	−10,580
	European Economic Community (9), balances on:[d]						
6	Merchandise trade[b]					1,034	2,733
7	Goods and services					−2,269	−169
8	Goods, services, and remittances					−2,360	−283
9	Current account					−2,360	−283
10	Current account and long-term capital[c]					−2,193	−2,001
	United Kingdom, balances on:						
11	Merchandise trade[b]	−42	329	−70	−216	244	574
12	Goods and services	−712	−431	−716	−964	−305	−226
13	Goods, services, and remittances	−758	−484	−778	−1,019	−377	−301
14	Current account	−758	−484	−778	−1,019	−377	−301
15	Current account and long-term capital[c]	−1,065	196	−809	541	−77	−1.269

	European Economic Community (6), balances on:[e]						
16	Merchandise trade[b]	966	1,644	412	−459	892	2,347
17	Goods and services	−129	453	−751	−2,678	−1,761	255
18	Goods, services, and remittances	−174	409	−787	−2,643	−1,746	252
19	Current account	−174	409	−787	−2,643	−1,746	251
20	Current account and long-term capital[c]	1,596	459	−1,354	−2,280	−1,819	−234
	Other Western Europe, balances on:[f]						
21	Merchandise trade[b]	478	913	436	16	709	1,732
22	Goods and services	−51	47	−356	−1,136	−857	271
23	Goods, services, and remittances	−263	−170	−609	−1,411	−1,133	11
24	Current account	−298	−199	−637	−1,351	−1,055	−17
25	Current account and long-term capital[c]	445	145	−99	−121	−193	−1,254
	Eastern Europe, balances on:						
26	Merchandise trade[b]	54	150	184	494	1,321	515
27	Goods and services	68	158	194	496	1,360	629
28	Goods, services, and remittances	50	137	174	471	1,333	597
29	Current account	47	128	170	471	1,332	596
30	Current account and long-term capital[c]	85	132	167	373	704	584
	Canada, balances on:						
31	Merchandise trade[b]	−812	−1,645	−1,735	−1,897	−1,612	−1,301
32	Goods and services	111	−476	−292	−298	367	1,036
33	Goods, services, and remittances	44	−580	−420	−418	249	888
34	Current account	44	−580	−420	−418	249	888
35	Current account and long-term capital[c]	−1,369	−1,631	−1,004	−1,612	−605	−1,110
	Latin American Republics and Other Western Hemisphere, balances on:						
36	Merchandise trade[b]	324	603	330	173	305	−2,868
37	Goods and services	1,778	1,952	1,843	1,341	2,156	−425
38	Goods, services, and remittances	1,533	1,682	1,571	1,054	1,800	−728
39	Current account	1,312	1,420	1,302	821	1,566	1,016
40	Current account and long-term capital[c]	402	187	59	−502	414	−4,930
	Japan, balances on:						
41	Merchandise trade[b]	−1,416	−1,244	−3,209	−4,101	−1,308	−1,809
42	Goods and services	−1,738	−1,497	−3,413	−4,741	−1,580	−1,172
43	Goods, services, and remittances	−1,777	−1,541	−3,461	−4,784	−1,632	−1,220
44	Current account	−1,777	−1,541	−3,461	−4,782	−1,630	−1,218
45	Current account and long-term capital[c]	−2,132	−1,579	−4,317	−4,340	195	−1,142

	Australia, New Zealand, and South Africa, balances on:						
46	Merchandise trade[b]	206	465	555	140	397	1,743
47	Goods and services	791	1,135	1,128	744	1,234	2,676
48	Goods, services, and remittances	769	1,112	1,104	720	1,206	2,649
49	Current account	769	1,112	1,104	720	1,206	2,649
50	Current account and long-term capital[c]	763	779	662	438	1,192	2,334
	Other countries in Asia and Africa, balances on:						
51	Merchandise trade[b]	745	961	399	-1,062	-375	-6,626
52	Goods and services	1,842	2,435	2,969	2,539	4,253	625
53	Goods, services, and remittances	1,238	1,730	2,257	1,761	3,248	-219
54	Current account	-12	451	703	38	1,672	-5,068
55	Current account and long-term capital[c]	-1,711	-1,382	-2,031	-1,957	-101	-1,771
	International organizations and unallocated, balances on:						
56	Merchandise trade[b]	—	—	—	—	—	—
57	Goods and services	-70	-147	201	90	-328	-280
58	Goods, services, and remittances	-70	-147	201	90	-328	-280
59	Current account	-204	-302	13	-187	-530	-557
60	Current account and long-term capital[c]	-108	-461	-922	-409	-510	-1,268

[a]Balance of payments by area on the net liquidity basis and the official reserve transactions basis lack validity because liquid dollar holdings of private and official foreigners may be affected not only by their transactions with the United States but also by transactions among themselves. The balances shown by area here have some shortcomings due to statistical discrepancies including errors, ommissions, and incorrect area attributions. The balance on current account and long-term capital with "all areas" includes changes in long-term liabilities to all private foreigners reported by U.S. banks; with "international organizations" includes only liabilities to International Bank for Reconstruction and Development and affiliated organizations; and with other areas includes only liabilities to regional organizations. Increases in the long-term liabilities to other private foreigners included in the total, but not in the areas, amounted to (millions of dollars): 1971 year, 95; 1972 year, 33; 1973 year, 71; 1973-I, 36; 1973-II, 6; 1973-III, 39; 1973-IV, -10; 1974-I, -68.
[b]Adjusted to balance of payments basis; excludes exports under U. S. military agency sales contracts and imports under direct defense expenditures.
[c]Includes some short-term U. S. government assets; area data exclude long-term liabilities reported by U. S. banks other than those to international organizations (see tablenote [a]).
[d]The "European Economic Community (9)," includes the "European Economic Community (6)," the United Kingdom, Denmark, and Ireland.
[e]The "European Economic Community (6)" includes Belgium, France, Germany, Italy, Luxembourg, and the Netherlands.
[f]"Other Western Europe" excludes the United Kingdom and the "EEC (6)" through the fourth quarter of 1972. Beginning in the first quarter of 1973, "Other Western Europe" excludes the "EEC (9)."
[p]Preliminary.
Note: Details may not add to totals because of rounding.
Source: U.S. Department of Commerce, Bureau of Economic Analysis, *Survey of Current Business*, June 1974, p. 58, March 1975, p. 46

As Exhibit 3.1 showed, the United States has a strong net export position in capital goods. This is the type of good one would expect to respond to changes in income promptly. Using the concept of elasticity, one may say that the goods for which the United States has a trade advantage tend to be *income elastic.* Likewise, the goods for which the United States has a strong net import position—industrial supplies—tend to be *income inelastic.*[8] However, the decline in the growth of oil imports while the United States was experiencing a slow-down in 1974 reflects a certain degree of income elasticity for these goods.

A complete analysis of the relationship between national income, or aggregate demand, and foreign trade would require a disaggregation of goods traded between the United States and each of its major trading partners. Short of this analysis one can make some inferences from the information in the preceding two paragraphs on the U. S. trade position with major partners and types of goods traded. For example, other things remaining constant, when the trade partners of a country are in an expansionary phase of their business cycle while the country is experiencing a slow-down in its economy, the balance of trade of this country is likely to improve. The country's exports will increase in response to the higher demand from abroad. Its imports will decrease as national income declines.

Exhibit 3.4 shows comparative rates of change in industrial production (a proxy for change in aggregate demand) for selected developed countries. Different phases in the business cycle are considered to be one of the factors underlying the U. S. balance of trade deficit in 1971 and 1972. During those years the United States was undergoing an expansion while its major trading partners, Western Europe and Japan, experienced a lull in their economies. By 1973 all the major developed economies were in an expansionary stage which reversed itself by 1974 when the rates of change in industrial production became negative.

Other Factors

In addition to the economic considerations mentioned above, there are other elements that affect trade accounts. Among these, tariffs and non-tariff barriers to trade occupy a central position. Though the trend in the postwar period has been towards liberalization of barriers, protectionism is still a strong deterrent to trade. Some of the movements toward liberalization of trade have taken place through the creation of custom unions and free trade areas such as the European Economic Community (EEC) and the European Free Trade Association (EFTA). The entry of the United Kingdom into the EEC in 1973 and the association of other EFTA countries with the EEC promise an eventual total integration of trade policies between

---

[8] More specifically, income elasticity is measured by the percentage change in imports associated with a given percentage change in national income. This is equivalent to the ratio of the marginal propensity to import to the average propensity.

$$\eta Y = \frac{\Delta M}{M} \div \frac{\Delta Y}{Y} = \frac{\Delta M}{\Delta Y} \times \frac{Y}{M} = \frac{\Delta M}{\Delta Y} \div \frac{M}{Y} = \frac{MPM}{APM}$$

where Y =   national income
   M =   imports
   MPM =   marginal propensity to import
   APM =   average propensity to import.

EXHIBIT 3.4 Comparative Rates of Change of Industrial Production, 1968-1975

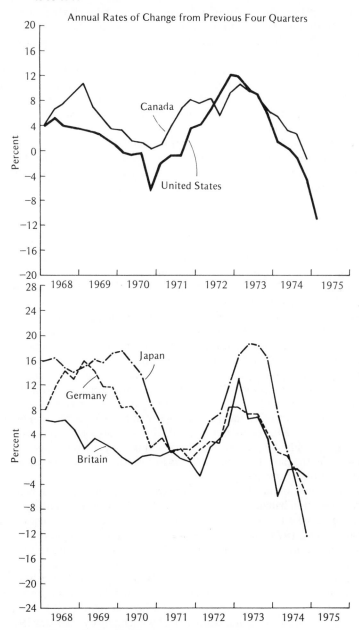

Source: Federal Reserve Bank of St. Louis, *Review,* May 1975, p. 12; compiled from statistics of *Canadian Statistical Review,* The Ministry of Industry, Trade and Commerce; *Industrial Financial Statistics,* IMF; *Economic Trends,* U.K. Central Statistical Office; and the Federal Reserve Board.

EEC and EFTA countries. The recent oil price increases promise either greater integration or a reversion to protectionism, depending on which policies the countries choose in handling the problem. Free trade areas have not achieved much success so far among developing countries.

Another important factor in the trade accounts is provided by the multinational corporation. Companies with a high degree of rationalization in their world production provide continuous trade flows in and out of various countries. These flows accommodate changes in demand throughout the world in general and the production plans of multinational companies in particular.[9]

One more item affecting the trade accounts is "tied" aid. When governmental foreign aid is granted on the condition that funds be used to buy the donor's goods, the export account will benefit unless these exports substitute for exports that would have taken place in any case.

SERVICES

The two major categories in this group of accounts are travel and transportation and income from foreign investment. (See lines 5-6 in Exhibit 2.2.) The travel figure is composed of the expenditures made by tourists visiting a country. Transportation involves passenger fares as well as shipping fees. The income from foreign investment is composed of interest, dividends, investment fees, royalties, and branch earnings (but not reinvested earnings in a subsidiary incorporated abroad). In addition to these transactions, the service accounts include other services such as the fees charged by financial institutions.

The determinants of these accounts are easy to identify. Tourists' expenditures are primarily a function of income. Citizens of rich countries tend to travel abroad more than those of poor countries. Transportation figures are related to the amount of travel in which the country's citizens are involved and to the volume and nature of its merchandise trade. This figure also depends on the transportation facilities that the country possesses. Finally, the returns on foreign investment are a function of investments made in the past. Large investments in foreign assets should produce relatively high investment income in the future.

The service account in the U. S. balance of payments shows a large deficit in the travel and transportation balance for the period 1962-74. However, contrary to statements made to the effect that this account is very insensitive to changes in relative income and prices, 1973 and 1974 witnessed a reversal in the trend towards larger deficits. The deterioration in the value of the U. S. dollar relative to the currencies of most developed countries during the early 1970s, together with the recession at home and the increases in the cost of transportation, reduced U. S. travel abroad and encouraged residents of other countries to visit the United States. For example, 1974 witnessed the first year since 1961 when the number of U. S. visitors to Europe failed to increase, with the figure actually declining by 6% from 1973.

[9] See Raymond Vernon and Louis T. Wells, Jr., *Manager in the International Economy,* 3rd edition (Englewood Cliffs, N.J.: Prentice-Hall, Inc., 1976).

Exhibit 2.2 shows travel and transportation with a deficit of $3.1 billion in 1972 and an estimated deficit for 1974 of only $2.4 billion.

The major source of foreign exchange in the service account of the United States is the income on investments. Although the bulk of the receipts of investment are concentrated on income from direct investment, the payments are mainly for liabilities of a portfolio nature. From 1973 to 1974 the investment income accounts have almost doubled in size. American residents have been repatriating an increasing amount of earnings ($9.4 billion in 1973 and $18.2 billion in 1974) and receiving more income in their portfolio investment abroad. Payments to foreigners also almost doubled between 1973 and 1974 ($8.6 billion in 1973 and $16.3 billion in 1974). This is partly because of the accumulation of U. S. liabilities in foreign hands as a result of protracted past balance of payments deficits.

Another peculiarity of the trade in goods and services of the United States is the large importance of military items. Excluding military grants of goods and services, the United States spent $2.1 billion abroad in 1974 in defense items. Part of this figure represents the cost of U. S. troops in Europe under the NATO agreement.

In terms of the service balances by major areas, Exhibit 3.3 shows a large deficit of the United States with the European countries, and a surplus against almost all other areas, including Canada and Japan. The travel of U. S. residents to Europe, the income European countries receive from their large holdings of U. S. liabilities, and European receipts for NATO forces make the United States a net importer of services from European countries. For the rest of the world the United States is primarily a net exporter of services.

UNILATERAL TRANSFERS

Traditionally, unilateral transfers are separated between those of the government and those of private citizens. Transfers initiated by the government are of two types: military and others. In the case of the United States, both categories play an important role. (Military grants are not included in the U. S. balance of payments account since the grant account is fully compensated in the export account. See line 14 in Exhibit 2.2.)

The nature of private unilateral transfers is very much a function of the immigration profile of the country. Countries that are net "importers" of people, like the United States, have a negative figure in this account. (See line 12 in Exhibit 2.2.) Countries that are net exporters of people (Spain, for example) have a positive figure.

LONG-TERM CAPITAL FLOWS

In the absence of legal restrictions and other barriers, capital tends to flow until its rate of return is equal in all locations. Although other factors must also be considered, economists often think these other factors can be combined into the rate of return. The major types of long-term capital movements are government flows, direct investment, and portfolio investment.

Government Flows

The motivation behind the changes in loans among governments is similar to that behind government grants. Some of these loans are for development projects, others are associated with defense, and others simply reflect the government's foreign policy. Although all of these loans carry interest, not all have a fixed repayment schedule. The U. S. government is traditionally a net lender to other governments. In 1973 it lent a net amount of $2.9 billion to foreign countries. However, in 1974 for the first time in many years, the United States had a net inflow of funds in this account, after taking into account the repayment of debt by foreigners. (See lines 16-18 in Exhibit 2.2.)

Direct Investment

Direct investment, broadly speaking, is the purchase of capital goods in one country by residents of another country when substantial ownership and management are involved. Substantial ownership has been arbitrarily defined as 10% or more. Direct investment takes three different forms: intercompany accounts, equity contributions, and retained earnings. Examples of intercompany transactions are shipment of machinery to a foreign subsidiary or a loan from a subsidiary to the parent company. The purchase of equity is any contribution of capital to a foreign subsidiary as long as the owner possesses more than 10% ownership of the foreign company. Finally, the type of foreign direct investment that does not involve a capital outflow is retained earnings in a foreign subsidiary. It is important to note the different treatment that the United States gives to earnings of foreign branches and subsidiaries. For balance of payments purposes, earnings of foreign branches are treated as declared dividends regardless of whether or not they are sent to the U. S. parent company. However, earnings of foreign subsidiaries do not enter the balance of payments unless repatriated.

The general motivation for international investment is a higher anticipated rate of return in the foreign country than in the home country. A mature country tends to increase its investment abroad as its own stock of capital grows and its rate of return falls relative to other countries. Economists who have found this explanation too general have looked for more specific explanations, such as a cheaper labor or raw material source, or economies of scale in large production units. Some of the factors inducing direct investment are discussed later, in Part Three.

Direct foreign investment of the United States is considerably larger than that of foreigners in this country. However, 1973 and 1974 have witnessed an increase in direct investment by foreigners in the United States. (See lines 20-21 in Exhibit 2.2.) Most of these investments are in subsidiaries incorporated in the recipient country rather than branches. (See Exhibit 3.5.) Of the funds invested in foreign subsidiaries, about half were in intercompany accounts and the other half new equity contributions other than retained earnings.

U. S. foreign direct investment tends to be cocyclical. It increases during domestic expansions and decreases during domestic contractions. From 1965 through 1973 these investments were affected by the controls on foreign direct investment imposed by the U. S. government. These controls were imposed initially

EXHIBIT 3.5   Direct Investment and Securities Transactions, 1969-74 (millions of dollars)

Line	(Credits+; debits–)	1969	1970	1971	1972	1973	1974
1	U. S. direct investments abroad (Exhibit 2.2, line 20)	−3,254	−4,400	−4,765	−3,517	−4,872	−7,268
2	Transactions with foreign incorporated affiliates	−2,987	−3,541	−3,677	−2,201	−3,549	−5,736
3	Intercompany accounts: short-term	−203	−691	−1,132	−200	−1,719	−3,705
4	long-term	⁻573	−278	−586	−55	−30	−238
5	Capital stock and other equity, net	−2,099	−2,339	−1,932	−1,890	−1,771	−1,793
6	Increase[a]	−2,407	−2,666	−2,310	−2,376	−2,637	−2,391
7	Decrease[b]	308	327	378	486	866	598
8	Miscellaneous[c]	−112	−233	−27	−55	−28	——
9	Branch accounts	−267	−859	−1,088	−1,317	−1,324	−1,532
	By industry of foreign affiliate[d]						
10	Mining and smelting	−76	−383	−519	−382	−201	——
11	Petroleum	−934	−1,460	−1,940	−1,603	−1,417	−971
12	Manufacturing	−1,164	−1,295	−1,468	−1,100	−1,820	−2,712
13	Other	−1,080	−1,262	−837	−433	−1,434	−3,585
14	Foreign direct investments in the United States (Exhibit 2.2, line 21)	832	1,030	−67	383	2,537	2,224
15	Transactions with U. S. incorporated affiliates	794	994	−153	306	2,305	1,915
16	Intercompany accounts	273	206	−384	−384	818	540
17	Capital stock and other equity, net	521	788	232	690	1,487	1,375
18	Increase[a]	538	796	255	773	1,537	1,477
19	Decrease[b]	−17	−8	−23	−84	−50	−102
20	Branch accounts	38	36	86	77	232	308
21	Of which: manufacturing affiliates[d]	567	545	231	192	725	1,009

[a]Acquisition of capital stock of existing and newly established companies, capitalization of intercompany accounts, and other equity contributions.

[b]Sales and liquidations of capital stock and other equity holdings, total and partial.

[c]Includes security issues placed with outside interests in the United States, the amortization of these security issues, and verified transactions of non-reporters not classified by type of transaction.

[d]Mining and smelting includes the exploration and development of mining properties, the extraction of raw ores and the processing necessary for basic refined metals. Petroleum includes the exploration, development, and production of crude oil and gas, and the transportation, refining, and marketing of petroleum products exclusive of petrochemicals. Manufacturing excludes petroleum refining and the smelting operations of mining companies. "Other" industries includes all industries except those previously listed, the major ones being agriculture, public utilities, transportation, trade, insurance, finance, and services. For 1974, "Other" also includes mining and smelting.

Source: U. S. Department of Commerce, Bureau of Economic Analysis, *Survey of Current Business*, various issues.

on a voluntary basis, but became mandatory from 1968 through 1973; although some reporting requirements remain, the controls were terminated for all intents and purposes in January 1974.

Portfolio Investment

Portfolio investment involves claims among nations in the form of stocks, bonds, and long-term loans provided the investor does not hold a controlling interest in the foreign company (10% according to U.S. regulations).

The most important factors affecting the behavior of long-term portfolio investments are the levels of interest rates and the expected performances of stock prices in the countries involved. Since the return on foreign securities has to be measured in terms of local currency, the exchange risk of currencies involved also plays an important role. Foreign stocks and bonds are usually exposed to exchange risk. A devaluation in the foreign currency vis-à-vis the local currency will reduce return to the investor. In cases of devaluation-prone currencies, the nominal yield on the investment has to be high enough to compensate for the potential devaluation.

Other factors also affect the relative rate of return on foreign investments. These factors are policies on taxation and regulations that affect foreign investment in particular. The best example is the withholding tax levied by most countries on dividends and interest paid to foreigners. These withholding taxes differ among countries and, in addition, are subject to variations according to special bilateral agreements between particular countries. Other regulations imposed on foreign investments are designed to control them because of balance of payments reasons or nationalistic considerations. Two examples are the former interest equalization tax of the United States and the bardepot tax in Germany during the 1960s and early 1970s. The interest equalization tax was an attempt to deter capital outflows resulting from foreigners borrowing at lower rates in the U. S. market, which caused a drain on U. S. foreign reserves. Any U. S. holder of a foreign security was subject to a tax on the income from the security. To remain competitive, borrowers would have had to pay a very high interest rate to compensate the security holder for the tax (s)he had to pay. The bardepot tax was designed to accomplish the opposite, to deter foreigners from investing in German securities; such investment would create a capital inflow, further increasing the level of foreign reserves. In this case the German government imposed special charges on any foreign funds brought into the country. Both these taxes were almost totally eliminated in January 1974.

Exhibit 2.2 (lines 22-25) showed the long-term portfolio investment in securities between the United States and the rest of the world. Since 1967, purchase of U. S. long-term securities by foreigners has been considerably larger than the purchase of foreign securities by U. S. residents, a situation that contrasts with the earlier 1960s. However, in 1974 the purchase of U. S. securities by foreigners declined substantially. The leveling-off of U. S. purchases of foreign securities was greatly influenced by the U. S. interest equalization tax. The increase in foreigners' purchase of U. S. securities has followed the fluctuations in the U. S. stock market. In 1967 when this market peaked, so did foreign purchases of U. S. securities. The decline in foreigners' purchases of U. S. securities between 1969 and 1971 and in 1974 was affected by the increased risk of devaluation that foreigners attached to the the U. S. dollar. As foreign exchange risk decreased, 1972 and 1973 saw a renewed interest in the U. S. market. For the whole period, interest rates in the United States have been among the lowest in the developed countries, as shown in Exhibit 3.6.

EXHIBIT 3.6   Comparative Government Bond Yields, 1966-1974

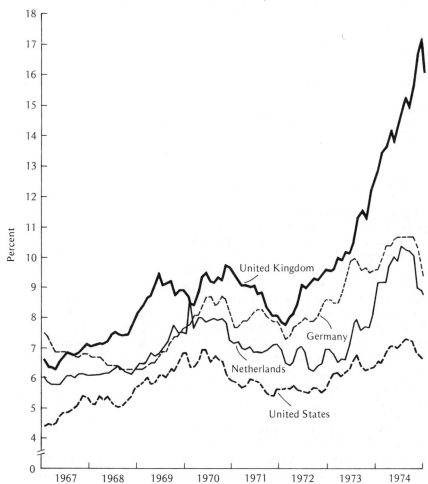

Source: Federal Reserve Bank of St. Louis, *U. S. Balance of Payments Trends,*
April 24, 1975.

SHORT-TERM CAPITAL FLOWS

Short-term capital flows represent claims of less than one-year maturity. The classification is on the basis of the instrument rather than on the intentions of the investor. The instruments usually are bank deposits and currency, short-term government securities (although the United States also considers its long-term treasury securities held by foreigners as a liquid liability), commercial paper, export loans, and bankers' acceptances.

Short-term capital flows can be subdivided according to the motivation behind them into three categories: trade capital, flows on a covered basis (arbitrage), and speculative flows.

Trade Capital

All trade transactions are associated with a capital movement, most of them of a short-term nature. When an exporter sells merchandise, (s)he either gets paid immediately, in which case demand deposits (usually in the foreign currency) increase. (S)he may extend credit in the form of accounts receivable or a banker's acceptance. So whenever the level ot exports of a country increase, short-term claims on foreigners are likely to increase.

Flows on a Covered Basis (Arbitrage)

Capital movements due to interest differentials have the sole purpose of earning a higher yield in one country than is possible in another. If the investor is not interested in speculating on the value of the currency at the time the security matures, (s)he covers the investment against possible exchange loss by an offsetting transaction in the future or forward market.[10] So, the yield comparison is based on the yields net of the cost of covering in the forward market. Obviously, the yields being compared must be for securities with the same risk in each country involved—usually treasury bills and bankers' acceptances. The incentive for short-term capital to flow to the country with the highest yield will last only until the discount in the forward market increases enough to compensate for the interest rate differential. The discount in the forward rate will take place in response to increased sales of the currency in that market to cover the transaction of repatriating the investment. When the forward discount is equal to the interest rate differential, there is no advantage in moving hedged funds to the high-interest-rate money market.

To the extent that an efficient market exists in the currencies involved, the opportunities for realizing a gain in covered foreign investment are small and, by and large, short-lived. In the cases where the apparent opportunities persist for a long time, i.e., interest differentials not compensated for in the forward market, these are usually due to governmental controls that impede the free flow of capital in and out of the country, in which case the opportunity for gain exists only to a limited degree.

Speculative Flows

Speculative capital movements take place when exchange risks are deliberately undertaken in conjunction with the capital movement. Speculative flows fall into four major groups:

[10] In the case of a U.S. investor who buys a three-month security in Germany in search of a higher interest rate, (s)he will "cover" the transaction by selling deutsche marks for dollars for delivery at the end of the three months at a prearranged exchange rate, thus "freezing in" the amount of dollars (s)he will receive for the deutsche marks when the security matures. This topic will be discussed in detail in Chapter 5.

1. *Flows in the search of higher yield in another currency without foreign exchange.* These flows are undertaken on the assumption that the exchange rate will remain fairly constant so the higher yield can be converted back into the local currency without much loss in foreign exchange. Governments which increase their discount rate in the hope of attracting short-term capital flows to help their balance of payments position do this in the expectation that individuals are willing to take a speculative position.

2. *Flows in response to temporary fluctuations in a foreign exchange rate which is expected to go back to its normal level.* In this situation capital inflows will take place in a country with a temporary balance of payments deficit. A temporary balance of payments deficit will produce a small downward pressure in the exchange rate. If this is considered to be only temporary it will attract capital flows to take advantage of the expected increase in the exchange rate. The opposite is true in the case of a temporary balance of payments surplus. Both these movements are stabilizing; they help to correct the balance of payments disequilibrium.

3. *Capital flows in anticipation of a permanent movement in the exchange rate.* In this case capital will flow into the currencies that are expected to be upvalued and away from currencies expected to be devalued. If a balance of payments surplus is expected to lead to an upvaluation, capital inflows will take place in that country. If a deficit in the balance of payments is expected to lead to the devaluation of the currency, capital outflows will take place. In contrast with the second type of speculative capital flow, this type is destabilizing.

4. *Speculative flows associated with trade, usually known as "leads and lags."* If a currency is expected to appreciate in value, foreigners making payments in that currency will accelerate payment of their obligations in that currency (*a lead*). Likewise, if a currency is under pressure, foreigners making payments in that currency will delay payment as long as possible (*a lag*).

Short-term capital movements are the hardest to measure. Particularly in periods of heavy foreign exchange speculation, many end up in the all-encompassing category "errors and omissions." In the sections of the balance of payments discussed earlier, the analysis was simplified as the nature of the flow was properly identified. Once the level of exports, for example, was identified, it was explained in terms of alternative variables. In the case of short-term capital movements, however, the analysis is more difficult. The nature of the capital flow must be derived from the attending circumstances. That is, capital flows in response to trade and capital flows initiated by other considerations are not properly segregated. The problem is not a trivial one since the impact on the future of the country's balance of payments and its foreign exchange rate is completely different depending on the nature of the short-term capital flow. Trade capital is stable; speculative flows can be not only highly unstable but also cumulative and subversive to the foreign exchange rate of the country's currency.

Exhibit 3.7 shows all the short-term capital accounts for the United States regardless of the definition of deficit. The exhibit presents all the changes in claims

EXHIBIT 3.7 United States Short-Term Capital Flows, 1962–1974 (millions of dollars, yearly changes in accounts)

(+ = decrease in claims or increase in liabilities, a source of funds)
(− = increase in claims or decrease in liabilities, a use of funds)

	1962	1963	1964	1965	1966	1967	1968	1969	1970	1971	1972	1973	1974
Claims													
Nonliquid													
United States banks	−358	−747	−1333	−200	−220	−645	−44	−658	−1023	−1802	−1457	−3940	−12,223
Nonbanking institutions	187	−198	−422	−103	−180	−376	−485	−73	−361	−530	−305	−1240	−2,453
Liquid													
United States banks	34	−34	−191	525	136	−85	−61	−209	−99	−586	−742	−1103	−5,445
Nonbanking institutions	−35	193	−201	532	−150	−122	−497	371	351	−531	−505	−841	−19
Allocation of Special Drawing Rights									867	717	710		
U.S. official reserve assets	1533	377	171	1222	568	52	−880	−1187	2477	2348	32	209	−1,434
Total change in claims on foreigners	987	−409	−1976	1976	154	−1176	−1967	−1756	2212	−384	−2267	−6915	−21,574
Liabilities													
Nonliquid liabilities													
Reported by nonbanking institutions	−112	−23	113	149	296	499	759	91	902	−15	221	904	1,721
Reported by U.S. Government	199	−125	139	123	15	452	1806	−162	535	341	189	−475	655
Liquid liabilities													
Liabilities to private	215	620	1654	131	2384	1472	3810	8658	−6240	−6691	4749	4246	15,732
Liabilities to official agencies													
Liquid	918	1673	1075	−18	−1595	2020	−3101	−554	7637	27615	9734	4452	8,253
Marketable	—	9	149	−38	793	894	534	−836	−810	−551	399	1118	596
Total change in liabilities to foreigners	1220	2154	3130	347	1893	5337	3808	7197	2024	20699	15292	10245	26,957
Net known short-term capital flows	2207	1745	1154	2323	2047	4161	1841	5441	4236	20315	13025	3330	5,383
Errors and omissions, net	−1179	−418	−978	−494	64	−439	94	−1805	−458	−9776	−1790	−2303	5,197
Balance on current account and long-term capital	−1028	−1327	−176	−1829	−2111	−3722	−1935	−3636	−3778	−10539	−11235	−1026	−10,580

Source: Exhibit 2.2

on foreigners, including changes in reserve assets, in the upper section. The lower section of the exhibit shows the changes in liabilities of the United States to foreigners. Finally, the line for "errors and omissions" is included as if it were composed mostly of short-term capital flows. If so interpreted, this account shows a steady increase in holdings of short-term foreign assets until 1973. However, in 1974 a surprising large positive "errors and omissions" for the first time in the recent past appeared. The algebraic sum of the changes in claims, plus changes in liabilities, plus errors and omissions, produces the same amount as the "balance on current account and long-term capital" (except for rounding errors).

The major reason behind the increase in claims of the United States on foreigners since 1964 is the Voluntary Credit Restraint Program initiated in 1965 to curtail the credit extended from the United States to foreigners. In 1971 a modification in this program exempted loans to foreigners associated with U. S. exports and the loan figure increased for the first time in seven years. In early 1974 the Voluntary Credit Restraint Program was eliminated altogether and the claims of the United States on foreigners soared. A world in dear need for credit to pay for oil imports provided the other element in the substantial lending of the United States to foreigners that year.

The account of U. S. official reserves is truly a compensating item and reflects more than any other account the "deficits" in the U. S. balance of payments. With the exception of 1968, 1969, and 1974, the United States decreased the level of its reserve assets in all years in the exhibit. The exceptions for 1968 and 1969 are partly due to the efforts to defend the U. S. dollar during periods of heavy speculation on an upvaluation of the deutsche mark and a devaluation of the French franc against the U. S. dollar. The increase in reserves during 1974 was largely due to special international agreements with the International Monetary Fund (IMF, which is discussed in the following chapter). Foreign countries borrowed substantial amounts in U. S. dollars from that institution in 1974 and this entitled the United States under the present agreement to increase its unconditional borrowing rights from the IMF. These borrowing rights are considered part of reserves.

The allocation of Special Drawing Rights was the result of an international agreement to provide world liquidity. This is explained further in the next chapter.

The changes in liabilities of the United States are more telling of the nature of international capital flows that prevailed during the 1962-74 period. In every year there was an increase in the liabilities of the United States to foreigners. These increases were kept under $3 billion until 1966, but they acquired very large proportions in the subsequent years and reached unparalleled magnitudes in 1971 and 1974. In analyzing the composition of the liabilities to foreigners, the most notable fact is the very large increase in liabilities to official agencies at the expense of the private sector during 1970-71. As the U. S. dollar came under increased attack during those years, the private sector sold its dollar-denominated assets to the public sector. It is to be noted that the errors and omissions account, with the exception of 1974, is almost a mirror image of the changes in liabilities account although at a lower level. The positive "errors and omissions" for 1974 may be associated with a reflux of unrecorded capital outflows during the preceding years, 1971 in particular (a record-high errors and omissions of −$10 billion).

Two factors can be used to explain the behavior of short-term flows: (1) the strength of the dollar against other currencies, and (2) the relative levels of interest rates. As shown in some examples above, the relative strength of the dollar finds a one-to-one correspondence with the fluctuations in short-term capital flows. Almost

EXHIBIT 3.8   Comparative 3-Month Interest Rates, 1971-1974

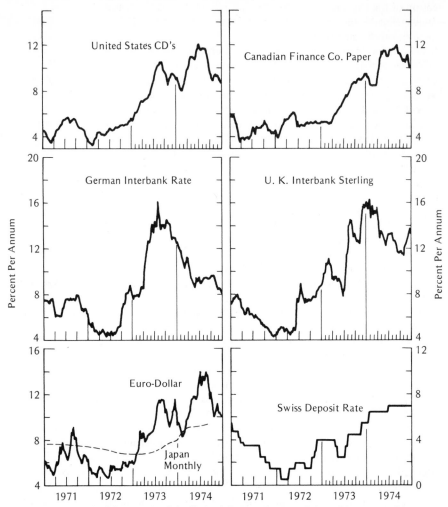

Source: Board of Governors of the Federal Reserve System, *Selected Interest and Exchange Rates*, December 2, 1974 and June 2, 1975.

every time the U. S. dollar has weakened in the foreign exchange markets, the liabilities of the United States and the "errors and omissions" (indicating an acquisition of foreign assets by Americans) have increased almost commensurately. Exhibit 3.8 shows that overall the United States has maintained lower interest rates than most of the other developed countries with the exception of Switzerland, particularly in 1971 and 1972. On the basis of relative interest rates alone, there was an incentive for investing in currencies other than the U. S. dollar. So if one must choose which is the autonomous transaction, acquiring foreign assets or borrowing from foreigners, then acquiring foreign assets makes more sense in economic terms.

Financing vs. Autonomous Cash Flows

So far we have discussed the various categories of short-term cash flows reported in the U. S. balance of payments and offered some heuristic explanation of the variables that contribute to understanding the behavior of these accounts. However, still to be considered is the distinction between autonomous and compensating transactions. To the degree that short-term capital flows are of a financing or compensating nature, we have a barometer of the pressures being built towards a change in the value of the currency in question relative to other currencies. For example, if autonomous transactions produced a deficit, then the short-term capital accounts will have to change to finance this deficit. In this case the financing will take the shape of either a decrease in reserves or an increase in borrowings from foreigners. If reserves continue to decrease and liabilities to foreigners continue to increase, pressures to devalue the currency in question relative to other currencies will mount. On the other hand, if the deficit in autonomous transactions excluding short-term capital accounts is compensated by an autonomous surplus in the short-term capital accounts, there will not be any pressure for the value of the currency to change. This will be the case if the liabilities that the country issued were desired by foreigners as financial investments in their own right. Foreigners might want to hold those financial assets, the liabilities of the country in question, if they thought that the foreign exchange rate would remain constant and that the interest rates and/or liquidity of the securities issued by the given country were higher than what foreign investors could obtain elsewhere. Alternatively, foreigners would want to hold the securities issued by that country, regardless of the yield, if they were expecting the value of the currency in which the securities are denominated to appreciate relative to other currencies.

If we analyze the figures in Exhibit 3.7, we see that the balance of what may be called autonomous transactions excluding short-term capital flows, the balance on current account and long-term capital, has been in a deficit position consistently through the period. This deficit reached astronomical proportions in 1971-72 and in 1974.

What about the variables which an investor would study before purchasing a financial asset: relative interest rates and foreign exchange risk? As shown before, the interest rates in the United States have tended to be among the lowest in the world (Exhibit 3.8). It is true that the liquidity offered by the money markets in the United States is unparalleled in any other financial market. This fact was actually used by Professor Kindleberger during the 1960s to argue that the increment in the U. S. liabilities to foreigners was of an autonomous nature.[11] Foreigners were willing to sell long-term financial assets to Americans (foreign direct investment by Americans abroad) in exchange for the short-term securities that the U. S. financial markets had to offer. From this point of view, the U. S. balance of payments was in balance. If short-term capital outflows are considered autonomous, these flows compensate for the deficits in the basic balance. However, the liquidity of the U. S. financial market notwithstanding, as the deficits in the basic balance of the United States mounted, many of the securities issues by the United

---

[11] Charles P. Kindleberger, "Equilibrium in the Balance of Payments," *Journal of Political Economy*, December 1969.

States must have become less and less desirable to hold as the possibilities of a dollar devaluation increased. The shift in foreign-owned U. S. securities from private to official hands in 1970 and 1971 has to be interpreted as the decision of investors not to hold U. S. dollar denominated securities any longer in contemplation of an imminent devaluation of the U. S. dollar relative to other currencies. Exhibit 3.9 shows that such fears were amply justified by the successive events that brought

EXHIBIT 3.9   Nominal and Effective Dollar Devaluation

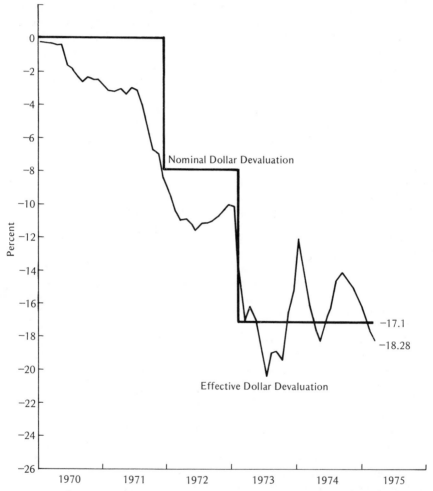

Note: Nominal devaluation is measured by the change in the dollar price of gold. Effective devaluation is measured by the appreciation of eleven major currencies relative to the par values which prevailed as of May 1970. The appreciation is then weighted by separate export and import shares with the United States based on 1972 trade data.

Latest data plotted: March

Source: Federal Reserve Bank of St. Louis, *U. S. Balance of Payments Trends,* April 24, 1975; compiled from data of the IMF and the Federal Reserve Bank of New York.

down the relative value of the U. S. dollar. Obviously, to the extent that investors anticipated the devaluation and sold their dollar denominated financial assets, they created additional pressures in the foreign exchange market to bring about the forecast devaluation. The only way to reduce the possession of dollar denominated assets is to change the denomination of such assets. For example, exchange U. S. dollar deposits for deutsche mark deposits. In the exchange market, this means an · increase both in the supply of dollars and in the demand for deutsche marks. Other things equal, these pressures will tend to decrease the value of the U. S. dollar relative to the deutsche mark.

Thus we can say that, particularly during the 1970s, speculation on the U. S. dollar's value and relative interest rates reinforced one another to induce capital flows out of the U. S. dollar and into other currencies. Because of the reserve currency status of the U. S. dollar, the United States was able to finance the deficit in the autonomous accounts by issuing more liabilities on itself.

Notice that this avenue of issuing liabilities to finance balance of payments deficits is open only to reserve-currency countries; only they can issue liabilities (financial assets) that creditors consider to be foreign exchange reserves. Other countries must reduce foreign exchange reserves to finance a deficit in the autonomous accounts of the balance of payments. Even for a country like the United States, one must examine the ability of the country to continue issuing liabilities upon itself before the foreign exchange market decides to penalize the value of the currency. For a developing country, the ability to issue liabilities is much more limited. In these cases, an evaluation of the size of the country's reserves relative to its needs is essential to forecasting the future exchange rate of the currency in question.

The above discussion of reserve assets is of great importance in a system of fixed exchange rates where the government is responsible for maintaining the external value of its currency. In such a system, the government exercises its responsibilities by accumulating reserves when it has a surplus in the balance of payments and selling reserves when it has a deficit. In a system of floating rates, market forces determine the external value of the currency, so the government does not have to accumulate reserves to defend the value of the currency when the value is under attack. The international monetary system in operation since 1973 reflects more a system of floating rates than one of fixed rates. These issues are explained in the following chapter.

THE BALANCE OF INDEBTEDNESS

While the *balance of payments* measures the *flows* of economic transactions that take place between the residents of a given country and the rest of the world, the *balance of indebtedness* measures the *levels of assets and liabilities* that the country has vis-à-vis the rest of the world. That is, the changes occurring between two balances of indebtedness drawn at two different points in time are measured by the balance of payments for the period.

The emphasis in the analysis of the international value of a country's currency has been centered around the balance of payments. However, it stands to reason that the two figures, the balance of payments and the balance of indebtedness, should be analyzed in conjunction. Although it is true that a business would go

EXHIBIT 3.10 International Investment Position of the United States at Year-end (millions of dollars)

Line	Type of Investment	Total				Western Europe		Canada		Japan[c]		Latin American Republics and Other Western Hemisphere		Other Foreign Countries[c]		International Organizations and Unallocated	
		1960	1971	1972	1973	1972	1973	1972	1973	1972	1973	1972	1973	1972	1973	1972	1973
1	Net international investment position of the United States	44,718	57,668	51,224	63,005	−37,801	−45,559	29,382	32,501	−11,548	−2,278	23,501	25,631	29,868	33,367	17,821	19,342
2	U.S. assets abroad	85,577	180,790	200,596	226,132	50,908	58,925	44,138	47,328	9,843	12,255	34,241	38,440	40,202	45,907	21,265	23,277
3	Nonliquid assets	66,218	164,659	181,813	204,177	48,584	56,321	42,490	45,520	9,233	11,023	33,262	36,959	39,800	45,438	8,355	8,907
4	U.S. Government	16,908	34,165	36,135	38,835	7,915	8,089	78	142	900	639	7,099	7,587	18,656	20,732	1,488	1,646
5	Long-term credits: Repayable in dollars[a]	14,016	25,593	28,444	30,650	6,919	7,124	75	140	762	554	6,398	6,896	12,808	14,294	1,483	1,641
6	Other[b]		6,183	5,697	5,571	849	842			94	40	654	651	4,099	4,038		
7	Foreign currencies and other short-term assets	2,892	2,389	1,994	2,614	147	123	3	2	44	45	47	40	1,749	2,400	5	5
8	Private, long-term	44,497	115,867	128,975	143,459	37,062	43,546	41,143	43,940	4,311	4,373	21,154	23,029	18,438	21,310	6,867	7,261
9	Direct investments abroad	31,865	86,198	94,337	107,268	30,817	37,218	25,771	28,055	2,375	2,733	16,798	18,452	13,833	15,493	4,743	5,317
10	Foreign securities: Foreign bonds	5,574	14,654	15,866	16,633	478	461	9,531	10,032	258	247	1,151	1,210	2,324	2,739	2,124	1,944
11	Foreign corporate stocks	3,984	7,050	9,049	8,538	3,329	3,163	4,136	3,967	1,188	1,003	141	151	255	254		
12	Other claims, reported by U.S. banks	1,608	3,647	5,029	5,862	803	959	406	489	353	247	2,016	2,076	1,451	2,091		
13	Other claims, reported by U.S. nonbanking concerns[d]	1,376	4,318	4,694	5,158	1,635	1,745	1,219	1,397	137	143	1,048	1,140	575	733		
14	Private, short-term nonliquid	4,813	14,627	16,703	21,883	3,607	4,686	1,269	1,447	4,022	6,011	5,009	6,343	2,796	3,396		
15	Claims, reported by U.S. banks	3,594	10,872	12,355	16,295	1,891	2,447	814	948	3,686	5,469	4,015	5,005	1,949	2,426		
16	Claims, reported by U.S. nonbanking concerns	1,219	3,755	4,348	5,588	1,716	2,239	455	499	336	542	994	1,338	847	970		
17	Liquid assets	19,359	16,131	18,783	21,955	2,324	2,604	1,648	1,799	610	1,232	979	1,481	312	469	12,910	14,370
18	Private	(e)	3,964	5,632	7,577	2,084	2,597	1,648	1,799	609	1,231	979	1,481	312	469		
19	Claims, reported by U.S. banks	(e)	2,400	3,321	4,424	1,086	1,431	1,100	1,012	466	931	468	856	201	194		

58

EXHIBIT 3.10 International Investment Position of the United States at Year-end (millions of dollars) (cont.)

Line	Type of Investment	Total 1960	Total 1971	Total 1972	Total 1973	Western Europe 1972	Western Europe 1973	Canada 1972	Canada 1973	Japan[c] 1972	Japan[c] 1973	Latin American Republics and Other Western Hemisphere 1972	Latin American Republics and Other Western Hemisphere 1973	Other Foreign Countries[c] 1972	Other Foreign Countries[c] 1973	International Organizations and Unallocated 1972	International Organizations and Unallocated 1973
20	Claims, reported by U.S. nonbanking concerns	(e)	1,564	2,311	3,153	998	1,166	548	787	143	300	511	625	111	275		
21	U.S. monetary reserve assets	19,359	12,167	f13,151	f14,378	240	7			1	1					12,910	14,370
22	Gold	17,804	10,206	f10,487	f11,652											10,487	11,652
23	SDR		1,100	f1,958	f2,166											1,958	2,166
24	Convertible currencies			241	8	240	7			1	1						
25	Gold tranche position in IMF	1,555	585	f465	f552											465	552
26	U.S. liabilities to foreigners	40,859	123,122	149,372	163,127	88,709	104,484	14,756	14,827	21,391	14,533	10,740	12,809	10,334	12,540	3,444	3,935
27	Nonliquid, liabilities to other than foreign official agencies	19,830	55,275	66,454	70,497	48,123	49,300	7,891	7,843	903	2,258	4,783	4,838	2,449	3,953	2,307	2,306
28	U.S. Government[g]	793	1,548	1,786	2,910	1,307	1,619	31	18	19	328	2	56	428	889		
29	Private, long-term	18,418	49,792	60,177	62,193	43,906	44,486	7,612	7,542	667	1,633	4,150	3,972	1,536	2,255	2,307	2,306
30	Direct investments in the United States	6,910	13,655	14,263	17,748	10,516	12,159	3,422	4,003	−129	307	309	424	146	856		
31	U.S. securities: Corporate and other bonds	649	8,647	10,939	11,938	8,780	9,552	375	414	58	177	273	337	33	24	1,420	1,434
32	Corporate stocks	9,302	21,429	27,827	24,843	19,722	17,851	3,598	2,833	254	644	2,822	2,263	1,040	881	391	321
33	Other liabilities, reported by U.S. banks	7	758	925	1,177	258	277	1	9	1	4	132	217	37	119		
34	Other liabilities, reported by U.S. nonbanking concerns	1,550	5,303	6,223	6,487	4,630	4,647	216	233	483	501	614	731	280	375	496	551
35	Private, short-term nonliquid, reported by U.S. nonbanking concerns	619	3,935	4,491	5,394	2,910	3,195	248	283	217	297	631	810	485	809		

EXHIBIT 3.10 International Investment Position of the United States at Year-end (millions of dollars) (cont.)

Line	Type of Investment	Total				Western Europe		Canada		Japan[c]		Latin American Republics and Other Western Hemisphere		Other Foreign Countries[c]		International Organizations and Unallocated	
		1960	1971	1972	1973	1972	1973	1972	1973	1972	1973	1972	1973	1972	1973	1972	1973
36	Liquid liabilities to private foreigners and liquid, other readily marketable, and nonliquid liabilities to foreign official agencies	21,029	67,847	82,918	92,630	40,586	55,184	6,865	6,984	20,488	12,275	5,957	7,971	7,885	8,587	1,137	1,629
37	To private foreigners	9,139	16,613	21,362	25,798	6,359	9,445	2,586	3,131	n.s.s.	n.s.s.	4,222	5,420	n.s.s.	n.s.s.	1,137	1,629
38	To foreign commercial banks[h]	4,818	10,949	14,665	17,643	5,047	7,816	2,024	2,439	n.s.s.	n.s.s.	1,374	2,066	n.s.s.	n.s.s.		
39	To international and regional organizations	1,541	1,523	1,627	2,003	10	7			n.s.s.	n.s.s.	334	318	n.s.s.	n.s.s.	1,137	1,629
40	To other foreigners	2,780	4,141	5,070	6,152	1,302	1,622	562	692	n.s.s.	n.s.s.	2,514	3,036	n.s.s.	n.s.s.		
41	To foreign official agencies	11,890	51,234	61,556	66,832	34,227	45,739	4,279	3,853	n.s.s.	n.s.s.	1,735	2,551	n.s.s.	n.s.s.		
42	Liquid	11,888	47,610	57,344	61,939	33,533	45,047	1,439	1,313	n.s.s.	n.s.s.	1,735	2,551	n.s.s.	n.s.s.		
43	Other readily marketable		144	543	1,661												
44	Nonliquid, reported by U.S. Government[g]	2	3,480	3,669	3,232	694	692	2,840	2,540	n.s.s.		n.s.s.		n.s.s.			

[a] Also includes paid-in capital subscription to international financial institutions (other than IMF) and outstanding amounts of miscellaneous claims which have been settled through international agreements to be payable to the U.S. government over periods in excess of 1 year. Excludes World War I debts that are not being serviced.

[b] Includes indebtedness which the borrower may contractually, or at its option, repay with its currency, with a third country's currency, or by delivery of materials or transfer of services.

[c] The Ryukyu Islands are included with Japan in 1972; in previous periods they are included with other foreign countries.

[d] The long-term position data given here include estimates for real estate, insurance, estates, and trusts.

[e] Liquid claims are not available separately and are included with nonliquid claims.

[f] Total reserve assets include increases from changes in the par value of the dollar, as officially implemented; on May 8, 1972, the increase totalled $1,016 million, consisting of $28 million gold stock, $155 million SDR, and $33 million gold tranche position in IMF; and on October 18, 1973, the increase was $1,436 million, consisting of $1,165 million gold stock, $217 million SDR, and $54 million gold tranche position in IMF.

[g] U.S. Government liabilities are broken down into those to foreign official reserve agencies in line 44 and those to others in line 28, including foreign official agencies other than reserve agencies.

[h] As reported by U.S. banks; ultimate ownership is not identified.

Note: Details may not add to totals because of rounding or because certain items cannot be shown separately.

n.s.s. = Not sufficient statistics.

bankrupt for lack of liquidity or inability to pay its current debts, it is also true that continuous deficits in operations can be sustained for a much longer period when the business has a large equity base.

Exhibit 3.10 presents the international investment position of the United States, the balance of indebtedness. The United States has a large surplus of assets over liabilities in its accounts with the rest of the world. However, this surplus has tended to erode during the period covered by the exhibit. An upturn from this downward trend appeared in 1973. Exhibit 3.10 also shows that although only 10% of its assets abroad were in liquid form in 1973, 57% of its liabilities to foreigners had a maturity of less than a year. This fact points to the concern for liquidity in the U. S. balance of payments.

Many of the changes in international exchange arrangements in the last decade will be discussed in the next chapter, together with a review of proposals currently under study.

Exercise on Forecasting the Balance of Payments of the United States

Collect the latest data on the U. S. balance of payments. This can be found in *Survey of Current Business* published by the Department of Commerce in March, June, September, and December.

Collect data on the variables relevant to explain the behavior of the various accounts in the balance of payments. Some possible sources are the following:

Department of Commerce, *Survey of Current Business,* special articles balance of indebtedness (October issue), and international economic indicators.

Morgan Guaranty Trust Company, *World Financial Markets,* monthly issues

Various Federal Reserve Banks, *Monthly Bulletins,* and special weekly reports

Board of Governors of the Federal Reserve System, *Monthly Bulletin* and *Weekly Report on Exchange Markets*

International Monetary Fund, *International Financial Statistics* and *Balance of Payments Yearbook* (pages for major trade partners of the United States)

OECD, *World Trade Statistics*

The Economist (weekly magazine)

The London Financial Times (daily newspaper)

For each account in the balance of payments, do the following:

1. Describe its behavior
   a. Performance over the last decade and recently, e.g., fast growth with large fluctuations
   b. Composition of account, e.g., types of goods traded
   c. Countries participating in the account, e.g., to whom does the United States export goods?
2. Why did the account behave in that way?
   a. What factors determine the performance of the account? e.g., foreign income
   b. How did these factors behave during the period analyzed? e.g., foreign income grew less fast than in the U. S.
3. How do you expect these accounts to behave in the future?

Bibliography

Balassa, Bela, "The Purchasing-Power Parity Doctrine: A Re-Appraisal," *Journal of Political Economy,* 72 (1964) pp. 584-596.

Caves, Richard E. and Ronald W. Jones, *World Trade and Payments*. Boston: Little, Brown and Company, 1973.

Gailliot, Henry J., "Purchasing Power Parity as an Explanation of Long-Term Changes in Exchange Rates," *Journal of Money, Credit and Banking*, Aug. 1970, pp. 348-357.

Gray, H. Peter and Gail E. Makinen, "Balance of Payments Contributions of Multinational Corporations," *Journal of Business*, July 1967, pp. 339-343.

Heller, H. Robert, *International Monetary Economics*. Englewood Cliffs, N.J.: Prentice-Hall, Inc., 1974.

Kindleberger, Charles P., *International Economics*. Homewood, Ill.: Richard D. Irwin, Inc., 1973.

Vernon, Raymond, "A Skeptic Looks at the Balance of Payments," *Foreign Policy,* Winter 1971-1972, pp. 52-65.

Vernon, Raymond and Louis T. Wells, Jr., *Manager in the International Economy,* 3rd Edition. Englewood Cliffs, N.J.: Prentice-Hall, Inc., 1976.

Walter, Ingo, *International Economics.* New York: The Ronald Press, 1968.

Ward, Richard, *International Finance*. Englewood Cliffs, N.J.: Prentice-Hall, Inc., 1965.

Appendix: Checklist for Evaluating the External Position of a Developed Country

A. Environmental and policy factors
  1. Political situation
     a. Goals of ruling party
     b. Permanency of present party. Upcoming elections?
  2. Institutional relationships
     a. Power of central bank to enforce monetary policy
     b. Use of fiscal policy
     c. Relationship between government, financial institutions, and business
  3. Industrial characteristics
     a. Major raw materials
     b. Major outputs
  4. Economic conditions
     a. Unemployment and industrial capacity utilization
     b. Inflation rate
     c. Economic growth: income, industrial production
     d. Currency exchange rate
  5. Government appraisal of economic conditions: to the extent that choices must be made in selecting desired objectives, which ones are likely to be the government preferences? e.g., reduce inflation rate or reduce unemployment?
  6. What tools is government likely to use to achieve goals?
     a. Monetary policy
     b. Fiscal policy
B. Trade account: Exports and imports
  1. Product composition - price and income elasticity
  2. Trade partners
  3. Relative prices
     a. Consumer demand relative to supply
     b. Wages
        (1) Labor organization
        (2) Unemployment rate
        (3) Future labor demands, strikes?
     c. Productivity
        (1) Technological developments
        (2) Labor skills
        (3) Capital investments
     d. Government policy

   (1) Expansionary vs. contractionary
   (2) Importance of the export lobby
   (3) Export subsidies
 4. Relative incomes
   a. Growth in national income
     (1) Consumption
     (2) Investment
     (3) Government expenditure
   b. Distribution of income-consumption patterns
   c. Government policy
 5. Trade barriers
C. Service account
 1. Any important item?
 2. Why?
 3. Permanency
D. Unilateral transfers
 1. Is it important?
 2. Will it continue?
E. Long-term capital accounts
 1. Countries involved
 2. Direct investment
   a. Need for raw materials
   b. Product cycle
 3. Portfolio investment
   a. Stock market performance
   b. Long-term interest rates
   c. Economic outlook for profits
   d. Demand for funds: private and public
   e. Monetary policy: money supply and interest rates
   f. Savings patterns: sectoral financing
   g. Controls on international capital flows
F. Short-term capital accounts
 1. Countries involved
 2. Trade-associated flows
 3. Monetary policy, money supply, and interest rates
 4. Need for funds: private and public
 5. Flows in speculation of foreign exchange parities
 6. Savings patterns: sectoral financing
 7. Controls on international capital flows
G. Reserves
 1. Involuntary changes resulting from changes in previous accounts
 2. Voluntary changes due to government intervention to support foreign
    exchange values.
 3. How long can they continue doing it?
   a. Reserve levels and borrowing power
   b. Economic consequences

Appendix: Checklist for Evaluating a Developing Country[12]

Size	Population
	GNP
Development	GNP/capita
	Percent GNP from industry
	Percent population in agriculture
Growth	Real growth per capita
	Trend
	Industrial growth
Potential	Investment ratio
	Minerals
U. S. Involvement	Percent with U. S. (imports, exports)
	U. S. investment
Political	Stability
	Relations with U. S.
Ability to Generate Foreign Exchange	Export/import ratio
	Expected trend of export/import ratio
	Percent major market(s)
	Balance of goods, services, and transfers
	Major factors in balance of payments
	Foreign aid
External Debt Reserves	Reserves
	Reserves, months of imports
	Net foreign assets
	Total external debt
	Debt servicing ratio
	Debt servicing trend
	Structure of debt
Financial Management	Budget revenues,
	Current expenditures
	Investment budget
	Plan

[12] This list was prepared by Mr. Antoine W. van Agtmael, Vice President, Bankers Trust, New York.

CHAPTER 4

How Do You Repair the Balance of Payments?

As economic pressures start to build up imbalances in the external position of a country, an outlet for these forces must be found. Two roads are available: (1) an adjustment in the exchange rate to compensate for the imbalances or (2) a taming of the initial economic pressures through explicit governmental economic policies or through automatic economic mechanisms. The adjustment in the exchange rate can take place automatically under the gold standard or a flexible rate system. Alternatively, the exchange rate may be altered by decree under a system of fixed rates. Taming the economic forces that lead to external imbalances will require the employment of specific government economic policies. Some abatement of the initial forces will take place naturally under automatic adjustment mechanisms based on price and income changes.

Each strategy or combination of strategies will have a different impact on the exchange market and the domestic economy. Therefore, there will be varying impacts upon individuals operating in various capacities in the international markets. For example, a multinational corporation which borrows funds denominated in Swiss francs but which does not have any other business operation in that currency has a very clear preference for how Switzerland should handle any pressure for the Swiss franc to appreciate against other currencies. Since this firm has no other operations in Swiss francs, it cannot generate Swiss francs to pay the debt except by converting another currency, say U. S. dollars, into Swiss francs. If Switzerland chooses to let the exchange rate reflect built-up pressures and the Swiss franc appreciates relative to other currencies, the multinational company will have to use more U. S. dollars to pay the debt. If, on the other hand, Switzerland chooses to resist the pressures for an appreciation of the Swiss franc and instead allows domestic prices to increase, the multinational company would not be affected. It would pay back the same amount of U. S. dollars as the Swiss francs were worth when the loan was received. Thus, there is a premium not only in assessing the pressures that will develop in the balance of payments, which is to say in the foreign exchange markets, but also in forecasting how economic authorities will handle the problem. This chapter presents the alternatives available and the trade-offs that government authorities have to make in choosing a course of action when problems emerge in the external balance of the country.

AUTOMATIC MECHANISMS

These automatic mechanisms operate through certain economic relationships which have at their core two variables: prices and income.

Price Mechanism

This mechanism works through changes in interest rates and commodity prices. In the case of a deficit in the balance of payments, money tends to flow from the deficit to the surplus country to finance the deficit. Unless the central bank acts to counteract these flows, money supply in the deficit country will contract, putting upward pressure on interest rates. In the surplus country, the money supply will increase and dampen interest rates. The new relative yields will encourage capital flows toward the deficit country and away from the surplus country, helping to bring the payments back into balance.

The price mechanism also operates through changes in quantities demanded and supplied. A deficit in the balance of payments caused by an excess of imports over exports implies an increase in demand for the products of the surplus country and a decrease in demand for the products of the deficit country. To the extent that prices are flexible, the increase in demand will cause prices in the surplus country to rise. Meanwhile, the decline in demand in the deficit country will push prices down. This change in relative prices will tend to restore the balance in the balance of payments by stimulating the demand for the products of the deficit country (which has lower prices now) and curbing the demand for the products of the surplus country (where prices have increased).

Whether these tendencies are sufficient to correct the original imbalances depends on the responsiveness of quantity demanded to changes in prices, i.e., the price elasticity of demand for imports. If these elasticities are high, a successful adjustment process is guaranteed. There will be a large increase in the exports of the deficit country and in the imports of the surplus country. However, if the price elasticities are low, the tendencies would be insufficient to adjust the balance of payments deficit. If the sum of the two countries' respective price elasticities of demand for imports exceeds one, the price adjustment will work. This is known as the Marshall-Lerner condition.[1]

[1] In cases where the supply elasticities in the countries involved are very low (i.e., a given increase in demand can be met only by a very large increase in prices or a given change in price produces a very small change in quantity supplied), the price adjustment process could work even if the sum of the price elasticity of demand for imports were less than one. The Marshall-Lerner condition is sufficient to guarantee the operation of the price adjustment; it is not necessary. A. Marshall, *The Pure Theory of Foreign Trade* (London: The London School of Economics and Political Science, 1930). Abba Lerner, *The Economics of Control* (New York: Macmillan Co., 1946).

Income Mechanism

The income adjustment works through the relationship between imports and income, and through the relationship between domestic investment and interest rates. An increase in national expenditures automatically becomes income to the various factors of production—labor, capital, entrepreneurship, and land. When these factors of production spend their increased income, there is a secondary increase in national income and the income-expenditure-income cycle continues. However, each time that the cycle is repeated the increments in income are smaller. This is because there are two major leakages in the system: savings and imports. When consumers have an increase in their income, they do not spend all of it—part of it is saved. Of that part of income that is spent, not all of it is spent in the domestic market—part is spent in foreign markets in the form of imports. This tends to produce a balance of trade deficit, other things remaining equal.

The income changes in the first country affect other countries. An increase in one country's imports is tantamount to an increase in another country's exports. This has an expansionary effect in the exporting country's economy, including secondary income effects. As a result, there is an increase in imports in the second country. This will affect the initial country which finds its exports increasing, thus compensating its initial tendency to a balance of trade deficit. The final outcome for the two balances of payments depends on the size of the "leakages" (savings and imports) in each country.

The other way in which the income change contributes to the restoration of equilibrium in the balance of payments is through the impact of changes in interest rates on domestic investment in real assets. Investment in assets such as plant and equipment is considered to be an inverse function of the level of interest rates. As interest rates in a deficit country start to increase because capital is being exported, investment in real assets will tend to decrease. So will national income and imports. The reverse occurs in the surplus country where the decline in interest rates produces an increase in investment in real assets and, therefore, in national income and imports. When these two forces are combined, the decrease in imports in the deficit country and the increase in imports in the surplus country contribute to balance the country's external accounts.

INTERNATIONAL MONETARY ARRANGEMENTS

As long as the balances of payments of the countries in the world remain in balance, the exchange rates among currencies can be considered adequate. However, when balance of payments deficits and surpluses develop around the world, it becomes necessary to correct the condition. Through history, countries have agreed on certain prescriptions to bring equilibrium into their balances of payments. These can be classified into two groups: (1) those that rely to a large extent on automatic mechanisms—the gold standard and flexible rates and (2) those that rely on government policy—the fixed rates system.

The Gold Standard

Under this system, international settlements of payments imbalances are made exclusively in gold, and domestic money supply is tied to the amount of gold the country possesses. Foreign exchange (key currencies such as the U. S. dollar) is excluded from international reserves. The exchange rate for each currency is fixed in terms of gold into which each currency is fully convertible. In the case of a balance of payments deficit, a gold outflow will take place to finance the external deficit. This would produce, in succession: a contraction in the domestic money supply, an increase in interest rates, a decrease in investment, a decrease in income, and a decrease in prices. As a result, capital inflows will take place in response to the higher interest rates; imports will decrease because of the reduction in income and the increase in foreign prices; and exports will increase because of the increase in foreign income and decrease in domestic prices. The opposite forces would be at work in the surplus country. After a while the balance of payments equilibrium would be restored.

In the preceding adjustment of the balance of payments disequilibrium, note that the burden of the adjustment is carried by the domestic economy. It is expected that the domestic economy will expand and contract, with the associated employment and inflation rates, in response to changes in the external balance. In addition, the rules of the game prescribe that monetary policy should not be used to offset gold flows. Governments are expected to sit quietly while the economy goes through a period of high unemployment to reduce incomes and adjust a balance of payments deficit, or a period of high inflation to adjust a balance of payments surplus.

The gold standard was implemented to some extent before the first World War and during the interwar period, 1925-31. Its proponents exalt the virtues of leaving the adjustment process to automatic forces instead of to the hands of policymakers. In addition, sole reliance on gold for international payments has the additional advantage that all currencies are the same and no country has to incur a deficit to provide the world with its currency, and therefore liquidity. This is usually the argument raised in the context of the present situation, in which the U. S. dollar is an international currency. Before 1971, when the role of the U. S. dollar as the world's reserve currency was not even contested by any other currency, countries had to possess additional dollars to meet the needs of an expanding world trade. This could be accomplished only by deficits in the U. S. balance of payments. Gold advocates point to this fact as a potential source of inflationary pressures when reserve-currency countries implement expansionary policies.

Opponents of the gold standard, when confronted with the above list of its virtues, mention that the independence from reserve-currency countries' economic policies is gained only at the expense of putting the system at the mercy of natural resources instead. Gold supplies certainly would not be responsive to the world needs for liquidity. In addition, the discipline imposed by this standard on domestic economies is not feasible politically. Today's governments are held responsible for maintaining full employment and reasonable growth in an environment of price stability.

Flexible Exchange Rates

This system, like the gold standard, relies on automatic mechanisms to adjust disequilibria in the balance of payments. Unlike the gold standard, however, flexible exchange rates do not require the domestic economy to carry the burden of the adjustment. Adjustments in the balance of payments are made through changes in the price of foreign exchange.

If a country has a balance of payments deficit, the supply of its currency to foreigners will exceed their demand for it. Alternatively, the country's demand for foreign exchange will exceed the supply of foreign exchange. The result of such tendencies will be to lower the price of the domestic currency in terms of foreign exchange, or, what is the same thing, increase the price of foreign exchange in terms of the local currency. That is, the currency of the deficit country depreciates in value, and the currency of the surplus country appreciates.

A reduction of the value of the local currency in terms of foreign exchange means that domestic goods become cheaper to foreigners, and foreign goods become more expensive to domestic consumers. Such changes in prices will tend to increase the country's exports and decrease its imports. This will help to restore equilibrium to the balance of payments. However, the extent to which this restoration is achieved depends on the responsiveness of imports and exports to price changes. As stated before in the discussion of the price adjustment mechanism, if the sum of the price elasticities of demand for imports of the countries involved exceeds one, the price adjustment will be successful.[2]

Before 1973, the system of flexible exchange rates had been implemented only occasionally, when the value of a particular currency was allowed to float. That occurred for the Canadian dollar between 1950 and 1961 and since 1971, and for the British pound since June 1972. However, since 1973 several major currencies have joined the list of "floating currencies." But the currencies have not always been allowed to float completely freely. Governments have intervened frequently to maintain orderly markets and often to support the external value of their currencies—the so-called "dirty" or managed floating. Surplus countries such as Germany have been more successful in restraining themselves from intervening in the foreign exchange market.

The greatest benefit of flexible exchange rates, its proponents argue, is that the adjustment of balance of payments disequilibria can be done with very little sacrifice of the domestic economy. Most of the burden is carried by changes in the exchange rate. Therefore, domestic economic policy can be shielded from the problems of the balance of payments; i.e., domestic policy can be implemented with little regard for its impact on the balance of payments. However, the danger of making the exchange rate one of the economic targets is always present. This is particularly so where the export sector is a substantial part of the economy. In addition, one can argue that the adjustments carried out by the exchange market, such as induced capital flows, will clearly have repercussions in the domestic economy with which policy makers will have to contend.

Critics of the flexible exchange rate system believe that the exchange rates under a pure version of this system would be highly unstable. As a result, the risk

___

[2] It should also be recalled that if supply price elasticities are low, a sum of import demand elasticities of less than one would be sufficient.

of operating in the foreign exchange market would rise and international trade and capital movements would be deterred. Defenders of flexible exchange rates contend that there is no reason to suspect that this would be the case. Fluctuations in the exchange rate would reflect basic economic conditions which are not unstable by definition. The evidence for 1973-75 is one of sizable fluctuations with decreasing amplitudes.

The predicted volatility in exchange rates is based on the potentially erratic short-term capital flows that might occur under a system of flexible rates. Real or imaginary changes in political and economic factors, the opponents of flexible rate contend, would find a large response in short-term capital movements. The response usually made to this argument is that there is no reason why well-informed speculators should generate destabilizing speculation that would work against their own interests.

The issue of low elasticities in demand for imports, which will make price adjustments ineffective, remains an untested question. Empirical data has tended to support the view that import price elasticities are low. However, these studies have been full of statistical problems. One of the bases on which they have been contested is that these studies measure short-term responses only; in the long-term these elasticities are probably much higher. This point is supported by the analysis of price changes and the U. S. trade accounts in the preceding chapter.

Fixed Rates: The Bretton Woods System

The monetary system that prevailed in the postwar period through 1971 was initiated in 1944 at Bretton Woods, New Hampshire. It was a system of fixed exchange rates based on a modified gold standard. In addition to gold, international reserves in this system included foreign currencies and the right to borrow from an institution created by the system and still alive—the International Monetary Fund (IMF).

The resources of the IMF are composed of money received from member countries. These resources constitute a pool which participant countries can draw upon during short-term balance of payments difficulties. Each country's contribution to IMF resources is determined by its "quota." A country's quota must be deposited in the IMF 25% in gold and 75% in its own currency. Up to the amount of the gold subscription, countries have an absolute claim on the IMF, i.e., they can draw this amount from the IMF at any time: this is called the *gold tranche position* and is counted among the countries' reserves. Beyond this point a country can draw upon its *credit tranche*—the additional credit the IMF can grant.[3] However, approval from the IMF is necessary for a country to draw on its *credit tranche*. This approval is usually accompanied by restrictions which become increasingly tight as the drawings on this credit rise. Approval from the IMF used to be required to alter the "par value" of a currency; this has not been the case since 1973 when major currencies joined in the present system of "managed floats."

In this monetary system the foreign exchange rate for each currency was initially fixed in terms of its par value vis-à-vis the U. S. dollar or gold. The value of the U. S. dollar, however, was defined in terms of gold only. The market exchange

---

[3] The *credit tranche* is the amount of drawings beyond the gold tranche that would bring the Fund's total holdings of that currency to 200% of quota.

rate for each currency was allowed under the IMF rules to fluctuate only within a narrow margin around the par value of the currency. When the exchange rate of a currency approached the limits of the band within which it was allowed to fluctuate, the country was expected to intervene in the foreign exchange market by buying or selling the given currency. When the market stepped up the volume of the given currency offered for sale, thus putting downward pressure on the foreign exchange rate of that currency, the monetary authorities of that country were expected to buy the currency by offering other foreign exchange in return. Similarly, when market forces indicated upward pressure on the value of the currency, the monetary authorities were expected to offer more currency for sale in return for other foreign exchange. That is, fixed rates in this system were maintained by monetary authorities using the official reserves of a country as a buffer against market fluctuations.

In this system of adjusting short-term imbalances in the external accounts, a country with a deficit in its balance of payments lost foreign reserves; a country with a surplus in its international accounts accumulated foreign reserves. However, if the imbalance in payments persisted over a long term, this short-term method of adjustment became ineffective. It was certainly not available to the deficit country (which might run out of reserves), and it was very undesirable to the surplus country (which accumulated an excessive amount of low-return assets). At this point the system offered two avenues to correct a disequilibrium in the balance of payments. In the case of a deficit, a country could choose either to deflate the domestic economy or to devalue its currency. In the case of a balance of payments surplus, a country could choose either to inflate the domestic economy or upvalue its currency. In either case, the corrective mechanism was operated at the discretion of the country with the imbalance.

If a country with a deficit in its balance of payments chose to correct its imbalance through adjustments in the domestic economy, it would apply measures similar to the ones that would occur automatically under the gold standard. The difference here is that the changes would take place according to an explicit government policy instead of an automatic mechanism. The government could use either monetary policy or fiscal policy, or both, to accomplish its objectives.

The problems with using special policies to correct a balance of payments disequilibrium arose when the measures required to improve the balance of payments ran counter to measures that domestic objectives would indicate. For example, it is easier to conceive of a deliberate deflation of the economy when the balance of payments deficit is accompanied by an overheated economy than when the economy is in a recession. The other avenue open to a government to correct a continuous imbalance of payments in this system was to change the foreign exchange rate of its currency: devaluation for a country with continuous deficits in the balance of payments, upvaluation for a country with continuous surpluses. The adjustment mechanism here was similar to that under flexible exchange rates. It worked through a change in price and it avoided adjusting the domestic economy. However, in this case the mechanism did not work automatically but was manipulated by the government like any other policy instrument. Its success, however, depended on the same conditions as the success of the flexible exchange rate system: a certain degree of price elasticity must exist in the demand for imports in the country involved.

Historically, the difficulty with relying on governmental decisions to change the foreign exchange parity of currencies has been the reluctance of governments to take such steps. For surplus countries, an upvaluation of their currencies has exposed their governments to the wrath of the export industry and of labor in general. For deficit countries, a devaluation has been considered a loss of international economic power. In addition, the Bretton Woods system appeared to impose the burdens of adjustment in a biased fashion. Surplus countries were under less pressure to correct their imbalances than deficit countries. The accumulation of reserves in the surplus countries failed to induce any sense of urgency in the need to correct the imbalance, for excessive reserves only have an opportunity cost. And, while deficit countries had to ask for the collaboration of the IMF to continue borrowing from it, little pressure would be applied by the IMF on a surplus country which chose neither to adjust its domestic economy nor to upvalue its currency. When the surplus countries refused to carry their part of the adjustment burden, the total adjustment process had to be carried by the deficit country alone, making the required deflation or devaluation in that country larger than if the adjustment process had been shared by the surplus country.

During the first twenty-five years of the Bretton Woods system, the tendency was for countries to try to defend their exchange rates through adjustments in the domestic economy, and to use changes in the exchange rate only as a last resort measure. England was a classical example in the 1960s, for its "stop-go" policies delayed the devaluation of the pound for four years at a very high cost to domestic objectives. Since 1971, however, there appears to have been a change in attitudes of participants in the system. Countries, including the United States, appear to be more willing to use the devaluation route than to sacrifice their domestic economies. The British pound, which was allowed to float in the exchange market in June 1972, while its foreign reserves were at record heights, provides an example of the new tendencies in the system. The larger number of floating currencies in subsequent years indicates that fixed rates as envisaged by the Bretton Woods system might not be seen again for a while.

NEW APPROACHES

New approaches have addressed three major problems of the Bretton Woods system: (1) difficulties in achieving adjustment of persistent imbalances in the payments positions of individual countries; (2) continuous deficits in the U. S. balance of payments necessary to meet demands for liquidity for an increasing volume of international transactions; and (3) severe periods of crisis resulting in a lack of confidence in reserve media. These problems obviously are interrelated. The slower the adjustment mechanism, the higher the volume of liquidity required, and vice versa. The higher the amount of liquidity available to the country, the easier it is for the adjustment mechanism to operate without creating problems of confidence.

In recent years there have been four major changes in the international monetary system: the introduction of Special Drawing Rights (SDRs), the Smithsonian Agreement on December 18, 1971, the establishment of the European monetary union, and the abandonment of fixed rates of European currencies vis-a-vis the U. S. dollar. There are a number of people who think that further changes are required; such proposals for change can be grouped between those which give more flexibility to the system (wider bands, crawling pegs, or crawling bands) and those that would entail complete departures from the present system.

Reforms to the Bretton Woods System

Special Drawing Rights. The machinery of SDR creation was activated on August 6, 1969, when the required majority of IMF members became participants in the SDR system. SDRs are international paper money created and distributed by the IMF in the quantities and at the times dictated by special agreements among member countries. This paper money is used only in transactions among governments and between the IMF and these governments. The first allocation was made in January 1970, with the creation of $3.5 billion for that year. Another $3 billion was allocated at the beginning of each of the two following years. No allocations were made for 1973-75.

Allocations of SDRs are made for "basic periods" normally five years in duration, and they are allocated to IMF members on the basis of IMF quotas at a uniform rate throughout the "basic period." The amount of SDRs allocated at any time is intended to meet a long-term global need for liquidity, and not the requirements of specific participants. The decision to allocate SDRs must be approved by a majority of the IMF participating countries with 85% of the weighted voting power of the Fund.

When a participating member receives an allocation of SDRs, it is not required to deposit an equivalent amount of gold or currency for the purpose of any subsequent transaction, as it must when drawing on its IMF borrowing rights. SDRs are a permanent addition to the stock of international liquidity. Countries are expected to maintain a balanced relationship between their holdings of SDRs on one hand, and their holdings of gold, foreign exchange, and IMF borrowing rights on the other.

SDRs were initially expressed in terms of a fixed amount of gold, equivalent to the gold content of the U. S. dollar. In June 1974, the value of SDRs was redefined and tied to the value of sixteen major currencies. The value of each of the currencies in the "basket" is weighted according to the country's participation in world trade, subject to some modifications. This new approach to the valuation of SDRs created a relatively stable measure of value in a time when the values of independent currencies were fluctuating widely in the foreign exchange market. As a result, many participants in the international financial markets who were looking for some stability in the value of international financial transactions began to use the SDR as a unit of account. In 1975 the first Euro-bond denominated in SDRs was issued. In addition, the ministers of the Organization of Petroleum Exporting Countries (OPEC) agreed to price oil in SDRs effective October 1, 1975. Also in 1975, Saudi Arabia, Iran, and Burma decided to state the value of their currencies in terms of SDRs.

The Smithsonian Agreement. On December 18, 1971, the Group of Ten nations agreed on a new set of parity rates (called *central rates* because they lacked the approval of the IMF). The U. S. dollar was still defined in terms of gold (although not convertible into gold) and the other currencies were defined in terms of either the U. S. dollar or gold. This followed a period after August 15 of the same year when all major currencies had been allowed to float in the exchange markets and the U. S. dollar's convertibility into gold was suspended.

In addition to the new set of central rates, two new features were introduced in the system. Currencies were allowed to fluctuate over a band wider than the past,

2.25% on either side of the central rate, without requiring government intervention. Previously, a currency had been allowed to fluctuate only within a margin of 1% (¾% in practice) on either side of par value. Under the new band, a currency could fluctuate 4.5% from floor to ceiling with reference to the U. S. dollar. This implied that a currency could fluctuate by as much as 9% against a currency other than the U. S. dollar. That would be the case if before the change occurred one of the currencies was at the lower limit against the U. S. dollar and another currency was at the upper limit. If they reversed positions completely, each currency would have changed by 4.5% against the dollar and by 9% against one another. This was expected to make speculation more expensive and to reduce the amount of control on the foreign exchange that a government would have to exert. The other feature of this agreement was the end of convertibility of the U. S. dollar into gold. Contrary to the previous twenty-five years, the United States refused to return to the convertibility into gold suspended the previous August 15. The United States required additional trade concessions before discussing convertibility. The need for a reform in the system was apparent and a committee of twenty nations was created to draft a proposal for a new system.

The European Monetary Union. The members of the European Common Market[4] agreed in early 1972 to keep their currencies fluctuating within a band narrower than the one allowed by the IMF. When the agreement was reached in 1972, the EEC countries, the United Kingdom, and Denmark agreed to allow their currencies to fluctuate only a maximum of 2.25% among themselves. However, the group as a whole could fluctuate against other currencies within the larger band provided by the Smithsonian Agreement. This created what has been called a "snake within a tunnel." The snake was the narrower band allowed among the EEC currencies; the tunnel was the wider band allowed by the Smithsonian Agreement.

The Events of March 1973. 1973 opened with the enlargement of the European Common Market to include the United Kingdom, Ireland, and Denmark. This was followed by a series of international monetary crises during the first quarter that led to a devaluation of the U. S. dollar in February, the floating of several other currency rates, and the elimination of the "tunnel" binding the "snake" created by the European monetary union. In mid-March, after a couple of weeks when the values of all the major currencies were allowed to fluctuate according to market forces, the foreign exchange market opened again with a new set of rules. The European currencies participating in the narrow margins of the European monetary union were to continue maintaining the parities with small fluctuations among themselves. However, all the currencies as a group were to be allowed to fluctuate in value with regard to the U. S. dollar according to market forces. But the range of the power of market forces was to be limited by the intervention of the monetary authorities in the foreign exchange market to maintain the range of the "floating" within certain, not specified, limits.

Subsequent Developments. Attempts to maintain the European monetary union have continued, and the original participants have been joined by non-EEC mem-

---

[4] The initial European Common Market included France, West Germany, Italy, Belgium, Luxembourg, and the Netherlands.

bers such as Sweden. However, participant countries have allowed the value of their currencies to float from time to time outside the limits imposed by the monetary union. In some cases the floating period has been brief and the currency has reentered the monetary agreement at a new rate established during the floating period, e.g., the Dutch guilder in September 1973. In other cases the floating period has been protracted, e.g., the pound sterling.

The floating of the European currencies as a group against the U. S. dollar (the agreement of March 1973) allowed a large upvaluation of the European currencies against the U. S. dollar in the summer of 1973. These forces tended to abate towards the end of that year, but started anew in 1974.

In June 1974, proposals for a reform in the international monetary system abounded, but no agreement among the members of the Group of Twenty, created in December 1971, appeared possible. As a result, the Group of Twenty disbanded and transferred its assignment to the IMF, with no permanent monetary system in sight.[5]

The build-up of funds in the hands of oil-producing nations as a result of the increase in oil prices added additional difficulties to the task of developing a workable new international monetary system. A special $3 billion IMF fund to help countries whose balances of payments were especially disrupted by the increase in oil prices was created in June 1974. An additional $6 billion was added in 1975. This was based on funds from the Arab nations, but with the IMF guaranteeing payment of principal and interest, thus easing the recycling problem of the oil producers. The lenders receive 7¼% with the borrowers paying an average of 7¾%. Higher rates are applied to loans of a longer maturity. Objecting to this insurance of the oil rich by the oil poor, the United States successfully argued for the members of the Organization for Economic Cooperation and Development (OECD) to make contributions to a $25 billion "safety net" to be made available to the oil-importing countries of the OECD.

Proposals for Additional Flexibility

Three proposals have been made to provide greater flexibility in the adjustment of the exchange rate: a wider band, a crawling peg, and a crawling band.

A Wider Band. This has been implemented by the Smithsonian Agreement. Instead of the 1% fluctuations around par value initially allowed by the Bretton Woods Agreement, the Smithsonian Agreement approved a band of 4.5%. Proponents of a wider band would prefer to see the band expanded to 10% at least. The objective is to retain some of the discipline that can be expected of a system of fixed exchange rates, while achieving the greater freedom and smoother adjustment process of more flexible rates.

Like flexible exchange rates, a wider band would permit the monetary authorities greater freedom to pursue independent monetary policies, and a greater scope for short-term intervention in the exchange market. The misgivings about the system are the same ones raised against a system of flexible rates. In addition, there is the question of how wide the band should be.

[5] An excellent review of the period 1973-74 can be found in Marina v. N. Whitman, "The Payments Adjustment Process and the Exchange Rate Regime: What Have We Learned," *American Economic Review*, May 1975.

The Crawling Peg. This proposal would provide for regular revision of each exchange rate according to an agreed formula. Under this system any parity change
would be implemented slowly, making the adjustment process continuous for all
practical purposes. This proposal would provide reasonably stable exchange rates
for those who consider this stability necessary for international transactions, while
also establishing a smooth adjustment mechanism. This is the Bretton Woods system except that under that system the change in the pegged rates has been used
only as a weapon of last resort. The changes have been made infrequently and by
large amounts. Smaller, more frequent adjustments in the pegged rate would avoid
the currency crises that have characterized the Bretton Woods system, would give a
larger scope to monetary policy for domestic purposes, and would reduce the incentives for countries to impose controls to delay a change in a foreign exchange
rate which is eventually inevitable. The major criticisms of this system are that it
would not secure a major adjustment with much rapidity and that it would remove
the discipline from the monetary authorities to control inflation. Brazil has used
this system for the last few years while the rate of inflation has been reduced.

The Crawling Band. This proposal combines the wider band and the crawling peg.
It provides that each parity could be revised upward or downward as a moving
average of the actual exchange rates that could fluctuate within a wider band. The
wider the range of a band, the smaller the size of crawling of the peg necessary.
However, the wider the range of a band, the greater the degree of allowable fluctuations and uncertainty. On the other hand, the narrower the range of a band, the
more reserves a country would require to support its exchange rate within limits.
Therefore, a way should be found to strike the proper balance between the conflicting interests. Economists have suggested a crawling band with 4% or 5% band
range and 1% or 2% yearly crawling.

Other Proposals

These other proposals are based on a system of fixed exchange rates. They
focus either on extending the reserve currency system or creating some supranational institution that would centralize the management of international reserves.

The proposals concerning an extension of the reserve-currency system suggest
the enlargement of the number of reserve currencies to include other currencies
in addition to the dollar and the pound sterling. It is expected that this would
spread the reserve-currency burden more evenly and render the monetary system
less vulnerable to attack. In a way, this proposal changes the dependency on balance of payments deficits for world liquidity from one country, the United States,
to a group of countries. This proposal is hardly a long-term solution to the present
problems.

There have been several proposals for the creation of a supranational institution
to manage the international monetary system. The earliest one of these proposals
was by John Maynard Keynes in 1944, who proposed the creation of an International Clearing Union which would have the power to create an international money,
bancor. The value of gold and each national currency would be fixed in terms of
bancors. In addition, each country would agree to accept bancors for settlements of
international payments on a par with gold. A country in deficit could borrow

bancors to finance the deficit. Deficit countries would transfer bancors to the surplus countries. As the bancor balance of the deficit countries approached depletion while the balance of the surplus countries continued to increase, there would be a penalty imposed on both the surplus and the deficit countries to encourage both countries to restore payments balance. The Clearing Union would control the volume of liquidity in the system by its management of the bancor overdraft account. Adjustment through the exchange rate would be allowed when circumstances warranted it.

Other proposals presented by Robert Triffin, Maxwell Stamp, Edward M. Bernstein, and others run along the lines of the Keynes plan.[6] They try to improve upon several of its characteristics, especially the mechanism by which liquidity is created in the system.

For the immediate future, managed floating is likely to continue. The term *dirty floating* is actually a misnomer, for what is involved is a form of controlled floating. Whatever chances a pure floating exchange system had prior to the OPEC actions, they were reduced to zero with that embargo, for large amounts of loose funds in the hands of a few individuals strengthens the arguments that central banks should not permit their currencies to fall to unreasonable levels in the face of purely speculative demands for funds. In the end, there will probably be international agreements on when intervention will occur, such as with the conferences among authorities from central banks of various nations who meet almost daily under the umbrella of the Bank for International Settlements.[7] These agreements may be on an *ad hoc* basis, so there will not be the formal "rules" such as a crawling band, crawling peg, or some other variant. However, it will mean that intervention will be sanctioned by international agreement and that a true float will not exist. On the other hand, such an intervention would be seen as following agreement on the specifics of that case, as opposed to fixed rate systems where intervention is expected (and required) as part of the agreement to keep currencies within certain parities.

Questions

1. At the end of the preceding chapter you were asked to analyze the current U. S. balance of payments. In light of recent events in the international financial

[6] Robert G. Hawkins, ed., *Compendium of Plans for International Monetary Reform,* New York University, Graduate School of Business Administration, C.J. Devine Institute of Finance, *The Bulletin,* Nos. 37-38, December 1965.

[7] The Bank for International Settlements (BIS) was created after the second World War to facilitate the transfer of funds among countries whose currencies were not then convertible into one another in Europe. Since free convertibility was established for most of these currencies in the late 1950s, the major function of the BIS became providing a forum for the monetary authorities of various countries to meet and exchange ideas.

markets, what is your forecast for the future value of the U. S. dollar relative to other major currencies within a year? In five years?

2. What changes would you make in the present international monetary system? Why?

3. What changes in the present international monetary system do you consider *likely* to occur in the near future? Why?

4. What role will the U. S. dollar play in international financial markets in the future? Why?

Bibliography

Ando, Albert, Richard Herring, and Richard Marston, eds., *International Aspects of Stabilization Policies.* Proceedings of a Conference at Williamstown, Massachusetts, June 1974, sponsored by the Federal Reserve Bank of Boston and the International Seminar in Public Economics. Boston: The Federal Reserve Bank of Boston, 1974.

Bhagwati, J. and A. Krueger, "Exchange Control, Liberalization, and Economic Development," *American Economic Review,* May 1973, pp. 419-427.

de Vries, Tom, *An Agenda for Monetary Reform.* International Finance Section, Department of Economics, Princeton University, Princeton, N. J., *Essays in International Finance,* No. 95, September 1972.

Hawkins, Robert G. and Sidney E. Rolfe, *A Critical Survey of Plans for International Monetary Reform.* New York University, Graduate School of Business Administration, C. J. Devine Institute of Finance, *The Bulletin,* No. 36, November 1965.

Hufbauer, G. C. and F. M. Adler, *Overseas Manufacturing Investments and the Balance of Payments.* U. S. Treasury Tax Policy Research Study No. 1,. Washington, D. C.: U. S. Government Printing Office, 1968.

Johnson, Harry G., *The Problem of International Monetary Reform.* University of London: Athlone Press, 1974.

Johnson, Harry G. and John E. Nash, *U. K. and Floating Exchange: A Debate on the Theoretical and Practical Implications.* London, Institute of Economic Affairs, 1969 (Hobart papers, 46).

Kindleberger, Charles P., *Europe and the Dollar.* Cambridge, Mass.: M.I.T. Press, 1966.

Kindleberger, Charles P., *International Economics,* 5th ed. Homewood, Ill.: Richard D. Irwin, Inc., 1973.

Polk, Judd, *et al., U. S. Production Abroad and the Balance of Payments.* New York: The Conference Board, 1966.

Triffin, Robert, *Our International Monetary System: Yesterday, Today, and Tomorrow.* New York: Random House, Inc., 1968.

Britannic International Shipping Limited [c]

On March 25, 1969, the Board of Directors of Britannic International Ship-ping, Limited (BIS) decided to increase their shipping business in crude oil cargo, and to acquire a VLCC (Very Large Crude Carrier), popularly called a "super-tanker." BIS had been considering purchasing a Swedish tanker for £8.5 million in kronor to avoid the risk of exchange losses. However, fears that the Swedish shipyard would go bankrupt before the tanker could be built had made the Board of Directors concentrate its analysis on the other two alternatives: a German vessel for £7 million, and a Japanese vessel for £7.5 million. (See Exhibit 1.)[1] Both proposals involved exchange risks associated with a possible revaluation of these currencies. This risk was an extremely important consideration since 80% of the cost of the ship was financed in the country—and therefore the currency—where the shipyard was located.

It was common understanding at the time that the deutsche mark and per-haps the yen were likely to be upvalued vis-à-vis the pound. If this happened, both vessels would carry a much higher price because of the higher exchange rate of the yen and the deutsche mark that would prevail when payments for the loan were made. It was not clear how much higher the final price in sterling would be.

The members of the Board acknowledged that they were not experts in the foreign exchange market. Indeed they wondered if such a person existed. The BIS executive who seemed most competent in these matters was Mr. Hugh F. E. Cooper, so he received the task of analyzing in detail the foreign exchange risks involved in the Japanese and German proposals. His report was due at the next Board meeting on April 3. A summary description of the background to the March 25 decision is contained in the appendix to the case.

Mr. Cooper knew he should first focus on forecasting the future develop-ments in exchange rates for the yen and the deutsche mark vis-à-vis the pound. Then, he had to show clearly how each of the two proposals would be affected if his forecasts were accurate and what hedging policy, if any, he should recom-mend to the Board. He also had to consider how the financial reporting would be affected under different combinations of financing options and behaviors of the currencies involved.

Forecasting Exchange Rates

In order to make the necessary forecasts, Mr. Cooper asked his assistants to compile economic data for Japan, Germany, and the United Kingdom. Their find-ings are contained in Exhibits 3-12. Mr. Cooper wanted to analyze these data in

---

[1] The problems of the Swedish shipyard originated for the most part from inflation in con-struction costs. These costs had soared in the last couple of years, and companies which had contracted many years in advance of ship construction on a firm-price basis had been subject to severe pressures. In addition, in contrast to the situation in other countries, Swedish shipyards did not receive much direct support from their government. One Swedish shipyard had fallen into bankruptcy, and others were near it.

the context of the comments he had heard in the City[2] or read in the papers
about the present international monetary situation. These comments are summarized below.

Germany. Less than a year before, in May 1968, the Germans had indicated
that by letting their economy grow faster than initially planned, they would solve
their huge balance of payments surplus which originated primarily in the trade
sector. (See Exhibit 3.) The speculation on a deutsche mark upvaluation which
had intensified during the gold crisis in the previous March was expected to recede. However, by September the president of the Bundesbank was admitting
that an upvaluation might be necessary in the future.

German trade surpluses continued, and in November, speculation on a
deutsche mark upvaluation again mounted, with $1½ billion flowed into Germany
in a single week. Foreign exchange markets closed, and the Group of Ten
finance ministers met in Bonn to discuss the crisis. Germany refused to upvalue
and instead imposed a 4% border tax on exports and an equal subsidy on imports.

For a few months, trading and fluctuations remained reasonably quiet on the
deutsche mark market, but it became even clearer that eventually this currency
would have to be upvalued. Germany's Finance Minister, Herr Strauss, recently
had talked of a possible 8% to 10% upvaluation in the deutsche mark as part of
a package in which Switzerland, the Netherlands, and Italy would upvalue their
currencies as well, and the French franc would be devalued by 10% or 15%. This
statement combined with the recent de Gaulle resignation (de Gaulle was a strong
opponent of French devaluation) placed considerable pressure on the currencies
involved. The French franc was trading at or near its floor and so was the pound.
Yet, the situation was not hectic as at the time of the gold rush in March, 1968,
or during the November crisis. It was thought that one reason the situation was
not worse was that the usual movers of large amounts of funds across the exchanges had already taken their positions in November. Another reason was a
rumor that Herr Kiesinger, the German Chancellor, opposed an upvaluation of
the deutsche mark. Herr Kiesinger's position was supported by a public poll that
showed 87% of the Germans against upvaluation. In the upcoming election on
September 28, 1969, the Finance Minister, Herr Strauss, in spite of his personal
views, was likely to support any decision that the Chancellor took on these matters. However, the Economics Minister, Herr Schiller (a Social Democrat), was
outspokenly for upvaluation. The consensus appeared to be that the deutsche
mark would have to be upvalued by the end of the year, particularly if the
Social Democrats won the September elections.

Japan. This country was in its longest postwar boom, and Mr. Cooper viewed
its economy and currency as being very strong indeed. He even felt that with the
furor over the deutsche mark, the increasing balance of payments surplus of
Japan had not been given appropriate attention. After a slow period in 1967 and
the first four months of 1968 when Japan's balance of trade surplus had been
relatively small, Japan had been increasing its reserves by about $100 million a
month. (See Exhibit 4.) Even the most pessimistic sources were forecasting well

---

[2] The financial district of London is referred to as "the City."

over a $1 billion surplus in Japan's balance of payments for fiscal 1968 (April 1968-March 1969), in sharp contrast to the $535 million deficit for the year ended March 1968. The year just ending had experienced a 24% increase in exports and better than 10% increase in real GNP. (See Exhibit 6.) The influential Japan Economic Research Center (JERC) was forecasting a further increase in foreign reserves. These increases in reserves were caused by a buoyant export trade, a moderate recovery of imports from the previous recession, and an enormous injection of foreign capital. The increase in reserves was in agreement with a recent announcement from the Tokyo government that it had raised its reserve target level from $3 billion to $4 billion.

Even though the consensus in the market was that the yen was a strong currency, there had been no wild speculative currency movements into the yen induced by expectation of an imminent upvaluation. One reason for this may have been that the Bank of Japan exercised very stringent controls over the yen and over the inflow and outflow of foreign currencies.

United Kingdom. The November 1967 devaluation of the pound had been followed by a wage-price control measure called the "Prices and Income Bill" in May 1968. Its goals were to eliminate the balance of payments deficits by the second half of 1968 and to achieve a balance of payments surplus of $1.2 billion for 1969. Control on foreign exchange was exercised by granting it only to people who could prove that they were performing a bona fide business transaction abroad. However, the outcome had fallen short of the desired targets: the balance of payments deficits continued, for even though exports performed well, imports increased even more. (See Exhibit 5.) Expectations of an upvaluation in the deutsche mark had attracted speculative money away from the pound. A continued high interest differential in favor of New York produced a large amount of short-term money to flow into New York away from the pound. Moreover, large long-term capital outflows continued. (See Exhibit 5.) Finally, the forecasts for the rest of 1969 did not anticipate any change for the better.

In addition to the intrinsic problems of the British situation, there was fear that even if currency realignments took place in an otherwise neutral fashion vis-à-vis the pound, the international nature of the pound would attract problems to this currency. It was particularly feared that if another speculative flow into the deutsche mark took place, it would be out of either French francs or British pounds, whichever was weaker at the time.

On the other hand, there were political pressures to maintain the pound at the $2.40 level. A devaluation of the pound would increase the pressure on the U. S. dollar which was considered to be overvalued. The position of the British government also appeared to be one of holding to a $2.40 rate. Their attitude seemed to be that they had done their part by devaluing in 1967; it was now up to the other currencies to make the remaining adjustments.

Hedging Policies

There were two policies Mr. Cooper was contemplating to protect BIS against an upward revaluation of the currencies involved. One possibility was to borrow pounds in England at 9½%, convert them to deutsche marks or yen, and invest them in Germany or Japan at the prevailing low market rates in those countries. However, it was highly doubtful that the Bank of England would agree to withdrawal of currency for this purpose.

The other alternative was to sell pounds for deutsche marks or yen in the forward market. Mr. Cooper thought that it would be very hard to buy a single forward contract to cover the life of the loan from the shipyard. Instead it would be necessary to buy a ninety-day, or perhaps a six-month contract and renew it at the end of that time period if a hedging policy was still considered appropriate. He estimated that the cost of the forward contract would be approximately 3% per annum if no currency crisis took place; however, in the event that crisis did occur, the cost could even run to infinity if the market dried up. As a working hypothesis, Mr. Cooper decided to use 15% as the cost of forward contracts in times of monetary turmoil.

In any case, the amount hedged at each point in time would be the cost of the ship still to be paid (both equity and loan) plus the full amount of future interest payments, less the 20% of cost covered by the investment grant from the British government (see Appendix).

Taxation and Financial Reporting

The treatment of hedging costs and valuation of assets for taxation and financial reporting purposes depended heavily on whether a currency revaluation actually took place or not and whether it took place before or after the ship had been delivered.

If *upvaluation occurred before the ship was delivered and began operation,* British Inland Revenue regulations and accounting practices provided both for increasing the asset cost for depreciation purposes and also for increasing the loan payable. Interest charges would be higher based on the increased size of the loan outstanding. In addition, since ships involved progress payments to be made from the cash/equity accounts as construction proceeded, these accounts would be adjusted. The British Investment Grant was also adjusted to correspond to any upvaluation of currencies.

If *upvaluation occurred after the ship was delivered and began operations,* there would be no write-up in assets (ship) or liabilities (loan payable). Instead, the differential in loan repayment required because of the upvaluation was added to the interest accrued for the year, and the total amount of revised interest would be expensed for tax purposes. For reporting purposes, exchange losses would be shown as a separate line entry annually.

If *hedging* took place, the hedging costs would *not* be deductible for tax purposes nor could they be capitalized for amortization at a later date *before the delivery of the ship.* Hence, these hedging costs would be deducted from the cash and equity accounts each year prior to the commencement of ship operations. Should upvaluation occur when the firm's position was hedged, there were taxes payable equal to 42½% of any proceeds of the hedge which exceeded the cost of the hedge in that year. Proceeds were then credited directly to cash and equity accounts. *After delivery of the ship,* then both hedging costs and the proceeds (if any) from a successful hedge were considered as an expense or income item, respectively, for both Inland Revenue and reporting purposes. They would net to a reserve against which the annual exchange loss would be charged.

A summary of the effects of these rules is contained in Exhibit 2.

EXHIBIT 1 Financing Proposals (thousands of dollars)

	German	Japanese
Total cost	£7,000	£7,500
Delivery date	April 1973	December 1972
Cost per DWT	£33.2	£32.6
Percentage of cost financed		
by shipyard	80%	80%
Interest rate	6%	6%
Currency	Deutsche mark	Yen
Loan Covenants		
		Bank Guarantee
Standby guarantee	$1,500	of £2,000
Minimum cash balance	£300	£300
Capital base of firm	£1,500	£2,000

Payment Schedule

German   10% on order, 5% on keel laying, balance on delivery. Loan to be repaid over ten years, payments semi-annually beginning six months after delivery.

Japanese   5% on order, 10% when propulsion system in place, balance on delivery. Loan to be repaid over eight years, payments semiannually beginning six months after delivery.

EXHIBIT 2 Taxation and Financial Reporting of Selected Items

	Upvaluation Does Not Take Place		Upvaluation Takes Place	
	Before Ship Delivery	After Ship Delivery	Before Ship Delivery	After Ship Delivery
Asset and loan	—	—	Written up	Remain fixed
Depreciation	—	—	Increases	Unchanged
Interest expense	—	—	Increases	Unchanged
Exchange losses	—	—	None	Realized as loan is paid up if hedged
Hedging costs	Reduce cash and equity—not tax deductible	A business expense	Reduce cash and equity—not tax deductible	A business expense
Gain from upvaluation if hedged	—	—	Netted against cash and equity. If greater than hedging costs, it is taxed	Create reserve and net it against exchange losses as loan is paid up

EXHIBIT 3 Germany: Balance of Payments (millions of dollars)

				1968 First Quarter	1968 Second Quarter	1968 Third Quarter	1968 Fourth Quarter	1969 First Quarter
	1966	1967	1968					
A. Goods, Services, and Unrequited Transfers								
Exports f.o.b.[a]	20,138	21,741	24,851	5,826	5,701	6,159	7,165	6,397
Imports c.i.f.	−18,024	−17,352	−20,150	−4,695	−4,819	−5,110	−5,526	−5,677
Other merchandise	−236	−223	−211	−60	−39	−58	−54	−5
Trade balance	1,878	4,166	4,490	1,071	843	991	1,585	715
Paid services to foreign troops	1,224	1,310	1,337	322	330	344	341	313
Other services (net)	1,419	−1,436	−1,193	−205	−279	−496	−213	−341
Total goods and services	1,683	4,010	4,634	1,188	894	839	1,713	687
Unrequited transfers (net)	−1,564	−1,576	−1,796	−410	−119	−391	−576	−381
Total	119	2,464	2,838	778	475	443	1,137	306
B. Long-Term Capital								
Private liabilities	1,096	414	434	62	55	93	224	52
Private assets (increase−)	−654	−830	−2,961	−459	−684	−1,024	−794	−1,454
Advance debt redemption	−235	−	−	−	−	−	−	−
Other government long-term capital	−409	−385	−386	−65	−63	−117	−141	−72
Total	−202	−801	−2,913	−462	−692	−1,048	−711	−1,474
C. Total (A plus B)	−83	1,663	−75	316	−217	−600	426	−1,168
D. Short-Term Capital, n.i.e. (including net errors and omissions)								
Government short-term capital	−42	49	329	64	38	212	15	−36
Other short-term capital	470	−409	134	16	−32	127	23	125
Net errors and omissions	149	−	733	378	217	326	−188	444
Total	577	−360	1,196	458	223	665	−150	533
E. Commercial Bank Short-Term Capital								
Liabilities	−102	297	1,493	−27	180	590	750	−741
Assets[a]	−41	−1,503	−879	−365	151	−346	−319	−438
Total	−143	−1,206	614	−392	331	244	431	−1,179
F. Total (C through E)	351	97	1,735	392	337	309	707	−1,814
G. Official Monetary Movements								
Net IMF accounts	−181	205	−163	−82	−466	44	41	161
Bundesbank investment in U.S. and U.K. Treasury paper (increase−)	−	−250	−675	−125	−175	−125	−250	−
Freely usable assets (increase−)	−537	−143	−345	−435	637	−81	−466	1,584
Miscellaneous claims (net)	249	27	60	5	7	−3	51	71
Monetary gold (increase−)	118	64	−312	255	−340	−144	−83	−2
Total	−351	−97	−1,735	−382	−337	−309	−707	1,814

[a]U. S. dollars put at the disposal of the commercial banks by the Bundesbank through swap arrangements are included in the commercial banks' assets in Group E and excluded from Bundesbank assets in Group G.

Source: International Monetary Fund, *Balance of Payments Statistics*, various issues.

EXHIBIT 4   Japan: Balance of Payments (millions of dollars)

				1968				1969
	1966	1967	1968	First Quarter	Second Quarter	Third Quarter	Fourth Quarter	First Quarter
A. Current and Long-Term Capital Transactions								
Exports f.o.b.	9,641	10,231	12,751	2,569	3,112	3,327	3,743	3,283
Imports f.o.b.	−7,366	−9,071	−10,222	−2,451	−2,566	−2,482	−2,723	−2,676
Receipts for services								
Transporation	816	908	1,110	238	268	291	303	277
Investment income	244	284	324	86	79	83	76	115
Military	474	523	589	130	147	144	168	145
Other	397	467	594	134	139	157	164	172
Payments for services								
Transportation	−1,422	−1,724	−1,969	−471	−485	−486	−527	−509
Investment income	−432	−462	−578	−145	−126	−151	−156	−181
Other	−963	−1,168	−1,366	−326	−332	−355	−353	−396
Private unrequited transfers (net)	−6	−23	−26	−25	−2	2	−1	−28
Central government unrequited transfers								
(net)	−129	−155	−149	−34	−43	−26	−46	−25
Long-term capital								
Direct investment	−77	−78	−144	−21	−14	−8	−101	−12
Trade credits and loans extended	−550	−702	−823	−192	−215	−198	−218	−232
Other	−181	−32	728	103	211	213	201	291
Total	446	−1,002	809	−405	173	511	530	224
Trade balance	2,275	1,160	2,529	118	546	845	1,030	607
Services and unrequited								
transfers	−1,021	−1,350	−1,481	−413	−355	−341	−372	−430
Long-term capital	−808	−812	−239	−110	−18	7	−118	47
B. Net Errors and Omissions	−45	−75	84	44	68	−1	−27	61
C. Short-Term Capital, n.i.e.								
Nonmonetary sectors								
Trade credits (net)	−29	486	140	75	−19	−5	89	9
Other (net)	−35	20	69	39	−1	36	−5	−16
Commercial banks								
Liabilities	−276	989	486	170	7	1	308	−63
Assets (increase−)	−113	−478	−724	37	−219	−166	−376	104
Total	−453	1,017	−29	321	−232	−134	16	34
D. Official Monetary Movements								
Net IMF accounts	−66	82	−50	14	−46	−7	−11	3
Other reserves (increase−)								
Foreign exchange	100	16	−809	31	47	−372	−515	−314
Gold	−1	−9	−17	−3	−14	−	−	−1
Other (net)	19	−29	12	−2	4	3	7	−7
Total	52	60	−864	40	−9	−376	−519	−319

Source: Same as Exhibit 3.

EXHIBIT 5 United Kingdom: Balance of Payments (millions of dollars)

	1966	1967	1968	1968 First Quarter	Second Quarter	Third Quarter	Fourth Quarter	1969 First Quarter
A. Goods, Services (net), and Unrequited Transfers (net)								
Exports f.o.b.	14,302	13,882	14,647	3,595	3,564	3,574	3,914	3,789
Net adjustment for recording of exports	168	229	312	77	74	79	82	84
Imports f.o.b. (excluding U.S. military aircraft)	−14,590	−15,326	−16,322	−4,140	−4,013	−4,010	−4,159	−4,255
Payments for U.S. military aircraft	−115	−270	−262	−55	−75	−84	−48	−79
Trade balance	−235	−1,485	−1,625	−523	−450	−441	−211	−461
Transporation	85	130	204	17	70	79	38	22
Travel	−219	−112	27	14	−2	−24	39	29
Investment income	1,164	1,156	1,005	288	319	283	115	456
Government services, n.i.e.	−812	−759	−681	−166	−174	−173	−168	−165
Other goods and services	837	1,048	1,048	264	256	259	269	269
Private transfers	−137	−173	−187	−60	−43	−38	−46	−48
Government transfers	−504	−517	−427	−139	−106	−91	−91	−129
Total	179	−712	−636	−305	−130	−146	−55	−27
B. Long-Term Capital, n.i.e.								
Private investment (net)								
In United Kingdom	762	1,031	1,375	199	264	610	302	324
Abroad	−851	−1,253	−1,766	−481	−410	−325	−550	−444
Official long-term capital								
U. S. Export-Import Bank loans received (net)	143	207	177	53	67	55	2	41
Other	−367	−354	−127	−89	31	−38	−31	−108
Total	−313	−369	−341	−318	−48	302	−277	−187
C. Total (A plus B)	−134	−1,081	−977	−623	−178	156	−332	−214
D. Net Errors and Omissions	−225	442	−311	−309	−62	38	22	432
E. Exchange Equalization Account Losses on Forward Commitments	−	−252	−602	−287	−199	−55	−61	−
F. Short-Term Capital, n.i.e.								
Miscellaneous capital	−260	−186	−58	36	77	−55	−116	245
U. K. banks' net liabilities in overseas sterling area currencies	−126	68	−110	2	84	−143	−53	14
U.K. banks' net liabilities in non-sterling area currencies								
Euro-dollar financing of new private investment abroad	34	135	372	71	53	84	164	84
Other	−482	−17	−288	8	−12	−10	−274	−118
Sterling liabilities (net) other than to central monetary institutions								
Sterling area countries	143	−27	−149	41	−211	211	−190	−24
Other countries	−546	−320	−878	−321	−274	−41	−242	−242
International institutions	36	−43	29	−12	9	10	22	29
Total	−1,201	−390	−1,082	−175	−274	56	−689	−12
G. Total (C through F)	−1,560	−1,281	−2,972	−1,394	−713	195	−1,060	206
H. Official Monetary Movements								
Net IMF accounts	−42	−851	1,262	10	1,413	−75	−86	−304
Gold deposit liabilities to IMF	35	1	−3	−	−3	−	−	−
Sterling liabilities (net) to central monetary institutions								
Sterling area countries	−129	−299	−192	204	−533	−209	346	490
Other countries	867	1,111	1,589	902	−400	413	674	−212
Official liabilities in foreign currencies	39	424	43	305	197	−290	−169	−132
Transfer of securities from dollar portfolio to reserves	885	490	−	−	−	−	−	−
Convertible currency reserves (increase−)	−420	−245	456	175	20	−22	283	−46
Gold reserves (increase−)	325	650	−183	−202	19	−12	12	−2
Total	1,560	1,281	2,972	1,394	713	−195	1,060	−206

Source: Same as Exhibit 3.

EXHIBIT 6   Gross National Product

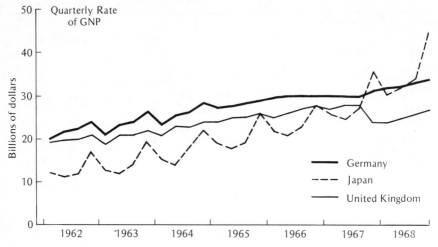

Source: International Monetary Fund, *International Financial Statistics,* various issues.

EXHIBIT 7   Earnings Per Employee in Manufacturing

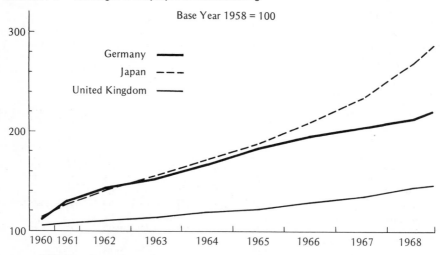

Definitions in each country are not strictly comparable.
Source: United Nations, *Monthly Bulletin of Statistics,* various issues.

EXHIBIT 8   Industrial Productivity

ªDefinitions of employment differed from country to country: industrial employment, manufacturing employment, etc., but are believed comparable.
Source: International Monetary Fund, *International Financial Statistics*, various issues.

EXHIBIT 9   Consumer Prices

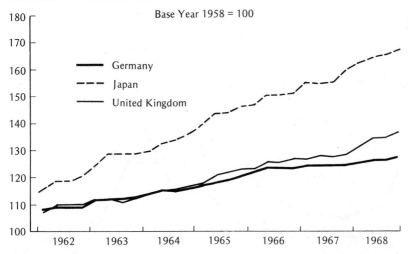

Source: International Monetary Fund, *International Financial Statistics*, various issues.

EXHIBIT 10   Net Barter Terms of Trade

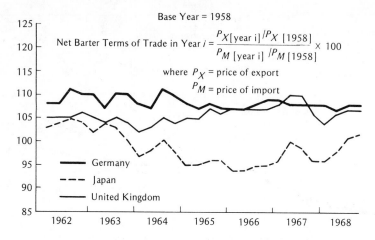

Base Year = 1958

$$\text{Net Barter Terms of Trade in Year } i = \frac{P_X[\text{year i}] / P_X [1958]}{P_M[\text{year i}] / P_M [1958]} \times 100$$

where P_X = price of export

P_M = price of import

—— Germany

- - - Japan

—— United Kingdom

Source: International Monetary Fund, *Interntional Financial Statistics,* various issues.

EXHIBIT 11   Short-Term Interest Rates

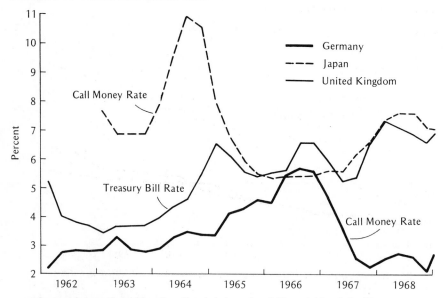

—— Germany

- - - Japan

—— United Kingdom

Call Money Rate

Treasury Bill Rate

Call Money Rate

Percent

Source: International Monetary Fund, *International Financial Statistics* (Germany and U.K.), various issues.

The Bank of Japan, *Economic Statistics Monthly* (Japan), various issues.

EXHIBIT 12   Long-Term Interest Rates

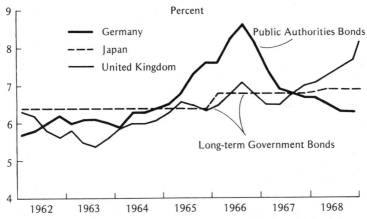

Source: International Monetary Fund, *International Financial Statistics*
(Germany and U. K.), various issues.
The Bank of Japan, *Economic Statistics Monthly* (Japan), various issues.

Appendix: Summary of Brittanic International Shipping Limited [A] and [B] [1]

A publicly-traded British Corporation, Britannic International Shipping (BIS), started operations in 1948. By 1969, the company had expanded to a twenty-three vessel fleet exceeding 500,000 tons, composed of eleven tankers, five dry cargo ships, and seven bulk carriers.

Expected Operating Profits

BIS's estimates of cash flows associated with a supertanker of the type the company was considering are presented in Exhibit 13. These estimates had been prepared by Mr. Cooper's staff and were the ones on the basis of which the Board had decided to proceed with the purchase of a supertanker. One critical assumption in these estimates was the shipping rate. The estimates were based on a rate

[1] This appendix is essentially a summary of the (A) and (B) cases of Britannic International Shipping Limited available from Intercollegiate Clearing House, case numbers 9-272-023 and 9-272-024, prepared by E. Eugene Carter.

of Worldscale 45.[2] This was one of the figures hardest to forecast given the instability of prices that plagued the industry. Recently these rates had fluctuated between a peak of approximately Worldscale 200 with the closing of the Canal and a low of Worldscale 17.5 in periods of excess supply of tankers. The average rate during the early 1960s had been around Worldscale 40-50. Current crude voyage rates for 100,000 DWT tankers were Worldscale 60 (a $2.74 time-charter equivalent). Longer-term time-charters for 250,000 DWT tankers were currently averaging $1.10 for a three-year charter, corresponding to Worldscale 34. The spread between these two rates was explained on two accounts. First, present voyage rates were still somewhat abnormally high as a result of the undercapacity that developed in 1967 with the closing of the Suez Canal during the Arab-Israeli war. Second, the shipping industry had a large amount of capacity ordered which was expected to depress rates when it came on stream. The company contracted shipping rates in sterling to avoid exchange risks on this account.

Another source of concern in the estimates in Exhibit 13 was the operating cost figures. Inflation in the past had produced fast rates of growth in these expenditures. This was particularly critical in the face of the forecast for excess capacity and depressed rates. Still another source of uncertainty was the cost of returning the ship to classification standards after each "Special Survey" every four years.[3]

Financing Provided Through the British Government

The British Investment Grant effective at the time entitled the shipping industry to a 20% refund on the cost of a new ship. This grant was payable twelve months after each payment by the firm on the ship. In addition, the firm also could take advantage of United Kingdom Inland Revenue regulations permitting "free depreciation" for ships owned by British corporations. The option allowed the firm to charge annually whatever yearly tax depreciation it wished, subject to the restriction that, if the Investment Grant were received, only the balance (i.e., 80%) of the ship could be depreciated. Once the cost of the ship had been set off against profits, normal tax would have to be paid on profits. The current rate of taxation was 42½%.

[2] Two rate systems existed in the industry. The chartering of a vessel *for a particular voyage* (voyage charter) was usually based on Worldscale rates. The chartering of a vessel *for an agreed period of time* in operating conditions with crew and operating expenses included but excluding fuel and port costs (time charter) was based on rates expressed in dollars (US$) per deadweight ton (DWT) per month. The Worldscale rate was an attempt to provide the owner of one sample tanker the same net per diem income for a voyage between any pair of ports allowing for a non-revenue earning voyage in ballast on the return leg. Therefore, the operating margin for the basic tanker was identical regardless of the ports between which the ship operated. Worldscale rates could be converted to a dollar per DWT rate by multiplying the Worldscale rate for the voyage times the deadweight tonnage, subtracting the fuel and port costs, and dividing this figure by the tonnage and time period involved.

[3] Classification of ship standards was done continually by any one of the seven or eight major classification services, with major reviews every four years. The Classification Report given then required the owner to remedy such defects as were cited in order to maintain classification. Two main rating services were the American Bureau of Shipping (ABS) and Lloyds. Employment conditions, acceptance in ports, insurance rates, and chartering were dependent on the vessel being fully classified.

EXHIBIT 13   Cash Flow of Swedish 252,000 DWT Very Large Crude Carrier (thousands of pounds sterling)

	1969	1970	1971	1972	1973	1974	1975	1976	1977	1978	1979	1980	1981	1982	1983	1984	1985	1986	1987
Payment for Ship	(415)	(830)	(7255)																
Investment Grant	83		166	1451															
Loan Receipt (Repayment)[a]			6640	(830)	(830)	(830)	(830)	(830)	(830)	(830)	(830)								
Operating Revenues[a]				1810	1810	1810	1653	1810	1810	1810	1653	1810	1810	1810	1653	1810	1810	1810	1810
Operating Expenses[b]				(456)	(456)	(456)	(456)	(456)	(456)	(456)	(456)	(456)	(456)	(456)	(456)	(456)	(456)	(456)	(456)
Interest on Loan[c]				(405)	(351)	(297)	(243)	(189)	(135)	(81)	(27)								
Special Survey							(200)				(200)				(200)				
Net Income Before Depreciation				949	1002	1057	754	1165	1219	1273	972	1354	1354	1354	997	1354	1354	1354	1354
Depreciation (Inland Revenue)[d]				(949)	(1002)	(1057)	(754)	(1165)	(1219)	(654)	0	0	0	0	0	0	0	0	0
Taxable Income				0	0	0	0	0	0	619	972	1354	1354	1354	997	1354	1354	1354	1354
Tax Payments[e]				0	0	0	0	0	0	(263)	(413)	(575)	(575)	(575)	(424)	(575)	(575)	(575)	(575)
Depreciation (Book)[f]				(404)	(404)	(404)	(404)	(404)	(404)	(404)	(404)	(404)	(404)	(404)	(404)	(404)	(404)	(404)	(404)
Net Income Before Tax (Book)				545	598	653	350	761	815	869	568	950	950	950	593	950	950	950	950
Net Income After Tax (Book)[e]				313	345	376	201	438	469	500	327	546	546	546	341	546	546	546	546
Salvage (Net of Tax)																			196
Equity	2250	2250	2250	1500	1500	1500	1500	1500	1500	1755	2352	2120	1888	1656	1424	1192	960	728	0
To (From) Shareholders[g]	(2250)			1213	345	376	201	438	469	245	(272)	779	779	779	573	779	779	779	1275
Ending Cash Balance[h]	1908	1205	786	1144	973	825	548	446	367	300	300	300	300	300	300	300	300	300	0

[a]Based on $1.50 DWT per month (Worldscale 45) for 11½ months. An extra four weeks of revenue is lost every 4th year during the Special Survey.

[b]Based on £1250 per day for 365 days.

[c]At 6½% per annum on balance..

[d]The "free depreciation" option is used on a cost basis of 80% of ship (£8,500,000 x .8 = £6,800,000). Depreciation to the extent of all income is taken each year until the ship is fully depreciated. A small part of the ship's cost is not covered by the 80% financing arrangement.

[e]Inland Revenue tax rate of 42½%

[f]Straight line on balance of ship after Grant for 16 years, 5% residual (£6,800,000 − £340,000)/16) = £404,000 yearly depreciation charge for book purposes.

[g]Cash payments to shareholders are maximum permitted. Equity must not decline below £1,500,000 and cash balance must not fall below £300,000 prior to full loan repayment. After loan repayment, equity may decline to £500,000.

[h]For 1969-1971, cash balances are invested in short-term securities to net 4% after tax, and the proceeds are added to the ending cash balance figure. Accumulated interest of £149,000 is paid out with return of capital in part in 1972 after the first year's trading and the receipt of the final Investment Grant.

Financing Provided Through the Shipyard

Each of the shipyards with which BIS was dealing was willing to arrange for 80% of the cost of the ship to be financed. This was facilitated by the existence in each of these countries of an institution that provided a guarantee for the loans and/or provided part of the loan at subsidized rates on a first mortgage on the ship.

In every case, the loan covenants contained various restrictions. These covenants referred to a minimum cash balance and capital base of the firm. In addition, the lender required the shipowner to provide a standby guarantee. The Japanese proposal required a bank guarantee in contrast to the company's guarantee in the other proposals. This guarantee entitled the lender to have recourse to shareholders' funds or bank funds in case of bankruptcy. The other loan terms (interest rate, installment payments, and so on) were somewhat different for each proposal. But in every case, the 20% equity contribution had to be made during the period of construction, and the loan repayment would begin six months after the ship's delivery.

An Introduction to
the Foreign Exchange Market

Every international financial officer must deal in a variety of currencies that do not keep their value constant relative to one another. The earlier chapters analyzed the forces that make currency values change; this chapter will look at the specific places where these changes take place: the money markets and the foreign exchange markets for each currency. The international manager needs to see the relationships that regulate these financial markets and to understand the behavior of participants in them.

The relationships that would prevail in the absence of interferences with the market such as governmental controls are discussed first. Although this review might appear too theoretical, it is the situation that prevails in the markets where currencies are traded outside national regulations, such as the market for Eurocurrencies. Discussing the free-market situation will establish the nature of the interrelationships among the money markets and the foreign exchange markets. Deviations from the prescribed behavior can then be identified as opportunities for profit.

NATURE OF THE FOREIGN EXCHANGE MARKET

Background

The foreign exchange market is where buyers and sellers of currencies meet. This market is somewhat similar to the over-the-counter market in securities. There is no centralized meeting place (except for a few places in Europe), and no fixed opening and closing time. The trading in foreign exchange is done over the telephone or through the telex. The currencies and the extent of participation of each currency in this market depend on local regulations which vary from country to country. Of the more than one hundred member countries of the International Monetary Fund, only a few have established full convertibility of their currencies for all transactions. The currencies with restricted convertibility play a very small role in the foreign exchange market.

Foreign exchange markets may be *spot* or *forward.* In the spot market currencies are bought or sold for immediate delivery, although in practice delivery and payment occur two days following the conclusion of the deal. In the forward market currencies are bought or sold now for future delivery. In this market payment is made upon delivery, but the exchange rate is agreed upon at the time of the contract. The date of the delivery is called *value date.*

The major participants in the foreign exchange market are large commercial banks that actually "make the market." In the United States about a dozen banks in New York and another dozen banks located in other U. S. cities maintain a position in twelve or fifteen major currencies and to a lesser extent in other currencies. These banks operate in the foreign exchange market at two levels. At the retail level they deal with their customers—corporations, exporters, etc. At the wholesale level banks maintain an interbank market. Contact in this market in the United States is usually made through a foreign exchange broker who receives a small commission. In this country there are about six of these brokers. By preserving the anonymity of the parties until the deal is concluded, the broker's function is to provide a fuller market than if the banks were to contact other banks directly. However, when dealing with institutions in other countries, banks usually deal directly with each other without the intermediation of brokers.

The other important participants in the foreign exchange market are the various countries' central banks. These institutions frequently intervene in the market to maintain the spot rates of their currencies within a desired range and to smooth fluctuations within that range. The permissible range of fluctuations in the past was defined by various arrangements such as the Smithsonian Agreement. Where an agreement existed and the market rate of a currency reached the upper limit ("upper intervention point") of the agreement, the central bank of that currency was obliged to increase sales of its currency in exchange for other currencies. Likewise, the central bank was obliged to sell foreign exchange and to buy its own currency when the market rate reached the "lower intervention point." Under a system of flexible exchange rates, central banks are not supposed to intervene in the foreign exchange market. However, historically, every time that a country has "floated" its currency, the central bank has continued to intervene in the foreign exchange market. This behavior of the central banks has led to the creation of "managed floating" as noted in Chapter 4.

The other participants in the foreign exchange market are nonfinancial businesses and individuals. These parties deal in the market through commercial banks.

Reading Foreign Exchange Quotations

A foreign exchange quotation, the price of a currency expressed in terms of another currency, is usually hard to understand for those who do not exchange currencies frequently. The difficulty arises from two sources. One is the fact that a quote is for the purchase of a given currency and the sale of another one. Identifying which currency is being sold and which is being bought creates some confusion. The other source of difficulty is the technical way in which foreign exchange quotes are given. Although a foreign exchange quote involves two currencies, the formal quote is given in terms of a single number without establishing explicitly the role that each currency plays in the quote. These two problems are interrelated and their solution requires a relatively simple approach: (1) make the role of each currency in the quote explicit; (2) establish the name of the currency whose unit the quoter is buying or selling.

In a foreign exchange quote, one currency plays the role of unit of account in terms of which the price is given; the other currency is the unit for which the price is being quoted. Actually, these two roles are always present in the quote of price for any article. When we say that "the price is $3.00 per pound of beef," the quote for beef is $3.00. In this quote the unit of account is the dollar and the unit for which the price is offered is a pound of beef. Likewise, when the price for one deutsche mark is given as $0.35, the dollar is the unit of account and one deutche mark is the unit for which the price is offered. To make these two roles explicit, one writes the currency used as unit of account before the quoted number, and the currency whose unit is being purchased or sold after the number. For example, $0.35/DM means $0.35 per deutsche mark.

A foreign exchange trader will usually quote two numbers: the price at which (s)he is buying and the price at which (s)he is selling a given currency. The first price is the "bid" price; the second price is the "offer" or "ask" price. In either case, the currency for which the bid or ask price is given is the unit of the item priced. In the bid quote $0.35/DM the trader is saying (s)he is willing to *buy deutsche marks* at the price of $0.35 per deutsche mark. However, this is tantamount to saying that (s)he is willing to *sell dollars* at the price of $0.35 per deutsche mark. Implicitly, the quote also establishes the offer price for the currency used as unit of account. Likewise, when the trader quotes an *offer* price per *deutsche mark,* (s)he implicitly quotes the rate at which *dollars* would be *bought* per deutsche mark. This point is elaborated further in the following sections.

Spot Market. Quotations in the foreign exchange spot market are generally made in terms of the amount of local currency required to buy a unit of foreign currency. This is called the *direct way*. In the United States, exchange rates are quoted in terms of dollars required to purchase one foreign monetary unit, while in France the quotations are made in terms of French francs per unit of foreign exchange. The major exception to this practice is the United Kingdom where foreign exchange prices are quoted in terms of foreign monetary units required to purchase one pound sterling. This is called the *indirect way* of quoting foreign exchange rates. Obviously, what is a direct quotation for a trader may or may not be a direct quotation for the listener. Thus, when an American trader quotes $0.35/DM in a direct fashion, this will be an indirect quote for a German trader and an *American direct quote* for a French trader.

One usually expects to hear a higher number when the price of an item increases. This may or may not appear to be true in a foreign exchange quotation depending on the terms in which the quote is expressed. If the currency in whose price we are interested is the one used as the unit for which the quote is given, the latter currency will appreciate relative to the currency used as unit of account when the quoted price increases. For example, if we are interested in the price of the deutsche mark relative to the U.S. dollar and the price moves from $0.35/DM to $0.38/DM, we can say that the deutsche mark has appreciated relative to the U. S. dollar by $0.03. However, this is the same as saying that the U. S. dollar has depreciated relative to the deutsche mark. That is, when the quoted number increases, this implies an appreciation in the value of the currency used as the item purchased or sold (deutsche mark), but a depreciation for the currency used as the unit of account (dollar).

Given that we are used to associating appreciation with larger numbers and depreciations with smaller numbers, it is useful initially to express the quote in a fashion where the currency whose price we want is used as the unit of the item priced. If the original quote is not given in these terms, a conversion can be achieved by simply taking the reciprocal of the given quotation. For example:

$$U. S. \$0.3534/DM^{1} \text{ is the same as}$$

$$U. S. \$1.00 = \frac{DM 1}{0.3534}$$

$$= DM\ 2.8296/\$$$

In the same fashion, the rate between two currencies can be obtained from the rates of these two currencies in terms of a third currency. This is called the *cross rate.* For example, suppose an American trader gave the following quotations in New York:

$$\text{The price of deutsche mark} = \$0.3534/DM$$
$$\text{The price of pound sterling} = \$2.4845/\pounds$$

To find the price of a deutsche mark in terms of pound sterling in New York:

First. Convert both quotations to a common denominator, i.e., use as the unit priced the currency present in both quotes, the U. S. dollar.

$$\$0.3534/DM = DM \frac{1}{0.3534} /\$ = DM\ 2.8296/\$$$

$$\$2.4845/\pounds = \pounds \frac{1}{2.4845} /\$ = \pounds\ 0.4845/\$$$

Second. Given that $1.00 equals $1.00, then:

---

[1] Algebraically, this is equivalent to stating:

.3534 US$ = 1 DM

and then solving for US$.

$$DM/\pounds = \frac{2.8296/\$}{0.4025/\$} = DM\ 7.030/\pounds;\quad \text{(i.e., the price of one pound in terms of DMs)}$$

Likewise $\pounds/DM = \dfrac{0.4025/\$}{2.8296/\$} = \pounds\ 0.1422/DM$; (i.e., the price of one DM in terms of pounds)

When a foreign exchange dealer receives a call asking for a quote, (s)he is under a general moral obligation to quote and to deal at the rate quoted. (S)he need not deal for unlimited amounts, but if the dealer is asked the price at which (s)he will buy a given currency and (s)he offers to transact only on a small amount, it is clear that (s)he prefers to be at the other end of the transaction—in this case, to sell that currency. A good dealer will provide a prompt response (to avoid giving the caller the opportunity to shop around) and narrow spreads. Otherwise, it is obvious what side of the transaction (s)he wishes to be. Quotations are stated both to buy and to sell. Given the narrow spreads, a dealer will very often sell when (s)he really wants to buy, and vice versa.

When given a quotation, the first number is always the buying rate, the *bid price*; the second number is the selling rate, the *offer* or *ask price*. Usually, in transactions among traders, only the last digits are quoted and the rest is understood. These last digits are called *points*. For example, the quotation of the spot dollar-lira rate might be 30/40. For one who knows the prevailing $/lit rates, this means:

willing to buy liras at $0.0016930 and sell at $0.0016940

which is the same as

willing to sell U. S. dollars at $0.0016930 per lira and buy U. S. dollars at $0.0016940 per lira.

Forward Market. The quotations for forward rates can be made in two ways. They can be made in terms of the amount of local currency at which the quoter will buy and sell a unit of foreign currency, like the quotes on spot rates. This is called the *outright rate* and is used by traders in quoting to customers. The forward rates also can be quoted in terms of points of discount and/or premium from spot, called the *swap rate,* and is used in interbank quotations. The outright rate is the spot rate adjusted by the swap rate.

A foreign currency is at a *forward discount* against a given currency when the forward price of the foreign currency (expressed in terms of units of the given currency required to buy a unit of the foreign currency) is lower than its spot price. The opposite is true in the case of a forward premium. For example, if the spot rate of the French franc is $0.2186 per French franc, then the quote of U. S. $0.2180 for three-month French francs shows a discount in the forward rate of the French franc against the U. S. dollar. That is, a unit of French francs buys fewer dollars for delivery in three months than for immediate delivery. This quote also shows that the U. S. dollar is at a forward premium against the French franc. One U. S. dollar buys more French francs for delivery in three months than for immediate delivery.

The percentage of discount (−) or premium (+) in a forward quote is computed by the following formula:

$$\text{Forward premium (discount)} = \frac{(\text{Forward rate} - \text{Spot rate})}{\text{Spot rate}} \times \frac{12}{\text{No. months forward}}$$

In a free market, if a three-month U. S. dollar deposit is yielding 5% per annum and a comparable deposit in pounds is yielding 7% per annum, the three-month forward rate of the U. S. dollar will sell at a 2% premium, and the three-month pound will sell at a 2% discount. If the spot rate for the pound is \$2.40/£, then the three-month forward pound will sell at:

$$\frac{(\text{Forward} - \text{Spot})}{\text{Spot}} \times \frac{12}{\text{No. of months forward}} = \frac{\text{Forward premium}}{\text{(discount)}}$$

$$\frac{(F - 2.40)}{2.40} \times \frac{12}{3} = -.02$$

Then: F = \$2.3880/£

Notice that the forward rate has to be adjusted by the actual fraction of the year to which the discount refers to convert it to an annual basis comparable to the one used to express the yield on deposits.

To find the outright forward rates when the premiums or discounts in quotes of forward rates are given in terms of *points* (swap rate), the points are *added* to the spot price if the foreign currency is trading at a forward *premium;* if trading at a forward *discount,* the forward quotations are *subtracted* from the spot price. The resulting number is the outright forward rate

It is usually well known to traders whether the quotes in points represent a premium or a discount from the spot rate, and it is not customary to specifically refer to the quote as a premium or discount. However, this can be readily determined in a mechanical fashion. If the first forward quote (the bid or buying figure) is smaller than the second forward quote (the offer or selling figure) there is a premium, i.e., the quotes are added to the spot rate. Conversely, if the first quote is larger than the second it is a discount.[2] This procedure assures that the buy price is lower than the sell price, and the trader profits from the spread between the two prices. Example: When asked for spot, one, three, and six month quotes on the French franc, a U. S. based trader might quote the following:

$$.2186/9 \qquad 2/3 \qquad 6/5 \qquad 11/10$$

In outright terms these quotes would be expressed as follows:

Maturity	Bid	Asked
spot	.2186	.2189
1-month	.2188	.2192
3-month	.2180	.2184
6-month	.2175	.2179

[2] A 5/5 quote would require further specification as to whether it is a premium or a discount.

Notice that the one-month forward is at a premium whereas the three- and six-month forwards are at discounts.

The remaining sections of this chapter and most parts of the book will ignore the existence of bid and ask prices. Instead, there will be only one rate, which can be treated as the *mid-rate* between bid and ask prices.

Determinants of Foreign Exchange Rates

Spot Rate. The major determinant of the spot rate is the basic condition of the country vis-à-vis the rest of the world. Continuous balance of payments deficits will eventually lead to a depreciation of the currency in question; continuous balance of payments surpluses will cause an appreciation of the currency. In addition to the basic economic forces, there are factors of a technical nature that influence the spot rate. These factors include seasonal fluctuations, publication of important statistics, and the movements in related currencies.

In principle, the rate quoted for a given currency should be the same in any market dealing in that currency. However, temporary discrepancies among various markets may occur. These discrepancies provide an opportunity to profit by buying the currency in the market where it is selling at a lower price and selling the currency in the market where a higher price prevails. The nature of these transactions is called *arbitrage*. The individual who performs them is the *arbitrageur*.

For example, assume that the quotes of the pound sterling against the U. S. dollar in New York and London are as follows:

New York	London
$2.4038/£	$2.4039/£

The pound commands a higher price against the U. S. dollar in London than in New York. As a result, one can benefit by buying pounds with U. S. dollars (selling U. S. dollars in exchange for pounds) in New York and selling the pounds in exchange for U. S. dollars (buying U. S. dollars with pounds) in London. This arbitrage tends to eliminate the incentive that initially triggered it. The purchase of pounds in New York will tend to increase the price of the pound against the U. S. dollar in that market. In London, opposite pressures will occur, for the continuous sale of pound sterling in London will tend to reduce the price of the pound against the dollar. This process will tend to continue until the price of the two currencies is the same in both locations.

The arbitrage transaction of buying and selling currencies in two different locations follows the basic finance principle of "buy low—sell high." However, confusion can arise when this principle is applied to foreign exchange. Always keep in mind the answer to three questions:

1. Which is the currency whose unit is being priced? Assume currency A.

2. Which is the currency used as the unit account? Assume currency B.

3. What are the B currency prices per unit of A currency in each geographic location?

Then compare the price of A in the two locations and act accordingly.

Consider these questions in a slightly more complex example. Take the following data:

New York	Frankfurt
$0.3540/DM	DM 2.8296/$

Following tradition, each rate is expressed in local currency per unit of foreign currency. Then,

1. *Q.* Which is the currency whose unit is being priced?
   A. Dollar

2. *Q.* Which is the currency used as the unit of account?
   A. Deutsche mark

3. *Q.* What are the quotes in each market in terms of DM/$?

New York	Frankfurt
DM 2.8248/$ (=1÷0.3540)	DM 2.8296/$ (as originally given)

It is clear that the dollar commands a higher price in terms of deutsche marks in Frankfurt than in New York. Therefore, buy dollars against DMs in New York and sell dollars against DMs in Frankfurt.

The questions presented above serve just to organize thoughts. If Question 1 were answered with deutsche marks and Question 2 with dollars, then the quotes should be expressed in terms of $/DM:

New York	Frankfurt
$0.3540/DM	$0.3534/DM

So, buy DMs against dollars in Frankfurt and sell DMs against dollars in New York. This is the same conclusion as in the previous paragraph when the quotes were expressed in terms of DM/$.

This principle of establishing mental discipline becomes particularly necessary when more than two currencies are involved. For example:

New York	Zurich
$0.3540/DM	SF 1.0600/DM
$0.3381/SF	SF 2.9580/$

In this case there are three relationships to be analyzed: $/DM, $/SF, and SF/DM. One could add three more relationships by also considering the reciprocals of the previous relationships, *i.e.*, DM/$, SF/$, and DM/SF. The three relationships in the two markets produce the following quotes:

	New York	Zurich
$/SF	$0.3381/SF	$0.3380/SF[3]
$/DM	$0.3540/DM	$0.3583/DM[4]
SF/DM	SF 1.0470/DM[5]	SF 1.0600/DM

Reading down the list of quotes, notice that:

1. there is little arbitrage incentive between the Swiss franc and the dollar;

2. the DM against the dollar is higher in Zurich than in New York;

3. the DM commands a higher price in terms of SF in Zurich than in New York.

Therefore, buy DMs in New York with dollars, sell the DMs against SFs in Zurich, and convert SFs to dollars in either New York or Zurich.

Forward Rate. In a completely free market, the relationship between the spot and the forward rates of a currency will be determined by the relationship between interest rates in the given country and in the rest of the world.

In a free market, the currency with the higher interest rate will sell at a discount in the forward market; the currency with the lower interest will sell at a premium in the forward market. This outcome will be brought about by the individuals who engage in *covered interest arbitrage,* the interest arbitrageurs. For example, if interest rates on one-year deposits in U. S. dollars are 4% while in DMs they are 6%, the investors in search of a higher yield will tend to move funds from U. S. dollars into DMs. In order to avoid the foreign exchange risks of converting the deutsche marks back into dollars, the investors will cover the transaction by selling deutsche marks for dollars for one-year delivery. The only way in which the 2% interest differential in favor of DMs would not induce an international flow of funds would be if the deutsche mark for one-year delivery were selling at a 2% discount.

[3] In Zurich
SF 2.9580/$

then $/SF = $\dfrac{1}{2.9580}$ = $0.3380/SF

[4] In Zurich
$/SF = $0.3380/SF (from footnote 3)
We know SF/DM = SF 1.0600/DM

then DM/SF = $\dfrac{1}{1.0600}$ = DM .9434/SF

So then $/DM = $\dfrac{\$/SF}{DM/SF}$ = $\dfrac{0.3380}{.9434}$ = $.3583/DM

[5] In New York
$0.3540/DM = DM 2.8248/$
$0.3381/SF = SF 2.9577/$

SF/DM = $\dfrac{2.9577/\$}{2.8248/\$}$ = SF 1.0470/DM

Consider the sequence of events when the interest differential and the premium or discount in the forward market are not the same. Assume the following data for April 23, 1973, for DMs and U. S. dollars:

Spot rate	$0.3534/DM
1-year forward rate	$0.3500/DM
Interest rates:	
DM	6%
U. S. $	4%

Then compute the percentage discount on the one-year DM by using the formula presented before:

$$\text{Forward premium (discount)} = \frac{\text{Forward rate} - \text{Spot rate}}{\text{Spot rate}} \times \frac{12}{\text{No. months forward}}$$

$$= \frac{0.3500 - 0.3534}{0.3534} \times \frac{12}{12} = -.0096 = \sim -1\%$$

That is, the discount of the forward DM is only 1% as compared to the interest differential in favor of DMs of 2%.

To benefit from this situation the following transactions would take place:

Spot Market		Forward Market	
April 23, 1973			
1. Buy 100,000 DM		3. Sell 106,000 DM	
at $0.3534	$35,340	one-year delivery	
		at $0.3500	$37,100
2. Buy 1,000,000 DM			
worth of one-year			
DM deposits			
paying 6% per			
annum. Expected			
interest is			
6,000 DM			
April 23, 1974			
4. Collect principal,		5. Deliver the 106,000 DM	
100,000 DM,		against the	
and interest,		forward position	
6,000 DM, on			
DM deposit for			
a total of			
106,000 DM			
		Profit in the transaction	
		Dollars on April 23, 1974	$37,100
			35,340
			$ 1,760

Alternative investment: $35,340 are invested in U. S. deposits at 4% rate of return:

Investment	$35,340
Rate of return	X.04
	$1,413.60

In this case there is an advantage in investing in DMs ($1,760.00 − $1,413,60 = $346.40 or 1%). As more investors are attracted by the higher net yields in DMs there will be two tendencies: (1) the spot rate of the DM will tend to appreciate as the demand for the spot DM increases; (2) the forward rate of the DM will tend to decrease as the supply of future DMs increases. As these tendencies continue, the returns on the two alternative investments tend to become the same. At that point there will be a 2% discount on the forward deutsche mark against the U. S. dollar. The 2% difference in interest in favor of DMs will be fully offset by the 2% discount in the forward mark.

In general, under covered interest arbitrage there is an incentive to invest in the higher interest currency to the point where the discount of that currency in the forward market is less than the interest differential. If the discount on the forward market of the currency with the higher interest rate becomes larger than the interest differential, then it pays to invest in the lower-interest currency and take advantage of the excessive forward premium of this low-interest currency.

A word of warning before leaving this subject. In calculating the opportunities for covered interest arbitrage, or estimating rates from other available information, two types of mistakes are frequently made. To avoid them, it is well to keep in mind the following concepts:

1. A "covered" transaction must begin and end with the same currency;

2. Only rates applicable to the same period of time (e.g., quarters) can be compared.

It is essential to note that except for cases such as the Euro-currency market, financial markets are usually not completely free. In these cases the forward discounts and premiums reflect other factors in addition to interest differentials. This is particularly so in periods of heavy speculation about a future change in the spot rate. The theory presented above applies only to *net accessible interest rates.*

THE ACTORS IN THE FOREIGN EXCHANGE MARKET

The previous section presented a panoramic view of the mechanics of the foreign exchange markets.

The behavior of one of the participants in these markets, the arbitrageur, was described. The motivation of these individuals to realize a profit in the financial markets without incurring foreign exchange risks makes them behave in a way that serves as a lubricant to maintain the relationships in the financial markets.

If one divides the other participants in the foreign exchange markets according to motivation, one can distinguish four major actors. (Note, though, that a given actor may play more than one role at one point in time or through time.) Two of these actors operate based on considerations of a purely financial nature. The other two add the financial considerations to basically nonfinancial business concerns.

The two types guided by purely financial considerations are: (1) *the outright speculator* who speculates on a change in the spot rate of a currency or currencies; and (2) *the commercial banks* who not only "make the market" and take positions in this market, but also engage in "swap transactions" (a seemingly-hedged speculation) based on anticipations of changes in interest rate differentials or premiums and discounts in the forward rates.

The actors with nonfinancial business enterprises approach the foreign exchange market in two different fashions: (1) *the merchandise trader* wants to protect a given cash flow in the future from fluctuations in the foreign exchange market, and therefore *covers* the transaction; (2) *the corporation with assets and liabilities in foreign countries* (and therefore in foreign currencies) wishes to protect the value of future foreign earnings by *hedging* in the foreign exchange market.

Please note that each of the four actors listed above can achieve his or her goal through either the forward exchange market or the money market. In a perfect market, both approaches produce similar results. The relationship between interest rate differentials and forward rates discussed in the previous section guarantees this identity. However, in practice this outcome is rarely the case. Therefore, in the following presentation notice the steps that the given actor could follow in either the forward market or the foreign exchange markets. (In this chapter we present the behavior of the outright speculator and the commercial bank. The behavior of the nonfinancial business enterprises will be discussed in the following two chapters.)

Whenever the maturity and the currency of cash inflows and outflows are matched one-to-one, e.g., a planned inflow in pound sterling in one year is matched with a planned outflow in the same currency for the same date, there is a *square* position. In this case the eventual gains or losses can be computed at the beginning because all the relevant rates are *locked in.* However, when a square position as to maturity and/or currency does not exist, the gains or losses in the transactions cannot be ascertained with certainty in advance. When this "matching" process does not take place, the final outcome of a gain or a loss depends on the movements in the market in the intervening period. For example, if there is a planned inflow in pound sterling one year hence and a planned sterling outflow fifteen months from now, then for three months a use must be found for the pound sterling received and not needed. The return for that investment is unknown at the present time. Likewise, if there is a planned inflow in pound sterling one year from now and a planned outflow for the same date in Swiss francs, one does not know with certainty the gain or loss in this transaction at the beginning. To determine the profit or loss in this transaction requires a knowledge not only of the interest rates associated with the known inflows and outflows for the intervening year (assume that the inflow is the product of the maturity of an investment on a British security, and the outflow the result of borrowings in Swiss francs), but also what happens to the value of the pound sterling against the Swiss franc at the end of the year. If the pound sterling devalues relative to the Swiss franc in the intervening year, a gain that might have been anticipated because of interest differentials could be wiped out by the fluctuations in the exchange market.

In general terms, any time the cash flows of a unit are not squared as to maturity and currency, speculation about the future of the money and exchange markets takes place. That is, the final gain and loss of the transaction can be computed initially only by making assumptions about how the markets will behave in the future, which is something no one knows with certainty at the beginning of the period. Therefore, financial institutions such as commercial banks which have liabilities (future outflows) of a much shorter maturity than their assets (future inflows) are in the business of speculating on the future of the money and capital markets. In similar fashion, when an individual or a financial institution has more assets (future inflows) than liabilities (future outflows) in a given currency, performance depends on the ability to anticipate the movements in the foreign exchange markets. This individual or financial institution must speculate as to the future value of the currencies involved at the end of the transaction period to estimate net gains or losses. Obviously, speculation in both the money market and the foreign exchange markets may be carried out simultaneously when neither the maturity nor the currency of the cash inflows and outflows is matched.

Perhaps some of the stigma attached to the word "speculation" has been dispelled in the previous paragraph. In its simplest sense, speculation is nothing more than an educated guess as to the future of the financial market from which the forecasting entity tries to profit. Conceptually, this is not very different from manufacturing a new product based on the existence of an anticipated demand for the product which may or may not materialize. In the financial world the word "speculation" has usually been used in a derogatory manner. In the mind of the individuals who consider speculation an "evil" thing, speculation is only a financial phenomenom, usually centered around the foreign exchange market and leading to instability. There is no evil intention in the mind of the speculator; like other members of a capitalist society, (s)he is merely trying to make a profit. Whether the actions of the speculator do or do not contribute to the well-functioning of the exchange markets is an empirical question that has not yet been settled.

Speculation in the foreign exchange market takes place when an individual or institution has an amount of assets (a future inflow) different from the amount of liabilities (a future outflow) in a given currency. If there is a change in the par value of the currency in question the value of the net holdings of the individual in that currency will change. In this case, the individual or institution has a "net position" in that currency. This position is called "long" if there are more assets (future inflows) than liabilities (future outflows). The net position is called "short" if there are more liabilities (future outflows) than assets (future inflows). A net position is called *outright speculation.*

The other situation that allows for speculation in the foreign exchange market can occur when the aggregate inflows and outflows for a currency over a period of time are the same; that is, the net position is zero. However, *for given dates,* the inflows and the outflows of the currency may not be the same. In this case the speculation is not based on forecasts about the spot rate. No matter what happens to the spot rate, overall the speculator will break even; what (s)he gains (loses) on the long positions, (s)he loses (gains) on the short positions since at any time additional transactions will always take place to make the net position square. In this case the speculation is based on forecast changes in the rates in the money market and (therefore) on the premium or discount in the forward markets. This case is called a *swap position* (seemingly-hedged speculation).

Outright Speculation

What are the steps one must take to benefit from a forecast of a change in the spot value of a currency? The speculation can be in the money market or in the forward exchange market. If a devaluation is expected, speculation suggests borrowing the currency in the money market or selling it in the futures market, i.e., moving into a "short position" in the currency. If the speculation is successful, the borrowed funds will be repaid with a devalued currency or the forward contract will be closed by purchasing the currency in the spot market at a lower price. If an upvaluation is expected, speculation suggests purchasing assets denominated in that currency in the money market or buying the currency in the futures market, i.e., moving into a "long position" in that currency.

Speculation in the Forward Market. If the speculator anticipates that the value of the pound will go from a current \$2.50/£ to \$2.40/£ within a year, this individual will try to be short in pound sterling in the forward market. The speculator will sell pounds for delivery in one year against another currency which the pound is expected to depreciate against (assume U. S. dollars). At the end of the one year the speculator will purchase pounds with dollars in the spot market to fulfill the forward contract. The extent of the gain (or loss) in this transaction will depend on the eventual value of the pound in terms of dollars in the spot market as well as the price specified in the forward contract for the pound against dollars.

Case 1: Forward pound is sold at \$2.50. One year later the spot rate is \$2.40. The *gain* will be \$0.10 per pound sold in the forward market.

Case 2: Forward pound is sold at \$2.50. One year later the spot rate is \$2.60. There will be a *loss* of \$0.10 per pound sold in the forward market.

Case 3: Forward pound is sold at \$2.40. One year later the spot rate is \$2.45. In spite of the depreciation, there will be a *loss* of \$0.05 per pound sold in the forward market.

If the speculator is expecting an appreciation of the currency, (s)he will want to be long in that currency. The speculator will enter the forward market offering to buy the currency in the future. Thus, if it were expected that the value of the pound will move upward from \$2.50/£ to \$2.60/£, the speculator will offer to buy pounds for future delivery at any price below \$2.60. This will produce a profit between the price at which the pounds are bought in the forward market and the \$2.60 expected to prevail in the spot market. As in the previous example, the profits of the speculator depend on the eventual price of the pound in the spot market as well as the price at which the pounds are bought in the forward market.

Speculation through the Money Market. If the speculator anticipates a depreciation in a currency and wishes to speculate through the money market, (s)he will borrow that currency, convert it into some harder currency, and wait until the depreciation takes place. The cost of this strategy is the interest differential between the cost of borrowing and whatever return can be obtained in the harder currency, plus transaction costs. The potential return depends on the eventual depreciation of the currency in question.

In the case of an expected appreciation, operations in the money market will reverse the pattern described above. The speculator will increase assets denominated in the currency expected to appreciate by borrowing in softer currencies. The cost is the interest differential between the interest on the loan and the return on the asset, plus transaction costs. The potential return depends on the final parity of the currency in question.

Swap Positions (Seemingly-Hedged Speculation)

This situation arises when each buy operation is matched by a sell operation in the same currency, i.e., a hedge, so that there is no net position in that currency. However, the maturity of each buy and sell is not perfectly matched; i.e., speculation. This type of transaction is often practiced by traders in commercial banks, and is called a *swap.*

The opportunity for this type of speculation arises when a change in interest rates and (therefore) forward premium or discount is anticipated.

For example, take the following situation:

	Money Market	Foreign Exchange Market
Initial interest rates:	United States—4%	3% discount per annum on pound (premium on U. S. dollar)
	United Kingdom—7%	
Forecast rates in one month:	United States—4%	2% discount per annum on pound (premium on U. S. dollar)
	United Kingdom—6%	

Swap through the Money Market. This is the easier transaction to undertake. It can be done without using the foreign exchange markets. If a decline in interest rates is anticipated the speculation in the money market will take the following form:

Day 1:   Borrow £ for 1 month at 7%. Invest in one year at 7%.
Day 31:   Refinance borrowing at 6%.

Therefore the investor will enjoy the interest differential of 1% for eleven months.

In this transaction, the total volume of outflows and inflows in pounds is the same, i.e., the amounts invested and borrowed are the same. The net position in pounds is zero and changes in the spot rate of the pound cannot affect the results of this transaction. For example, if the pound depreciated on day 25 by 10%, the value of the one-year investments in pounds will decrease by 10%, but so would the value of the borrowings incurred in pounds.

The risks involved in this transaction arise from the nature of the forecast. What if interest rates do not decline? Worse still, what if interest rates in the United Kingdom go above the 7% return on the investment? In the first case no profit will be made; in the second case there will actually be a loss for the whole transaction.

Swap in the Forward Market. To take advantage, of an anticipated change in interest rates and the associated forward premium or discount through the foreign exchange market, one must assume that any change in interest differentials will be translated to changes in the forward market. If this is the case, as it should be in an efficient market, then cash flows generated in the exchange markets must be similar to the ones generated through swaps in the money market. The complication in understanding this transaction arises from the basic nature of the foreign exchange market where there are always at least two currencies and two markets, spot and forward.

Assume that the same rates or interest differentials prevail for all maturities within a year and make the following basic calculations for the discounts on the pound sterling:

Spot rate $2.4000

		Forward rate	12-month point disc.	Points disc./ month
12 months	3% discount	2.3280	.0720	.0060
12 months	2% discount	2.3520	.0480	.0040

That is, if there is an expected decrease in interest differentials in favor of the pound, there is also an expected decrease for the discount of the pound in the forward market. If that is the case, the forward pound will command a higher price in terms of dollars after the interest rates in the United Kingdom decline. By the same token, the price of the forward pound is lower while interest rates in England are kept high. Thus, looking only at what happens to the prices of the pound in the forward market and applying the simple rule of buy low—sell high, buy forward pounds while interest rates in England are high and sell them after the interest rates come down and the forward price of the pound increases.

However, in a swap transaction, the net position in that currency must be zero. That is *not* the case suggested in the previous paragraph. If forward pounds are bought with the hope of selling them one month later, and the spot rate of the pound changes before the sale, there might be a loss, in spite of the expected reduction in the forward discount taking place. The loss will originate if the pound depreciates. In that case, even if the change from 3% to 2% discount materializes, the absolute value of the forward pound will be lower than the initial purchase price (2% discount on a small number produces a smaller value than 3% discount on a large number). To avoid the foreign exchange risks introduced by having a net position in the forward pound, each buy must be matched by a sell and vice versa.

Therefore, in order to take advantage of the forecast and avoid risks of changes in the spot rate, take the following steps:

Day 1:	Sell 1 month £ at (2.4000 − .0060)	$2.3940		Buy 1 year £ at	$2.3280
Day 31:	Buy spot £ at	2.4000		Sell 11-month £ at 2.4000−(11×.0040)	2.3560
	Loss	$0.0060		Gain	$0.0280

Net Profit:	Gain	$0.0280
	− Loss	0.0060
		$0.0220

The right-hand side of the transaction is the section showing the profit from the anticipated reduction in the discount of the forward pound. The left-hand side of the transaction is the counteracting sell and buy that assure that the net exchange position in pounds is zero throughout.

Although at each point in the swap "buy" equals "sell," at the beginning the buy is for thirty days, while the sell is for one year, a clearly speculative situation. The profit in this transaction arises from the decline in the discount of the pound, 20 points per month (from 60 to 40 points). Since the trader enjoyed a 60-point discount for the twelve-month buy, at a cost of 60 points for one month and 40 points for eleven months, (s)he netted 20 points for eleven months, or 220 points. *Notice that even if the spot rate had changed during the intervening month, the profit would still be the same.* Both the component loss and gain will be larger, but the net of the two will still be 220 points.

The risks in this transaction arise from a misassessment of future interest rates. For example, the forecast of the British interest rates might have been correct; however, if the U. S. interest rates also decline, the discount at the time of closing the transaction might be even larger than at the beginning of the swap, and there will be a loss.

These examples of speculation are related to forecasting rates, and in this era of managed floating, forecasting which way rates will move is highly speculative. Central banks may change policies, recognizing always the conflicts between stimulating exports and improving employment versus accepting more inflation. Likewise, they have to make judgements about the reaction of the central banks of their major trading partners. Hence, the speculator making sharp judgements about the natural course of currency in the future does so at his or her own peril!

SUMMARY

Trades in currencies take place in the foreign exchange market for immediate exchange (spot) or future exchange (forward). The market itself is a world-wide network of traders, usually operating from commercial banks, who communicate via telephone or telex. Transactions primarily focus on a dozen or so major currencies. Central banks also operate in the foreign exchange market to adjust the value of their nation's currencies.

Spot quotations are usually in terms of the amount of local currency to buy one unit of foreign currency, with the United Kingdom a major exception to this practice. This is the *direct* quotation. The quotient of two foreign currencies in terms of the local currency (cross rate) can be used to find the price of one foreign currency in terms of the other.

The forward quotations can be made at the *outright rate,* which is done in the same terms as the direct price quotation for spot trades. Among dealers, quotes are usually at bid/ask premiums or discounts from spot, called the *swap rate.* The forward premium (discount) of a currency is computed as:

$$\frac{(\text{Forward Rate} - \text{Spot Rate})}{\text{Spot Rate}} \times \frac{12}{\text{Number of Months Forward}}$$

These exchange rates in the forward market reflect interest rate differentials. *Arbitrageurs* operate to equilibrate the rates for a currency in various parts of the world by buying and selling the same currency for the same maturity at different places. *Covered interest arbitrage* is the process by which the forward exchange rates are brought into equilibrium with differing interest rates in various countries. Through its operation, the total return in a period for all currencies from interest plus exchange gain or loss is the same. When the markets are not completely free or when there are major expectations about revaluations of currencies, this covered interest equilibrium will not be based on interest differentials alone.

There are four major actors in the foreign exchange market. Two actors with straight financial goals are the outright *speculators,* gambling on changes in spot exchange rates, and the *commercial banks,* which create the foreign exchange market and may speculate as well. The other two actors have nonfinancial business concerns which create their interest in the market. These are the *merchandise trader,* who wants to protect a future cash flow from exchange rate fluctuations, and the *corporation with net exposed assets in foreign currencies,* which wishes to hedge the value of those assets. The behavior of these two actors is detailed in the next two chapters.

A *square position* occurs when both the *maturity* and *currency* of cash transactions are perfectly matched. Speculation occurs whenever a square position does not exist. The *net position* in a given currency for an individual or institution is *long* if future inflows in a currency exceed outflows and *short* if future outflows exceed inflows. *Outright speculation* refers to a net long or short position. One can speculate in the forward market using forward contracts or in the money market by borrowing and lending different currencies.

In a *swap,* the total net position is zero but it is not zero for specific dates in the future. In the money market, a short debt to be rolled over at an expected lower interest rate can be loaned long. Here the speculation on interest rates is clear. The currency can be revalued and there is no effect on the speculation outcome. When the swap involves the foreign exchange market, then the gamble is that the forward premiums or discounts will move in line with the changes in interest rates. Different maturities of forward contracts are used so the net position in a given currency can be zero, yet the expected change in interest rates will result in a gain if the forward discount/premium moves parallel to the interest rates.

Exercises on Foreign Exchange Mechanics

1. On April 30, 1973, the buying rate for deutsche mark spot in New York was $0.352350.

   a. What would you expect the price of the U. S. dollar to be in Germany?

   b. If the dollar were quoted in Germany at DM 2.8400, how is the market supposed to react?

2. On the same date that the DM spot was quoted $0.352350 in New York, the price of the pound sterling was quoted $2.4890.

   a. What would you expect the price of the pound to be in Germany?

   b. If the pound were quoted in Frankfurt at DM 7.00/£, what would you do to profit from the situation?

3. On August 2, 1974 the DM was quoted $0.3876/DM, and the French franc was quoted $0.2133/FF, in New York. If on this same date Paris was quoting FF1.7500/DM, and FF4.6875/$, what are the incentives for arbitrage?

4. You have called your foreign exchange trader and asked for quotations on the Belgian franc spot, one-month, three-month, and six-month. The trader has responded with the following:

$$\text{\$0.02479/81} \qquad 3/5 \qquad 8/7 \qquad 13/10$$

   a. What does this mean in terms of dollars per Belgian franc?

   b. If you wished to buy spot Belgian francs, how much would you pay in dollars?

   c. If you wanted to purchase spot U. S. dollars, how much would you have to pay in Belgian francs?

   d. What is the premium or discount in the one-, three-, and six-month forward rates in annual percentages? (Assume you are buying Belgian francs.)

5. The spot Danish krone is selling for $0.15985, and the three-month forward is selling for $0.15900. The three-month treasury bill rate in the United States is 6.25% and in Denmark 7.50%.

   a. Are the forward rates and interest rates in equilibrium? Why?

   b. If not, what would you do to take advantage of the situation?

   c. If a large number of individuals take similar action, what will be the impact in the market? (Assume interest rates remain constant.)

6. Ms. LeRoy is convinced that the Japanese yen is presently undervalued. She wants to profit from her analysis.

Spot rate–day 1	$0.0037660
Forecast rate–day 30	0.0041426
30-day forward	0.0037816

Interest rates–1 month
  United States   7.50%
  Japan   6.30%

a. What is the premium or discount on the forward yen?

b. What choices does Ms. LeRoy have to profit from her forecast of the future value of the yen?

c. What are the potential costs and gains of each alternative?

	Case A	Case B	Case C
Spot rate–Day 30	$0.0037660	$0.0041426	$0.0043309

d. What course of action would you advise Ms. LeRoy to follow?

7. Mr. Morales, a trader at one of the major banks in New York, has received information from the economic research department of his bank that short-term interest rates in the United States are bound to increase by 100 basis points within a month. (100 basis points equal 1%.)

1-year treasury bill rates
  United States   6.45%
  Canada   4.46%

Spot rate: $0.996800/Canadian dollar

Forward rate:
  1 year $1.016636
  1 month $0.998453

a. What is the premium or discount on the Canadian dollar?

b. What does the new information mean in terms of future rates? If the trader is bound by the rule "buy equals sell," what opportunities does he have to profit from the information given to him by his economic research department?

c. What are the costs or gains of such alternatives:
  i. if the U. S. interest rate increases to 7.45% within a month?
  ii. if interest rates remain constant?
  iii. if spot Canadian dollars on day 30 were $0.9500?

d. What course of action would you advise the trader to follow?

Bibliography

Aliber, Robert Z., "Exchange Risks, Yield Curves, and the Pattern of Capital Flows," *Journal of Finance,* May 1968, pp. 361-370.

Aliber, Robert Z., ed., *The International Market for Foreign Exchange.* New York: Praeger, 1969.

Einzig, Paul, *A Textbook on Foreign Exchange.* London: Macmillan, 1966.

Einzig, Paul, *The Dynamic Theory of Forward Exchange,* 2nd edition. London: Macmillan, 1967.

Foreign Exchange Exposure Management. New York: Chemical Bank, 1972.

Foreign Exchange Handbook for the Corporate Executive. New York: Brown Brothers Harriman and Co., 1970.

Ken and Joan Morse

On Thursday, June 22, 1972, the ancient city of Florence could be seen clearly from the hillsides surrounding its valley. The lovely view was lost on Ken Morse and his wife, Joan, as they were seated rather nervously by a fountain at the Villa le Rondini, waiting for a phone call to get through to their broker at Merrill Lynch in New York.

"If we do nothing," thought Ken, "we'll miss a fantastic opportunity to speculate on sterling. If we are right, we'll double everything that we own. But if we're wrong, we could be in debt for the rest of our lives." "We've run all the numbers," said Joan. "I think we should take the risk and hope like hell that we're right!"

*   *   *   *   *

The June crisis in the British pound had not come entirely unexpected to the Morses because they had been following sterling closely during the spring of 1972. Ken, who had just completed the second year of an MBA program, had written on his final exam for International Finance that he expected a devaluation of the pound to be forced upon the United Kingdom before the end of that year. During March, April, and May, 1972, he made several efforts to take a short position on sterling for their personal account. Initially, he contacted some major banks in Boston and proposed to sell £100,000 eighteen months forward at about U. S. $2.6060, the then prevailing rate for that type of contract and a slight discount from the spot rate.

The Response of the Banks

Ken's first telephone call in early March 1972 was to the First National Bank of Boston. The head of the foreign exchange department, Mr. Hartwell, refused even to discuss the possibility of allowing an individual to take a short position on any currency. He stated that it was the strict policy of the bank not to assist individuals to take positions in foreign exchange and that such had been the bank's policy for as long as he could remember.

The same day, Ken contacted Mr. Arthur Snyder, a senior officer at New England Merchants Bank (NEM). Ken thought his chances would be better because Art had a very good reputation with the New Ventures Department at the school, and Ken had worked with him before. Art said that the bank had no "formal" policy against allowing individuals to take foreign exchange positions through the bank and that several "friends" of the bank had done so. This had been allowed in part because the individuals were also treasurers of major corporate clients of the bank who were very familiar with the mechanics and risks of dealing in the foreign exchange market. Mr. Snyder said that he would let Ken take a position provided he backed it up with 10% collateral.

Mr. Meehan, the NEM foreign exchange trader, explained that the 10% figure was established in the days when countries had to request permission from the IMF to devalue more than 10% so that the most that could be lost due to a "surprise" change in an exchange rate was 10%. Asking for 10% collateral was tantamount to refusing to help Ken because he did not have $26,000 in ready cash to cover a £100,000 contract, and most of the banks in the Boston area were completely unwilling to loan him more than $1,000 without a guarantee other than his signature. When an officer of one of the popular banks in Harvard Square heard what Ken wanted to do with the funds, he said, "Can you imagine how the bank examiners would roast us if they found out we loaned you money to do that!"

An Approach to a Brokerage Firm

Leaving NEM on the back burner for the moment because of the collateral constraint, Ken next approached Paine, Webber, Jackson and Curtis, a nationwide brokerage firm where he and his wife kept their small but active account. He asked Mr. George Gardner, the Boston office partner, if they would either:

1. execute a short trade position in British pounds for him; or

2. allow him to use his present stocks (mostly over-the-counter or highly speculative securities) as collateral for a transaction at NEM.

Mr. Gardner replied that he was unwilling to help because, first of all, they did not recommend that their clients speculate in the commodities market, and secondly, there was no precedent for them to use a person's stock holdings as collateral for another institution. Although the Chicago Mercantile Exchange had announced that it was going to begin dealings in foreign currency futures, Mr. Gardner said that Paine Webber had no intention of participating in that segment of the Exchange.

They did, however, allow their customers to take positions in other commodities on the Chicago Exchange, such as wheat, corn, and sugar.[1]

A Return to the Bank

A bit dizzy from the run-around (it was now early April), Ken went back to the New England Merchants Bank and met with their head trader, Mr. Meehan, explaining his desire to go short on the pound even though he didn't have the cash necessary for 10% collateral:

Ken: You and I both know that the 10% collateral figure was arbitrarily chosen. Once it may have been an easy "rule of thumb," but now it seems inappropriate for the particular transaction my wife and I have in mind. The spot and forward pounds are trading close to the middle of their bands (parity is $2.6057). Unless the United States devalues again, for all practical purposes the absolute worst case would be if the pound went to the top of its band, exposing me to a risk of about 2¼%.

Meehan: That's absolutely right, Ken, and it makes a lot of sense to me that your collateral should only be about 2½% which means you would need to put up only $6500 instead of $26,000 for a transaction of £100,000. We could put the collateral in a certificate of deposit (CD) at 4% for you until you close out your position. I'll talk with Art Snyder and the other powers that be to see what we can do for you. However, because of the weakness in the U. S. dollar, we see sterling as quite strong at this time, and we think it will get stronger. You might consider waiting until maybe June or July to take your position.

Ken: Well, the most I could gain by waiting is about 2%, but if I take an eighteen-month forward contract *now*, I eliminate any risk of missing the devaluation in case the British are forced to do it early. Sure, I might miss a few basic points, but I'm betting on a quantum jump. They just have to devalue before entering the Common Market [January 1, 1973], I think.

Meehan: Well, I guess what we're saying is that we really see the pound as quite strong, and the dollar as relatively weak, and we're not really sure that it's such a good idea to short the sterling at this time

*   *   *   *   *

Several weeks later, the coalminers' strike in the United Kingdom was settled, and sterling was firm. Ken was convinced that the time was right to take an eighteen-month short position. He called Mr. Meehan at NEM and said that he and his wife had agreed to liquidate all the stocks they owned, if necessary, and get the maximum

[1] By September 1972, Paine Webber reversed its policy. Boston office clients may now take positions in the International Monetary Market of the Chicago Mercantile Exchange.

loan possible on each of their checking accounts so that they could put up the collateral in order to take a short position. It wasn't enough cash to cover a £100,000 contract but it was certainly every cent they could lay their hands on.

"Well, Ken," said Mr. Meehan, "in the meantime, I've talked with the bank's president, and we've decided that even with 10% collateral, we just can't help you out. Our reasoning is that this may be a risk that you shouldn't take and we've now made it bank policy that we're not going to let any individuals take currency positions even if they're well known to the bank and can pay up if the deal goes sour. Besides, you'll probably be glad. With Britain's strong reserve position and another whopping U. S. deficit expected, I'm really not sure that this is a good idea anyway."

The Chicago Mercantile Exchange—His Last Hope

By mid-May, Ken was convinced that his only opportunity to go short on pounds would be through the newly established International Monetary Market of the Chicago Mercantile Exchange—called the IMM of the CME. The IMM was founded, in part, because of the exhortations of Milton Friedman, the didactic economist. A few years earlier, he had faced frustration similar to Ken's when he had tried to go short on sterling and no bank in Chicago would assist him to make the short transaction he had wished to make before the 1967 pound devaluation.

Because Paine Webber said they would not participate in the IMM, Ken asked some friends to recommend another broker. They suggested a man at Merrill Lynch in New York who seemed to have a less moralistic attitude towards speculation.

Ken and his wife explained to their new broker what they wanted to do and waited impatiently while he and the IMM tried to get organized. During that time, before the IMM began functioning, they watched frustratedly as the forward and spot rate of pounds depreciated relative to the dollar. A major factor in this depreciation had been the United Kingdom's announcement of unfavorable trade figures resulting from the coalminers' strike.

After some negotiations, Merrill Lynch allowed Ken and Joan to operate with the *minimum* collateral requirements of the CME—$2,500 per contract. The IMM specifies that a "contract" equals £50,000[2] and charges a slight fee per contract traded. Ken and Joan scraped together everything they could, bought a $10,000 three-month treasury bill, and offered four sterling contracts for eighteen months forward at $2.6060, the then prevailing rate among New York banks for that type of contract. They did not buy a longer Treasury bill because they thought rates were going to go up.

*   *   *   *   *

The following is a summary of the events which Ken and Joan felt were significant in assessing the future rate of the pound:

December 1971:   The Smithsonian Agreement. After four months of floating, the U. S. dollar and other major currencies return to a fixed

[2] One contract also equals 50,000,000 Italian lire, 25,000,000 Japanese yen, 1,000,000 Mexican pesos, 500,000 Swiss francs, 50,000 deutsche marks, or 200,000 Canadian dollars. The size of these contracts was reduced subsequently.

rate within wider bands (2¼% either side of parity). Sterling parity is set at $2.6057, up from $2.40 in the previous May. Exhibit 1 shows the Smithsonian parities and presents data on the movement of spot rates after September 1971.

January 1972: U. K. balance of trade surplus for 1971 is announced: $750 million (Exhibit 2, pages 124-25, presents the U. K. balance of payments for the period 1968-1971). The British government starts pursuing an expansive monetary and fiscal policy. Many experts feel that the United Kingdom's strong reserve position is evidence of a strong pound.

February 1972: Three-month U. S. treasury bills at all-time low, below 3½% (see Exhibit 3, page 123). Low U. S. interest rates lead to massive outflows of "hot" money. Japan and France establish tighter controls on capital flows.

March 1972: Citibank Financial Letter asks, "When will the dollars come home?" All EEC currencies are at the top of their new bands relative to the dollar (Exhibit 4 shows the spot and forward exchange rates relative to their central rates for various key currencies).

March 9-12: European central bankers meet in Basel and agree that their present parities with the dollar are appropriate. Arthur Burns assures them that U. S. short-term rates will rise further soon.

Ken and Joan decide this is a good time to go short on the pound, before exchange markets react to upcoming changes in interest rates. Ken contacts First National Bank of Boston and New England Merchants Bank for the first time.

March 15: Three-month U. S. Treasury rates are up to around 3¾%. Europe adds more controls. United Kingdom forced to import large amounts of coal due to miners' strike. Cuts in electric power force industry to produce below capacity.
[Exhibit 5 shows the impact of the strike on the United Kingdom's capital utilization, unemployment, and international trade.]

March 25: Mr. Barber, Chancellor of the Exchequer, in his budget message states:
"It is neither necessary nor desirable to distort domestic economies in order to maintain unrealistic exchange rates, whether they are too high or too low. Certainly, in the modern world, I do not believe there is any need for this country, or any other, to be frustrated on this score in its determination to sustain sound economic growth." *The Economist,* March 25, 1972.

March 30: OECD working group states that the U. S. dollar's new parity is sound and that central bankers accept it as such. Furthermore, despite the expectation of further sizable U. S. trade deficits, some hidden reflow of funds is already taking place.

Early April: Cost of apartments in London seen as considerably higher than New York following spiraling rents in the United Kingdom. Annual consumer price increases in April 1971–March 1972 announced:

United States	3.7%
Japan	5.0%
Italy	5.0%
Germany	6.0%
United Kingdom	9.0%

U. S. interest rates begin to rise while many European rates remain sluggish (see Exhibits 3, 6, and 7), indicating that business is picking up in the U. S. before in Europe.

Ken and Joan decide this is a good time to go short on the pound before inevitable bad news from miners' strike is announced and before the U. S. rates rise further. Ken contacts NEM for the second time.

Mid-April: United Kingdom announces a March trade deficit of $208 million but emphasizes heavy reserve position.

April 24:   Europe takes major step toward monetary union (for details see Exhibit 8).

End of April: United Kingdom pays off all loans to the IMF and is now free of short and medium term debt for first time since May 1964. During April, the price of gold jumps from $48 to $58 per ounce as South Africa announces a reduction in output.

The report to the Club of Rome, *The Limits to Growth,* estimates that if the present increase in the rate of demand for gold continues, the world's total supply will be exhausted in less than four years (data on gold price movements are presented in Exhibit 9).

May: United States announces a massive trade deficit for the first quarter of 1972. Japanese and European central banks are frequently forced to intervene in support of the dollar.

May 5:   *The Wall Street Journal* reports, "More workdays were lost through strikes in Britain in 1971 than in any year since 1926 (the year of a general strike)."

The Events of June

After he finished his exams, Ken and Joan left for a trip to Europe on a combination of business and pleasure. In mid-June when they were in London, they could almost "feel" that a devaluation was coming, sometime. At parties some of their British friends laughed, "Don't worry about us—Britain will always be Britain." But in the City, a banker confided, "We never would try to benefit from a devaluation. But while we were long on sterling earlier this week, we have moved to a more balanced pound position today."

Ken promptly dialed his New York broker and was surprised to hear the following:

Merrill Lynch: We haven't been able to sell your contracts yet. Nobody seems to want to take an eighteen-month position in any currency on the IMM. There just isn't any market that far out.

Ken: Well go ahead and offer at a price below what the New York banks are quoting, and I'll check back with you when we get to Florence.

Merrill Lynch: O.K., Ken. We'll do what we can to generate interest in your offer.

On June 22, 1972, as Ken and Joan waited to talk with Merrill Lynch again, they reflected on recent events which they had been following in the *International Herald Tribune* and local magazines as they traveled by train through Europe:

June 1-21:   Bank of England *Quarterly Bulletin* states that United Kingdom cost of inflation is "serious." Bank of England spends $1.5 billion of its reserves to keep the pound inside the EEC "tunnel" (see Exhibit 8). EEC central banks also are forced to intervene to maintain sterling (see Exhibit 4) with the result that their spot rates weaken against the dollar. In London, students carry signs saying "Devalue Now."

It was 7:15 p.m. local time in Florence, about one hour before the IMM was scheduled to close in Chicago. Ken and Joan had stopped at a local bank after lunch and learned that spot sterling had gone down almost 1% from the Friday before. Presumably the 30-, 90-, and 180-day forward rates were discounted an even greater percentage. The price of the pound sterling had been slipping since early June. However, the decline had accelerated during the most recent week.

Selling Price of Bank Transfers in U. S. for Payment Abroad at 4 P.M.

	Spot	30-days	90-days
Thursday, June 1	$2.6128	$2.6122	$2.6096
Thursday, June 8	2.6114	2.6113	2.6089
Thursday, June 15	2.5976	2.5964	2.5926
Friday, June 16	2.5940	2.5916	2.5861
Monday, June 19	2.5914	2.5886	2.5822
Tuesday, June 20	2.5875	2.5765	2.5575
Wednesday, June 21	2.5725	2.5575	2.5375

If their eighteen-month contracts had not been sold, should they offer shorter term contracts (30, 90, 180 days) which had a greater probability of being sold? What discount should they sell them at?

"It all depends on the timing and the extent of the devaluation," said Joan, as the owner of the Villa appeared and said, "Telephone for you Mr. Morse. I believe it's about your call to New York. . . ."

EXHIBIT 1   Spot Exchange Rates, September 1971-February 1972

Left scale: U. S. cents per unit, weekly average of daily rates in New York
Right scale: Percentage change from parties existing as of April 1971
Solid line: Old parity before August
Dotted line: New parity of December

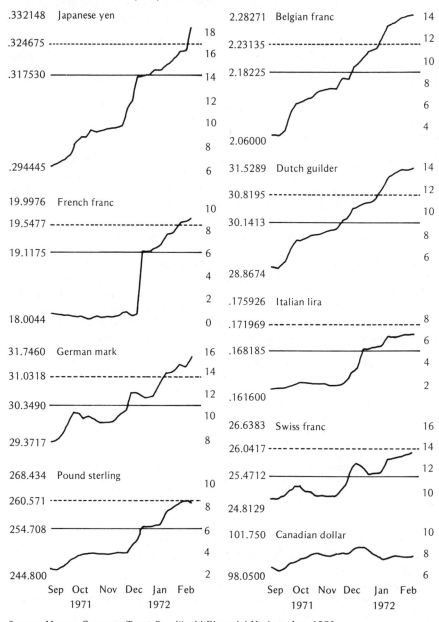

Sep Oct Nov Dec Jan Feb
1971   1972

Source: Morgan Guaranty Trust Co., *World Financial Markets.* Jan. 1972.

EXHIBIT 3   Short-Term Interest Rates, December 1970-June 1972

Treasury Bill Rates

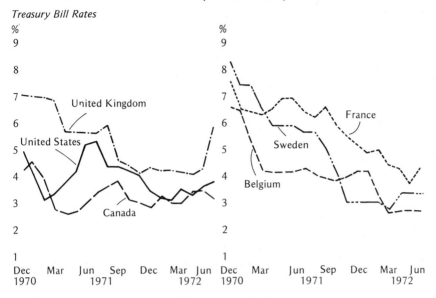

Representative Money Market Rates

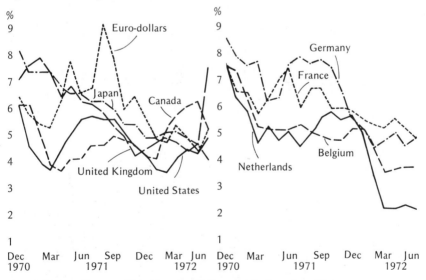

Source: Morgan Guaranty Trust Co., *World Financial Markets.* July 1972

EXHIBIT 2 U. K. Balance of Payments 1968-1971 (millions of pounds)

	1968 Year	1969 Year	1970 Year	1971 Year	1971 1st quarter	1971 2nd quarter	1971 3rd quarter	1971 4th quarter	1972 1st quarter
Seasonally adjusted									
Current account									
Exports (f.o.b.)	6,273	7,061	7,886	8,882	1,994	2,286	2,322	2,280	2,218
Imports (f.o.b.)	6,916	7,202	7,879	8,585	2,060	2,173	2,146	2,206	2,336
Visible balance	−643	−141	+7	+297	−66	+113	+176	+74	−118
Interest, profits, and dividends (net)	+341	+502	+490	+506	+117	+134	+140	+115	+124
Services and transfers (net):									
Government	−466	−467	−486	−521	−121	−125	−141	−134	−151
Private	+480	+549	+600	+697	+170	+161	+179	+187	+175
Total invisibles (net)	+355	+584	+604	+682	+166	+170	+178	+168	+148
Current balance	−288	+443	+611	+979	+100	+283	+354	+242	+30
Not seasonally adjusted									
Currency flow									
Current balance	−288	+443	+611	+979	+51	+338	+331	+259	−50
Investment and other capital flows:									
Official long-term capital	+17	−98	−204	−274	−45	−43	−35	−151	−42
Overseas investment in the United Kingdom	+583	+673	+739	+1,161	+443	+286	+209	+223	+236
U.K. private investment overseas	−727	−667	−761	−762	−223	−211	−185	−143	−359
Foreign currency borrowing (net) by U.K. banks to finance U.K. investment overseas	+155	+72	+189	+255	+35	+120	+50	+50	+175
Other foreign currency borrowing or lending (net) by U.K. banks	−124	−108	+290	+240	+55	+35	−1	+151	−44
Exchange reserves in sterling:									
British government stocks	−22	+237	+63	+55	+57	+36	−40	+2	+64
Banking and money market liabilities	−158	+77	+126	+638	+159	+234	+145	+100	+134

EXHIBIT 2 U. K. Balance of Payments 1968-1971 (millions of pounds)

	1968 Year	1969 Year	1970 Year	1971 Year	1971 1st quarter	1971 2nd quarter	1971 3rd quarter	1971 4th quarter	1972 1st quarter
Investment and other capital flows: *(cont.)*									
Other external banking and money market liabilities in sterling	−128	−53	+262	+734	+74	+2	+235	+423	+1
Import credit	+83	+156	+25	+76	+29	−5	+29	+23	+71
Export credit	−331	−328	−237	−337	−79	−120	+14	−152	−56
Other capital flows	−102	−58	+86	+72	+121	−28	+53	−74	−126
Total investment and other capital flows	−754	−97	+578	+1,858	+626	+306	+474	+452	+54
Balancing item	−117	+397	+98	+391	+296	−10	−137	+242	+53
Adjustment for maturing pre-devaluation forwards	−251	—	—	—	—	—	—	—	—
Total currency flow	−1,410	+743	+1,287	+3,228	+973	+634	+668	+953	+57
Allocation of Special Drawing Rights	—	—	+171	+125	+125	—	—	—	+124
Gold subscription to I.M.F.	—	—	−38	—	—	—	—	-	—
Total affecting official financing	−1,410	+743	+1,420	+3,353	+1,098	+634	+668	+953	+181
Official financing Net transactions with:									
I.M.F.	+506	−30	−134	−554	−287	−8	−259	—	−10
Other monetary authorities	+790	−669	−1,161	−1,263	−607	−500	+167	−323	+20
Official reserves (drawings on +/ additions to −)	+114	−44	−125	−1,536	−204	−126	−576	−630	−191
Total official financing	+1,410	−743	−1,420	−3,353	−1,098	−634	−668	−953	−181

Source: Bank of England, *Quarterly Bulletin,* June 1972.

EXHIBIT 4   Spot and Three-Month Forward Exchange Rates, March–June, 1972 (percentage deviation from central rates)

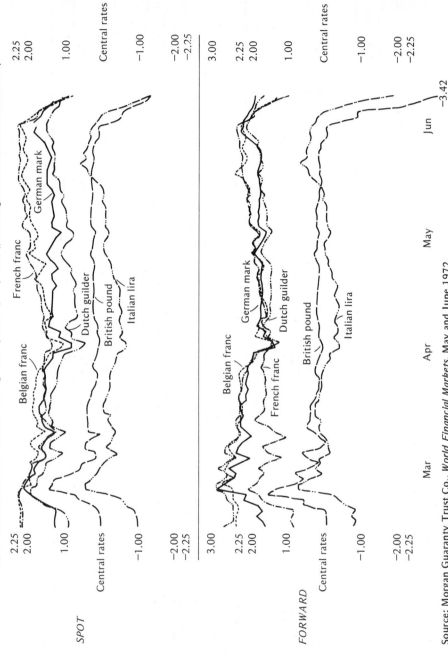

Source: Morgan Guaranty Trust Co., *World Financial Markets,* May and June 1972.

EXHIBIT 5

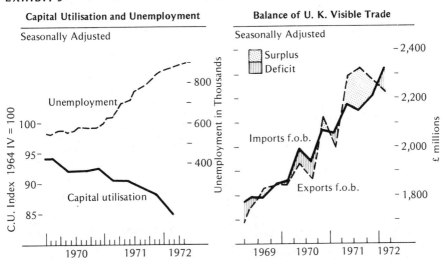

Capital Utilisation and Unemployment	Balance of U. K. Visible Trade

The growth in unemployment showed signs of slackening but capital utilisation fell sharply as a result of the miners' strike.

	Capital Utilisation Index			
	I	*II*	*III*	*IV*
1969	94·8	95·7	94·9	94·4
1970	94·4	92·3	92·3	92·6
1971	90·8	90·7	89·4	88·1
1972	85·8			

Source: Bank of England, *Quarterly Bulletin.* June 1972.

EXHIBIT 6   Commercial Bank Deposit Rates and Prime Lending Rates, January
1971-June 1972

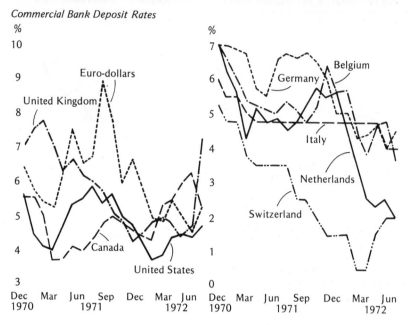

Commercial Bank Deposit Rates

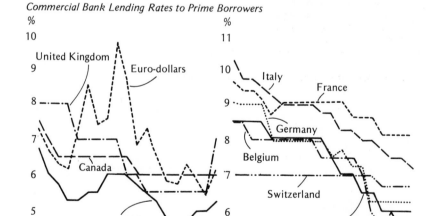

Commercial Bank Lending Rates to Prime Borrowers

Source: Morgan Guaranty Trust Co., *World Financial Markets.* July 1972.

EXHIBIT 7   Domestic Government and Corporate Bond Yields, January 1971-
June 1972

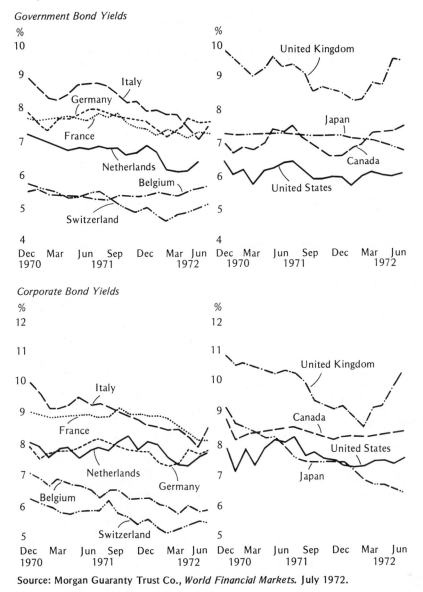

Source: Morgan Guaranty Trust Co., *World Financial Markets.* July 1972.

EXHIBIT 8 Sterling and the EEC "Snake" in the "Tunnel"
(percent premium/discount against US$)

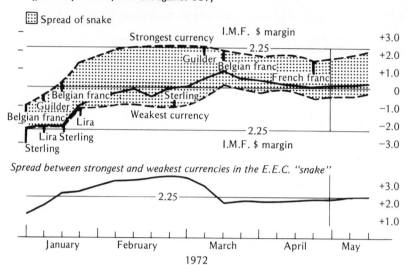

Spread between strongest and weakest currencies in the E.E.C. "snake"

After the E.E.C. currency arrangements took effect on 24th April, most E.E.C. exchange rates and sterling were at a premium against the U.S. dollar.

E.E.C. currency arrangements

Under the Washington Agreement of last December which permitted the rates for currencies to fluctuate between margins of 2¼% on either side of their parities or central rates against the U.S. dollar, it was possible for the rate between any two other currencies to vary by 4½% from their cross parity. On 24th April the central banks of the countries of the European Economic Community took steps to halve this possible divergence between any two of their own currencies from 4½% to 2¼%, *i.e.*, to ensure that the rates between any two of their own currencies could not diverge from their cross parities by more than 2¼%. This move was part of a general agreement by these countries to co-ordinate their policies in the foreign exchange markets, and represented an early step towards monetary and economic harmonisation in the enlarged Community. The measures flowed from an E.E.C. Council Resolution of 21st March accepted by the United Kingdom. The central banks were linked by direct telephone lines to allow rapid discussion and concerted action. At the invitation of the founder members, the Bank of England, together with the central bank of Denmark, joined the scheme on 1st

May, and the central bank of Norway followed on the 23rd.

The scheme has been put into operation by each participating country quoting buying and selling rates for its currency not only against the U.S. dollar as before but also against the currencies of the other participants at 2¼% on either side of their cross parities. The effect is that, within a total range of fluctuation of 4½% ("the tunnel"), the rates for the participating currencies at any one time are restricted within a community band of 2¼% ("the snake"). When the community band is within the tunnel, intervention at the limits of the community band must take place in community currencies. Intervention may also take place in U.S. dollars when a currency reaches its official U.S. dollar buying or selling rates at the limits of the tunnel. A mechanism for the short-term financing of interventions in community currencies and for subsequent settlement in various reserve assets had been established. Since the scheme came into operation the margin between the strongest and weakest member currencies has ranged between 2% and 2¼%, with sterling in the lower half of the band.

Source: Bank of England, *Quarterly Bulletin.* June 1972.

EXHIBIT 9   London Gold Price, January 1969-June 1972

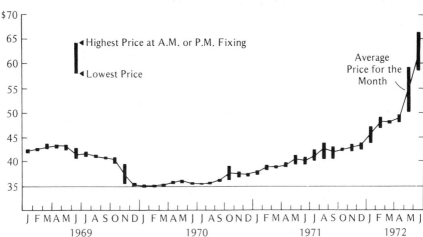

In late 1969 and early 1970, the free market gold price actually average at or below the official price of $35 per troy ounce. The price began to rise steadily in September 1970, however, and continued upward throughout last year. The tremendous surge in the price this year—to an average of $62.13 in June—appears to be the result not only of strong demand but also of a reduction in supplies. Moreover, the outlook is not very favorable for a change in this situation in the near-term.

Source: First National Bank of Chicago, *Business and Economic Review,* July 1972.

Citibank's Foreign Exchange Problems

In June 1965, the First National City Bank announced that a loss of four million dollars had been experienced in foreign exchange operations. It was later revealed that this loss had been incurred by one trader in the bank's Brussels branch who had engaged in forward transactions in the British pound.

As a stimulus for your thinking about the operations of the forward exchange market, you are being given a selection of the published reports on this situation. From these accounts you should develop an explanation of exactly how this loss occurred. This explanation should include timing of transactions and trends in prices and forward market spreads. Useful background information can also be obtained from the articles by Charles A. Coombs on the foreign exchange operations of the U. S. government and excerpts from the Bank of England, *Quarterly Bulletin* for the period when Citibank sustained the loss.

Newspaper Reports [1]

CITY BANK STOCK SHOWS PRICE DIP[2]

First National Issue Falls After Loss is Disclosed

The price of First National City Bank stock slipped ¾ point yesterday to 52⁷/₈ following the bank's disclosure that its second-quarter net operating earnings would be affected by a $4 million loss of "nonrecurring character."

George S. Moore, the bank's president, confirmed reports that the loss had been caused by foreign exchange transactions.

The stock, which is traded in the over-the-counter market, opened at 52¹/₈, down 1¼ points, in heavy trading, but then recouped part of its loss following comments by bank stock analysts that its first half earnings would at least equal those of the 1964 period.

Although the prices in the foreign exchange markets here appeared unaffected by the news, a number of traders reported that customers were hesitant to make commitments until there had been a more complete disclosure of the mechanics of the loss.

Walter B. Wriston, executive vice president of the bank's overseas division, would only say, however, that the loss had been incurred by an overseas branch office that had engaged in "foreign exchange transactions in excess of authorized limits."

Leading bank officials emphasized that as far as could be determined there was no evidence of fraud. . . .

International bankers here and abroad continued to conjure up ideas as to how First National City, with 114 branches in thirty-nine countries, could have lost that much on just foreign exchange transactions.

There was also some concern as to why stockholders had not been told of the loss at a special meeting last Thursday to approve the notes offering.

Bernard T. Stot, a vice president and the controller of the bank, explained that the stockholders weren't told because "we were resolving the problem at the time.". . .

The bank's officials refused to say what overseas offices or foreign exchange currencies were involved.

Foreign exchange experts expressed serious reservations that the loss could have been incurred by one office. One well-informed source noted: "It's hard to lose more than 1 percent in a convertible currency."

FIRST NATIONAL CITY FOREIGN EXCHANGE LOSS
LAID TO $800 MILLION SHORT SALES IN POUND[3]

First National City Bank's recently announced $4 million loss in foreign exchange transactions came as a result of about $800 million in "short sales" of British pounds, it was learned yesterday.

---

[1] Reprinted by special permission of *The Wall Street Journal, The New York Times,* and *Business Week.* These articles were originally collected under the supervision of Professor Eli Shapiro.

[2] *The New York Times,* June 16, 1965.

[3] *The Wall Street Journal,* July 20, 1965. Reprinted with the permission of *The Wall Street Journal,* © Dow Jones & Company, Inc., 1965.

The sales of British pounds, which weren't hedged in the "forward market," were executed for dollars by a trader in the bank's Brussels branch. He apparently was acting in the expectation that the pound would be worth less as a result of possible devaluation when the time came to deliver the sterling to the purchasers. But by delivery time, pounds were selling for a higher dollar exchange rate in the spot market and the trader had to spend more dollars than he anticipated to make good the contracts, it was explained.

The dollar loss to First National City from the transaction was $7.5 million before taxes, resulting in an after-tax loss of the $4 million.

Secrecy Spurs Guesswork

First National City, New York City's largest bank and the second biggest in the United States, first reported the loss in mid-June in a prospectus covering its recent sale of some $266 million of convertible capital notes. The bank at the time said only that the loss resulted from foreign exchange transactions in one of the bank's foreign branches. It wouldn't identify the kind of currency or the branch.

The bank's secrecy prompted considerable speculation in banking circles as to the exact nature of the transaction; bank officials refused to comment publicly. One early guess was that the heavy commitment had been made in the foreign exchange of a Latin American country, possibly Colombia or Uruguay, and had involved that nation's foreign central bank. But a number of bankers surmised from the start that the transactions had been in pounds sterling on the ground that the magnitude of the bank's loss suggested the dealings had been in a heavily traded currency.

First National City officials yesterday again declined to comment on any particulars of the foreign exchange loss. The bank, however, previously stated that the trader involved had violated its guidelines when he persisted in maintaining an "uncovered" position in his trading accounts.

Trader Loses Job

A trader covers his positions, for example, by offsetting sales of a currency in the forward market by purchasing roughly the same amount of the currency on a similar "futures" basis. Thus, to the extent that the trader sold pounds forward for dollars, he would have been considered in the desired "square position" if he had purchased approximately the same amount of pounds for dollars in the futures market.

The First National City trader, who is understood to be a Belgian national, is no longer in the bank's employ. The manager of the Brussels branch, it was learned, has been transferred to another post.

Foreign exchange transactions on a "forward" basis are entered into fairly frequently as a means of protecting the holder of a foreign currency from a possible loss in the event the money should depreciate in value by the time the owner repatriates the funds. This has been particularly true in the case of the pound, which for months has been the target of devaluation rumors.

Two Versions of Trader's Role

A company that goes into the forward market to protect its sterling holdings from possible devaluation can have a bank, for a small outlay, buy for sterling a specified amount of dollars for future delivery, say in 90 days. If the company sold pounds for dollars yesterday, it would have received a "spot" rate of $2.7904 for each pound. But if it sold for delivery in 90 days the exchange rate fixed at the time the forward contract is made, would have been $2.7775. Should there be a devaluation in the intervening 90 days, making the pound worth, say, $2.56 at the end of the 90 days, the company still would get its $2.7775 a pound.

Two versions of the Brussels trader's transactions have been circulating in banking circles in the U. S. and abroad. One holds that he sold the pound short as much as six or seven months in the future late last year. This was at about the time the British government barely staved off devaluation by resorting to an emergency $3 billion line of credit made available by 11 countries. Bankers who subscribe to this view theorize that the trader expected the pound to weaken sharply after a "disappointing" budget message by the Labor government in April 1965. The Labor government, instead, presented a stern "austerity" financial plan aimed at defending the pound.

Procedures Being "Tightened"

The other version is that the trader went short initially for only 30 or 60 days in the future. When he had to spend more dollars than he had anticipated in the "spot" market to cover these short positions, he entered into additional futures contracts, again for at least 30 days, "doubling up on his commitments as he went," in the words of one knowledgeable banker.

Bankers noted that if a 10% devaluation had pushed down the dollar value of the pound, he stood to make a profit for the bank of about $50 million. But as it was, the bank absorbed a $4 million after-tax loss, which it was required to divulge in the full glare of publicity surrounding its capital notes issue.

A First National City official said in answer to a reporter's question that the bank didn't plan to alter its reporting procedures on foreign exchange traders' positions as a result of the Brussels episode. But a spokesman conceded current procedures were "being tightened up" as a consequence.

There were also two versions as to how the sizable short position was detected. One is that institutions with which the trader dealt on the opposite side of foreign exchange transactions felt he was involving the bank in unusually large commitments, and asked bank officials about it. From another source, however, it was learned that the trader's position was discovered in a routine bank audit.

It was also pointed out that the $800 million in short sales, while sizable in an absolute sense, was relatively small when compared with the total foreign exchange transaction conducted by the bank in a year; this totaled a record $150 billion last year.

The Brussels trader, it was understood was on salary and didn't receive any commission based on profit he might bring in. One banker observed that he had taken the large short position "for the prestige, perhaps, if everything had worked out all right."

CITY BANK'S LOSS WAS IN STERLING[4]

First National's Deficit in Foreign Exchange Area
Laid to Brussels Unit, By Robert Frost

The First National City Bank confirmed yesterday that the $4 million net loss in its foreign exchange operations, which it reported last month, was the result of forward market operations in sterling at its Brussels branch.

At a hastily called press conference at the bank's headquarters here, Edwin A. Reichers, vice president in charge of the bank's foreign exchange operations, explained that the bank's trader in Brussels had persistently overextended his position in forward contracts.

Mr. Reichers said the trader was "operating independently, working on his own initiative and without the authority of the bank."

Contrary to reports the bank had gone short, or sold sterling it did not have in anticipation of covering its sales later at a lower price, Mr. Reichers emphasized the bank had been long on sterling forwards.

Use of Contracts. A forward contract calls for delivery at a future date of a specified amount of currency against a fixed dollar exchange rate agreed upon by the buyer and seller at the time the contract is made. Contracts may be made for one month up to one year into the future.

If there is any risk of downward price fluctuations or changes in the exchange rate, the forward contract is bought at a discount from the price of the currency in the spot, or immediate delivery, market. Otherwise, there may be a premium.

Prices for the pound sterling in the spot market here were quoted at $2.7904 yesterday. Sterling for delivery in three months could be bought at $2.7776, or at a discount of 1.28 cents a pound from the spot quotation.

First National City's foreign exchange problems began last September at a time when there were doubts about the future value of sterling, Mr. Reichers said. He explained the events that led to the loss as follows:

Confidence in Pound. Despite the gloomy market outlook for sterling, the bank's Brussels trader was still confident in the currency's future.

The apparent reasoning behind his transactions was his expectation that the spot price of the British pound would rise faster than the forward price. Thus, at the time the contract fell due, the bank would have a substantial profit.

As the forward contracts began to fall due, however, the trader found himself short of dollars. To insure that he would have the dollars on the due date, he sold sterling in the near-term market for delivery in 10 to 15 days at discounts considerably below what he had originally paid for the sterling.

Since he still needed the sterling for everyday business, he "rolled over," or renewed, the near-term contracts. Each time, he sold at a price below that which he had originally paid.

[4] *The New York Times,* July 21, 1965.

He was also forced to sell sterling in the spot markets, often at a price below that which he had originally paid.

In addition, where possible, the trader "rolled over" his forward contracts and continued to add new forward contracts as well.

Apparently, he hoped that in the end the profits from his operations would more than offset the initial spot losses.

At the end of April, the trader's dilemma was discovered by the branch's manager, Arthur Worthington, who directed the trader to reduce his forward position. According to bank sources, Mr. Worthington's directive went unheeded.

The loss itself was discovered at the end of May during a branch examination. It was estimated to be a pre-tax deficit of $8 million and was made public in the bank's June 10 prospectus, which accompanied its $266 million offering of convertible notes. The net loss was $4 million.

Because the branch still had a large position in sterling forwards that it was trying to liquidate, Mr. Reichers said, the bank decided not to announce the details publicly for fear the disclosure would scare off potential buyers of forward contracts or create a scarcity of spot sterling.

Although the bank declined yesterday to disclose the amount of the total forward contract commitment at the time the loss was discovered, it has been reported to have been as high as $800 million.

Position Liquidated. The bank's silence over details of the loss reported on June 10 stirred speculation and rumor in financial circles over the site and mechanics of the event.

However, the bank had steadfastly refused to say anything except that the loss involved foreign exchange transactions at an overseas branch until the forward position was liquidated. This was done on Monday.

Since the trader apparently was not buying to meet customer needs, a generally accepted practice in banking, the question was raised at yesterday's press conference whether he was speculating with the bank's money.

Mr. Reichers answered: "Draw your own conclusions."

The bank officer, who is considered to be one of the leading foreign exchange experts in the country, was at a loss to explain what gave the trader confidence in the pound at a time when few were optimistic.

Mr. Reichers asserted that "complete steps have been taken to insure that this situation will not come up again." He would not elaborate.

Accounting Procedures. It was assumed that some of these steps would insure proper accounting practices, which he said had not been enforced at the Brussels branch.

The trader's position at the end of the day was being reported as a "net" balance rather than as a breakdown of forward and spot balances.

A spokesman for the bank confirmed that Mr. Worthington, who has managed the Brussels office since August 1962, was being transferred to Paris. Reportedly, there is no tie between the loss and the transfer.

The trader, a Belgian whose name was not disclosed, resigned from the bank, the spokesman said, although under Belgian law, he is still technically employed, but on vacation.

Despite the foreign exchange loss, First National City was able to report record first-half earnings of $1.70 a share, compared with $1.57 for the 1964 period. The foreign exchange loss amounts to about 15 cents a share for the year.

A PLAUSIBLE LOSS[5] By Vartanig G. Vartan

Despite lingering skepticism in Belgian banking circles, the monetary authorities and commercial bankers in Brussels have accepted the First National City Bank's $8 million foreign-exchange loss as technically plausible, but hardly believable.

During the eight-month period when the bank's branch built up its heavy position in forward sterling, the monetary authorities there were aware of the increase, but since there appeared to be no violations of banking laws they left the bank to its business.

HOW TO LOSE $8-MILLION ON STERLING[6]

New York's First National City Bank Tells How—
and Takes Steps So It won't Happen Again

The Foreign Exchange Market, its devotees like to explain, is like a mirror—a currency transaction in one place is reflected by another currency transaction elsewhere. This week, New York's big First National City Bank explained how it let that mirror crack while losing $8-million.

Citibank's foreign exchange loss was revealed a month ago [B.W. Jun. 1965, p. 134]. But the bank has kept details hidden until it was able to close out a massive position in sterling that a trader in its Brussels branch had taken. That position—reported to be $800-million, though the bank denies the figure is right—was closed this week. Ironically, the trader had bet that sterling would be saved from devaluation, and had not "beared" the pound. It was a good bet, but, given the trickiness of foreign exchange markets, he lost anyway.

Election Effect. Starting last September, the man—a Belgian national, whose name is being kept secret—began selling spot sterling, while buying forward contracts of sterling. A forward contract calls for delivery on a future date at a rate fixed at the time the contract is made. For some time, forward sterling has been selling at a discount to the spot price (now $2.7904), and the Brussels trader was betting that the discount would shrink and bring a profit on the forward sterling when the pound strengthened.

This bet was taken before the British elections, and the maturity of the forward contracts went beyond that time. In the trade, it is regarded as a routine swap deal—you sell sterling for dollars, then use the dollars to buy forward positions. As it turned out, however, the forward purchase commitments had to be closed out at a loss.

[5] *The New York Times,* Aug. 5, 1965.
[6] *Business Week,* July 24, 1965.

As the months rolled on, the trader kept at it, selling spot or near forwards, simultaneously buying forwards or longer maturities, and constantly rolling over his swaps. According to Edwin A. Reichers, vice president in charge of Citibank's foreign exchange operations, the man "exceeded his trading limits on his own initiative."

Hard to Detect. Citibank puts overnight limits on its foreign exchange traders, though they vary from branch to branch. At the beginning, the trader's moves would not have aroused much anxiety: Citibank, along with most other New York banks, was confident sterling could weather an immediate storm, and the trader was bullish on the pound, too. He was on salary, and though he was clearly speculating, the profits would have gone to the bank. The size of his deals, though, soon got out of hand, and controls in the Brussels office broke down.

The Belgian branch kept track of its foreign exchange transactions only on a net basis—for example, over-all sterling sales and purchases would be toted up and only the balance, plus or minus, would be shown. Each man's trades were not shown and thus a sizable loss could go undetected for some time. Exchange transactions of a branch also appear on its books only, not in New York. Reichers says, too, that "prescribed accounting procedures were not followed by the Brussels office."

According to Reichers, the manager of the Brussels office did not become aware of the size of the trader's position until May. Then, he moved to have the trader close the position, and the losses became apparent. The New York office wasn't notified until early June.

Two-way Loss. The losses came about in two ways: first, in the trading itself, and second, in liquidating the position.

The bulk of the loss, says Reichers, came in trading. The Brussels man was betting that the discount on forward sterling would shrink; but confidence in sterling waned during the British election and after, and even the move to a 7% bank rate didn't help much. At times, the forward discount widened sharply—sometimes it was 3½¢ below the spot price. The trader was whip-sawed by the market's gyrations. He was buying forward contracts at only a tiny discount, and sterling didn't strengthen enough for the forward price to narrow—and thus produce a profit.

The bank also took a loss in closing the position. To do this, Citibank had to buy spot and then sell forward—just the reverse of what the trader had done in building his position. The loss here resulted from the fact that the forward still sells at a discount to the spot price. This week, sterling for delivery in three months could be bought at $2.7776, or a discount of 1.28¢ from the spot price.

The bank insists that it has taken steps to assure that such a mishap does not recur, though it won't spell them out.

Central Bank Reports

STERLING SITUATION: 1964–1965[7]

Early in 1964 sterling showed weakening tendencies as a result of the deteriorating trade position of the United Kingdom and various uncertainties connected

---

[7]Excerpts from Charles A. Coombs, "Treasury and Federal Reserve Foreign Exchange Operations." Federal Reserve Bank of New York, *Monthly Bulletin,* March 1965, pp. 43-45.

with the general election to be called sometime during the year. A timely increase of the Bank of England discount rate from 4 per cent to 5 per cent in late February temporarily relieved market pressures, while delay of the general election until October induced some short covering by commercial interests.

Late in May, however, tight conditions in several Continental money markets exerted new pressure on sterling. These pressures became strong toward the end of June because of heavier-than-usual midyear window dressing by Continental banks. To temper the impact of these movements of funds on official reserves, the Bank of England on June 30 drew $15 million against its $500 million swap line with the Federal Reserve; it repaid the drawing on July 13.

As the credit squeeze in the Continental money market centers extended into July, moderate selling of sterling continued, and the spot rate moved downward with a minimum of official support to a low for the month of $2.7874 on July 20. The decline in the spot rate was taken in stride by the market without any speculative re-action developing. Indeed, market confidence in the sterling parity at that time was such that the discount on forward sterling tended to narrow as the spot rate declined.

As the discount on forward sterling was reduced, the covered interest-arbitrage differential on Treasury bills in favor of London became correspondingly more at-tractive and by July 13 had reached 0.44 per cent per annum. To forestall private covered outflows in response to this arbitrage inducement, the Federal Reserve, with the agreement of the Bank of England, intervened in the market to reduce the arbitrage differential. This intervention, amounting to a total of $54 million equiva-lent in mid-July and again in late August, was accomplished by swap transactions in the New York market, with the Federal Reserve buying sterling spot and selling sterling forward against United States dollars. These operations had the dual effect of protecting the dollar against short-term flows of funds from New York to London while at the same time lending useful support to the spot rate on sterling.

In September, sterling came under increased pressure, mainly owing to increas-ingly widespread recognition of the mounting balance-of-payments deficit of the United Kingdom, which became further aggravated by the usual seasonal weakness during the autumn and early winter months. Uncertainties connected with the general election called for October 15 further unsettled the sterling exchange market, and the problem of maintaining confidence in sterling seemed likely to become in-creasingly difficult. In anticipation of reserve losses, the Bank of England in mid-September made timely arrangements to supplement the $500 million swap line with the Federal Reserve by another $500 million of short-term credit facilities with other central banks in Europe and with the Bank of Canada. This reinforcement of the British reserve position cushioned the impact of recurrent, and increasingly forceful, waves of selling during September and October. Net drawings by the Bank of England on the Federal Reserve swap line and on short-term facilities provided by other central banks rose to $415 million by the end of October.

The new Labor government elected on October 15 was thus immediately con-fronted with a grave balance-of-payments situation. The announcement on October 26 of emergency surcharges of 15 per cent on a wide range of imports brought only brief relief as critical reactions appeared among Britain's trading part-ners world wide, more particularly the European Free Trade Association (EFTA) group. In a formal budget presented to Parliament on November 11, the government proposed certain new welfare benefits, to be financed by tax increases, and an-nounced that it intended to introduce a capital gains tax and to substitute a new corporation tax for the existing application of the income tax to corporations.

These proposals created uncertainty in business circles, in part because the immediate deflationary influence of the increased tax on fuel as well as the import surcharge was to some extent obscured by the other measures. These uncertainties in domestic financial markets were, in turn, communicated to the exchange market. During this period, the exchange market began to anticipate bank rate action on each successive Thursday, and thus a pattern developed of a strengthening of sterling prior to Thursday of each week, followed by a major selling wave on Friday as the bank rate remained unchanged. When the bank rate remained unchanged on Thursday, November 19, reserve losses by the Bank of England on the following day reached such proportions that action could no longer be postponed. On Monday, November 23, the Bank of England raised its discount rate from 5 per cent to 7 per cent.

Perversely enough, market reaction to such forceful use of monetary policy by the Labor Government quickly degenerated into fears that the threat to sterling must have reached a truly crisis stage. Whether these reactions might have been averted by earlier bank rate action, more particularly on the usual Thursday date for bank rate announcements, may be debated for some time to come. In any event, the market seized on rumors that the $1 billion of short-term central bank credits at the disposal of the Bank of England in September had now been exhausted; that the $1 billion standby credit from the IMF secured by the British Government in August had accordingly been fully committed to repayment of such central bank credits; and, hence, that the United Kingdom would have to fall back in defense of sterling upon its reserves of roughly $2 billion. (The still-substantial unused drawing rights on the IMF would have required longer to mobilize than events at that time allowed.)

This situation assumed increasingly grave significance on the London afternoon—and the New York morning—of November 24 when a virtual avalanche of selling developed. If sterling were to be rescued, it was clear that a major package of international credit assistance would be required. On the afternoon of the 24th, the Federal Open Market Committee—meeting through a telephone conference—committed itself to an increase in the Federal Reserve-Bank of England swap line from $500 million to $750 million if credit assistance on a roughly corresponding scale could be secured from other central banks. That evening the Export-Import Bank gave assurance of a $250 million standby facility. Beginning early on the morning of November 25, the Bank of England, the Federal Reserve Bank of New York, and the central banks of other major countries were in almost continuous telephone communication. At 2 p.m., New York time, it was announced that a $3 billion credit package provided by eleven countries and the BIS was at the disposal of the Bank of England.

As a result of the heavy reserve losses, the $500 million Federal Reserve swap and the additional $500 million of other central bank credit facilities made available to the Bank of England in September were not only fully exhausted, but immediate drawings of $200 million on the new credit facilities were also required. From the end of October figure of $415 million, recourse by the Bank of England to central bank credit facilities thus rose by $785 million during November to a total of $1.2 billion. Of this total, the Federal Reserve share was $675 million.

In early December the British Government drew the full amount of its $1 billion standby facility with the IMF and so repaid an equivalent amount of the central bank credits outstanding, including $500 million of the Federal Reserve credit.

At the same time, Switzerland, which although not a member of the IMF, is associated with the General Arrangements to Borrow, provided the United Kingdom with a three-year credit of $80 million; $50 million of the Swiss credit was used to repay an earlier loan from Switzerland, outstanding from the sterling crisis of 1961.

With its exchange reserves thus heavily reinforced, the British Government could face with confidence further temporary pressures on sterling during December. Selling was particularly heavy just prior to the long Christmas week end, and during the month the Bank of England increased its use of short-term central bank credit facilities from the $200 million outstanding early in December to $525 million at the year end. Of this $325 million increase, $25 million was secured by an increased use of the Federal Reserve swap line, raising the total outstanding from $175 million to $200 million, while $300 million was drawn from other central banks.

Beginning in late November, heavy selling of sterling appeared in the forward market, mainly by commercial interests insuring their future exchange transactions. This selling threatened to move the forward sterling rate to an excessive discount and hence intensify sales of sterling in the spot market. Accordingly, the Bank of England gave firm support to the forward rate. This support not only served to lessen the drain on reserves from spot transactions at the time, but more generally helped to buttress confidence in sterling by providing official reassurance that the sterling parity would be maintained. The operation was comparable to the determined stand taken in the forward market by other central banks in recent years and promised to achieve the same useful results.

After the turn of the year, both the spot and forward markets for sterling returned to a more balanced position. Since then, sterling has shown an increasingly buoyant trend. On February 10 it was announced that those of the central bank credit facilities made available last November which were shortly due to expire would be replaced by new facilities, available to the end of May, thus reconstituting the entire $3 billion credit package. By the end of February the Bank of England was able to start repaying these debts.

STERLING SITUATION: 1964–1965 (continued)[8]

By mid-January 1965, sterling began to show signs of recovery from the speculative onslaught of late 1964, and this improvement continued through February. In March, however, the market once again became beset by doubts as to whether the British Government's pledge to defend the sterling parity would be matched by truly effective measures to curb excessive domestic demand and to restrain the inflationary trend of wage settlements. New complications arose as the United States Voluntary Foreign Credit Restraint Program led to some withdrawal of funds from London. Large forward commitments previously entered into by the Bank of England also began to mature, but firm defensive operations in both the spot and forward markets facilitated the rolling-over of most of these commitments. For those interested in the technical complexities of official intervention in the forward markets, a useful summary may be found in the Bank of England's *Quarterly Bulletin* for June 1965, pages 107-108.

[8] Excerpts from Charles A. Coombs, "Treasury and Federal Reserve Foreign Exchange Operations." Federal Reserve Bank of New York, *Monthly Bulletin,* Oct. 1965, pp. 202-203.

   With the announcement of new restraint measures in Chancellor Callaghan's budget message on April 6, sterling moved strongly upward and this trend was reinforced as the Bank of England on April 29 introduced special deposit requirements for the London clearing and Scottish banks and on May 5 requested the London clearing banks to limit the increase in their advances to the private sector to no more than 5 percent during the year ending March 1966. The other banks operating in London and a wide range of other financial institutions were also asked to exercise comparable restraint. However, following the announcement in mid-May of disappointing trade figures for April, the sterling rate once more began to drift downward. The British drawing on May 25 of $1.4 billion equivalent from the IMF and full repayment with the proceeds of $1,097 million of short-term central bank credits did little to bolster market sentiment. On the contrary, publication of figures showing a continuing deterioration in the British trade position during the second quarter further undermined market confidence, and substantial support had to be given to both the spot and forward markets. By late July the market had become convinced that a new crisis was shaping up for the autumn months. Against this ominous background, the British Government took further corrective action on July 27, announcing cutbacks and deferments in public sector spending programs and a further tightening of instalment credit.

   Unfortunately, an initially favorable market reaction to the July 27 measures was quickly swamped by the report on August 3 of a reserve loss for July that was much larger than the market had anticipated. As a result, sterling was again heavily offered in both the spot and forward markets, requiring substantial official support. By mid-August, however, the market began to take on a more balanced look, no doubt reflecting in part the improved July trade figures but also suggesting that sterling had become grossly oversold. From time to time, the market gave clear evidence of a squeeze for sterling balances.

   Against these mixed developments during August, the British Government on September 2 announced its intention to seek statutory authority to require advance notification and, if deemed appropriate, temporary deferment of wage and price increases. This basic policy action went a long way toward relieving the market's apprehension of a progressive undermining of the sterling parity by wage and price inflation. Meanwhile, negotiations were progressing among the central banks with the objective of providing additional facilities in order to further the recovery of confidence. On Friday, September 10, the Bank of England announced that these negotiations had been completed, stating that:

   > There is increasing evidence that the measures taken by Her Majesty's Government to restore the United Kingdom balance of payments are having their effects. Sentiment towards sterling in the exchange markets is improving. To further this trend the Bank of England with the full authority of Her Majesty's Government has entered into new arrangements with the central banks of Austria, Belgium, Canada, Germany, Holland, Italy, Japan, Sweden, Switzerland, the United States, and the Bank for International Settlements who cooperated in the support of sterling last November.
   >
   > These new arrangements take various forms and will enable appropriate action to be taken in the exchange markets with the full co-operation of the central banks concerned.

Immediately following this announcement concerted market action was initiated. As the spot rate for sterling moved up, short covering developed causing a further jump in the rate. The recent measures thus appeared to be yielding good results.

EXHIBIT 1   Foreign Exchange and Money Market Rates

	U. S. dollars		Interest on U.S. $ deposits in London (3 months)	Interest on £ deposits in Paris (3 months)
	Spot	3 months' forward (cents)		
	2.80		per cent per annum	
Last working days: 1964 June	2.7917	0.39 pre.	4.31	4.75
July	2.7882	0.47 pre.	4.25	4.88
Aug.	2.7839	0.43 pre.	4.25	4.75
Sept.	2.7833	0.54 pre.	4.44	5.13
Oct.	2.7850	0.59 pre.	4.50	5.19
Nov.	2.7912	2.01 pre.	5.00	7.75
Dec.	2.7901	1.90 pre.	4.50	7.63
1965 Jan.	2.7920	1.87 pre.	4.50	7.00
Feb.	2.7941	1.98 pre.	4.56	7.25
Mar.	2.7905	2.04 pre.	4.81	8.00
Apr.	2.7991	1.65 pre.	4.81	7.06
May	2.7927	1.89 pre.	5.25	7.75
June	2.7917	1.25 pre.	4.81	6.19
July	2.7920	1.47 pre.	4.63	6.56
Aug.	2.7907	1.73 pre.	4.44	6.88
Sept.	2.8018	0.98 pre.	4.94	6.50

Source: Bank of England, *Quarterly Bulletin*. Oct. 1965.

EXHIBIT 2 U. K. Balance of Payments (millions of pounds)

| | Current Account | | | | | | Long-Term Capital Account[a] | | | |
| | Imports (f.o.b.) | Exports and Re-exports (f.o.b.) | Visible Balance | Govern-ment (net) | Other Invisibles (net) | Current Balance | Official Capital Trans-actions | Private Investment | | Balance of Long-Term Capital |
								Abroad (net)	In the United Kingdom (net)	
1961	4,041	3,892	−149	−338	+473	−14	−45	−304	+426	+77
1962	4,092	3,994	−98	−362	+553	+93	−104	−236	+247	−93
1963	4,366	4,287	−79	−382	+566	+105	−105	−335	+278	−162
1964	5,005	4,471	−534	−439	+561	−412	−116	−398	+170	−344
1964 1st quarter	1,249	1,126	−123	−123	+190	−56	−26	−99	+39	−86
2nd quarter	1,254	1,153	−101	−109	+147	−63	−19	−110	+22	−107
3rd quarter	1,217	1,030	−187	−102	+97	−192	−28	−89	+60	−57
4th quarter	1,285	1,162	−123	−105	+127	−101	−43	−100	+49	−94
1965 1st quarter	1,227	1,141	−86	−111	+156	−41	−14	−110	+35	−89
2nd quarter	1,270	1,211	−59	−113	+197	+25	−10	−48	+61	+3

Monetary Movements[a]

	Balance of Current and Long-Term Capital Transactions	Balancing Item	Gold and Convertible Currency Reserves	Account with I.M.F.	Other Liabilities (net)				Balance of Monetary Movements
					In Sterling	In Overseas Sterling Area Currencies	In Foreign Currencies	Miscellaneous Capital, etc.	
1961	+63	−24	−31	+374	−356		−15	−11	−39
1962	—	+89	+183	−379	−23		+40	+90	−89
1963	−57	−68	+53	+5	+150	−6	−17	−60	+125
1964	−756	+35	+122	+359	−6	+8	+210	+28	+721
1964 1st quarter	−142	+58	−1	—	+49	+4	+35	−3	+84
2nd quarter	−170	+7	−16	−1	+85	+4	+55	+36	+163
3rd quarter	−249	+2	+59	+1	+80	−5	+95	+17	+247
4th quarter	−195	−32	+80	+359	−220	+5	+25	−22	+227
1965 1st quarter	−130	—	−5	−6	−34	−3	+175	+3	+130
2nd quarter	+28	−19	−165	+503	−169	+9	−195	+8	−9

[a]A decrease in liabilities or an increase in assets is shown —, an increase in liabilities or a decrease in assets +.
Source: Bank of England, *Quarterly Bulletin*. Oct. 1965.

PART TWO

We can now discuss some of the specific financial problems that a nonfinancial business manager faces when operating in the international markets. Where Part One created a foundation to aid the international financial officer in evaluating the financial markets and discussed the behavior of some major international financial institutions, Part Two will turn to major problems of the international financial officer of a nonfinancial business. Although the dividing line is not always easy to draw, particularly for large multinational companies with huge financial resources to manage, nonfinancial businesses, in general, come to financial markets more as "market takers" than as "market makers."

One major problem for the nonfinancial business is the financing of international trade. Chapter 6 discusses methods of covering to protect against foreign exchange risks, the institutions and procedures involved in financing international trade, and the risk/return tradeoffs in credit and foreign exchange decisions in this area.

Chapter 7 introduces the tools for evaluating some of the major decisions that the financial officer must make. These decisions include raising the necessary funds to finance the business operations, investing any excess funds that the business generates, supervising the flow of intercompany accounts, and protecting the foreign operations against foreign exchange risks.

The various problems discussed and evaluated in Chapter 7 are combined in Chapter 8 which presents a framework of specific steps in the analysis of the finance function of a nonfinancial business enterprise in the international markets. Although simplifying assumptions are made to keep the presentation within a manageable size, the issues of risk and the outcomes of alternative strategies under various future states of the world are brought together into a final interacting summary. This summary should serve as a digest of ground rules for management in choosing policies with which it feels comfortable, given attitudes towards risk and the implications of each policy under alternative market outcomes.

CHAPTER 6

Financing
International Trade

With the evolution of a greater world marketplace, the trading caravans and ships of many centuries past have been replaced by major air and ship cargo carriers. Likewise, the simple direct exchange of goods for money between buyer and seller has developed into an indirect payments mechanism that often involves several financial institutions.

In earlier periods of international trade, exporters relied on working capital loans and advances against shipment from their own banks to finance their operations prior to receipt of payment from their customer, the importer. In some cases, the importer paid cash in advance. The importer, in turn, was usually financed by loans from a local bank. Where the importer and exporter were well known to each other, open account arrangements were used just as one may use a charge account at a local department store. Periodically, the importer was billed for goods which had been shipped, and (s)he remitted payment in a form and to a location which had been agreed upon. Consignment shipping was used: the exporter retained title to the goods and was paid as the importer resold them to his/her local customers. All of these patterns are still present in the world marketplace. However, in later years, additional financing devices have been used. For example, a bank in the exporter's country may make a direct loan to the importer to finance his/her purchases or the bank may purchase the importer's liability from the exporter. In either case, the exporter would receive immediate payment and a large number of documents would be generated.

Although many recent developments in the financial markets have facilitated international trade, two basic factors continue to affect the assessment of trade financing options and the institutions that have evolved in the field: credit risk and foreign exchange risk. Like any other sale which is not paid immediately, international trade has to deal with the problems imposed by credit risks. Credit risks often present a larger problem in international than in domestic trade because of the greater distance between the trading parties in the international setting. The other problem, which is peculiar to international trade, derives from the potential fluctuations in the relative values of the currencies of the trading parties. In a system of foreign exchange rates such as the gold standard, this aspect of the transaction did not pose any problem. Under such a system foreign exchange problems would arise only if governments chose to impose foreign exchange controls that impeded the flow of trade. However, in a system where the relative values of currencies are subject to change, at least one of the trading parties has to deal in a foreign currency and, therefore, is subject to an uncertain outcome in terms of his or her domestic currency. For example, the importer who promises to pay in foreign currency will not know the exact cost of merchandise in terms of local currency until the payment is effected or insurance measures are taken.

The remainder of this chapter is divided into three major sections. The first section concentrates on the problem peculiar to international trade, foreign exchange risk, while assuming a simple open account credit arrangement. In international trade, the party to the transaction who incurs foreign exchange risks may wish to insure against these risks by covering the transaction in either the forward exchange market or the money market. The methods and tradeoffs in making this insurance decision are presented in this section.

The second section of the chapter removes the simplifying assumption of open account credit and introduces some of the procedures and accompanying documents that are used to deal with more complex credit arrangements. These procedures also offer alternative ways to handle the problem of foreign exchange risk. (Some of these financial procedures are also used in domestic trade. However, when dealing in domestic trade these procedures are only concerned with the issue of credit terms.)

Finally, the third section consolidates the two preceding sections by analyzing the issues of risk and return in international trade from the point of view of both the exporter and the importer.

INTERNATIONAL TRADE AND FOREIGN EXCHANGE RISKS

Whenever there is foreign exchange to be received or paid in the future because of a trade transaction on open account, there is a risk that the relative value of the currencies will change in the intervening time. If an Italian exporter sells on credit to U. S. residents and invoices them in dollars, there is a risk that three months later when payment is due the value of the dollar may have deteriorated relative to the Italian lira. In that case the exporter will have a loss in foreign exchange that might well erase the trade gains. In this example, (s)he can make sure of the amount of liras to be received at the end by covering in the forward market or by borrowing in the U. S. money market and investing in liras.

Assume that the export transaction takes place on April 23 and that it is payable in U. S. dollars on July 23. The export transaction is in the amount of $10,000. On April 23 the following rates prevail in the market:

Foreign Exchange Market

Spot rate: $0.0016940/lira (lira 590.3188/$)
3-month
        forward rate: $0.0017154/lira (lira 582.9544/$)

That is, the three-month lira is trading at a premium of 5.05% per annum against the U. S. dollar.[1] (The U. S. dollar is trading at a discount against the lira.)

Money Market

3-month lira: 9%
3-month U. S. dollar: 4%

That is, except for 0.05% per annum that can be attributed to transaction costs, the foreign exchange market and the money markets are in equilibrium and there is no incentive for interest arbitrage. Other than 0.05%, interest differentials equal the premium/discount in the forward market.

Covering in the Forward Market

In the preceding example, if the exporter chooses to cover export revenues in the forward market, (s)he will sell dollars in the forward market for delivery in three months in exchange for liras. The sequence of events will be as follows:

April 23:   Deliver $10,000 worth of shoes to a U. S. department store. Payment is due on July 23 in U. S. dollars. At April 23 spot prices of $0.0016940 per lira (lira 590.3188/$), the export sale is worth 5,903,188 liras.

In order to protect against an adverse change in the value of the dollar against the lira, the exporter sells $10,000 against liras for delivery on July 23 at $0.0017154 per lira (lira 582.9544/$), the market price for 3-month liras against U. S. dollars. That is, the forward contract will provide 5,829,544 liras.

July 23:   Exporter receives check for U. S. $10,000.

Exporter delivers $10,000 against forward contract and receives 5,829,544 liras.

From the beginning of the transaction the exporter knew exactly the amount of liras to be received when the payment was finally realized, i.e., 5,829,544 liras. This policy makes good sense, particularly if the Italian exporter expected the U. S. dollar to weaken against the Italian lira. If the exporter is uncertain as to the behavior of the U. S. dollar, the coverage transaction represents a purchase of insurance against a weakening of the U. S. dollar relative to the Italian lira. However, if the dollar actually strengthened against the lira by July 23, the Italian exporter would have suffered an opportunity loss by having sold the $10,000 against liras in the forward market in April.

$$[1]\ \frac{\text{Forward rate} - \text{Spot rate}}{\text{Spot rate}} \times \frac{12}{3} = \frac{0.0017154 - 0.0016940}{0.0016940} \times 4 = .0505$$

More specifically, the price of the liras was locked in by the forward contract at $0.0017154/lira (lira 582.9544/$). The spot rate for the lira in April, when the trade took place, was $0.0016940/lira (lira 590.3188/$). So, by locking in the forward price, the exporter was accepting a discount of 5.05% on the dollar against the Italian lira (a premium on the forward lira against the dollar). However, this action assured that if the spot rate at the end of the period turned out to be more than $0.0017154/lira (less than lira 582.9544/$), i.e., the dollar weakened against the lira below the initial forward price, the exporter would not incur the extra loss. This is the objective of the insurance bought by the forward contract. On the other hand, if on July 23 the dollar had strengthened against the lira and the spot rate was less than $0.0016940/lira (more than lira 590.3188/$), the exporter would have an opportunity loss. If (s)he had not bought the insurance of the forward contract the transaction would have been more profitable. As an illustration, compare the three cases below:

	Case A	Case B	Case C
1. Spot rate on July 23	$ 0.0016940	$ 0.0018634	$ 0.0015246
2. Less contracted forward rate	−0.0017154	−0.0017154	−0.0017154
3. Gain or loss (−) on forward transaction	$− 0.0000214	$+ 0.0001480	$− 0.0001908
4. Opportunity foreign exchange gain or loss (−): Lit 5,903,188 × (line 3)	$− 126.33	$ + 873.67	$ − 1,126.33

In this example, Case A shows the initial insurance price that the exporter is willing to pay to avoid paying a higher price for liras, since the April and July spot rates are identical. In Case B the dollar has weakened against the Italian lira below the point at which the forward contract was entered. By having the forward contract, the exporter avoided a loss of $873.67; i.e., an opportunity gain was realized or an opportunity loss avoided.[2] On the other hand, in Case C the exporter would have been better off by not covering in the forward market. In this case the exporter suffered an opportunity loss of $1,126.32. This loss was created because the forward contract had the U. S. dollar at a discount against the lira in April when actually the dollar strengthened against the lira by the day of payment in July.

It must be emphasized that the preceding foreign exchange gains and losses are of an *opportunity* nature. These gains and losses can be calculated only after the eventual spot rate prevailing on the date of the final payment is known. Then, with the benefit of hindsight, one can establish the losses that the forward contract

[2] If the exporter were operating solely on an expected value basis, then the minimum probability of the Case B outcome (assuming Case A and Case B were the only two outcomes evaluated) would be .13, since $(1-.13) \times (-\$126) + (.13) \times \$874 = 0$. As long as the exporter believes that the probability of the weakening of the exchange rate depicted in Case B is at least as great as .13, then the covering transaction will take place. In fact, given a risk averse exporter, the covering transaction will occur even for much lower values of the probability for Case B, because the lower expected value for the transaction is offset by eliminating the possibility of receiving a very low exchange rate.

avoided or the gains that were foregone because of the covering transaction. These opportunity gains and losses are *not* the actual cost of covering the forward market. The cost of covering in the forward exchange market in this example is the 5.05% per annum discount on the 3-month dollar against the lira that prevailed at the beginning of the transaction in April.

The actual cost of covering in the forward market can be understood better if one realizes that, in effect, there are two transactions that take place almost simultaneously on the date of final payment, July 23. One transaction is the delivery of U. S. dollars by the American importer in payment for the goods, regardless of whether or not a forward contract exists. These dollars converted into liras at the spot rate prevailing on the date of payment produce a foreign exchange gain or loss. That gain or loss depends on the difference between the spot rate at the end of the period, July 23, and the one prevailing when the export bill was drawn, April 23. The other transaction, which takes place if a forward contract is outstanding, is the delivery of dollars against liras by the exporter to fulfill the forward exchange contract. The foreign exchange gain or loss in the forward contract is the difference between the rate in the contract and the spot rate prevailing on the closing date, July 23. In the absence of the dollar proceeds from the export transaction, the Italian exporter would have to purchase U. S. dollars in the spot market at the rate prevailing on that date, July 23. Since the gain or loss in each component transaction in a covered export sale is calculated by comparing in one case the initial spot rate, and in the other case the initial forward rate, with the spot rate at the end of the period, July 23, the net gain or loss from the combined transactions must be the difference between the initial spot and forward rates; i.e. the 5.05% per annum discount on the dollar against the lira. We can illustrate this point further with specific calculations for the case of the Italian exporter:

	Case A	Case B	Case C
1. Spot rate, July 23	$ 0.0016940	$ 0.0018634	$ 0.0015246
2. Spot rate, April 23	0.0016940	0.0016940	0.0016940
3. Appreciation or depreciation (−) of the U. S. dollar against lira	———	$−0.0001694	$+0.0001694
4. Contracted, forward rate in April	$ 0.0017154	$ 0.0017154	$ 0.0017154
5. Gain or loss (−) on April forward vs. July spot (line 1 less line 4)	$−0.0000214	$+0.0001480	$−0.0001694
6. Gain or loss (−) from converting dollar proceeds into liras: Lit 5,903,188 × (line 3)	———	$− 1,000.00	$+ 1,000.00
7. Gain or loss (−) on closing forward contract: Lit 5,903,188 × (line 5)	$− 126.33	$+ 873.67	$− 1,126.33
8. Total costs	$− 126.33	$− 126.33	$− 126.33

In every case, the actual cost to the Italian exporter is $126.33. In every case the gain (loss) in converting the dollar proceeds into liras at the new spot rate when netted against the loss (gain) from the forward contract valued at the final spot rate produces the same net cost of $126.33. This cost is 1.26% of the total amount of export proceeds, $10,000. Since the cost was sustained over only three months, this is equivalent to 5.05% on a per annum basis—the initial discount of the 3-month dollar against the lira.

Covering through the Money Market

In the case of the Italian exporter, another way to insure against a large devaluation of the dollar against the Italian lira would be to borrow $10,000 in the United States for three months. The proceeds from this loan would then be converted into liras and invested in the Italian money market at the going rate. Thus, when July 23 arrives, if there is a devaluation in the dollar against the lira the loss in the receipt from exports will be compensated by the gain in the payment of the loan. The sequence of events in this case will be as follows:

April 23: Deliver the $10,000 worth of shoes to a U. S. department store. Payment is due on July 23 in U. S. dollars. At April 23 spot prices of $0.0016940 per lira (lira 590.3188/$) the export sale is worth 5,903,188 liras.

In order to protect against an adverse change in the value of the dollar against the lira, the exporter borrows $10,000 from a New York bank at 9%, discounts the loan, converts the proceeds, $9,775, into liras (5,770,366 liras), and invests them in a three-month bill in Italy at 4%. That is, after three months the bill will be worth 5,828,070 liras.

July 23: Exporter receives check for U. S. $10,000.

U. S. dollar proceeds from export sales are used to pay the $10,000 loan from New York bank.

3-month lira bill is liquidated and it yields the anticipated 5,828,070 liras.

The net cost of this covering transaction is the interest differential between the cost of the loan in U. S. dollars at 9% and the return on the lira investment, 4%. The net cost is 5%. The initial export sale is 5,903,188 liras. After the sale of the lira bill at the end of the transaction the exporter nets 5,828,070 liras. The covering transaction has cost 75,118 liras. This cost represents 1.27% of the original export sale in liras. Since this cost was incurred over only three months, it represents 5.08% on an annual basis. On an opportunity cost basis, the exporter is insuring that (s)he does not incur a loss larger than the one implied by the interest differential. However, if the dollar actually appreciates against the lira by the time the payment is due, the exporter would have been in a better position by not covering the transaction. Again, these last statements refer to the opportunity gains or losses from covering the export sale in the money market.

The cost of covering in the money market can be dissected in the same fashion as the cost of covering in the forward market. In effect, it is as if two transactions took place on July 23. One, the export proceeds in dollars are converted into liras; two, the proceeds from the lira investment are converted into dollars to pay for the loan in New York. Both of these conversions take place at the spot price prevailing on the date of payment, July 23. The following table presents the gains and losses for the Italian exporter from various parts of the export transaction covered in the money market:

	Case A	*Case B*	*Case C*
1. Spot rate: July 23	$0.0016940	$0.0018634	$0.0015246
2. Spot rate: April 23	0.0016940	0.0016940	0.0016940
3. Appreciation or depreciation (−) of the U. S. dollar against lira	——	$− 0.0001694	$+0.0001694
4. Proceeds from bill in lira:[a] (5,770,366) + (5,770,366 × .04 × 3/12 = Lit 5,828,070			
5. Conversion of proceeds from lira bill into dollars: 5,828,070 × (line 1)	$ 9,872.75	$10,860.02	$ 8,885.48
6. Loan due in dollars	10,000.00	10,000.00	10,000,00
7. Gain or loss in money market operation (line 5 less line 6)	$− 127.25	$+ 860.02	$−1,114.52
8. Gain or loss (−) from converting dollar export proceeds into liras Lit 5,903,188 × (line 3)	——	$ −1,000.00	$+ 1,000.00
9. Total cost	$− 127.25	$− 139.98	$− 114.52

[a]Assumes that the $10,000 loan was discounted before being converted into liras and invested in the lira money market.

The discrepancy in total costs is a function of the conversion of the differential between the interest paid on the loan at the beginning of the period and converted from dollars into liras at the April 23 spot rate, and the interest received in lira and converted into dollars at the end of the period at the spot rate on July 23. If the interest had been paid and received on the same date at the same prevailing spot exchange rate, the cost of covering in the money market would have been the same under every outcome, $127.25. That is, the cost is about 5% per annum—the interest differential.

If the costs of covering in the money market in the preceding computations are compared with the costs of covering in the forward exchange market computed earlier, the figures are very similar. Besides rounding errors and technical variations based on when the interest rates are converted, the costs differ only by the amount that the interest differential, 5%, differs from the premium on the three-month lira against the dollar at the beginning of the period, 5.05%. If the markets are in equilibrium (discounts or premiums in the forward market equal the interest differentials), the two approaches to covering a cash flow in a foreign currency should produce similar results, as was the case in our example.

When the export transaction was covered in the *forward market*, the *forward rate* for the lira against the U. S. dollar was locked in (0.0017154) at the beginning of the transaction. When the export transaction was covered in the *money market*, the *spot rate* for the lira against the U. S. dollar ($0.0016940/lira) was locked in at the beginning of the period. At a cost of approximately 5% per annum, both approaches to covering the cash flow generated from the export transaction accomplish the objective of locking in a foreign exchange rate at the beginning of the transaction to eliminate all uncertainty about the total proceeds from the sale. Both approaches also eliminate the possibility of an additional gain of 10% if the dollar strengthens against the lira as indicated in Case C.

Choosing a Cover

The analysis in the preceding two sections showed that if a decision to cover the proceeds from an international transaction is made, it does not make much difference in terms of cost whether the forward exchange market or the money market approach is followed, if the financial markets—money markets and foreign exchange markets—are in equilibrium. However, if the markets are not in equilibrium at the beginning (interest differentials and premiums or discounts in the forward markets are not the same), then even if the spot rate remains constant throughout the period, the forward market and money market outcomes will vary. If the spot rate remained constant but there was an interest differential of only ¾%, then the money market alternative would be superior. If the spot rate remains constant, the forward market approach still costs $126.33, but the cost in the money market is only $18.75, that is, ¾% × 10,000 × 3/12. If on the other hand, interest differentials in favor of the United States were much larger than the forward discount on the dollar, the forward market alternative would be the most attractive approach. As mentioned before, these disequilibrium situations exist in the presence of two parallel markets, domestic and external, separated from one another by the barriers of government control. Government controls apply only to transactions within the country boundary, i.e., Italy. However, currencies traded outside the country, e.g., Euro-lira, are not subject to these controls. The subsidiary located in the foreign country has access to its own domestic market. The parent company always has access to the external markets.

It is disequilibrium situations that are appealing to the corporate treasurers of firms which are major importers and exporters. The costs of covering in each of these markets may diverge, and when large sums are involved it is worthwhile for the treasurer to have sufficient knowledge of the differentials. Once the basics are mastered, the costs can be computed rapidly under each approach to covering. Then, the comparison of costs under the two alternatives can be made and the best option chosen.

Using the previous example of a ¾% interest differential (while maintaining a 5.05% discount on the U. S. dollar against the lira), the costs of the money market cover under *any* of the three outcomes outlined here would be lower by approximately the same $108 per $10,000 transaction ($126.33 − $18.75). Thus, the insurance policy's "cost" would be reduced by approximately 85% ($108 ÷ $126.33) by choosing the money market route to covering instead of the forward exchange market.

One more consideration to be kept in mind when choosing one approach to covering over another is the matter of financial reporting. The money market cover will appear directly on the balance sheet: an investment on the asset side and a liability on the liabilities- plus-equity side. The forward transaction will appear only as a footnote. To the extent that the financial officer is concerned about ratios such as the debt-to-equity ratio, financial reporting considerations introduce a bias against using the money market route to cover international trade and in favor of using the forward exchange market.

One other potential risk which we have avoided in the preceding discussion is that which can result from a mismatch of the maturities of various cash flows involved in a covered trade transaction. The previous calculations assumed that the investment in the Italian money market matured (could be converted into cash) on the same date that the proceeds of the export sale were received. However, in many cases it becomes impossible to find a security with a maturity to match the date of payment for the trade transaction. In these cases there is an additional risk: the value of the security at the time of the receipt from the export sale. If the level of interest rates increases during the investment period, and the security bought has a maturity longer than the trade account, the investor will be able to liquidate the debt security only by offering it at a discount on the closing date—a capital loss. On the other hand, if interest rates decline during the investment period, the exporter will have a capital gain on the investment. A similar risk is incurred if the security bought to cover the foreign exchange risks has a maturity shorter than the length of time until the receipt from the trade transaction is expected. In this case the exporter has to speculate on the interest rate that (s)he will be able to obtain on the security purchased after the initial security matures. If the initial security has only a one-month maturity, at the end of the first month the exporter will have to make another investment for the remaining two months of the trade transaction to continue on a covered basis.

To Cover or Not To Cover

Although the issue of opportunity gains and losses from covering was mentioned in the discussion of protection against foreign exchange risks in international trade, the emphasis so far has been on the computation of the actual costs of covering. Before we leave the topic of covering we should again consider its basic desirability.

In the example of the Italian exporter, the actual cost of covering was about 5% under the initial assumptions, regardless of what covering method was used. In some industries, 5% may appear to be a small price to pay for insurance against negative fluctuations in exchange rates. However, in other industries 5% may be more than the usual profit margin. In the latter case, covering for foreign exchange risk would make the trade transaction a loss, and international trade will take place only if one of the parties is willing to bear the uncovered foreign exchange risk. This willingness is a function of how likely and how large the people involved in the trade perceive the potential change in spot rates to be. If the expected negative fluctuation in the exchange rate is more than the profit margin, trade will not occur unless the profit margin can be increased accordingly. In a fiercely competitive market, the decision to cover or not to cover may make the difference between whether the company stays in business or not.

The likelihood and possible magnitude of an adverse foreign exchange rate fluctuation, and therefore the willingness of one of the parties to accept the risk, depend to a large extent on whether fixed or floating exchange rates prevail. Under a system of fixed rates, the decision to cover is typically made only when there is a "substantial" probability of loss. Unfortunately, this situation involving a high probability of a devaluation usually coincides with the most severe discounts in the forward market. Even assuming this coincidence, the exporter may rationally cover a loss based on a utility function which accepts a lower return with certainty in exchange for a higher expected return in an uncertain world. This is the typical situation, for the exporter knows that a rational market would prevent a gain on a less risky alternative (the covered position) from exceeding the return on the riskier alternative (the uncovered position).

In a world of fluctuating exchange rates, however, the situation becomes much more complex. A currency is subject to many more random outcomes in intervening periods so that, while the imposition of a fixed covering cost resolves the uncertainty, it may be worth the corporation's time and expense to consider in detail the opportunity costs and gains foregone. In a system of flexible rates, in contrast to a fixed rate system, it is likely that there will be fewer large changes in the relative value of currencies during the typical period involved in trade financing. However, under the flexible rate system there will also be many more changes over all currencies, though of a smaller amount, than the usual changes under a fixed rate system. Given these complexities, and the response of the financial intermediaries to them, major corporations can certainly be expected to consider their covering decisions with much greater care under the present managed floating exchange rate system than in the past. The alternative covering sources and the means of computing gains or losses from covering which we have discussed are essential in this analysis.

INTERNATIONAL TRADE: SPECIAL FINANCING ARRANGEMENTS

There is a whole series of documents that have been developed to facilitate the financing of trade. Among the major instruments involved are the letter of credit, the draft, and the banker's acceptance. Sources of financing for both importers and exporters who use these instruments have been primarily commercial banks and to a lesser extent governments. However, factoring firms and finance companies are involved in this field as well.

Letter of Credit

Suppose Zebracorp, a U. S. manufacturer of widgets, has agreed with Chao-widgets, a distributor of the product in Chaolandia, to sell a certain quantity of widgets to the firm. Although Zebracorp knows that Chao-widgets wants the product, the firm's credit is not well known to Zebracorp, and the firm wonders about the process by which it can assure itself of payment.

In the most typical use of the *letter of credit* (l/c), the buyer, Chao-widgets, will go to its local bank and ask for that bank to issue a letter of credit. In this letter the bank agrees to honor the demand for payment resulting from the import transaction described in the document. In exchange, the importer promises to pay to the bank the required amount plus fees on mutually accepted terms.

Here, Chao-widgets, which applied for the l/c, is the *account party*, and its local bank is the *issuing* bank. Zebracorp is the *beneficiary* of the l/c and receives its money from the *paying* bank, also called the *drawee* bank, whom the issuing bank instructs to make the payment upon presentation of appropriate documents.

It is easiest to see this behavior in a few examples of l/c's such as might occur between firms around the world. The bank in the importer's country may well operate through its own affiliate in the exporter's country, but often it will deal through one of its *correspondent* banks. The documents certifying shipment of the goods will be presented to the paying bank—an affiliate of the issuing bank or its correspondent. This situation is shown in Exhibit 6.1. Here, the exporter, Africa Patterns, Ltd., is informed by the issuing bank, Bankers Trust, that Africa Patterns will be paid by the Bank in Manchester when documents certifying shipment of goods are accepted by the Bank in Uganda. The account party is the importer, Mainwaring Frocks, Inc.

Here, once the documents are accepted in good order by the Bank in Uganda and the payment is made through the Bank in Manchester, Bankers Trust reimburses the Bank in Manchester. Bankers Trust then has the problem of collection from Mainwaring Frocks. Thus, the exporter knows that Bankers Trust guarantees that (s)he will be paid upon certification of shipment by various documents as noted in the draft (explained below). (S)he can be relatively unconcerned about the payment eventually made by Mainwaring Frocks to Bankers Trust.

The bank serves as a *guarantor of payment*, and that is the main value of the letter of credit. Where the buyer and seller are not known to each other, where the credit of the buyer is unknown, or where the seller demands quick payment, the letter of credit can be a useful device.

The security of the bank involved is of concern to the exporter, of course. Hence, there are several varieties of letters of credit depending on the relationships among the account party, the issuing bank, and the paying bank.

Confirmed Irrevocable Letters of Credit. Notice in Exhibit 6.1 the last paragraph where Bankers Trust has added its *own* confirmation to the letter of credit, meaning that both Bankers Trust and the Bank in Manchester are obligated to pay Africa Patterns once the documents specified in the letter are furnished and accepted by Bankers Trust.

Unconfirmed Irrevocable Letters of Credit. Where the local bank rewrites the letter but does not add its name as a confirming bank, it sends an *advice of an irrevocable letter of credit*. In Exhibit 6.2, the Bank in Tokyo is the issuing bank and guarantees the credit. Morgan Guaranty will pay upon presentation of the documents to it by Tewig Spice, the beneficiary. However, should the importer/account party, Lantern Trading Company, not pay the issuing bank, then the Bank of Tokyo must bear the entire loss of the transaction.

Revocable Letters of Credit. In some cases, neither bank guarantees payment. Here the advisory statement at the bottom of the letter indicates that there is no guarantee on either of the banks' part. In Exhibit 6.3, once the documents are ac-

EXHIBIT 6.1

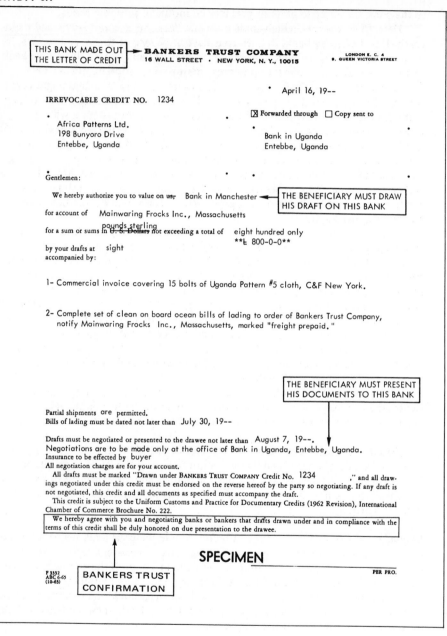

THIS BANK MADE OUT THE LETTER OF CREDIT → **BANKERS TRUST COMPANY**
16 WALL STREET · NEW YORK, N. Y., 10015

LONDON E. C. 4
9. QUEEN VICTORIA STREET

April 16, 19--

IRREVOCABLE CREDIT NO.   1234

[X] Forwarded through   [ ] Copy sent to

Africa Patterns Ltd.
198 Bunyoro Drive
Entebbe, Uganda

Bank in Uganda
Entebbe, Uganda

Gentlemen:

We hereby authorize you to value on ~~us,~~ Bank in Manchester ◄— **THE BENEFICIARY MUST DRAW HIS DRAFT ON THIS BANK**

for account of   Mainwaring Frocks Inc., Massachusetts

for a sum or sums ~~in U. S. Dollars~~ pounds sterling not exceeding a total of   eight hundred only
£ 800-0-0

by your drafts at   sight
accompanied by:

1- Commercial invoice covering 15 bolts of Uganda Pattern #5 cloth, C&F New York.

2- Complete set of clean on board ocean bills of lading to order of Bankers Trust Company, notify Mainwaring Frocks Inc., Massachusetts, marked "freight prepaid."

THE BENEFICIARY MUST PRESENT HIS DOCUMENTS TO THIS BANK

Partial shipments are permitted.
Bills of lading must be dated not later than July 30, 19--

Drafts must be negotiated or presented to the drawee not later than August 7, 19--.
Negotiations are to be made only at the office of Bank in Uganda, Entebbe, Uganda.
Insurance to be effected by buyer
All negotiation charges are for your account.
    All drafts must be marked "Drawn under BANKERS TRUST COMPANY Credit No. 1234   ," and all drawings negotiated under this credit must be endorsed on the reverse hereof by the party so negotiating. If any draft is not negotiated, this credit and all documents as specified must accompany the draft.
    This credit is subject to the Uniform Customs and Practice for Documentary Credits (1962 Revision), International Chamber of Commerce Brochure No. 222.

We hereby agree with you and negotiating banks or bankers that drafts drawn under and in compliance with the terms of this credit shall be duly honored on due presentation to the drawee.

SPECIMEN

F 3352
ABC 6-65
(10-65)

BANKERS TRUST CONFIRMATION

PER PRO.

Source: *Letters of Credit,* Book 2. The American Bankers Association. Washington, D.C., 1968, p. 23.

EXHIBIT 6.2

9-66-6M

FORM 11-4-945

MORGAN GUARANTY TRUST COMPANY
OF NEW YORK
INTERNATIONAL BANKING DIVISION
23 WALL STREET, NEW YORK, N. Y. 10015

February 10, 19--

Tewig Spice Company
568 Mott Street
New York, New York

On all communications please refer to
OUR REFERENCE NUMBER
K-2000

Dear Sirs:
          We are instructed to advise you of the establishment by
• Bank in Tokyo
of their IRREVOCABLE Credit No L3-8120
in your favor, for the account of   Lantern Trading Company

for   U.S. $1,000.00 (ONE THOUSAND U. S. DOLLARS)

available upon presentation to us of your drafts at sight on us, accompanied by:

Commercial Invoice.

Full set of on board ocean steamer Bills of Lading to order of Bank in Tokyo, marked
"Notify Lantern Trading Co.,"

evidencing shipment of PLASTIC CHOP STICKS, C.I.F. Tokyo, From New York to Tokyo.

    Except as otherwise expressly stated herein, this advice is subject to the Uniform Customs and Practice for Documentary Credits
(1962 Revision), International Chamber of Commerce, Brochure No. 222.

Your drafts must indicate that they are drawn under the aforementioned
Advice . . . . , number K-2000   of the
Morgan Guaranty Trust Company of New York   and must be presented
to our Commercial Credits Department, 15 Broad Street, New York, N. Y. 10015 with
specified documents, not later than August 3, 19--   on which date this
advice expires.

THIS LETTER IS SOLELY AN ADVICE AND CONVEYS NO ENGAGEMENT BY US.

Yours very truly,
SPECIMEN
Authorized Signature

    Immediately upon receipt please examine this advice, and if its terms are not clear to you or if you need any assistance
in respect to your availment of it, we would welcome your communicating with us. Documents should be presented promptly
and not later than 3 P.M.

161

EXHIBIT 6.3

Irving Trust
Company

ONE WALL STREET
NEW YORK, N.Y. 10015

DATE March 1, 19--
REVOCABLE ADVICE
NO. 123456

Morgan T. Burns, Inc.
1421 Elm Road
New York, New York 10012

GENTLEMEN:

WE ARE INFORMED BY { Bank of Finance
London, England }

THAT YOU WILL DRAW ON US AT   SIGHT TO THE EXTENT OF

$10,400.00

FOR ACCOUNT OF   John Brown Ltd., London, England

YOUR DRAFTS MUST BE ACCOMPANIED BY THE FOLLOWING DOCUMENTS (COMPLETE SETS UNLESS OTHERWISE STATED) EVIDENCING SHIPMENT(S) OF:

Pump Parts, F.O.B. Vessel New York, from New York to Southampton

Commercial Invoice

On board ocean bills of lading issued to order of shipper and endorsed in blank, marked "Notify John Brown Ltd., London, England."

Insurance covered by buyer.

Description of the engagement of the issuing and advising banks to the beneficiary.

DRAFTS MUST CLEARLY SPECIFY THE NUMBER OF THIS ADVICE, AND BE PRESENTED AT THIS COMPANY NOT LATER THAN   June 1, 19--

THIS ADVICE IS SUBJECT TO THE UNIFORM CUSTOMS AND PRACTICE FOR DOCUMENTARY CREDITS (1974 REVISION) INTERNATIONAL CHAMBER OF COMMERCE PUBLICATION 290

THIS ADVICE, REVOCABLE AT ANY TIME WITHOUT NOTICE, IS FOR YOUR GUIDANCE ONLY IN PREPARING DRAFTS AND DOCUMENTS AND CONVEYS NO ENGAGEMENT OR OBLIGATION ON OUR PART OR ON THE PART OF OUR ABOVE-MENTIONED CORRESPONDENT.

NOTE   YOURS VERY TRULY

DOCUMENTS MUST CONFORM STRICTLY WITH THE TERMS OF THIS
ADVICE. IF YOU ARE UNABLE TO COMPLY WITH ITS TERMS, PLEASE
COMMUNICATE WITH US AND/OR YOUR CUSTOMER PROMPTLY WITH   **SPECIMEN**
A VIEW TO HAVING THE CONDITIONS CHANGED.

150/70 (R-75) Rev. R-75   AUTHORIZED SIGNATURE

Source: Irving Trust Company, One Wall Street, New York, New York 10015

cepted by Irving Trust showing that Morgan T. Burns, Inc., has shipped the goods as ordered by John Brown Ltd., then payment is made. However, Morgan T. Burns, Inc. the beneficiary, has no guarantee that John Brown Ltd. will not cancel his letter of credit at any time. The only guarantee the exporter/beneficiary has is that, once the documents are accepted by Irving Trust, if the letter of credit has not been cancelled, (s)he will be paid.

These examples point to the importance of the *date* of the letter of credit, which is indicated at the bottom of the l/c. In the case of the irrevocable l/c, this date gives the beneficiary a firm date prior to which (s)he knows the credit is guaranteed by one or more banks.

A summary of the terms and arrangements concerning these three types of letters of credit is shown in Exhibit 6.4. As suggested in the exhibit, l/c's can have their terms altered at the initiation of the account party, subject to approval of certain other involved parties.

EXHIBIT 6.4   Summary: Terms of Letters of Credit

	Revocable l/c	Unconfirmed irrevocable l/c	Confirmed irrevocable l/c
Who applies for l/c	account party	account party	account party
Who is obligated to pay	none	issuing bank	issuing bank and confirming bank
Who applies for amendment	account party	account party	account party
Who approves amendment	issuing bank	issuing bank and beneficiary	issuing bank, beneficiary, and confirming bank
Who reimburses paying bank	issuing bank	issuing bank	issuing bank
Who reimburses issuing bank	account party	account party	account party

Source: *Letters of Credit*, Book 2. The American Bankers Association. Washington, D. C., 1968, p. 116.

Negotiable Letters of Credit.   In some cases, the beneficiary of the l/c may not find it convenient to present documents to a particular paying bank. In other cases, where foreign exchange rates quoted by the banks differ, it may be hard for the beneficiary to know before payment date what bank would be most desirable as the paying bank. In these cases, the *straight* l/c can be replaced by a *negotiable* l/c which could be used with any bank willing to act as paying bank. The difference in wording specifies which form of l/c is involved, as shown in Exhibit 6.5. Note that Ⓐ requires under a separate paragraph that drafts drawn against that l/c must be endorsed and marked with reference to Credit No. 1234. This is a negotiable l/c. This statement is not necessary in Ⓑ, a straight l/c, since the draft can only be presented to the paying bank designated in the l/c. In addition, Ⓐ, the negotiable l/c, says specifically that the "Drafts must be negotiated or presented to the drawee not later than. . . ." In contrast, Ⓑ, the straight l/c, does not mention the word "negotiated." In the negotiable l/c, the expiration date is the

EXHIBIT 6.5

Ⓐ

Drafts must be negotiated or presented to the drawee not later than August 7, 19--.
Insurance to be effected by buyer
All negotiation charges are for your account.
    All drafts must be marked "Drawn under BANKERS TRUST COMPANY Credit No. 1234   ," and all draw-
ings negotiated under this credit must be endorsed on the reverse hereof by the party so negotiating. If any draft is
not negotiated, this credit and all documents as specified must accompany the draft.
    This credit is subject to the Uniform Customs and Practice for Documentary Credits (1962 Revision), International
Chamber of Commerce Brochure No. 222.
    We hereby agree with you and negotiating banks or bankers that drafts drawn under and in compliance with the
terms of this credit shall be duly honored on due presentation to the drawee.

SPECIMEN

PER PRO.

F 3352
ABC 6-65
(10-65)

Ⓑ

THE ABOVE MENTIONED CORRESPONDENT ENGAGES WITH YOU THAT ALL DRAFTS DRAWN UNDER AND
IN COMPLIANCE WITH THE TERMS OF THIS CREDIT WILL BE DULY HONORED ON DELIVERY OF DOCU-
MENTS AS SPECIFIED IF PRESENTED AT THIS OFFICE ON OR BEFORE   February 13, 19--   WE CONFIRM
THE CREDIT AND THEREBY UNDERTAKE THAT ALL DRAFTS DRAWN AND PRESENTED AS ABOVE SPECIFIED WILL
BE DULY HONORED BY US.
THIS CREDIT IS SUBJECT TO THE UNIFORM CUSTOMS AND PRACTICE FOR DOCUMENTARY CREDITS (1962 RE-
VISION), INTERNATIONAL CHAMBER OF COMMERCE BROCHURE NO. 222.

YOURS VERY TRULY,

SPECIMEN

ASST TREAS /PER PROCURATION

Source: *Letters of Credit*, Book 2. The American Bankers Association. Washington, D.C., 1968,
pp. 23, 137.

last date the letter of credit can be negotiated. Thus, in Ⓐ, the expiration date is August 7.

Time Letters of Credit.   In all the examples presented above, the issuing bank promises to pay a certain amount "at sight" of a draft (explained in the following section) and certain other documents. However, if the exporter wishes to extend credit to the importer, the exporter would require only a *time l/c*. In a time l/c the issuing bank promises to pay at a specified date *after* the presentation of certain documents. This way the exporter provides more lenient credit terms while retaining the payment guarantee of a major bank.

Transferable Letters of Credit.   In many cases, a trading house or intermediary may be aware of a possible transaction. In this case, the account party (buying importer) will open a *transferable letter of credit* between the firm and the trading house. The trading house can then tell prospective sellers that the buyer has a bank that guarantees the payment for the purchase. When the trader finds the seller, (s)he instructs the advising bank to transfer the letter of credit to the seller, letting the seller become the new beneficiary. The creation of a transferable letter of credit is noted by simply having a line such as, "This credit is transferable," added to the documentation.

Documents Required by Letters of Credit.   The various documents described in letters of credit are usually standard commercial forms. Thus, the *commercial invoice* is simply a bill for the goods which have been shipped. It details the banking arrangements and the product shipped, specifies any charges which are to be paid (such as insurance, freight, handling, and so on), and usually the shipper and ports involved. The *bill of lading* is a control form of the goods. It is issued by the common carrier transporting the goods. It is usually issued to the exporter or to the bank issuing the letter of credit. This document shows that the merchandise has been received by the carrier who agrees to deliver it according to special conditions. Possession of this document often establishes the ownership of the merchandise. Thus, it can be used to ensure payment before delivery of goods, and also as collateral against loans. Various insurance policies, consular/custom forms, or invoices may also be required by terms of the l/c.

When there are irregularities in the documents, the paying bank has the choice of asking to have the l/c amended, asking the beneficiary to complete the documents in a specified manner, or receiving an indemnification from the beneficiary holding the bank not responsible if the account party later refuses to pay. In this situation, the beneficiary has lost most of the benefit conveyed by the letter of credit.

However, if the documents are in proper order but do not conform to the facts, e.g., description of color of merchandise, the paying bank is *not* responsible for this variance. In this case the importer has to refer to the commercial legal code to determine the party responsible for the irregularity. If the documents are *not* in order when submitted, the exporter can guarantee the paying bank and receive payment as per terms of the draft. In other cases, the paying bank will seek to have the issuing bank agree to the payment. Alternatively, it may reject the beneficiary's claim until the documents are in order.[3]

Import/Export Drafts

The final payment in the trade-financing process is accomplished by a *draft*. When you write a check to someone, that is one form of a draft, drawn against your account with a commercial bank, with payment to another party.

In exporting, when the l/c has specified certain terms as agreed upon by the importer and the exporter, then the exporter/beneficiary will include a draft with the documents. A draft is a written order to pay a specified amount of money at a specified point in time to a given person or to the bearer. A draft is a formal version of the account receivable that the exporter possesses as a result of the sale. The parties involved in a draft are the drawer, the drawee, and the payee. The *drawer* is the exporter who signs the document. The *drawee* is the entity to which the draft is addressed (the importer or his/her bank), who makes the payment on the document. The *payee* is the importer who ultimately pays for the goods. The payee and the drawee may be the same.

For example, from Exhibit 6.6 one may presume that G.T. Tyler, the drawer, (B), exported goods to (say) XYZ GmbH. XYZ had previously arranged a letter of credit with the Bank in Switzerland, the l/c's issuing bank. Morgan Guaranty may have confirmed the l/c, or it may have been only the agent or the advisor of the l/c. In any case, G.T. Tyler completes the documents required under the Bank in Switzerland's l/c and hands them over to Morgan Guaranty, the drawee, with this draft. If all the documents are in order, Morgan Guaranty pays $1,000 to G.T. Tyler. Note that the draft is made payable in this case to the Tyler Company (A). Unlike a draft on one's personal checking account, an import/export draft is written by the person or company to whom the money is owed. They could have made the draft payable to the bank or to some other source.

Payment Terms. The draft in Exhibit 6.6 is labelled "At sight." When the documents have been found to be in good order, the draft is honored by Morgan Guaranty and the Tyler Company has its account credited. (Morgan Guaranty, if it is only a paying bank, will examine the documents carefully. Should the issuing bank, the Bank in Switzerland, find them faulty after Morgan Guaranty has paid the Tyler Company, then Morgan Guaranty will not be reimbursed even though it did not confirm or advise on the l/c).

---

[3] The letters of credit shown here all have a standard clause at the bottom which is typical of the U. S.-issued letters of credit. Until recently, that phrase was: "This credit [or, advice] is subject to the Uniform Customs and Practice for Documentary Credits (1962 Revision), International Chamber of Commerce Brochure No. 222." As you may note on the updated form used for Exhibit 6.3, this phrase now reads: "This advice is subject to the Uniform Customs and Practice for Documentary Credits (1974 Revision), International Chamber of Commerce Publication 290." This clause indicates the regulations under which shipment disputes or any arguments between any of the parties are to be settled. They are available from banks, from chambers of commerce, and from other sources. In addition, the *Revised American Foreign Trade Definitions—1941* specifies common terms for adjudication of disputes arising under most U. S. letters of credit if buyer and seller agree to abide by them. (The definitions were adopted on July 30, 1941 by a Joint Committee representing the Chamber of Commerce of the United States, the National Council of American Importers, Inc., and the National Foreign Trade Council, Inc.

EXHIBIT 6.6

```
    Bank in Switzerland Credit ABZ-6033

 $  1,000.00 (U.S.)            New York,  September 1,    19 --

    At sight                               Pay to the order of

                  Ourselves        (A)

    One thousand and 00/100 - - - - - - - - - - - - - -   Dollars

  To:
                                   G. T. Tyler Company      (B)
        Morgan Guaranty Trust
        Company of New York
        New York, N.Y SPECIMEN  —
```

Source: *Letters of Credit*, Book 3. The American Bankers Association. Washington, D.C., 1968, p. 77. By permission of the American Bankers Association and Morgan Guaranty Trust Company of New York.

The *sight* draft is paid on presentation when the documents are in good order. An alternative arrangement which the two parties may have agreed upon and confirmed in the letter of credit is a *time draft*. Time drafts will specify payment typically 30, 60, 90, 120, or 180 days after *date* (after the date the draft is drawn) or after *sight* (after the draft has been presented and accepted by the paying bank). The terms of payment are often called the draft's *tenor*. These terms are agreed upon by the importer and the exporter as part of their business arrangements pursuant to the sale of the product. If a letter of credit is part of the transaction, the paying terms in the l/c must be the same as those in the draft; i.e., a time l/c. A time draft is a way for the exporter to extend credit to the importer.

Often, firms well known to each other will not find the l/c necessary. Instead, the exporter will use a bank as a collection agency, sending a draft drawn according to terms agreed upon by the two parties together with required documents and a letter of instruction to the bank for collection. The exporter's local bank typically will then deal with a bank in the importer's land, arranging for collection of the funds which are due the exporter.[4]

The collecting bank will turn over the documents certifying title to the goods to the importer when the importer pays (when it is a sight draft) or when the importer accepts the draft liability (when it is a time draft). Although the collecting bank can submit the drafts for payment or acceptance at receipt, usually the bank withholds presentation of the drafts until the goods have arrived in the importer's

---

[4] There is also a documented discount note that is sometimes used. Essentially, it is a corporate note to which is attached a bank's irrevocable letter guaranteeing payment on the note to any purchaser.

port. As part of the letter of instruction to the local bank, the exporter will specify the fees to be collected (if any), the means and currency for remission of the funds, and so forth.

Documents Required. Drafts are also classified according to the documents that are required to accompany the draft. A *clean draft* does not require any other document. A *documentary draft* requires accompanying documents such as bill of lading, commercial invoices, insurance certificates, and so on.

Lending by Financial Institutions

Trust Receipts. Sometimes goods are shipped under a time letter of credit and a time draft. In this case the importer usually signs a trust receipt for the goods, collateralizing the draft by the goods. Under a trust receipt, the bank retains title to the goods, with the importer operating as a trustee. As the goods are sold, proceeds are to be remitted to the bank in most cases. When the time draft is due, the importer pays the bank which sends the funds to the exporter's account specified in the draft. If the documents are *not* in order when submitted, the exporter can guarantee the paying bank and receive payment according to the terms of the draft.

Loans to Exporters. When the exporter wants immediate payment and the terms of the sale involve a time draft, there are several means for reimbursement. The bank may lend against a set percentage of the drafts outstanding. This process is similar to receivable financing, and is based on the credit history of the exporter's customers. In other cases, the exporter may collateralize a note as needed by the drafts. A third form, and a popular one when a major exporter can convince the bank to agree, is through the banker's acceptance.

Banker's Acceptances. Suppose the exporter and the importer have agreed to "ninety-day sight" terms. This arrangement means that the exporter will be paid ninety days after the bank certifies that the documents are in good order. In Exhibit 6.7 the exporter, John Doe and Co., has drawn a ninety-day sight time draft against an l/c from the Bank in Lima, presumably arranged by the importer of goods from Doe and Company. When Morgan Guaranty, the paying bank, acknowledges the forms as being in good order, it then stamps "ACCEPTED" across the face of the check, dates, and signs it. This is a guarantee that Morgan will pay the draft as noted ninety days from the date of the draft, or December 23.

     With this acceptance in hand, the exporter may sell the draft/acceptance (now called a *banker's* acceptance) to an investor at a discount. The investor knows that the bank will pay the face amount at some future date, and the discount represents the going interest rate for banker's acceptances. Alternatively, the bank may buy the draft/acceptance from the exporter at a discount, repaying itself when the importer's bank remits funds. Finally, the importer, as the account party to the draft, may have agreed to pay the discount when the beneficiary presents the draft. The beneficiary receives the full face amount and the paying bank receives the discount from the importer. Later, when the banker's acceptance matures, the bank collects the full amount of the draft (which is what it had paid the beneficiary).

EXHIBIT 6.7

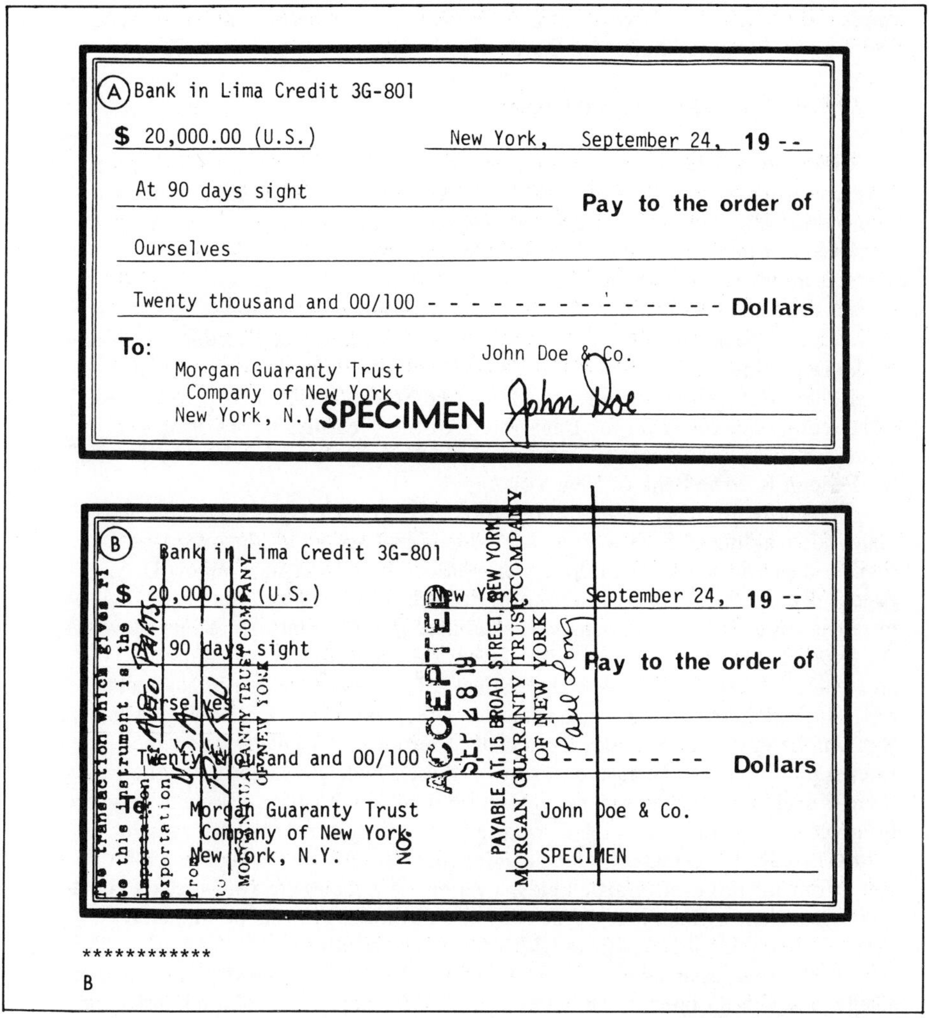

(A) Bank in Lima Credit 3G-801

$ 20,000.00 (U.S.)   New York,   September 24, 19 --

At 90 days sight   **Pay to the order of**

Ourselves

Twenty thousand and 00/100 - - - - - - - - - - - - - - - Dollars

To:
Morgan Guaranty Trust   John Doe & Co.
Company of New York
New York, N.Y **SPECIMEN**   *John Doe*

(B) Bank in Lima Credit 3G-801

$ 20,000.00 (U.S.)   New York,   September 24, 19 --

90 days sight   **Pay to the order of**

Ourselves

Twenty thousand and 00/100 - - - - - - - Dollars

To: Morgan Guaranty Trust   John Doe & Co.
Company of New York
New York, N.Y.   SPECIMEN

ACCEPTED
SEP 28 19
PAYABLE AT 15 BROAD STREET, NEW YORK
MORGAN GUARANTY TRUST COMPANY
OF NEW YORK
NON

****
B

Source: *Letters of Credit*, Book 3. The American Bankers Association. Washington, D.C., 1968, p. 35.

Banker's acceptances tend to be especially popular in periods of tight money, and have expanded rapidly in total amount in recent years. One reason is that a bank which sells an acceptance to another bank is not required to count the contingent liability of that sale in computing its reserve requirements. In mid-1974, over $12 billion of U. S. banker's acceptances were outstanding, an increase of over 40% from a year earlier. Acceptances solely related to U. S. exports were $5 billion in early 1975.

Loans to Importers. In many cases, the importer will arrange financing through a local bank, notifying the exporter. Usually, the bank will lend against the *import draft* in conjunction with a trust receipt arrangement, so that the loan from the bank supports the import draft which in turn is collateralized by the goods themselves. This instrument is the reverse of the export draft in terms of which party "creates" it, but the purpose is the same.

Other Aspects of Trade Credit

Commercial attachés of embassies as well as export financing institutions in most countries are well-trained to provide interested exporters and importers with information about regulations and restrictions on the movement of various merchandise. For instance, in the United States, the Department of Commerce oversees movement of merchandise out of the country. Most goods for export are not controlled, but some strategic goods or items with particular legislation may require special licenses. The Government Printing Office distributes copies of the Department's *Export Control Bulletins* and *Control Regulations* which detail these restrictions. Imports to the United States usually involve duty, and some require licenses from the Department of the Treasury. Information and forms for these imports are available from the Foreign Assets Control Division of the Federal Reserve Bank of New York.

The United States Export-Import Bank (Eximbank), created in 1934, is a major force aiding U. S. exporters. An independent agency of the executive branch, it provides billions of dollars of credit to help foreigners import U. S. goods. The credits often are in the form of insurance or a guarantee. For instance, for a fee the Eximbank will guarantee the payment of a receivable which the exporter has sold to a local bank, where the receivable is from a foreign customer. The guarantee covers all political risk and portions of normal business risk. The Eximbank will also guarantee the direct loan by a U. S. bank to a foreign purchaser of a U. S. good, often capital equipment. In many cases, the foreign purchaser will be a government. In these financial guarantees to the bank, there is usually a 100% guarantee against political and business risk including all principal and interest up to 1% above the U. S. Treasury rate on comparable debt. Through the Foreign Credit Insurance Association, involving more than sixty firms in various insurance fields, a variety of policies are available to exporters to protect them against nonpayment by their overseas customers. In many cases, Eximbank will participate with commercial banks and/or the exporter in a direct loan to a foreign customer. Eximbank will take the loans of longer maturity, leaving the shorter ones to the banks and the exporter. For a comprehensive discussion of various financing alternatives, the exporter will want to consult financial sources, such as banks and finance companies, in the involved nations. Other countries have financial institutions similar to those for the United States discussed above in order to encourage the export of their goods.

FOREIGN EXCHANGE RISKS AND CREDIT RISKS: SOME TRADE-OFFS

The first section of this chapter concentrated on analyzing the foreign exchange risk that international trade involves and offering a framework for evaluating the price of buying insurance against these risks. The second section introduced a series of documents and financing procedures and focused on the terms of these documents as well as the protection they afford to various parties. However, these documents also indicate the foreign exchange risks for each party through the currency in which the l/c and drafts are drawn and the time period involved in the payment. For example, for the Italian manufacturer that exported shoes to the United States, there was an assumption that this transaction was made on open account and that the payment was to be made by the U. S. buyer in U. S. dollars three months after delivery. Modifications to these assumptions involve three major issues: (1) How much foreign exchange risk does each party bear? (2) How much credit risk does each party bear? (3) Who is providing the financing of the transaction?

Abstracting from the complications of the special commercial documents, one can answer the three questions for the Italian exporter in the following manner:

1. The foreign exchange risk is at a maximum to the exporter if (s)he sells in terms of U. S. dollars for payment in the future and does nothing else but wait. The foreign exchange risk is eliminated if the billing is made in Italian liras or if a U. S. dollar billing is covered in the financial markets.

2. The credit risk is at a maximum to the exporter when dealing on open account. The credit risk is at a minimum if an irrevocable confirmed letter of credit is required from the importer.

3. The exporter provides the maximum amount of financing to the importer if it sells the merchandise on time on open account. The exporter does not provide any financing to the importer in the case of a sight draft or a requirement of payment before shipment.

Obviously, the exporter would like to keep these three risks at a minimum. But so would the importer. In this example the Italian exporter would prefer to be paid in liras at presentation of a sight draft drawn against an irrevocable confirmed letter of credit. On the other hand, the U. S. importer would rather have the transaction as initially presented—denominated in U. S. dollars to be paid later and on open account. How are these conflicting interests reconciled?

When we discussed the foreign exchange risks in international trade and how to insure against them, the focus was on the explicit costs associated with covering a cash flow as well as the opportunity gains and losses of the two alternatives of covering or not covering. To the extent that time elapses between the entering of the transaction and the receipt or payment of a foreign currency, there is a foreign exchange risk. If this risk is considered high enough to require insurance, somebody is going to have to pay for the price of that insurance. The first section showed how to calculate the cost of covering a cash flow. Whether the exporter bears this cost or whether it is passed on in terms of higher prices or explicit extra charges depends on the bargaining power of each party. An apparent alternative is to bring in a financial intermediary to pay the Italian exporter in liras and extend a loan to the U. S. importer in dollars. Now the risk is shifted to a financial institution. However, this action has not necessarily shifted the cost of buying insurance. The financial intermediary has had its foreign exchange position altered as a result of this transaction. So it is not difficult to imagine that the costs of changing its foreign exchange position back to the original one will be passed to the parties involved in exchange and interest rates. If the market is working efficiently, the situation is virtually the same as that of trading under open account, except that now the necessary fees for the financial intermediary are added!

The amount of credit risk incurred by the exporter also has a cost attached to it. Such credit risk can be minimized by bringing in the largest possible number of financial institutions to share the responsibility for payment of the merchandise. However, each of these institutions will testify that payment will be forthcoming only because it receives a fee from the importer as a charge for the letter of credit. This fee effectively increases the price of the merchandise to the importer, therefore minimizing the competitiveness of the exporter's prices.

The solution to the problem of how much credit the exporter will provide to the importer is similar to the evaluation of how much foreign exchange risk each party assumes. To the exporter, the extension of trade credit is similar to the acquisition of a financial asset. The account receivable has an explicit return to the extent that it is a substitute for lower prices or higher quality goods. However, the account receivable has an opportunity cost that can be measured by the net return that the exporter could make were those funds not used in financing the importer. Notice that this is a *net* return. In order for the exporter to extend this credit a source of funds must be found, and these funds have a cost attached to them. So the other consideration in extending credit to the importer is the cost of money to the exporter, who in this regard is operating as a financial intermediary. Obviously, if the exporter refuses to extend this credit the problem is only shifted to the importer who must find a source of funds to finance inventories until sold. This loan also has an interest rate attached to it that can be translated into higher cost of goods purchased.

In not every case are the interests of the exporter and the importer diametrically opposed. On occasions the alternatives appear to be somewhat biased. This bias comes from the fact that most business enterprises consider their local currency as the unit of account. An Italian considers the Italian lira as the unit of account; an American considers the U. S. dollar as the unit of account. So there is some tendency to ignore the opportunity gains from dealing in a currency other than the local one. Thus the Italian exporter might be very happy to be paid in liras. If the American importer, and even the market, actually thinks that the Italian lira is likely to devalue by the time that payment is due, the importer will be glad to have the import liability denominated in Italian liras, and might even be willing to pay the interest charges for term credit. In these cases of different appraisals of the market or different assessment of the opportunities, a compromise is easy to achieve. Given the market facts, the final word will be determined by the bargaining power of each party.

SUMMARY

Credit risks occur for the international trader as for the domestic trader, but they are accompanied by foreign exchange risks when the payment for the goods at a future date will be in a currency different from the currency the trader desires. The trader may specify the home currency, in which case the buyer faces the foreign exchange risk.

To resolve this risk, buyer or seller may use the forward markets. The actual costs will depend on the price of the forward contract relative to the spot price.

The opportunity gain on loss depends on what happens to the spot rate in the future versus the date the forward contract was entered into.

The parties may also use the money market. An exporter may borrow the foreign currency, convert to the local currency, and invest the funds. When the receivable from the customer is paid, the gain or loss in the exchange rate of the foreign currency applied to the receivable is balanced by the loss or gain in repayment of the loan. The actual cost is simply the interest differential between the currencies, plus or minus the small impact that any foreign exchange rate change may make on the interest payment.

The cover in the forward market locks in the forward rate of the currencies. Covering in the money market locks in the spot rate. If the markets are in equilibrium, then covering in either market will produce similar results.

An importer, as the account party, may arrange with a bank to issue a letter of credit in which the bank guarantees payment subject to successful production and certification of shipment of goods. This letter of credit assures the exporter that there will be reimbursement for goods shipped to the importer. The local bank of the exporter may advise of the l/c or may confirm it, in which case the local bank becomes a co-guarantor of the payment. When not confirmed by either the issuing bank or the local bank, l/c's are revocable at the direction of the account party. However, once the documents and the draft going with them are accepted by the paying bank, they cannot be cancelled. Letters of credit may be transferrable (which facilitates the use of a trading intermediary who has found a buyer with credit but is still seeing a supplier) and may be negotiable (which permits the exporter to seek the best rate of foreign exchange, or simply to select the bank for collection at a later point).

The actual payment is completed by means of a draft. It is simply a demand for payment by the drawer (the exporter, or beneficiary of the l/c), sent to the collecting bank against the l/c of the issuing bank. The draft may be on sight, in which case there is immediate payment once the paying bank has acknowledged receipt of the draft and certifying documents. It may be a time draft, in which case payment will be so many days beyond the date of the draft or from sight when the draft is accepted by the bank. When a time draft is accepted by the bank, it becomes a banker's acceptance, and may be negotiated. Hence, the holder of the draft may sell it to the bank or to an investor at a discount, receiving payment immediately. Upon the maturity of the acceptance, the account party pays the holder of the draft the full face amount. In some cases, the beneficiary/drawer of the draft will receive the full amount immediately with the account party paying the discount plus the full face amount to the bank at a later date.

In many cases, drafts are used by exporter and importer on terms which they have agreed upon without the l/c of an issuing bank. In these cases, the banks usually act as collecting parties, remitting funds to the exporter subject to completion of certain requirements as specified by the importer.

Most countries have various regulations governing imports and exports of certain products. In the United States, restrictions on exports are noted in the Department of Commerce's *Control Regulations* and *Export Control Bulletins.* Restrictions on imports, in addition to duty collected by the Department of the Treasury, are noted in publications of the Foreign Assets Control Division of the New York Federal Reserve Bank.

The U. S. Export-Import Bank is a major force for helping U. S. exporters sell their goods to foreign importers. Through a program of guaranteed loans; direct loans to foreign buyers who may be individuals, firms, or governments; loans to exporters; insurance programs and other items; this independent government agency encourages the growth of U. S. exports. Other countries have similar institutions to facilitate the financing of exports of their goods.

The nature of the foreign exchange risk and the financing arrangements between importer and exporter fundamentally depend on the relative bargaining power of the parties where their interests conflict. When financial intermediaries are involved to absolve the participants of some risks, the fees for these intermediaries must be added to the costs of the transaction.

Questions

1. An English exporter scheduled to receive payment in Italian liras sells the liras on a forward contract, so that she knows the sterling value of the receivable. How will she know the cost of this cover? When will she know the cost?

2. "As long as the forward rate for the currency is below the spot rate, I should cover my transactions if I have receivables in that currency; the forward discount shows that the currency is likely to devalue." Do you agree with this statement? Why?

3. A U. S. distributor purchases perfume from France in the amount of French francs 22,850 (approximately $5,000). Payment is due in three months in French francs.

		Day 90		
	Day 1	Case A	Case B	Case C
Exchange rates:				
Spot	$0.218850	$0.218550	$0.240735	$0.196965
3-month forward	$0.218140			
Interest rates:				
United States	6.00%	6.00%	6.00%	6.00%
France	7.30%	7.30%	6.80%	7.80%

a. On Day 1 what is the premium or discount on the forward French franc? What is the interest differential between the U. S. and France? Is there an incentive for interest arbitrage?

b. If the importer wants to cover its transaction against foreign exchange risks, what alternatives are open?

c. What is the cost of each alternative? (i) if a three-month treasury bill is bought; (ii) if a one-year bill is bought (do not make specific calculation in the latter case).

d. Would you advise the importer to cover the foreign exchange transaction? Why?

4. If there is no change in the spot rate of a currency in a given period, does it make any difference whether one covers a transaction in the forward market or the money market? Give an example to support your answer.

5. What is the purpose of a letter of credit? What are the major types of l/c's?

6. How may an exporter use a letter of credit to extend credit to an importer?

7. Who are the parties involved in a draft? Why is a check you write to your department store a draft? Who are the parties in that "draft"?

8. What is meant by a draft's tenor? What are examples of different tenors? Why do these differences exist?

9. Can a banker's acceptance be sold to another party? Since it does not pay interest, why would a person buy it? Who guarantees payment?

10. Edward M. Graham, a United States wholesaler of specialty clothes for men and women, hopes to expand his operations considerably by emphasizing a new line of leisure wear to be marketed through various clothing boutiques. As part of this plan, he has contacted three exporters with a view toward supplying his needs. He considers the products and offerings of each comparable in terms of his business, although each reflects certain national styles and trends.

Assume the three potential suppliers have offered him various terms. Mary Freed Ltd. of London has suggested that an appropriate financial arrangement would would involve a revocable letter of credit since she knows his general reputation. They agree that, if Mr. Graham can arrange the letter of credit through a bank, Ms. Freed will draw a time draft payable 60 days after sight, in sterling.

Tomas Rodriguez of Spain has an interest in supplying Mr. Graham, but indicates that he would expect a confirmed irrevocable negotiable letter of credit, with drafts drawn under the l/c payable at sight. Credit would be available, he suggests, at a rate of 2% per month, but should not exceed 90 days after shipment.

Finally, Heinz Riehl of Geneva manufactures an Austrian style of aprè-ski lounging clothes, and has indicated that he has long wished to have an American distributor. He suggests that an appropriate method of operation would be for Mr. Graham to deposit funds to the Riehl account in Basel 30 days prior to a shipment, with the deposit equal to 50% of the invoiced value of the goods. After shipment, the balance would be due within 10 days of receipt by Mr. Graham. Mr. Riehl noted that his general impressions of Mr. Graham's business were sufficient to commend the Graham firm as a customer, and he has no need for a letter of credit arrangement.

If you were to help Mr. Graham with this decision, what data would you need? How would you analyze the decision. In addition to any factors you believe are particularly important, consider the following elements, and how they would alter the decision. Give an example of how Mr. Graham might favor one supplier over the others depending on the facts surrounding each item noted below:

    a. The currency prospects of each of the exporters vis-à-vis Mr. Graham's currency, the U. S. dollar.

    b. The cost of funds for payable financing by Mr. Graham.

    c. The option to accept or reject the Spanish credit terms as each order is due.

    d. The cost of different letters of credit from the banks involved.

Bibliography

Eiteman, David K. and Arthur I. Stonehill, *Multinational Business Finance.* Reading, Mass.: Addison-Wesley Publishing Co., 1973, Ch. 6.

The Financing of Exports and Imports. Morgan Guaranty Trust Company of New York. New York, 1973.

Foreign Exchange Exposure Management, Chemical Bank, New York, 1972.

Foreign Exchange Handbook for the Corporate Executive, Brown Brothers Harriman and Co., New York, 1970.

Greene, James, *Organizing for Exporting.* National Industrial Conference Board Business Policy Study Number 26. New York, 1968.

Harrington, J. A., *Specifics on Commercial Letters of Credit and Bankers Acceptances.* Jersey City, N.J.: Scott Printing Corporation, 1974.

Hollis, Stanley E., *Guide to Export Credit Insurance.* Foreign Credit Insurance Association. New York, 1971.

Letters of Credit, Books 2 and 3. The American Bankers Association. Washington, D.C., 1968.

Overseas Private Investment Corporation, *An Introduction to OPIC.* Washington, D.C., 1973.

Syrett, W. W., *A Manual of Foreign Exchange,* 6th edition. London: Sir Isaac Pitman and Sons, Ltd., 1966.

U. S. Government, Department of Commerce, *Control Regulations.* Government Printing Office, Washington, D.C.

———, *Export Control Bulletins.* Government Printing Office, Washington, D.C.

Weston, J. Fred and Bart W. Sorge, *International Managerial Finance.* Homewood, Ill.: Richard D. Irwin, Inc., 1972. Chs. 4, 8, and 9.

The AP&M Trading Company

In preparation for his upcoming trip to Japan in early October 1972, Mr. H. Hinson, President of the AP&M Trading Company, was reviewing his company's position in the Japanese import business.

Mainly importers of synthetic fabrics from Japan, the AP&M group had 1971 sales of $14 million. Their success was based on the service they performed and the low cost and excellent quality of the Japanese goods. Since the 1971 monetary crisis, however, the yen upvaluation, the quotas on Far Eastern textile imports, and the increasing European aggressiveness in exports of certain fabrics to the United

States had caused severe problems for the smaller U. S. import businesses dealing in Japanese textile products. Several of AP&M's less well-managed competitors had already been forced to discontinue their operations. Mr. Hinson had successfully shepherded his group through the several 1971-72 crises, but critical questions regarding the future were troubling him. The likelihood of another yen upvaluation and the cost of hedging were only two of several key issues Mr. Hinson had to deal with in formulating his tentative strategies prior to his meeting with the Japanese in October.

Company Background

The AP&M Trading Company was incorporated in New York in 1948 by Mr. H. Hinson and Mr. R. Kroner, two Polish refugees who arrived in the United States in 1945. From 1948 to 1951, the firm imported $6 to $8 million annually of surplus Japanese silk fabrics left from before the war. These unfinished dyed fabrics (grey goods) were sold to converters for the ladies' garment industry.[1] AP&M commissioned Far Eastern Exporters (Japan) Ltd., a branch of a large U. S. trading and shipping concern owned by Mr. Hinson's relatives, as AP&M's export agents in Japan. Far Eastern's functions were to handle all dealings with suppliers, shippers, foreign exchange dealers, Japanese banks, and the several official Japanese agencies involved.[2] Mr. K. Yokoma was put in charge of handling the AP&M account. For its services, Far Eastern Exporters charged AP&M 2% of the f.o.b.[3] value of the goods shipped.

In the early fifties, AP&M diversified into other segments of the growing U. S. market for Japanese silk imports. In 1952, Dept. F was opened to import fancy, high-priced silk fabrics such as brocades, chiffons, and organzas on a custom order basis for selected East Coast couturiers.

By the late fifties, silk fabrics were on the decline in the U. S. apparel market. Synthetics, meanwhile, were making large inroads into the dresswear market. The Japanese mills moved rapidly into the new synthetics. In late 1961, AP&M began importing the more expensive lines of quality and fancy-finish rayon, nylon, and acrylic fabrics. Several new technical sales experts and stylists were hired to promote the new synthetics with customers, and to work with the Japanese mills on the technical aspects of the new design-oriented fabrics.

Financial data for the company are contained in Exhibit 1.

AP&M contained three departments: Dept. F (25% of sales), ladies' sportswear fabrics (60%), and odd lots (15%). The market for ladies' sportswear fabrics

---

[1] Converters are key middlemen in the textile industry. They buy many different kinds of fabrics in large volumes from varied domestic and foreign sources, print or otherwise finish the fabrics as required by the manufacturers, and resell the goods to the many producers in the apparel, home furnishings, and industrial textile industries. Aside from some purchases by the largest U. S. apparel manufacturers direct from U. S. or European mills, the bulk of the fabrics consumed in the U. S. dresswear is distributed through converters.

[2] Japanese regulations required that all exports be routed to the foreign buyer through a licensed Japanese exporting agent.

[3] F.o.b.—free on board (excluding transportation, insurance, and so on); c.i.f.—cost, insurance, and freight (including these costs).

was more price conscious than the one for the specialty lines of Dept. F. As a consequence, the average price markup in the sportswear lines was only 12% as compared to 25%-30% in Dept. F lines. However, in spite of the large supply provided by the U. S. and European producers of synthetic fibers, there was a large degree of quality differentiation in the market. In 1971, Japanese imports accounted for approximately one-fifth of the U. S. market in the type of fabrics handled by AP&M. (The U. S. and European producers provided most of the rest.) In some of these lines, especially in polyester woven fabrics, the Japanese products were considered to be the best in the world in their price range.

Customer Relationships

Due to the fluctuations in the dollar price of the yen and the high obsolescence factor in fabrics, AP&M's policy was to minimize ordering for inventory. As a result, only the more standard items were stocked in anticipation of customers' orders. All other items were purchased on the basis of confirmed orders received from customers.

For goods bought through Mr. Yokoma and paid for in yen, prices to AP&M's customers were quoted in dollars based on the f.o.b. yen price converted at the spot rate on the day of the customer's order. However, the contracts with the customers stipulated that all fluctuations in the yen's parity from the date of order were to be absorbed by the customers. (Many contracts were renegotiated, however, especially during the period from August 15 to December 18, 1971, when the 10% U. S. import surcharge was also being passed on to the buyers.)

Shipment of these goods ordered from Far Eastern generally took place within 120 to 150 days of the order date. The ocean voyage, clearing through customs and distribution to the customers, required another forty-five days. Receivables were due ninety days following the customer's receipt of the goods.

Import Financing

Of the approximately $12.5 million of AP&M purchases in 1971, $5.5 million were from the New York representatives of several major Japanese trading companies. The other $7 million were ordered from Mr. Yokoma of Far Eastern Exporters.

Purchases from the New York offices of the Japanese traders were payable in dollars upon delivery to AP&M in New York. The prices quoted were fixed in dollars and included ninety-day credits. Mr. Hinson had been unable to obtain price quotations from the Japanese which excluded the cost of financing. It was believed that during periods of severe currency fluctuations the Japanese were basing their dollar quotations on yen costs converted at a forward rate midway between the spot rate on the day of order and the best available sixty-day forward rate at that time. The assumption was that the cost of the traders' ninety-day credits approximated the cost of such financing available to AP&M from its U. S. banks, i.e., 1.25% to 1.75% above prime rate.

On goods ordered from Mr. Yokoma, the f.o.b. price to AP&M was always fixed in yen. Payment in yen was due upon Mr. Yokoma's presenting of a sight draft, the bill of lading, and other stipulated documents to AP&M's paying agent in Japan.

The means of financing the orders from Mr. Yokoma were limited by several factors. The Japanese Ministry of Finance required that all foreign exchange payments for export orders be remitted to Japan immediately upon transfer of the ownership documents from the exporter to the buyer's agent.[4] Also, in order to be licensed as "receipts for exports" (one of the processes required before the exporter could obtain the necessary export permits) all such foreign exchange remissions had to be linked to a specific commercial transaction. As a result, AP&M made use of only two modes of financing its purchases from Far Eastern Exporters. One method of financing employed was the direct transfer of dollars to the special "export receipts" account of Far Eastern Exporters held in a Tokyo bank. Dollars cabled to this account were immediately validated as export receipts and converted at that day's telegraphic transfer (TT) rate.[5] Mr. Yokoma had indicated several times that no interest was paid on this special account due to its revolving short-term nature. Mr. Hinson obtained these dollar advances from his New York banks at a cost of 1.5% above prime rate.

The second means of financing employed by Mr. Hinson was the opening of letters of credit (l/c's) in favor of Far Eastern Exporters. The l/c's were "negotiated" through a Japanese bank designated by Yokoma.

The banks indicated that, on a normal basis, AP&M's need for continual short-term funds which were secured by fabric inventories alone could be met only under an l/c arrangement. The conventional loan advances mentioned above were made available only for specific emergencies. Mr. Hinson understood that banks enjoyed several advantages in l/c financing as opposed to regular short-term loans. The banks, however, had never elaborated on this point with Hinson.

Since mid-1971, AP&M had had lines of credit of $2 million with each of two New York banks. The "lines" represented contingent liabilities of the banks and were utilized in two parts: letters of credit (l/c's) and trust receipts.

The dollar l/c's were opened with AP&M's New York banks who then advised the "negotiating" banks in Japan of the dollar credits in favor of the exporter (Far Eastern Exporters). To receive payment in yen, Mr. Yokoma presented a sight draft (bill of exchange), a bill of lading, a commercial invoice, and a consular invoice (for customs purposes) to the negotiating bank. This bank paid Yokoma in yen the face amount of the draft and forwarded the documents to AP&M's bank. In times of currency fluctuations, AP&M could request that the Japanese bank cable New York immediately, advising of the negotiation of the draft and the equivalent amount in dollars at that day's spot rate. The New York bank credited the dollars to the Japanese bank's account that same day, even prior to the arrival of the documents in New York. Mr. Hinson could opt to instruct his banks to await receipt of the documents. In that case, however, the negotiating bank in Japan converted the

---

[4] Under certain circumstances (such as a letter of credit) a bank guarantee of the future remission was accepted.

[5] Slightly more favorable than that day's spot rate at the time.

dollar l/c's at a rate based on the quotation for contracts five days forward. The increase in the dollar cost was borne entirely by AP&M.

Upon receipt of the documents by airmail at the New York bank, some three days later, the second phase of the credit was initiated. AP&M was issued a trust receipt under which the New York bank retained title to the imported goods while AP&M was commissioned as the selling agent. Receipts were due in 120 days. The costs to AP&M were .25% of the l/c plus cabling charges (approximately $8) for opening the l/c, and 1.25% above prime rate for the 120-day trust receipt loan. The bank could then guarantee the trust receipt loan and discount it in the money market. Exhibit 2 summarizes the steps of the l/c process.

An alternative to the above system was the "time l/c" and "banker's acceptance." The time l/c instructed the negotiating bank to pay the exporter 120 days (or other specified period of time) following his presentation of a "time draft." The interest was borne by the exporter, who could, of course, simply raise the f.o.b. cost of the goods. AP&M could obtain the bank l/c for 1.25% while Yokoma could have his time draft "accepted" by the Japanese bank and discounted at a rate slightly above the Japanese discount rate. All exchange rate risk, however, was clearly borne by the buyer who might choose to cover in the forward market.

A variation of the time l/c and the banker's acceptance described above was an instrument instructing the negotiating bank to pay Mr. Yokoma the face value of his "time draft" immediately. Upon receipt of the documents, the New York bank immediately credited the Japanese bank's account. A 120-day fixed dollar loan was then automatically credited to AP&M's account. Thus, AP&M avoided the exchange risk during the credit period. The New York bank could then "accept" the time draft by countersigning it, and discount it in the money market. The cost to AP&M for the loan was the banker's acceptance rate plus a 1.5% per annum commission for the bank's "accepting" or guaranteeing the draft. If the time draft had been issued in yen, the U. S. bank would have a yen liability against a dollar asset (the loan to AP&M). In this case the bank would make an additional charge to AP&M for the additional risk involved.

Mr. Hinson had not investigated the possibility of borrowing yen in Japan to finance the purchases. AP&M had no direct credit relations with banks in Japan, nor could Mr. Hinson be sure that the payments to the exporter under such an arrangement would qualify as "export receipts."

Factoring of accounts receivable provided another reliable source of short-term liquidity when needed. Factors guaranteed payment of receivables for 1.25% and discounted them, if cash was needed before the due date, for 2% to 3% above the "banker's acceptance" rate.

Selected U. S. and Japanese financial market rates are presented in Exhibit 3.

The 1971 Monetary Crisis

Following President Nixon's August 15, 1971 announcement that the U. S. dollar's value against gold would not be supported and that the U. S. dollar would not be convertible into gold any longer, the Japanese attempted to support the yen

at 360 units per dollar. By August 28, the billions of dollars pouring in forced the
Japanese into a managed floating of the yen. The yen floated upward until
December 18, 1971, as shown below:

Yen/U. S. $ Rates, 1971

Aug. 30	Sept. 30	Oct. 30	Nov. 30	Dec. 18
338.9	334.1	329.2	327.5	320.5

The Smithsonian Agreement that weekend reset the yen/US$ parity at 308 within
a 301-315 band. The rate continued to float upward from 314.8 on December 20
to 310 in late January 1972 and to almost 300 by early August 1972.

The December 1971 monetary agreements had terminated the U. S. dollar float
and the 10% surcharge, but had raised the dollar cost of Japanese goods 17% and
had forced the main Far Eastern textile exporters to levy quotas on their exports to
the United States. Many less resourceful importers were forced out of business. Mr.
Hinson, by a combination of pressures on the mills to reduce their yen prices and
several shrewd financial maneuvers, was able to carry AP&M through the entire
crisis period until August 1972 with all its customers and suppliers intact.

AP&M's Financial Tactics During the Monetary Crisis

In order to take into account the floating exchange rates during the period from
late August until mid-December 1971, AP&M contracts with the mills and customers
had called for renegotiation in the event of unacceptable adjustments in costs to
either party due to the floating of the yen. Rather than tolerate the serious disrup-
tions that would ensue under such arrangements, Mr. Hinson engineered a triangular
agreement with the mills and customers. In this agreement, the first 6% increase in
the yen's parity above 360 would be immediately absorbed by the mills who would
lower their yen prices proportionately. Any further increase in the yen's value
would be shared between AP&M and its customers—the latter having already accepted the burden of the 10% surcharge.

In addition to the previous arrangements to absorb the actual increase in Japanese prices, AP&M was able to execute several specific financial transactions. This
was done in spite of the increasingly tighter Japanese controls on dollar transfers
of all types. The transactions described below were possible only as a result of the
close daily telegraphic contacts Mr. Hinson maintained with Mr. Yokoma in Japan.

1. A total of $2 million was transferred by cable to Far Eastern's special ex-
port account in Japan in late August and early September to cover shipments in the
first quarter of 1972. This money was transferred to the account at the telegraphic
transfer (TT) rate, slightly more favorable than the day's spot rate. $1.3 million of
the funds was received from AP&M's two banks as an advance against future l/c's.
The banks insisted, however, that all these advances be converted into l/c's by the

end of the first quarter of 1972. The rate on the loan was the same as for the trust receipt loans—1.25% above prime. Of particular importance in these transactions was the fact that the transferred funds were then licensed by the Bank of Japan as "export receipts," applicable, however, only to exports routed from Far Eastern to AP&M. The remaining $700,000 were "borrowed" in yen from surplus funds in Far Eastern's noninterest bearing yen account in Japan in a special arrangement with the Bank of Japan. Title to the yen was retained in Far Eastern's hands, but forms were issued stating that the funds had been earmarked for payment of future AP&M shipments. AP&M issued promissory notes to Far Eastern for an equivalent amount of dollars calculated at that day's TT rate. The interest was set at 6% per annum.

2. To cover shipments from August 1971 through January 1972, several l/c's were opened in favor of Far Eastern within thirty days prior to shipments during that period. By special agreement with the Bank of Japan, several major banks in Japan were authorized to issue contracts guaranteeing the conversion rate on the l/c's, if negotiated within thirty days. The rates on these contracts varied, but were always less than 5 yen per dollar lower than the spot rate prevailing on the day of the contract. Approximately $2 million in credits were transferred under these forward contracts during the period.

3. In late December 1971, the Japanese government became concerned over the plight of the smaller manufacturers whose export sales were being severely curtailed by the effects of the revaluation, quotas, etc. By special proclamation, the Bank of Japan authorized negotiating banks to accept pro forma invoices submitted by exporters on behalf of importers. The Bank of Japan guaranteed conversion of the future l/c's at the TT rates prevailing on the day the pro forma invoices were submitted. The contracts were to be valid for shipments through June 15, 1972, only. Mr. Yokoma drew up pro forma documents for $3.0 million in orders through June 1972 and submitted them along with guarantees from the New York banks stating that they would open l/c's in that amount to cover the shipments. In this manner, Yokoma guaranteed the conversion of the $3.0 million at rates of 319 to 315. For each thirty days forward, the rate was reduced by 1 yen per US$. As with other transactions, the yen obtained subsequently were for use only in payment for goods shipped from Far Eastern to AP&M.

By the end of March 1972, these forward contracts were still unused due to the existence of the TT yen which the banks were still demanding be converted into l/c's. By June 15, 1972, the date of the contract's deadline, $1.4 million of the forward contracts still remained unutilized. The Bank of Japan agreed to extend their guarantees, but discounted the guaranteed rates by 1 yen per dollar for each thirty days beyond the original contract date. Thus, an unused February contract for 318 could be sold in September 1972 for 311.

The Situation in August 1972

With only $0.5 million left out of the $3.0 million pro forma invoices negotiated by Mr. Yokoma, and with requirements for the remaining part of the year in the neighborhood of $3.0 to $4.0 million, Mr. Hinson worried about the increasing number of rumors concerning an impending second yen upvaluation by year-end, 1972. The only avenue open to protect himself against a further upvaluation of the yen appeared to be the purchase of forward yen against dollar l/c's. In addition, Mr. Hinson had to negotiate with Japanese trading companies to use some of their export quota, since Far Eastern's quota appeared to be already at its limit.

The Forward Contracts. Mr. Hinson had received a letter from Mr. Yokoma on July 15, 1972 indicating that two large banks in Japan were quoting rates on dollar l/c's sold forward. On l/c's to be negotiated in 60 days, one bank guaranteed conversion at 287 yen per dollar. The second bank quoted 281 yen for the same contract.[6]

A phone call to his own New York bank the first week of August had yielded Mr. Hinson the following quotations for such l/c's sold forward:

Forward Yen Rates per Dollar 1/c

Term	30 days	90 days	120 days
Rate	285.5	272.1	272.7

The decision whether to use these contracts had to be made within a few days as the banks had indicated that such contracts were rapidly becoming harder to come by.

The Export Quotas. The quotas imposed by Japan on her textile exports in late December of 1971 limited annual growth in exports of many major synthetic fabrics to 5%. By March 1972, Far Eastern had used up its allocation for polyester tie fabric exports. The large Japanese traders, on the other hand, had been allotted permissible volumes well in excess of their needs. Mr. Hinson instructed Far Eastern to implement the following procedures:

1. Polyester fabrics were invoiced out to AP&M by Far Eastern under the description "polyester-rayon blends." This exempted Mr. Yokoma from the quota limitations for polyesters.

2. A bargain was struck with two large Japanese traders that specified polyester shipments would be invoiced out to AP&M on the traders' forms, relieving Far Eastern of accountability for those shipments. For their service, the traders charged 6 cents per yard shipped under these arrangements. (The average price per yard was $1.50.)

Mr. Hinson was uncertain as to how the new quotas to be announced in September 1972 would affect his company's operations. His assumption was that his

---

[6] The market for these instruments was much narrower than the regular forward market. The entire contract was conditional on the on-time delivery of the goods by the exporter. Rates on these contracts mirrored much more closely the perceived risk of a parity change.

quota would be increased or, alternatively, that other arrangements could be set up with the large traders. In any case he had to be prepared to negotiate again with the Japanese trading companies.

To aid him in his analyses of future financial strategies, Mr. Hinson had compiled data on the Japanese balance of payments. See Exhibit 4. Reflecting on the general status of Japanese textile exports, Mr. Hinson posited that the Japanese would maintain their competitiveness in textiles by controlling raw material prices, developing new fabrics, introducing subsidies at various levels in the textile industry, and continuing to maintain the technical and design superiority they now enjoyed in several synthetic fabric classes.

EXHIBIT 1   AP & M Trading Company: Financial Data

Sales, Expenses, and Net Income, 1964-1971 (thousands of dollars)

	1964	1966	1968	1969	1970	1971
Sales	$9,338	$8,098	$9,446	$8,598	$9,782	$14,124
Cost of goods	8,376	7,068	8,366	7,572	8,564	12,544
Other expenses	840	912	924	920	1,114	1,394
Taxes	32	36	64	46	32	72
Net Income	$ 90	$ 82	$ 92	$ 60	$ 72	$ 114

Balance Sheet, December 31, 1971 (thousands of dollars)

Assets		Liabilities & Equity	
Cash	$ 224	Accounts payable	$1,382
Accounts receivable	4,264	Acceptance and loans payable	3,662
Inventory	2,254	Accrued taxes	62
Notes receivable	306	Accrued expenses	132
Total current assets	$7,048	Total current liabilities	$5,238
Long-term investments	51	Notes payable	310
Net fixed assets	39	Capital stock	546
		Retained earnings	1,044
Total assets	$7,138	Total liabilities and capital	$7,138

EXHIBIT 2 AP & M Trading Company: Letter of Credit Process

	Description				Accounting								
	AP & M	U.S. Bank	Japanese Bank	Far Eastern	AP & M Dr.	AP & M Cr.	U.S. Bank Dr.	U.S. Bank Cr.	Japanese Bank Dr.	Japanese Bank Cr.	Far Eastern Dr.	Far Eastern Cr.
1.				Advises Hinson of particulars of shipment								
2.	Requests l/c from U.S. bank	Issues l/c against Far Eastern on the basis of AP & M's line					Contingent claims on AP & M ↑	Contingent l/c payable ↑ (Far Eastern)				
3.		Sends l/c to Japanese bank	Notifies Far Eastern									
4.			Pays Far Eastern. Notifies U.S. bank. Sends documents to and debits U.S. bank	Presents sight draft and other documents to Japanese bank. Receives payment					Deposits in N.Y.↑	Demand deposits ↑ (Far E.)	Inventory ↓	Cash ↑
5.		Credits account of Japanese bank and cancels l/c						Demand deposits ↑ (Jap. bank) Contingent l/c payable ↓ (Far Eastern)				
6.	Accepts promissory note. Receives merchandise on consignment	Issues trust receipt and promissory note to AP & M			Merchandise on consignment ↑	Notes Payable ↑	Contingent claim on AP & M ↓ Advances ↑ (trust receipt to AP & M)					

EXHIBIT 3   Selected Financial Market Rates,
1968-1972

Ratio Scale
of Yields

U. S. 4- to 6-Month
Prime Commercial Paper[a]

Japan—City
Banks' Regular
Lending Rate[b]

U. S. Banker's Acceptances[a]

[a]Monthly averages of daily figures.
[b]End of the quarter figures.
Sources: Federal Reserve Bank of St. Louis and Bank of Japan.

EXHIBIT 4   Japan Balance of Payments, 1962-1972 (millions of dollars)

Year or Month	Current Balance	Trade Balance	Exports	Imports	Services	Credits	Debits	Transfers	Credits	Debits	(a) Long-Term Capital	Assets	Liabilities	(a)(b) Short-Term Capital	Errors & Omissions	Overall Balance	Gold & Foreign Exchange Reserves	Others
Calendar Year																		
1962	△48	401	4,861	4,460	△420	1,088	1,508	△29	68	97	172	△309	481	107	6	237	355	△118
1963	△780	△166	5,391	5,557	△569	1,134	1,703	△45	68	113	467	△298	765	107	45	△161	37	△198
1964	△480	377	6,704	6,327	△784	1,323	2,107	△73	72	145	107	△451	558	234	10	△129	(c)121	△70
1965	932	1,901	8,332	6,431	△884	1,563	2,447	△85	63	148	415	△446	31	△61	△51	405	108	297
1966	1,254	2,275	9,641	7,366	△886	1,931	2,817	△135	69	204	△808	△706	△102	△64	△45	337	△33	370
1967	△190	1,160	10,231	9,071	△1,172	2,182	3,354	△178	74	252	△812	△875	63	506	△75	△571	△69	△502
1968	1,048	2,529	12,751	10,222	△1,306	2,607	3,913	△175	83	258	△239	△1,096	857	209	84	1,102	886	216
1969	2,119	3,699	15,679	11,980	△1,399	3,261	4,660	△181	85	266	△155	△1,508	1,353	178	141	2,283	605	1,678
1970	1,970	3,963	18,969	15,006	△1,785	4,009	5,794	△208	98	306	△1,591	△2,031	440	724	271	1,374	(d)903	593
1971	5,898	7,900	23,650	15,750	△1,748	4,842	6,590	△254	124	378	△1,161	△2,317	1,156	2,993	△53	7,677	(e)10,836	△3,031
1968 1~3	△295	118	2,569	2,451	△354	588	942	△59	23	82	△110	△237	127	114	44	△247	△42	△205
4~6	191	546	3,112	2,566	△310	633	943	△45	20	65	△18	△243	225	△20	68	221	13	208
7~9	504	845	3,327	2,482	△317	675	992	△24	21	45	7	△252	259	31	△1	541	384	157
10~12	648	1,020	3,743	2,723	△325	711	1,036	△47	19	66	△118	△364	246	84	△27	587	531	56
1969 1~3	130	560	3,236	2,676	△377	709	1,086	△53	20	73	49	△286	335	△7	106	278	322	△44
4~6	551	913	3,794	2,881	△309	779	1,088	△53	22	75	80	△323	403	△17	23	637	△124	761
7~9	672	1,067	4,155	3,088	△357	873	1,230	△38	19	57	△106	△320	214	61	31	658	137	521
10~12	766	1,159	4,494	3,335	△356	900	1,256	△37	24	61	△178	△579	401	141	△19	710	270	440
1970 1~3	55	579	4,036	3,457	△465	896	1,361	△59	23	82	△438	△670	232	185	182	△16	(d)△372	△266
4~6	373	845	4,586	3,741	△422	974	1,396	△50	24	74	△463	△435	△28	149	△36	23	△99	122
7~9	599	1,105	4,939	3,834	△458	1,072	1,530	△48	23	71	△315	△392	77	244	122	650	△213	863
10~12	943	1,434	5,408	3,974	△440	1,067	1,507	△51	28	79	△375	△534	159	146	3	717	843	△126
1971 1~3	450	1,071	4,932	3,861	△541	1,079	1,620	△80	26	106	△194	△649	455	131	222	609	(e)1,059	△322
4~6	1,292	1,778	5,765	3,987	△433	1,123	1,556	△53	32	85	177	△445	622	660	159	2,288	2,141	147
7~9	2,127	2,516	6,261	3,745	△354	1,300	1,654	△35	39	74	△304	△507	203	1,991	246	4,060	5,785	△1,725
10~12	2,029	2,535	6,692	4,157	△420	1,340	1,760	△86	27	113	△840	△716	△124	211	△680	720	1,851	△1,131
1972 J	△18	180	1,539	1,359	△186	388	574	△12	8	20	△275	△175	△100	465	24			
F	390	623	2,004	1,381	△198	471	669	△35	8	43	△118	△174	56	469	△100			
M	588	887	2,474	1,587	△197	537	734	△102	10	112	△366	△487	121	△127	23			
A	510	722	2,219	1,497	△159	449	608	△53	10	63	△261	△310	49	△68	△24			
M	183	515	2,085	1,570	△191	486	677	△141	12	153	△250	△300	50	△23	112			
J	531	759	2,169	1,410	△206	438	644	△22	11	33	△227	△325	98	△113	49			
JP	750	971	2,390	1,419	△202	477	679	△19	10	29	△483	△545	62	198	△63			
AP	626	729	2,374	1,645	△95	594	689	△8	10	18	△346	△397	51	325	△48			
SP	719	918	2,583	1,665	△164	594	758	△35	10	45	△315	△462	147	159	16			

a △shows outflow of capital (an increase in assets or a decrease in liabilities).
b Excluding transactions which belong to monetary movements.
c Gold tranche of 180 million dollars at the end of March 1964 is included.
d Including the allocation of Special Drawing Rights, 122 million dollars.
e Including the allocation of Special Drawing Rights, 128 million dollars.
P Preliminary

Source: Bank of Japan

CHAPTER 7

Exchange Risk and the Multinational Enterprise

When a firm carries on activities overseas, it immediately makes itself vulnerable to possible gains and losses on the value of its monetary holdings denominated in various currencies. A British firm that decides to sell a product to customers in Italy who insist on being invoiced in liras will be concerned about the value of the lira vis-a-vis the pound until the receivable is paid. Often, the U. K. firm can be expected to have very short terms on its receivables. If longer terms are desired, the English firm may require that the Italian customer bear the exchange risk beyond a certain amount or pay a higher price to compensate for the risk. This is the type of problem discussed in Chapter 6.

When the firm expands its operations abroad to include direct investment in a foreign subsidiary (or branch), the issue becomes more complicated. Financing for the foreign operations must be found and a decision on the exposure of the firm to foreign exchange risks must be made. In a foreign subsidiary there are receivables due from the foreign customers in the foreign currency. However, part of these receivables may be financed with debts payable by the subsidiary to locals. In a simple case, if the subsidiary has receivables of $100 and it is financing them partially with payables of $50 in the local currency, then the amount of foreign exchange risk it must worry about vis-à-vis the parent currency is $50. Regardless of what happens to the local currency, the receipt from the local customer is in part protected by the debt to the local supplier. It is only the difference ($50) which is subject to revaluation if the relative values of the currencies of the parent and the subsidiary change. Notice that the amount of foreign exchange risk is partially determined by the manner in which assets are financed.

In the short-term, the financial officer is endowed with a set of investment and operating decisions made in the past that result in the firm's having a diversity of assets in various countries. These assets generate three major types of problems for the financial officer:

1. Some assets *require financing;* funds must be raised.

2. Some investments become *cash generators;* a proper use for these "excess" funds must be found.

3. The location of the assets, as well as the decisions taken under (1) and (2) above, generates *foreign exchange positions;* they must be evaluated and altered if necessary.

In approaching these problems, the financial officer operates in the money market and in the foreign exchange market for each currency. These financial transactions can be accomplished *directly* by having the excess funds or the financing of a given subsidiary handled directly by that subsidiary interacting with the market. Alternatively, these transactions can be made *indirectly* by using intercompany accounts; e.g., one subsidiary may borrow from the market and loan the proceeds to another subsidiary.

Finally, the financial officer may want to interfere with the normal operations of the business and attempt to affect the size and the currency of various assets and liabilities associated with trade. This approach usually encounters resistance from the executives in the field, particularly when intercompany pricing and terms of trade are involved.

This chapter presents a methodology for evaluating both the cost of financing and the return on investments in the international markets; it then proceeds to deal with the problems of foreign exchange exposure that foreign direct investment generates. The objective here is simply to describe the major considerations faced by the international financial officer in the evaluation of decisions. The next chapter will present an integrated framework to analyze the whole function of this officer. Similarly, while this chapter is concerned with responding to the fluctuations in currencies where there are assets fixed in nominal terms such as debt issues or receivables, the more complicated issues of fundamental changes in operating revenues and costs because of currency realignments are dealt with in Part Three in the framework of capital budgeting.

We will use the terms "devaluation/depreciation" and "upvaluation/appreciation" somewhat interchangeably. Under the adjustable peg system prior to the recent managed floating experience, currencies could devalue or upvalue. Today, it is more appropriate to speak of depreciation or appreciation of many currencies even though the other terms are often used synonymously and many currencies have their value fixed officially in terms of the U. S. dollar.

Since much of the concern over exposure is because of accounting concepts, this chapter concludes with a brief appendix which reviews some of the differences in accounting standards around the world, suggesting where major conflicts may arise. There is a brief discussion of the impact various price-level adjustments may have on the value of a firm's income statement and balance sheet.

THE VALUE OF MONEY IN INTERNATIONAL FINANCE

For the financial officer of a multinational company, the value of money represents specific costs and returns to the firm. The costs and returns involve the costs of raising funds to finance foreign operations and the returns from investing excess funds temporarily in financial assets in the international markets. Costs and returns from operating in the forward exchange markets must also be considered.

Financial costs and returns traditionally have been measured in terms of interest rates and percentage discounts or premiums. In international finance one can use the same units, as has been done in preceding chapters. When the finance function is evaluated within the scope of solely domestic operations, only one currency in one financial market is involved. However, when the scope of the finance function is expanded to the international arena, there is a large variety of currencies and financial markets. In order to be able to make comparisons among the options offered in various markets, one must establish a currency as a common denominator; this base currency is usually the currency of the parent company. Then one can proceed to compute what may be called "effective interest rates." The following sections deal with the means of computing the effective interest rates. The role of time and the impact of inflation are also included in these computations.

Effective Interest Rate

For simplicity's sake, these examples will use returns in the money market; however, the same approach applies to borrowing costs in that market. Assume the following quotes for one-year deposits:

pound sterling	18%
U. S. dollar	13%
Swiss franc	11%
Italian lira	22%

Where should funds be invested? Based on the figures for interest rates alone, the answer is to invest funds in Italian liras. However, what would happen if the Italian lira depreciated 15% against each of the other three alternatives? In terms of liras, there would have been a larger percentage return than any alternative. But converting the proceeds of such an investment into any of the other three currencies would create a loss of 15% on both the principal and the interest.

As a rough approximation, in terms of the other three currencies the Italian lira's *effective interest rate or yield* would be only 7% (22% − 15%),[1] that is, *the nominal interest rate less the percentage change in the value of the currency.* (Notice that the analysis is for one year, so adjustments for fractions of year or compounding after one year are not necessary.)

---

[1] This formula provides a good approximation for the effective interest rates as long as the interest differentials are not large. If interest rates differ by large amounts then the impact of variations in exchange rate on interest received or paid will alter the results obtained by this simple formula. An elaboration of this formula is presented later in the chapter.

When one says "percentage change in the value of the currency" one must establish "against what other currencies." The previous example assumed that the exchange rates for the other currencies remained constant throughout the period with the exception of their value against the Italian lira. These currencies appreciated in value against the Italian lira, or the Italian lira depreciated against the other three currencies. If at the same time that the lira depreciated, the Swiss franc appreciated 4% against the U. S. dollar and the pound sterling, and 19% against the Italian lira (15% depreciation of the lira plus 4% appreciation of the Swiss franc against every other of the three currencies), what would be the effective interest rates? In order to answer this question, decide first upon what currency we wish to measure the effective yield.

This is illustrated in the following table. On the left are the nominal rates for investments in each of the four currencies. As before, the Italian lira offers the highest nominal return. The numbers in the following four columns state the *net effective yield* in terms of each of the currencies involved. For example, in terms of Swiss francs, investing funds in pounds sterling would produce a net effective yield of 14%. This is composed of the nominal 18% return on a pound sterling investment less the 4% lost when converting the pound proceeds into Swiss francs which have appreciated 4% against the pound sterling. If the funds were invested in U. S. dollars the net effective yield would be 9%. The nominal yield for the dollar is 13% and there is a 4% foreign exchange loss when converting into Swiss francs. Investing in Swiss francs and measuring the net effective return in terms of Swiss francs, then the nominal and the effective interest rates are the same. Finally, if Swiss francs were invested in Italian liras, the net effective interest rate would be only 3%. Although the Italian lira offers the highest nominal return, 22%, when the lira proceeds are converted into Swiss francs, there is a foreign exchange loss of 19%.

Currency	Nominal Rates	Effective Rates in Terms of			
		£	US$	SF	Lit
Pound Sterling	18%	18%	18%	14% (18 − 4)	33% (18 + 15)
U. S. Dollar	13%	13%	13%	9% (13 − 4)	28% (13 + 15)
Swiss Franc	11%	15% (11 + 4)	15% (11 + 4)	11%	30% (11 + 19)
Italian Lira	22%	7% (22 − 15)	7% (22 − 15)	3% (22 − 19)	22%

The columns for the net effective rates in terms of pounds and U. S. dollars produce the same results because there has not been any change in the value of the pound against the U. S. dollar (or the U. S. dollar against the pound); if one invests funds with the same nominal rates and there is no change in the foreign exchange value between two specific currencies, the net effective yield will be the same whether measured in one or the other base currency. Another point to notice is that the diagonal of the table shows the nominal rates. This is to say that if funds are invested in the same currency used as unit of account, the nominal rates and the net effective rates are the same. Dealing with only one currency, foreign exchange considerations do not enter the analysis. Finally, ranking of the investments yields the same list of priorities regardless of the currency used as unit of account or base currency. In between are the U. S. dollar and the Swiss franc investments, in that order. Notice that the ranking is the same although the absolute numbers for rate of return obviously are different. These differences in interest rates in a competitive market are maintained by the discounts and premiums in the forward exchange market, as explained in Chapter 5.

The computations of future effective rates involve an element of speculation, and, consequently, risk. The speculation is on the future exchange rates of the currencies being considered. The previous example took this as a given; however, in real life one would have to make forecasts that are subject to risks. To act on the basis of these forecasts (e.g., in the previous example, to invest the funds in pound sterling) and not cover the flow means to undertake foreign exchange risks. If the forecasts turn out to be wrong, then, with the benefit of hindsight, we may see that the approach chosen—which we thought was optimal—was actually sub-optimal. The following section discusses financial transactions without foreign exchange risks, usually referred to as covered transactions.

Time Factor and the Effective Interest Rate

The remarks above have dealt with investments and borrowings of a one-year maturity. Once longer maturities are introduced, explicit assumptions must be made for repayment of principal in the case of borrowings, or for intended changes in the amount of financial investment. (Actually one would have to make the same refinements within a year, but the results will not alter the decision very much.)

The question of what happens to the size of the borrowings or investments is relevant when the transaction is made on an open basis, without coverage in the foreign exchange market. Without foreign exchange cover, when borrowing in a currency that appreciates against the base currency, the appreciation loss will be the most damaging the sooner the appreciation happens. Likewise, investing in a currency that depreciates against the base currency, the depreciation loss will hurt the most the earlier the depreciation takes place.

Specifically, look at the net present value (NPV) of the cost of borrowings. In the stream of cash flows, first are the inflows for the proceeds from the borrowings, and subsequently there are cash outflows for the payment of interest and repayment of principal:

$$\text{NPV} = \text{Borrowing} - \frac{\text{Interest} + \text{Principal Repayment}_1}{(1 + r)} - \frac{\text{Interest} + \text{Principal Repayment}_2}{(1 + r)^2} - \frac{\text{Interest} + \text{Principal Repayment}_n}{(1 + r)^n}$$

where r is the interest rate on the loan and only one currency is considered. The timing of principal repayment will have no effect on the NPV to the extent that interest is charged only on the loan balance outstanding. NPV will be zero. However, to compute the cost of borrowing in a foreign currency in terms of the unit of account, the home currency, another factor is included in the calculations: the change in relative value between the two currencies, the borrowed one and the home one. In this case r is unknown and finding its value, while holding NPV = 0, will produce the net effective interest cost.

The denominator in the above equation, regardless of the size of r, becomes larger with time because every year the exponent in the denominator increases by one. The value of whatever happens in later years when discounted by the appropriate factor expressed in the denominator tends to be small. Therefore, the sooner the appreciation takes place in a borrowed currency, the greater the impact on the effective interest rate, r.

Whether the loan is a level principal payment loan or a balloon note also affects the impact of the appreciation or depreciation. Generally, appreciation of the currency in which the loan must be paid hurts a balloon payment loan more than a level principal payment loan if the appreciation takes place in early years. As an example, the table below shows the different effective interest costs for a 10% loan and a 5% appreciation under the two different types of borrowings.

	Effective Interest Cost	
	Level Principal Payment	Level Principal and 50% Balloon Payment
Year of Appreciation		
1	11.7%	12.0%
2	11.3	11.5
3	11.0	11.0
4	10.8	10.6
5	10.6	10.3

Inflation and the Effective Interest Rate

This topic will be explained in more detail in Chapters 9 and 10. However, there are a couple of issues to clarify. The first point is the effect of inflation on interest rates in the domestic market. It is well established that the interest rates in a given currency have two elements: one is the "real return" that the investor expects; the other is the expected rate of inflation that will erode the value of money received in the future. To the extent that the borrower has reason to believe that his or her forecast of the rate of inflation is higher than the forecast that the market is making, the borrower in effect is anticipating payment of a "real rate" below what the market expects. Given that the repayment of the debt and interest are contracted in advance, to the extent that inflation proceeds at a rate faster than what the market anticipated, the lender will be hurt. The lender's purchasing power will be less than expected initially. However, the borrower will benefit. It is this type of thinking that gives rise to the prescription: "Borrow as much as possible in inflationary situations."[2]

The second point to make regarding inflation has to do with the relationship between inflation and the foreign exchange rate. It is true that there is a general tendency for relatively high inflation rates to be followed eventually by a devaluation of the currency in question against other currencies. However, in this general tendency, notice that there are two factors that must be evaluated carefully before translating the effect of the rate of inflation into a net effective rate. One is the phrase *relative inflation.* To the extent that all the countries are experiencing a similarly large rate of inflation, there is no cause for one particular currency to devalue relative to the other, other things remaining constant. The other factor is derived from the word "eventually." This eventuality might take a long time to materialize, and it might not ever materialize if the government can smooth the external implications of the domestic inflation until a turnaround situation arises; e.g., other countries catch up with the country's rate of inflation. It is only by ignoring these two considerations that the usual recommendation holds that lending in a foreign currency with a high interest rate does not pay if the inflation rate is also high. The assumption of such a statement is that a devaluation commensurate with the rate of inflation will take place and that this will erode the gains from the high rate of interest. This ignores the fact that as long as one removes the investment from the country before the devaluation actually takes place (if it takes place at all), one will realize a high rate of return regardless of the rate of inflation in the local markets.

Financial Transactions on a Covered Basis

Covered Transactions in Perfect Markets. If the markets are in equilibrium one would expect in our previous example the following premiums and discounts to prevail for one-year forward currencies:

Currency with Premium or Discount (–)	Nominal Rate	Currencies Against Which Premium or Discount Is Maintained			
		£	U.S.$	SF	Lit
Pound Sterling	18%	–	–5% (13 – 18)	–7% (11 – 18)	+4% (22 – 18)
U. S. Dollar	13%	+5% (18 – 13)	–	–2% (11 – 13)	+9% (22 – 13)
Swiss Franc	11%	+7% (18 – 11)	+2% (13 – 11)	–	+11% (22 – 11)
Italian Lira	22%	–4% (18 – 22)	–9% (13 – 22)	–11% (11 – 22)	–

[2] Brazil, Finland, France, and Israel, among other countries, have offered a number of bond issues that have provisions for adjustment of principal and interest payments by some cost level. Usually these indexed bonds are linked to a general level of prices, although sometimes the adjustment is made to particular cost indices. Indexed bonds are not unknown in the United States. The only issue after World War II was in 1959 by the municipality of Carlsbad, New Mexico. It offered a $3M conventional issue with a 7% coupon and a twenty-year maturity. At the same time, it offered a $4M issue with a 6% coupon and a thirty-year maturity, but with an increase in the coupon as well as the redemption value by the annual percentage rise in the cost of living.

For example, this table shows that the pound sterling is at a discount of 5% against the U. S. dollar (the U. S. dollar is at a premium of 5% against the pound). The discount on the pound, or the premium on the U. S. dollar, is reflected by the interest differentials for one-year money. The interest rate on the pound is 18%; the interest rate on the U. S. dollar is 13%. Therefore, there is a 5% discount on the pound and 5% premium on the dollar. In this table each side of the diagonal is a mirror image of the other except for the sign. This only means that the premium of currency A against currency B is the same as the discount of currency B against currency A. These principles of the relationships between the money market and the foreign exchange market were explained in Chapter 5.

The table shows that if one wishes to invest in a foreign currency without incurring foreign exchange risks one earns the same return everywhere if the markets are in equilibrium as assumed here. For example, a sterling investor can invest in the pound sterling market and earn 18%. Alternatively, the investor can convert the pounds sterling into liras and invest in liras at 22%. To insure the price at which the liras are converted back into pounds, the investor would sell liras in the forward market against pounds sterling. This forward sale would carry a 4% discount on the lira. So the net return of this "covered transaction" is the same as leaving the funds in pounds sterling. The extra 4% that is made by investing in liras is lost in the forward transaction when selling the liras to return to pound sterling.

What if there were a depreciation of the Italian lira as postulated in our first example? The net effective return would still be 18%, for the return was locked in by the forward contract to sell liras at a 4% discount. This forward transaction, in effect a loss of 4%, protected the investor against an 11% greater loss (if the 15% depreciation had occurred). On the other hand, the forward contract also eliminated the possibility of increasing the return over 22%, and certainly over 18%, if an opposite outcome occurred and the lira actually appreciated against the pound sterling.

Covered Transaction in Imperfect Markets. Imperfect markets arise when the arbitrageurs who keep the interest differential equal to the premiums or discounts in the forward markets are not allowed to operate. In these cases the markets for a given currency are segmented between the domestic market regulated by the country's governmental authorities and the external markets traded outside the reach of government control. In these situations the equilibrium in the markets will exist only in the external markets. The domestic money market will present a situation of disequilibrium when compared with the foreign exchange market. When this type of situation arises, opportunities to profit appear for those individuals who have access to both markets. This is typically true for the multinational company with a subsidiary within the country's boundaries but with access to international markets.

An example of the situation described will occur when the domestic markets are restricted to domestic users in one way or the other. For example, only domestic entities can borrow in the domestic market; outsiders are not allowed to borrow in that market. At the same time if that currency is important enough (such as the pound sterling), there will be an external market in both the money and foreign exchange markets. These external markets will be in equilibrium. Assume the following with the U. S. dollar as the alternative borrowing source:

Domestic borrowing rate for pound sterling	18%
External borrowing rate for pound sterling	20%
External borrowing rate for U. S. dollar	12%
External discount on the pound against the U. S. dollar	8%

The option of borrowing in the U. K. domestic market and covering in the external market is measured as follows:

Cost of borrowing in the United Kingdom	18%
Returns on the covering transaction:	
Purchase pounds against U. S. dollars for one year delivery in the external market at 8% discount on the pound (8% premium on the dollar)	8%
Net cost of borrowing on a covered basis	10%
Cost of the alternative "borrowing in U. S. dollar" (the unit of account)	12%

Clearly the option of borrowing local pounds and covering in the external market is preferable to borrowing U. S. dollars. (Dollars do not need to be covered because they are used as the unit of account. The covering operation would be done on the dollars if the pound were the unit of account.) Notice that this transaction involves two separate legal entities operating in a centralized manner. The subsidiary incurs the borrowing costs in pounds. The parent company does the forward transaction and realizes the gain.

An opportunity for investment by the domestic subsidiary while the parent company does the covering in the external market will occur when interest rates in the domestic market are higher than in the external market. (Remember the two markets are segmented by regulations.) Example:

Domestic investment rate for deutsche mark	12%
External investment rate for deutsche mark	10%
External investment rate for U. S. dollars	12%
External discount of the U. S. dollar against the deutsche mark	2%

In this case the domestic subsidiary will invest its funds in the domestic market for deutsche mark at 12%. Using the dollar as the unit of account, the covering transaction to be made by the parent company will involve selling deutsche marks against U. S. dollars at a premium of 2%. The net effect of the transaction covered in this fashion is a yield of 14% (12% realized by the subsidiary, 2% by the parent). This alternative dominates the opportunity of investing in the base currency, U. S. dollars at 12%, and the foreign exchange risks are the same in terms of U. S. dollars—zero.[3]

---

[3] Using daily data from the Reuters' telex from February through May, 1973, Agmon and Bronfeld (1975) confirmed that opportunities to profit from covered interest arbitrage generally did not exist; i.e., the market is efficient. Some opportunities seem to exist for longer maturities (six and twelve months) but they suggest that the data for these maturities are not particularly representative since it is not clear that transactions could take place at the quoted price. They ar-

DIRECT INVESTMENT AND FOREIGN EXCHANGE EXPOSURE

The above comments dealt with financial assets and liabilities. The discussion presented the foreign exchange risks that these assets and liabilities generated and how to cover against such risks. Now one must consider the foreign exchange risks that are generated from less liquid assets, those produced by direct investment.

As a foreign subsidiary begins to acquire assets other than financial ones, the definition of which assets are *exposed* to the risks of fluctuations in the exchange rate between the subsidiary's currency and the parent's currency becomes more difficult to determine. Likewise, the policies which the firm will follow to protect itself (to cover or to hedge its exposure) will vary depending on the amount of the exposure and the cost of various alternatives which are available.[4]

Foreign Exchange Exposure

The Concept of Accounting Exposure. Suppose Bongo Corporation, a U. S. company, has a South American subsidiary, Bongo Latino, which carries on manufacturing and distribution activities in Latin America. At the end of one period, the balance sheet of Bongo Latino translated into U. S. dollars is as follows:

BONGO LATINO: Balance Sheet for End of Period
(thousands of U. S. dollars)

Assets		*Liabilities and Net Worth*	
Cash and Securities	$ 40	Accounts Payable	$ 60
Receivables	80	Taxes Payable	20
Inventory	80	Total Current Liabilities	$ 80
Total Current Assets	$200	Long-Term Debt	120
Plant and Equipment,		Equity	100
Net	100	Total Liabilities	
Total Assets	$300	and Equity	$ 300

---

gue that perceived opportunities which are claimed to exist are the result of misspecification. First, traders average the bid and asked rates for forward contracts, which is not relevant for the actual trader who would pay the asked rate for a forward contract. Second, there is often a misspecification of the relevant opportunity rate for the home currency's return. Thus, a U. S. dollar *owner* would have to cover the opportunity cost of lending the money in the United States plus gain from the foreign covered arbitrage. A U. S. dollar lender would have to net even more from a covered foreign interest arbitrage transaction, since (s)he would have to cover the U. S. borrowing cost as well. This borrowing cost is higher than the U. S. lending rate. Their study shows the owner could rarely profit. Hence, the lender could profit from only a subset of the owner's profit opportunities. When transaction costs are included, the opportunities would be further reduced. See Tamir Agmon and Saul Bronfeld, "The International Mobility of Short Term Covered Arbitrage Capital," *Journal of Business Finance and Accounting,* Spring 1975.

[4] In all these examples, we operate on the basis of some standard or numeraire, such as dollars or pounds or liras. The issue is vastly more complicated if the local firm's shareholders are not local citizens. Hence, protecting assets in terms of local purchasing power may not be their relevant concern. This issue is dealt with in Part Three, where we examine the issue of a reference currency in the context of capital budgeting.

At the time of this balance sheet, the peso is worth $.14. That is, there are about seven pesos to the dollar.

Suppose the management of Bongo Corporation foresees that a 10% depreciation of the peso is very likely in the coming year. At the end of that year, what would be the loss from translating the now-cheaper peso investment of Bongo Corporation in Bongo Latino?

First, this balance sheet is convenient, but to accurately determine Bongo Latino's loss from depreciation of the peso the flow of funds in the future should be merged with this balance sheet. This is a point often overlooked in the analysis. For our purposes, however, assume that Bongo Corporation wants to know what its accounting peso exposure is as of the date of the balance sheet.

If the peso depreciates, then the value of the cash and securities shown on the balance sheet and the receivables collectable from the customers should presumably be valued at the new, current exchange rate. If they were exchanged for dollars, their value would be less by the amount of the depreciation. Likewise, the bill from the suppliers would also be less in dollars since the payables would be paid in "cheaper" pesos.

But the basis for most accounting concepts is cost, so the historic cost based on the historic exchange rate for many of the other balance sheet accounts may be relevant. For example, the depreciated book value of the plant may have little relationship to any current market value. Thus, if the value does not match market value, why should one worry about whether the translation rate used for converting its historic book value to dollars is the current one? After all, the depreciation charges are simply a method to expense the original (historic) cost over a period of time, so there is no point (in this logic) in translating the plant at the current rate.

But what of inventory? If inventory is thought of as historically produced goods not yet sold, or as goods in process, why should their dollar value be adjusted? If they are destined for sale in the Latin economy then the price may not change with the devaluation, so their future value will likely be less in dollar terms. On the other hand, if they are for export, the new depreciation may make the goods more competitive. Hence, total revenues might actually be higher in the future in pesos so that to translate the inventory at the current value would be too severe a decrease in value. Likewise, if we retain an historic cost basis for goods, then their historic cost (in dollars) should not be changed simply because of fluctuations in the peso.

A similar conflict develops for long-term debt. Some people would argue it should not be considered on a current basis. Including the long-term debt, which will only be repaid in the future, lowers the subsidiary's exposure to a foreign exchange loss from a devaluation just as including the current liabilities reduces the exposure. These accountants would argue that the future payment of the liability is many years away, perhaps after other currency revaluations. Furthermore, long-term liabilities often were incurred to purchase fixed assets; if the plant and equipment valuation is not lowered because of the currency depreciation, then the funds supporting it should not be. Other students of the subject argue that long-term debt should be included; the gain to the parent from financing its subsidiary in a devalued currency occurs when the currency depreciates, regardless of when the debt is paid.

If the accounts are rearranged to include only those translated on a current basis, and the liabilities are subtracted from the assets to compute a net exposure, then one might complete a table as follows. Three different measures of exposure are calculated depending on what the managers of the firm wished to include or to exclude in the definition of exposure. The first method includes current accounts only, and is usually called the Current/Non-Current method (also referred to as Net Current Asset or Net Working Capital method). The Monetary/Non-Monetary method excludes inventory but includes the long-term debt. Finally, the Net Financial Asset method includes all current accounts as well as the long-term debt.

| | METHOD | | |
	Current/ Non-current	Monetary/ Non-monetary	Net Financial Asset
Current Assets, except Inventory	$120	$120	$120
Inventory	80	80	80
Current Liabilities	80	(80)	(80)
Long-Term Liabilities	120	(120)	(120)
Exposure	$120	($ 80)	0

Where there is a blank, the account is not included when the determination of exposure is made. The final exposure is the sum of the positive and negative figures. Under the Current/Non-Current method, the exposure is $120. This means a 10% devaluation of the peso would result in a $12 translation exchange loss to the parent. Conversely, an appreciation of the peso would result in a $12 exchange gain to the parent. Under the Monetary/Non-Monetary method of calculating exposure, there would be an $8 gain from a 10% peso depreciation, for the firm owes $80 more in the now-cheaper currency than it has in cash and other current assets. But there would be an $8 loss if the peso upvalues by 10%. Finally, there is no net exposure under the Net Financial Asset method.

When the complex real-world balance sheets of firms are studied, there are as many methods of translating the foreign subsidiary accounts as there are firms. All of the above methods were acceptable for U. S. firms prior to January 1976, and highly variable treatments were accorded prepayments, local liabilities of varying types, and other accounts. However, a new ruling by the Financial Accounting Standards Board now requires the Temporal method for consolidating foreign operations. Under this method, the relevant exchange rate is that which was in effect at the time the foreign currency value appearing on the balance sheet was established. Current assets (except inventory), current liabilities, and long-term debt are translated at current exchange rates. Other accounts are translated at historic rates in most cases. For accounts such as marketable securities or inventories, either cost at historic exchange rates or market at current rates is used. Further arguments on the methods are contained in the appendix to this chapter and in various accounting publications.[5]

[5] For examples, see the *Accounting Research Bulletin No. 43*, American Institute of Certified Public Accountants, 1953; the *National Association of Accountants Research Report No. 36*, 1960; and the exposure draft of the Financial Accounting Standards Board, *Accounting for the Translation of Foreign Currency Transactions and Foreign Currency Financial Statements*, Stamford, Connecticut, 1974.

Report of Exchange Losses and Gains. Whatever the concept of exposure the firm uses, the actual reporting of the exchange gain or loss by the parent is also a highly variable practice. In the United States, the general procedure in the case of foreign subsidiaries is to report the gain or loss on the parent's income statement, adjusting net income for the period by the amount involved. Whether it is treated as an extraordinary item is a function of materiality. Often, losses are reported in the period when they occur, with gains reported only as realized.

In other lands, the process is more varied. In some cases, the U. S. practice of entering the loss/gain through the income statement is practiced. In other nations, the normal procedure is to charge the loss directly to the equity account, reducing the consolidated asset and liability accounts to reflect the new exchange rates; the equity account is the balancing item. Sometimes, the asset and liability accounts are not reduced but the surplus account is. The difference is then a reserve account on the liability side, "Reserve for Foreign Exchange Gains and Losses." In most situations where this practice is followed, the income statement will have reflected the creation of this reserve as well. These are but a few examples of the highly divergent accounting practices throughout the world business community.

Effective with fiscal years beginning in January 1976, firms have been required to show foreign exchange gains and losses currently. To restate historical accounts shown for comparison purposes, firms use the Temporal method of consolidation. Exchange gains and losses as calculated with that method are taken in the appropriate year. Differences in what was reported to shareholders in those years are taken as a direct charge to surplus. The inevitable result of this new ruling is rather erratic profit performance for subsidiaries which have large amounts of debt in volatile currencies when there are floating rates, especially if the assets are large in relation to profits. For example, assume a firm whose sales are five times its total assets, whose after-tax margin on sales is 5%, and whose local long-term debt is 80% of its capital structure. Further assume that current liabilities and current assets translated at current exchange rates cancel each other, and that inventory and fixed assets are the remaining assets, all translated at historic rates. Shareholders would find profits up by 32% with a 10% depreciation of the local currency. The next year, should the currency appreciate by 15% against the parent's currency, profits would be down by 33% regardless of operating performance. Both calculations ignore the additional changes induced by altered interest values.

Economic versus Accounting Exposure. There is difficulty in agreeing upon a single standard for exposure, and in setting the process by which the gain or loss on whatever assets are deemed exposed is to be recorded. A more fundamental difficulty concerns the mixture of the accounting cost concepts with the idea of value.

Consider the present value of the surviving firm in the country which has just devalued its currency. That value may be more or less following the devaluation and it is a function of future cash flows. With lower export prices now possible, sales for exports may increase and the expected profits of the firm may have increased for the coming years over and above the percentage of initial devaluation. Likewise, if the devaluation increases domestic income, local sales may increase substantially enough to compensate for the effects of the devaluation on price per unit. On the expense side, if the cost of the goods sold arise largely from within the local country, those costs should not necessarily increase because of the devaluation.

The whole consideration of the issue of price and income elasticity of demand for the products in both the domestic and the export market, and the sensitivity of the cost components to the devaluation, combine to complete the increase or decrease in the firm's present value. Yet, the result of this increase or decrease in future cash flows is likely to have very little to do with the accounting exposure. One must also notice that if the company never intends to pay dividends from the foreign operations, the translation gain or loss may never materialize in terms of cash flows to the parent company.

The accountant is unlikely to accept management's appraisal of an adjustment to the firm's present value derived from a devaluation. The accountant is concerned with an historical reporting of what has happened to the firm, and resists most attempts to forecast or to certify management's forecasts. However, the fact that the profession is reluctant to certify statements regarding the change in future value of the firm because of currency realignments does not mean that the reader of the statements should not recognize the possibly great divergence between the accounting exposure (and possible foreign exchange loss or gain) and the economic exposure of the firm.[6]

The Firm's Response to Exchange Risk

When the firm finds that it has an unwanted net exposure to foreign exchange risks, there are a variety of steps it can take. It may try to adjust its operations to change the exposure. Alternatively, it may accept the exposure as a given and try to counteract it by operations in the money and foreign exchange markets.

Adjustment in Operations. The level of exposed assets and liabilities associated with the operations can be altered to accomplish the desired exposure. In these adjustments one should separate the adjustments in operations involving third parties from the adjustments in operations among units of the same multinational company—intracompany accounts.

1. Operations with Third Parties. In the context of the subsidiary's relationship with other firms, the general policy is to eliminate obligations in upvaluation-prone currencies and convert assets from weak currencies into hard currencies. That is, borrow in weak currencies and invest in hard currencies. In the case of an expected depreciation, local suppliers' terms of credit may be stretched and local customers' receivables reduced if at all possible. Either transaction would reduce the amount exposed to a devaluation of the local currency. Inventories also could be reduced if that account is translated on a current basis. A conscious effort to reduce sales or size of operations may be the second line of attack if reducing receivables through less favorable credit terms does not result in a sufficient decrease in exposed current asset accounts. However, these measures are bound to encounter very strong oppo-

---

[6] Fredrikson (1968) argues that the relative expected exchange rate at the time of completion of a transaction should be forecast and used in the income statement, rather than the exchange rate in effect at the end of the year for (say) receivables with a foreign exchange loss charged on the financial statement. A related break with accounting convention is in Heckerman (1972), who notes that the value of the firm depends on the discounted value of future cash flows. Changing price levels for the parent and the subsidiary economies and the changing exchange rate affect this discounted value; he compares the adjustments to the balance sheet under this approach with normal accounting standards.

sition from the people in the operating line. No manager ever likes to have the size of his or her operations reduced in size. A tightening in credit terms would be perceived as a direct threat to sales, and lax payments to creditors could result in problems in sourcing materials in the future.

    2. Intracompany Accounts. When there are several subsidiaries in the same parent's orbit, intracompany accounts can often be used to great advantage. While the subsidiary in the devaluation-prone country might attempt to remit funds to the parent in the form of dividends or royalties (or withhold these payments in the case of an upvaluation-prone currency), usually this route is restricted to some degree by the local authorities. However, intracompany trade offers other opportunities to achieve desired transfers of resources. Although the term "intercompany" is commonly used in referring to legally separate corporations, we are here using the term "intracompany" to emphasize a common central control within a broadly defined company.

    The objective of altering intracompany payments practices is simply to reduce the amount of resources exposed in a devaluation-prone currency and increase the resources in an upvaluation-prone currency. The change in the level of the intracompany accounts is only a device to accomplish an exposure objective. Given a level of intracompany accounts receivables and payables, the desired objectives will be accomplished if:

    1. Subsidiaries in devaluation-prone countries pay intracompany accounts payable as soon as possible and delay collecting intracompany accounts receivable for as long as possible;

    2. Subsidiaries in upvaluation-prone countries delay paying intracompany accounts payable as long as possible and collect intracompany accounts receivable as soon as possible.

In the case of the devaluation-prone subsidiary the company is effectively removing cash from the country through the mechanism of fast payment of intracompany payables, and delaying the entry of additional resources into that currency by extending the collection terms for sister subsidiaries. The opposite is accomplished with the suggestions for the subsidiary in the upvaluation-prone currency.

    Although the logic behind these procedures is relatively simple, confusion often arises when the subject is discussed. There are two major sources of puzzlement. One source is the fact that at any point in time the intracompany accounts receivable and accounts payable net to zero. The intracompany account receivable of one subsidiary is the account payable of another. When the two given subsidiaries are consolidated into one reporting unit the receivable of the first subsidiary cancels the payable of the other. This is the standard procedure in consolidations of financial statements for reporting purposes. However, this misses the point that the manipulation of the size of these intracompany accounts is nothing else than a tool to move resources from one currency into another. The statement as to the impact of consolidation of intracompany accounts at one point in time is correct. However, if one can affect the level of these intracompany accounts, one is effectively redeploying resources.

    The other source of confusion in the use of intracompany accounts to achieve exposure objectives is the question of currency denomination of the intracompany accounts. Actually the currency of denomination has an impact only on taxes of foreign exchange gains and losses after the revaluation takes place. Assume two subsidiaries that trade with one another. One subsidiary is in Germany, the other is in France. Further assume that the German subsidiary sells products to the French one. That is, the German subsidiary has an account receivable from the French subsidiary and the French subsidiary has an account payable to the German subsidiary. Now examine the impact from an appreciation of the deutsche mark relative to the French franc when payment is made under alternative billing currencies. If the bill is extended in deutsche marks at the time of payment the French subsidiary will have a foreign exchange loss; it will have to generate more French francs than anticipated to pay the deutsche mark debt. In this case nothing happens to the German subsidiary. If the bill had been invoiced in terms of French francs, when the payment is made there is no foreign exchange effect on the French subsidiary. However, the German subsidiary now receives fewer deutsche marks than anticipated at the the exchange rates prevailing at the time of the sale. The German subsidiary experiences a foreign exchange loss. Thus, regardless of the currency used in the denomination of intracompany trade, one of the units will have a foreign exchange loss if the payment to the German subsidiary (with the stronger currency) is not made before the appreciation of the deutsche mark. If such a loss must be accepted, for example because of goverment controls in remittances from France into Germany, the choice of a specific currency for invoicing is inmaterial if the tax rate is the same in the two countries. If that is not the case, then one will want to have the foreign exchange loss fall in the country with the higher tax rate so the highest tax shelter benefit from the loss can be reaped.

As the reader will notice, we have suggested that in the case of an upvaluation-prone currency, debts to third parties in that currency should be decreased while intracompany accounts payable of the subsidiary operating in the country of that currency should be increased. Both are debts of the subsidiary in the upvaluation-prone country. Why decrease one type of debt and increase the other? Both accomplish the desired objective of increasing the net amount of resources in that currency. If asset levels are maintained constant, the reduction of payables to third parties in the upvaluation-prone currency must be accompanied by an increase in financing in a weaker currency. By increasing the intracompany payables, the upvaluation-prone subsidiary is able to keep the resources it has in the relatively harder currency. Both approaches preserve, and might even increase, the resources in that currency.

All the prescriptions we have just mentioned had one goal in mind: reduce exposure to foreign exchange risk. However, each of the actions discussed above has certain costs attached to it. Only if the costs of these measures are less than the impact of the unwanted exposure will they be worthwhile. Otherwise, in economic terms, the firm could be avoiding the appearance of an ugly foreign exchange loss in the financial statements only at an expense higher than the extent of the exchange loss. However, in certain cases financial reporting considerations may be such an overwhelming concern that management might choose to follow economically suboptimal strategies to avoid the appearance of a foreign exchange loss in the financial statements—even at the expense of much higher costs elsewhere in the income statement.

As indicated earlier, the reduction in the size of accounts receivable and inventory can have repercussions in the volume of sales. The profits lost on the foregone sales are a clear cost of these approaches. Likewise, denominating export sales in hard currencies might be accomplished only at the expense of a reduction in price—the buyer also has foreign exchange considerations to take into account. This decrease in price might neutralize and even decrease the net effect of billing in a hard currency. On the liability side, extending the terms on which suppliers are paid may be accomplished only by foregoing discounts for prompt payment and by facing higher prices in the future from the supplier to compensate for the larger financing. There is an increase of the funds provided by this source, and that has a price.

The cost of leads and lags in intracompany transactions can be assessed only by making clear who is the final holder of the merchandise (including cash) and who is providing the financing. Once these facts are established, one can proceed to evaluate the interest payments that the financing involves, the net effective cost of the debt, and the returns obtained by the holders of the merchandise. When the merchandise is a financial asset the return is easy to measure; it is simply the effective interest rate in that market. When the merchandise is goods then one has to consider inventory carrying costs as well as profit margins.

Finally, in evaluating the cost of these operating adjustments to compensate foreign exchange risk one must consider the factor of time. If these measures are necessary for a very short period because the change in currency values is imminent, then they might be worthwhile even if the net cost is very high in terms of annual interest rates. One would be paying a very high cost for a small period of time, while the devaluation impact would last much longer.

Hedging in the Financial Markets. When a devaluation of a currency is feared, the excess of exposed assets over exposed liabilities in that currency (a net asset position) implies a potential loss. Likewise, if exposed liabilities exceed the amount of exposed assets in that currency and an upvaluation occurs there will be a loss.[7] These are the situations that give rise to the need for hedging.

The transactions described in Chapter 6 as "covering" are sometimes also called "hedging" operations. Technically, however, covering and hedging have different meanings.[8] Covering implies the protection of the value of an identifiable and quantifiable *cash flow* that could give rise to a foreign exchange loss in the *conversion* from one currency to another, *e.g.,* proceeds from export sales or dividends to be received in a foreign currency. Covering involves a "self-liquidating transaction." Hedging, on the other hand, refers to the protection of the value of *assets* located in foreign countries and their financing. That is, hedging attempts to protect the value of future profits generated in foreign currencies. However, as discussed earlier, the corporation is primarily concerned with protecting against the foreign exchange loss that might arise from the *translation* of financial statements of foreign subsidiaries into the currency of the parent company.

The objective of hedging an unwanted foreign exchange exposure is to generate foreign exchange gains in the forward or money market that will compensate for the losses produced by the translation of the accounts from foreign currency to local

---

[7] The alternative definitions of exposure were discussed earlier in this chapter.

[8] These technical differences in the meaning of hedging and covering were established by Paul Einzig, *A Textbook on Foreign Exchange* (London: Macmillan, 1966).

currency in the parent's accounting books. That is, in practice exposure is an accounting concept which is not directly related to economic cash flows; the measures taken to hedge an accounting exposure are based on specific cash flows in the financial markets. The cash flows associated with the accounting exposure may only be realized in the distant future. The cash flows of the hedging measures have very specific dates attached to them in the financial markets. These hedging operations can be conducted in the forward exchange or the money markets.

Hedging in the Forward Market. For example, in April, year 1, a U. S. company has a subsidiary in the United Kingdom which is expected to have a *net asset* exposure of £500,000 by April, year 2.

Exposure of £500,000 at April rate of $2.50	$1,250,000
If value of pound declines to $2.40,	
Exposed assets £500,000 at $2.40	1,200,000
Loss in exposed assets in parent's books	$ 50,000

If the parent company wishes to fully protect against the $50,000 loss in British assets through the exchange market, it will have to make a $50,000 gain in that market.

Notice that *the anticipated $50,000 loss will initially occur only in the books of the parent company.* The British subsidiary will continue having a net asset position of £500,000. What this position will mean to the parent company in terms of cash flows received from the British subsidiary in the future is not directly reflected in the definition of net exposure and expected translation gain or loss. On the other hand, to hedge this exposure there must be an *actual gain.* Hedging involves a financial transaction designed to produce a *realized* gain. The objective in this example is to net the *unrealized loss* reflected by the translation of the net asset position against a *realized gain* in the foreign exchange market.

In this example a gain in the forward market will be realized only if the price contracted for future delivery of the pounds against dollars is higher than the eventual spot price at the time of the delivery. To fulfill the forward contract the hedger will have to buy the pounds with dollars in the spot market at the time of delivery (the net asset position in the books is not going to be liquidated to fulfill the contract) and sell them at the price established by the forward contract. To make a gain, the price at which the pounds are bought in the spot market at the end of the period must be below the price at which the holder promised to sell them in the forward contract.

Consider how the translation and the foreign exchange operations interact under a variety of situations.

Case 1: In April, year 1, the one-year forward pound is selling at $2.50, at par with the spot rate. If in April, year 2, the pound sterling sells at $2.40 in the spot market, the calculations will be as follows:

April, year 1: Sell £500,000 for 1-year delivery at
           $2.50/£ = $1,250,000

April, year 2: Buy £500,000 on spot market
                    at $2.40/£   ($1,200,000)
                Deliver £500,000 on forward
                    contract at $2.50/£   1,250,000

                Gain in foreign exchange market $50,000
                Loss in exposed assets   (50,000)
                Net effect   0

    Case 2: The pound sterling for one-year delivery is selling at $2.45, a 2% discount from the spot rate. The spot rate in April, year 2 is expected to be $2.40. In this case two possible hedging strategies are available: (1) generate a foreign exchange gain in the same amount as the expected foreign exchange loss from the translation of the British operation; or (2) lock in a known loss if the forward pound is selling at a discount (or a profit if the forward pound is selling at a premium) against the U. S. dollar.

    If we attempt to generate a foreign exchange profit of exactly $50,000, it will be necessary to sell future pounds in an amount larger than the exposure. This amoung can be determined according to the following formula:

$$(\text{Amount})\ 2.45 - (\text{Amount})\ 2.40\quad =\quad 50{,}000$$

$$\text{Amount}\quad =\quad \frac{50{,}000}{.05}\quad =\quad £1{,}000{,}000$$

Therefore, the transactions will be as follows:

April, year 1: Sell £1,000,000 for 1-year delivery at
                    $2.45/£ = $2,450,000

April, year 2: Buy £1,000,000 on spot market at
                    $2.40/£   ($2,400,000)
                Deliver £1,000,000 on forward
                    contract at $2.45/£   2,450,000

                Gain in foreign exchange market $50,000
                Loss in exposed assets   (50,000)
                Net effect   0

These cases assume that the forecast depreciation of the pound took place to the extent anticipated. What will happen if the depreciation is larger than forecasted? Assume the pound sterling is selling in April, year 2, for $2.35/£.

Case 1A: *Gain in foreign exchange market*

                Buy £500,000 on spot market at
                    $2.35/£   ($1,175,000)
                Deliver £500,000 on forward contract
                    at $2.50/£   1,250,000

                Gain in foreign exchange market $75,000

                Loss in exposed assets:
                    £500,000 × $0.15 (depreciation)   (75,000)
                Net effect   0

In the cases when the forward currency is selling at par with the spot rate, the gains in the forward market will be sufficient to cover the losses on the exposed assets, regardless of the extent of the depreciation.

Case 2A: *Gain in foreign exchange market*

Buy £1,000,000 on spot market at $2.35/£	($2,350,000)	
Deliver £1,000,000 on forward contract at $2.45/£	2,450,000	
Gain in foreign exchange market		$100,000
Loss in exposed assets: £500,000 × $0.15/£ (depreciation)		(75,000)
Net gain from depreciation		$25,000

When the hedged amount is larger than the exposed amount and the depreciation is larger than anticipated, the net gain from the hedging operation depends on the initial forward discount and the eventual spot price.

What will happen if, instead of the anticipated depreciation, there is actually an appreciation of the pound with regard to the U. S. dollar? Suppose that in April, year 2, the pound sterling is selling at $2.60/£.

Case 1B: *Loss in foreign exchange market*

Buy £500,000 on spot market at $2.60/£	($1,300,000)	
Deliver £500,000 on forward contract at $2.50/£	1,250,000	
Loss in foreign exchange market		($50,000)
Gain in exposed assets: £500,000 × $0.10/£ (appreciation)		50,000
Net effect		0

Since the forward rate was at a par with the spot rate, the unanticipated change in the value of the pound was completely hedged against once again.

Case 2B: *Loss in foreign exchange market*

Buy £1,000,000 on spot market at $2.60/£	($2,600,000)	
Deliver £1,000,000 on forward contract at $2.45/£	2,450,000	
Loss in foreign exchange market		($150,000)
Gain in exposed assets: £500,000 × $0.10/£ (appreciation)		50,000
Net loss		($100,000)

When the hedged amount is larger than the exposed amount and there is a change in the value of the currency in the opposite direction from the one expected, there will be a net loss in the operation depending on the initial discount on the forward rate and the appreciation in the spot rate.

As mentioned before when Case 2 was introduced, there is another approach to hedging the pound exposure. In Case 2 the pound sterling is selling at a 2% discount against the U. S. dollar. In the preceding approach an attempt was made to calculate the amount of pounds that will have to be sold forward to produce a foreign exchange gain exactly comparable with the anticipated loss from translating the exposure in the British subsidiary in April, year 2. As a result the amount of pounds sold forward in the hedging operation was double the amount planned to be exposed in April, year 2. In this case, if the forecast of the spot rate in April, year 2, turns out to be incorrect, the combined effect of the translation of the financial statements and the gains or losses in the foreign exchange market can generate substantial net gains or losses. This risk is perceived by many companies as being too high. Therefore, these companies may choose to accept a certain 2% loss ($25,000) in advance, the discount at which the pound is selling against the U. S. dollar in April, year 1. This will be the case if the amount of pounds sold forward is exactly the amount that the firm expects to have exposed at the end of year 2, £500,000. This procedure guarantees a 2% foreign exchange loss but it avoids the risk of the $100,000 loss in Case 2B. On the other hand, it also makes sure that the $25,000 foreign exchange gain in Case 2A cannot be realized. The following tables illustrate the effect of such action.

Initial situation in April, year 1
       Spot rate: $2.50/£
       1-year forward rate: $2.45/£

Case 2A: Spot rate in April, year 2: $2.35/£
(Revised) *Gain in foreign exchange market*
       Buy £500,000 on spot market at

$2.35/£	($1,175,000)	
Deliver £500,000 on forward contract at		
$2.45/£	1,225,000	
Gain in foreign exchange market		$50,000
Loss in exposed assets:		
£500,000 × $0.15/£ (depreciation)		(75,000)
Net loss		($25,000)

Case 2B: Spot rate in April, year 2: $2.60/£
(Revised)
   Loss in foreign exchange market
       Buy £500,000 on spot market at

$2.60/£	($1,300,000)	
Deliver £500,000 on forward contract at		
$2.45/£	1,225,000	
Loss in foreign exchange market		($75,000)
Gain in exposed assets:		
£500,000 × $0.10/£ (appreciation)		50,000
Net loss		($25,000)

By simply reversing the signs in the previous computations, one can see that if instead of a 2% discount the pound had been selling at a 2% premium against the U. S. dollar in April, year 1, the hedging operations would have netted a gain of $25,000. In this situation the company not only eliminates the risk involved in foreign exchange fluctuations, but can do so at a profit. Unfortunately, devaluation-prone currencies usually sell at a discount.

In this approach, where only the amount of pounds exposed is sold in the forward exchange market, the calculations of hedging costs appear to follow the same pattern as that followed to estimate the costs of covering trade transactions discussed in Chapter 6. The cost of hedging in the forward market, like the cost covering trade transactions in that market, is the discount of the currency in the exchange markets. However, we must remember that the nature of hedging is intrinsically different from covering. In covering, the item covered generates the necessary cash flows to pay for the forward contracts. In hedging future profits, there is no cash flow generated from the simple translation of financial statements of the British subsidiary to match the real cash flow generated by the forward exchange contract.

Hedging through the Money Market. The objective of using the money market for hedging purposes is to generate a gain which will compensate for the expected loss in the translation of the exposed position in the books. Returning to the previous example, the company has a net asset position in pound sterling while expecting a devaluation in that currency and, therefore, a translation loss of $50,000. To counteract that loss by operating in the money market, the company would have to borrow pound sterling (the currency expected to devalue) and invest the proceeds in another currency that is expected to remain constant in price relative to the currency of the parent company (assume the U. S. dollars). The principle is that the proceeds of the investment in the harder currency will produce an exchange gain when used to pay the borrowed funds in a currency that has devalued. The problems and risks associated with this type of transaction derive from the interest differentials which are likely to be in favor of the devaluing currency. If the amount of hedge is roughly the amount of anticipated exposure, *the cost of the transaction will be roughly the interest differential.*

Consider how the translation and the operations in the money market interact under a variety of situations.[9] Let's assume first that only the amount of the exposure is involved in hedging.

Case 1′: The one-year forward pound is selling at $2.50, at par with the spot rate. The interest rates for one-year money are 7% in both the United Kingdom and the United States. Therefore, the markets are in equilibrium, for there is zero interest differential and zero discount or premium in the forward values of the two currencies. The spot rate for the pound in April, year 2, is expected to be $2.40/£. Then to hedge in the money market the following steps will take place:

April, year 1: Borrow £500,000 at 7% for one year. Convert the proceeds into dollars at $2.50/£($1,250,000). Invest proceeds of loan in one-year dollar security at 7%.

---

[9] For easier comparisons, money market cases corresponding to forward market cases will be designated with the same number and letter, but with an added prime (′) sign, e.g., Case 1 ′ is the money market case describing a revaluation situation like that in forward market Case 1.

April, year 2:   Sell dollar-denominated security. Proceeds are:

($1,250,000) + ($1,250,000 × .07) $1,337,500	
Convert dollar proceeds into pounds:	
$1,337,500 ÷ $2.40/£	£557,292
Pay the loan in pounds:	
(£500,000) + (£500,000 × .07)	(535,000)
Gain in money transaction in pounds	£22,292
Gain in money transaction in dollars:	
£22,292 × $2.40/£	$53,500
Loss in exposed assets:	
£500,000 × $0.10/£	(50,000)
Net gain	$3,500

The gain of $3,500 in this transaction, in spite of the zero interest differential, is due to the foreign exchange gain realized on the payment of interest on the loan. The interest on the loan is £35,000 (£500,000 × .07). In each pound paid in interest the hedging saved $0.10 because of the devaluation from $2.50/£ to $2.40/£. So the savings are $3,500 (£35,000 × $0.10/£).[10]

Case 2':   Now, assume the spot pound is quoted at $2.50 while the one-year pound is quoted at $2.45, a 2% discount from the spot rate. Interest rates in the United Kingdom are 9% and in the United States 7%. Therefore, the markets are in equilibrium, for the interest differential of 2% is the same as the 2% discount in the forward pound. The spot rate for the pound in April, year 2, is expected to be $2.40. The hedging steps will be as follows:

April, year 1:   Borrow £500,000 at 9% for one year. Convert the proceeds into dollars at $2.50/£ ($1,250,000). Invest proceeds of loan in one-year dollar security at 7%.

April, year 2:   Sell dollar-denominated security. Proceeds are:

($1,250,000) + ($1,250,000 × .07) $1,337,500	
Convert dollar proceeds into pounds:	
$1,337,500 ÷ $2.40/£	£557,292
Pay the loan in pounds:	
(£500,000) + (£500,000 × .09)	(545,000)
Gain in money transaction in pounds	£12,292
Gain in money transaction in dollars:	
£12,292 × $2.40/£	$29,500
Loss in exposed assets:	
£500,000 × $0.10/£	(50,000)
Net loss	($20,500)

[10] A formula to derive the exact amount of pounds needed for the hedging transaction to result in no residual gains or losses on the payment of interest will be presented in the following case. Subsequent examples of Case 1 will continue to use the £500,000 base.

   The net gain of $3,500 can also be eliminated if the pound loan is taken on a discounted basis; i.e., borrowing proceeds amount to only £467,290, though the amount to be paid back is £500,000.

The net loss in the operation of $20,500 in this case is the result of the interest differentials against the United States of $25,000 (.02 × $1,250,000) less the foreign exchange gain on interest paid on the pound loan of $4,500 (£45,000 × $0.10/£). To compensate for these factors one would have to hedge more than £500,000, actually £847,456, as shown below.

In the preceding hedges in the money market the amount hedged was the same as the amount of expected exposure, £500,000. As with the case of hedging in the forward market, this approach locks in a certain loss, which is the magnitude of the interest differentials (discount on the currency). The discrepancies we found in the net cost of the hedges were due to the impact of the revaluation on interest rates. An alternative approach would be to try to generate sufficient profits in the money market transactions to fully cover the losses expected on the translation of the operations of the British subsidiary. In this case, as suggested in the previous paragraph, if the pound is selling at a discount against U. S. dollars, the amount of pounds borrowed will have to be larger than the amount of the expected exposure. The exact amount which should be borrowed and loaned may be found from solving the equation below:

$$\text{Amount } (1 + R_I) - \text{Amount } (1 + R_B)(1 + \text{Reval}_B) = \$50,000$$

Here, the first part of the equation represents the investment in the "dearer" currency with the investment rate (R_I). The second part represents borrowings, i.e., the repayment of the borrowed principal plus interest (R_B) in the new value of the currency (Reval_B). The purpose of the exercise is to produce a $50,000 foreign exchange gain. In the example, the goal is to borrow pounds and invest in U. S. dollars so:

$$
\begin{aligned}
R_I &= 7\% \text{ (U. S. dollar interest rate)} \\
R_B &= 9\% \text{ (pound interest rate)} \\
\text{Reval}_B &= -4\% \text{ (devaluation of £} = \frac{.10}{2.50} \text{)}
\end{aligned}
$$

Solving the previous equation:

$$
\begin{aligned}
\text{Amount} &= \frac{\$50,000}{(1 + .07) - (1 + .09)\,[1 + (-.04)]} \\[2mm]
&= \frac{\$50,000}{0.236} \\[2mm]
&= \$2,118,640 \\
&= £847,456 \text{ at } \$2.50/£
\end{aligned}
$$

A hedge in this amount will compensate for the $50,000 expected translation loss in Case 2′ as follows:

April, year 1: Borrow £847,456 at 9% for one year. Convert the proceeds into U. S. dollars at $2.50/£ = $2,118,640. Invest proceeds of loan in one-year dollar security at 7%.

April, year 2: Sell U. S. dollar-denominated security. Proceeds are:

($2,118,640) + ($2,118,640 × .07)	$2,266,949
Convert dollar proceeds into pounds:	
$2,266,949 ÷ $2.40/£	£944,562
Pay the loan in pounds:	
(£847,456) + (£847,456 × .09)	(923,727)
Gain in money transaction in pounds	£20,835
Gain in money transaction in dollars:	
£20,835 × $2.40/£	$50,004
Loss in exposed assets:	
£500,000 × $0.10/£	(50,000)
Net effect	~0

So far in our money market examples, the assumption has been that the pound devaluation took place to the extent anticipated. What will happen if the actual depreciation is larger than the one anticipated? Suppose that in April, year 2, the pound sterling is selling for $2.35/£, instead of the expected $2.40/£.

Case 1A': *Gain in money market.* Amount hedged is £500,000; interest rates are 7% in both the United States and the United Kingdom.

Sell U. S. dollar-denominated security. Proceeds are:	
($1,250,000) + ($1,250,000 × .07)	$1,337,500
Convert dollar proceeds into pounds:	
$1,337,500 ÷ $2.35/£	£569,148
Pay the loan in pounds:	
(£500,000) + (£500,000 × .07)	(535,000)
Gain in money transaction in pounds	£34,148
Gain in money transaction in dollars:	
£34,148 × $2.35/£	$80,250
Loss in exposed assets:	
£500,000 × $0.15/£	(75,000)
Net gain	$5,250

The small gain is similar to the gain of $3,500 that would have occurred if the pound only depreciated to $2.40/£ and is due to the revaluation impact on interest payments.

Case 2A': *Gain in money market.* Amount hedged is £847,456; interest rates are 9% in the United Kingdom, 7% in the United States.

Sell U. S. dollar-denominated security. Proceeds are:	
($2,118,640) + ($2,118,540 × .07)	$2,266,949
Convert dollar proceeds into pounds:	
$2,266,949 ÷ $2.35/£	£964,659
Pay the loan in pounds:	
(£847,456) + (£847,456 × .09)	(923,727)
Gain in money transaction in pounds	£40,932

Gain in money transaction in dollars:
£40,932 × $2.35/£ $96,190
Loss in exposed assets:
£500,000 × $0.15/£   (75,000)
Net gain $21,190

Since we hedged an amount much larger than the amount exposed and the pound devalued more than anticipated, the hedging operation produced a net gain.

What would happen if, instead of the anticipated depreciation, there is an appreciation of the pound against the dollar? Suppose, that in April, year 2, the pound sterling sells at $2.60/£.

Case 1B': *Loss in Money Market.* Amount hedged is £500,000; interest rates are 7% in both the United States and the United Kingdom.

Sell U. S. dollar-denominated security. Proceeds are:
($1,250,000) + ($1,250,000 × .07) $1.337,500
Convert dollar proceeds into pounds:
$1,337,500 ÷ $2.60/£   £514,423
Pay the loan in pounds:
(£500,000) + (£500,000 × .07)   (535,000)
Loss in money transaction in pounds   (£20,577)
Loss in money transaction in dollars:
£20,577 × $2.60/£   ($53,500)
Gain in exposed assets:
£500,000 × $0.10/£   50,000
Net loss   ($3,500)

The small loss results in the same way as the small gain that would have occurred if the pound fell to $2.40/£, as shown before, and is due to the revaluation impact on interest payments.

Case 2B': *Loss in Money Market.* Amount hedged is £847,456; interest rates are 9% in the United Kingdom, 7% in the United States.

Sell U. S. dollar denominated security. Proceeds are:
($2,118,640) + ($2,118,640 × .07) $2,266,949
Convert dollar proceeds into pounds:
$2,266,949 ÷ $2.60/£   £871,903
Pay the loan in pounds:
(£847,456) + (£847,456 × .09)   (923,727)
Loss in money transaction in pounds   (£51,824)

Loss in money transaction in dollars:
£51,824 × $2.60/£   ($134,742)
Gain in exposed assets:
£500,000 × $0.10/£   50,000
Net loss   ($ 84,742)

The excess of amount hedged over the size of the exposure produces very large losses when the exchange rate moves opposite to the direction anticipated; i.e., a devaluation (depreciation) was anticipated, and instead an upvaluation (appreciation) took place.

Thus the choice in the example is to have a guaranteed loss of approximately 2% which corresponds to the interest differentials in favor of the pound on a hedge of only £500,000; or, alternatively, management may try to reduce the loss to zero by increasing the amount of the hedge to £847,456. However, this last alternative carries the risk of large losses if the currency turns in a direction opposite to the one forecast. But it also has the chance of realizing some profits if the devaluation is larger than the one expected.

In these hedging examples, the basic model presumed a 4% depreciation of the pound and a net exposure of £500,000 to produce a $50,000 foreign exchange loss. Money market hedges involved borrowing pounds, so on an accounting basis there was no longer any exposure when £500,000 was borrowed and converted into dollars because liabilities in sterling were increased. This approach to exposure does not count in generating a gain from the money market transactions; it just allows us to net the net asset position in pounds against the increased borrowings in that currency. However, the drawback of this position is that the increased borrowings may affect basic financial ratios in the company such as the debt-equity ratio. If this is a serious concern, the money market hedge will have to be liquidated between balance sheet dates and the gains generated in that fashion used to neutralize the losses that will be generated from the translation of the British financial statements into U. S. dollars.

We have examined two different initial positions: (1) interest differentials equal to zero and no premium or discount on the pound (Cases 1, 1A, and 1B); and (2) an interest differential in favor of the pound that produced a 2% discount on the forward pound against the U. S. dollar (Cases 2, 2A, and 2B). With these initial assumptions and a forecast that the spot rate will move from $2.50/£ to $2.40/£, we have looked at the outcome of alternative strategies when the forecast was correct, when we underestimated the amount of the devaluation, and when instead of a devaluation an upvaluation of the pound took place. The two strategies followed were to hedge only the amount of the exposure, £500,000, or to overhedge to compensate for the discount on the pound in the cases where an interest differential prevailed. If only the amount of exposure was hedged the cost of the hedge was nothing if there was no interest differential or 2% when there was a discount on the pound in that magnitude. (The money market results present small gains or losses because of the impact of converting interest payments at the end of the period.) When overhedges were utilized in an attempt to have zero foreign exchange gains or losses, the objective was achieved only when the forecast spot rate was correct. In the other cases substantial gains or losses occurred depending on the direction of the miscalculation. These results are summarized in Exhibit 7.1.

Multi-Currency Money Market Hedges. When the decision on the use of the money market is being investigated and there are more than two currencies, one must use the Net Effective Interest Differential (NEID). It is essential either to bring all the currencies to a common denominator, one currency, or to compute effective interest differentials.

Suppose Bongo Latino, the U. S. corporation discussed earlier in the chapter, adopts a policy of assuming its accounting exposure coincides with its economic ex-

EXHIBIT 7.1 Gains or Losses After Hedging Transaction and Translation of Gains or Losses on Exposed Assets

Case	Interest Differential = 0 Discount on Pound = 0			Interest Differential = 2% in favor of the United Kingdom 2% Discount on Pound against U.S. Dollar					
	1	1A	1B	2	2A	2B	2	2A	2B
Year 1 Forward Rate for Year 2 Delivery ($/£)	2.50	2.50	2.50	2.45	2.45	2.45	2.45	2.45	2.45
Spot Rate Anticipated for April, Year 2 ($/£)	2.40	2.40	2.40	2.40	2.40	2.40	2.40	2.40	2.40
Actual Spot Rate in April, Year 2 ($/£)	2.40 Hedge £500,000	2.35 Hedge £500,000	2.60 Hedge £500,000	2.40 Over-hedge	2.35 Over-hedge	2.60 Over-hedge	2.40 Hedge £500,000	2.35 Hedge £500,000	2.60 Hedge £500,000
Forward Market Gain (Loss)	0	0	0	0	$25,000	($100,000)	($25,000)	($25,000)	($25,000)
Money Market Gain (Loss)	$3,500[a]	$5,250[a]	($3,500)[a]	0	$21,190	($84,742)	($20,500)[a]	($20,500)[a]	($20,500)[a]

aBecause of an approximation to the amount to be hedged in the money market rather than the use of the exact amount computed by formula, and the conversion of interest payments at the end of the period, these results are not consistent with the forward market results. See text.

posure, and has a policy *never* to operate (speculate) in the money market unless there is a need to hedge a potential exchange loss. If there are foreign exchange controls in the South American country where Bongo Latino is operating and there is not an external market in pesos, then the hedging operation will have to be conducted through currencies other than pesos.

Assume that the interest rate for one-year pounds is 16% and for guilders 10%. If management thinks that the pound will depreciate by 8% and the guilder appreciate by 4% against the U. S. dollar, then the *effective interest rates* in the two currencies are 8% for the pound (16% − 8%) and 14% for the guilder (10% + 4%). If the borrowing rates and the lending rates are comparable within a given currency, then management can earn the difference in the effective interest rates (the net effective interest differential) by borrowing pounds and lending guilders in the Euro-markets. There is a 6% differential. Accordingly, if management foresees a 10% depreciation of the peso, and has $120,000 exposed in pesos under the Current method example shown earlier, then it anticipates having an accounting and an economic loss of $12,000 (10% × $120,000). It will then want an economic gain to offset this loss. Accordingly, with a 6% NEID between pounds and guilders, it can compute the amount it wishes to hedge in these markets.

$$\text{Amount hedged} = \frac{-\text{Amount Exposed} \times \text{Devaluation}}{\text{NEID}}$$

or

$$A_H = \frac{-\$120,000 \times -10\%}{6\%}$$

$$= \$200,000$$

Thus, $200,000 should be switched between two markets (pound and guilders) to produce a gain under the forecasted currency realignments to offset the economic loss from the net peso exposure. As in the simpler example with only two currencies, pounds and dollars, this formula is only roughly accurate. Its lack of accuracy is due to the effect of foreign exchange fluctuations on interest payments. Using the $200,000 as the amount to be hedged the results will be as follows:

	Lend Guilders		Borrow Pounds	
Principal		$200,000		$200,000
+ Interest	(10%)	1.10	(16%)	1.16
= Total		220,000		232,000
+ or − Exchange Rate Change	(+4%)	1.04	(−8%)	.92
= Ending Dollar Value		$228,800		$213,440
Net Gain = $15,360[11]				

[11] Given the superior forecasting ability of the managers, a profit could be made *regardless* of Bongo Latino's existence. However, this pure speculation, discussed in Part One, was precluded as part of the policy of the firm, as noted earlier.

The exact amount which should be borrowed and loaned can be found by using the formula presented earlier modified to take into account third currencies; i.e., currencies other than the parent's or the subsidiary's. The formula is as follows:

$$\text{Amount } (1 + R_I)\,(1 + \text{Reval}_I) - \text{Amount } (1 + R_B)\,(1 + \text{Reval}_B) = \text{Potential loss}$$

The term $(1 + \text{Reval}_I)$ is added to the determination of the gain in the loan. This is done because the deposit is in guilders, while the base currency is the dollar. The values to substitute in the formula are as follows:

$$R_I = 10\%\ (\text{DFl rate})$$
$$\text{Reval}_I = 4\%\ (\text{Upvaluation of DFl})$$
$$R_B = 16\%\ (\text{Pound rate})$$
$$\text{Reval}_B = -8\%\ (\text{Devaluation of £})$$
$$\text{Potential loss} = \$12,000$$

Solving,

$$A_H = \frac{\$12,000}{(1 + .10)\,(1 + .04) - (1 + .16)\,(1 - .08)}$$

$$= \frac{\$12,000}{.0768}$$

$$= \$156,250$$

This amount will produce the required $12,000 gain. Note that it is 78.125% of the $200,000 calculated under the NEID method. The gain of $12,000 is also 78.125% of the $15,360 realized gain under the $200,000 transaction, as would be expected.

The success of this four-way action depends on the collinearity of the changes in the dollar/peso parity and the guilder/pound action. How well these four currencies will react in relation to each other is a critical point. If the peso fails to depreciate vis-à-vis the dollar and the guilder/pound realignments are as forecast, then the company makes money, and is charged by some sources with "speculating." On the other hand, if the peso devalues and the guilder-pound realignment fails to take place, then the firm loses the difference in the nominal interest rates since it borrowed at 16% and loaned at 10%. The merits of the policy further depend on access to these markets, for this may be restricted by the government of the subsidiary. However, the parent of Bongo Latino will likely be able to operate as anticipated here.

A final difficulty with the policy is the sharp increase in the amount which must be borrowed and lent as the NEID narrows. For example, assume that the dollar rate is 8% and that the peso rate is 16% and the firm is allowed to hedge using these two markets. With the expected 10% depreciation of the peso the strategy would be to borrow pesos and lend dollars. Using the formula, then the amount hedged would be:

$$A_H = \frac{\$12,000}{(1 + .08)\,(1 + 0) - (1 + .16)\,(1 - .10)}$$

$$= \$333,333$$

Yet, the gross exposure is only $120,000 in pesos. That is, increasing liabilities by $120,000 would neutralize the *accounting* exposure, but hedging to produce a gain of $12,000 would increase peso liabilities by $333,333, which is far larger than the amount needed. However, the $333,333 peso debt is needed if (1) $120,000 is the economic exposure, (2) there is to be a peso/dollar trade, and (3) the hedging transaction is to be completed within the accounting period. In this case, if the NEID dropped to 2%, then the amount calculated with the NEID method which must be borrowed and loaned in the Euro-market would be $600,000:

$$\frac{-\$120,000 \times -10\%}{2\%}$$

When the NEID is 0, of course, no amount of money market action can offset the expected loss from the currency depreciation.

All of these techniques are examined in more detail in an extended example in Chapter 8. However, we have already seen some of the difficulties in determining accounting exposure and in relating that accounting exposure to the economic exposure faced by the firm. A further problem relates to the fact that the parent company may not be aware of a variety of accounting practices that are used in other countries. Likewise, a manager reviewing a foreign corporation may be quite surprised to learn that the accounting standards (s)he thought were being applied were not in fact employed. Some of these differences are noted in the appendix on Comparative Accounting Practices.

SUMMARY

The corporation with assets and liabilities in more than one currency, together with cash flow surpluses and deficits in various currencies, faces a compounded problem in foreign exchange rates. Initially, the effective interest rate may be considered as the nominal yield plus any foreign exchange gain or loss in a given currency. The *net effective yield* in any currency is thus related to the base currency used as a numeraire; two currencies depreciating in concert against all other currencies would create no foreign exchange gain or loss vis-à-vis each other. In free markets at equilibrium, the forward premium or discount in currencies should bring the *net effective interest differential* on various currencies to zero. In imperfect markets, especially where there are domestic and external markets for given currencies to which the parent or subsidiaries may not have equal access, the net effective yields on various currencies will differ. Standard discounting techniques can compute the yield for longer maturity issues where the currency revaluation takes place at various points in time.

Local interest rates in nominal terms combine a real rate and an anticipated inflation factor. Relative inflation vis-à-vis the rest of the world may result eventually in depreciation of the currency, but there is not a one-to-one mapping of relative inflation and depreciation in each time period.

A firm's accounting exposure is the balance of assets less liabilities translated at current exchange rates. Definitions of which accounts are translated at current rates and which are translated at historic or other rates are highly varied. Until recently, the three most popular variations found in the United States have been the Current/Noncurrent method (current assets less current liabilities), the Monetary/Nonmonetary method (current assets except inventory less current and long-term liabilities), and the Net Financial Asset method (current assets less current and long-term liabilities). New accounting rules now require the Temporal method for U. S. firms. In the United States, exchange gains and losses usually are a one-line entry in the income statement. In other nations, exchange gains or losses may be charged directly to the equity account with the assets/liabilities reduced, or gains or losses may be segmented as a reserve liability account with reduction in the equity account but no adjustment in the asset/liability accounts.

The actual *economic* exposure of the firm may be quite different from the accounting exposure, depending on whether the present value of the future cash flow is increased or decreased as a result of revaluations.

Firms may reduce exposure by adjusting the exposed accounts through business operations with customers, suppliers, or other members of the same corporate family. The firms also may hedge in the forward or the money markets. When there is an expected foreign exchange loss, a gain may be created by operating in various currencies to offset the anticipated loss. It is particularly important in a hedging situation to correctly predict the relative movements of the currencies in order to have the expected gains and losses cancel each other. In a covering transaction, gains and losses will tend to match closely regardless of revaluation outcomes.

When many decisions are based on accounting data, the manager should be aware of the variety of accounting conventions throughout the world, as discussed in the appendix. Wide variations in disclosure arrangements, in the principles of consolidation, in the creation and depletion of reserves under (seemingly) arbitrary rules, in the depreciation and revaluation of assets, and in the use of the surplus account create a dangerous environment for the manager attempting to compare firms in different lands, even if both have certified financial statements. The impact of inflation on corporations has caused a variety of price-level adjustments. In some nations, adjustments are made by government decree and are considered in tax liability calculations. In most lands, the auditor determines the acceptability of an adjustment, and the practices are highly varied.

Our emphasis in this chapter has been on the similarity in hedging postures which are available under money market and forward exchange market opportunities. Firms may reach a decision on which instrument to use from a variety of factors.

1. There may be sharply different intermediary costs. Banks usually control the forward market whereas the money market is more openly competitive. However, to use the money market requires greater sophistication on the part of the treasurer. The forward market is the simpler alternative, for it merely involves obtaining one or more telephone bids on the forward contract rate and making the decision.

2. There may be different access routes. The foreign subsidiary does not have access to the domestic money markets of the parent or other subsidiaries. However, the parent, acting through subsidiaries, does have access to many markets, and this increases the opportunity for a less costly hedging option but also increases the analysis required for a decision.

3. Borrowing and lending rates as well as spot rates differ, and often these differentials eliminate some of the benefits of the money market or forward market options. These differentials in part reflect the intermediary fee.

4. In terms of evidence to shareholders, we have noted that the money market activities are usually accomplished between balance sheet periods. If these accounts remain on the firm's balance sheet at the end of the accounting period, then the debt ratio of the firm is increased. This could alter the riskiness of the firm in the minds of the public, even though there is an offsetting marketable security account. The forward contracts, on the other hand, are rarely revealed, and only appear in footnotes to the financial statements.

5. If there is no differential between forward and money market rates, it is reasonable for the firm to use the simplest and cheapest alternative, often the forward market. However, if differentials do exist (a particularly likely situation for major currencies, which have segmented domestic and external markets), then the firm should evaluate the costs of the alternatives, taking into account both the disequilibrium costs/gains and the intermediation costs.

Multinational treasurers must be aware of these alternatives, and must use simple computer time-sharing systems and forecasts of future action to calculate which way to hedge. The final decision, of course, is related to the costs to the treasurer for his firm's using the two different markets.

Questions

1. MNC Corp. will have a net liability position in Switzerland in the amount of 162 million Swiss francs (approximately $50 million).

Exchange rates	
Spot rate—Day 1	$0.308500
Expected future spot rate	0.333180
1-year forward	0.320840
Interest rates—1 year	
United States	7.50%
Switzerland	2.00%

a. What is the premium or discount in the forward Swiss franc?

b. What would be the consequences of the Swiss net liability position if the forecast changes in the spot rate take place? What are the choices that MNC Corp. has to hedge its liability position in Switzerland?

c. What is the cost of each of these alternatives if the actual spot rate at the end of the period is as follows:

Spot rate—Day 360	*Case A*	*Case B*	*Case C*
	$0.308500	$0.320840	$0.339350

d. What course of action would you advise MNC Corp. to take?

2. "The rough effective interest rate in a currency is the nominal interest rate for the period adjusted by any change in the value of the currency. This valuation is independent of the other currencies involved in the discussion." Is this true? Explain.

3. What is a quick definition of exposure that applies regardless of the accounting method used by the company? What are some of the different accounting exposure measurements? Which do you think is most realistic? Would your statement hold for all corporations, or would it be specific to particular types of business? To particular countries?

4. Why might accounting exposure differ from economic exposure? Do you believe there exists a difference for most corporations? Why?

5. Consolidated Corporation instructed its subsidiary in Devaluland to remit funds to the parent as soon as possible when a new devaluation was likely. This action was completed, and the parent was surprised to see that there was still a large foreign exchange loss on the funds, even though they were owned by the parent. How could this happen? Who should be held accountable?

6. What options are open to reduce exposure in a devaluation-prone subsidiary? How might each of these options affect the business and the management incentives of the subsidiary?

7. How can a firm, which covered itself completely in the forward market based on its expected balance sheet as of the end of the period, still have a foreign exchange loss to report?

8. To hedge an expected $90,000 loss in foreign exchange, a firm intends to borrow $2,000,000 in lira at 12% and invest it in the deutsche mark short-term market at 6%. How much of a devaluation in the lira is the firm expecting in order to cover the anticipated $90,000 loss?

Bibliography

Berg, Kenneth, *et al.*, ed., *Readings in International Accounting.* Boston, Mass.: Houghton Mifflin Company, 1969.

Eiteman, David K. and Arthur I. Stonehill, *Multinational Business Finance.* Reading, Mass.: Addison-Wesley Publishing Co., 1973, Ch. 11, 12, and 13.

Fredrikson, E. Bruce, "On the Measurement of Foreign Income." *Journal of Accounting Research,* Autumn 1968, pp. 208-221.

Goudeket, A., "An Application of Replacement Value Theory." *Journal of Accounting,* July 1960, reprinted in Berg, *et al.,* (1969) pp. 142-159.

Heckerman, Donald, "The Exchange Risks of Foreign Operations." *Journal of Business,* January 1972, pp. 42-48.

MacNeill, James H., "Accounting for Inflation Abroad." *Journal of Accounting,* Aug. 1961, pp. 67-73.

Olstein, Robert A., "Devaluation and Multinational Reporting." *Financial Analysts Journal,* Sept.-Oct. 1973, pp. 65*ff.*

Queenan, John W., "Problems in International Auditing." *New York Certified Public Accountant,* July 1966, reprinted in Berg, *et al.* (1969), pp. 66-76.

Treuherz, R. M., "Re-evaluating ROI for Foreign Operations." *Financial Executive,* May 1968, pp. 64-71.

Wells, Michael T., "Devaluation and Inflation and their Effect on Foreign Operations." *Accountancy,* Aug. 1965, reprinted in Berg, *et al.* (1969), pp. 262-275.

Weston, J. Fred and Bart W. Sorge, *International Managerial Finance.* Homewood, Ill.: Richard D. Irwin, Inc., 1972, Ch. 6 and 11.

Wheelwright Steven C., "Applying Decision Theory to Improve Corporate Management of Currency-Exchange Risks." *California Management Review,* Summer 1975, pp. 41-49.

Appendix: Comparative Accounting Practices

THE VARIATIONS IN INTERNATIONAL ACCOUNTING STANDARDS

Although this text is not primarily concerned with accounting differences among countries, any financial analyst must assure comparability of reports from firms in different lands. The difficulty is that two firms may both have financial statements which have an auditor's statement that the reports were prepared "in conformity with generally accepted accounting principles applied . . . consistently." Yet the principles may be quite different in the two lands. In reviewing and comparing statements from different firms, the reader must confirm that:

1. All the relevant data are present from which one can judge the results of the firm;

2. The standards are consistent across firms and within a given firm over the years; and

3. The principles of accounting are acceptable to the analyst.

Varying principles which might not be acceptable include practices on consolidation, definition of income, and price level adjustments for inflation.[1] These inconsistencies must be resolved in order to compare firms.

[1] See the discussion by Gordon Shillinglaw, "International Comparability of Accounts." *Accounting,* Feb. 1966; or, Edgar Barrett, *et al.,* "Japan: Some Background for Security Analysts," Parts 1 and 2. *Financial Analysts Journal,* Jan./Feb. and March/April 1974, for examples.

Some of the differences among various nations relate to the function of the auditor. In some cases, the auditor is concerned with certifying statements which are in compliance with a body of principles and standards. In other nations, the auditor merely agrees to management's statement that the reported figures conform with some governmental rules; the statements may have little to do with economic reality or previous financial statements of the firm. Firms in some nations have only one set of published statements (in contrast to the sharply different income statements often prepared for taxation purposes in the United States), so the firms also have to resolve conflicts between high earnings for the public (or simply "fair" earnings) and low earnings to reduce taxability. Given a desire to minimize taxes, firms will often generate just sufficient profits to pay dividends that seem "reasonable," with the remainder of the earnings reduced by various reserves.

Perhaps the largest difference between the U. S. and non-U. S. systems derives from the basic issue of *disclosure.* Secrecy of operations is almost a watchword among many international corporate officers. For example, in 1966 the huge Swiss pharmaceutical house, F. Hoffmann-LaRoche, published a statement that showed record profits of 39.7 million Swiss francs. There were no sales figures, no asset figures, and no cost comments. The board of directors noted that the results were an improvement over previous years. "Sales and earnings have increased in approximately equal proportions. . . . The volume of investment was again large and will hardly diminish in the foreseeable future." The report was sent only to shareholders; all other requests were denied.

Such secrecy is related to the reserve of the businessmen, the reluctance to alert tax authorities and labor unions, and other causes. One could speculate that the reluctance is often based on a disinclination to alert competitors to the size of the firm's operations. Sometimes management itself does not know what the consolidated profits and losses are, or knows and does not like to reveal the results. This process of extreme secrecy (viewed from the American shareholder's standpoint) is diminishing with time and greater demand from shareholders in all lands for information about the corporate holdings. The case presented above is extreme, but discrepancies in disclosure compared to U. S. standards remain quite large.

Other critics of non-U. S. financial statements have said that the critical problem is *consolidation.* Many of the foreign statements are not consolidated, or consolidation is optional from subsidiary to subsidiary. The foreign firm may mark-up goods sold to unconsolidated sales subsidiaries in order to realize a high reported income for the parent (or at least some income!). The unconsolidated sales subsidiary, inventorying goods at inflated prices, may not be able to sell the goods at all, or at least not able to sell them to recover cost. The first big Japanese bankruptcy in the economic success of that nation after World War II came in the mid-1960s when the Sanyo Special Steel Company, with capital of only $22 million, went bankrupt after "adjustments" showed the accumulated losses totaled over $222 million. Yet, these losses had been hidden in part by the unconsolidated subsidiary device.

A third major problem relates to the creation of *reserves,* secret or not. These reserves are charges against income in a particular year, and mean that the definition of "income" is highly variable from year to year within a given firm and across firms in a given year. Generally, they level income over time, with high reserves created in good years and vice versa. The reserves have a variety of purposes. Many of the definitions parallel the previous practice in the United States, where the term denoted any number of different accounts. Thus, reserves may be contra-accounts to reduce the value of a wasting asset, such as a reserve for depreciation. They may represent a contingency payment or future liability, such as a legal settlement or future costs for employee health insurance programs. They may be segmented retained earnings, sometimes earmarked for a particular project by vote of the shareholders or the board of directors ("reserve for future expansion"), or may be general ("free reserves") in the form of the American pattern of "retained earnings." Finally, the reserves may be from special government tax programs, such as the British investment program of some years ago in which extremely rapid write-offs of some ships would be permitted when a certain portion of earnings were segmented as reserves for future construction outlays.

Another problem area relates to *depreciation and the revaluation process.* In periods of high inflation, many firms feel forced to revalue assets, as discussed below. Yet this process, which is often most dramatic in its effect on inventory and fixed asset values, can have sharp effects on the income statement through large depreciation charges or through great increases in the net worth of the company. Hence, the application of the depreciation schedule from year-to-year on a given asset as well as the process of revaluation of assets will often alter the income statement from what a U. S. reader would expect. Furthermore, the nature of the disclosure in footnotes on non-U. S. statements often masks the changes which have been made. The assumptions on which the charges are based are often unstated.

The translation of foreign accounts varies internationally, and the impact can be seen in the U. S. practice prior to 1971. Prior to that date, U. S. firms could consolidate subsidiaries in which the firm had more than a 50% interest, but ownership of less than 50% could be reported using the equity method or the cost method. Under the equity approach, the pro rata inclusion of profits and losses of the subsidiary would be included in the parent's income statement each year (hence, it is often referred to as "one-line consolidation"). Under the later method, the initial investment of the firm in the subsidiary is retained as the value of the investment. Dividends as received are the income.

Under the cost method, the gain or loss from currency fluctuations would never be shown. In 1966, the accounting regulations in effect in the United States required that domestic subsidiaries be included on either a consolidated basis or an equity basis, but foreign subsidiaries were excluded from this regulation. As a result, by 1970 the American corporations treated foreign subsidiaries in a wide range of ways. IBM and others consolidated all foreign subsidiaries. Some firms used the equity or the cost method exclusively. Many firms used a mixture of cost and equity, translating subsidiaries in relatively risk-free areas on an equity basis and others on a cost basis.[2]

Most managements had given little attention to accounting for foreign exchange gains and losses from their foreign subsidiaries until the U. S. dollar's devalu-

---

[2] Exemptions to the rule requiring equity or full consolidation for over 50% ownership occurred when the investor could not have "significant influence" over the policies of the subsidiary and when the subsidiary was operating under particular exchange controls. As will be discussed in Chapter 10, the current requirement is consolidation for more than 50% ownership, equity consolidation for more than 20% ownership, and dividends as received for 20% or less ownership.

ation in 1971, the first devaluation in almost forty years. The devaluation coincided with a new requirement for the equity accounting method for *most* subsidiaries, creating sharp impacts in the reported profitability of many corporations. Thus, one sampling of companies reporting exchange gains and losses in 1971 indicated that those reporting such gains or losses realized them to the extent of almost 10% of net income. For example, the losses and the respective percentage of operating income for several firms in 1971 included $1.345 million for Amerada Hess (10%), $1.360 million for Braniff Airways (14%), and $9.2 million for Continental Oil (6%). Most of these figures would have been far lower under the previous method of accounting for foreign subsidiaries since the subsidiaries were not consolidated. Other companies had sizable foreign operations but did not report the losses, largely because of the creation of prior reserves against which the losses would be charged, or because of the deferment of the realization of the loss (which is permissible when long-term liabilities are involved under some methods of translation). (See, for example, Mary M. Wehle, *Note on the Profit Impact of Accounting for Foreign Operations,* Harvard Business School, Boston, Mass., 1973.)

Some companies in 1974 had the practice of recognizing losses as they occur, but deferring gains to a reserve for future losses. International Harvester and Rockwell International followed this pattern. The Financial Accounting Standards Board has ended this flexibility for U. S. firms by requiring all losses and gains to be taken in the year they occur.

A final major difference is the concept of *retained earnings* or *earned surplus.* To the American shareholder in recent years, *clean* surplus is an accepted fact. It means that adjustments to the retained earnings or surplus account are made only through the income statement: there is no charge directly to the retained earnings account. Yet, from a review of many foreign financial statements, charges deemed not to be related to operations or not related to the current period's operations are often charged directly to the earned surplus account without the intermediary appearance in the income statement. Hence, the retained earnings account is sharply different from the American corporation's account under the same name.

Treatments of inventories, tax liabilities, stock dividends, and other accounts also differ from nation to nation, but the preceding comments highlight some of the major difficulties. The form of presentation of financial statements also may differ greatly, since firms may use different conventions in reporting income compared to the U. S. form. However, the reader can often interpret the figures to recast them roughly in the form of the U. S. income statement. The greater difficulty, however, is in the valuation process by which the accounts were determined, as noted above. Accounting firms periodically brief their clients and publish small booklets that outline some of the more pervasive differences in accounting statements.[3]

ACCOUNTING STANDARDS FOR FOREIGN EXCHANGE EXPOSURE

The text presented three of the most widely used standards for calculating the exposure of foreign subsidiaries. In fact, anyone discussing this topic needs to con-

---

[3] For example, see the *Guide to Foreign Financial Statements* published annually by Price Waterhouse, New York.

firm that the title has the same meaning for the speaker and for the audience with whom (s)he is discussing the issue. As noted, what is called the Current/Non-Current method in the United States is often referred to as the Current Asset approach in other countries. Likewise, what is called the Monetary/Non-Monetary approach in the United States is also called the Financial Asset method. The Current Rate method is widely used in the United Kingdom; this approach (which is often called the Net Asset method in the United States but is rarely used) translates all accounts on a current basis, using equity as the residual balancing account. Additional variations are quite possible.

The fundamental issue to most managers is what their accountant translates at current rates. The difference between those assets and those liabilities translated on a current basis represents the accounting exposure, regardless of the name applied. The income statement is constructed based on the average exchange rate prevailing for the period, except for those items that are derived from the balance sheet. These expense figures would relate to depreciation charges and cost of goods sold (where there is some production and some selling from inventory accounts).

PRICE-LEVEL ADJUSTMENTS (INDEXING) IN ACCOUNTING STATEMENTS

In the wake of relatively large U. S. inflation in recent years, many of the arguments advanced after World War II (when the nation also had relatively high inflation) have been resurrected to justify indexing of assets. The main argument is essentially that the diminishing value of the dollar means that depreciation charges for fixed assets are inadequate to provide for a recovery of cost based on purchasing power of the dollars invested in the equipment. Outside the United States, there has been increasing frequency of adjustment in the balance sheet for changes in the purchasing power of the local currency. This action has been most prevalent in many Latin American countries. Indexing in Brazil has resulted in formal adjusting of both the liabilities and the asset values of corporate accounts based on a government price index factor.

In most lands, however, indexing varies considerably in practice. Usually, the local accounting firm selects some price index which is then applied to the relevant assets. These assets are principally inventory and the plant/equipment accounts. Liabilities are usually unchanged. The difference between the revised asset accounts and the old figures then increases the liability and equity side in the form of a *revaluation reserve*. However, the effect is usually to diminish reported income in a given year because the depreciation expense is larger. Likewise, income taxes paid are usually very large in relation to income reported to shareholders when the revaluation of assets is not permitted for tax purposes. In that case, a larger net income is subject to tax because of historic cost depreciation.

U. S. auditors have rendered opinions on some foreign statements along these lines. This action is justified on the basis of various Accounting Research Bulletins for dealing with severe price inflation situations. Thus, Chapter 9 of ARB No. 43 notes that, "Should inflation proceed so far that original dollar costs lose their practical significance, it might become necessary to restate all assets in terms of the depreciated currency, as has been done in some countries."

One dramatic example of the effects of indexing is found in Brazil. The managing partner of Haskins and Sells cites the example of a firm whose plant was mainly constructed in 1958 and 1959. The annual average price index in Brazil had proceeded as follows:

1958	1959	1960	1961	1962	1963	1964
229	316	407	559	848	1,465	2,814

This result represents a compounded inflation rate of 52%. In fact, at year end for 1964, the index stood at 3,649. The client's financial statements for 1963 showed a net *income* of 145 million cruzeiros on a historical cost basis, yet a net *loss* of 540 million cruzeiros on a price-level basis. However, a large tax payment was still required at that time in the Brazilian economy since the government did not recognize price-level adjustments for tax reporting (depreciation) purposes.

In the following year, the historical basis showed a loss of 6,827 million cruzeiros, yet the price-level basis showed a loss of (only) 2,592 million cruzeiros, since the historical basis included a large adjustment for exchange losses on U. S. dollar liabilities. Even here the historical basis accounting resulted in a large tax liability since the exchange loss on the dollar liability was not deductible for tax purposes.

Voluntary price-level accounting has been included in Shell's financial statements in the United States. The actual adjustment is based on the index applied to nonmonetary assets. When these are increased in value, as in inflationary times, the depreciation charges also are increased. The price-level adjustment plans usually call for a one-line entry on the income statement reflecting the net effect of the price-level adjustments on the monetary assets and liabilities. The idea behind this adjustment is that firms with relatively large amounts of debt in relation to current (monetary) assets gain from paying off their debt in relatively cheaper dollars. Hence, there is an incentive under this standard to use debt in larger amounts.

Adjustment could also be made according to current value accounting, which values the assets not at an index-related current valuation of historic costs but rather on the basis of current replacement value of like assets, i.e., replacement cost accounting. The Financial Accounting Standards Board has proposed requiring all U. S. firms to provide supplemental financial statements which will present price-level-adjusted balance sheets and income statements. The price index will be a general one, such as the GNP deflator. The FASB would also apply the deflator to the net of monetary assets and liabilities. The Securities and Exchange Commission, however, has proposed requiring replacement cost accounting instead of the GNP deflator index and not adjusting for price change effects on the real value of monetary items.

Some of the variations in international accounting may be removed as a result of the International Accounting Standards Committee formed in 1973. This committee has representatives from 22 nations that are pledged to adopt the standards agreed upon. Although most western European nations are included, two significant nonmembers are Switzerland and Italy.

The first standard adopted required disclosure of significant accounting policies, a disclosure of changes in accounting standards where the change had material effect, and the inclusion of comparable figures for the prior period in all financial statements. Although these standards were not changes for U. S. practitioners, they represented a change for several nations. The next two standards dealt with inventory valuations and the rules for consolidation. Other standards scheduled for adoption through 1976 and 1977 deal with depreciation policies, the translation of foreign accounts, inflation accounting, and research and development outlays.

Bibliography to Appendix

Berg, Kenneth, *et al.*, eds., *Readings in International Accounting*. Boston, Mass.: Houghton Mifflin Company, 1969.

Mueller, Gerhard G., "Accounting for Multinational Companies." *Cost and Management*, July–Aug. 1971, pp. 28–34.

Taylor, Natalie Tabb and M. Edgar Barrett, *Introduction to European Accounting*. ICH 9–174–043, Harvard Business School, Boston, Mass., 1974.

Wilkinson, Theodore L., "International Accounting: Harmony or Disharmony." *Columbia Journal of World Business,* March-April 1969, pp. 29-36.

Marwick Home Products, Inc.

On December 27, 1971, Mr. George Rosenthal, Treasurer of the International Division of Marwick Home Products (MHP), had four days left to reach a decision regarding the company's exposure in pound sterling. Mr. Rosenthal's position was summarized in the following quote.

For the sixty years that MHP has been operating in the international market, our policy has been to keep our exposure to foreign exchange risks at a minimum. To a large extent, we have accomplished this by financing our subsidiaries with funds raised in the countries where they are located. There are times, however, when borrowing in foreign markets is not sufficient to protect us against currency devaluations. In these cases, other means have to be used—some of which can be very expensive if our judgment proves to be wrong.

In the case of the pound sterling, in spite of our efforts to borrow as much as possible in the United Kingdom, we found the size of our exposure in this currency at the end of 1970 to be too high. In addition, we thought that the possibility of a devaluation in the pound vis-à-vis the dollar during 1971 was significant. So we decided to hedge this risk by buying one-year forward commitments to sell pounds at a discount. Well, a year has now gone by, the pound has not been devalued, but the U. S. dollar has, and we have to go to the market to buy pounds at a high price to fulfill our contract.

The most interesting part of this story, however, is that the present situation is roughly similar to the one we faced last year. The decision to hedge our exposure in pounds at that time has proved to be expensive, but it is not clear to me that we should not take the same course of action now. At the present time, the pound is not in the spotlight of international financial markets, but I do not think England will be able to afford the present exchange rate though the coming year.

If the forward market route to hedging in pound sterling were used again, the options at this point appeared to be: (1) buy forward contracts to deliver pounds in a year, (2) leave the exposure situation uncovered through next year, and (3) do nothing now, but if the risks of a pound devaluation increase, then sell pounds forward at that time. The previous trading day, the price of bank transfers in sterling had closed at the following prices: $2.5485 for spot transactions, $2.5550 for thirty-day contracts, and $2.5560 for ninety-day contracts.

The International Operations

MHP manufactured a wide variety of household products—deodorants, toothpaste, hair spray, detergents, window cleaners, plastic storage bags, and so on. In 1971, its operations were divided into five major regions: United States, Europe, Africa, Western Hemisphere, and the Far East. The four non-U. S. regions reported to Mr. Johnson, President of Marwick Home Products International, and Corporate Vice-President in charge of international operations. Mr. Rosenthal also reported to Mr. Johnson. See the organization chart in Exhibit 1. Consolidated financial statements are presented in Exhibit 2.

The present organization extended through fifty countries and had developed during the previous fifty years. MHP followed a strategy of cautious penetration of each country. It first exported to a country; then, as the market in the new country expanded, MHP established a distributor in the country. Finally, only when the market expanded sufficiently to warrant it, MHP would start manufacturing in the new country. Often, this manufacturing was first done by a local manufacturer while MHP did the marketing. Later, MHP undertook the manufacturing. This manufacturing sequence was particularly common in the case of products requiring large investment in fixed assets. Once the company decided to undertake manufacturing operations in a country, the whole process was done there. No transfer of goods in process existed among the various subsidiaries because, for the most part, the preparation of the final goods was a one-step production process which was best performed in a single location.

All MHP subsidiaries were 100% owned by the parent company. There were two rationales for this strategy: the zeal in protecting the company's trademark names and the flexibility of sole ownership. The pressures for joint ventures from the host country had been resisted even in the case of Japan where the company preferred to be classified as an "unvalidated company" (unable to repatriate earnings) rather than to share ownership with Japanese interests.

Financial Management

MHP's decision to start operations in a new country was based on the analysis of market potential and production costs in the specific country. The decision of the size and form of the parent's investment was then guided by two general principles: (1) limit capital investment to the minimum that will be acceptable to the host country and to its financial institutions, and (2) use as much local borrowing as possible. From here on, the company gave subsidiaries' management freedom, subject to financial controls.

The Budget. The budget was the instrument by which MHP controlled its subsidiaries. Every year around September, each subsidiary submitted two detailed budgets for the following year: one for operations and one for capital expenditures. To make the budgets for subsidiaries from different countries comparable, the estimates were converted into U. S. dollars. The exchange rates used in these conversions were the quoted rates (not the official rates) at the end of the month. These quoted rates were adjusted to reflect the parent's evaluation of the strength of the currency in the subsidiary's country, thus anticipating the impact of currency devaluations.

By the time that the subsidiary submitted a proposal to the corporate level, a close screening had preceded it—a screening that included the availability and cost of local funds to finance the project. At the home office, the marketing, the production, and the financing aspects of the proposal were studied closely by the respective staff members. A rough measure used to discriminate among various proposals was a required payout of seven years. A longer payout, however, could also be accepted, especially when the project involved savings in labor.

Profits Remittance Policy. The general policy of MHP regarding remittances was to repatriate an average of 65% of annual foreign profits. The form that these remitted funds took was subject to the negotiations between the company and the host country when the subsidiary was first established. The company tried to have these remittances take the form of royalties to the extent allowed by the host company and to use dividends as a complement to reach the desired 65%. The emphasis on royalties was on two accounts. First, quite often royalties were considered business expenses by the host country and were therefore tax deductible. Second, in cases of foreign exchange controls on remittances, it was more likely to get permission from the host country to obtain foreign exchange to pay for royalties than to pay for dividends to the parent company.

The 65% rule of thumb was subject to modifications depending on the subsidiary's ability to pay and on its requirement for funds. Nevertheless, the underlying policy was to remit as much cash as possible. A new subsidiary was expected to have an initial period of three to five years when it was not possible to remit funds to the parent company. But once it started remitting profits, it was expected to continue doing so—even if it involved borrowing in the local country—unless it had a heavy program of expenditures.

The dividend schedule was set at the time the budget was approved in September. At this time, calculations of the tax on dividends in the foreign country and in the United States were done before a final decision was made as to the size of the dividend payments from each subsidiary. Dates for specific remittances based on monthly cash flow estimates were agreed upon at the beginning of the year.

Parent-Subsidiary Business Relationships. After the headquarter's office approved the subsidiary's budget for the following year, most business transactions between parent and subsidiary were conducted at arm's length. These transactions were largely restricted to the sale of some special raw materials by the parent company to the subsidiary. Such sales were billed in dollars at standard cost plus a surcharge to cover handling costs. The debt was expected to be paid as promptly as possible according to industry terms—usually 30 days.

This arm's length policy also applied to the financing of the subsidiaries. It was the parent's policy not to lend money to a subsidiary for its operations. Moreover, there were virtually no lateral relationships; one subsidiary did not borrow from another. Once the subsidiary was established, the financing of new projects had to be done out of retained earnings and local borrowing power which had been approved initially by the board of directors. If needs for funds exceeded this limit and the local market was willing to provide the funds, permission still had to be obtained from the board to increase the borrowings.

Management of the Foreign Exchange Position

As Mr. Rosenthal's earlier quote indicates, MHP felt that the best policy in dealing with foreign exchange risks was to minimize its exposure to them. If Mr. Rosenthal's assessment of the possibilities and the size of a devaluation in a currency, when combined with the net exposure in that currency, indicated a potentially significant loss, MHP tried to reduce it by increasing local borrowings, and if this failed, by covering in the forward exchange market.

MHP computed the exposure to foreign exchange risk in a given currency by taking the subsidiary's net worth and subtracting fixed assets from it. Adjustments for current assets and liabilities denominated in U. S. dollars were then made. In this method, long-term debt, to the extent it did not apply to specific fixed assets, and inventories were valued at current exchange rates. The rationale for treating inventories on a current basis was that, although on some occasions prices of goods in inventory could be increased to take into account the new exchange rates, more often than not price control measures in the country made this impossible to accomplish. Long-term liabilities were translated at current rates except where these liabilities had been created to finance the purchase of specific plant and equipment. In the latter case, both the asset and the debt were translated at historical rates. In case of devaluations, when exposed assets exceeded exposed liabilities, debt in terms of dollars was overstated for a while until payment in the depreciated currency took place and a gain in exchange was realized. This gain was used to offset the unrealized exchange losses that year. That is, foreign exchange gains were reported only when they were realized. However, foreign exchange losses were reported as soon as they were incurred, and they appeared on the income statement as extraordinary items. (In computing taxes, both losses and gains were recognized when they were realized.)

Inventory and accounts receivable combined averaged about 20-25% of sales. When the parent company believed a change in the value of the foreign currency was about to occur, it tried to influence the size of these accounts. Another MHP policy was to keep the cash account at a minimum consistent with the size of overdraft facilities available to the subsidiary and the schedule for cash payments in the subsidiary. When sizeable amounts of cash were left in the accounts of the subsidiary because of an impending payment, this cash was invested in short-term securities in the local country until payment was due. Under no condition was the subsidiary allowed to invest these funds in another country. To the extent that there was some question about the possibility of devaluation of the subsidiary's local currency, remittances were covered in the forward market. To the extent that an upvaluation of the local currency was possible, an attempt was made to delay the remittance of funds as long as possible, given present regulations.

Control of the operations in foreign exchange was exercised by regular computations for each subsidiary of the cost of borrowing in local markets as compared with the alternative of being financed from headquarters. The after-tax interest cost in the subsidiary plus the actual exchange losses incurred were compared with the cost of money after taxes to the parent plus the exchange losses under this second course of action. The performance of the foreign exchange operations as measured by this system had been highly successful. The exchange losses saved in every devaluation had proved more than enough to compensate for the higher interest rates paid in the local borrowing market. As one can see in Exhibit 3, the average loans in local currencies held in the various subsidiaries for particular time periods were computed (column 1) together with the total exchange losses realized in that period (column 2). Had these loans been completed by the parent and submitted to the subsidiary, then the loans would have been in dollars. Where the local currencies on the average devalued relative to the dollar, then the foreign exchange losses shown by the parent would have been greater under this policy, because the net exposure in non-dollar currencies would have been larger in the absence of local currency loans. Under this policy, the exchange losses can be determined, and the savings in avoiding these losses (versus column 2) are reported in column 3. The local interest cost on the loans is in column 4, and the dollar interest cost had the home loans been used are in column 5. Finally, the firm's computation of the net savings by using foreign loans is shown in column 6, and is the sum of the exchange loss reduction (column 3) and the dollar interest costs which are avoided (column 5), less the local loan interest cost (column 4).

The British Subsidiary

By the early 1920s, MHP was conducting business in England through its office in London. However, not until after World War II did it commence manufacturing operations in that country. Significant expansions took place in the late 1940s and early 1950s.

MHP's line of products in England was similar to the one in the United States, although some formulas had been modified to take into account the British tastes. As of late, the company's growth in England was similar to growth in the United States; although not exceptional, it was commensurate with the growth in the economy. Exhibit 4 presents the balance sheet of Marwick's British subsidiary for selected years.

Before taking a final course of action, Mr. Rosenthal decided to review once more the information he had on the British economy and on the stability of the pound. A few days before, the Group of Ten key industrial nations had put an end to the period of floating rates initiated by President Nixon the previous August 15. In a policy designed to curb U. S. inflation, increase employment, and control the balance of payments, the Nixon administration had cut the U. S. dollar loose from the historic $35-an-ounce gold price. In the four months that world currencies were allowed to float before fixed "central rates" were agreed upon on December 18, the pound had been subject to continuous inflows of speculative funds. These inflows, which brought the British reserves to record levels, continued unabated in spite of the Bank of England's decision to slash its discount rate by a full percentage point to 5%. In the week that the pound had been working under the new fixed rates, its price had remained well within the wider bands now allowed. The feeling in the financial markets appeared to be one of optimism for the pound, at least in the short run. However, some economists did not have such a sanguine view and thought that the pound would not be able to hold its new price for any length of time. These views were reflected in a recent editorial in *The Economist* (see Exhibit 5). Additional basic economic data for the United Kingdom are contained in Exhibits 6 and 7.

EXHIBIT 1 Organization Chart for Marwick Home Products International (Fully-owned subsidiary of Marwick Home Products, Inc.)

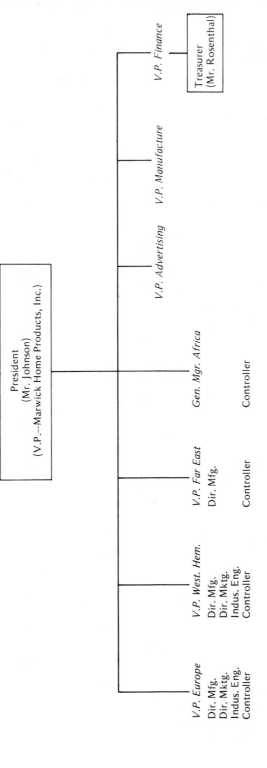

EXHIBIT 2   Marwick Home Products, Inc.: Consolidated Balance Sheets as of December 31, 1966-1970 (thousands of dollars)

			Assets		
	1966	1967	1968	1969	1970
Current Assets					
Cash	$ 42,500	$ 45,600	$ 44,850	$ 56,450	$ 49,300
Marketable securities at cost	51,100	54,500	84,800	86,600	104,000
Receivables	84,250	97,500	99,700	98,200	108,600
Inventories	135,200	130,500	149,500	154,400	170,500
Total current assets	$313,050	$328,100	$378,850	$395,650	$432,400
Fixed Assets, at Cost					
Land	13,690	13,520	13,710	14,520	14,720
Buildings	113,900	115,700	120,000	125,300	129,900
Equipment	193,500	206,400	220,000	237,000	254,000
	$321,090	$335,620	$353,710	$376,820	$398,620
Accumulated depreciation	138,000	153,000	168,000	183,400	202,000
Net fixed assets	$183,090	$182,620	$185,710	$193,420	$196,620
Other Assets					
Miscellaneous investments	2,624	3,452	5,430	3,110	1,905
Goodwill trademarks	13,580	13,550	13,550	13,550	9,820
Prepaid items	9,095	10,790	11,090	7,610	9,000
	$ 25,299	$ 27,792	$ 30,070	$ 24,270	$ 20,725
TOTAL ASSETS	$521,439	$538,512	$594,630	$613,340	$649,745

			Liabilities		
	1966	1967	1968	1969	1970
Current Liabilities					
Bank loans of foreign subsidiaries	$ 16,170	$ 17,670	$ 29,600	$ 24,550	$ 22,400
Current portion of long-term debt	5,300	4,870	6,910	4,420	6,440
Accounts payable	45,500	36,800	47,950	45,450	43,300
Dividends payable	3,420	4,240	4,240	4,670	5,100
Miscellaneous	37,800	46,400	53,700	63,500	72,200
Accrued taxes	25,450	22,800	25,100	28,400	40,800
Total current liabilities	$133,640	$132,780	$167,500	$170,990	$190,240
Noncurrent Liabilities					
Long-term debt	54,350	53,300	49,300	50,600	44,300
Deferred taxes	5,990	7,330	10,400	15,160	17,250
Reserves	7,980	11,000	14,680	16,400	21,780
	$ 68,320	$ 71,630	$ 74,380	$ 82,160	$ 83,330
Shareholders' Equity					
Preferred stock	15,000	15,000	15,000	15,000	15,000
Common stock at par value	42,300	44,900	43,600	49,000	48,300
Capital surplus	37,100	34,500	34,800	28,350	24,400
Earned surplus	225,079	239,702	259,350	267,840	288,475
Total shareholders' equity	$319,479	$334,102	$352,750	$360,190	$376,175
TOTAL LIABILITIES	$521,439	$538,512	$594,630	$613,340	$649.745

Source: Annual reports of the company, 1966-1970.

EXHIBIT 3   Marwick Home Products, Inc.: Net Reduction in Exchange Loss Due to Loans (thousands of dollars)

Period	Average Loans (1)	Recorded Exchange Losses (2)	Exchange Loss Reduction Due To Loans (3)	Interest Cost on Loan (Net)[a] (4)	Cost of Money to Replace Loans (Net)[a,b] (5)	Net Reduction (6) (3) + (5) − (4)
1/1/48-12/31/52	12,366	4,303	1,582	1,413	927	1,095
1/1/53-12/31/57	27,136	5,581	4,558	4,125	2,036	2,469
1/1/58-12/31/62	41,181	6,408	8,129	7,415	3,089	3,803
1/1/63-12/31/67	44,702	3,155	2,075	8,698	5,301	(1,322)
Total	31,485	19,447	16,344	21,651	11,353	6,045
1/1/68-12/31/68	42,901	57	100	1,853	1,287	(466)
1/1/69-12/31/69	54,084	176	2,016	2,430	1,840	1,426
Total 22 Years	33,543	19,680	18,460	25,934	14,480	7,006

[a]Net after taxes.
[b]1.5% net for 1948/62   2.7% net for 1966
1.8% net for 1963   3.0% net for 1967
2.1% net for 1964   3.0% net for 1968
2.25% net for 1965   3.4% net for 1969

EXHIBIT 4   Marwick—U. K. Balance Sheets as of December 31, 1965-1971
(thousands of pounds sterling)

	Assets			
	1965	*1967*	*1969*	*1971*
Current Assets				
Cash	£ 858	£1,846	£1,615	£ 184
Receivables (trade)	1,362	983	980	1,627
Intracompany accounts	339	170	267	493
Prepayments	none	288	116	126
Inventories	2,760	2,460	2,085	2,210
Total Current Assets	£5,319	£5,747	£5,063	£4,640
Net Fixed Assets	3,395	3,440	3,570	3,790
Investment in Non-consolidated Subsidiaries	102	102	102	102
TOTAL ASSETS	£8,816	£9,289	£8,735	£8,532

	Liabilities			
	1965	*1967*	*1969*	*1971*
Current Liabilities				
Bank overdrafts	£ none	£2,298	£ 23	£1,000
Accounts payable (trade)	1,742	1,595	1,795	2,130
Intercompany accounts	73	132	102	89
Miscellaneous	125	none	none	none
Accrued taxes	1,109	1,101	719	192
Total current liabilities	£3,049	£5,126	£2,639	£3,411
Noncurrent liabilities				
Deferred taxes	819	650	1,090	681
Shareholder's Equity				
Issued capital	1,330	1,330	1,330	1,330
Earned surplus	3,618	2,183	3,676	3,110
Total shareholders' equity	£4,948	£3,513	£5,006	£4,440
TOTAL LIABILITIES AND EQUITY	£8,816	£9,289	£8,735	£8,532

EXHIBIT 5   "The Dirty Fixing"

To help the dollar, sterling is now probably overvalued again, but the DM is almost certainly undervalued. Fortunately, upward pressure on the DM is likely to bring us back to dirty floating once more.

The most important point about the new pattern of world exchange rates is that it will not last for long. That is why all statesmen are having to say the opposite very loudly. President Nixon called it "the most significant monetary agreement in the history of the world." The Group of Ten's communiqué talked about "assuring a new and lasting equilibrium in the international economy," although, unless one makes the odd assumption that all rates of inflation between all countries will always be equal ever after as from midnight last Saturday, "lasting equilibrium" and fixed exchange rates have to be a contradiction in terms. Mr. Barber said that during last weekend's bargaining Britain's competitive position had been preserved. Actually, Britain's exports have been made dearer than they were last week in every important country except Japan and France (which do not buy many of our exports); in such main markets as America South Africa and, probably, Australia, British exports are being made much dearer.

Since August 15, the Americans have won a bigger depreciation of the dollar than anybody outside America thought possible then, and they have won it mainly at the expense of the Japanese and the "weaker Europeans" (such as Britain, France, and Italy). Incredibly, the DM and Swiss franc have been devalued against us. This is shown by column 3 of the accompanying table, which is set in bold type because it lists the new parities' appreciations against the dollar since exchange markets closed on the eve of Mr. Nixon's August measures. The argument that Britain has maintained its competitive position comes from citing the change since the old May 1 parities, shown in column 2 of the table; but by May those parities were already in total disequilibrium, which is why the DM and guilder floated up (and the Swiss franc was hoisted up). What the ten ministers have managed to do in Europe is to march us back from last August's near equilibrium towards May's disequilibrium, so that all the reequilibrating panics that were necessary in May will slowly become necessary all over again.

Percentage upvaluation against the dollar

	(1) *New parity*	(2) *Since May 1*	(3) **Since August 13**	(4) *Since December 17*
Yen	308	+16.9	**+15.9**	+1.9
Sterling	2.6057	+ 8.6	**+ 7.8**	+3.0
French francs	5.1157	+ 8.6	**+ 7.8**	+7.8
Liras	581.5	+ 7.5	**+ 6.2**	+3.3
Swiss francs	3.84	+13.9	**+ 5.9**	+1.0
Deutsche marks	3.223	+13.6	**+ 5.1**	+1.1

The main trading consequence is that the German and American balances of payments are likely to do much better in the period ahead than anybody could previously have supposed.

Source: *The Economist*, December 25, 1971.

For Germany this probably means that there will not be a relapse into recession in 1972, but a recovery from the threat of recession by the usual German escape route of large export sales and a very favorable balance of payments. By some time in 1973 it is therefore rather likely that there will be another so-called currency crisis, and yet another upward floating of the mark. There should not be loud complaint about this. For 1972-73 it may well be better that there should be another familiar and ridiculous German slump. Since the new and unmaintainable pattern of fixed rates is going to be bust anyway, the best way for the busting to come is probably this old and well-known way of the mark thumping irresistibly up against the ceiling. The more agonising way of destroying the new pattern would be by one of the overvalued rates—such as sterling—coming crashing down irresistibly against the floor; some people might then expect British Chancellors to cause chaos by resisting the irresistible for a while.

Back to a dollar gap?

There may be more reason to worry about the coming improvement in America's external payments. Although the top ten finance ministers and central bank governors hate to recognize this, the equilibrium position for the world economy is that America should be running a balance of payments deficit of a quite easily specifiable amount: namely, the amount of deficit where it is just pumping out into the world the number of dollars that other countries want to hold newly in their reserves. Just before August, America was running a bigger deficit than this. Now it may run a deficit smaller than this world equilibrium level, and a greedy lion's share of the reduced number of dollars that it pumps out is likely to be gobbled up by Germany. The danger is that other countries, feeling indigent in their dollar reserves, may then start to squeeze their internal economies or to impose restrictions on their trade. Contrary to the guff spoken by the top ten finance ministers and central bank governors last weekend, there is obviously a slightly greater risk of this happening under this week's regime of dirtily fixed exchange rates than there was under last week's regime of dirtily floating rates.

Fortunately, there are two reasons why these gloomy possibilities are not really likely to lead to an unnecessary world recession or trade war. First, although the top ten finance ministers and bank governors believed themselves last weekend when they said that they were restoring "stability" by returning to nominally pegged exchange rates, they are now happily likely to unpeg them pretty sharply rather than meet future balance of payments troubles by stopping all economic growth. America's strongman action this year has made devaluation respectable. There is a small worry that there may be some undesirable deflationary influence for the now-probably overvalued countries in the early stages. Because Britain has unhappily pitched its rate at a level from which it is rather more likely to go down than up, there may now be a movement of money out of London: this will probably and temporarily cause the Bank of England to keep British interest rates higher than they logically should be. As an insufficient mitigation for this the Bank has wisely adopted the full permitted margin of 2¼% on either side of sterling's unmemorable new parity of $2.6057 (so that the permitted range round that figure, which every sensible person should now forget as quickly as he forgets every telephone number except his bookmaker's, is from $2.5471 to $2.6643). The original proposal was that the permitted margin of fluctuation should be 3% on either side of parity; it is a symptom of mindless restrictionism that the Group of Ten has whittled this down. Mr. Barber should have fought harder for the 3%.

The second principal hope of the optimists is that the drain on world liquidity through a new dollar gap could be staunched by a major extension of the use of Special Drawing Rights in the International Monetary Fund. Here Mr. Barber has played a very constructive part, by the excellent proposals in his speech to the IMF last September. Unfortunately, the recent experience in the Group of Ten does raise doubts about whether intelligent settlements can be made on complicated matters in the multilateral negotiations that are now deemed to be required. When all the experts from all the countries were present at these meetings of the Ten, too many experts had too many different points of view for the discussions to proceed sensibly; when, as in the Rome meeting of the Ten, the ministers and governors turned the experts out into the corridors, there was too inexpert a majority among the twenty gentlemen left in the room for sensible discussions to start. After fixing exchange rates at the wrong levels, the Ten's communiqué last weekend set out this agenda for the coming talks.

The Ministers and Governors agreed that discussions should be promptly undertaken, particularly in the framework of the IMF, to consider reform of the international monetary system over the longer term.

It was agreed that attention should be directed to the appropriate monetary means and divisions of responsibilities for defending stable exchange rates and for ensuring a proper degree of convertibility of the system; to the proper role of gold, of reserve currencies, and of Special Drawing Rights in the operation of the system; to the appropriate volume of liquidity; to reexamination of the permissible margins of fluctuation around established exchange rates, and other means of establishing a suitable degree of flexibility; and to other measures dealing with movements of liquid capital. It is recognized that decisions in each of these areas are closely linked. . . .

Is there any way in which the international monetary system can be rescued from the ministrations of muddled meetings of this kind? Probably only by restoring the ministration to the market. Under the admirable system of dirty floating, into which the so-called currency crisis of last August precipitated us, the value of each currency was set at whatever the market was willing to pay for it—except that nearly all individual governments intervened to cheapen their currencies in dollar terms, by just sufficiently enough to enable the Americans to run the desirable level of deficit where they were pumping out as many dollars as the outside world wanted to hold. It is a pity that the ten countries have spent so many meetings rescuing us from it; luckily they have done the job so very botchedly, chiefly by making the mark too cheap, that their new system is exceedingly unlikely to stand.

EXHIBIT 6. United Kingdom: Balance of Payments (not seasonally adjusted, millions-U. S. dollars)

	1965	1966	1967	1968	1969	1970	1971	1971 First Quarter	Second Quarter	Third Quarter	Fourth Quarter
A. Goods, Services (net), and Unrequited Transfers (net)											
Exports f.o.b.	13,558	14,582	14,227	15,122	16,946	18,926	21,654	4,742	5,589	5,445	5,878
Imports f.o.b. (excluding U. S. military aircraft)	-14,140	-14,627	-15,359	-16,368	-17,138	-18,909	-20,921	-5,071	-5,263	-5,064	-5,523
Payments for U. S. military aircraft	-33	-115	-270	-261	-146	—	—	—	—	—	—
Trade balance	-615	-160	-1,402	-1,507	-338	17	733	-329	326	384	355
Transportation	67	85	121	214	50	-139	-60	-91	-5	51	-15
Travel	-272	-218	-109	25	84	115	64	19	17	-32	60
Investment income	1,238	1,064	1,015	760	1,202	1,176	1,263	370	398	342	153
Government services	-549	-594	-532	-465	-696	-753	-818	-166	-197	-225	-230
Other goods and services	501	585	792	866	1,311	1,572	1,691	446	409	408	428
Private transfers	-90	-137	-161	-231	-132	-108	-97	-14	-26	-29	-28
Government transfers	-495	-304	-517	-429	-425	-413	-453	-137	-106	-110	-100
Total	-215	121	-793	-766	1,056	1,467	2,323	98	816	786	623
B. Long-Term Capital, n.i.e.											
Private investment (net)											
In United Kingdom	616	745	979	1,392	1,615	1,774	2,818	1,063	686	511	558
Abroad	-991	-848	-1,267	-1,764	-1,601	-1,826	-1,851	-535	-506	-452	-358
Official long-term capital											
Intergovernmental loans (net)	-185	-172	-97	-15	-115	-428	-461	-94	-91	-78	-198
Other	-53	-53	-48	55	-120	-62	-213	-14	-12	-7	-180
Total	-613	-328	-433	-332	-221	-542	293	420	77	-26	-178
C. Total (A plus B)	-828	-207	-1,226	-1,098	835	925	2,616	518	893	760	445
D. Net Errors and Omissions	87	-72	510	-193	960	274	864	706	-46	-274	478
E. Exchange Equalization Account Losses on Forward Commitments	—	—	-252	-602	—	—					

EXHIBIT 6. United Kingdom: Balance of Payments (not seasonally adjusted, millions-U. S. dollars) (cont.)

	1965	1966	1967	1968	1969	1970	1971	1971 First Quarter	Second Quarter	Third Quarter	Fourth Quarter
F. Short-Term Capital, n.i.e.											
Nonmonetary sectors' capital—											
Trade credit	202	-320	-92	-62	-413	-509	-672	-103	-288	42	-323
U. K. banks' net liabilities in overseas sterling area currencies	20	-126	68	-110	-5	-17	-34	-14	7	-27	—
U. K. banks' net liabilities in non-sterling area currencies											
Euro-dollar financing of new private investment abroad	25	42	}118	422	173	454	583	84	276	98	125
Other	-174	-490		-338	-259	696	628	132	96	22	378
Sterling liabilities other than to central monetary institutions											
Sterling area countries	462	81	7	-256	-115	391	945	163	34	237	511
Other countries	-120	-512	-337	-930	-12	192	873	14	-19	352	526
International institutions	-17	37	-43	38							
Other	—	—	—	—	-209	175	351	300	-65	191	-75
Total	398	-1,288	-279	-1,236	-840	1,382	2,674	576	41	915	1,142
G. Total (C through F)	-343	-1,567	-1,247	-3,129	955	2,581	6,154	1,800	888	1,401	2,065
H. Allocations of SDRs	—	—	—	—	—	410	300	300	—	—	—
I. Total (G plus H)	—	—	—	—	955	2,991	6,454	2,100	888	1,401	2,065
J. Official Monetary Movements (increase in assets—)											
Gold reserves	-129	325	650	-182	3	122	574	226	319	26	3
SDRs	—	—	—	—	—	-266	-325	-216	-6	-65	-38
Convertible currency reserves	-560	465	245	456	-108	-156	-3,837	-499	-617	-1,355	-1,366
Other claims	—	—	—	—	—	—	-2,109	-500	-1,200	400	-809
Use of fund credit	1,391	-42	-851	1,262	-34	-412	-1,332	-688	-22	-622	—
Gold deposit liabilities to IMF	8	35	1	-3	-2	-9	-4	-1	-2	-1	—
Official liabilities in foreign currency	-202	39	424	43	-146	-360	—	—	—	—	—
Sterling counterpart of official borrowing	510	786	1,291	1,852	-1,458	-2,427	-957	-957	—	—	—
Other sterling liabilities to central monetary institutions											
Sterling area countries	-456	-75	-333	-73	900	507	1,099	509	475	185	-70
Other countries	-219	34	-180	-226	-110	10	437	26	165	31	215
Total	343	1,567	1,247	3,129	-955	-2,991	-6,454	-2,100	-888	-1,401	-2,065

Source: Bank of England, *Monthly Bulletin.*

EXHIBIT 7 United Kingdom: Basic Financial Data

		1965	1966	1967	1968	1969	1970	I	II	III	IV	Aug.	Sept.	Oct.	Nov.
								1971					1971		
Exchange Rates							US Dollars per Pound Sterling: End of a Period								
US Dollar: Spot Rate	a	2.8025	2.7900	2.4065	2.3844	2.4006	2.3938	2.4169	2.4194	2.4850	2.5525	2.4525	2.4850	2.4912	2.4938
Forward Rate	b	2.7950	2.7850	2.3900	2.3606	2.3975	2.3881	2.4012	2.4138	2.4969	2.5656	2.4619	2.4969	2.4875	2.5031
London Gold Price (US$ per ounce)	c	35.11	35.19	35.20	41.90	35.20	37.38	38.88	40.10	42.60	43.62	40.65	42.60	42.34	43.60
International Liquidity							Millions of US Dollars: End of a Period								
Monetary Authorities	1	3,004	3,099	2,695	2,422	2,527	2,827	3,316	3,620	5,015	6,583	4,808	5,015	5,211	5,574
Gold	1a	2,265	1,940	1,291	1,474	1,471	1,349	1,123	804	778	842	778	778	778	778
SDRs	1b						266	482	488	553	542	528	553	588	591
Fund Gold Tranche Position	1c														
Foreign Exchange	1d	739	1,159	1,404	948	1,056	1,212	1,711	2,328	3,684	5,099	3,502	3,684	3,845	4,205
Dollar Assets Reported by US	9a	3,277	4,165	5,047	6,534	11,801	5,978	5,286	6,642	6,799	7,702	6,588	6,799	7,766	8,230
Short-Term	9aa	2,714	3,817	4,667	6,184	11,394	5,505	4,776	6,152	6,367	7,379	6,128	6,367	7,339	7,868
of UK Government and Banks	9ab	2,450	3,607	4,470	5,880	11,146	5,236	4,472	5,919	6,135	7,135	5,879	6,135	7,094	7,618
Long-Term	9ad	553	348	380	350	407	472	510	490	432	323	460	432	427	362
Dollar Liabilities Reported by U.S.	9b	212	191	244	318	418	379	454	532	459	564	785	459	493	681
Financial Survey							Millions of Pounds Sterling: Changes during Period								
Foreign Assets (net)	51	−194	22	−331	−655	698	728	645	−65						
Domestic Credit	52	3,131	2,571	4,055	4,147	1,916	3,916	232	1,668						
Claims on Government	52a	765	453	1,292	963	−851	−431	−938	451						
Claims on Official Entities	52b	410	310	495	449	403	878	264	231						
Claims on Private Sector	52c	1,956	1,808	2,268	2,735	2,364	3,469	906	986						
Money	54	919	471	1,340	1,129	494	1,554	−11	509						
Domestic Dep. with Other Fin. Inst.	55	835	902	1,252	954	1,053	1,649	412	510						
Life Insurance and Pension Funds	56a	1,163	1,241	1,381	1,525	1,535	1,755	425	495						
Capital Issues, etc.	56b	104	226	154	410	305	152	46	62						
Other Items (Net)	57r	−84	−247	−403	−526	−773	−466	5	27						
Interest, Prices, Production							% or Index Numbers (1963=100): Period Averages								
Bank Rate (End of Period)	60	6.00	7.00	8.00	7.00	8.00	7.00	7.00	6.00	5.00	5.00	6.00	5.00	5.00	5.00
Treasury Bill Rate	60c	5.91	6.10	5.82	7.04	7.64	7.01	6.75	5.67	5.39	4.52	5.76	4.84	4.63	4.49
Euro-Dollar London	60d	4.81	6.12	5.45	6.36	9.76	8.52	5.54	6.73	7.71	6.33	8.21	8.46	6.60	6.28
Gov't Bond Yield: Short Term	61a	6.57	6.77	6.66	7.59	8.81	7.89	7.63	7.09	6.66	6.10	6.71	6.55	6.28	6.00
Long-Term	61	6.56	6.94	6.80	7.55	9.04	9.22	9.30	9.05	8.69	8.12	8.82	8.45	8.23	8.07
Industrial Share Prices	62	100.4	101.2	108.1	152.8	151.0	133.8	131.6	152.9	172.5	173.4	171.3	176.9	172.6	168.7
Prices: Industrial Output	63	106.8	109.6	110.9	115.3	119.8	127.7	134.4	137.1	139.2	140.2	139.3	139.5	139.7	140.0
Consumer Prices	64	108.2	112.5	115.3	120.7	127.2	135.3	142.8	147.9	149.9	151.8	149.9	150.1	151.0	151.8
Wages: Avg. Mo. Earn., All Indust.	65	107	115	123	127	137	147	178	183						
Industrial Production, Seas. Adj.	66	112	113	114	120	123	124	124	126	126	125	126	127	125	125
Employment, Seas. Adj.	67	102.3	102.9	101.9	100.1	99.9	99.0	97.6							
International Transactions							Millions of Pounds Sterling: Millions of Pounds Sterling								
Exports	70	4,901	5,255	5,230	6,434	7,389	8,063	2,020	2,385	2,307	2,468	719	785	784	829
Imports, cif	71	5,751	5,950	6,437	7,897	8,315	9,052	2,434	2,488	2,386	2,599	732	831	837	853

EXHIBIT 7 United Kingdom: Basic Financial Data (cont.)

1963=100

Item	Code														
Volume of Exports	72	107	112	110	126	139	144	136	159	152	160	144	155	154	163
Volume of Imports	73	112	114	123	136	139	147	154	153	145	155	135	151	152	155
Export Prices	74	105	108	110	118	122	131	138	140	143	146	143	144	145	146
Import Prices	75	104	106	106	117	122	128	129	133	134	133	134	135	134	133
Freight Rates: Tramps, Voyages	76	116.1	104.1	110.6	113.6	114.7	205.6	153.3	98.8	85.2	85.2				

Balance of Payments *Millions of US Dollars; Minus Sign Indicates Debit*

Item	Code								
Goods and Services	70	378	801	-115	-118	1,613	1,911	223	915
Trade Balance fob	70a	-664	-204	-1,446	-1,543	-338	7	-329	319
Transportation	70b	81	84	120	125	50	-139	-98	-14
Investment Income	70c	1,218	1,100	1,018	818	1,202	1,229	379	398
Government n.i.e.	70d	-756	-812	-750	-689	-696	-753	-175	-194
Other	70e	499	633	943	1,171	1,395	1,567	446	406
Transfers: Private	71a	-20	-64	-161	-144	-132	-108	-14	-17
Central Government	71b	-496	-504	-769	-1,032	-425	-413	-127	-106
Capital Flows	72	-625	-1,558	-719	-1,377	-1,001	973	901	34
Private Investment	72a	-398	-11	-233	-346	14	-7	34	55
Official Long-Term Flows	72b	-238	-224	-147	41	-235	-490	542	-101
UK Bks'-For Curr. Liab. (Net)	72c	-81	-412		74	-86	-108	216	374
Trade Credit	72d	-137	-484 }	-339 }	-595	-413	-506	-91	-331
Other Short-Term Flows	72e	229	-427 }		-551	-281	812	342	37
Allocation of SDRs	75						410	300	
Official Financing	76	704	1,532	1,254	2,952	-955	-2,996	-2,108	-882
Monetary Gold	76a	-129	325	650	-183	3	122	226	320
SDR Holdings 76b	76b						-266	-216	-6
IMF General Account	76c	1,399	-7	-850	1,259	-36	-421	-690	-24
Convertible Currency Reserves	76d	-560	465	245	456	-108	-156	-499	-617
Other Claims	76e							-500	-1,200
Liabilities in Foreign Currency	76f	-202	39	424	43	-146	-360		
Sterl. Counterpart of Borrowing.	76g	510	786	1,291	1,852	-1,458	-2,427	-957	
Other Sterling Liab. to Authorities	76h	-314	-76	-506	-475	790	512	528	645
Net Errors and Omissions	77	59	-207	510	-281	900	223	825	56

Government Finance *Millions of Pounds Sterling; Calendar Years and Quarters*

Item	Code									
Deficit (−) or Surplus	80	-610	-530	-1,155	-759	1,112	678	722	6	-451
Revenue	81	10,457	11,638	12,760	14,781	17,131	18,168	5,535	4,534	722
Expenditure	82a	9,832	10,652	12,262	13,753	14,477	15,786	4,369	4,204	
Net Lending	83	1,235	1,516	1,653	1,782	1,542	1,704	444	324	
Domestic Borrowing	84a	499	72	663	-405	-423	663	76	480	

National Accounts *Billions of Pounds Sterling*

Item	Code										
Exports	90c	6.56	7.03	7.23	8.79	9.84	11.21	2.83	3.26	3.27	1,111
Net Factor Income from Abroad	90e	.44	.39	.38	.34	.50	.52	.15	.17	.14	
General Government Consumption	91f	6.05	6.58	7.28	7.74	8.13	9.08	2.45	2.47	2.54	
Gross Fixed Capital Formation	93e	6.32	6.72	7.26	7.88	8.12	8.89	2.37	2.31	2.42	
of which: Central Government	93gu	.30	.33	.39	.46	.49					
Increase in Stocks	93f	.39	.27	.22	.21	.37	.45	-.07	-.01	.02	
Private Consumption	96f	22.94	24.32	25.45	27.24	28.80	31.24	7.72	8.57	8.88	
Less: Imports	98c	-6.86	-7.14	-7.68	-9.18	-9.67	-10.90	-2.88	-3.04	-3.05	
Gross National Expenditure—GNP	99a	35.88	38.16	40.13	43.02	46.10	50.49	12.71	13.74	14.22	
Gross Domestic Product	99b	35.39	37.77	39.75	42.68	45.60	49.97	12.56	13.57	14.08	
National Income	99c	28.71	30.17	31.82	33.59	35.35	38.69				

Source: International Monetary Fund, *International Financial Statistics Monthly.*

CHAPTER 8

A Framework for Analyzing the Finance Function in the Multinational Enterprise

Previous chapters have shown the various financing opportunities and challenges that may appear for a firm that first engages in simple international trade and then expands into major operations abroad. The use of the foreign exchange market and the money markets as financing vehicles and opportunities for adjusting the currency risk and return position of the firm was outlined. Each of the problems that the international finance officer faces was examined in isolation. However, in the real world all these problems appear simultaneously and interact with one another.

The goal in this chapter is to develop a framework that will incorporate the separate problems studied earlier. The unifying element in this framework is management's foreign exchange policies. In a domestic environment an analysis of forecast cash flows would suffice. However, for the international financial officer one more step becomes necessary: the adoption of a foreign exchange management posture. The purpose of the coherent scheme developed here is to enable the international finance officer to evaluate alternative exchange policies.

The approach will include a simple three-country, three-alternative, three-outcome analysis, but the process can be easily adapted to large numbers of variables with the aid of a computer system. Preprogrammed alternatives would require the manager to insert only the current cost assumptions and rough probabilities of various outcomes in order to have a rapid computer presentation of the relevant returns. However, the concern here is not so much with an exact analysis, but with a framework that is useful in looking at the problem and that permits rough conclusions about the magnitude of the returns or costs involved.

The chapter is divided into two major parts: (1) a presentation of the steps in the analysis of foreign exchange policies; and (2) an application of the suggested framework of analysis to a simple example. A summary of the approach and a discussion of the management application concludes the chapter.

The premises of this chapter are the following:

1. Every single move of the multinational company abroad has foreign exchange implications; and

2. There is no simple formula to evaluate the costs of alternative policies in foreign exchange management. The costs of each of the components of the policy must be evaluated under alternative *scenarios* (outcomes in the foreign exchange market) before the financial officer may choose the most desirable policy, given the officer's perceptions of the world.

As discussed in Chapter 7, the cost of altering the size of a firm's assets or liabilities is measured by the impact of such a decision on profits as well as by the potential effect of a currency revaluation. For example, contracting accounts receivable by reducing the credit terms may decrease the amount of sales (and profits), but it will also reduce the amount of assets exposed to a devaluation in that currency. Likewise, while an increase in the size of accounts payable may anger a few creditors and make the company lose the advantage of a discount for prompt payment, it can increase the amount of liabilities in a currency prone to devaluation.

ANALYZING ALTERNATIVE FOREIGN EXCHANGE POLICIES

Assumptions

In the following analysis, there are a few assumptions. Some of them are essential, others merely simplify the presentation.

Necessary Assumptions

1. There exists a centralized treasury function.

2. Reliable forecasts on the cash flows of the business are available.

Simplifying Assumptions

1. Economic and accounting exposures are assumed to be the same. Accounting exposure in each currency is defined here as cash plus accounts receivable less debt.

2. One year is the time horizon. This avoids complications with calculations of the time-value of money and refinancing decisions. It also avoids dealing with fractions of annual interest figures.

3. The U. S. dollar is the unit of account. (Any other currency would do as long as one is consistent.)

4. External financial markets are close to equilibrium. The forward market and the money market approaches to hedging produce similar results.

Data for the Analysis

There are three types of data which one must have before starting to analyze the implications of a given foreign exchange policy.

1. A forecast of business operations.

2. Present actual market conditions.

3. A variety of scenarios for the market's situation at the end of the planning period.

Data Forecasting Business Operations and Describing Actual Market Conditions. In this category, the officer needs:

1. A forecast of assets and liabilities per currency.

2. A forecast of flow of funds per currency.

3. The rate of return on business assets in each currency.

4. Initial interest rates in the domestic and Euro-markets, spot exchange rates, and forward exchange rates for each currency.

(1) normally appears at the end of a period during financial consolidation. However, it must be linked with the expected *changes* in those asset and liability positions (combining (1) and (2)) in order to consider covering policies. The data from (3) and (4) provide information required to evaluate the costs (and returns) of various strategies while (1) and (2) indicate the amount of funds involved. For our purposes here, one can eliminate the possibility of wrong forecasts on the operations of the business, and proceed as if (1)-(3) were known with certainty. A wide range of values could be incorporated in the analysis. Again, this broader analysis involving risk considerations in one or more of the above data sets could be handled operationally on a computer with ease.

Data on Future Market Scenarios. Various strategies can be analyzed under a number of different *scenarios*. These scenarios may be thought of as possible *outcomes* or future *states of the world*. In this example, the number of scenarios is reduced to three, which we will call:

1. The *most likely* outcome.

2. *No change* from the present situation.

3. A change *opposite to* the one anticipated in the *most likely* scenario.

Since there is a simplifying assumption of a one-year planning horizon, only the spot rates at the end of the period are needed. Interest rates and forward rates for multiple horizons would be relevant if the firm manager were thinking in terms of sequential financing. That consideration is omitted here for the sake of simplicity.

Steps in the Analysis

1. Choose a foreign exchange strategy. Find what transactions this exchange management will generate in answering the three basic problems of the financial officer:
   a. In what currency should excess funds be invested?
   b. In what currency should funds be raised to meet financing requirements?
   c. After (a) and (b) are answered, what more could be done to achieve the desired foreign exchange exposure?

2. Establish the returns and costs of the financial transactions initiated under step 1 with a variety of scenarios. For each scenario disaggregate the costs/returns of financial transactions into three major components:
   a. Incremental financing.
   b. Translation of foreign operations.
   c. Hedging.

3. Repeat the analysis presented under steps 1 and 2 for alternative policies. In this example, there will be three types of policies:
   a. *Aggressive.* Make the best estimate possible of currency changes and interest rates and act accordingly. Some positions might be "overhedged" where there are likely to be substantial gains from the cover to fully offset the translation losses.
   b. *Zero exposure.* Reduce the exposure to revaluation effects in all non-parent currencies to the minimum. This strategy implies that the initial financing should be designed to minimize all exposed positions.
   c. *Do nothing.* Let the chips fall where they may! Finance in the cheapest currencies, accept any translation losses in the remaining assets, and do no covering.

4. Select a decision criterion, or criteria (e.g., "maximize expected value").

5. Evaluate the results of the impacts of each policy under alternative scenarios.
   a. How likely is each scenario?
   b. What is the return or cost, given the decision rule from step 4?

6. Run the previous analysis backwards.
   a. What scenario would render a given policy unacceptable?
   b. How likely is that scenario?

APPLICATION OF THE SUGGESTED FRAMEWORK

The Business and Market Environment

The example is based on data for three subsidiaries of a U. S. company; i.e., the dollar is the base currency. Subsidiaries are located in the United Kingdom, the Netherlands, and France. The outline will follow the form detailed earlier for obtaining and analyzing the various data items. In this section are (1) a forecast of business operations, (2) the actual foreign exchange and money market rates, and (3) the impact of alternative market scenarios on the effective rates.

1. Forecast Business Operations

Balance Sheets—Today

	United Kingdom			Netherlands			France	
Cash	$ 45		Cash	$ 10		Cash	$ 2	
A/R	100		A/R	75		A/R	50	
Inv.	50		Inv.	75		Inv.	50	
P&E	100	Equity $295	P&E	20	Equity $180	P&E	5	Equity $107
	$295	$295		$180	$180		$107	$107

Forecast Balance Sheets—One Year Later

	United Kingdom			Netherlands			France	
Cash	$ 45	New	Cash	$ 30		Cash	$ 2	New
A/R	160	Funds[a] $ 70	A/R	75		A/R	75	Funds[a] $ 50
Inv.	90	Equity[b] 325	Inv.	75	Equity[b] $200	Inv.	95	Equity[b] 127
P&E	100		P&E	20		P&E	5	
	$395	$395		$200	$200		$177	$177

[a]Financing to be raised, which will be done with some debt issue. The topic of the change in capital structure implied by this action will be discussed in Part Three.
[b]Includes retained profits from the year's operations, as detailed in the next table.

Assuming initial cash balances are minimum amounts required for operations, then the flows of funds through the period are:

Sources	United Kingdom	Netherlands	France
Profits	$ 30	$ 20	$ 20
Required Financing	70	———	50
	$100	$ 20	$ 70
Uses			
↑A/R	$ 60	$ 0	$ 25
↑Inventories	40	0	45
↑Cash	0	$ 20	0
	$100	$ 20	$ 70

Summary of Forecast Flow of Funds

Excess cash to be invested:	Netherlands	$ 20
Funds to be raised:	United Kingdom	70.
	France	50

2. *Actual Foreign Exchange and Money Market Rates*[1]

	US$	£ $\left(\begin{array}{c}\text{Pound}\\\text{sterling}\end{array}\right)$	DFI $\left(\begin{array}{c}\text{Dutch}\\\text{guilder}\end{array}\right)$	FF $\left(\begin{array}{c}\text{French}\\\text{franc}\end{array}\right)$
Spot rates		$2.3820/£	DFI 2.6275/$	FF 4.6925/$
Forward 1-year rates		$2.3025/£	DFI 2.6095/$	FF 4.9525/$
Forward premium (discount) against US$		−3.3%	+0.7%	−5.5%
Interest rates				
Euro-market[2]	12.5%	16.5%	11.7%	17.5%
Domestic	9.0%	14.0%	12.5%	14.0%

3. *Alternative Market Scenarios and the Effective Rates*[3]

a. The Most Likely Outcome (in one year)

	US$	£	DFI	FF
Spot rates		$2.20/£	DFI 2.50/$	FF 4.80/$
% revaluation		−7.6%	+4.8%	−2.3%
Effective interest rates				
Euro-market	12.5%	8.9%	16.5%	15.2%
		(16.5 − 7.6)	(11.7 + 4.8)	(17.5 − 2.3)
Domestic	9.0%	6.4%	17.3%	11.7%
		(14.0 − 7.6)	(12.5 + 4.8)	(14.0 − 2.3)

b. No Change from the Present Situation

Spot Rates—same as actual market rates shown earlier.
Effective interest rates—same as actual market rates shown earlier.

c. Changes Opposite to the Most Likely

	US$	£	DFI	FF
Spot rates		$2.50/£	DFI 2.65/$	FF 4.60/$
% revaluation		+5.0%	−0.9%	+2.0%
Effective interest rates				
Euro-market	12.5%	21.5%	10.8%	19.5%
		(16.5 + 5.0)	(11.7 − 0.9)	(17.5 + 2.0)
Domestic	9.0%	19.0%	11.6%	16.0%
		(14.0 + 5.0)	(12.5 − 0.9)	(14.0 + 2.0)

[1] These rates represent midpoint rates. In practice, one would deal with bid and offer rates as discussed in Chapter 5. Notice that the quotes are expressed in terms of $/£, DFl/$, and FF/$, the standard procedure for the currency of each country.

[2] External markets for the given currency.

[3] As in Chapter 7, effective interest rates are calculated as nominal rates plus the percentage change in the value of the currency. This is accurate only if borrowings are made on a discounted basis. In addition, one must take into account the impact of changes in spot exchange rates on interest payment.

Prescriptions of an Aggressive Policy

The returns (or costs) of various policies depend on the outcome (i.e., which scenario turns out to have been the accurate forecast) as well as the actions taken. One return/cost factor is the effective interest rate times the funds involved. A second cost is the translation loss or gain on exposed assets. (Again, the example arbitrarily assumes that the *accounting* exposure of cash, receivables, and debt measures the true *economic* exposure.) Finally, if some of the exposures are covered, then the cost evaluations must include the results of these coverage returns under each scenario. These three components of return (or cost) are shown below under the prescriptions of one specific policy: the aggressive policy. The implications of this policy under three different scenarios are computed. Its prescriptions are divided into three parts: (1) suggested sources for incremental financing, (2) impact of this financing together with forecast of operations on translation foreign exchange gains and losses; and (3) suggested hedging policies. The three components are then combined. By segregating the costs/returns of the finance function into the three major components, one obtains a better grasp of the implications of alternative financing strategies. Given that management may have different risk attitudes toward each of the components in the finance function, the segregation should be useful in choosing the desired financial strategy.

1. Sources for Incremental Financing. The objectives of the financial officer in managing cash flows are to invest excess funds at the highest possible effective rate and borrow at the lowest possible effective rate. Under the aggressive policy the decision maker will take the estimates of the "most likely" outcome as if this were a certain outcome and act to maximize profits accordingly. In the example, this rule would dictate: "borrow domestic £'s as much as possible, and invest excess funds in domestic guilders as much as possible."

This conclusion is derived from the effective interest rate calculations shown above. The cheapest *source* of financing is the domestic £ at 6.4%. If external markets must be used for borrowing because of foreign exchange controls, the £ is still the cheapest currency at 8.9% versus 16.5% for the Euro-guilder and 15.2% for the Euro-franc. The effective Euro-pound rate is actually lower than the domestic rate for each of the other currencies. On the other hand, the best *use* of funds is the domestic guilder (17.3%), if it is possible to deposit or lend funds there. Alternatively, the best use of funds in the external markets is the Euro-guilder at 16.5%.

If all these opportunities are available *but domestic markets can be used only by local subsidiaries and if transactions between subsidiaries are avoided,* then the Summary of Forecast Flow of Funds would indicate that the parent should direct the subsidiaries to complete the following transactions:

United Kingdom: −$70—Raise funds in domestic pounds.

Netherlands: +$20—Invest the funds in the domestic guilder market.

France: −$50—Raise funds in Euro-pounds.

These transactions will maximize revenues (or minimize costs) in the management of incremental financing needs under the most likely scenario, given the two restrictive assumptions above.

Now one can compute the return (cost) of this policy by combining decisions with the effective interest rates calculated earlier for each scenario.

Incremental Financing

	Most Likely	Scenario No Change	Opposite to Likely
United Kingdom (£) −$70 @ 6.4% = $4.5	−$70 @ 14.0% = −$9.8	−$70 @ 19.0% = −$13.3
Netherlands (DFI) + 20 @ 17.3% = 3.5	+ 20 @ 12.5% = 2.5	+ 20 @ 11.6% = 2.3
France (Euro-£)−50 @ 8.9% = −4.4	− 50 @ 16.5% = − 8.3	− 50 @ 21.5% = − 10.7
−$5.4	−$15.6	−$21.7

2. Return (cost) on Translation.   Combining the initial forecast exposure (cash and accounts receivable at the end of the period) with the financing decisions taken in the previous section will produce the forecast exposure after financing for the three subsidiaries in combination.

	£	DFI	FF
Forecast exposure before incremental financing (Cash + A/R)	$205	$105	$77
Impact of financing	− 70		
	− 50[a]		
Total forecast exposure after financing	+$ 85	+$105	+$77

[a]For France

Now one can join the forecast accounting/economic exposure after incremental financing with the changes in spot rates specified under each scenario. Although the firm has borrowed to meet its incremental financing needs in the currency expected to devalue, pounds, an exposure to fluctuations in the value of that currency remains. In spite of the additional pound borrowings, the company still has a net asset position in pounds. It also has a net asset position in French francs, another currency expected to depreciate against the U. S. dollar. The incremental financings, however, have helped to bolster the asset position in the currency expected to appreciate against the dollar, the guilder. The combination of the initial balance sheet positions and incremental financing, in the absence of any other action in the exchange markets, will provide translation foreign exchange gains and losses which can be computed as follows:

Translation

Most Likely	Scenario No Change	Opposite to Likely
(£) $ 85 × −7.6% = −$6.5	Nothing	(£) $ 85 × +5.0% = +$4.3
(DFI) $105 × +4.8% = + 5.0		(DFI) $105 × −0.9% = − 1.0%
(FF) $ 77 × −2.3% = − 1.8		(FF) $ 77 × +2.0% = + 1.5
−$3.3		+$4.8

3. Return (cost) on Covering Undesirable Exposures. Under an aggressive policy the decision maker will not be happy with the exposures in devaluation-prone currencies. (The manager might even want to profit from the expectations for upvaluations; however, this approach is omitted here.) Under the expected outcome, there will be a foreign exchange loss of $3.3, when the gains and losses in the three currencies are combined as shown in the preceding table. However, the manager may look at this table and decide to engage in hedging transactions, to compensate for the translation losses with foreign exchange gains. Again, recall that this analysis focuses upon accounting exposure which is assumed to equal economic exposure.

Using the money market examples (assuming that the forward market would provide similar results), suppose that the manager first looks at the largest loss, which is in sterling. Using the formula developed in the last chapter to target the exchange gains to be equal to the translated losses under the expected scenario, one can compute the amount which would have to be switched from Euro-pounds to Euro-DFl. The latter yields 16.5% while the cost of the former is 8.9% on a most likely basis after revaluations. In this case, the amount borrowed in pounds and loaned in the Euro-DFl market would be $68, actually less than the exposure of $85.[4] In light of the British subsidiary's equity base even with the additional debt financing, this amount seems small enough to avoid a foreign exchange loss in sterling.

The FF loss is $1.8, but the amount which would have to be borrowed in Euro-FF at an effective interest rate of 15.2% and loaned in Euro-DFl at 16.5% would be $78.[5] For simplicity's sake let's assume that management, in consideration of the potential loss from the franc's devaluation, decides not to hedge this exposure.

Notice that in this example the hedging decision moves in the same direction as the incremental financing decision. In both cases, effective rates on a most likely basis suggest borrowing funds in pounds and investing them in guilders. A more difficult situation arises when the hedging decision actually indicates moves opposite to those dictating the incremental financing decision. This would be the case if the effective interest rates calculated initially included a devaluation, instead of an upvaluation, of the guilder. Under these assumptions the incremental financing decision might still dictate borrowing funds in pounds and investing them in guilders. However, the expected translation gain in guilders of $5.0 in the example would instead become a translation loss of $105 (the exposure) times the percentage devaluation. In economic terms one might say that this is a translation loss worth having

---

[4] Using the net effective interest differential formula developed in Chapter 7:

$$\frac{\text{Amount}}{\text{Hedged}} = \frac{\text{Expected loss}}{(1 + R_I)(1 + \text{Reval }_I) - (1 + R_B)(1 + \text{Reval }_B)}$$

where R_I = nominal interest rate on currency of investment
$\quad\quad R_B$ = nominal interest rate on currency borrowed
$\quad\text{Reval}$ = % revaluation

$$\frac{\text{Amount}}{\text{Hedged}} = \frac{\$6.5}{(1 + .117)(1 + .048) - (1 + .165)(1 - .076)} = \$68$$

[5] Again, from the formula,

$$\frac{\text{Amount}}{\text{Hedged}} = \frac{\$1.8}{(1 + .117)(1 + .048) - (1 + .175)(1 - .023)} = \$78$$

if the gain in interest differentials in the financing more than compensated for the loss in translation. However, the manager might still feel that, although the long exposure in guilders might make sense economically, the implications of the guilder exposure for financial reporting (translating foreign exchange losses) would be unacceptable. In that case, hedging would have an additional cost because the cost associated with incremental financing will be higher. Management's ability to explain foreign exchange losses reported explicitly versus interest differential costs submerged in the financial charges account will dictate the amount of "irrational" hedging that management will contract.

Now the firm can compute the difference in costs from this decision to cover the pound exposure under the three outcomes. By the calculations of the amount to be hedged, the gain from hedging will be exactly the amount of the pound loss under the most likely alternative, $6.5. Under the no change outcome, the cost of hedging will be the differential interest rates 4.8% (11.7 − 16.5) times the $68 hedged. Under the opposite to likely the cost of hedging can be found by multiplying the adjusted interest rate differential by the $68.[6] The results are shown in the table below.

Hedging

	Scenario	
Most Likely	_No Change_	_Opposite to Likely_
+$6.5	−$3.3	−$7.9

If the forecast is correct, there are hedging gains. Otherwise, the hedging operation produces losses.

4. Total Cost of Aggressive Policy Under Each Scenario. One can then combine the dollar costs of the three components under the aggressive strategy with the three different scenarios to find the total cost or return under each scenario.

		Scenario	
	Most Likely	_No Change_	_Opposite to Likely_
Incremental financing	−$5.4	−$15.6	−$21.7
Translation	− 3.3		4.8
Hedging	+6.5	− 3.3	− 7.9
	−$2.2	−$18.9	−$24.8

[6] Gain (Loss) = $\dfrac{\text{Amount}}{\text{Hedged}}$ $[(1 + R_I)(1 + \text{Reval}_I) - (1 + R_B)(1 + \text{Reval}_B)]$

where R_I = nominal interest rate of investment currency
R_B = nominal interest rate of borrowed currency
Reval = Revaluation

Gain (Loss) = $68 × $[(1 + .117)(1 − .009) − (1 + .165)(1 + .05)]$
= −$7.9

Final Evaluation of Alternative Strategies

If the analysis shown above is completed for *each* of the strategies under consideration, it is then possible to review the outcome of each policy or strategy in comparison with the others on each scenario. The results of these computations for the two other alternatives ("zero exposure" and "do nothing") may be combined with the return/cost figures of the "aggressive" policy to produce the following table:

| | Scenario | | |
Policy	Most Likely	No Change	Opposite to Likely
Aggressive	−$2.2	−$18.9	−$24.8
Zero exposure	− 9.6	− 16.0	− 20.6
Do nothing	− 8.7	− 15.6	− 16.9

Under the policy of zero exposure, we assume that the firm will first finance in local currency up to the point where zero exposure is achieved using the cheaper of domestic or Euro-currency markets. Beyond that exposure level, the firm would finance with the parent's reference currency, dollars. If the required financing leaves an exposure to foreign exchange risk, the exposure will be hedged in the money market. An amount equal in size to the amount of the exposure will be used in the hedging operation. Borrowings for hedging purposes will be made in the local or the Euro-market, whichever is less expensive. Proceeds from the borrowings for hedging purposes will be invested in the highest yielding dollars. Since the amount used in the hedging operation is the same as the amount exposed, the cost of hedging is the interest differential. Excess funds are also converted into dollars. Thus, the total cost of this financing strategy is the cost computed under its prescriptions for incremental financing plus the impact of interest differentials.

Under the do nothing strategy, funds are raised in the cheapest source and invested in the highest yielding currency, as with the aggressive strategy. In this three-part analysis, do nothing will require proceeding only as far as step one, selecting the optimum incremental financing mix. This policy will not take into account covering of foreign exchange exposure. Foreign exchange risk will enter into the calculations only to the extent required to calculate the net interest yields (nominal interest rate plus foreign exchange expectations). In essence, this strategy is not quite as passive as it might seem. It presumes consideration of foreign exchange rates when financing is done (like the aggressive strategy) but refuses to consider doing anything about the translation losses on the remaining exposed assets.[7]

From this table summarizing the implications of alternative financing strategies under various outcomes in the market, one has then to reach a decision on the policy to follow. Here the important variables are management's attitude towards *risk* and the *size* of the funds involved. Thus, the management might be willing to gamble on a 50-50 proposition if the sum is $1. The same odds and the same gamble would not

---

[7] The actual calculation of the results under the do nothing and zero exposure strategies are included in the questions at the end of the chapter.

be so appealing if there is $1 million involved. The principle applies to the corporation as well as to the individual.

Even though one might argue that perfect markets mean that in the long run one would break even on average from making no adjustments for foreign exchange exposure, it does not necessarily follow that the corporation would avoid hedging or covering. (Of course, if there *are* imperfections in the market, it would certainly be to the firm's advantage to hedge.) Even granting the restrictive assumptions of perfect capital markets, the rational corporation officer may hedge in a number of situations; the fact that an exposed position would probably be more profitable in the long run might not be sufficient to compensate for the possibility of a large loss to which superiors and shareholders would react very sharply. This is merely a form of insurance, in which individuals sacrifice a small amount with certainty to avoid the small possibility of a large loss.

Among the criteria that management may use to select the desired financial strategy is a rule dictating the choice of the strategy with the highest expected value (least cost). To use this expected value decision rule, assign probabilities to each scenario. For example, we can assign .6 to the most likely alternative, .3 to no change, and .1 to the opposite to likely scenario. With these probabilities, one can compute the expected value for each policy. For example, under the aggressive policy the expected return under the three scenarios is −$9.47, that is, .6 × −$2.2 + .3 × −$18.9 + .1 × −$24.8. Similarly the expected values for the zero exposure policy and do nothing policy are −$12.62 and −$11.59 respectively. This analysis indicates the dominance of the aggressive strategy on an expected value standard.

One can alter the probabilities, searching for the break-even point at which there must be a "greater-than-$x\%$" expectation for the most likely outcome and below which $x\%$ the aggressive strategy is no longer dominant.[8] In addition, manage-

---

[8] If the ratio of no change to opposite to likely scenario probabilities remains at 3 to 1, then the strategy which would eventually come to dominate would be do nothing. Combining these two scenarios we can solve algebraically for the probability (P), below which the aggressive policy is no longer dominant, using the following system of simultaneous equations:

Expected value of do nothing

$$P \left\{ \begin{array}{l} \text{Outcome} \\ \text{of "do nothing"} \\ \text{under most likely} \end{array} \right\} \quad + \quad (1-P) \left\{ \begin{array}{l} \text{Weighted outcome of} \\ \text{"do nothing" under no change} \\ \text{and opposite to likely} \end{array} \right\}$$

Expected value of aggressive

$$P \left\{ \begin{array}{l} \text{Outcome} \\ \text{of "aggressive"} \\ \text{under most likely} \end{array} \right\} \quad + \quad (1-P) \left\{ \begin{array}{l} \text{Weighted outcome} \\ \text{of "aggressive" under no} \\ \text{change and opposite to likely} \end{array} \right\}$$

Using the results from the table summarizing the impact of various strategies under alternative outcomes we can calculate the weighted values as follows:

Weighted outcome of "do nothing" under no change and opposite to likely:

$$\frac{3 \times (-\$15.6) + (-\$16.9)}{4} = -\$15.9$$

Weighted outcome of "aggressive" under no change and opposite to likely:

$$\frac{3 \times (-\$18.9) + (-\$24.8)}{4} = -\$20.4$$

ment may want to examine other probabilities, reviewing how the trade-offs vary under alternative policies and different probability assessments.

For the reasons indicated above on the $1-versus-$1-million gamble, expected value may not be the main criterion. Management might not be willing to live with even a .1 probability of a $24.8 loss, which would be possible given an opposite to likely outcome and the aggressive strategy. It may be that such a loss would not be tolerated, rendering the expected value of this strategy unimportant. Other such *loss functions* could be designed and considered after discussion with management.

ISSUES IN GENERATING ALTERNATIVE STRATEGIES

The above framework has been used to evaluate three popular strategies for dealing with the situation proposed. Based on effective interest costs from various financing sources, the raising and deployment of funds was assigned a net cost or profit. Then a charge for translation gains or losses was inserted based on fund raising and deployment, where the economic gain or loss to the units was linked directly to an accounting exposure evaluation based on cash plus accounts receivable. Finally, a charge for hedging certain unacceptable exposure positions was included where what was unacceptable varied depending on the alternative strategies under evaluation.[9] The aggressive strategy was selected from among three strategies examined as the one that minimized the expected cost of the finance function, given assigned probabilities for different eventual states in the foreign exchange markets.

This example has dealt mainly with the short-term financial planning of the international firm, analogous to working capital management in traditional domestic corporation finance. It is useful to contrast this situation with operations in a single domestic environment, where, generally, there are no problems in providing financing for a given subsidiary if the parent (or the consolidated firm) has surplus cash. When facing international financing, there are limits on the mobility of funds. There are tariff rules which alter the pricing structure that can be used to move funds from subsidiary to subsidiary. There are differential tax considerations. There are absolute limits on the removal of profits and/or cash transfers between firms. There are local borrowing limits. There are exposure complexities. All of these represent restrictions that simply do not apply in the totally domestic operation. Note that even if the consolidated international firm were in total balance, external transactions for the sake of local tax and tariff considerations and the exposure situation would still be required in many cases.

Substituting in the simultaneous equations above, we have:

$$P \; (-\$8.7) + (1 - P) \; (-\$15.9)$$
$$P \; (-\$2.2) + (1 - P) \; (-\$20.4)$$

These are equal at the breakeven P. Solving for P we find $P = .41$.

Below this probability of the most likely outcome, do nothing is a superior policy on an expected value basis.

[9] Notice that the assumption is that $1 of exchange loss would be considered equivalent to $1 of interest cost. In fact, the utility of exchange losses may be different from that of interest. Thus, a firm might have Financing Option A with higher net interest costs, lower foreign exchange losses, but total cost equal to Financing Option B. Yet, Option A would be preferred by management which weighed the foreign exchange loss more heavily. This management preference could be built into the table explicitly.

There are some parallels in domestic conglomerates, where lenders to a given subsidiary and the decentralized incentive system for local managers influence cash transfers within the family, but these situations are not as constraining as most international examples.

In the preceding example we also followed a preestablished sequence of financial problems. We first solved the problem of providing incremental financing, then evaluated the impact on translation of foreign operations, and finally decided whether to cover or not and in what amount. An alternative sequence could result in different results, given that the actions under the alternative strategies would be changed. For example, if instead of the sequence used in the preceding example, the initial decision were based on creating a zero exposure in certain currencies, after which funds could be raised or deployed within a subset of the "approved" (i.e., nondevaluation-prone) currencies, then the cost/return results would differ in some cases.

In other situations, there could be restrictions on quantities of funds which can be invested or borrowed in certain currencies by particular subsidiaries. These "outer limits" could be built into the analysis, if necessary.

The issue of intracompany transactions among sister companies was avoided, forcing each subsidiary to operate in the open markets and not having access to the domestic markets of other subsidiaries' national economies. In fact, this assumption could be eased in many organizational settings. The complexity of the analysis would be increased, together with problems of incentives and organizational rewards to the various subsidiary managers whose interests in a given situation would often conflict. The "arm's length" guideline is a good operational rule for these transactions. The difficulty arises in dividing any extra savings one subsidiary realizes from having access to the domestic market of another subsidiary. Thus, the transfer price problem encountered in many firms (when one division sells a good to another division, and each division manager seeks a price which will maximize the division's profits) is encountered here as well.

Had the initial balance sheets included some debt for these three subsidiaries, then the firm would also have had the option of changing some of its debt exposure. This could have been done either by changing the currency of the debt or borrowing funds in another currency which then would be converted to the same currency as the existing debt. Either of these options might have been used under the zero exposure strategy or under possible interpretations of the aggressive strategy. The all-equity assumption in the initial balance sheets is used here for simplicity. If there had been existing debt and the firm was unwilling or unable to make changes in the currency or to borrow additional amounts for conversion to an asset which would offset the existing debt in currency, then the all-equity assumption is still valid for considering incremental costs and revenues of various strategies under various outcomes.

Ultimately, the computer models suggested would permit evaluation of a number of alternative strategies considered by management. In addition, mathematical formulations under certainty could optimize strategies given certain cost and revenue functions together with limits on the amount of funds which may be channelled around the firm. These formulations can be run under different expectations about the effective interest cost figures (pivoting on what happens to the various currencies involved), and management can see how the optimum strategy alters with various scenarios. Each formulation provides an optimum under a given scenario. Management could then evaluate each "optimum" for its return under the alternative scenarios. An "expected value" weighting system or a complex utility formulation could be introduced to aid management in finding a reasonable strategy for dealing with its currency environment.

Of course, when the one-period model above is replaced with a multiperiod analysis, the computational difficulties are vastly increased. More serious than the mathematical programming, computer programming, and computer capacity problems are the difficulties in forecasting: (1) subsidiary funds flow, (2) currency effective interest rates, and (3) currency spot and forward rates for many periods of varied lengths many years into the future. Although the use of more sophisticated analyses will increase in future years, the practicality of the forecasting is a serious obstacle.

CONCLUSION

Part Two has reviewed the instruments of foreign trade financing, evaluating the costs of some sources of funding as well as the difficulties surrounding the definition of "foreign exchange exposure." This last chapter has offered a relatively simple approach for combining costs associated with particular financing options, evaluating those costs for several popular strategies under alternative outcomes of the world. It has been suggested that the most useful approach to this problem will ultimately involve a computer simulation under many "states of the world" and/or a mathematical programming model under uncertainty, in which the optima for given states of the world are found for various scenarios and compared by the manager. Multiperiod models of analysis vastly complicate the entire cost/return evaluation. Whatever the ability of the programming staff and the computer facility, the applicability of these models has been limited in practice by the forecasting problems associated with multiple subsidiaries under various outcomes, the expected spot and forward rates at many points in the future, and the variety of possible outcomes. Some versions, however, are implemented in some corporations.

Part Three will turn to the problems associated with capital budgeting in the broader sense, analyzing the returns from projects in various nations over a longer period.

Questions

1. How does a strategy for dealing with foreign exchange risk differ from an outcome?

2. Why might a foreign exchange manager reject a strategy even though (s)he concedes it is optimal on an expected value basis?

3. Why may there be different interest rates in the local and the Euro-markets of a given currency? How can a multinational corporation take advantage of these differentials?

4. One multinational firm has a policy of making each subsidiary within a given currency area responsible for its foreign exchange losses. What are some of the costs of this strategy? How would you decide upon a better strategy? What example would you suggest as a more desirable policy for the firm?

5. "I don't care what happens to the currency vis-à-vis our parent's currency. My job is to make a profit here." If the head of your subsidiary in a country with a devaluation-prone currency had this reaction, how would you deal with it?

6. Calculate the cost of hedging shown in the text example for the opposite to likely outcome and the aggressive strategy. Show how the cost is computed.

7. Show the costs for a do nothing and a zero exposure strategy for the example given in the text. Note the description of these strategies in the text for an indication of how the calculations should be done.

Bibliography

Folks, William R., Jr., "The Optimal Level of Forward Exchange Transactions." *Journal of Financial and Quantitative Analysis,* Jan. 1973, pp. 105-110.

Heckerman, Donald, "The Exchange Risk of Foreign Operations." *Journal of Business,* Jan. 1972, pp. 42-48.

Hoyt, Newton H., Jr., "The Management of Currency Exchange Risk by the Singer Company." *Financial Management,* Spring 1972, pp. 13-20.

Lietaer, Bernard A., *Financial Management of Foreign Exchange Risk: An Operational Technique to Reduce Risk.* Cambridge, Mass.: MIT Press, 1971.

Rutenberg, David P., "Maneuvering Liquid Assets in a Multinational Company." *Management Science,* June 1970, pp. B671-B684.

Schydlowsky, Daniel, foreign exchange model described in Sidney Robbins and Robert Stobaugh, *Money in the Multinational Enterprise.* New York: Basic Books, Inc., 1973.

Shapiro, A. C. and David P. Rutenberg, "When to Hedge Against Devaluation." *Management Science,* Aug. 1974, pp. 1514-1520.

Farmatel, S. A.

In October 1972, Mr. de Chomereau, the treasurer of Farmatel, was analyzing the problems associated with the company's financial policies. Farmatel was a French company selling pharmaceutical and chemical products worldwide. During

1972, the foreign subsidiaries had increased their accounts payable to the parent company substantially, and additional large increases were planned in 1973. These increased demands on the parent company's financial resources coincided with an increase in working capital needs and a large decrease in profits at the parent company during 1972. These internal pressures promised that 1973 would be a difficult financial year. In addition, the French government had decided to follow a tight monetary policy to combat the country's high inflation rate. The amount of credit available to the economy was to be limited and the cost of short-term and medium-term credit was to be increased.

Mr. de Chomereau was wondering what might be done to improve the coordination between the financial policies of the foreign subsidiaries and the parent company to achieve a reduction in the amount and cost of financing required for the group. He was particularly puzzled by the fact that he had no financial control whatsoever over these subsidiaries. As the treasurer of Farmatel, his tasks mainly were to manage the cash position and the short- and medium-term financing of the parent in France. The subsidiaries were controlled only by Farmatel product divisions and by Farminter, the subsidiary in charge of the international operations of Farmatel. The major concern of both Farminter and the product divisions was sales growth. As a consequence, not much attention was paid to the financial practices of the subsidiaries even though their actions had a direct bearing on Farmatel's sources and uses of funds.

Company Background

Farmatel was created between the world wars by an M.D., M. Daubarede, whose research had produced some patentable products. In 1950, his son, Michel Daubarede, who had made a career within the firm, took over the presidency. Farmatel was composed of three parts: the parent operating and holding company, the French subsidiaries, and the foreign subsidiaries. Very often the ties between some of the French subsidiaries and the product divisions of the parent company were much stronger than the ties between the product divisions of the parent company. The French subsidiaries retained a higher degree of autonomy than plant or sales branches inside a divisionalized American firm. The firm was research-and-development oriented, and patents protected a high profit margin. As a result, the pressure to control subsidiaries was low. Control was mostly informal through discussions between parent company headquarters and the subsidiaries' management. A high degree of autonomy was given to the subsidiaries' top management and great reliance was placed on tradition. The decision to consolidate accounts in 1968 and the profitability crises of 1967 and 1969, however, were pushing headquarters toward an increased centralization. Since 1969, rumors of a new formal control system had been circulating at Farmatel.

Top management had pursued a consistent strategy of:

1. *Research and Development.* The firms had patented many products. More than 50% of sales were represented by products less than five years old. Between 6% and 9% of sales had been consistently allocated to R&D.

2. *Internationalization.* Exports and the creation of foreign subsidiaries were emphasized. The first foreign subsidiary, Farmatel-Brazil, had been created in 1935. By 1972, foreign sales were 54% of total sales. This policy of internation-

alization had proved to be extremely helpful during periods of instability in France, such as in 1968. The contribution of foreign operations had been fundamental to Farmatel's growth and profitability (see Exhibit 1).

3. *Diversification.* The firm's R&D capabilities were used in related fields, such as pesticides. In 1963, chemical products were 8% of total sales; by 1972, chemicals represented 20%. Furthermore, the distribution channels and the knowledge of special markets (M.D.'s, hospitals) also were used to sell other products such as medical equipment. In 1963, these miscellaneous products represented 6% of total sales; by 1972 this percentage was up to 9%.

In 1972 the major product lines accounted for the following percentages of total sales:

Drugs	53%
Therapeutic chemical products in bulk	18%
Chemicals	20%
Miscellaneous	9%

The results of this policy had been a fast and profitable growth, but relative disorder from the organizational standpoint. Total sales for the group[1] grew tenfold between 1965 and 1972, while profits increased nine times and R&D expenses fifteen times. In 1972, sales were FF 1,320,000,000 ($259,000,000), profits were FF 62,000,000 ($12,000,000), and R&D expenses were FF 121,000,000 ($24,000,000). The financing of the growth had been largely achieved through retained earnings (see Exhibit 2). In 1970, long- and short-term debt was less than 30% of total liabilities and equity.

Organization

In 1972, the parent operating and holding company sales were FF 320,000,000 ($63,000,000), French subsidiary sales were FF 370,000,000 ($72,500,000) and foreign subsidiary sales were FF 630,000,000 ($124,000,000). A diagram of the organization of the company is presented in Exhibit 3.

The Operating-Holding Company. Within the operating-holding parent company, there were three product divisions: pharmaceuticals, chemicals, and miscellaneous. Each of these divisions was then organized on a functional basis. For instance, the pharmaceutical division was split into sales and manufacturing. The sales function was itself split into two departments: specialties and active principles. Specialties were finished products; active principles were semifinished products that were to be transformed by the subsidiaries.

The French Subsidiaries. These subsidiaries were in pharmaceuticals (ten large subsidiaries), chemicals (six large subsidiaries), and medical instruments and other business (two subsidiaries). In addition, Farminter, an independent French subsidiary, operated as a sort of International Division for Farmatel. In general, the French sub-

---

[1] Farmatel sales, plus French subsidiary sales, plus foreign subsidiary sales, less intragroup sales. These same principles of consolidation apply to group profit and R&D figures.

sidiaries reported directly to the top management of Farmatel, but they communicated widely with the corresponding product divisions of the operating-holding company (e.g., subsidiaries in the chemical business with Farmatel chemical product division, and so on) or with the R&D division (for laboratories). Their financial autonomy was variable. Some of them had a fairly independent borrowing policy. Others (especially laboratories) were heavily dependent on Farmatel funds.

The Foreign Subsidiaries. The international operations of Farmatel were organized in an intricate fashion. Direct exports were channeled through Farminter. This subsidiary was the link between the product divisions of Farmatel (or the exporting French subsidiaries) and the foreign clients. To have better access to some markets, Farmatel had created several wholly owned sales subsidiaries in these markets. Some of these sales subsidiaries, like the Brazilian one, had then set up limited manufacturing or packaging operations because of tariff problems, patent necessity, or governmental pressures. The supervison of these subsidiaries had originally been given to Farminter. But the transformation in the nature of the foreign operations from free export to limited manufacturing had made it necessary to create additional links with the product divisions that sent the goods to the foreign subsidiaries. The increased coordination requirements had pushed the product divisions at Farmatel to bypass Farminter and to communicate directly with the individual managers of the foreign subsidiaries.

In case of conflict between a subsidiary and Farminter, Farmatel's top management had an arbiter's role. The line of authority between Farminter and the foreign subsidiaries was thus rather dubious. The true role of Farminter was apparently to "control" the subsidiaries, i.e., to collect reports sent by the subsidiaries, and to "discuss" with the subsidiaries when a variance in budget appeared. Farminter also had an advisory role on commercial matters. Its influence was very important in the area of direct export sales from France. The international experience of its executives was an advantage that allowed them to have a clear picture of the group situation worldwide, to detect opportunities internationally, and to discuss informally the marketing performance of subsidiaries as related to local opportunities. Farminter also played a role in the collection of royalties, and in the setting of royalty rates.

The sales departments of the French product divisions and French subsidiaries were responsible for product quality, delivery dates, selling prices, and the terms of sale (e.g., length of accounts receivable of the subsidiaries). The product divisions were anxious to have the foreign subsidiaries absorb a regular and growing volume of production since they were judged mainly in terms of sales growth, and because this contributed to the good relationships between the sales and manufacturing department (which depended on a regular and planned growth in sales).

The nature of the relationship between Farmatel and the foreign subsidiaries depended also on the size and nature of these subsidiaries. Three kinds of subsidiaries could be distinguished:

1. Export sales subsidiaries (mainly in Europe and Japan) sold Farmatel finished products.

2. Captive manufacturing subsidiaries bought active principles from Farmatel and transformed these basic materials into specialty products (Latin America, and so on).

3. Integrated subsidiaries bought bulk chemicals outside the group and transformed them into finished products (e.g., the U. K. subsidiary, which also had its own R&D facility).

The third group of subsidiaries (United Kingdom, United States, Mexico) were often large in size. They were relatively autonomous and managed by general managers who regarded Farmatel as an associate more than a parent company. These managers reported directly to the Farmatel president. Other subsidiaries generally reported to Farminter's president, although the largest ones (Brazil, Japan) were directly supervised by the Farmatel president.

Control System

The foreign subsidiaries sent detailed reports to Farminter containing:

1. Monthly sales forecasts for the next year.

2. Income statement for the current year and for the next five years.

3. Investment budget—current year and next five years.

4. Balance sheet for the current year and pro forma balance sheets for the next five years.

From these annual forecasts, Farminter computed monthly forecasts of purchases by subsidiaries, which were used by the manufacturing departments to schedule production. Farminter's second task was to compute variance between actual and budgeted figures each month and to indicate corrective actions to small subsidiaries. The focus of Farminter was mainly on commercial variables, especially sales volume.

The budget evaluation process was very simple with very little feedback from subsidiaries to headquarters during the budgeting phase. In fact, the subsidiaries' budget was not discussed as long as sales and profit showed an increase over the previous year's performance. Partly accounting for this behavior was the fact that no one at Farminter (or Farmatel) was particularly competent in international finance and accounting. The impact on the subsidiaries of different financial policies and accounting principles, of local environmental variables, or of variables such as currency parity changes was rarely considered.

The managers of the large subsidiaries reporting to the president sent the same kind of financial information as the small ones. Their sales were less carefully monitored because they had no direct impact on the sales or manufacturing operations of the parent company. Their forecasts were accepted without discussion as long as profitability and sales were growing.

Financial Policies

The situation was very different depending on the nature of the subsidiaries. Big, integrated subsidiaries were financially independent of the parent company. The managers of these subsidiaries tried not to depend on the parent company for their financing needs to avoid giving Farmatel any leverage on them. Their high profitability and the relatively low payout to Farmatel allowed them to finance their expansion from retained earnings. When external financing was necessary, they dealt with local banks with whom they had developed banking relationships for a long time. This was especially true of the U. K. subsidiary, controlled by Farmatel since 1946.

The smaller subsidiaries, buying finished products or raw materials, were much more dependent on Farmatel. An important part of their financing came from Farmatel's accounts receivable. When the had additional financial needs, they asked Farmatel for a lengthening of their credit terms or for a loan. In these cases, the decision taken by Farminter and the product departments was generally positive.

Some conflicts had arisen in the past about devaluation losses. Subsidiaries having an important volume of accounts payable to Farmatel were severely hit when a devaluation in the local currency suddenly increased the local currency value of these accounts. As a result, some had asked to be invoiced in local currency, and this change was accepted. In other cases, the burden of the devaluation had been split on a 50/50 basis between Farmatel and the subsidiary.

Mr. de Chomereau's Position

Mr. Boutrolles, the financial vice president, was responsible for determining the long-term financial policy of Farmatel. This policy included financial structure, availability of funds for major R&D investment projects, and dividend policy. Mr. de Chomereau negotiated with banks about terms of the loans and managed the short-term financial needs of Farmatel.

At the end of 1972, Mr. de Chomereau, the treasurer who reported to Mr. Boutrolles, felt very uneasy about the financial needs for the coming year. The local subsidiaries' increase in the length of accounts receivable was imposing a heavy financial strain on Farmatel. Simultaneously, the working capital requirements of Farmatel had increased due to an increase in inventories and a slight increase in domestic accounts receivable. This situation was expected to continue into 1973. Furthermore, price increases for finished products were blocked by the government, but labor and material costs were increasing steadily. Therefore, the profit margins in 1973 were expected to be lower than in 1972.

Because of governmental restrictions, it was difficult to obtain short-term loans in France. Also, the cost of Euro-dollar or Euro-mark financing was uncertain. Mr. de Chomereau had dealt with the Euro-currency market, but he was apprehensive about the reaction of Mr. Boutrolles to the high interest rate on Euro-dollars or to the eventual exchange loss from possible upvaluation of the deutsche mark or devaluation of the French franc. Furthermore, to borrow on the Euro markets was complicated by the necessity of obtaining authorization from the French government.

Taking the delicate present financial situation of Farmatel as a stimulus, Mr. de Chomereau had tried to demonstrate to Mr. Boutrolles that the financial autonomy of the subsidiaries was detrimental to the group interest. He pointed out that the sales people were not always acting in the best interest of the company by granting the subsidiaries very favorable financial terms. Mr. de Chomereau asked Mr. Boutrolles whether some form of financial coordination between different units of the group would not be an improvement over the present situation. Mr. Boutrolles' reaction had been relatively cold. He explained to Mr. de Chomereau that their task was already complicated enough, and that to advise the sales department of Farminter on such matters would make this task even more complex. Furthermore, nobody in the finance department had experience and competence in the area of international financial management. He stated that the subsidiaries were growing fast and profitably, and that it would be unwise to disturb such a satisfactory situation.

Mr. de Chomereau was annoyed by this answer. He perceived the antagonism of Mr. Boutrolles to his proposal, but he thought that Mr. Boutrolles had failed to give solid contrary arguments against a change in the actual situation. As far as expertise was concerned, he felt that he had some insight in international matters (Farmatel had borrowed two times on the Euro-dollar market—in 1967 and 1969). Anyway, he thought that worldwide financial coordination could be established progressively, allowing him to learn the intricacies of the matter. He decided to write a report using four subsidiaries as an example. This would give Mr. Boutrolles and Mr. Daubarede a basis for a realistic decision regarding the foreign operations' financial policy. If Farmatel decided to move towards financial centralization, then other factors should also be taken into account. For example, he thought the possibilities of establishing a holding company in a tax haven should be considered. According to French law, the profits of such a holding company would not have to be consolidated with the parent for tax purposes. Increased centralization also opened the door for a more tax-conscious management of transfer prices.

In the process of writing this report, Mr. de Chomereau became increasingly aware of the complexity of computing gains from worldwide financial centralization. Since the main objective of these computations was to illustrate and reinforce his standpoint, he decided to make some simplifying assumptions:

1. Half of long-term debt for the parent company and the subsidiaries was one-year debt that could be borrowed at the beginning of the year and repaid with interest at the end of the year.

2. Accounts receivable by the parent from foreign subsidiaries were in local currencies.

3. Parental tax rate (50%) should be applied to foreign subsidiaries. (The actual differences were not so high if taxes on remittances were included. Furthermore, local profits were to be eventually repatriated.)

4. Inventories of foreign subsidiaries were not exposed to exchange risk, for a change in parity was in general matched by a roughly equal change in price.

5. Since Farmatel consolidation was not for tax purposes, foreign exchange losses were not tax deductible and foreign exchange gains were not taxable.

With these assumptions in mind, Mr. de Chomereau decided to estimate the optimum financing for 1973 using the cost figures (interest, taxes, and so on) for the end of 1972, and to compute the overall savings for the group of a more centralized financial policy.

Data on the selected subsidiaries and their countries are presented in Exhibits 4 through 7.

EXHIBIT 1 FARMATEL S.A.: Financial Data on Foreign Subsidiaries, 1972

Country of Incorporation	% of Ownership	Sales	Profit (Loss)	Dividends to Farmatel	Purchases From Farmatel and French Subsidiaries		
					Finished Products	Semifinished or Raw Materials	Royalties
West Germany	100	$ 4,500	$ 250	–	$ 200	$ 270	$ 180
Belgium	100	2,000	80	$ 60	600	1,500	60
Spain	90	5,000	400	–	–	2,500	70
Italy	100	8,900	150	30	–	5,100	450
Portugal	90	2,000	200	–	–	700	110
United Kingdom	95	58,000	3,900	–	900	3,300	2,300
Argentina	55	2,900	50	–	–	2,100	200
Brazil	100	5,700	(200)	–	–	3,800	–
Mexico	80	13,300	507	–	–	2,000	600
Peru	70	4,900	50	45	–	1,700	350
Uruguay	100	1,000	60	–	–	560	55
Venezuela	100	2,900	150	–	–	2,000	–
India	60	400	(5)	–	–	60	–
Japan	100	10,000	(280)	–	6,000	1,000	–
Vietnam	100	1,500	(150)	–	–	900	–
Thailand	100	20	1	–	–	12	–
United States	100	5,000	150	30	–	15	–
		$128,020	$5,313	$165	$7,700	$27,517	$4,375
Direct Export (Farminter)		18,000					

EXHIBIT 2   FARMATEL S.A.: Unconsolidated Balance Sheets 1969/1973 (million dollars; translation rate: 1$ = FF5.10)

Assets

	1969	1970	1971	1972	1973 Forecast
Fixed Assets	$160	$171	$189	$211	$237
Accumulated depreciation	48	63	74	89	110
Net fixed assets	112	108	115	122	127
Long-term loans and equity investment in subsidiaries	68	73	77	101	106
Inventories	20	22	27	40	58
Accounts receivable	19	24	28	39	67
Cash	6	2	1	2	1
Total	$225	$229	$248	$304	$359

Liabilities

	1969	1970	1971	1972	1973 Forecast
Common stock	$ 30	$ 30	$ 30	$ 40	$ 40
Reserves and retained earnings	160	165	172	187	191
Long-term debt	12	9	8	27	113
Short-term debt	13	14	29	38	
Accounts payable	10	11	9	12	15
Total	$225	$229	$248	$304	$359

Source: Disguised company data.

EXHIBIT 3   FARMATEL S. A.: Organization Chart

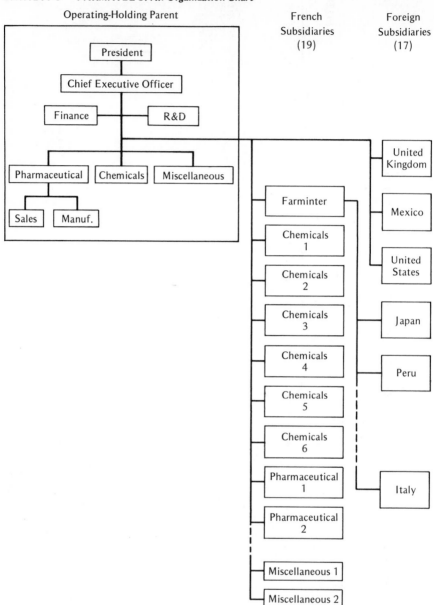

EXHIBIT 4 FARMATEL S.A.: Balance Sheets—Selected Subsidiaries (thousands of dollars)

1. United Kingdom (Pound @ $2.34/Pound)

Assets	1972	1973 (Forecast)	Liabilities	1972	1973 (Forecast)
Fixed Assets	$30,900	$32,800	Common stock	$ 7,000	$ 7,000
Accumulated depreciation	9,600	10,100			
			Reserves and retained earnings	21,100	23,400
Net fixed assets	21,300	22,700			
Inventories	6,600	6,800			
			Long-term debt	7,500	7,100
Accounts receivable					
Other Farmatel subsidiaries	5,600	4,700	Short-term debt	4,900	3,000
Others	7,300	7,500			
Cash	2,100	1,200	Accounts payable	2,400	2,400
Total	$42,900	$42,900	Total	$42,900	$42,900

2. Germany (DM @ 3.20 DM/$)

Assets	1972	1973 (Forecast)	Liabilities	1972	1973 (Forecast)
Fixed Assets	$ 2,300	$ 2,300	Common stock	$ 400	$ 400
Accumulated depreciation	1,000	1,000	Reserves and retained earnings	900	1,000
Net fixed assets	1,300	1,300			
			Long-term debt	600	700
Inventories	400	500			
			Short-term debt	100	100
Accounts receivable	300	400			
Cash	100	100	Accounts payable	100	100
Total	$ 2,100	$ 2,300	Total	$ 2,100	$ 2,300

3. Italy (Lira @ 582.5 Lira/$)

Assets	1972	1973 (Forecast)	Liabilities	1972	1973 (Forecast)
Fixed assets	$ 429	$ 438	Common stock	$ 343	$ 343
Accumulated depreciation	34	34	Reserves and retained earnings	206	326
Net fixed assets	395	403	Long-term debt	670	644
Inventories	635	687	Short-term debt	275	258
Accounts receivable	1,785	2,077	Accounts payable (Farmatel)		
Cash	21	17		1,342	1,614
Total	$2,836	$3,185	Total	$2,836	$3,185

4. Brazil (Cruzeiro @ 6.21 (Cz/$)

Assets	1972	1973 (Forecast)	Liabilities	1972	1973 (Forecast)
Fixed assets	$ 177	$ 242	Common stock	$ 81	$ 80
Accumulated depreciation	19	24	Reserve and retained earnings	290	129
			Long-term debt		
Net fixed assets	158	217	Farmatel	161	274
			Others	80	—
Inventories	338	548			
			Short-term debt	110	145
Accounts receivable	950	1,304	Accounts payable		
			Farmatel	709	1,409
Cash	32	48	Others	48	81
Total	$1,478	$2,118	Total	$1,478	$2,118

EXHIBIT 5   Cost of Borrowing (End 1972)

	Central Bank Discount Rate	(Prime Borrowers) Call	Short-Term	Long-Term
France	7.5	7.5	8.0	8.4
Germany	4.5	6.	8.75	8.5
Italy	4.0	—	8.0	8.5
United Kingdom	8.0	9.	9.0	9.5
Brazil	12./24	—	34.	36.
Euro $	—	7.	6.25	7.5
Euro Pound	—	—	10.25	9.75

Source: Morgan Guaranty Trust Company, *World Financial Markets.* various issues.

EXHIBIT 6   Exchange Rates, 1971 and 1972

		1971	1972 I	II	III	IV
French Franc/$	Spot	5.53	5.028	5.002	5.012	5.125
3-month forward		5.44	5.028	4.994	5.002	5.150
Deutsche mark/$	Spot	3.31	3.168	3.150	3.202	3.202
3-month forward		3.31	3.152	3.125	3.178	3.188
Italian Lira/$	Spot	612	582.5	580.75	581.88	582.50
$/U. K. Pound[a]	Spot	2.48	2.615	2.44	2.42	2.34
3-month forward		2.48	2.61	2.42	2.40	2.32
Brazil[b] Cruzeiro/$	Spot	5.50	5.845	5.915	6.025	6.215

[a]For the United Kingdom, unlike all other countries, the exchange rate is given in dollar per unit of national currency (and not in units of national currency per dollar).

[b]Between 1967 and 1972, the value of the dollar in terms of cruzeiros went from a basis of 100 to 217 ($\sim$ 25% depreciation/year).

EXHIBIT 7 Tax Rates and Exchange Controls (End 1972)

	Corporate Tax	Tax on Dividends, Royalties Paid	Maximum Remittances	Other Exchange Control
France	50%	No	No limit in theory.	Transfer of funds (other than for imports)[a] has to be authorized by Finance Ministry.
Germany	52.53% (undistributed profit) 15.45% (distributed profit)	50% of royalties added to taxable income	Should be "fair"; maximum around 10%.	No
Italy	38.39%	Royalties: 16.5% tax Dividends: 30% tax	No limit in theory.	If remittances less than 8% capital: exchange at official rate; if amount greater than 8%: use "account in lira" (more expensive).
United Kingdom	40%	Royalties: 0% tax Dividends: 15% tax	No limit in theory.	No
Brazil	30% (undistributed profit) 35% (distributed profit)	Royalties: 25% tax Dividends: 25% tax Interest: 25% tax	Royalties should be less than 5% of sales. If three year average remittances are greater than 12% of equity, then there is an additional tax on the amount greater than 12%. Tax is usually around 40% to 60%. Management fees should be less than 5% of sales.	In balance of payments "emergency," remittances may be limited to 10% of capital.

[a] Or debt amortization, dividends, royalties.

Sola Chemical Company [1]

ORGANIZING THE INTERNATIONAL FINANCE FUNCTION

The year was 1970. The subject before Sola Chemical's board of directors was a set of proposals by Multinational Consultants, Inc., recommending a drastic overhaul in the organization of Sola's overseas business. The board had already agreed, albeit a bit uncertainly, that the International Division would have to be abolished and that its responsibilities for overseas production and overseas marketing be distributed among some new regional divisions. Now the question was: What to do about the finance and control functions for which the International Division had been responsible?

Origins

Ever since World War II, Sola had been doing what came naturally in the expansion of its foreign business. In the years just after the war, Sola thought of itself as one of five or six companies that made up the leadership in the industrial and agricultural chemicals industry in the United States. At that time, a company with annual sales of $150 million could claim a leadership position. Besides, sales of the company at that time were reasonably well concentrated in only four main product groups. From the perspective of 1970, after nearly twenty-five years of growth and diversification into new products and markets, operations in the immediate postwar period seemed extraordinarily neat and tidy.

In the first years after the war, the foreign business of Sola was limited. Historically it had consisted of the sales that a small export department could drum up in Western Europe and Latin America, relying largely on commission merchants, wholesalers, and industrial buyers in those areas. From time to time, Sola would discover that one of its newer products had taken hold in some country, generally at a time five or six years after it had found a market in the United States. After a few years of expansion in any foreign market, however, the attractiveness of the particular line in the area would generally fall away as quietly as it had appeared.

Apart from the seemingly episodic and sporadic lines of business of this sort, Sola's main "foreign" commitment in the years up to World War II was a manufacturing subsidiary in Canada, a subsidiary that Sola had set up in the late 1920s in response to a sharp increase in Canada's industrial tariffs. Except for a few shares nominally held by Canadian directors, this subsidiary was wholly owned by Sola. When the Imperial Preference tariff system was established in 1932, the Sola management had congratulated itself on its foresight in establishing a subsidiary inside the Commonwealth so that it could meet British competitors such as Imperial Chemical Industries on equal terms. From Sola management's viewpoint, however, the Canadian subsidiary could hardly be called "foreign." Situated not far from

---

[1] This case is based on interviews conducted under the direction of R. B. Stobaugh as part of the Harvard multinational enterprise study. The case itself was prepared by Raymond Vernon.

Windsor, Ontario, it was close enough to Sola's midwest headquarters to be run like any other branch plant. The product policies and marketing policies of Sola seemed to apply about as well to the Canadian plant as any other. True, there were some occasional crises of an unfamiliar sort, as when the Canadians tinkered with the value of their currency in relation to the U. S. dollar, or when they set up unfamiliar provisions in relation to the taxation of profits. But an occasional consultation with the company's bankers and tax attorneys was generally sufficient to deal with crises of this sort.

Quite different from Sola's relationship to its Canadian subsidiary in the years immediately after World War II were its ties to a French subsidiary which had been set up at about the same time. Unlike the Canadian subsidiary, only 53% of the equity of this company was owned by Sola, the rest being in the hands of Cie. Chimie Tricolor, a leading French manufacturer whose product lines fell largely within two of Sola's four product groups. Nobody at Sola could quite recall how this particular liaison had first developed. But there was an impression that Sola had been confronted with an ultimatum by the French chemical industry at one point in the 1920s: either it must invite a French business interest to join it in the creation of a French manufacturing subsidiary or it must risk losing a lucrative market that was being supplied by exports from the United States. There was some recollection among Sola's oldtimers that the ultimatum had been backed up by hints from the French ministry of industry that the threats might not prove hollow. In any event, whatever the origins of the French partnership might be, the subsidiary had grown away from Sola over the years. By the late 1940s it was thought of as almost an independent entity, operating under the stewardship of the French partner and negotiating with Sola for product information and technology very much on an arm's-length basis.

So much for the situation at the beginning of the postwar era.

Between that time and 1970, the foreign business of Sola had expanded at an astonishing rate, considerably faster than the business in the United States. And as the foreign business grew, not only the policies and strategies but even the very structure of Sola was greatly affected. Step by step, additional locations had been selected for the establishment of new manufacturing subsidiaries: the United Kingdom in 1952; Germany in 1955; Mexico in 1956; Brazil in 1960; Italy in 1962; Australia in 1965; and so on, until Sola's manufacturing facilities covered fifteen different countries. At the same time, operations in Canada had been considerably expanded, covering more of Sola's product lines. In each of these cases, Sola had preferred to go it alone, without local partners. And after a nasty confrontation or two with the French partners over the management of the French facility, a friendly divorce had been arranged, leaving Sola with a wholly owned manufacturing facility in France in lieu of the old partnership.

Although Sola had not set up more than a portion of the U. S. product line in any one country, the total number of products manufactured overseas was widening every year. In fact, there were even three or four cases in which the U. S. plants had suspended operations on an old staple item, assigning what was left of the business to one of the foreign facilities where the product still seemed to command a market. When that happened, the foreign facility took over Sola's third country markets as well.

While the manufacturing subsidiaries were spreading over the globe, Sola was setting up other units to facilitate the handling of its foreign business. Sola had discovered very early the tax advantages of a Western Hemisphere trade corporation and had set up a company in Delaware to qualify under the U. S. tax code. A corporation could qualify if it derived practically all its income from trade or business (as distinguished from investment), and confined its business to the Western Hemisphere outside the United States. The profits of such a corporation were taxed at a rate 14 percentage points less than the standard U. S. rate. To exploit this advantage, U. S. Sola billed its exports to Western Hemisphere countries from the United States through its Western Hemisphere trade corporation. As a rule, such exports were billed out by U. S. Sola to the trade corporation at the lowest possible appropriate figure, which Sola calculated in accordance with a formula that included an 8% mark-up over cost. This formula had the effect of placing most of the profit on such sales in the trade corporation.

Other arrangements to minimize taxes had been made as well. Back in 1958, before the Revenue Act of 1962 had restricted the use of foreign-based holding companies as "tax havens"—that is, as vehicles for postponing the payment of U. S. taxes on foreign income—Sola's treasurer and tax attorney had pushed through the establishment of a Swiss holding company. U. S. Sola owned Sola-Switzerland, which in turn held nominal ownership over Sola's subsidiaries outside the United States. In those days, Sola-Switzerland could perform all kinds of useful services for U. S. Sola. For one thing, like the Western Hemisphere trade corporation, it could act as an intermediary in export sales from the United States. When Sola-Switzerland was used as an intermediary, the tax benefits to U. S. Sola were rather different from those associated with the use of the Western Hemisphere company. Sola-Switzerland's profits were subject to normal tax rates once they got into the U. S. tax jurisdiction. But that did not occur until the profits were declared to U. S. Sola in the form of dividends. Meanwhile, Sola-Switzerland could shuttle the cash generated by export profits to any point in the Sola system that required it.

Sola-Switzerland's cash flow could be built up not only by exports but also by the dividends, royalties, interest, and fees generated in the Sola subsidiaries that Sola-Switzerland nominally owned. As long as Swiss law did not tax the income of the Swiss holding company and as long as U. S. law did not classify the funds as taxable in the United States, Sola-Switzerland was a highly useful mechanism.

That particular arrangement had deferred quite a lot of tax payments for a few years. Subsidiaries could declare dividends and could pay interest, agency fees, administrative charges, and royalties to the holding company without subjecting the income to U. S. taxation; the U. S. tax bite would come only when the income moved upstream as dividends to the U. S. parent. Although the U. S. system of tax credits on foreign-earned income ensured that the income would not be taxed twice when it finally appeared on the U. S. parent's books, still there was something to be gained at times from deferring the U. S. tax. The tax advantage was especially important when the subsidiary's payments to its parent had not been taxed locally because they represented expenses to the subsidiary, or when the subsidiary's income had been taxed at rates well below those in the United States. In those situations, when the payments finally were received as dividends in the United States, some U. S. taxes would be due.

When the Internal Revenue Code was amended in 1962 to restrict the use of tax haven companies, many of the tax advantages involved in the maintenance of such a company disappeared. The provisions that expose the income of such tax haven companies to U. S. taxation are exceedingly complex. But Sola's Swiss holding company clearly fell within its terms. It was controlled by U. S. Sola, and it derived more than 70% of its income from the dividends, interest, royalties, and other fees received from Sola's operating subsidiaries located in third countries. Accordingly, the income of Sola-Switzerland was fully taxable under U. S. law just as if it had been paid directly to U. S. Sola itself.

One tax advantage associated with foreign holding companies still remained, however. Loath to discourage exports from the United States in any way, Congress had exempted from the new provisions such income as the tax haven companies were garnering from their role in the handling of U. S. exports. As long as a spread could exist between the price at which U. S. Sola invoiced its goods for export and the price at which the goods were invoiced for import in the foreign country of destination, there were still tax advantages in assigning the spread to an intermediate company located in a tax-free area.

Despite the fact that Sola-Switzerland had lost much of its original purpose, there was some hesitation about liquidating the Swiss company. It would entail the transfer of the equity of many underlying operating subsidiaries, the transfer of the Swiss company's claims to the long-term and short-term debt of some of the operating subsidiaries, and the shift of the Swiss company's title in patents and trade names abroad that were being licensed to the subsidiaries. Numerous contractual ties between the Swiss company and the subsidiaries also would have to be dissolved, such as the right of the Swiss company to receive payment for administrative and technical services and for sales agency services. All these rearrangements were bound to generate administrative and legal problems in a number of different countries, where the increasing curiosity and sophistication of the regulatory authorities could be counted on to stir up difficulties.

Accordingly, Sola decided to leave the Swiss holding company in existence and to create several other intermediate companies besides. One would be a Luxembourg company, set up to capture some of the profits on U. S. exports, which still were entitled to tax deferral treatment. Another enterprise would be set up to segregate the income generated by subsidiaries in advanced countries. Under the 1962 law income originating in subsidiaries in the less developed areas, unlike income from the advanced countries, could still be kept beyond the reach of U. S. tax collectors to the extent that it was reinvested in less developed areas. Accordingly, a holding company was set up in Curacao to own Sola's subsidiaries in less developed areas and to receive the income of such subsidiaries for routing to destinations where the income was needed. Curacao's virtue as a holding company headquarters consisted *inter alia* of its willingness to leave such income virtually untaxed as it passed through the holding company on its way to a new destination.

As if this complex cluster of intermediate companies was not enough, Sola decided in 1966 that another intermediate structure would be useful, namely, a holding company created under the laws of Delaware to act as Sola's alter ego in floating bond issues in the European market.

Well before 1966, it was clear to U. S. Sola that its European subsidiaries' voracious appetite would have to be fed by more borrowing from abroad. Sola itself was under a handicap when raising money in Europe, because U. S. internal revenue requirements obliged it to withhold 30% of interest or dividend payments to non-resident recipients. That provision placed a heavy handicap on the securities of U. S. issuers in Europe. Sola's Swiss holding company had been used two or three times before as the nominal borrower of dollar-denominated funds from European sources. Operating under the umbrella of a guarantee from U. S. Sola, the Swiss holding company had been able to borrow medium-term money at reasonable rates from private European sources. Though the interest costs had run a little higher than they would have in the United States, these flotations had saved the bother of registration with the Securities and Exchange Commission, the problem of qualification under the "blue sky" laws of the state regulatory agencies, and so on; the difference in costs, therefore, was not as great as the interest rates indicated. At the same time, Sola had developed some excellent European banking ties that might help out in the event that the U. S. government really clamped down on the export of capital from the United States. As early as 1958 or 1959, that contingency had become something to worry about, as U. S. officials began to express their misgivings over the condition of the U. S. balance of payments.

By 1965, contingency had turned to reality. "Voluntary" controls had been imposed over the outflow of funds from the United States to subsidiaries in Europe. Although the controls were very loose and left many different ways in which Sola could arrange for the generation of cash flows in its overseas subsidiaries, Sola tried to respond to the spirit of the regulations by raising a larger proportion of its needed funds outside the United States.

One possible step to that end was to continue using the Swiss holding company, as it had been used in the past, to borrow from European sources. But Sola was not eager to expand the use of the Swiss holding company, now that it had lost most of its usefulness as a tax haven. True, such a holding company still had some advantages that U. S. Sola did not share, such as the fact that its payments of dividend and interest to non-U. S. recipients were not subject to the reporting and withholding requirements of U. S. tax law. But the use of such a company also had some disadvantages when compared with a Delaware company, such as the fact that losses, if any, could not be consolidated in U. S. Sola's income tax return in the United States.

The upshot was that Sola decided in 1966 to create a second Delaware holding company, with functions carefully designed to retain the advantages of a Swiss holding company as a financing intermediary while avoiding some of its disabilities. The main purpose of the second Delaware holding company was to borrow funds outside the United States with the guarantee of U. S. Sola and to lend those funds to Sola's foreign subsidiaries. As long as the new holding company confined itself to this sort of operation, its only significant income—namely, interest payments from the subsidiaries—was regarded as of foreign origin. Since 80% or more of its income was of foreign origin, the Delaware company, like the Swiss company, was not required to withhold any sums in connection with interest payments to non-U. S. recipients. Such profits as the Delaware company might have were within the reach of the U. S. and Delaware tax jurisdiction. But profits were likely to be trivial, given the purpose of the company. Besides, Delaware tax provisions were traditionally benign in such matters, and U. S. tax provisions, ever since the adoption of the 1962 amendments, made only small distinctions between the profits of domestic holding companies and those of foreign holding companies of U. S. taxpayers.

The creation of the Delaware finance company proved to be a very wise step indeed. On January 1, 1968, the so-called "voluntary" program of capital export controls became mandatory. At the same time, the program was tightened up so that the various alternative means of transferring funds abroad became more restricted. Under the new program, Sola's right to transfer funds abroad was tied to its historical record of investment in the years just prior to 1968. Investment for that base period was defined as capital transfers in cash or in kind made to foreign subsidiaries plus profits retained in the subsidiaries during the period. Once that base figure was calculated, its application was variously defined for different groups of countries. Subsidiaries in the less developed countries, the "Schedule A" countries, were allowed to continue receiving investment from U. S. Sola at their old levels, even a little higher. There was also a "Schedule B" group, which the U. S. regulators thought of as being especially dependent on U. S. capital flows—the oil countries, the United Kingdom, Japan, and a few other areas. Added investments from the United States in these areas was cut down but not eliminated; capital flows to these areas were restricted to 65% of the base period. Canada, originally in this group, was exempted from the regulations altogether.

The real problem for Sola, therefore, was financing the European subsidiaries, that is, the subsidiaries located in "Schedule C" countries. Drastic cuts were made here. At first, added investment from U. S. Sola could only take place through retained earnings. Even the retained earnings could not be used under the rules if this meant a retention rate higher than base period rates or if it meant an investment rate higher than 35% of the base period.

If it had not been for the fact that borrowings outside the United States were exempted from the restrictions, Sola would have been in real trouble at first. That exemption carried the company through 1968. And in 1969 and 1970, the restrictions were eased somewhat. But the experience impressed on the minds of Sola's management more than ever the need to have an intimate knowledge of the world's sources of capital and to have the flexibility in organization to use the sources as needed. This heightened recognition centered attention on just how decisions were taken on such matters inside the organization.

The Financial Organization

As Sola expanded its overseas operations, the legal instrumentalities and national environments that concerned it increased rapidly in number. From World War II until 1970, therefore, there was a constant need to restructure the internal organization and procedures that were responsible for formulating and executing financial policies and for controlling financial operations. That restructuring was tied in intimately, of course, with other changes in Sola's organization, including changes in the marketing and production systems associated with a growing overseas operation.

In the early 1960s, the foreign business had grown to such proportions that it was thought advisable to create an international division. The first executive in charge of that division, an aggressive and ambitious manager, decided that one of his major needs was to pull together the haphazard structure which up to that time had been formulating financial policy for the foreign areas. With the approval of Sola's top management, therefore, a new structure was created. Some of the essential elements of the organization tying together the financial function at that stage are suggested by the diagram in Exhibit 1. A word or two of elaboration is needed in order to relate this chart of Sola's structure in the early 1960s to financial decisions taken at that time.

EXHIBIT 1   Financial Offices in the Structure of Sola Company, 1962

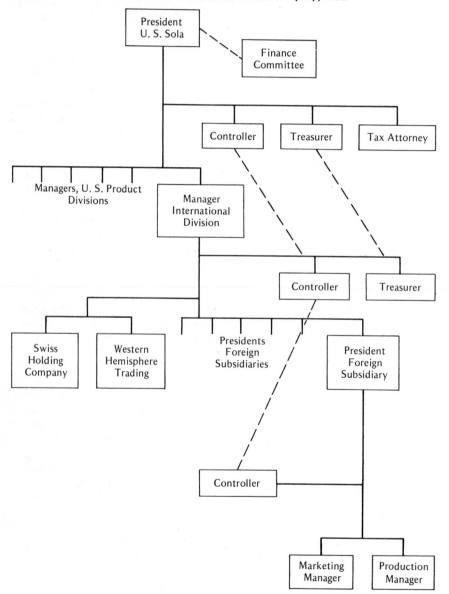

Major investment decisions, such as decisions to create a new foreign subsidiary or substantially to increase its capitalization, were generally recommended in the first instance by the international manager to Sola's president; he, in turn, usually sought the advice of his board of directors, as well as the advice of many other sources.

Major policies aimed at reducing taxes on overseas operations were usually initiated by the international treasurer, discussed with U. S. Sola's treasurer and tax attorney, then cleared with the finance committee.

Policies with regard to borrowing by foreign subsidiaries were no problem. Apart from accounts payable and accrued liabilities and except for a rare local loan initiated by the international treasurer, such transactions did not arise. Subsidiaries were not authorized to borrow; indeed they were not thought of as managing their own cash flow. Funds were channelled to the subsidiaries by the international treasurer as needed. Before 1965 these funds had come mainly from the parent or the Swiss holding company, in the form of short-term dollar debt. Later on, after the Delaware company was formed and had begun to raise dollars through the sale of Eurobonds, it became the principal creditor for Sola's foreign subsidiaries.

Apart from decisions on whether and how to provide the subsidiaries with their working capital needs, the other major area of financial operating policy was the withdrawal of funds from a subsidiary that held surplus cash. In this case, the main problem was viewed as minimizing the tax burden associated with withdrawal, and the main policy variable was the choice between dividends, royalties, interest and management fees. That choice was made by the tax attorney, on the basis of data provided by the international treasurer.

The international controller, as Exhibit 1 suggests, bore a somewhat different relation to the organization than the treasurer. Unlike the treasurer, the controller had representatives in each of the subsidiaries. This difference reflected the fact that the treasurer saw his function as that of managing the money flows of the system, whereas the controller saw his function as that of monitoring the performance of its various parts. The first function, so it seemed, could be performed well enough from the bridge of the enterprise, whereas the second function required getting down into the various holds below.

Proposals for Reorganization

As a rule, the international treasurer's problems were not the sort of subject that got discussed very much among Sola's directors. When a major investment abroad was involved, that of course was fairly well explored. But most discussion involved questions of strategy, rather than financing and cash flow problems. These were left pretty much for the finance committee and the treasurer's office to worry about. As far as the finance committee was concerned, that group freely admitted that its ability to second-guess the treasurer's office on overseas financing was quite limited. The subject was just too specialized, it appeared. And so, the international treasurer proved to be performing a vital function.

Fortunately for Sola Chemical, it had filled that post very well indeed. Milray Thaler had been international treasurer ever since 1958 when the post was first created. He had come out of the old export department, seasoned by years of selling in a world of inconvertible currencies. He had learned all about the ways in which blocked currencies could be turned into usable cash, and ways in which avoidable taxes could be avoided. As international treasurer, he ran a tight organization. He kept close touch with the problems of every subsidiary, especially their problems of cash flow. As far as he could see, the foreign subsidiaries had been well provided for, without having to worry about money and credit questions for which they were hardly equipped. And as far as taxes were concerned, the foreign side of Sola had done marvellously well in avoiding the avoidable.

Despite that fact, by 1970 the financial organization was showing certain signs of strain. By that time, Thaler's unflagging efforts to hold down taxes and to generate money where it was most needed had made a shambles of the periodic profit and loss statements of the subsidiaries. The U. S. system of controls over the export of funds to subsidiaries had increased the complexities of financing. The objective of holding down the total tax bill was now constrained by restrictions on the outflow of capital from the United States. The importance of distinguishing between the treatment of subsidiaries in different countries also was increasing. The differences between less developed countries and advanced countries, and between countries in Schedules A, B, and C, were important. Added wrinkles, such as Canada's special status under the U. S. capital export control program, had to be kept in mind. The difficulties were heightened further by the fact that some countries, especially the United States and Germany, were beginning to take seriously their various fiscal provisions relating to the international pricing of goods and services. Provisions such as Section 482 of the U. S. Internal Revenue Code, authorizing the tax authorities to use arm's-length prices in interaffiliate transactions, were beginning to be applied seriously. Thaler's consultations with the tax people and his demands on Sola's treasurer were constantly rising in number and urgency.

In addition, Thaler's difficulties with the controller's area seemed on the increase. The more strenuous the efforts of the treasurer, the more difficult the problem of the controller. If the reported profit and loss statements of the manufacturing subsidiaries could be taken at face value, most of them were operating at practically no profit; the only exception was the subsidiary in Canada. What actually was happening depended on what the word "actually" meant. Profits were appearing in the Western Hemisphere trading company, in the Swiss holding company, and in the holding companies in Luxembourg and Curacao. Whether these profits were "actual" or not depended on what one thought of the validity of the prices charged for products traded among the affiliates, as well as the royalty charges and administrative fees. Sometimes there was a basis for testing these prices and fees against analogous arm's-length transactions. But more often, the goods or services involved were sufficiently distinctive so that no independent arm's-length standard could readily be found, assuming an effort were made to find one.

On top of this problem was the fact that Sola's subsidiaries in Europe, facing the elimination of trade barriers in the EEC and EFTA, found themselves competing in one another's territory with similar product lines. Here and there, the problem had been reduced by the timely intervention of the international manager. Once or twice, where specialty items were involved, the subsidiaries had agreed to allocate production tasks between them without bothering to involve the international office. In situations of that sort, the transfer price was fixed according to the bargaining strength of each subsidiary and the transaction was recorded as if it were undertaken with an outside vendor. But as the number of subsidiaries and the number of product lines kept rising, this *ad hoc* approach was beginning to prove inadequate.

For the controllers in the local subsidiaries, all these problems presented growing headaches. The performance reports were beginning to make less and less sense, unless adjusted in various ways. Adjustments, however, required the refereeing role of the international controller when it involved a decision affecting the relative performance of two foreign subsidiaries, and it required the involvement of U. S. Sola's controller when the decision affected the U. S. company's reported performance. As a result of the accumulation of decision rules arising out of these adjudications, controllers' reports were beginning to bear less and less relation to the financial statements.

With these considerations and others in mind, Multinational Consultants, Inc., a prominent international consulting firm, was called in to advise on the reorganization of Sola's foreign business. After studying the operations of the company for a number of months, Multinational Consultants produced a voluminous report covering the problems of the foreign side of Sola's business. Among other things, it had a number of observations regarding the operation of the financial function, observations that boiled down to three propositions:

1. The treasurer's function had become much too complex and diffuse to be managed effectively from the center. Opportunities were being missed and errors committed. Among the errors cited, for instance, was the failure of the international treasurer to develop a systematic policy toward the threat of currency fluctuations. The opportunities missed as a result of the absence of such a policy were not the sort that were necessarily visible in Sola's financial statements. But once in a while, missed opportunities could be detected. One of these was the failure to hedge against a sterling devaluation in 1967, when the likelihood of the devaluation seemed extraordinarily high; this alleged oversight was said to have cost the company $350,000 in translation losses. Other opportunities overlooked, according to MCI, were those inherent in the possibilities for borrowing in local markets. The tight cash flow controls from headquarters, MCI guessed, reduced the likelihood that such opportunities were being recognized and exploited.

2. The treasurer was much too preoccupied with tax savings and too little concerned with reducing the cost of funds.

3. The financial data essential for the use of the treasurer's office was markedly different from the data needed for the performance of the controller's function, more so than in the case of complex operations within the United States proper. This difference was due to the fact that the units of Sola were in so many different jurisdictions with different rules covering taxation, access to capital, and so on. Essentially, the controller would be obliged to develop a separate score card, gauging the performance of profit centers on the basis of data that were compiled primarily for control purposes.

As a first step toward achieving the needed shifts in direction, Multinational Consultants, Inc., proposed a number of major organizational changes. It was proposed that the international division should be broken up into several foreign area divisions, each of which would have status on a par with a U. S. product division. The international treasurer and the international controller would be moved upstairs into the offices of Sola's treasurer and controller respectively. A new layer of treasurers, controllers, and tax attorneys would be created at the area division level.

Under the new system, the lowest control center on the foreign side would be a given product line in a given area. Where more than one subsidiary in an area was involved in the product, the control center would combine the activities in the product of all such subsidiaries. Presumably, the treasurer could not ignore the performance of the subsidiary, since that performance would affect its tax liability. But for the controller's needs, an area-product approach to performance would be taken. Exhibit 2 indicates how the financial offices would sit in the revised Sola structure after reorganization.

Practically everyone on the foreign side of the Sola organization reacted to the proposals with some degree of hostility or reserve. The international manager saw himself as risking a major demotion: either he would be moved upstairs into the staff of Sola's president, or would be placed at the head of the "Europe and Africa" area. In either case, his status would be a notch lower. Of all the officers reacting to the change, however, it was Milray Thaler, the international treasurer, who felt most threatened.

Thaler was furious at the report of Multinational Consultants. A few days after it had been circulated in Sola, Thaler produced a twenty-six page reply, refuting the report point by point. Some of the extracts from his rebuttal were especially provocative.

. . . . .

2. Of course, the international side of the treasurer's function is growing more complicated. Governments get smarter every day. Regulations get more complicated. With Section 482 on one side and the Office of Foreign Direct Investment on the other, it is not easy to do business abroad. But what kind of an answer is MCI offering us? To set up a treasurer in every area, so one area doesn't know what the other is doing? Who will tell German-Sola to stop trying to make a record for itself by gouging Argentine-Sola with its high invoice prices for petrochemicals? And who will stop the subsidiaries from always trying to build up their equity, instead of building up accounts payable? Much better to give me a few more high-level assistants who have had a little experience with such complicated matters so that we can stay on top of such problems.

3. Maybe production and marketing need some decentralizing at the regional level. After all, the users of industrial chemicals in Nairobi are not exactly the same types you find in Hamburg or Rio. But the management of money is another matter; that should be centralized. Money is money once you get it out of the clutches of a country and make it convertible. A dollar out of Peru is a dollar out of Turkey, and it ought to be managed that way.

. . . . .

5. How would a regional treasurer know how to use the Curacao or Luxembourg companies, or why? Today, if Sola-Switzerland needs to pay a dividend to U. S. Sola, I can easily drum up the money by way of Curacao. I can do it because I

EXHIBIT 2   Financial Offices in Proposed Reorganization of Sola Company, 1970

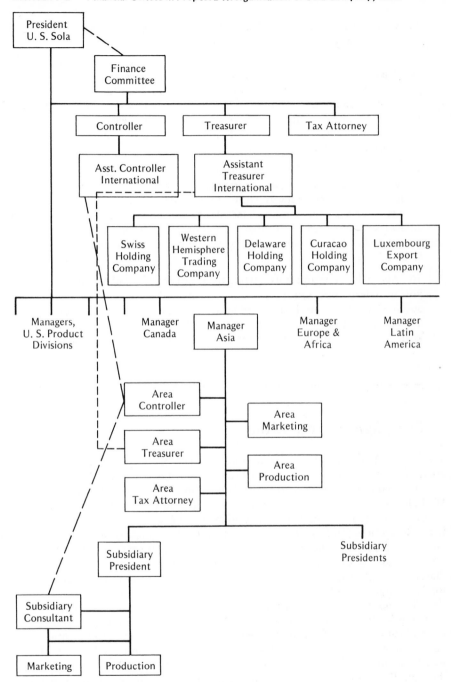

know just what to expect in Curacao and I know how to compare it with Berne's cash flow prospects.

. . . . .

14. That famous $350,000 translation loss from the devaluation of sterling is getting a little ridiculous. Translation losses are not money, they are bookkeeping. They mean nothing to Sola's cash flow. Tax payments are a different matter. Real money can be saved there. If I were to worry about every currency that might devalue tomorrow, I would eat up the time of the company and the office chasing paper butterflies.

15. Once the controller starts making up his own score card and the treasurer makes up a separate one, it will be impossible to know where we stand. The controller has everything he needs, without the headaches of a special set of books, if he gets copies of the treasurer's instructions to the subsidiaries. If he wants to adjust his records because of these instructions, so that the effect of tax transactions and cash flow transactions are cancelled out, it is easy enough for him to do it.

16. Above all, once you start putting the profit centers in the regional offices, you are a dead duck. Europe is not yet a country. Neither is Latin America. The authorities in the central banks and in the national tax administrations are not about to give up their powers and go away. These are the offices you have to keep your eye on if you are going to survive in the international business.

Burroughs Corporation

In April 1971, Mr. Charles Exley, Vice-President of Finance for Burroughs Corporation, was reviewing the financial situation facing the company. Despite confirmed forecasts that both domestic and foreign growth in 1971 could be financed internally, Mr. Exley was going to have to consider borrowing additional long-term money from external sources. This situation arose from regulations set by the Office of Foreign Direct Investment (OFDI). OFDI was insisting that the company limit its reinvestment overseas to a sum not to exceed 40% of the previous year's foreign earnings. The remainder of 1971 earnings was to be remitted to Burroughs in the United States. Thus, although total earnings overseas would be sufficient to finance 1971 foreign operations, not all the earnings would be available for this purpose.

The controls on U. S. foreign direct investment had been imposed on a compulsory basis in 1968. Although initially envisaged as a short-term measure to cope with the problems of the U. S. balance of payments, three years had gone by without any indication that the controls would be removed in the near future. Therefore, Mr. Exley was concerned with developing a strategy to cope with OFDI regulations, in the event that they were maintained on a permanent basis. In addition, Mr. Exley had to take into account in his financial planning the possible acquisition of International Computers Ltd. (ICL), a British computer company.

COMPANY BACKGROUND

Burroughs's business was defined by the President, Ray W. Macdonald, as "data recording, communications, computation, and processing." Originally the manufacturer of quality adding machines, Burroughs evolved its product line to include a broad selection of electronic equipment from $100 calculators to $20 million computers. By 1971, the company's operations had extended throughout the world with forty-seven manufacturing and engineering plants in nine countries. The Burroughs product line was marketed in six continents through 797 sales offices. In 1970, 33% of the company's revenues and more than 45% of its earnings came from the overseas operation. Exhibit 1 compares Burroughs's foreign and domestic operating performance for the years 1965-1970. As Exhibits 2 and 3 demonstrate, Burroughs had enjoyed extensive growth since 1965. The company had succeeded in meeting or exceeding its goal of 15% annual increase in revenues from 1968 to 1970.

The company employed a centralized organizational structure headquartered in Detroit. Its operations were divided along both product and geographical lines with seven operating groups, each headed by a vice president. Burroughs's subsidiaries were 100% owned by the parent.

Production

Taking advantage of economies of scale was of primary importance. To a large extent, only one factory in the world produced each of the company's product lines. With the high value-to-volume ratio for most Burroughs products, it was more economical to produce in a single plant and ship throughout the world than to produce in several plants closer to individual markets. This policy gave rise to a large volume of intracompany trade.

A major factor in the success of Burroughs was a continuing emphasis on research and development and a deep awareness of users' applications. For example, in 1961 Burroughs pioneered the development of virtual memory, a feature later acquired by many other computer manufacturers. This innovation greatly increased the apparent real memory available to the user, improving programming flexibility and convenience.

Like most other computer manufacturers, Burroughs rented to customers a large portion of the electronic data processing (EDP) equipment it made. Since almost half the company revenues in 1970 came from EDP system equipment and accessories, the rental nature of these items played a large part in the cash flow and earnings behavior of the company. The early years of a rental contract showed small or no earnings as the depreciation of the machine (four years straight line for book, five years sum-of-digits for tax purposes) offset the annual rental payment. After the four-year book life, however, the "zero" value machine was often still producing revenues. Thus, the later stages of the computer's life showed substantially larger earnings. The cash flow pattern was one of substantial outlay at the start of the contract with a steady annual inflow from there on. About 65% of Burroughs's computer systems were installed as rentals in 1970.

The product composition of Burroughs's sales in the United States and abroad, though increasingly similar, still showed some differences. Traditionally, sales patterns outside of the United States lagged behind those in the United States. An example was the proportion of business represented by leasing. Even in 1971, leasing was less significant in Europe than in the United States. Another example was the relative importance of accounting machines and EDP in total sales. In both the United States and abroad, EDP represented an increasing percentage of total sales. However, the percentage of sales represented by EDP was lower outside the United States than in the United States. These facts were also reflected in the historical figures for capital requirements in each sector:

	1968	1969	1970	1971
				(est.)
		(millions of dollars)		
Capital additions—Rental				
North America	$ 90.4	$132.4	$143.8	$ 68.3
Affiliated companies	11.8	38.3	61.2	43.1
Capital additions—Other				
North America	42.6	68.3	44.9	27.4
Affiliated companies	7.6	7.9	21.2	13.7
	$152.4	$246.9	$271.1	$152.5

Financial Management

Burroughs's financial controls were highly centralized. All long-term loans as well as major revolving credit agreements were approved and often initiated by Mr. Exley in Detroit. All capital expenditures in excess of $50,000 required the approval of the Detroit financial office. Cash management was also centered in Detroit, where cash flows were monitored carefully to arrange for cash availability where and when it was needed.

The extent of the latest surge of Burroughs expansion was reflected in the quantity of external financing utilized. In order to finance new rental equipment and additional plant capacity, Burroughs had required over $500 million in new debt and stock between 1968 and 1970. Exhibit 4 shows a six-year history of the company's long-term liabilities. In 1970, about $250 million (approximately half in debt, shown in Exhibit 4, and half in equity, shown in Exhibit 2) was raised for capital additions. Of the $250 million raised, $195 million was used in new rental equipment.

Planning and control of the company's extensive subsidiary network was achieved primarily by five-year plans and yearly operating budgets. Each of the seven operating groups annually prepared a current budget and a five-year plan according to company guidelines. Paramount among these guidelines was the goal of achieving an annual 15% revenue growth. Upon approval of the group's plans, the operating units of each group received their individual budgets which had been incorporated into the approved group budget.

Two major financial policies regarding overseas operation were those concerning exchange rate exposure and overseas borrowing. Burroughs took a "neutral" stance toward exchange rates and tried to minimize the impact of their fluctuations. No conscious attempt was made to profit via changes in exchange rates. All overseas invoices were written in the local currency with provision for adjustment if the currency was devalued. For example, in Brazil invoices were written in cruzeiros. With large devaluations occurring frequently, the amounts were often adjusted according to Brazilian price indices.

Borrowings were analyzed in light of future expectations for the currency in which the loan agreement was written. Rates were compared from all available world sources. For instance, recently the Brazilian subsidiary, needing funds for plant expansion, was offered a loan by a local bank at 22%. Burroughs could borrow elsewhere overseas at 7% in a harder currency. Management in Detroit decided to borrow at 7% and send the funds to Brazil, judging the risk of exchange deterioration to be less serious than the interest differential. These funds were charged to the Brazilian subsidiary at 11%, the legal limit for intercompany lending set by the Brazilian government.

CAPITAL NEEDS

Mr. Exley classified cash needs into three categories: operating expenses and investment, OFDI requirements, and acquisition capital.

Operating Expenses and Investment

Capital needs were derived from forecasted cash flows, budgets, and the company's five-year plan. Mr. Exley, upon reviewing these statements, could see no need for additional domestic capital for quite some time, unlike the tight cash situation of the recent past.

OFDI Compliance

OFDI regulations were quite complex. In short, the regulations and their rationale could be summed up as follows: the United States wished to discourage net export of capital from the States due to the country's balance of payments situation. Thus, the OFDI was established to monitor the flow of capital in the form of direct investment across U. S. borders.[1] OFDI basically monitored two kinds of transfers: (1) purchases of equity or loans to foreign ventures, including increases in intracompany trade accounts receivable; and (2) the amount of foreign earnings *reinvested* outside the United States. The regulations stipulated that the total of the two types of transfer (called "direct investment") be restricted to a specific level. For example, a U. S. company that reinvested $1.0 million of its foreign earnings in its foreign subsidiaries and that, in addition, lent another $1.0 million to these subsidiaries from funds obtained in the United States would have accumulated a total direct investment of $2.0 million. If its limit on direct investment, according to OFDI, was $1.5 million, this company would have to produce a capital inflow of $0.5 million into the United States. This remittance could take one of two forms: (1) a decrease in direct investment, either through a repatriation of earnings in the form of dividends or a decrease of loans to the foreign subsidiaries; or (2) proceeds of foreign borrowings.

[1] Direct investment has been arbitrarily defined as investment where more than 10% of the ownership belongs to the U. S. investor.

When proceeds of foreign borrowings were used to meet the requirements of OFDI, a further problem arose when the debt was paid back. When funds were transferred abroad to pay for the borrowings, OFDI considered this capital outflow an increase in direct investment, except under certain circumstances. Assuming everything remained constant, the repayment of the debt required additional capital inflows into the United States to compensate for the repayment outflow. In many cases this meant a need to refinance the debt. The exceptions to this OFDI rule were the cases when repayment of principal did not commence until seven years after the debt-issue date; or when convertible bonds, with an initial maturity of more than seven years, were converted into a U. S. company equity.

In 1971 the *estimated* limit on direct investment for Burroughs had been established at 40% of 1970's earnings. This percentage was determined on the basis of calculations done according to OFDI guidelines. There were a number of valid ways for Burroughs to compute the limit on direct investment but the 40%-of-previous-year-earnings method offered the best solution.[2]

Accordingly, Mr. Exley tentatively estimated Burroughs's direct investment situation vis-à-vis OFDI requirements for 1971 as follows:

Transfer of Capital		
Estimated increase in receivables from affiliated companies		$31.5 million
Repayment of borrowings:		
Eurodollar term loan:	$10.8 m	
Other:	10.0 m	20.8
Total transfer of capital		$52.3
Reinvested Earnings		
Estimated net income for 1971		34.7
Direct Investment		$87.0
Allowed Direct Investment		
40% of 1970 net income ($33.0)		$13.2
Excess of Expected Over Allowed Direct Investment		$73.8

If Burroughs proceeded with its planned direct investment abroad, Mr. Exley would have to remit $73.8 million into the United States. This would have to be done by December 31, 1971.[3]

Acquisition Capital

One important large demand for capital was expected to arise if Burroughs acquired International Computers Ltd., of England (ICL). The financially weak company subsidized by the British government was thought to be looking for a partner.

[2] The other two most important methods are (1) minimum allowable, where up to $2 million is allowed as direct investment; and (2) historical allowable, where a fixed amount based on a percentage of average direct investment in 1965-66 is allowed.

[3] After November 1971 the compliance date was shifted from December 31 to February 28. Previously a U. S. company had to *guess* the extent to which repatriation was necessary based on an estimate of the current year's earnings in order to remit funds by the December 31 deadline. With the establishment of the new date, a company could wait until the year's total earnings had been determined and then calculate the necessary remittance.

No price or terms for an acquisition were available but on December 31, 1970 the book value of ICL assets exceeded $372 million and the company's net worth was $116 million. ICL's 1970 earnings were about $10.9 million.

The computer industry in Europe consisted basically of a single domestic company per country competing with a number of U. S. firms dominated by IBM. Each of the European firms, like Siemens in West Germany, CII in France, and ICL in England, was subsidized in some manner by the national government. The products provided by the local companies were often more expensive and sometimes of lower quality than their American counterparts. The advantages enjoyed by the American companies stemmed primarily from their large size and technological advantage. The large expanding customer base enjoyed by the U. S. firms at home and abroad permitted economies of scale in production and distribution that had not been available to the European companies. Realizing the importance of these economies, many European companies had been trying to establish partnerships among themselves.

One recent attempt at partnership, however, had already failed. A consortium of computer companies consisting of ICL, Philips, CII, and other European firms was assembled to produce a £10 million computer system for the European Space Research Organization (ESRO). The consortium was dissolved when the German government which provided part of ESRO's budget rejected the group's proposal. IBM could provide the necessary system for £2 million less.

ICL, which had been selling 40% of its machines to the British government or government-related organizations, was already the product of many mergers. The company had evolved from what was once nine separate British firms. If ICL did seek an American partner, Burroughs was thought to be a likely candidate. Burroughs had been producing and selling machines in England since 1898 and had established fine relations with many British banks and institutions. The American firm would be interested in such an acquisition both to gain access to existing ICL accounts and to gain a better foothold for establishing new European customers. The relatively undeveloped European market provided numerous opportunities for market share expansion, a task which had become increasingly more difficult in the United States.

FINANCING OPTIONS

A number of foreign capital sources were being examined. Mr. Exley was considering the possibility of a Swiss loan or a public debt issue. A Belgian loan was pending and the company had recently been asked to participate in a parallel loan. Other possibilities included the Euro-bond and sterling bond markets. Also, a newly expanded overseas revolving line of credit was available if necessary.

Swiss Capital Market

Burroughs had enjoyed excellent relations with Swiss bankers and had made use of Swiss capital markets on several occasions. Mr. Exley had received a call in February from a Swiss bank advising him that Burroughs had come up in the "queue" for public issues. Fully aware of the Swiss queue system, Mr. Exley knew he would have to either act on this issue soon or wait about two more years when Burroughs's turn in the line would come up again. The terms of this issue would yield 60 million Swiss francs ($13.8 million)[4] at $6\frac{1}{2}$% due on June 15, 1985, or sooner at a premium. Another Swiss alternative could be a loan of 50 million Swiss francs ($11.5 million) for 5 years at $6\frac{7}{8}$%, 50% due at the end of the fourth year, 50% at the end of the fifth year. Both these sources stipulated repayment in Swiss francs, although the proceeds of either alternative had to be converted into U. S. dollars almost immediately after the borrowing took place. A table presenting the effective interest rate under various combinations of coupon rate and upvaluations of the loan currency is presented in Exhibit 5.

Belgian Loan

A ten-year term loan of $4 million at 5% with two Belgian banks had been requested and was currently being negotiated. The loan would be repayable in five equal annual installments, beginning six years from the receipt of the loan. The Belgian government, eager to promote investment in Belgium, was subsidizing this loan, making the relatively low 5% rate possible. However, government paperwork had delayed the loan so far. Mr. Exley was optimistic about the consummation of this loan agreement during the next month.

Parallel Loan

One instrument often utilized by international companies operating under rules of foreign exchange control was the parallel loan. This involved simultaneous loans made by two companies based in different countries to each other. The concept worked best if each business required funds in the other's country and both were constrained by their own country's capital export regulations. There was typically a broker's fee of approximately $\frac{3}{8}$%. Mr. Exley had been approached by an English company's broker with a parallel loan possibility. The terms of the agreement involved $10 million for 10 years and would give the English firm a spread of $\frac{3}{4}$%, given that interest rates in England at the time were higher than in the United States. That is, if Burroughs provided $10 million at 6%, the English firm would provide $10 million in sterling at $6\frac{3}{4}$%. The exact rate was to be determined relative to the U. S. prime rate upon acceptance of the proposal. The OFDI watched these agreements closely and allowed only those exchanges which, in their opinion, permitted a positive contribution to the balance of payments *which would not have been possible otherwise.* Mr. Exley knew that in addition to satisfying OFDI, the proposed exchange undoubtedly would be subject to U. K. government controls. However, in the past these deals had been approved by both authorities without much trouble.

Euro-bond and Sterling Bonds

In addition to the specific options mentioned above, the Euro-bond and sterling bond markets offered other sources of foreign capital. Mr. Exley wanted to compare the available rates (see Exhibit 6) with his other alternatives. Rates on recent specific international bond issues were as follows:

---

[4] At the April foreign exchange rate of SF 4.3478/$.

Month (1971)	Company	Amount (millions)	Coupon	Yield	Maturity
Jan.	Texaco	SF 60	6.75	6.61	15
	Int'l Std. Electric	$25	8.25	8.09	15
Feb.	Continental Telephone	$20	8.25	8.09	15
	Ford Motor	$50	6.00	5.91	15
March	Std. Oil of New Jersey	$50	7.50	7.64	7
	Std. Oil of New Jersey	$50	8.00	8.19	15
	American Brands	SF 60	6.50	6.40	15
	Corning	$20	8.50	8.33	15
April	American Metal Climax	$20	8.75	8.80	15

These bonds usually included provisions for repayment not to start before seven years. This guaranteed that the repayment would not be treated as a transfer of capital by OFDI.

Short-Term Credit

A significant source of short-term funds was soon to be available overseas. Burroughs was currently negotiating a $75 million Euro-dollar revolving credit agreement through the overseas branches of a group of fifteen U. S. banks. This source of short-term funds would allow the company more flexibility in the timing of its long-terms issues. The rate on this loan was to be set at $\frac{1}{2}$% over the London interbank deposit rate of comparable maturity. This revolver would be for no more than three to five years, with the interest rate re-set every six months. The $75 million overseas line of credit was to supplement an already existing $75 million Euro-currency revolving credit and $100 million in domestic lines. The domestic credit had been expanded to $300 million in 1970. It was now being reduced since it had become clear that the company would not soon be in a position to utilize the larger facility.

Short-Term Investment

It seemed apparent to Mr. Exley that with no funds actually needed for operations in 1971 but with additional debt likely to be raised overseas for remittance to the United States, excess liquidity would be mounting in the United States. Various alternatives were being considered to utilize this liquidity:

1. *Pay Down Notes Payable.* The company could reduce outstanding bank debt when allowed.

2. *Contribute to Pension Fund.* Burroughs could make tax deductible payments into the pension fund up to certain limits. The return to Burroughs on these payments would be $5\frac{1}{2}$% after tax.

3. *Purchase of Burroughs's Securities on the Open Market.*

4. *Commercial Paper, etc.* The conventional short-term domestic money market was, of course, another viable investment alternative.

THE PROBLEM

Burroughs, after a considerable growth period which involved extensive external financing, had reached a point where operations and growth could be financed from internally generated sources of funds, except for the appearance of the OFDI regulations. With a limit placed on its foreign direct investment, Burroughs had to bring funds into the United States. The estimated funds inflow necessary in 1971 could be achieved by issuing a dividend to the parent, by raising debt abroad with remission of the proceeds, by reducing the trade credit to affiliates, or by a combination of the three. The issues of liquidity, taxes, money market rates, and future financial flexibility were among those to be considered in approaching this problem. Whereas, in the past, OFDI regulations had been considered temporary, it was now clear that they had a longer life span. Assuming OFDI requirements to be temporary, Burroughs had met them in the past with dividends which had to be increased each year.

Dividend payments in Burroughs' foreign operations in recent years had been as follows:

1968 . . . . 38.7%
1969 . . . . 62.0
1970 . . . . 81.5

A strategy had to be established to satisfy the OFDI while optimizing the present and future earnings of the company.

EXHIBIT 1 Burroughs Corporation: Overseas and Domestic Performance, 1965-1970

	1965	1966	1967	1968	1969	1970
Domestic Revenue ($ millions)	334.9	339.7	391.0	491.4	542.7	604.6
Domestic Earnings ($ millions)	5.4	15.2	19.7	30.5	32.8	36.3
Earnings/Revenue	1.6%	4.5%	5.0%	6.2%	6.1%	6.0%
Overseas Revenue ($ millions)	124.5	154.1	162.9	164.1	216.7	288.9
Overseas Earnings ($ millions)	12.2	15.8	15.2	12.8	22.4	30.2
Earnings/Revenue	9.8%	10.2%	9.3%	7.8%	10.3%	10.5%
Overseas Revenue/Total Revenue	27.1%	31.2%	29.4%	25.0%	28.5%	32.4%
Overseas Earnings/Total Earnings	69.5%	50.9%	43.5%	29.5%	40.5%	45.5%

Source: Burroughs Stock Prospectus.

EXHIBIT 2 Burroughs Corporation: Comparative Balance Sheets as of December 31, 1965-1970 (millions of dollars)

	1965	1966	1967	1968	1969	1970
Assets						
Cash	$ 17.8	$ 23.2	$ 17.1	$ 39.7	$ 35.3	$ 16.3
Accounts and notes receivable	100.7	115.0	141.2	177.9	227.7	310.1
Inventories	169.7	192.9	218.3	238.7	363.1	424.4
Prepaid expenses	14.3	11.3	15.0	17.0	23.5	31.0
Total current assets	302.5	342.4	391.6	473.3	649.6	781.8
Net fixed assets	129.7	157.3	191.5	286.8	445.7	619.8
Other	11.3	9.5	19.0	11.9	20.2	46.5
Total assets	$443.5	$509.2	$602.1	$772.0	$1,115.5	$1,448.1
Liabilities						
Notes payable within one year	$ 57.3	$ 51.1	$ 86.3	$116.5	$ 251.5	$ 263.0
Current maturity of long-term debt	1.4	1.0	2.8	3.4	3.0	13.4
Accounts payable and accrued expenses	51.2	58.9	68.8	92.1	127.5	135.6
Customer deposits and prepayments	39.8	30.2	18.3	18.8	21.7	34.5
Dividends payable	1.8	2.1	2.0	2.0	2.6	2.7
Estimated income taxes	21.0	25.0	37.8	30.5	47.4	48.6
Total current liabilities	172.5	168.3	216.0	263.3	453.7	497.9
Long-term liabilities	91.8	114.4	116.9	212.5	236.2	352.1
Other liabilities	11.7	5.0	15.1	–	–	–
Reserve for foreign operations	3.8	5.3	8.7	8.7	8.7	8.7
Total liabilities	279.8	293.0	350.7	484.5	698.6	858.7
Common stock	37.1	40.9	41.0	41.4	86.3	91.9
Paid-in capital	36.8	61.7	64.1	70.8	110.1	221.0
Retained earnings	91.2	114.1	140.7	175.8	221.0	227.0
	165.1	216.7	245.8	288.0	417.4	589.9
Less: Treasury stock	(1.4)	(0.5)	(0.4)	(0.5)	(0.5)	(.5)
Total shareholders equity	163.7	216.2	245.4	287.5	416.9	589.4
Total liabilities and net worth	$443.5	$509.2	$602.1	$772.0	$1,115.5	$1,448.1

Source: Burroughs Annual Reports.

EXHIBIT 3 Burroughs Corporation: Comparative Income Statements and Related Per Share Data For Years Ended December 31, 1965-1970 (millions of dollars)

	1965	1966	1967	1968	1969	1970
Income and Shareholders Equity						
Revenue	$459.4	$493.8	$555.9	$655.6	$759.3	$893.4
Cost of products & services sold & leased	279.3	272.4	309.3	369.8	399.3	450.1
Research & development expenses	15.8	18.8	22.2	26.1	37.1	45.0
Administrative, selling, & general expenses	120.8	134.0	146.5	155.5	189.1	220.5
Interest expense: Long-term debt	4.1	4.5	7.2	8.6	12.5	45.5
Short-term borrowings	2.7	3.2	3.3	6.6	11.8	
Total costs and expenses	422.7	432.9	488.5	566.6	649.7	761.1
Income before income taxes & provision for foreign operations	36.7	60.9	65.4	89.0	109.6	132.3
U. S. & foreign income taxes	16.9	28.4	29.3	45.7	54.4	65.8
Provision for foreign operations	2.3	1.5	1.3	–	–	–
Net income for the year	$ 17.5	$ 31.0	$ 34.8	$ 43.3	$ 55.2	$ 66.5
Shareholders equity at beginning of year	153.9	163.7	216.2	245.4	287.5	417.0
Dividends	(7.4)	(8.2)	(8.2)	(8.2)	(10.0)	(10.5)
Capital stock transactions during year	(0.3)	29.7	2.5	7.0	84.3	116.5
Shareholders' equity at end of year	$163.7	$216.2	$245.4	$287.5	$417.0	$589.5
Per Share Data[a]						
Average shares outstanding	14.8	16.1	16.4	16.4	16.6	17.84
Net income per share	$ 1.19	$ 1.93	$ 2.13	$ 2.64	$ 3.32	$ 3.83
Dividends per share	$ 0.50	$ 0.50	$ 0.50	$ 0.50	$ 0.60	$ 0.60
Shareholders equity per share	$ 11.08	$ 13.23	$ 14.96	$ 17.41	$ 24.20	$ 32.11

[a]Shares in millions of shares, per share data in dollars, both adjusted for 2-for-1 stock split in 1969.
Source: Burroughs Annual Reports.

EXHIBIT 4   Burroughs Corporation: Composition of Long-Term Liabilities
1965-1970   (thousands of dollars)

	1965	1966	1967	1968	1969	1970
In Non-U. S. Currency						
5½% Swiss Loan due 1983				13,800	13,800	13,800
6¼% Swiss Loan due 1985						9,200
8% British Sinking Fund Debenture due 1973-1992		5,600	4,800	4,800		
7% British Board of Trade Loan due 1969-1973		4,200	7,200	4,800		
5½% British Convertible,[d] at $190 due 1985						14,400
3¾% British Convertible,[d] at $140 due 1982				14,400	14,400	14,400
Other	810	18,750	16,967	14,586	25,727	21,029
In U. S. Dollars						
6% Sinking Fund Debentures due 1992			30,000	30,000	30,000	30,000
4½% Sinking Fund Debentures due 1988	25,000	25,000	24,000	22,993	21,968	21,000
4³/₈% Sinking Fund Debentures due 1983	20,694	20,000	19,000	18,000	17,000	16,000
3³/₈% Sinking Fund Debentures due 1977	16,650	15,815	14,980	14,145	13,310	12,256
4⁵/₈% Convertible Subordinated Debentures due 1994, convertible[d] into common stock at $159 a share					100,000	100,000
3¾% Convertible Subordinated Debenture due 1993, convertible[d] into common stock at $126.75 a share				75,000[c]		
4½% Convertible Subordinated Debentures due 1981, convertible into common stock at $37.42 a share	28,664[a]					
9% Note due 1975						100,000
5¼% to 6¼% U. S. Bank Loans Payable commencing in 1969		25,000[b]				
	$91,818	$114,365	$116,947	$212,524	$236,205	$352,085

[a]Converted, February 1966, into 1.5 million shares of common stock.
[b]Refinanced, December 1967, under revolving bank credit agreement.
[c]Converted, November 1969, into 1.6 million shares of common stock.
[d]All conversion prices are adjusted for 2-for-1 stock split in March 1969.

EXHIBIT 5   Burroughs Corporation: Effective Interest Rates

Change in Parity Occurs in Year	6.5% Coupon[a]		6.875% Coupon[b]		10.5% Coupon[a]	
	Upvaluation 5%	Upvaluation 10%	Upvaluation 5%	Upvaluation 10%	Devaluation 5%	Devaluation 10%
1	7.05	7.58	8.18	9.45	9.82	9.11
2	7.01	7.51	8.10	9.28	9.88	9.24
3	6.98	7.44	8.02	9.12	9.94	9.35
4	6.95	7.38	7.95	8.98	9.99	9.46
5	6.92	7.33	7.38	7.87	10.04	9.55
6	6.90	7.28			10.08	9.64
7	6.87	7.23			10.12	9.72
8	6.85	7.18			10.16	9.80
9	6.83	7.14			10.19	9.87
10	6.81	7.10			10.22	9.93
11	6.79	7.07			10.25	9.98
12	6.77	7.03			10.27	10.03
13	6.76	7.00			10.29	10.08
14	6.74	6.97			10.31	10.12
15					10.33	10.16

[a]Repayment at the end of the period.
[b]Repayment, 50% at the end of the fourth year, 50% at the end of the fifth year.

EXHIBIT 6   Burroughs Corporation: International Borrowing Rates

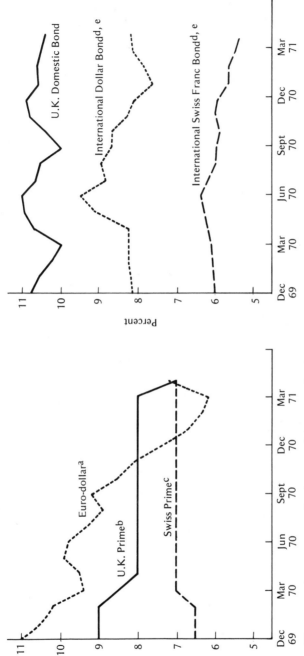

aRepresentative average rate for three-month loans to prime borrowers.
bUnsecured overdraft rate for prime borrowers.
cOverdraft rate for prime borrowers, including commission of .25% per quarter on highest debit balance in quarter.
dAn international bond issue is one sold outside the country of the borrower.
eIssued by U. S. companies.
Source: Morgan Guaranty Trust Company, *World Financial Markets*. June 24, 1971.

PART THREE

Capital budgeting is usually concerned with the rate of return from a particular project. This rate of return is often based on the future receipts from the project compared to the investment required to generate those receipts. The future receipts are discounted to reflect the cost of capital for the firm. Thus, the firm obtains funds at some rate, and a delay in the receipt of cash from an investment means that the cash receipts must be large enough to compensate for the time the funds were unavailable.

The next four chapters draw upon the basic capital budgeting analysis contained in most introductory finance texts. Chapter 9 discusses the determination of the cash flows relating to a single investment with emphasis upon the particular aspects which uniquely affect international investments. The appropriate mechanisms for evaluating those cash flows and an analysis of special types of risk attendant to international investments are reviewed.

Chapter 10 analyzes the acceptance criteria for projects. Building upon the traditional capital structure theory and cost of capital in differential capital markets, it presents the considerations for determination of the discount rate or acceptance criterion for risky investments.

Chapter 11 moves beyond the single project to address the issue of "strategic" investments, where intertemporal (multi-period) considerations are important. These considerations may include keeping the firm's market position over time or maintaining the firm's ability to compete in a particular industry in later years. The general philosophy of governmental taxation and contributions from economics, organization theory, business policy, and general management are brought forth to help in understanding the motivation for foreign investment. An extended example of a major project analysis by a multinational corporation is a conclusion to this chapter.

Chapter 12 discusses returns from investments for various markets within the framework of capital markets and portfolio theory. The concepts of portfolio risk for evaluating projects in a capital budgeting framework are introduced, and this framework provides information about international diversification opportunities. Empirical results based on security returns are also noted. This chapter will integrate concepts from the previous chapters and conclude this section on capital budgeting in the international corporation.

Although many of the examples will be based on a U. S. corporation operating abroad, the goal is to present general patterns of analysis which are independent of particular corporate considerations in the United States. Thus, students from other lands may read the text for the suggestions which bear on any business enterprise contemplating investment outside its home country. A summary of some international taxation policies and some particular references to the U. S. system is contained in an appendix to the book.

Cash Flows
in Capital Budgeting —
The International Elements

Although reported profits are used as a standard for many evaluations of management, materials and other costs are paid from cash, not earnings. Accordingly, in the international corporation one begins an appraisal of a given project by noting the expected cash flows attendant to the project. The determination of those flows in the international firm creates the usual difficulties found in a one-country corporation. However, the determination of the relevant incremental cash flows in the international setting is more complex than in the typical domestic project analysis. Although the analytical pattern follows the basic model suggested by good corporate financial practice, the multinational firm must also consider factors peculiar to multinational operations and their financing.

OPERATING CASH FLOWS—THE INTERNATIONAL ELEMENTS

Joint Consideration

Revenues from any proposed project must be reviewed carefully if the firm has the ability to realize some of the revenues *independent* of the project. For example, there is no problem if a truck manufacturer has decided to establish a car manufacturing plant in another country. On the other hand, often the proposed investment in the other country will affect the operations of other units in the system of the multinational firm through vertical integration, such as a mining operation in Bolivia for a U. S. metal firm, or a sales subsidiary in France for an Italian car manufacturer. The investment may also be a duplicate of the parent operation in major respects through horizontal combinations, such as a typewriter manufacturer creating a manufacturing and distribution outlet in another land.

When such joint effects exist, the firm evaluates the project by aggregating total demand for a common product. Then, the executives ask themselves, "How much extra business can we create from this foreign operation? For that portion of the business which is 'taken' from an existing operation, what are the savings involved?"

For example, the ability to compete more effectively in the Brazilian home furnishings market might suggest to Westinghouse that the firm locate a refrigerator manufacturing plant there. This plant will have some sales generated from a new market, some sales taken from other competitors who are already there, and some sales which are substitutions of Westinghouse products which are currently imported. The first two components of sales are clearly incremental revenue. The last component, substitution of Westinghouse-Brazil refrigerators for Westinghouse-World refrigerators, may have differential benefits because of different costs of production and importation. However, unless these savings are present, these sales are not relevant to the revenue considerations. In the typical case, the loss of the sales and profits to Westinghouse-World is a net cost which should be charged to the project.

Economies of Scale

If there is a policy of many small local manufacturing outlets versus world-wide manufacturing and there are substantial production economies of scale, individual projects should be charged for the additional costs involved in the diseconomies. Thus, while Honeywell manufactures computers in many nations, its major models tend to be manufactured in one location and shipped throughout the world. Clearly, management perceives total shipping costs of Honeywell's large 3500s to be less than the costs associated with diseconomies from small unit production if the machines were manufactured in more than one location.

Differences in Cost and Revenue Assumptions

Another special operating cash flow is the *supervisory fee or royalty* paid to the parent. Often, parents require supervisory fee arrangements with their subsidiaries as one means of remitting funds from foreign projects. In evaluating the cash flows of a project and the cash flows to the parent, several cautionary notes must be considered in relation to a supervisory fee. First, for the project, the relevant cash flow is the after-tax cost of what a real payment for the "supervision" would be worth in an arm's-length transaction. An arbitrarily high fee, created to permit remission of the funds from the project to the parent, has no relevance in evaluating the worth of the project *per se* if it is an accounting or political expediency designed for currency remission. Secondly, for the parent evaluating the cash flow to itself from this project, the supervisory inflow after subtracting any incremental costs is simply one more cash return. On the other hand, taxing and business authorities in the host country may question the propriety of this arrangement unless both sides initially recognize and accept it as a device to permit cash remissions.

Tie-In Sales

A variant of the supervisory/royalty fee is the tie-in sale, in which the subsidiary must buy certain items from the parent. Sometimes this purchase represents an implicit royalty; other times, it is simply a device to insure quality control and/or a low cost to all manufacturing facilities on an integrated, company-wide basis (the "economy of scale" argument for a component of the final product, for example). The conclusion on how to treat this item is the same as for the supervisory/royalty fee: it is the value of the product at an arm's-length level for the project.

Operating Cash Flow—An Example

One way to see the effect of several of the above items is to consider the following situation. Zebracorp currently exports 5,000 units per month to Country X at a price of $2.00. The variable cost of producing these units and delivering them to Palma, the capital and major distribution point of the country, is $1.00 per unit. The Minister of Development has approached Zebracorp with a proposal that the firm install a small manufacturing operation in Palma that would cost $300,000. In return for special tariffs against other firms, Zebracorp will agree to sell its product at $1.80, buy certain raw materials from local suppliers, and use local managers; total costs of local labor and materials will be $.50 per unit. Zebracorp will turn over the investment at the end of five years to a local investor for the sum of $1. Under this arrangement, Zebracorp believes it can sell about 10,000 units per month. Other materials can be purchased from the parent at $.30 per unit, and the parent will receive a direct contribution to overhead after variable costs of $.10 per unit sold. There is a five-year straight-line depreciation of the $300,000 of equipment. Taxes are 50% of profits in Country X and the parent country also has a 50% tax rate with direct credit for Country X's taxes. There is no restriction on cash flow repatriations and the exchange rates are expected to remain constant.

Should Zebracorp accept the Minister's proposal? Begin by looking at several sets of cash flows. For example, look at the figures in Exhibit 9.1.

After this analysis, the company decides to reject the project. The Minister then hints that Alphacorp, a major competitor, is probably interested in the proposal. Does this fact change the decision?

If Zebracorp believes the Minister's assertion, then it must accept a probable loss in sales of the 5,000 units it presently sells. Hence, the relevant cash flow in this case is the basic cash flow of the project, $96,000 per year for five years, and

Rate of Return:
$96,000 per year for 5 years,
$300,000 investment   18%

FINANCIAL CASH FLOWS—THE INTERNATIONAL ELEMENTS

There are three special elements in the financial aspects of the cash flows: the value of capital equipment contributed, the evaluation of taxes, and the remission of debt/equity funds provided by the parent.

EXHIBIT 9.1   Zebracorp—Palma Project

Cash Flow Generated by Project:

Revenues = 10,000 × $1.80	$18,000 per month	
Variable costs = 10,000 × $.80	− 8,000 per month	
Operating profit	$10,000 per month	
Operating revenues per year	$120,000	
Depreciation ($300,000/5)[a]	− 60,000	
Profit for tax purposes	$ 60,000	
Local taxes @50%	− 30,000	
Profit after taxes	30,000	
Depreciation[a]	+ 60,000	
Net annual cash flow in Country X		$90,000
Yearly profit on materials sold by parent =		
(12 × 10,000 × $.10 − 50% of total for taxes)		6,000
Net cash flow to parent with full repatriation		$96,000

Cash Flow Foregone:

Revenues = 5,000 × $2	$10,000 per month	
Variable costs = 5,000 × $1	− 5,000 per month	
Extra profits	$ 5,000 per month	
Extra taxes @50%	− 2,500 per month	
Extra cash flow	$ 2,500 per month	
Extra cash flow per year which is foregone		−30,000
Net incremental cash flow		$66,000

Rate of Return:[b]

$66,000 per year for 5 years,		
$300,000 investment		3.3%

[a]Depreciation is a non-cash expense, subtracted to compute taxable income, then added back to compute cash flow.

[b]For those readers unfamiliar with discounting and the calculation of the rate of return, a brief summary of these concepts may be found in the appendix to this chapter.

Contribution of Equipment

When there is manufacturing involved in the project, the contribution of used equipment from the parent is a central item. The equipment may cost $100,000 new, have a depreciated book value for tax purposes of $40,000 to the parent, and have a fair used market value in the project's host country of $60,000.[1] Transferring the

[1] Other than import duties and shipping charges, the used market price in the host country and the parent's home country should be the same. In the absence of this identity, the relevant price would be the higher charge, assuming the parent would operate to maximize its own return from sale of used equipment. From the project's standpoint, of course, the relevant price is the lower one. That is, the parent manager could first sell the equipment at the higher price, taking a profit. In a second transaction, the project manager could then buy similar equipment at a lower price.

equipment to the project at any price above $40,000 forces the parent to incur either a capital gains tax or ordinary income taxes on recapture of depreciation, depending on the situation and the interpretation. On the other hand, transferring at any price below $60,000 means that there is an implicit investment or subsidy in the project by the parent in the amount by which the nominal value differs from $60,000.

The *value* of the equipment to the project may be taken as the fair market price in the host country, $60,000. However, the *cost* of the equipment to the parent is the present book value, $40,000, plus shipping expenses, and plus any tax payment due because of the difference between the book value and the market value in the foreign country. Assume shipping costs paid by the parent are $5,000. This implies that there is a $15,000 difference between the book value of the equipment adjusted for transportation costs, $45,000, and the market value of $60,000. This $15,000 would be treated as excess depreciation subject to recapture by the taxing authorities in the parent's country. Using a 50% tax rate, the parent company would owe the tax authorities $7,500. Thus, the cost of the investment to the parent is $52,500. This figure is composed of the $40,000 book value plus the $5,000 shipping costs, plus $7,500 for incremental taxes. Since the host country accepted the value of the equipment at $60,000 as part of the investment, the parent company is making a "profit" of $7,500 ($60,000 − $52,500) which is part of the investment in the new project.

Because the economics of equipment are typically so intertwined with production, it may be difficult for the parent to look at a project in this light. However, the incremental cash flow associated with the project investment is the focus of the analysis, and the relevant price to the project is the fair market price, $60,000.

The parent can help the project in another way which eliminates the problem of the taxes imputed to the parent by depreciation recapture on a $60,000 sale. If tax authorities in the two countries permit it, the parent may well be able to claim a transfer of the equipment to the project at $40,000 in value (hence, incurring no tax by selling at book value), whereas the local taxing authorities may permit a higher valuation (e.g., $80,000) for purposes of depreciation and/or investment by the parent. A higher value for depreciation purposes permits the project to shelter more of its income from profitable operations from local taxes. A larger base for investment also increases the parent's claim on profits (as a percentage of investment) or loan repayments (in the event much of the investment is called a "loan"). This transaction is, however, often illegal in that taxing authorities may require a common basis for valuation.[2]

Taxation

Earlier it was noted that international taxation agreements are extremely complex. There is little merit in learning the details of particular covenants, for the tax treaties and enforcement practices change over time. At any point, these policies vary considerably from nation to nation. General institutional summaries of these provisions are available.[3] Information about the tax arrangements of a particular

---

[2] In the National Industrial Conference Board (1966) study, one of every eight companies interviewed said they contributed machinery to their foreign subsidiaries, usually to Latin American countries and less frequently to European subsidiaries.

[3] See Appendix 1 to this book, for example, which has an extended bibliography.

country can be furnished by local governmental, financial, and legal sources. In addition, popular business chronicles in many industrialized countries often feature several popularized articles on the latest "tax haven," which may stimulate search procedures for a desirable location. A summary of some tax issues is contained in Appendix 1 to this book. It is important that the manager be aware of the general framework of income taxation in the international setting.

Some of the basic concepts that one must examine in determining the general philosophy of taxation include the following: (1) the principle of equity; (2) the use of cash vs. accrual systems in the determination of taxable income; (3) the definition of a taxable entity; (4) the treatment of dual taxation; (5) the presence of special tax treaties; and (6) the existence of tax incentive programs.

It is generally accepted that *equity* dictates that persons in similar situations should pay a similar tax. However, the definition of similar situations is largely affected by some of the concepts discussed briefly below.

Foreign income can be taxed on a cash basis or on an accrual basis. On a cash basis foreign income is taxable only when received in the form of cash for dividends, royalties, etc. On an accrual basis income is taxed according to the period when sales and associated costs are incurred, even though cash receipts and expenditures may not have taken place or may have taken place in advance. Given the complexities associated with accrual systems there is a tendency for countries to tax foreign income on a cash basis instead of on an accrual basis. However, the result is also a function of how the taxable entity is defined.

A broader definition of the corporate *entity* reduces the merits of this argument vis-à-vis the multinational. Thus, if Shell is not just a corporation in the Netherlands, but in fact is a world-wide citizen, then taxes should be due on that world-wide income. Sometimes this broad entity concept is desired by the parent for tax purposes; the use of a branch for foreign operations makes it possible for the U. S. corporation to consolidate branch losses in earlier years, offsetting taxable profits in other operations. At other times, the parent prefers a separate subsidiary in another land, especially when such an arrangement delays or avoids imposition of taxes by the parent's home country. This avoidance is especially valuable when the firm wishes to transfer funds from one nation to another. If the home land taxes profits only when these profits are remitted home, then a "tax haven" subsidiary which receives funds from an operating subsidiary can reinvest these funds, tax-free, in some other land. Had this intermediate corporation not existed, the withdrawal of profits from the operating subsidiary might have created a home-country tax liability, reducing the amount which could be reinvested in the other land.

Once the entity is broadened to include operations in other lands, then there is a jurisdictional question. The policy among nations has been to recognize the injustice of *dual taxation* upon the same entity. Country X will tax the operations of Zebracorp in its land, perhaps withholding taxes on profits which are remitted to the home nation. The home land may permit Zebracorp to receive partial or total credit for the taxes paid to Country X. Typical choices involve the option either (1) to deduct the taxes paid to Country X from gross income taxable at home, or (2) to compute the taxes which would have been due at home had all income been received there, and then to deduct the taxes paid in Country X from the tax liability. Normally, Zebracorp will prefer the latter course; there is a full credit against the home country's taxes for the taxes previously paid as opposed to a simple deduction against taxable income.

Many nations also operate on the basis of special tax treaties which further adjust the amounts which may be paid or withheld in those countries. In these situations, the subsidiary may not even have to file a tax return in Country X if the operations are carefully kept within well-defined guidelines. For example, the United States presently has special tax treaties with more than twenty nations which permit this nonfiling.

Finally, tax laws are influenced by *special policies,* designed to achieve certain goals. The country may wish to sponsor particular types of development, granting major income tax concessions such as lower rates, a moratorium on taxes, or rebates. As part of its foreign policy, a nation may encourage investments by its corporations in Less Developed Countries (LDCs), providing special tax provisions to enable more of the profits to be kept by corporations operating in the LDCs, or permitting them to defer payment of the taxes (the U. S. approach). To meet competition from other nations, taxes may be deferred or reduced on trading companies or financing operations for exports. As an example of special governmental tax incentives for exports, Ireland eliminates all corporate income taxes until 1990 on firms' profits from export sales. Since Ireland is a member of the European Economic Community which provides free trade benefits to firms operating in the EEC nations, this benefit is substantial. Alternatively, special taxes may be imposed which force companies to repatriate earnings in consideration of the parent country's balance of payments.

Thus, the manager should develop a general awareness of tax policy approaches in various nations; consult a local accountant, lawyer, banker, and government representative; and determine the relevant cash flow considerations for the project analysis.

Remission of Funds

For the project, the relevant cash inflow is the return from operations after adjustment for local corporate taxes. From the parent's view, however, the crucial variable may be the remission of funds to the parent treasury in New York or London. Accordingly, from this point of view the cash flows are related to the investment; the supervisory payments net of cash costs to provide the supervision; royalties, interest, and dividend remission; and loan principal and equity return.[4] Here, the policies of many multinationals have been about one step (five years) ahead of local taxing authorities.[5] Anxious to preserve capital in their land and concerned about excessive profiteering by the outside parent, local officials began limiting the amount of profits which could be remitted. The multinational parents responded with greater parent loan participation, arguing that loan repayment was not part of profit; loans were then adjusted for very high interest rates. When this practice began to be challenged, the local authorities were confronted with large supervisory fees. And the fight still continues!

---

[4] Remitting royalties *may* be more lucrative than dividends. The royalties are considered deductible business expenses for local country taxes in most cases. However, the local country may tax these remissions at a lower rate than dividends. The local host nation often levies a *dividend withholding tax* in addition to the *corporate tax.* These taxes may total a very high amount. Hence, the royalty may be exposed to lower total taxes than the straight dividend from corporate profits. However, the United States taxes the royalty in full, whereas dividends can be given credit for some taxes.

[5] Government is the pursuit of Jackals by Jackasses . . . H. L. Mencken

In a study by Judd Polk and others at the National Industrial Conference Board in 1966, corporations noted that the key factor in considering a country's remittance policy was the *possibility* of remittance, whether or not the company had expectations of large remittances. The European countries' record of liberal policy on remittance was in their favor, although some experienced executives feared that recent restrictions might recur. Some firms attempted to negotiate formal agreements on withdrawals, although this approach typically applied to earnings and not to capital. Newer companies favored parent loans rather than equity to a greater degree than experienced multinationals, although the risk for long-term loans is similar to that of equity. Many new firms assumed these "loans" were more easily retrievable, while others felt that easy availability of equity from the parent was a poor motivator for the local manager when compared to a loan obligation with fixed principal repayment. Companies with an "international" appearance were not as concerned about remission as the "nationals with international operations." Some managers viewed earnings on a flexible approach, looking at each land individually. Others regarded earnings as a pool which should be remitted to a tax haven for the reasons we noted earlier.

Today, many local taxing authorities recognize the legitimate concern of parents about remission. On the other hand, they are also concerned about the development of their own nations. Accordingly, the typical investment contract for a major project will specify the capital structure of the firm and will limit supervisory fees or royalties to (say) 5% of gross revenues. However, the availability of alternative arrangements and the specifics of the particular proposal offered are factors that the manager must include in evaluating the project cash flows. The operating tactics used to cope with these restrictions on debt repayment or profit remission are contained as part of the capital structure discussion in Chapter 10.

WHOSE CASH FLOWS?

Although there will be more to say later on the issue of parent return versus project (subsidiary) return as the relevant criterion, note how this decision is central to the analysis. Without evaluating the cost of funds (which is done in the following chapter), consider the following example.

Recall the problem of Zebracorp's investing in Country X for five years. The cash flows generated by the project for Zebracorp as a whole were $96,000 if it is assumed that the current business will be lost unless Zebracorp establishes local operations. At the end of the period, the business is turned over to local managers. Suppose the Minister of Development then notes that it would be appropriate if all the cash were left on deposit locally at no interest. At the end of the five year period, the accumulated cash may be remitted to the parent. What is the rate of return of the project to Zebracorp?

First, segment the cash flows received and generated by the project (which includes both the local operations and the additional parent profit generated by purchase of materials from the parent) from the cash actually received by the parent. If the funds are blocked until later years, the only cash flow to the parent during earlier years relates to the profits in the materials produced, $6,000 per year. Hence, the calculations are:

Zebracorp–Palma Project: Profits Remitted to Parent Only at End of Period

	Project	Parent
Investment	$300,000	$300,000
Cash flow per year (5 years)	96,000	6,000
Terminal cash flow (5th year)	0	450,000
Rate of return	18.0%	10.2%

Notice that it is especially helpful in the international example to separate the operating cash flows generated by the project locally and the alternative channels by which that cash may be remitted to someone else in the corporate family. Tariff and tax considerations may dictate different approaches to the channelling of the cash throw-offs from a project, and it is useful to distinguish among these two types of flows as shown in the example.

If the example is altered to allow for a deterioration in the exchange rate of the local currency vis-à-vis the parent country's currency, and the analysis is computed in terms of local currency (LC), the cruzeiro, and parent currency (PC), the U. S. dollar, then the results change again. Suppose the expected deterioration is 5% per year after the first year.

The value of the raw material "profits" will deteriorate if the prices of raw materials purchased from the parent are fixed in cruzeiros. The stated receipt relates to the purchase *price* but the relevant cash flows to the parent are the variable *cash flows* above the manufacturing cost. With constant costs of operation, the margins shrink. The example included payment of $.30 per unit for variable profits of $.10. If the currency in which payment is made deteriorates by (say) 20% over several years, the value of the payment is really only 80% of $.30, or $.24. Hence, the margin of cash flow contributed, assuming parent production costs continue to be $.20, is $.04. Thus, after a 20% decline in exchange rates, the actual margin has declined from $.10 per unit to $.04 per unit, or 60%.[6]

In the example, the unit profits to the parent from selling raw materials after allowance for the 5% annual deterioration in the local currency, the cruzeiro, may be computed as follows:

	Year 1	Year 2	Year 3	Year 4	Year 5
Unit payment	$ .30	$ .285	$.2708	$.2572	$.2444
Cost	(.20)	(.20)	(.20)	(.20)	(.20)
Unit profit	.10	.085	.0708	.0572	.0444[7]
Yearly cash flows (120,000 units, 50% tax)	$6,000	$5,100	$4,248	$3,432	$2,661

[6] As a general formula in any simple inflationary evaluation, if x is the percentage change in gross revenues per unit and y is the initial profit margin, then the percentage decrease or increase in profits (z) is (x/y) times 100. Using the example, $x = -20\%$, $y = 33\frac{1}{3}\%$, and $z = (-20\%/33\frac{1}{3}\%) \times 100 = -60\%$.

[7] Our earlier rough approach ignored the effects of compounding. Thus, the 5% is applied to a smaller base each year, leaving $.044 per unit in year 5 rather than the $.040 we calculated before.

Using these figures, one may compute the dollar value of the project's cash flow to Zebracorp even though portions of the cash flow generated by the project are not remitted to the parent. These figures are:

Zebracorp-Palma Project: Total Cash Flows in U. S. Dollars

Project	Year 1	Year 2	Year 3	Year 4	Year 5
Operating cash flows	$90,000	$85,500	$81,225	$77,164	$73,306
Cash to parent on raw materials	6,000	5,100	4,248	3,432	2,661
Total	$96,000	$90,600	$85,473	$80,596	$75,967

Dollar Return on $300,000 Investment = 13.8%

For the parent, one may calculate the dollars on hand each year, assuming the currency is blocked until the fifth year except for the raw material purchases. These cash flows and the related return are:

Zebracorp-Palma Project: Cash Flow to Parent in U. S. Dollars

Parent	Year 1	Year 2	Dollar Values Year 3	Year 4	Year 5
Cash to parent on raw materials	$6,000	$5,100	$4,248	$3,432	$ 2,661
Terminal flow ($90,000 × 5 years × .95^4)					366,528
Total	$6,000	$5,100	$4,248	$3,432	$369,189

Dollar Return on $300,000 investment = 5.4%

Alternatively, the manager may wish to value the return to Zebracorp in terms of the local currency, the cruzeiro. The local currency values and the associated investment and cash flow normally would create the same value as the return calculated earlier for a constant exchange rate, 18.0%. However, the flows must be adjusted for the decline in profits to the parent associated with the depreciation of the cruzeiro. The cruzeiro value of those raw material profits will be lower than under no depreciative of the local currency against the parent's currency. As a result, the rate of return should be slightly lower. The local investment is Cr. 3,000,000 (assuming an initial exchange rate of 10Cr/$), local income is Cr. 900,000 per year, and the firm generates cruzeiro income for the parent as noted in the table.

Zebracorp-Palma Project: Total Cash Flows in Cruzeiros

	Year 1	Year 2	LC (Cruzeiro) Value Year 3	Year 4	Year 5
Exchange rate	10Cr/$	10.5Cr/$	11.03Cr/$	11.58Cr/$	12.16Cr/$
Raw material cash gain to parent, US$	$ 6,000	$5,100	$4,248	$3,432	$2,661
Raw material cash gain, cruzeiro value	Cr 60,000	Cr 53,550	Cr 46,834	Cr 39,730	Cr 32,345
Operating cash flows	900,000	900,000	900,000	900,000	900,000
Total	Cr 960,000	Cr 953,550	Cr 946,834	Cr 939,730	Cr 932,345

Cruzeiro Return on Cr 3,000,000 Investment = 17.5%

Thus, depending on the numeraire (cruzeiro or U.S. dollar) and whether one looks at total project cash flows or only the cash flows received by the parent, there are sharply divergent returns associated with this simple investment. These returns are summarized as follows:

Zebracorp-Palma Project: Comparative Rates of Return

	With Cruzeiro Devaluation	Constant Cruzeiro/Dollar Ratio
Total Project Returns		
In Local Currency (Cr)	17.5%	18.0%
In U. S. $	13.8%	18.0%
Return to Parent in U. S. $, with Profit Repatriation Blocked until Fifth Year	5.4%	10.2%

Thus, from the point of view of the parent company, there are two major problems. First, the currency is blocked. The parent has substantial cash flows from the project which remain idle because of restrictions of the host country's government. Second, evaluating the return in terms of the currency invested by the parent, the loss in dollar purchasing power of the local currency may be substantial. This is a problem similar to the external purchasing power of nations discussed in Part One.

These problems are particularly acute in this case where we have assumed an investment horizon of five years. Quite often the investment by the parent company in a subsidiary has a much larger time horizon, in which case initial controls on repatriation of earnings and changes in the relative value of currencies tend to be evened out over the long run. If the parent intends to continue expanding a profitable operation (in local currency), the restriction in repatriation of earnings is quite irrelevant to the evaluation of the project. The expansion of the operations would likely require that profits be retained and reinvested in the project anyway, instead of being remitted to the parent company in the form of dividends. On the other hand, a multinational company with all its foreign investments in countries that restrict the repatriation of earnings should analyze the impact on the liquidity of the parent company, e.g., its ability to pay dividends. The other major problem, the change in the relative value of currencies, also acquires a different dimension when a long period of investment is assumed. Some currencies that were considered to be very weak against the U. S. dollar in the 1960s have turned out to be very strong during the 1970s.

Although these problems will continually confront the parent, there are some elements which mitigate their impact. First, convertibility insurance is sometimes available from outside sources, as for example from the Export-Import Bank (Eximbank) and the Overseas Private Investment Corporation (OPIC). Lloyds and other large private insurers will insure against expropriation in some situations. Second, the restricted funds can be usually reinvested in some project. If there is no short-term project, bonds of the local government or local industries can be selected. These bonds are likely to be a little riskier than the currency of the country per se, but they do provide a positive rate of return. This topic is covered in the following section.

THE TERMINAL RATE OF RETURN

Ultimately, a firm does not invest in a single project, but invests in a series of projects over time. From the standpoint of the parent (which desires to have funds available for other projects) or the project (where there are blocked currencies created by the host country), management needs to focus on the *reinvestment rate* of the cash flows. In many cases, reinvestment will be in the project itself. The host country may have created high tariffs on imported goods, allowing the project's output to sell in a favored market. However, the condition attendant to this agreement may be that all domestic demand must be filled at a "reasonable" price. Alternatively, the original capital structure related to the project in this host country may have contained a large debt base linked to the financial cash flows discussed previously. In either case, the profits and cash flow from the project may have to be reinvested in the project both to protect the viability of the project by increasing output to meet domestic demand at a reasonable price and to provide normal funds for expansion given the initial low equity base.

Even if reinvestment in the project is not required because of these above considerations, the host country simply may block repatriation. Accordingly, a reasonable approach is the use of the Terminal Rate of Return (TROR) or Net Terminal Value (NTV). This approach is also helpful in any situation where there are unequal project lives.[8]

Essentially, the TROR requires the analyst to explicitly state the reinvestment rate for cash flows from a project. In the absence of this explicit statement, the computations of rate of return implicitly assume that any cash generated during the life of the project is reinvested at the same rate as the calculated rate of return. The reinvestment rate the firm assumes to compute TROR may be the firm's cost of

---

[8] Again, readers who wish to review discounting are referred to the appendix to this chapter.

capital or may be some lower rate based on investment of the idle cash in short-term securities. It may change over time, reflecting alternative reinvestment rate assumptions. Whatever the rate, the cash throw-offs from a project are compounded forward to some horizon point. The initial investment is compared to this summed horizon value (the sum of each year's cash flows compounded forward to the same point). Then the internal rate of return is computed which will equate the investment to that compounded horizon value.

Changing the example, assume Zebracorp considers another $300,000 project in Country Y, with a stable currency and similar returns of $96,000 per year for five years. The taxation policy is the same, but none of these returns is related to purchase of parts from the parent. Hence, all of the $96,000 is generated by the project in Country Y.

Again, assuming free repatriation, the rate of return to the parent is simply the discount rate which equates a $300,000 investment with $96,000 per year for five years, or <u>18.0%</u>.

If currency repatriation is blocked and cash must be kept idle, the rate of return must now be based on a $300,000 investment and 5 × $96,000 which is received at the end of the fifth year, and the return is <u>9.9%.</u>

Finally, assuming the money can be reinvested at a local account at 5% after taxes, then the parent may choose to compute a terminal rate of return. This is that return for which a $300,000 investment will provide the amount received by the parent after five years from the project's operating cash flow and reinvestment cash flows. This amount is:

$96,000 first year invested for 4 years at 5% compounded	=	$116,689
96,000 second year invested for 3 years at 5% compounded	=	111,132
96,000 third year invested for 2 years at 5% compounded	=	105,840
96,000 fourth year invested for 1 year at 5% compounded	=	100,800
96,000 fifth year received at the end of the year	=	96,000
Total at end of fifth year	=	$530,461
Terminal rate of return on a $300,000 investment	=	12.1%

The Net Terminal Value (NTV) is computed in similar fashion except that the investment is compounded forward at some opportunity (reinvestment) rate and subtracted from the compounded value of the accumulated operating cash flows. However, in the case where the discount rate is related to the cost of capital, this decision rule will provide the same accept/reject signal as a normal net present value evaluation. In the case of the project with low reinvestment rates the results may differ.

Accordingly, in evaluating a single project, a manager may need to use various assumptions for projects located in different countries as well as study a given project under alternative hypotheses about repatriation and reinvestment. Consider how the relative rankings of the projects vary (1) when there is free repatriation, (2) when the currency is blocked, and (3) when the currency is blocked but with a reinvestment assumption. A sample of such calculations is shown in Exhibit 9.2. The outlay for each of three projects is held constant at $1,000, the horizon period is five years, and the reinvestment rate assumed is 10%. Although these examples are simplified to provide level cash flows in most cases and changing parity rates are ignored, the student should be satisfied that (1) the pattern of analysis is valid (i.e., reinvestment rates are important); and (2) depending on the assumptions made regarding repatriation and reinvestment, the "return" to the parent from an investment will vary sharply.[9]

Notice in this example the following:

First, under a simple rate of return calculation, the project with a very short life and high flows in early years is favored.

Second, where the currencies are blocked, the returns for all projects decline. These declines are especially sharp for Projects B and C where the blocking period relative to the productive life of the investments is large.

EXHIBIT 9.2   Alternative Criteria for Determining Project Returns

| | | Projects | |
Cash Flows	A	B	C
Outlay	($1,000)	($1,000)	($1,000)
Year 1	0	700	400
Year 2	200	700	400
Year 3	300	0	400
Year 4	400	0	400
Year 5	800	0	0
Total inflows	$1,700	$1,400	$1,600
Terminal value of inflows @10%	$1,869	$1,957	$2,042
Rate of return (Cash received yearly, reinvested at rate of return)	14%	25%	22%
Rate of return (Blocked until year 5, No reinvestment).	11%	7%	10%
Terminal rate of return (Blocked until year 5, reinvested at 10%)	13%	14%	15%

Note: The preferred choices are circled. Figures are rounded to the nearest whole percentage.

Third, under TROR the final reversal of project rankings is obtained. A project which was never dominant under the other two evaluations becomes the most desired project.

Since the terminal rate of return calculations eliminate one of the main objections to the rate of return analysis (i.e., in the latter calculation the reinvestment rate is the same as the project's rate of return[10]), and since rate of return can be

[9] The zeros in later years for Projects B and C are for ease of calculation. They can be replaced with small values and the earlier flows adjusted to provide similar results.

[10] For example, create a cash flow and compute the ROR. Delay receipt of $1 from one year's cash flow to a later year and compound it at the rate of return of the project. This action will provide a new cash flow which has the same rate of return as that of the original project. Hence, the implicit worth of the earlier receipt is the ROR; i.e., the implied opportunity cost of the funds is independent of the firm's cost of capital.

more appealing to corporate executives than net present value, even though the latter is technically superior, this measure will also be included in future examples in this text. However, a full portfolio evaluation of the firm's projects requires much more than a simple project accept/reject decision. As the firm moves toward this portfolio evaluation, its managers must begin to consider risk. This is a topic which colors any but the most superficial analysis of project analysis in other nations. It is especially critical in the less developed nations with a history of rapidly changing governments.

TYPES OF PROJECT RISK

Whatever the return of a project, the corporate officers are likely to be very concerned with the risk associated with that return. The safest of government bonds still has risk. First, for a long maturity bond, changes in prevailing levels of interest rates will mean changes in the price of the bond before maturity. The price will decline if prevailing interest rates rise. Only with such a decline in price can a new purchaser of the bond receive a return from the coupon and from price appreciation as the bond approaches maturity which is equivalent to the coupon from a new issue brought out in the time of higher rates. Likewise, the longer the maturity, the greater the risk of changes in taxes affecting the net yield vis-à-vis other financing instruments. There are risks over the existence of the government itself which will affect the safety of the bond. Hence, even a relatively safe investment such as a government bond has risk.

When one focuses upon the operating projects of the typical corporation, the risks are compounded. First, there are the risks normally evaluated in domestic capital budgeting problems: *business* and *financial* risk. Second, there are risks associated with *inflation* and *currency* considerations. Finally, there are basic *political* risks relating to expropriation and other government policies.

Business and Financial Risk

The corporate financial officer typically must evaluate risk associated with a particular line of business as well as the capital structure of the firm which is under study. For example, the purchase of an established department store in a growing metropolitan area normally would be considered as having less risk than the decision to invest in an imaginative new computer terminal. This is a type of business risk: it relates solely to the particular characteristics of the industry and the firm in question. Cyclical businesses (capital goods industries such as steel, for example) have a higher business risk than noncyclical businesses. Newer businesses in an industry generally have higher risk than established firms, simply because of the extra risk attendant to choice of location and development of an effective organization.

The return to the equity investors is related to the business risk of the firm plus any financial risk. The latter is incurred by the presence of the senior financial securities (i.e., debt) in the capital structure. As a greater amount of debt or preferred stock is added to the capital structure, common equity holders require a higher return since their financial risk is increased by the larger principal and interest payments. The business risk associated with a firm and an industry will have some influence on the capital structure. Even the best established firms in a high-risk industry are unlikely to be able to have the same proportion of debt at a cheap price as a firm with many readily marketable current assets in a low-risk industry, for example. Beyond these industry characteristics, there is still a question of the *financial policies* followed by the corporate officers. Some nearly identical firms may choose a policy of relatively high debt (i.e., added financial risk) while others in the same industry and with an equally seasoned business may select a more conservative policy, perhaps with no debt. This issue in relation to capital structure will be covered in Chapter 10.

These issues are traditional in normal corporate financial theory and are well discussed in most introductory textbooks in the field. However, the impact of risk evaluations as they influence this judgement must be delayed until after a discussion of special uncertainties in the international setting: inflation/currency risks and political risks.

Inflation and Currency Risks

When the corporation is considering a project in another land, an issue which is often considered is the question of inflation. When the investment is in a nation noted for rapid inflation (e.g., Brazil), there are likely to be concerns about the value of the investment and the discounting procedures that should be applied.

For the United States, inflation has not been a domestic source of concern until recent years, and the issue of inflation has rarely been considered in capital budgeting. However, there are several important concepts.

First, consideration should be given to increased wages and general operating costs as well as the ability to pass on cost increases in the form of higher prices. The market may be such that price increases exceeding the net cost may be made. Alternatively, allowable price increases may be less than cost increases.

Second, differential rates may well apply. Labor may increase an expected rate of 5% per year and raw materials 4%; many of the fixed costs of the firm, such as depreciation or amortization of R&D costs, may not change. Accordingly, the rate of price increase needed to sustain standard profits will usually be much less than the inflation rate attendant to many of the costs. This is true because the costs apply to a fraction of the revenues whereas the sales price increase applies to all the revenues.

Third, the terminal value of the project should reflect gains on eventual sale of assets at the higher inflated price for used equipment.

The primary reason that inflation in another economy is likely to pose substantial problems in the evaluation of capital budgeting decisions is the potential effect on the currency exchange rates. Assuming that productivity, wage, and material cost increases are comparable among nations over time, and that the value of international trade is similar in each country, the inflation rate and the exchange rate in a given currency will be directly related over the long run. With a relatively high inflation rate and goods whose quantity demanded is sensitive to price changes, the country *must* devalue its currency. The country's relatively high inflation will make its goods less competitive on the world market and it will make the country's balance of payments run continuous deficits. Therefore, the nation loses reserves. As discussed in Part One, in the absence of major tariffs and other barriers, the exchange rate adjustment is the equilibrating method by which the international economy accommodates differential inflation rates given comparable productivity increases, and wage/material cost changes.

It is helpful to understand how the inflation effects and the currency effects may be separated in an analysis. Although these relationships are not independent, there are likely to be lags in the adjustment system. Consider a simple example ignoring taxes and repatriation restrictions. For convenience, it may be helpful to think of borrowing in the United States to buy a bond in a foreign country, although one would not advocate 100% debt financing for any corporation! Consider an asset with a one-year holding period. There is a cost of borrowing funds and expected return on the asset as follows:

	US$ Rate	LC Rate
Cost of borrowed funds	10%	20%
Return on investment		30%

From this table, a manager might infer that the local providers of capital are expecting a 10% rate of differential inflation (LC rate of 20% minus the U. S. rate of 10%) in the absence of major restrictions on the capital markets or other factors.

Assume that management wishes to consider two strategies:

1. One strategy is to raise all the capital in the United States, translate it to the local currency, invest, and repatriate profits and cash from the sale of the asset at the end of one year to the United States.

2. The other strategy is to raise the funds locally, invest, pay the lenders or investors at the end of the year following receipt of profits and sale of the asset, and repatriate funds to the United States again.

The results under each strategy are shown in Exhibit 9.3. The outcomes are listed under "No Inflation" and "10% Inflation" rates. It is assumed that government authorities adjust the value of investment to reflect the impact of inflation, a practice known as indexation. However, the cost of borrowing is fixed. Each of these situations is computed under both "No Devaluation" and "20% Devaluation." In all cases, the expected return of the asset is 30% of the original investment. The results are based on a $100 initial investment.

There are three major conclusions:

First, *with inflation,* the return on the project is greater everywhere regardless of where the financing for the project takes place. In the absence of devaluation, the excess return beyond the capital costs of the project is $13 whether financing is local or in the United States, reflecting the 10% inflation rate applied to the project and its income ($100 + $30 × 10% = $13). With devaluation, this extra return is reduced to $10.40, which is the $13 generated from inflation minus 20% devaluation ($13 × (1−.20) = $10.40). A large part of the advantage under the inflation situation derives from allowing the inflation rate to be reflected in the returns from the investment, but not on the local borrowings.

EXHIBIT 9.3 One-Period Project Evaluation under Inflation and Devaluation

	No Inflation		10% Inflation in Returns	
	No Devaluation	20% Devaluation	No Devaluation	20% Devaluation
Strategy 1				
(Funds raised in United States)				
Receive income on investment	$ 30	$ 24	$ 33	$ 26.4
Receive principal on investment	100	80	110	88
Pay interest on borrowings	−10	−10	−10	−10
Pay principal on borrowings	−100	−100	−100	−100
Total	$ 20	($6)	$ 33	$ 4.4
Strategy 2				
(Funds raised in LDC)				
Receive income on investment	$ 30	$ 24	$ 33	$ 26.4
Receive principal on investment	100	80	110	88
Pay interest on borrowings	−20	−16	−20	−16
Pay principal on borrowings	−100	−80	−100	−80
Total	$ 10	$ 8	$ 23	$ 18.4

Second, *with no devaluation,* the return is always greater by $10 for financing in the United States regardless of inflation. This differential reflects the 10% difference in financing costs which were initially assumed.

Third, *with devaluation,* the local financing is always superior to U. S. financing regardless of the inflation rate. This differential is always $14 regardless of whether there is a steady price level or a 10% inflation rate. This figure is a local cost of principal plus interest ($120) times (1 − .20) for devaluation, or $96. The U. S. financing cost was $110 for principal plus interest, and $110 − $96 = $14.

This example is simplified, and ignores mixed strategies, taxation effects which may differ for alternative conditions, and problems of multiple periods. It assumes a U. S. dollar standard (numeraire) and that both the income earned by the asset and the value of the asset itself (but not the costs of local borrowings) will increase by the amount of inflation. The example does illustrate the independence of the financing and the investment decision under these assumptions. Furthermore, it exemplifies most clearly the effect of lags in the adjustment process even if there is a relationship between high local inflation and the devaluation of the local currency over time.

The impact of inflation per company is highly divergent and is largely related to:

the rate of increase in revenues,

the rate of increase in variable operating expenses,

the size of depreciation charges relative to the revenues,

the tax structure,

the terminal value of the financial and real assets,

the financing strategy.

The complexities of this issue can best be seen in an extended example such as the Chaolandia Super Widgets case included at the end of Chapter 10. These items all relate to the effect of inflation on the cash flows, or the numerator of our rate of return analysis. The impact of inflation on the discount rate, or denominator, is covered in Chapter 10.

Political Risks

There are really only two political risks, both usually associated with investments in developing countries having unstable governments. These risks are related to *exchange* and *expropriation* (fractional or total!).

In addition to the problem of a deteriorating exchange rate discussed above,[11] another currency exchange problem associated with political risk is a temporary block on the currency. Black market operations, whatever the moral attitude the corporation may hold toward them, are usually not available for the relatively large size and highly visible transactions associated with a corporation from a major developed nation attempting to terminate its operations in a small developing land. Ownership may continue, but there is simply no way to remove funds from the country. This situation confronted many Indians in the wake of General Amin's actions in Uganda in 1972-74. Some of them felt they still owned their businesses, and nothing the Ugandan government did directly contradicted this premise. The Indians, many of whom were Ugandan citizens, operated from Kenya after widespread racial violence against them in Uganda, yet they had no means by which they might remove funds from their Ugandan operation.

These blocks can be evaluated in context of the example shown in Exhibit 9.2, where the effect on the terminal rate of return from blocking with and without reinvestment assumptions can be determined. Where such risk is substantial, then the effect of such a block on the return must be considered.

The more direct political risk is *expropriation.* Sometimes this action will be gradual with increasing demands for participation by locals or by the host government in the profits and ownership of the business. Initially, it may take the form of a high sales tax or the right to buy into the equity of the firm at some price. Often the price is extremely low and related to the book value of the firm. Later, formal plans for takeover may include a five-year phasing of nationals into key operating positions. The more dramatic course is a pure take-over, as for the American copper operations in Chile or the international petroleum corporations in Libya. At its extreme form, expropriation is a simple one-hour affair in which military forces with heavy armaments surround the offices and the corporate managers are given thirty minutes to evaluate the situation. They are provided with transportation to the airfield where a DC-3 removes them from the land after an unusual avoidance of baggage clearance and customs formalities. Where the situation warrants, the corporation's officers will consider the "worst case" assumption, calculating the maximum loss if expropriation occurs in various years.

---

[11] One survey of devaluations and upvaluations as they affect reported earnings is contained in Olstein and O'Glove (1973). This article also reports proposed changes in reporting standards, and contains a table of firms which derive at least 20% of their revenues from non-U. S. sources.

There is a variety of techniques which the firm may employ to alter the probabilities of expropriation no matter what the transition in governments might bring. One way of categorizing actions designed to lessen the probabilities or the effect of expropriation is shown in Exhibit 9.4. First, there are influences on the government in a positive vein. Second, there are negative inducements for the government to avoid expropriation. Finally, there are outside options which sometimes alter the probabilities, but more often alter the effect.

EXHIBIT 9.4   Coping with Political Risks: the Expropriation

Positive approaches–government		Negative approaches–government
Prior negotiation of controls and operating contracts	⎫	License/patent restrictions under international agreements
Prior agreement for sale	⎬ Direct	Control of external raw materials
Joint venture with government	⎭	Control of transportation to (external) markets
Use of locals in management	⎫	Control of downstream processing
Joint venture with local banks	⎪	Control of external markets
Equity participation by middle class	⎬ Indirect	
Local sourcing	⎪	
Local retail outlets	⎭	

External approaches to minimize loss

International insurance or
  investment guarantees
Thinly capitalized firms:
  Local financing
  External financing secured only by
    the local operation

The positive approaches (left column) involve indicating to the host government the firm's interest in the nation on a longer term basis. Careful negotiation may result in contracts addressing the firm's obligation to employ locals, and to accommodate various control agreements relating to management, profitability, and investment. Perhaps the agreements provide for eventual termination of the foreign ownership. There can be a joint venture with the host government, either now or in later years, with arrangements made for the government to have a long-run minority or majority position. These contracts indicate the firm's commitment to meet the government in achieving political, developmental, and financial goals for the project. Indirectly, the firm can provide for reinforcing the government's nonfinancial goals by sourcing capital equipment and operating supplies locally; by using locals for unskilled, skilled, and managerial roles; and by spreading equity throughout the local citizenry.[12]

---

[12] The last policy is usually operated in the form of using substantial investments by a few big banks controlled by the wealthier citizens of the country. An alternative approach, somewhat limited in the absence of a well-developed equity market, is to encourage investment by as many of the middle class as possible. The disadvantages of this indirect pressure on the government are the costs of handling small investors (many of whom may be relatively unsophisticated

Among the negative approaches to the government is control of the operation by restricting inputs or outputs. By having the local venture provide only one step in the process of selling a product (basic raw material development, or selling imported goods manufactured elsewhere, for example), nationalization of the operation prevents the government from retaining a viable business. Where there is a sizable producing operation which depends on external markets, control (1) of those external markets, (2) of the transportation to those markets, or (3) of intervening processing required to provide the final good to those markets all constrict the government.

For example, Mideast oil producers were limited in their abilities to nationalize local oil operations when most of the downstream refining capacity was controlled by their local partners (the international oil companies) who presumably would not be pleased by an expropriation. To the extent that the international oil producers could supply their refineries from other sources and no other refineries were available (the situation prevailing in the late 1950s and 1960s), the ability of the Mideast nations to profit from expropriation was reduced. In later periods, it was the limited availability to the oil companies of alternative economic sources of crude oil which increased the Mideast nations' position, even though most of the tanker fleets were either owned or under long-term charter to the oil companies. The benefit of nationalization to the oil-producing nations, of course, was greater influence in the whole production process from crude oil to consumer petroleum products.

A corporation which controls critical licenses or patents has influence on the government, for operating illegally without these licenses brings sanctions upon the nation. Many Western nations and companies have been reluctant to invest in the Eastern bloc for many years because of Soviet indifference to international copyright and patent agreements. Control of transportation, the situation of United Fruit (now United Brands) vis-à-vis various small Latin countries (also known in former days as "banana republics" for their main United Fruit product), prevented those nations from nationalizing plantations. Put simply, the bananas would rot before optional transportation could be developed, and unless all these nations acted in concert, the effect on United Fruit from one nationalization would have been relatively insignificant.[13]

Finally, as suggested at the bottom of Exhibit 9.4, the company has outside options. First, investment guarantees from OPIC (the Overseas Private Investment Corporation) or another source mean that any expropriation can be recovered to some degree. The determination of value may be very different for the corporation (which viewed the operation as a going concern) and the insurance agency (which may view it at book value). Such insurance programs

---

financially) coupled with the stockholder resentment created when a dividend is passed. The indirect pressure on the government, of course, is that nationalization forces the government to contend not just with workers who may be unhappy under government operation (the Chilean copper case), but also with a wide range of investors who either lose their investment or anticipate poor results from government ownership and operation. Hence, the joint venture or involvement of local middle class equity participation may be a direct way of responding to a government's goals, but may also be a very indirect way of forcing the government to reckon with higher domestic costs from an expropriation move.

[13] The merits of concerted action were learned well in the Middle East by the Organization of Petroleum Exporting Countries.

have a negative effect on the host governments, for inhospitable investment environments are well noted by these insurance organizations and are transmitted to potential investors who inquire about insurance and risks. Such insurance may eventually be developed through the United Nations or regional insurance banks, for the collective benefits to most developing countries would seem to be considerable.

Another strategy, followed by many investors in unstable environments, is to pay whatever price is required for local financing or for unguaranteed outside financing supported by the local investment. In the event of nationalization, the corporation negates any debt obligation, leaving the local lenders to fight with the local government about repayment. Alternatively, as occurred in the Freeport Cuban nickel operation, the major banks can be left to argue with the new government while the corporation goes on its way (home).[14]

THE EVALUATION OF RISK

After observing the types of international financial risk, the management must reach a decision on how to cope with that risk. In terms of the analysis suggested, contingency planning of a "what-if" variety can (1) reduce the probabilities of expropriation or repatriation restrictions beyond those known when the investment is made and (2) show the probable effects on the terminal rate of return should such blockages be encountered.

Chapter 10 will discuss the determination of the appropriate acceptance criteria when risk is present. However, in addition to the types of risk discussed earlier (business and financial risk, inflation and currency risk, and exchange and expropriation risk), a final question must be how to determine the composite risk that is present in a project.

After looking at historical information about the type of business in general and the profitability of business in that country in particular, the firm's managers may form reasonable judgments about the probable performance of a project in that country. Through interaction of the various factors, the final dispersion of terminal rate of return, earnings per share, sales, or whatever other values the management might be concerned about can be determined most effectively by a risk analysis simulation. This technique will be reviewed as part of Chapter 10, and an extended example of its use is part of Chapter 11.

SUMMARY

We may separate the determination of the project's cash flows into operating cash flows and financial cash flows. In the operating cash flow determination, the

[14] These examples, of course, actually reverse the conventional corporate finance evaluation where additional debt increases the financial risk to the equity holders. In these situations, local debt or unguaranteed debt permits the equity holders both to improve their return because of the leverage and to have less risk from expropriation. On the other hand, the higher debt burden increases the risk that inability to meet debt payments will force loss of equity in the business. In many cases, however, the increased risk of insolvency in no way compares with the benefit of avoiding substantial losses from expropriation.

importance of determining the relevant cash flows when there are substantial inter-dependencies or joint effects with the parent sponsor of the project was stressed. These interdependencies include vertical and horizontal combinations, alternative cost and revenue assumptions for the finished products, and economies of scale in production or distribution. The use of royalties or supervisory fees as they affect the return also must be considered.

In evaluating the financial cash flows, one aspect is the impact on the value of investment when there is a contribution of equipment from the parent. A brief introduction to the major concepts of taxation argued that the enlarged concept of the corporate entity has made governments increasingly believe that corporations in their land should pay taxes on profits earned anywhere in the world with some adjustment for local taxes paid in other lands. In response, a major motivation for tax havens has been to avoid the taxes on funds removed from one foreign subsidiary to be invested in another foreign subsidiary. Finally, there are special national or supranational policies designed to encourage foreign trade, to increase investment in less developed countries, or to protect a balance of payments position.

The issue of the remission of funds and the concern of companies for the return of cash to the parent has been raised but not resolved. This concern led to the discussion of whose cash flows are relevant: the parent's or the project's. This issue will return later, but there are sharply divergent returns depending (1) on the numeraire selected for evaluating the cash flows and (2) on the cash flows received by the project versus the parent.

In evaluating the returns, the familiar concepts of rate of return and net present value were used. These standards were supplemented by the terminal rate of return and net terminal value which permit an explicit consideration of the reinvestment rates for projects. This assumption is especially important where there are blocked funds which cannot be removed from a host country until a later period. The returns of a project may vary sharply depending on which standard of evaluation is considered. Tables of present values of one unit of a currency received at various periods and at different discount rates are in Appendix 2 of the book.

An introduction to project risk reviewed the business and financial risk concepts found in traditional corporate finance. Another type of risk results from the link between differential inflation rates and currency exchange rates. Political risks, relating to blocks on exchange or outright expropriation, are a third type of uncertainty. Finally, a variety of positive, negative, and independent actions which may be taken by the corporation to reduce these risks was offered.

Questions

1. What are the factors which make the cash flow from a project create different values for the parent and for the subsidiary which undertakes the project?

2. How does the terminal rate of return differ from the rate of return? How

would you use it in a project which has revaluations (appreciation or depreciation) likely for the local currency against the parent's currency? Does it make a difference if the funds are blocked or remitted?

3. "I don't worry about anticipating currency changes; all I care about is the absolute level of inflation. I just reduce the value of the funds by that amount to get the equivalent in German marks."—German corporate executive. Do you agree with this analysis?

4. How would you attempt to cope with the political risks in a country where you plan to locate a project when the government has a record of rapid changes in personnel?

5. "They claim we exploit them since we demand a one-year payout on all projects. But, you know, we have had so many things nationalized in Latin America in the last thirty years with all these revolving governments that a short life is all we can fairly anticipate. Now, one country may feel we exploit them if they do not have nationalization in a given decade, but we have to look at our portfolio of returns from all the nations over many years. So we have no choice." Comment.

Bibliography

Carter, William Gilbert, "National Support of International Ventures." *Columbia Journal of World Business,* Sept.-Oct. 1972, pp. 6-12.

Eiteman, David K. and Arthur I. Stonehill, *Multinational Business Finance.* Reading, Mass.: Addison-Wesley Publishing Co., 1973, Ch. 10.

Mikesell, Raymond F., *et al., Foreign Investment in the Petroleum and Mineral Industries.* Resources for the Future, Inc., Baltimore, Md.: Johns Hopkins Press, 1971.

Olstein, Robert A. and Thornton L. O'Glove, "Devaluation and Multinational Reporting," *Financial Analysts Journal,* Sept.-Oct. 1973, pp. 65-84.

Polk, Judd, *et al., U. S. Production Abroad and the Balance of Payments.* National Industrial Conference Board, New York, 1966.

Robock, Stefan H., "Political Risk: Identification and Assessment." *Columbia Journal of World Business,* July-Aug. 1971, pp. 6-20.

Truitt, J. Frederick, "Expropriation of Foreign Investment: Summary of the Post-World War II Experience of American and British Investors in the Less Developed Countries." *Journal of International Business Studies,* Fall 1970, pp. 21-34.

Appendix: Discounting-Net Present Value and Internal Rate of Return

Once the cash flows are determined for the project and for the parent, we seek a means to evalute what value to assign to the cash flows considering the time value of money. Net Present Value (NPV) and Rate of Return (ROR) are two means by which we discount cash flows. A brief review of these concepts is included for those who have not had an introductory finance course.

Suppose one has X dollars (e.g., $10) and the discount rate is r (e.g., 10%). At the end of one year, the value Y_1 of the holding is:

$$Y_1 = X(1 + r) \qquad\qquad Y_1 = \$10(1 + .10) = \$11.00$$

At the end of two years:

$$Y_2 = Y_1(1 + r) = X(1 + r)^2 \quad Y_2 = \$10(1 + .10)^2 = \$12.10$$

Y_2 represents the *terminal value* of investment X at the end of the second year compounded annually at the rate, r. One can reverse the procedure. Given Y_2 dollars at the end of two years, and the rate of discount, r, then X, the amount of money equivalent to Y_2 dollars two years hence, can be found.

$$X = \frac{Y_2}{(1 + r)^2} \qquad X = \frac{\$12.10}{(1 + .10)^2} = \$10$$

and X is the *present value* of Y_2.

In capital budgeting, we estimate the Y values (yearly net cash flows) for the investment. We select a discount rate which is the opportunity cost of funds to the firm (the cost of capital), r. Then X can be computed, where X is the *net present value* of the stream of cash flows. This stream includes the initial investment, Y_0, which is negative, and the other Y_i's which may be negative or positive.

$$X = Y_0 + \frac{Y_1}{(1 + r)} + \frac{Y_2}{(1 + r)^2} + \dots + \frac{Y_n}{(1 + r)^n}$$

If the present value is positive ($X > 0$), the the investment is considered desirable, as it covers the cost of funds to the firm.

The rate of return is also called the discounted rate of return, internal rate of return, or return on investment. The ROR is the rate at which the future cash flows can be discounted to equal the investment. It is obtained using the same equation but slightly different analysis. Instead of assigning a discount rate, r, the equation is solved for that rate for which the present value of the stream of cash outflows and inflows of an investment equals 0. That is,

$$0 = Y_0 + \frac{Y_1}{(1 + r)} + \frac{Y_2}{(1 + r)^2} + \dots + \frac{Y_n}{(1 + r)^n}$$

Y_0 is negative, representing the cash investment by the firm in the project.

These two standards will not always rank projects in the same way. Further, it is possible for a project to have more than one rate of return. One difficult assumption is that the project cash flows evaluated under a ROR calculation are presumed to continue to earn at that rate when they are reinvested. However, in evaluating single projects in the international setting, a general adjustment is useful which also happens to eliminate the limitations of some of the assumptions contained in these two models. This adjustment, the Terminal Rate of Return, was discussed in Chapter 9.

CHAPTER 10

The Appropriate Acceptance Criteria for Capital Expenditures

The previous chapter outlined how a manager determines the relevant cash flows in international investments. Now the manager needs to consider the return that should be demanded for a single project. First, there are the traditional corporate finance precepts on the cost of capital. But then, whose capital structure is germane: the parent's or the subsidiary project's? In resolving this issue, consolidated statements and their effect on the expectations of lenders and investors must be considered. This chapter will also comment on the practical tactics of international business operations and explain their presence in the basic capital budgeting model. From these topics which deal with the cost of capital and capital structure considerations, we turn to the specifics of a project, introducing both the techniques by which the probable risk associated with a project can be determined and the appropriate criteria for valuing that risk. Finally, we address directly the dilemma recurring in both these chapters: the corporation operates under certain policies to protect itself from excessive risk, yet these policies themselves contribute to a climate that often breeds the outcome of the most feared risk—expropriation.

THE COST OF CAPITAL

The cost of capital is the variable that financial theory uses as the minimum rate a project must yield in order to be accepted by the firm. Since the cost of capital refers to the average cost of funds (debt and equity) used to finance the firm, the project must yield at least that amount to be a worthwhile operation.

Chapter 9 discussed the concept of business (operating) and financial risk and built upon the traditional analysis offered in corporate financial theory. Debt has a lower cost than equity since it has priority claim in liquidation as well as first claim on earnings in each period. Equity requires a higher return because the investors face the business risks related to the corporation as well as the financial risks associated with the presence of debt.

For the firm, this combination of factors allows a cost of capital curve which may appear as presented in Exhibit 10.1. The overall cost of capital of the firm is a function of the cost of debt and equity and their relative proportions. The cost of capital initially declines as the relatively cheaper debt is substituted for the more expensive equity. At some point, the steadily increasing equity cost combined with the increasing cost of debt will cause the cost of capital to flatten and then to rise.

EXHIBIT 10.1   The Cost of Capital

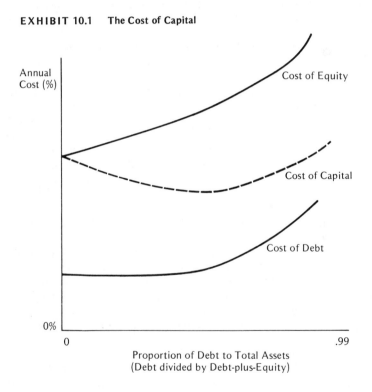

Proportion of Debt to Total Assets
(Debt divided by Debt-plus-Equity)

There is continuing controversy over whether there is a unique point or a range of points at which the cost of capital curve is low. Likewise, there is concern over how these curves differ for alternative industries (different business risks) and for more complicated financial structures than the simple debt-equity model suggested here. The most famous critics of this traditional model, Modigliani and Miller, would suggest that the only benefit of debt financing is the tax-deductibility of the interest.

However, later versions of their theory would still have the cost of capital curve turning upward at some point as the risk of financial insolvency increases.[1]

The job of the financial manager is to choose the best capital structure for the firm in the long run and then to time the issues of debt, equity, and preferred stock to minimize the company's cost of capital over time. There are periods in the market when a debt or equity issue is relatively favorable, so the financial officer should seek to avoid the periods of highest cost for issuing these securities. Expectations may change, of course. In the last few years, many firms that refused to issue debt at an interest cost of 9% were rapidly seeking funds eighteen months later at 9½%. The difference was that the 9% rate appeared at a time of rising rates which eventually reached over 10% for seasoned corporate debt issues. When the market turned down to "only" 9½%, many managers were happy to have these lower rates. The 9½% rate became more reasonable once the higher rates had been seen.

By focusing upon the capital structure concept, the executive can avoid the error of evaluating capital projects on the basis of the particular financing alternative considered at a point in time. Thus, if the company is issuing debt with an after-tax cost of 4%, it might use a discount rate of 4% in evaluating projects. Some years later, an exceedingly high debt ratio induced by following this policy over time would force an equity issue. Assume that the company believes equity costs 15%. The implication is that the projects being evaluated that year should meet a 15% hurdle rate. Such a mentality plays havoc with any sort of decentralized organization in which divisions must compete against each other for scarce funds. The motivation of a divisional manager would be to submit all the low return projects in debt-financing years, saving the higher return projects for equity-financing years and/or urging a competing division manager to meet the equity hurdle rate.

The conclusion is that the firm should decide on a cost of the combined components of the capital structure over time. This cost is used as the hurdle rate each year regardless of the particular financing which is undertaken that year.

Obvious as this conclusion is to most practicing financial executives, its subtlety is often missed when evaluating major projects or proposals which have particular mortgage debt attached to them. In most cases, a lender considers the overall capability of a business and not just the security of a mortgage on a proposed new building. Likewise, the presence of a mortgage on a building may in turn affect the potential availability of debt from other lenders. Hence, to give the new building the benefit of all the debt (resulting in a lower hurdle rate for the new building as a project) ignores the effect of lessened debt availability for the remainder of the corporation.

The cost of capital for the firm is one of the most unsettled issues in both theory and practice. When one turns to the assessment of the appropriate cost of capital for a project, the confusion increases. Essentially, the cost of capital to the firm is related to the return and risk of the firm's project investments. How does one determine the appropriate cost of capital for projects of varying risk classifications? The issue is important, for that cost of capital is reflected in the discount rate used in evaluating the project.

---

[1] For those readers interested in the assumptions beyond this analysis and for additional references, see an introductory text such as Weston and Brigham, *Managerial Finance*, 5th Edition, (Hinsdale, Ill.: Dryden Press, 1975) or Van Horne, *Financial Management and Policy*, 3rd Edition, (Englewood Cliffs, N.J.: Prentice-Hall, Inc., 1974). In particular, see Van Horne, ch. 9, for a discussion of the Modigliani and Miller position.

One can focus on the weighted cost of capital appropriate for this investment. Where the corporation is a holding company, in effect it may be viewed as owning separate corporations acting as a relatively passive investor. The weighted cost of capital may be computed for those subunits as separate entities either by looking at how the local market evaluates publicly-traded competitors of those subunits or by discussing with lenders and investors the appropriate capital structure of those entities.

Viewing the weighted average cost of capital argument shown in Exhibit 10.1, one might note that it has both theoretical and empirical foundations. The theoretical foundations are based on the existence of a rational (or "perfect") capital market. The empirical foundations are still subject to debate. On the other hand, in international capital markets we should assume *imperfect* capital markets. There are segmented capital markets, there is disequilibrium in the markets, and there are special financing arrangements unique to many projects depending on their location. Where these imperfections in the capital market exist, the determination of the lowest cost of capital is not possible theoretically. However, empirically, the manager must still find a hurdle rate by which to accept or reject projects in foreign countries. An approximation to the cost of capital under those imperfect conditions must be found. The way that local investors react to similar projects will provide some guidance in this endeavor, although not a theoretically optimal decision rule.

An alternative to the concept of the average cost of capital is the concept of return to equity, one of the components of the total cost of capital. This can be particularly useful when special financing arrangements are attached to the specific project.

An example of a situation where management usually concentrates its analysis on the return on equity is the shipping industry. In this case the shipyard which manufactures the ship traditionally supplies a substantial amount of the total funds required. The return to the equity holders is a function of the ship's cost, the revenues and operating expenses, and the timing of the particular financing scheme offered by a given shipyard. This last item is often a source of erroneous conclusions. Holding the cost, revenue, and operating cost assumptions constant, it is obvious that the shorter loan (faster payback) option will have a lower return to equity in normal settings. Essentially, the cheaper debt financing will be paid off sooner, meaning that the ship will be financed increasingly by larger portions of equity over its life. Without debt on which to lever the return to equity in later years, the return to equity will be lower than otherwise would be the case.

The analysis is valid, however, only if one assumes that no other financing is available in later years. One can argue that short-term financing might be used in later years to replace some or all of that debt. Alternatively, one needs to consider if the low-debt balance sheet afforded by the rapid repayment of debt under the shorter-lived debt option would not permit more debt from other lenders for financing additional projects.

In some situations the particular financing may be dominated uniquely and completely by the particular project at hand. Special joint ventures or subsidiaries in which the parent firm offers no guarantees may be regarded as unique projects with their own cost of capital. For example, Freeport Minerals traditionally operates in this manner. Nationalization of its huge Cuban nickel plant caused the parent to lose its equity in the subsidiary and several banks to lose huge amounts of loans to the project secured by that plant. However, the effect on the other lenders to Freeport and the rest of Freeport's operations was minimal. This case is probably atypical. Often the corporation will fulfill a moral obligation (perhaps induced by enlightened self-interest in assuring itself a welcome for future financing options) to pay off liabilities of legally separate entities. This behavior was seen when American Express repaid debts of its legally separate warehousing subsidiary in the wake of the salad oil scandal.

In the following discussion we will focus upon a number of returns when looking at cases, for the manager will appropriately review several different returns. On one hand, the overall operating return will be considered. In addition, the return to equity which may be affected by unique financing arrangements in particular settings will be reviewed, and judgments must be reached about whether returns to equity under sharply divergent financing arrangements are comparable. Will equity shareholders and other lenders perceive their risk as unchanged regardless of the local financing arrangements which are employed for a particular project? The terminal rate of return introduced in Chapter 9 allows us to interpose a particular reinvestment rate, but it mixes the operating and reinvestment returns in stating a project return. Accordingly net present value and rate of return results will be useful as well.

WHOSE COST OF CAPITAL?

In evaluting the cost of capital, particular projects may sometimes be evaluated on the basis of their appropriate capital structure when operating alone. This option is easy when the projects are operations in a major industry with publicly traded competitors. However, for the typical international project, one must evaluate the particular risk characteristics of the cash flow, a topic discussed later. There is a form of fallacious analysis that is sometimes encountered, which essentially is based on the use of pyramiding, as shown in Exhibit 10.2. Advocates of this position say the following: "We shall invest in that project in Country X, and we know our parent has a cost of capital of (say) 12%. Accordingly, we shall borrow as much local money as possible, and then invest the balance ourselves. As long as we can earn our 12%, we are in fine shape."

EXHIBIT 10.2   Pyramid Corporate Structure

Holding Corp
$2M debt at 4%   } 12% cost of capital
  2M equity at 20%

            Subsidiary 1
            $4M debt at 4%   } 8% cost of capital
              4M equity at 12%

                        Subsidiary 2
                        $8M debt at 4%   } 6% cost of capital
                          8M equity at 8%

Consolidated
Debt $30M   *Subsidiary 3*
Equity   2M $16M debt at 4%   } 5% cost of capital
                                  16M equity at 6%

Ignoring major risk considerations and differential inflation rates, assume the proposed project is comparable to other projects of the firm. What is the fallacy of this argument? Exhibit 10.2 indicates the problem. Assume the parent and all subsidiaries are able to obtain 50% debt and 50% equity with debt carrying a consistent cost of 4% after tax. Call the parent a holding company and let two of the subsidiaries act as holding companies. That is, they do nothing but invest their capital (raised by debt and equity issues) in the equity of other firms. In this example, they have invested directly in only one other firm. In the typical pyramiding example, the units invest in a variety of firms. An analysis of the conclusions drawn from this table may suggest why such "diversification" is used.

Consider the final operating company, Subsidiary 3. The lender to this firm is content, assuming the $16M in debt is reasonably secured by real assets. The lenders to the other firms are not concerned, for the firms only have a .5 debt-to-total-capitalization ratio. However, if these lenders go beyond the simplest of analysis, they see that their ultimate real assets for security are downstream. Furthermore, the lender to Subsidiary 3 would have first claim on the assets under normal circumstances. To take the first case, consider the lender to Holdingcorp. When this lender considers the consolidated statement, it is apparent that the real "firm" has $30M in debt and only $2M in equity. This lender's $2M of debt stands behind an additional $28M of debt, and all of the indebtedness is secured by the $32M of assets of Subsidiary 3. (For kindness' sake in this example, assume that the assets of Subsidiary 3 do exist and are reasonably valued, a situation that does not always occur.)

This exaggerated situation points out the fallacy of merely charging the subsidiary with the cost of capital of the parent when that investment is really equity. In fact, the subsidiary should be charged with the appropriate cost of equity for going into that business in that land. Typically, this charge for equity will be higher than the parent's cost of capital. Accordingly, the cost of funds to the usual subsidiary will be increased.

The local capital structures may differ sharply from the parent capital structure arrangements. For example, the debt load afforded most Japanese firms is grossly above the comparable debt load of an American firm in the same industry. Exhibit 10.3 shows tabulations of debt ratios in different nations. In part, this additional debt is because of the involvement of the government of Japan on both sides. The Bank of Japan (government-owned) provides debt via commercial banks to major industries on the government's favored list, as we elaborate upon in Chapter 15. Lenders know that the government is committed to protecting business. Hence, the risk of bankruptcy is lessened given the government commitment to preserve the major corporation as an economic force in Japan and throughout the world. The local capital structure considerations may provide a lower capital cost in some cases than the parent's home country would permit. Typically, the local capital structure will provide a higher cost to the project if the home country is an industrialized nation and the local country is a less developed land.[2]

Thus, one returns to the basic conclusion that the relevant starting cost of capital for business and financial risk should be based on what the subsidiary would have to earn operating on its own in its own environment. Bearing in mind currency

[2] From their survey in 1968, Stonehill and Nathanson found that 64% of their respondents who used a cost of capital concept did *not* vary it for foreign investments. In terms of income, the largest group counted cash flow plus retained earnings as "income." See Arthur Stonehill and Leonard Nathanson, "Capitol Budgeting and the Multinational Corporation," *California Management Review,* Summer 1968, pp. 39-54.

EXHIBIT 10.3 Debt Ratios in Selected Industries and Countries[a]

	Alcoholic Beverages	Auto-mobiles	Chemicals	Electrical	Foods	Iron and Steel	Non-ferrous Metals	Paper	Textiles	Total
Benelux	45.7	—	44.6	37.5	56.2	50.0	59.2	35.9	54.2	47.9
France	35.8	36.0	34.3	59.1	24.7	33.7	55.0	35.5	20.9	37.2
W. Germany	59.2	55.1	54.8	67.5	42.5	63.8	68.1	71.8	44.9	58.6
Italy	64.9	77.3	68.2	73.6	66.4	77.9	67.5	—	66.6	70.3
Japan	60.9	70.3	73.2	71.1	78.3	74.5	74.5	77.7	72.2	72.5
Sweden	—	76.4	45.6	60.1	46.8	70.0	68.7	60.7	—	61.2
Switzerland	—	—	59.7	50.8	29.2	—	26.3	—	—	41.5
United Kingdom	43.8	56.5	38.7	46.9	47.6	44.9	41.7	46.6	42.4	45.5
United States	31.1	39.2	43.3	50.3	34.2	35.8	36.7	33.9	44.2	38.7
Total	48.8	58.7	51.4	57.4	47.3	56.3	55.3	51.7	49.4	

[a]The number in the matrix represents average total debt as a percent of total assets based on book value. Each company is weighted equally, i. e., the individual company debt ratios are summed and divided by the number of companies in each sample.

Source: Stonehill, Arthur and Thomas Stitzel, "Financial Structure and Multinational Corporation." *California Management Review,* Fall 1969. Vol. 12, No. 1, pp. 91-96. U. S. corporations are the ten largest in each industry (four only for automobiles), ranked by 1965 sales and reported in *Moody's Industrial Manual* (New York: Moody's Investor Service, Inc., June 1966). Japanese corporations are the largest publicly owned corporations in each industry as reported in *Kaisha Shikiho* (Quarterly Reports on Corporations) (Tokyo: Toyo Keizai Shinpo Sha, July 1967). European corporations are all the publicly owned corporations reported in *Beerman's Financial Yearbook of Europe* (London: R. Beerman Publishers, 1967).

and political risks and possible imperfections in the capital markets which permit lower capital costs of the parent to be passed through, one can consider whether this investment is desirable from the standpoint of the parent.

INFLATION AND THE SELECTION OF THE DISCOUNT RATE

Coping with inflation within the capital budgeting framework is one of the most difficult topics to evaluate. *As a general rule, inflation that is widely accepted will be built into the cost of debt and equity for the firm.* Hence, the weighted cost of capital reflects such anticipated price changes, and the cash flow assumptions also can accommodate these expectations. Unless the manager has superior forecasting ability, it is unrealistic to add a further increase to the discount rate derived from the cost of capital to adjust for inflation. To the extent that lenders anticipate price increases, the cost of debt will reflect the cheaper currency in which they are repaid. Equity holders, too, should have a nominal return consistent with inflation and anticipated real returns, and the sensible calculation of the cost of equity should reflect this valuation. Accordingly, domestic inflation should already be included in the cost of debt and equity which together determine the cost of capital. By proper evaluation of the cost of capital based on current and future costs for the optimal capital structure for the firm as opposed to historical costs (sometimes called the "imbedded cost of capital"), the firm's managers already are considering inflation in the capital budgeting process.[3]

A local lender had no interest in lending money at 8% if there is 7% inflation. Assuming the real rate on debt is 8%, this individual knows that a borrower can invest those funds in an asset which will likely go up in value (either as a raw material or in terms of earning value). Hence, to give up the choice of doing this personally, the lender demands a return which will provide purchasing power parity (i.e., at least 7% increment), plus compensate for not having the use of the money (the real interest rate). Hence, the stated rate will reflect both inflationary expectations and the price of money.

Thus, in a highly inflationary economy, almost any project will have a positive rate of return. The increase in the value of the assets alone assures this appreciation. It is only when this inflationary cost is factored into the cost of capital that the firm can avoid being mesmerized by high nominal returns.

Fundamentally, using the local weighted cost of capital in evaluating projects is beneficial because that cost accounts for much of the inflationary pressures if

---

[3] Foster (1970) presents a model relating inflation rates to net present value, allowing for three differential inflation rates. There are changes in general price levels (adjusting the discount rate), increases in some revenues because of the ability to pass on higher costs, and an increase in variable costs. He notes that the general rate of inflation may differ from the revenue or cost increases. In the case of costs, labor market imperfections or considerations of capital intensive options may allow a lower rate of increase in costs. For revenues, the question is the elasticity of revenues with the general price increases. This elasticity reflects the ability to pass along general price increases. Foster also introduces the capital costs for fixed-debt obligations and adjusts for taxes in his formula. Again, as noted earlier in a criticism of ship financing, a fixed-debt formula relies on an "imbedded" debt cost, and does not insure that the capital structure remains in balance. This particular version of Foster's formula forces a unique matching of projects and debt which is not always practically or theoretically desirable.

properly computed. This viewpoint prevents the foreign corporation with a domestic cost of capital of (say) 12% from concluding that it would be much better off in Country X where almost any project earns 20%. It prevents this behavior simply by forcing the multinational corporation to reflect that much of those "earnings" in Country X are inflationary, and a local cost of capital would probably have a basic cost of (say) 15%.

When one considers the multinational firm and currency interactions, then the complexities of the inflation adjustment become much more severe. In this discussion, there are several simplifying assumptions to illustrate the basics of the issue, some of which will be relaxed later.

Inflation and Currency Realignments

The initial assumptions are:

1. World capital markets are efficient and productivity plus wage increases are relatively uniform among nations. (In fact, there are instances of capital scarcity because of many of the risks noted in Chapter 9, and productivity can change radically among nations.)

2. There is a one-year lending decision. At the end of that period, all of the business is terminated and the transaction closed.

3. The firm may separate the investment and financing decision. (Special incentives by particular governments mean this separation is almost impossible for evaluation of many projects in developing countries, an issue addressed in Chapter 12.)

4. One may ignore major differentials induced by taxation and reported earnings per share considerations. (Accounting vagaries and tax policies usually mean that the firm is not indifferent among alternative inflation rates even if offset by currency realignments.)

Working from these basic assumptions, one would expect, over time, that differential costs of capital reflect inflationary expectations, and those inflationary results (if realized) will correspond eventually to adjustments in the currency exchange rates among nations.

This conclusion implies that, for loans of comparable risk and maturity, a lender expects the same real return wherever the money is lent. Inflationary expectations of an unusually high order in any nation will force lenders to build expectations into their required loan rate. Likewise, for the nation to remain competitive in the international markets, the currency must adjust when the inflation in that land exceeds a world norm for any protracted period of time. Hence, arbitrarily high nominal rates for debt or equity in a country reflect inflationary expectations in part, and those inflationary forces will likewise have an effect on the parity of that nation's currency over time. Hence, the real return will not differ among nations.

As a simple example, consider Zebracorp investing in Country Z. The firm can borrow money in New York at 8% or borrow locally at 15%. What is the decision?

If it operates on a one-year planning period, look at this decision in terms of a 7% depreciation of the Country Z currency, the franc, vis-à-vis the U. S. dollar. Hence, one would assume what is saved by using the lower U. S. 8% loan is offset by the requirement to convert francs to dollars at the end of the period since there is a 7% loss in value of the franc vis-à-vis the dollar. The cost to Zebracorp is 8% on the U. S. loan plus 7% on the currency depreciation, or 15%. That 15% corresponds to the local borrowing rate.[4]

This pattern can be generalized to the returns demanded by other contributors to the capital structure. The pattern is generally that the inflationary rate will largely be reflected in the currency adjustments.

The key to the high local rate (15%) may be scarcity or other attributes of the capital market which were eliminated by the initial assumptions. The main cause of this differential is the internal inflation. If the higher financial costs in the local market are due to market imperfections, then the multinational company may be at a comparative advantage by having access to lower cost of funds elsewhere.

In the absence of a monetary correction policy as in Brazil, the taxation assumptions are important. The problem is that depreciation is usually based on historical cost. The increase in earning power of an asset caused by the inflationary effects on the currency are taxed heavily. Thus, part of the recovery of the currency erosion might be recovered by higher selling prices. Yet this recovery is accomplished by higher profits which are taxed using the original cost basis of depreciation.[5]

Moving to a time horizon of more than one year and considering the possibilities of lags in the exchange adjustment, there are additional complications. As the example in Chapter 9 showed, lags in the exchange realignment will justify alternative financing strategies. Even though the "benefits" of inflation are realized regardless of where the project is financed, delays in the impact of inflation on the currency exchange rate can have a sizable impact on the corporation's return from the project, as discussed in Chapter 7.

Many countries may have differential short-term productivity increases which lessen the accuracy sensibility of the assumption of equal world-wide increases. Furthermore, the policy of the International Monetary Fund or agencies of the United Nations to help certain countries may mean that rampant inflation is not checked by a forced devaluation of the currency (e.g., Ghana). Hence, the investing

---

[4] In fact, this calculation is slightly inaccurate even for the simple one-year loan model. The difficulty is that the firm must repatriate the loan *plus interest* using devalued trancs. Consider the loan at $1,000, and assume the exchange rate is 10fr/US$. At the end of the period, the Country Z operation must pay $1,000 plus $80 in interest, or $1,080. If the franc has devalued by 7%, then there are 10.7fr/US$, and the firm must remit

$$\begin{array}{lll} \$1,080 \times 10.7\text{fr/US\$} & = & 11,556\text{fr} \\ \text{The loan was } \$1,000 \times 10\text{fr/US\$} = & & \underline{10,000\text{fr}} \\ \text{So the total franc cost was} & & 1,556\text{fr} \end{array}$$

The cost of 1,556 francs is 15.56% on the original 10,000 francs. Hence, the firm could have committed itself to a 15% fr loan locally and had an extra 56 francs left at the end of this period. This topic was discussed in Part Two.

[5] See the appendix to Chapter 7 for additional comments on accounting practices, and see Appendix 1 to the book, which discusses general principles of international taxation.

firm needs to be very specific in considering both the local capital costs (which were discussed as the most relevant single discount rate for a project) and the lending options which are open to the firm.

Currency Realignments and Differential Long-Term Lending Rates

Inflationary expectations should be built into the cost of capital. Under a number of restrictive assumptions, differential national inflation rates will be reflected in currency exchange rate realignments over time. When one compares differential long-term rates, the implicit assumptions about currency realignments may seem very unrealistic. Consider a twenty-year loan, and the assumptions used earlier. That is, the local cost is 15%, the U. S. borrowing cost is 8%, and the expected depreciation of the franc to the dollar is 7%. In the case of the twenty-year loan, one must also note that the assumption presumes an average compounded depreciation of 7% per year for all twenty years.

This assumption is highly restrictive. In fact, it is because of such uncertainty that many lenders will not grant long-term loans in many currencies, or that the rate on such loans is a floating one.

To understand the reason for the lender's caution, consider Exhibit 10.4. The true interest cost is based on an internal rate of return calculation which considers principal and interest payments in varying currency parities. This interest cost is calculated for a level principal payment loan as well as for a 25% balloon payment ("bullet") loan.

EXHIBIT 10.4 Relative Costs of $100,000 Loan, 8% Local Currency Rate, 20-Year Maturity

| | Cost of the Loan in US$ | |
	Level Principal Payment	75% of Loan Level Principal 25% Balloon
7% Compounded Depreciation for		
20 Years	15.6%	15.6%
7% Compounded Depreciation for		
5 Years	12.4%	12.1%
10 Years	14.5%	14.2%
15 Years	15.3%	15.1%
5% Compounded Depreciation for		
10 Years	12.6%	12.4%
20 Years	13.4%	13.4%
9% Compounded Depreciation for		
10 Years	16.4%	16.0%
20 Years	17.7%	17.7%

In the first comparison, the interest cost on the 8% loan given a 7% compounded depreciation of the local currency is equal for the level loan and for the balloon payment. These results are consistent with expectations based on the previous one-year example.

Then look at the cost when the local currency depreciation is 7% per year only for the first 5, 10, or 15 years, shown in the middle of the table. There is a saving from borrowing outside the nation. For example, if the currency remained stable after five years of depreciation, then the rate of the loan over the full twenty years would only be 12.4% on the level payment and 12.1% on the balloon payment loan.

Perhaps that is too restrictive an assumption. Consider a depreciation of the currency that is only 5% compounded for all twenty years, shown in the lower part of Exhibit 10.3. Note that the cost of the level payment loan and the balloon payment loan are both lower than the 15% local rate. Of course, a higher compounded rate would increase the cost, as shown at the bottom of Exhibit 10.4. Depreciation of 9% compounded for ten years on a level loan costs 16.4%.

These simple examples illustrate the importance of the manager's being aware of the depreciation implicit in the high nominal lending rates in a country where inflation is a serious problem. The issue is not just inflation but inflation relative to the rest of the world, and the compounded depreciation of the local currency compared to the currencies in which the other loans are considered.

As these examples show, it is somewhat naive to note a local borrowing rate, compare it with some external borrowing rate, and then say, "Unless the currency depreciation is greater than the difference (assuming the local currency rate is higher than the outside rate), it pays to borrow outside." The nature of compounding and the particular structure of the loan repayment for other than the simple loan agreement prevent this analysis from giving a valid answer. In conclusion, when dealing with inflation and the local financing options compared to an external option, the manager should:

1. Compute the compounded devaluation rate implied by differentials in lending rates for comparable loans.

2. Verify the impact of local and parent tax considerations.

3. Decide if the differential, net of currency effects, justifies one option over another.

In fact, there are often compelling reasons for the firm to favor local financing even at a higher rate. These reasons relate to many of the political risks noted earlier. However, it is vital that the executive be aware of the implicit cost of this insurance policy.

THE ISSUE OF CONSOLIDATED STATEMENTS

The conclusions reached above are based on the awareness of lenders. Sometimes, this awareness is myopic. For example, some advocates of leasing continue to emphasize that it expands the debt capacity of the firm, an argument that depends largely on the assumptions that the lenders will not adjust for the lease commitments, which are every bit as mandatory for the going concern as debt payments. This is the issue argued about under the topic of "off-balance sheet financing." In fact many lenders acknowledge that they should adjust for lease commitments, yet the adjustments made are often cursory if they exist at all, and they differ from analyst to analyst within the same lending institution.

Likewise, rather spectacular bankruptcies when not based on fraud are often created by this same sort of analysis. Nearly half a century ago, Ivar Kreuger, the Swedish "match king,"and Samuel Insull, the American utility executive, both relied on massive pyramiding of corporate holding companies. Ultimately, of course, the smallest downturn in the operating concerns destroyed the financial viability of the other firms, a risk which the lenders to the various holding companies might have been expected to foresee. In addition, Kreuger had substantial elements of fraud through grossly overvalued assets.

In the context of a cost of capital analysis, it would seem that if the consolidated risk position of the firm is changed by the addition of a major subsidiary in a high-risk area, then the minimum expected return to shareholders and to lenders should be increased. This incremental charge, which applies not just to the incremental financing associated with the project but also to the firm's existing assets as well, should be charged in full to the subsidiary project.

From the standpoint of reported earnings, the Insull and Kreuger pyramiding examples and other more recent cases have helped stimulate more careful accounting standards for consolidation. Currently, the U. S. rules are as follows, as one goes from the consolidation based only on dividends (i.e., a one-line income item, dividends from subsidiaries) to a pro rata inclusion of profits and losses, to a full merging of the balance sheets with a minority interest shown where the subsidiary is not 100% owned:

Percentage of Beneficial Ownership by Parent in Subsidiary	Consolidation for Financial Reporting Purposes
0 – 20%	Dividends as received
20 – 50%	Pro rata inclusions of profits and losses
50 – 100%	Full consolidation

The actual structure the parent chooses for the subsidiary may be dictated by legal formalities, by the request of the host government, and by the protection afforded the parent if its investment is a loan. These are issues of practical tactics.

OPERATING TACTICS FOR THE CAPITAL STRUCTURE

One popular rule of thumb is for the parent to borrow locally as much as possible. This strategy is followed in order to limit the loss if nationalization takes place, to reduce the foreign exchange loss from currency devaluations in the host country (assuming the loans are denominated in the local currency), and to serve as a motivational device for the local manager (who can be told that the capital costs are dictated by that environment and not by simple parent policy).

However, the cost of this insurance must be considered. In some situations, the interest rate differential exceeds any reasonable expectation for currency alignment. A high local interest rate may compensate in part for the lender's reluctance to leave his money in the local currency which is likely to devaluate. Beyond this level, the rate charged may reflect the scarcity of the capital markets and the uncertainty which motivates the parent to investigate local financing sources and to operate on the assumption of maximizing local borrowings. Hence, the cost of the insurance is the differential over the life of the loan for local financing versus alternative external financing proposals.

As an example, if currency rates are stable and there are no major inflationary effects, borrowing locally at 20% versus externally at 10% really amounts to the borrower paying a 10% yearly premium on the amount borrowed to avoid expropriation risk on that part of the investment or to protect against the unlikely event of a devaluation in the local currency. If the plant is expropriated, that loan is just never repaid to the local sources. Of course, the expropriating government may make some token payment, and that payment will be given to the local lenders.

In addition to borrowing locally, many firms prefer local investors for reasons of risk-coping as discussed in Chapter 9. The local government may appreciate the efforts of the company to bring in local interests as well as they will recognize the anger of those local interests in the event that the operation is nationalized with little payment to the investors. However, the limitations of local capital markets coupled with the high costs of dealing with many small investors often limit this approach. In this situation, the local government may prefer the multinational which brings in all the hard currency needed for the project instead of absorbing local funds.

Just as supervisory fees and royalties are sometimes used to minimize disputes over the remission of some funds, so many parents prefer to term their equity investments in the local operation a "loan." The loan repayments are held by the parent as required by the conditions of the financing agreement. Accordingly, remission of interest plus principal is considered to have a better chance of approval from the local government.

When local governments complain about excessive amounts of parent loans to the subsidiary, these loans are sometimes converted to direct loans against inventory and accounts receivable. Although this policy reduces the security for the local senior lenders, it does give the parent a legitimate basis for lending. A disadvantage of this strategy is that with a growing business the inventories and accounts receivable are likely to expand. This expansion requires a greater debt commitment by the parent at the time when a withdrawal is desired. However, the growing business may be in a better position to substitute local debt for parent debt at this point, so that the financing may be quite reasonable. From the standpoint of the U. S. taxing authorities, Section 482 of the 1962 Revenue Act placed the burden of proof on the parent to show that these were bona fide loans. The IRS argued that much of the loan principal being remitted was a dividend payment, and as such was subject to tax. The U. S. parents, in the absence of such a ruling and with a favorable outcome of their project, would reduce most of their investment by tax-free loan repayments and then pay a capital gains tax on the sale of the small equity investment in the firm if and when that sale was made and became taxable.

In terms of the total debt on the consolidated corporate balance sheet, intercompany loans are eliminated. Thus, the effect on the debt-to-equity ratio of the consolidated firm is nil. However, from the standpoint of the debt-bearing capacity of the local firm, local lenders may be more skeptical of a parent's high debt obligation. Placing the parent's debt in a subordinated position dispels this local concern.

DETERMINING THE DISCOUNT RATE IN A RISKY PROJECT

After a risk analysis simulation is completed, or perhaps from some other analysis, the management may have a distribution of return on some criterion as shown in Exhibit 10.5. To calculate net present values with risky projects one has two options. One may adjust the returns to a "certainty equivalent" figure, as discussed in the appendix to this chapter. Alternatively, given the uncertainty attached to the returns of a project (the numerator in present value calculations), one can then search for the discount rate (the denominator in present value calculations) that would incorporate the riskiness of the project. Methods of searching for this discount rate adjusted for risk are presented below.

One approach is to evaluate the project in terms of what capital structure would be appropriate for a project with that risk profile. A capital structure appropriate for the industry, the country, and the risk attitude of management can be selected. This same approach can be applied to aid in determining an appropriate discount rate. Inductively, this same logic can be applied to projects within a given firm; if the project carries more risk than the normal project of the firm, the relevant cost of capital is higher. This reasoning leads to what is called the risk-adjusted discount rate.

An alternative to these approaches, which in practice should achieve a similar result, is to focus on discounting the project's cash flows at a rate appropriate for an all-equity investment of that riskiness, and then to adjust for various loads of debt. If this adjustment is made, then (1) the amount and cost of the debt, and (2) the amount and cost of the equity, will vary somewhat from the weighted cost of capital in practice.[6]

Another approach involves evaluating the standard deviation or variance of a project based on the risk analysis results. In Exhibit 10.6 Project B has one distribution of returns and Project C has another. By calculating the standard deviation of the returns, the manager has an index with which to compare the distribution of the two projects' returns. Others prefer the coefficient of variation of the return, which is a ratio of the standard deviation to the expected value of the return. There are recurring conflicts about the use of standard deviation as a measure for risk; many of these issues and the process of computing variance are discussed in the appendix.

Practically, the outcome from a project simulation model can provide information of returns and Project C has another. By calculating the standard deviation of the returns, the manager has an index with which to compare the distribution of the two projects' returns. Others prefer the coefficient of variation of the return, which profile of a restricted number of possible corporate portfolios is critical for the final decision. These issues and the application of the capital asset model to determine the relevant discount rate are discussed in the two final chapters concerning capital budgeting.

---

[6] Whatever the intellectual justification, higher hurdle rates are used for riskier projects. In Fremgen's survey, 54% of the 179 respondents indicated their firms used higher discount rates when evaluating riskier projects. See James M. Fremgen, "Capital Budgeting Practices: A Survey." *Management Accounting,* May 1973, pp. 19-25.

EXHIBIT 10.5   Probabilities of Rates of Return of Project A

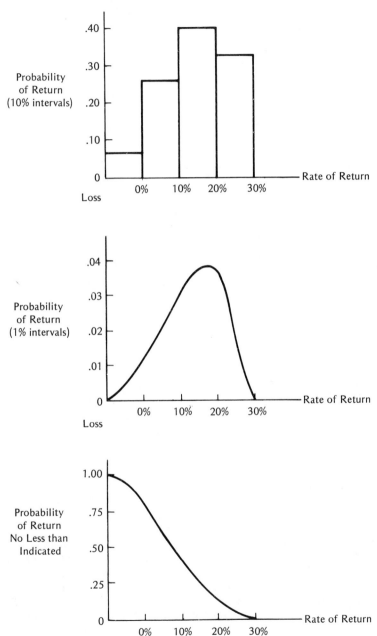

EXHIBIT 10.6   Probabilities of Rates of Return, Projects B
                and C

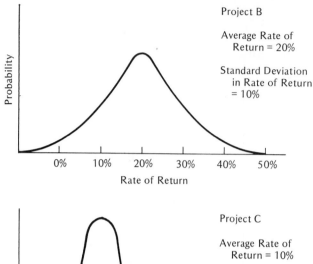

Project B

Average Rate of
Return = 20%

Standard Deviation
in Rate of Return
= 10%

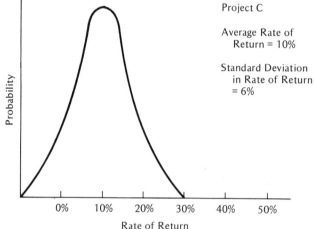

Project C

Average Rate of
Return = 10%

Standard Deviation
in Rate of Return
= 6%

THE RELEVANT RETURN

Both chapters 9 and 10 have noted the differentials when comparing
the return to the project and the return to the parent, and when comparing the returns in the project's or the parent's currency. Where there are dramatic currency
shifts or major delays in repatriation, the divergence of returns can be substantial,
as discussed in Chapter 9. Finally, then, whose return should be considered?

At the most basic level, the ultimate return and risk considerations should be
for the parent company's stockholders. Hence, dollar remittances for the U. S.
parent and a return consistent with the risk of operating in the foreign subsidiary
are appropriate for this example. However, two general issues complicate this view.

First, increasingly the investors in the parent are from a worldwide "family."

If the shareholder group wants only U. S. investments, the impact of their nationality on the external portfolio is not significant. However, these non-U. S. investors may want a "worldwide purchasing power" return, so that their concern is a currency basket weighted in some way, with the dollar only one part of the contents. In addition, just as many U. S. shareholders have increasingly emphasized a variety of noneconomic issues (South African operations, minority employment, the environment), so, too, may these non-U. S. shareholders demand increasing concern by the company management for the firm's operations worldwide, especially in the shareholders' lands.

Second, and more directly, many companies in the true multinational tradition accept their role as worldwide investors. Hence, the fact that funds are blocked in removal from Country X is about as relevant as knowing that a plant in (say) California is not readily marketable. The fact that assets are restricted in a nation on a temporary or a long-term basis is merely an additional inconvenience for the U. S. corporation, just as a low-skill labor force, poor commuter facilities, bad railroad connections, or limited banking associations may be part of operating in some parts of the United States. Obviously, blocked funds are more serious than weak communications or nonmarketable plants in California, but the difference is one of degree, not substance. The nonmobility of assets and the restrictions on business practice are a fact of corporate life not unique to operations in particular countries.

Hence, to the extent that the corporation views itself as a true multinational, the effect of restrictions on repatriation may not be severe. If the firm anticipates continued investment in a country which is in a growing market, the restriction is not even an issue to be addressed in the "good-citizen or bad-citizen" framework noted above. Rather, the commitment is made for long-term continuing portfolio investments in the country, and the restriction on repatriation is generally irrelevant.

In most cases, the firm will verify that the project return and the parent return are both agreeable. However, these are but two goals, and the firm will probably have a number of other goals or constraints of a financial nature, plus nonfinancial standards. Among the financial considerations beyond the return of the project and the return to the parent are:

Liquidity

Even if the returns are satisfactory, the parent may have stringent needs for cash in particular years which a given international project cannot meet. Hence, this constraint may be binding.

Reported Earnings

The consolidation standards may mean that the huge reported losses in the early years of a project will be too large to be acceptable to the current managers, who fear adverse shareholder reaction. Alternatively, relatively high reported earnings may be linked to a need for cash remissions if the parent wishes to maintain a particular dividend payout ratio of (say) 40% of reported earnings. Hence, the earnings reported may relate directly to the liquidity issue.

Alternative Uses of Cash

If the parent plans to invest the funds in the local country, then the project return and reinvestment rate may dominate. At the other extreme, reinvestments overseas mean the parent return in the parent currency will prevail. Hence, a multinational may emphasize different return standards for various nations depending on how a given project fits the corporation's portfolio of projects now and in the future.

Thus, the returns are but two financial aspects of international investments, and other financial values operate as constraints. In extreme cases, these other values become dominant goals.

PUBLIC POLICY AND THE ECONOMICS OF THE FIRM

Even these basic examples have illuminated the essential conflict between the developing nation's government—concerned with the growth of the country's economy and the welfare of its people, and the multinational corporation—preoccupied with earning a fair return on the shareholder's investment consistent with general corporate responsibility and a justifiable level of risk.

On the one side, the firm may segment proposed investments based on risk and rate of return. Classically, the firm will demand a higher return where there is greater risk whether that risk be economic or political. Accordingly, limitations on the firm's freedom to repatriate funds, the imposition of blocked or semiblocked currency restrictions, and the polite inquiry by the potential host country's negotiators about eventual sharing of the ownership of the proposed venture with the local government or other nationals all cause the assessment of the project's risk to increase.

On the other hand, the LDC is interested in a partner that will improve the country itself. The corporation is expected to bring in not just hard currency but a new business which will produce a good product at a fair price with suitable employment policies. It is only natural that the LDC negotiators will take strong interest in the intentions of the firm. They may understandably impose safeguards to prevent the rapacious devouring of the resources of the LDC by a corporate octopus whose single goal is to remove as much profit as rapidly as possible.

Thus, the firm wants stability and a hospitable environment, and is willing to continue investment in the country given that environment. The host country, concerned about the nature of some corporations, wants an enduring commitment not only to profits but to a reasonable corporate citizenship in terms of pricing, employment, and proper corporate demeanor. Worries on the part of the firm cause it to inquire about repatriation agreements. Worries on the part of the LDC negotiators cause them to seek plans for substantial national representation on the board or for restrictions on the pace at which the firm can remit its profits.

These issues, once raised, reinforce the concerns of the firm's envoys about nationalization or expropriation, at the most serious level, or minority voting blocks and repatriation restrictions at the least obnoxious level.

Hence, the cycle begins, and the cobweb created by this action-reaction-intensified action-intensified reaction creates not only ill will but very rigid contracts!

The result is the situation viewed today: the LDCs resent major corporations (often American) that have high returns from foreign operations which are remitted rapidly. The American corporation, in turn, worries about the increasing risks from longer term investments in nations where political instability and currency shocks are a yearly (if not monthly) fact of life.

Stated simply, worries about risk induce greater profiteering, usually translated into "high returns remitted rapidly." This action, in turn, supports the contention of LDCs that the multinationals are tempted to bleed their lands for a larger corporate goal of maximizing profits.[7]

To this end, private and public insurance schemes designed to minimize these possible shocks help the corporations feel more comfortable with the environment. However, limitations on the types of risk which are covered, together with careful considerations of the legality of the agreement, induce a cautionary attitude on the part of the multinational. The continuing hesitancy of OPIC to pay Kennecott and Anaconda for Chilean losses because of (legitimate) factual disputes, of course, has done nothing to reassure corporations.

There is also the conflict between the desire to be a good local citizen (whether from local economic self-interest or survival or from the view of responsible business practice) and the need to use global transfers of skills and resources which form the basis for the multinational firm. Hymer (1970) reviews many of the assumptions justifying the existence of a multinational firm, observing that one can reasonably argue whether the economies of scale offered by the multinational firm might be as well realized by crossing industries, placing the giant firm within a given political/societal border. Among other issues, there are difficulties imposed on local fiscal and monetary policy of a given nation-state by the existence of the multinational firm, since there is no multinational fiscal/monetary authority.

SUMMARY

This chapter has reviewed the corporate financial theory on the cost of capital and the impact of business and financial risk on the return to shareholders. The use of different discount rates for projects of varying degrees of risk was suggested as plausible, providing that discount rates were based on what firms active primarily in that type of project would require as a capital structure in the open market or on what is reasonable based on the general riskiness of the project.

We have examined the fallacy of pyramiding in which the local capital structure is used in conjunction with a low cost of equity from the parent-investor to justify a very low discount rate for a project in a foreign land. The appropriate discount rate for a project in another nation is generally no less than the discount rate implied by domestic financing of that project using domestic capital sources if available. The divergence of capital structures from nation to nation was noted.

Inflation, if anticipated, is built into the cost of capital for a project when domestic sources are used as the initial standards for evaluation. Local lenders have

---

[7] The possibility of a war between the host and parent governments further aggravates the situation. On the other hand, the American subsidiaries of the German I. G. Farben produced chemicals for the Allied war effort while General Motor's German subsidiaries manufactured trucks for the Wehrmacht in World War II. See *The New York Times,* March 13, 1974, p. 36.

very high charges for debt because they often anticipate substantial inflation which will reduce the nominal returns of the debt issue. In a frictionless perfect market, inflation and currency parity changes tend to accommodate each other. However, lags in the adjustment process and various rigidities in the system may make the impact less than perfectly compensating. In the long term, very high nominal local rates often imply an unrealistically high compounded devaluation of the local currency over time. In other cases, these high nominal rates for local loans are the result of capital market imperfections (i.e., limits on foreign investments and limited domestic capital availability).

Practical operating tactics for investing in some lands include maximum use of local debt and equity financing, denominating the parent's investment as a loan instead of equity, and use of royalty and supervisory fees paid to the parent.

After noting the alternative means by which managers may evaluate the risk of a project, once again the issue of whose returns are to be considered, appeared. The tradition of concern with the welfare of shareholders is blunted by two considerations. First, many shareholders are not citizens of the parent country, especially in the case of a U. S. parent. Second, a socially responsible corporation committed to a given region or area as a true multinational may not be preoccupied with bringing funds home.

Finally, the problem of insecure corporations confronting worried governments of developing countries was addressed. Each is concerned about undesirable actions of the other, yet each protective reaction by one reinforces the anxiety felt by the other. Supranational insurance schemes were suggested as one means to stop this cycle of mutual action and reaction.

Questions

1. "If the parent's cost of capital is 15%, its equity investment in a subsidiary only needs to be charged to the subsidiary at 15%." Why or why not?

2. "Regardless of the interest rate, we always borrow in a cheap currency with a likely devaluation, since that minimizes our financing costs." Give an example where this strategy would fail. Do you think it is a good rule of thumb?

3. What data would you desire in order to evaluate the risk of a project in a particular country? Why would one corporation find the same level of risk acceptable while another one might reject it? Does this indicate the irrationality of corporate management?

4. With worldwide operations, IBM has about 300 American nationals working for it outside the United States. Do you think this policy is a good one? What firms could use it more profitably than other firms, or do you believe it makes sense for all firms?

Bibliography

Adams, William T., "The Emerging Law of Dispute Settlement Under the United States Investment Insurance Program." *Law and Policy in International Business.* Vol. 3, No. 1, 1971, pp. 101-156.

Chenery, H. B., "Comparative Advantage and Development Policy." *American Economic Review,* March 1961, pp. 18-51.

Eiteman, David K. and Arthur I. Stonehill, *Multinational Business Finance.* Reading, Mass.: Addison-Wesley Publishing Co., 1973, Ch. 9 and 10.

Foster, Earl M., "The Impact of Inflation on Capital Budgeting Decisions." *Quarterly Review of Economics and Business,* Autumn 1970, pp. 19-24.

Hymer, Stephen, "The Efficiency (Contradictions) of Multinational Corporations." *American Economic Review,* May 1970, pp. 441-448.

Johnson, H. G., "A Theoretical Model of Economic Nationalism in New and Developing States." *Political Science Quarterly,* June 1965, pp. 169-185.

Keesing, D. B., "Outward Looking Policies and Economic Development." *Economic Journal,* June 1967, pp. 303-320.

Polk, Judd, *et al., U. S. Production Abroad and the Balance of Payments.* National Industrial Conference Board, New York, 1966.

Shulman, J. S., "Transfer Pricing in the Multinational Firm." *European Business,* Jan. 1969, pp. 46-54.

Weston, J. Fred and Bart W. Sorge, *International Managerial Finance.* Homewood, Ill.: Richard D. Irwin, Inc., 1972, Ch. 3.

Appendix: The Evaluation of Project Risk

The technique of risk analysis has been available for many years. Essentially, the technique requires estimates of the distribution of possible outcomes of a project's major components (e.g., sales, market share, advertising costs, wage rates, and so on). The crucial variables are linked together in a model (e.g., if market share increases by 8% in year 4, sales will increase by an expected value of $3,000,000 with a standard deviation of $50,000). Then the model is embedded in a computer program. Computer simulation can determine the range of possible outcomes on various criteria for the project.[1]

If the criterion is rate of return and the company is considering Project A and Project B as two mutually exclusive alternatives, there might be a distribution of returns as shown in Exhibit 1. Notice the greater risk in Project B. Although Project B

---

[1] Simulation involves repeated chance trials using calculations from a random number generator adjusted to provide various probability distributions.

EXHIBIT 1 Cumulative Rate of Return Distribution

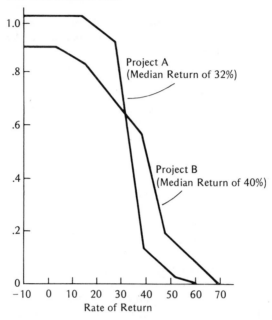

Probability of Return No
Less Than Indicated Rate

Project A
(Median Return of 32%)

Project B
(Median Return of 40%)

Rate of Return

has a higher rate of return than Project A, one management might prefer Project B, arguing that a higher risk is fully justified by the return, and another management might prefer the safer (and lower) return of Project A.

In addition, risk analysis reveals to the manager that some projects are not what they seem at first. Thus, in comparing the rate of return or net present value of two projects on the basis of the most likely single value (mode) for each of the many underlying variables, a manager might find one project has the higher value with certainty. However, on the basis of simulation, the executive might learn that the other project has a higher mode for rate of return or net present value because of the form of the underlying distributions which must be combined.

Finally, risk analysis and simulation may be used as part of sensitivity analyses which enable one to explore the effect of shifts in any or all of the underlying variables.

In addition to the problem of obtaining estimates of the variables, a basic drawback of risk analysis is in the indeterminacy of the technique. In some cases, a project will be eliminated if it is completely dominated (i.e., there are other alternatives which have a higher return for any level of risk). However, in most cases the manager now sees risk added to the analysis and the choice is based on an attitude toward risk. This weakness indeed may be a strength, for it allows the manager to include attitudes and values which are not so readily obtained by explicit questioning from a staff management scientist.

From a risk analysis simulation, a manager can derive a distribution of probable returns for a proposed project. These distributions may be quite varied, but a standard deviation and variance for each distribution can be calculated.[2] From these measures of dispersion, some managers impute requirements for the discount rates. For example, they may consider the coefficient of variation, the ratio of the standard deviation of the value to the expected value. Thus, if the standard deviation of a project is 7% and the expected terminal rate of return is 18%, the coefficient of variation of the terminal rate of return is $7/18$, or .4. When this project is compared with another project, the focus is not on return or variation *per se*, but the ratio. Another project with a return of 5% and a standard deviation of return of 2% would also have a coefficient of variation of .4. Likewise, a project with a 25% terminal rate of return but a standard deviation of 13% would have a coefficient of variation of .2, making it less desirable than the first project. The problem with this measure is that management's attitude toward risk is not necessarily uniform with regard to the ratio. An equally good measure may be to require that a project have a return minus the standard deviation which is at least 10%. Or perhaps a relevant measure is the return minus some constant times the standard deviation. Alternatively, management may focus simply on the probability of a loss. If the probability of a loss is greater than N%, no return will be sufficiently high to invest. Another standard is to say that the return must be reduced by a constant times the probability of a loss, and the resulting figure must be greater than say (10%). All these rules are only armchair standards for coping with risk.[3]

Risk aversion is a measure of one's disinclination to take risks. Risk aversion is expressed by index numbers that measure the willingness of an individual to gamble in given situations. If one assumes that most individuals prefer less risk to more risk for a given level of expected return, then one can see how the level of risk an individual is willing to accept in exchange for a potentially higher expected return changes with income or with wealth.

---

[2] Variance in algebraic terms is computed as follows. Let

Y_i be a return in category i,

P_i be the probability of category i occurring,

$\bar{Y}$ be the average of all Y_i values, weighted by the probability of occurring

$$(= \sum_{i=1}^{N} P_i Y_i, \text{ where } \sum_{i=1}^{N} \text{ means } P_1 Y_1 + P_2 N_2 + ... + P_N Y_N)$$

Then the variance is equal to

$$\sum_{i=1}^{N} P_i (Y_i - \bar{Y})^2$$

[3] Conrath found that executives analyzed projects consistent with a decision rule that P (loss) $\leqslant$ 10% and E (Return) = 30% + 3 × P (loss). See David W. Conrath, "From Statistical Decision Theory to Practice: Some Problems with the Transition." *Management Science*, April 1973, pp. 873-883. Alderfer and Bierman found that subjects in a gambling situation consistently had a strong aversion to loss and preferred an alternative with a lower mean and higher variance but with a lower probability of loss to another alternative with a higher mean, lower variance, and higher probability of loss. See Clayton T. Alderfer and Harold Bierman, Jr., "Choices with Risk: Beyond the Mean and Variance." *Journal of Business*, July 1970, pp. 341-353. From a field study of eight firms, Mao concluded that the negative semivariance (the variance of outcomes below the mean) was a far better measure of risk than variance. James C. T. Mao, "Survey of Capital Budgeting: Theory and Practice." *Journal of Finance*, May 1970, pp. 349-360.

Consider the investor who has a choice between a risky asset and a fixed income asset. (S)he can transform the expected income into some combination of the risky investment and the fixed income investment. Then, if (s)he increases the *absolute* dollar amount invested in the risky asset as wealth increases, the investor has decreasing *absolute* risk aversion. If the *percentage* of total wealth invested in the risky asset increases with wealth, then the investor has decreasing *relative* risk aversion. Pratt and others have indicated that it is plausible that individuals would show decreasing absolute risk aversion.[4] Intuitively, one can find plausible explanations for either increasing or decreasing relative risk aversion as wealth rises.

To replace the dependency on variance and its inadequacy as a measure of risk, one may substitute a more formal approach of charging each period's cash flow with the cost of reducing risk in that period. This adjusted cash flow then may be included in computing the adjusted terminal rate of return after this insurance premium has been included. This approach parallels the idea of a certainty equivalent which has been discussed in business decisions by Raiffa and others.[5] A rational and consistent decision maker will be indifferent between some certain value and a distribution of uncertain returns. For example, one may choose to accept 50¢ rather than a gamble with equal probabilities of nothing and $1. Depending on whether one is risk averse or risk prone, one might accept (for example) 45¢ or 55¢, respectively, rather than accept the gamble. Similarly, one can generalize this concept to (1) uncertain payments at some future time period and (2) a distribution of outcomes more detailed than the two possibilities (0 or $1) shown here. Hence, in analyzing a capital budgeting project or a portfolio, the manager must obtain a distribution of cash flows which may be expected in each year. Then, what payments would be acceptable with certainty in place of that uncertain cash flow in that year? This certainty equivalent value is then discounted at the appropriate rate.[6]

Apart from management specification problems, the disadvantage of this approach is selecting the combinations of portfolio cash flows and finding the probability of their outcome. The certainty equivalent of a portfolio distribution in the nth year is not the sum of the certainty equivalents of the projects within that portfolio unless the projects, individually and in total, are so small as to warrant the assumption of a linear utility function for the manager over that interval.

---

[4] See J. W. Pratt, "Risk Aversion in the Small and the Large." *Econometrica*, Jan.-April 1964, pp. 122-136.

[5] See Howard Raiffa. *Decision Analysis: Introductory Lectures on Choices Under Uncertainty.* (Reading, Mass.: Addison-Wesley, 1968).

[6] The rate would be a risk-free rate (U. S. government bonds, for example) since the risk of the project has already been considered. In making this decision operationally, several simplifications can be employed which somewhat distort the results from the theoretical values. Thus, one may assume a_i, a coefficient for transforming the expected value of the cash flows in year (Y_i) to the certainty equivalent ($a_i Y_i$). Under this simplification, the net present value of the certainty equivalents of an N-year project is

$$\sum_{i=1}^{N} \frac{a_i Y_i}{(1+r)^i} \qquad [0 \leq a_i \leq 1].$$

Essentially, the selection of a_i is designed to compensate for the parameters of the cash flow distribution other than the expected value.

Chaolandia's Super-Widgets

In early 1976, the Manager of Aggressive Enterprises in Chaolandia submitted the following project for approval by the parent company. Chaolandia was a developing country and Aggressive Enterprises operated there in the form of a locally incorporated subsidiary.

Product: Super-widgets. Aggressive Enterprises had been manufacturing widgets in Chaolandia. The new project would allow the country to produce more powerful widgets, super-widgets.

Investment Requirements: It was estimated that 100,000 Chaolandia pesos (CP) would be required for plant and equipment. There was no parent investment for working capital. However, 20,000 CP of the 100,000 CP required for plant and equipment could be provided by the parent out of obsolete equipment it maintained in its warehouse. Chaolandia's government was agreeable to this transfer. The government also agreed to a five-year straight line depreciation method for the 100,000 CP of plant and equipment.

Project Life: Although the market for super-widgets was expected to continue expanding at least for the next twenty years, Chaolandia's government insisted in making arrangements for the government purchase of the company after five years. In this case, the government proposed to purchase the super-widget plant for 155,000 CP at the end of five years, in December 1981.

Demand: At a price of 400 CP per unit, demand for super-widgets was estimated as follows:

	Domestic	Exports
	(units)	
1977	100	50
1978	150	75
1979	200	100
1980	200	100
1981	200	100

The domestic demand was considered to be price inelastic. That is, for the likely prices in the future, the quantity demanded appeared to be independent of the price charged. However, this was not the case with exports. Export demand was considered to be price elastic. It was thought that for each 1% increase in prices, the export quantity demanded decreased by 1.2%. Chaolandia's exports could affect the sales of some of the other divisions of Aggressive Enterprises. However, this impact was expected to be nominal at least during the first five years of the project.

Prices: The engineers had estimated that an initial price of 400 CP was quite appropriate, given the competition. However, historical inflation in the country made it possible to count on an annual 10% increase in prices. The 400 CP for 1977 already incorporated the rate of inflation between 1976 and 1977.

Variable Costs were estimated by the Engineering Department as follows:

Raw material	Domestic	50 CP per unit
	Imported	25 CP per unit
Labor		25 CP per unit

Domestic costs had recently been increasing at an annual rate of 12% because of inflation. Import prices were subject to fluctuations in the exchange rate. Cost estimates for 1977 already incorporated the rate of inflation between 1976 and 1977.

Fixed Costs were estimated as follows:

Supervisory fees to the parent	10,000 CP annually
Selling and administrative expenses	30,000 CP annually
Depreciation	20,000 CP annually

Selling and administrative expenses were also subject to a 12% inflation rate per annum. The supervisory fees were a form of royalty and they did not involve additional expenditures at home.

Exchange Rate: The economics department of Aggressive Enterprises had estimated the following exchange rates:

	CP per $
1976	4.00 CP
1977	4.00
1978	4.40
1979	4.40
1980	4.90
1981	4.90

There was no control on repatriation of earnings.

Taxes:

Chaolandia's Taxes:	25% income tax and no loss carry forward
	25% withholding tax on dividends
Parent Country Taxes:	Income: 50%, allowing tax credit for taxes paid abroad
	Capital gains: 25%

Remittances: It was expected that all the profits after taxes would be remitted to the parent company.

Cost of Capital Applicable to Chaolandia: 20%. Super-widgets production in Chaolandia was not expected to alter the risk profile of Aggressive Enterprises.

1. Would you accept the project? What assumptions do you consider to be critical in your analysis? Use Exhibits 1 and 2 for your projections.

2. How would you analyze the project if earnings repatriation were prohibited during the initial four years of the project?

3. How would you analyze the project if Aggressive Enterprises intended to continue operating Super-widget for the next twenty years (i.e., the government would not purchase it at the end of fifth year) and a control in earnings repatriation existed? Assume earnings repatriation at the present time is limited to 12% of annual earnings.

4. Chaolandia's government and financial institutions have offered several alternatives to finance the project. These alternatives include several degrees of leverage with local funds. These local funds, however, are much more expensive than the price Aggressive Enterprises has in the home country. How would you analyze the project if an independent financial package had to be created for its financing, and the relevant question became: what is the return on Aggressive Enterprises' equity?

EXHIBIT 1   Super-Widgets Project: Pro Forma Statement (Chaolandia pesos)

Receipts	1977	1978	1979	1980	1981
1. Sales (units)					
2. Domestic					
3. Exports					
4. Total					
5. Price per unit					
6. Gross revenue					
Expenses					
7. Raw material					
8. Domestic					
9. Imports					
10. Labor (per unit)					
11. Total variable cost per unit					
12. No. of units					
13. Total variable costs					
14. Supervisory fees					
15. Selling and administrative					
16. Depreciation					
17. Total expenses					
18. Profit before taxes					
19. Local taxes					
20. Profit after taxes					
21. Withholding taxes					

EXHIBIT 2: Super-Widgets Project: Cash Flow Analysis (parent country dollars)

Exchange Rate:	1976 4.00	1977 4.00	1978 4.40	1979 4.40	1980 4.90	1981 4.90
Cash Inflows						
1. Profit after taxes						
2. Depreciation						
3. Others:						
4.						
5.						
6. *Total Cash Inflows*						
Cash Outflows						
1. Initial investment						
2. Taxes:						
3. Chaolandia						
4.						
5. Parent country						
6. On dividends						
7. On fees						
8. On capital gains						
9.						
10.						
11. *Total Cash Outflows*						
12.						
13. Net cash flows						
14. Discount factors at 20%						
15. Discounted flows						
16. Net present value						

Corporate Strategy and the Decision to Invest Abroad

Although this book emphasizes the financial considerations relating to investment appraisal, prior to such analysis must come resolution of the issue of the corporation's strategy. Also called the question of "policy" or "corporate philosophy of operations," the issue centers about such concerns as:

"What is our primary expertise to be in ten years?"

"Where do we want to operate, by geographic region and by product line?"

"Without changes in our operating policies and business lines, where will we be in ten years?"

Thus, the heuristic the firm employs to reduce the number of projects which are subject to detailed analysis is a screening device based on an answer to the question:

"In terms of our corporate strategic plan, would this operation fit our desired future image of the firm?"

Only if there is an affirmative answer should the firm pursue an analysis of the project. This issue is explored after reviewing economic and organizational behavioral factors which influence the decision to invest abroad. Following the discussion of approaches to the strategy issue is a comprehensive financial analysis of a project, Freeport Minerals' decision to invest in an Australian nickel mine.

THE STIMULUS FOR INTERNATIONAL INVESTMENT

Economic Motivation

Comparative Advantage. A major economic motivator is comparative advantage. This basic concept of economics suggests that each productive asset is most effective in terms of the value of total output for the society if it is used in those tasks for which its relative advantage over other alternatives is greatest.

As an example, assume that there are two countries, A and B, both with one hundred labor weeks of time available at equal labor rates. A product can be produced in either nation, but it must have two processes completed for the finished version. The units per process for each nation are:

		Units Produced Per Week	
		Process X	Process Y
Country A	100 weeks	10/wk	5/wk
Country B	100 weeks	6/wk	2/wk

Comparative advantage suggests that each nation's workers should be used where they have the largest relative advantage or smallest relative disadvantage. In this example, Country A is more efficient in terms of units per week for both Processes X and Y. This fact relates to *absolute efficiency.* However, its relative efficiency is greater for Process Y, since the ratio $5/2$ is greater than $10/6$. A policy of completing as many units as possible of Process Y in Country A would result in production of 500 units. Those units are treated with Process X in Country B, and the remaining seventeen weeks of unused time in Country B are used to produce an additional $25\frac{1}{2}$ finished units (completing both Process X and Process Y for these extra units), for a total finished production from both nations of $525\frac{1}{2}$. Given the problem as defined, this is the maximum output possible from a division of the countries.[1]

Translated to international corporate operations, the impact of comparative advantage may be related to labor skills or unit costs, to transportation expenses for reaching the total market, and to capital markets, for example. In spite of much rhetoric about cheap foreign labor and its effect on American jobs, there are several aspects to the issue of relative labor costs and unit costs. These unit costs, in turn, are a function of capital (machinery and human training) and wage rates in conjunction with productivity. The wage rates paid in many countries appear low when compared with the wages paid in the United States. This fact is likely to make these other countries more attractive as an investment site for the multinational company when the goods to be produced require a large amount of labor. However, when the

[1] A strategy of completing all Process X in Country A would provide 1,000 units, but this is beyond the capacity of Country B for Process Y since the maximum in Process Y from Country B at 2 units per week is 200 units in 100 hours. Thus Country A would complete Process X on these 200 units, and complete both Process X and Process Y on an additional 266.7 units in the remaining 80 labor weeks, for a total finished production of *466.7 units.* If one were to produce finished products separately in each country (the "no-trade" situation in international exchange, for example), then Country A could produce 333.3 units and Country B could produce 150 units, for a total of *483.3 units.*

goods to be produced require a considerable amount of capital investment relative to labor, then the lower wages play a less important role in the final decision. Other factors such as the skill of the labor force may make investing in high-wage countries more desirable.

When there are limited economies of scale in producing a product which has relatively high transportation costs, the firm may favor establishment of several plants around the world. This policy allows lower transportation costs to customers and lower total unit costs. In this case, lower costs would result from distribution benefits: average miles per unit delivered are lower. In addition, special economies in transportation may exist if there is governmental aid or differential geographic elements (e.g., navigable waterways or mountainous terrain and no railroads).

In the capital markets, freedom of transactions among currencies means that rates adjusted for risk should reach equilibrium. However, limitations on capital export and import, alternative expectations about currencies, special tax considerations, and the political risks noted in Chapter 9 suggest rate differentials in capital markets. When the local government commits public policy toward encouragement of a particular enterprise, then special tax concessions and other arrangements mean that, even if the markets were in equilibrium, the special arrangements may offer attractive financing incentives for the multinational corporation. The studies relevant to this issue in the international securities example will be discussed in Chapter 12.

Operational Constraints. A second economic incentive for international operation is simply binding operational constraints or incentives. Independently of comparative advantage, certain raw materials may only be available in a particular region. Proximity to those supplies may induce a location of manufacturing operations at those points. Government political policies may force production operations in many lands in order to sell in those countries. Finally, the local government may tie availability of the resource (bauxite, nickel, and so on) to the establishment of a local plant beyond the scope required by the firm's basic operation. Hence, these economic constraints, induced by nature or by man, determine the location of international operations and may become a force for worldwide vertical integration.

Taxation. Among the most basic economic incentives to location decisions is taxation. Because management is charged with the responsibility of maximizing shareholder returns in the long run, the issue of lower corporate taxes in particular areas of the world becomes important.

The form of tax benefit differs. The absolute rate of taxes on profits may be low. The definition of taxable income may be more advantageous to the firm in some nations than in others; for example, the United Kingdom has periodically allowed free depreciation on some assets in particular industries, permitting the firms to take as much depreciation as desired in a given year to offset all profits until the asset is fully depreciated. Finally, some nations may have very low taxes on the receipt of dividend income or a very low withholding tax applied to dividend or interest payments outside the nation. Such an arrangement encourages the multinational firm to use this land as a base for a financing subsidiary which receives dividends from operating subsidiaries and remits payments to other firms in the same corporate family. These issues, and the basic rules of U. S. taxation of international income are addressed in Appendix 1.

Financial Diversification. One economic motivation often linked to the "acceptance of a good investment" philosophy is financial diversification, which is spreading the firm's risk throughout a wider range than any one nation will permit. By diversifying over basic markets, products, regions, and governments, the firm hopes to avoid dependence on the outcome of a single unique investment. This is the same intent as that which compels an investor to allocate a securities portfolio over many stocks.

Oligopolistic Markets. An oligopolistic market structure is often associated with a decision to invest abroad. When there is limited product differentiation, economies of scale, and a small number of sellers, then an oligopolistic market structure induces a follow-the-leader strategy among the competitors. To prevent one member from dominating local or world markets, the other members of the industry are compelled to match one company's expansion lead. Often, this is simply a "me, too" attitude. However, this attitude can also be rationalized as the result of an effective reduction in the risk that management perceives in the investment. An investment that once appeared extremely risky because of the large number of unknowns involved, could be perceived by the firm as less risky if a major competitor is investing in that area. In other cases, the reaction is part of a well thought-out strategy based on industry economics where the competitors believe the cost structure and economies of scale in marketing, production, sourcing, and so on, would permit one member to dominate if that firm could seize a large enough total market share.[2]

Potential Loss of Markets. Finally, there is the opportunity to invest because failure to invest would result in losses. Some business opposition to a particular anti-pollution device may be based on the belief it is uneconomic to the firm. However, if the mayor of a city makes it clear that unless the firm installs a residual fluid discharge precipitator he will close the plant, then the return on the investment in the precipitator is quite high. Likewise, a firm may establish foreign operations in order to supply the foreign market (or the original domestic market) when there is a belief that the market will be lost unless such an operation is established.[3]

Organizational and Behavioral Elements

Some researchers have focused upon concepts from organization theory and psychology to explain corporate investment decisions. Before turning to the descriptive studies which analyze why firms have gone abroad in the past, it is helpful to review the ideas from organization theory as they influence the investment process. One comprehensive structure which was developed to explain organizational decision making is *The Behavioral Theory of the Firm* by Richard M. Cyert

[2] For a detailed analysis of the impact of oligopolistic markets on the multinational enterprise see F. T. Knickerbocker, *Oligopolistic Reaction and Multinational Enterprise.* Boston: Division of Research, Harvard Business School, 1973.

[3] A review of the major economic elements which may contribute to a direct foreign investment decision is found in Richard E. Caves, "International Corporations: The Industrial Economics of Foreign Investment." *Economica,* Feb. 1971, pp. 1-27.

and James G. March.[4] In their work, Cyert and March treat the organization as a *coalition* of decision-making individuals. Decisions can be analyzed according to certain "relational concepts," which describe how individuals handle the problems of reaching decisions within the framework of an organization.

Elements of the Decisions. Cyert and March find three major components in the decision process—goals, expectations, and choice.

The *goals* in a decision are formed through formal and informal bargaining among the participants, and these goals evolve through time. A goal can be characterized by its "dimension"—the target of the goal, and its "aspiration level"—how far the goal is to be carried out. The dimensions of the goal are highly influenced by the nature of the changing membership in the coalition of individuals. For example the decision of a new president of General Motors to emphasize the production of small cars to offset the impact of imported compacts shows the goal of offsetting foreign competition. The level of aspiration may fluctuate from holding market share to wiping out foreign competition.

Expectations formed by the coalition members are a function of the information gathered. Accordingly, changes in the system of sampling information, in the presentation of information to the firm, and in the range of information available affect firm expectations. If the new GM president had a new information system installed, receiving daily selling data by model instead of weekly reports ten days after each week ended, then the expectations of the firm (i.e., its view of the automobile world) would probably be different at any given point in time than would otherwise be the case.

Cyert and March analyze *choice* as occurring in response to a problem, and affected by standard operating rules for coping with an uncertain environment. They assume multiple and changing goals, and the choice process was to obtain an "acceptable decision which met the minimum level for various goals."[5] Thus, the GM president may have seen a problem as "stop the erosion of GM world market share by foreign compacts." GM administration may have an alert system which triggers the response, such as any 10% decline in sales volume maintained more than two quarters in a row. A general task force may be assigned to review the situation and make recommendations, which is the normal response to a volume decline. The recommendation may be for a restyling of a certain body shell, even though all participants know there may be other options which additional intensive study might reveal as a superior choice. However, this restyle recommendation is consistent with the time frame, certain cost structures, and no more than a certain level of production disruption.

Relational Concepts. There are four relational concepts which Cyert and March believe affect the goals-expectations-choice decision framework:

---

[4] Richard M. Cyert and James G. March, *The Behavioral Theory of the Firm.* Englewood Cliffs, N.J.. Prentice-Hall, Inc., 1963.
    [5] Thus, a typical decision cycle involves a problem which forces the organization to enter a decision process. Standard operating procedures, rules of thumb, and the like are first used to handle the problem. A variety of alternatives are formulated or considered. With multiple standards which are themselves changing over time, the first alternative which meets the "minimum level of acceptability" on the entire range of standards is selected.

Quasi-resolution of conflict occurs in the Cyert and March framework because departmentalized rationality usually prevails over the single-mindedness of centralized decision making. By having local rationality (in which subunits operate with subgoals), by using acceptable-level decision rules ("minimum-or-better" standards rather than "maximization"), and by the occurrence of sequential attention to goals at various tiers in the organization, potential conflict is reduced. Decisions are made to accommodate and to resolve disagreement among coalition members for the time being. In this approach no formal or long-term conflict resolution is involved.

The *search* for problem solutions is influenced by the decision process in that search is (1) motivated, (2) simple-minded, and (3) biased. A problem evokes a search process to find an acceptable-level solution. A solution is sought by seeking alternatives within the neighborhood of the problem itself and in the area of the most obvious alternative. If this procedure fails, the search process is broadened until an acceptable alternative is found.

Organizational learning is the process by which organizations adapt over time. Firms adapt in *goals* based on past performance, past expectations, and past performance of comparable organizations. There is adaptation in *attention rules;* coalition members learn to study parts of their environment and to ignore other information. Organizations adapt in *search rules,* for if a search is unsuccessful, the search rules themselves are altered until a solution is found.

Uncertainty avoidance behavior is practiced by organizations which use short-run "fire-fighting" techniques to solve problems after they occur rather than to anticipate them. Cyert and March argue that firms typically do not anticipate the future by seeking a maximum expected value or a minimum level of operations. Rather, they ignore the problem and focus on short-run feedback as a response to problems which develop. They seek a "negotiated environment" in which standard pricing policies for members of the industry, normal business practices, and other such phenomena allow the firm to reduce the uncertainty present in its competitive environment.

One can expand on this basic Cyert and March framework to evaluate major capital budgeting decisions. Thus, one study suggested the following:[6]

Multiple Organizational Levels for Decisions. Within *The Behavioral Theory,* the emphasis upon unilevel or multilevel "coalitions" served to avoid the discussion of the influence that tiers of individuals have upon decision making. For example, the final consensus is the result of highly filtered goals in which a participant received a somewhat ordered goal system from above, modified it according to his/her interests and biases, and transmitted it lower in the organization. The requirement that decisions pass through many organizational levels itself influences the outcome of those decisions. Whatever the goals of the board of GM, the interaction of engineers, marketers, stylists, and so forth will all affect the decision process as decisions move through the various organizational levels.

Bilateral Bargaining. Related to the multiple level consideration is the two-party (superior-subordinate) formation of expected project performance. The final expectations of the coalition are the result of sequential bargaining at various levels in the firm rather than the result of any original group concensus or study. The auto-

[6] See Carter (1971).

mobile engineer concedes a certain engine performance in the compact car in order to gain approval of the marketing department; together they recommend a particular model for production to the group vice-president for that automobile division, for example.

Uncertainty and Goals. Goals found in a firm are related to the degree of uncertainty present in the firm's general environment and to the uncertainty present in a particular project's forecasts. In strategic decisions the firms may use a partial adjustment in goals to handle uncertainty. The number of goals adjusts to accommodate the degree of uncertainty. Thus, a simple goal of maximum rate of return may dominate a decision on which GM division would bring out a previously approved new model. On the other hand, a potential decision for GM to build a mass transit system in Seattle is likely to trigger many more issues as part of the discussion. How much does GM want to be in mass transit? What timetable is appropriate for this new venture? Will it detract from automotive and truck production?

Stimulus for Search. Many factors besides a problem generate search. Some of these stimuli might be:

1. The desire of an executive to meet a certain goal which is related to personal well-being.

2. A top executive's decision to have the firm enter a new area even though profits and sales are satisfactory in the current field. For instance, GM has an interest in mass transit. Hence, the problem is less important than a general philosophy of management to diversify.

3. A change in managers. The new manager may have fundamentally different beliefs on what the firm should be doing.

4. Opportunity-oriented search. The fact that a business operates in certain economic, geographic, and industrial markets means that particular opportunities will occur. In this situation, there is no problem. Rather, the nature of the business means that certain opportunities will come to management, regardless of any search effort.

The Pollyanna-Nietzsche Effect. Managers may operate as if decisions once made resolve all uncertainty present in the data on which the decision was based. A "think positive" mental attitude can be used to stimulate successful performance by the organizational participants. Thus, the new GM president could forget all the uncertainty surrounding a task force's recommendation of a particular restyled model intended to lessen the foreign compact car penetration of GM's world market share. The president could act as if the project will stop these competitors.

From this extended discussion of *The Behavioral Theory of the Firm,* one can judge the impact of these concepts upon the international operations of the firm. For example, the impact of changes in the coalition members on the goals and choice process of the firm is important. England and Lee (1971) found that there were different priorities among Japanese, Korean, and American managers in the degree with which they pursued such values as organizational harmony, growth versus earnings, and so on. The main maximization criteria for American managers were productivity, organizational efficiency, and profit maximization. For Japanese managers, the main criteria were productivity and organizational growth. Carter (1974) concluded that American managers were significantly less interested in cash flow as a decision criterion than European managers. Thus as the firm expands beyond its national borders, inclusion of other executives from different cultures may be expected to alter the decision criteria and the decision process.

Chapters 9 and 10 emphasized return on investment, yet the initial decision to go abroad is often based on some preoccupation with market share, especially for consumer product companies. The decision to go abroad may begin with a sales outlet in a foreign land. As the nationals are brought into the firm, they have a greater influence in the decision process. Their concern with larger operational and organizational significance may create an organizational impetus to expand the firm in that nation, perhaps adding manufacturing or assembly. Later, financing of major customers' purchases may occur with greater autonomy for the decisions given to the local managers.

All of these factors suggest the impact of the financial evaluation on a strict rate of return criterion may be diminished. These organizational realities are important, and often have great effect on the types of projects which are evaluated and the standards which are applied. The financial evaluations are important for a final decision, for the financial results provide the basis for the decision. The arguments within the organization then will be whether a project has a reasonable return given the organizational and environmental constraints. The impact of organizational or behavioral characteristics of the firm on its standards and strategy is considerable. However, those organizational elements influence the nature of the financial evaluations but do not negate them.

Other Studies of the Motivation to Invest Abroad

In one major analysis of the decision of U. S. firms to invest abroad, the National Industrial Conference Board (1966) survey by Judd Polk, et al., found that the main criterion dominating the decision was a concern for *markets*. [7] The companies usually also referred to some goal of return on investment, but the measurement of this return was usually quite simple and was often expressed as a percentage of sales. Leading U. S. consumer goods firms were especially oriented in this way.

Such a strategy is not inconsistent with some of the economic goals noted earlier: loss of markets may be the loss of a financial return, and the decision to invest abroad is made either to prevent economic losses or to profit from opportunities which are available in other lands.

---

[7] Other researchers confirm this motivation. Spitäller (1971) reviews various quantitative studies of both long-term portfolio capital and foreign direct investment. He concludes that the decision to invest abroad is primarily affected by the size of the foreign market, but notes the results are also consistent with the argument for differential rates of return. However, because of the aggregative nature of the data by which other researchers supported the importance of differential rates of return, Spitäller suggests that the other researchers did not consider the "unity of the investment decision of the international firm. This unity implies that the foreign investment decisions of a firm are interdependent." Hence, the broader strategy issue also appears in this conclusion.

Likewise, market dominance may be a reasonable companion to profitability under some circumstances. For example, Gale (1972) presents a cross-sectional regression analysis based on 106 companies for which he evaluated the impact of market share, firm size, and concentration as explanatory variables for rate of return. Defining rate of return as net income on book equity over a five-year period (1963-1967) and adjusting for leverage of different firms, he confirmed his hypotheses that positive relationships between market share and profitability were greater for: (1) high concentration industries versus low concentration industries, (2) moderate growth industries versus rapid growth industries, (3) relatively large firms versus smaller firms, and (4) large firms in high concentration industries with relatively moderate growth versus all other firms. He notes that "the findings of this study would seem to confirm our belief that interaction effects... play an important role in the determination of firm and industry performance." Thus, his conclusion is consistent with the strategy of a firm's seeking access to particular markets in the expectation of greater long-run profitability from obtaining a dominant market share.

A subset of this emphasis on the market strategy has often been referred to in the context of the *product life cycle* (or, in a related term that is less favorable and uses more ideologically-loaded words when applied to the United States, "American economic imperialism"[8]). Stated briefly, the product life cycle as presented by Raymond Vernon suggests that the corporation will be forced to seek untapped markets due to increasingly broad penetration of a market and development of competitive pressures sufficient to lessen the return on the company's incremental investment. Thus, this product cycle approach is a dynamic oligopoly theory, in which declining margins in one land induce the firm to go abroad. It may initially export, and then follow this policy with full manufacturing abroad as the export market is threatened by competition.[9]

Aharoni (1966) found that the decision process of major corporations to invest in Israel was heavily dominated by a combination of the product life cycle and the absorption of organizational uncertainty as projects filtered upward. The absorption of organizational uncertainty, observed in many firms by various researchers, is the filtering process by which successive individuals in the decision-making process condense and delete risk elements associated with a project or decision. This study reinforces the blending of financial/economic factors and organizational/behavioral characteristics in the foreign investment decision process.

Stephen Hymer (1966) for example, found the decision for foreign investment motivated by one or more forms of monopolistic advantage. The monopoly forms which may help the firm have an advantage abroad included technology, capital markets advantages, sourcing advantages, management, or some other variable.

---

[8] As Marxist economists note in the related issue of production, the commitment of capitalism to exploitation of labor eventually will stimulate labor organization, especially given the boom/bust nature of a capitalist economy with recurring commitments to excesses of capital equipment. As a response to the labor organization which increases labor costs, the (American) capitalist will seek foreign operations where labor is available at a much lower rate. Eventually this pattern was hypothesized to intensify world economic oscillations, forcing complete world revolution.

[9] Raymond Vernon, "International Investment and International Trade in the Product Life Cycle." *Quarterly Journal of Economics,* May 1966, pp. 190-207.

Robert Aliber (1970), among others, emphasized the advantages the major multinational may have in access to capital markets, arguing that such access permits a lower discount rate when evaluating projects, placing the firm at an advantage over the domestic corporation in many nations which may not have such a capital market opportunity.

A Normative Model for Evaluating Direct Investment

A large number of the factors considered in the decision to invest abroad have been studied in the preceding pages. Some of these factors were related to economic considerations, such as market structure. Other factors were related to the fashion in which business firms make decisions. In this section we attempt to unify these considerations into an analytical framework that may be useful to the financial manager who must evaluate investment proposals. Like any framework, only the skeleton of the analysis is given, but the specific details of any situation should be easily fitted into this analytical construct.

The following strategic analysis is presented on a general basis without any attempt to give a rigorous mathematical treatment. This approach consists of three basic steps: (1) statement of alternative strategies according to specific criteria, (2) evaluation of each strategy in terms of risk and return, and (3) selection of the strategy or combination of strategies that best suits management's preferences and capabilities.

Statement of Alternative Strategies. In order to limit the number of product and country combinations which a multinational company could consider, it will develop a series of criteria to select alternative strategies. These criteria could be designed by the managers who are acquainted with the characteristics that make a strategy worthy of further consideration. Consider four criteria: (1) product life cycle stage, (2) market characteristics, (3) replacement versus expansionary projects, and (4) financing constraints.

Using *product life cycle stages* as a criterion, Stobaugh (1969) classifies countries according to market size, investment climate, availability of local resources, and distance to major producing centers. Products, in turn, are classified according to freight costs, economies of scale in production, and consumers' need for the products. Under this scheme, a table is prepared containing an index number for each product in each country. The strategies implied by this table are usually based on expanding operations into those products and countries where the index numbers are high and where the competitors are not yet established.[10]

One way of using *market characteristics* to select strategies would be to classify the products according to potential market growth and present market penetration. This decision rule will select products in those countries where a large market share is held or where a promising stable growth may exist. An alternative way to use mar-

---

[10] An extremely simplified use of the transportation (linear programming) model of product/plant location decisions is contained in Zwick (1967). The informational requirements of the model also limit its use, as the author notes. Nevertheless, this simplified approach could be useful in a strategy evaluation. See Zwick, Jack, "Models for Multicountry Investment." *Business Horizons,* Winter 1967, pp. 69-74.

ket characteristics would be to classify the products according to income or price elasticity and favor those countries where income levels are such that the product has the best chance to enjoy a large market.

A *replacement/expansion* approach to selecting potential strategies would be based upon classification of investments into those which represent replacement of old projects (e.g., a plant to substitute a fully depreciated one) and those which involve an expansion. This latter group could conceivably be subdivided into those which are expansions of old ideas and those which are new ideas altogether. Again, a table of index numbers could suggest relative desirability of the projects.

Finally, *financing considerations* might dictate that only a certain percentage of total earnings may be kept in countries where controls on repatriation of earnings exist. Alternatively, management might consider that only a certain percentage of earnings can be maintained in countries where exchange losses are likely to occur.

The outcome of the exercise of screening the company's products and the world according to certain criteria is to derive a list of strategies (combinations of products and countries) which management then can proceed to evaluate. A composite index might be created by summing the weighted index scores of each country/product combination for all the tables above. The index number of some of these combinations will further reduce the number of strategies that management must consider. Hence, a reduced composite score for countries and products might suggest the family of strategies for final review.

Strategy Evaluation. Traditional financial theory evaluates projects along two dimensions: return and risk. In this context, risk has usually been measured by the size of the standard deviations of the returns of the project before financing considerations.[11] Once management has decided upon a reduced number of strategies (combinations of products and countries) it wishes to consider further, it is then possible to estimate the return and the risk associated with each of those strategies or combinations of strategies. If management does not wish to prepare a full risk evaluation for each broad strategy or potential product/country offering, then to adjust for risk it may attach a premium or discount to the return required from each strategy. Suppose the required return in traditional investments domestically is 15%. If the project is a new product in a less developed country (LDC) it may well be that the required return is raised to 26%. Once these adjustments are determined, they could be presented in tabular form as shown in Exhibit 11.1. For any given proposal, the adjustment to the required rate is taken from the table. From the example of the new product in an LDC, if it has low income elasticity of demand, high growth, a large market, and a stable government, then the premium is +4 +2 +3 +2, or 11%, for a total required return of 26%.

Note that this analysis assumes simple additive relationships for risk, although a correlation among various risks is presumed to exist. For example, in every case the premium requested for political instability is higher when the product has a low income elasticity or a low growth potential. The rationalization for this assignment of requested premiums may be that management believes that, regardless of the overall political stability of the country, local authorities are more bound to inter-

---

[11] Under the capital asset model, risk is linked to the covarability of the asset with some market, as will be discussed later in Chapter 12.

EXHIBIT 11.1   Increases in Returns Required to Adjust for Risk

Country		New				Old			
		Income Elasticity		Growth Potential		Income Elasticity		Growth Potential	
		High	Low	High	Low	High	Low	High	Low
Less Developed Countries									
Effective Mkt. Size	Large	+2	+4	+2	+4	+1	+3	+1	+3
	Small	+4	+6	+4	+6	+3	+5	+3	+5
Political Instability	High	+5	+8	+5	+8	+5	+7	+5	+7
	Low	+2	+3	+2	+3	+1	+2	+1	+2
Developed Countries									
Effective Mkt. Size	Large	+1	+3	+1	+3	0	+1	0	+1
	Small	+2	+4	+2	+4	+1	+2	+1	+2
Local Competition	High	+2	+4	+2	+4	+1	+2	+1	+2
	Low	+2	+3	+2	+3	0	+1	0	+1

fere with the operations of a foreign-owned plant producing staple commodities with low income elasticity in a stagnant economy of low growth potential than with the operations of a plant producing a product with the opposite characteristics. Obviously, this is a very crude approach to the assessment of these premiums. More sophisticated mathematical approaches are easy to envisage once the basic concept is accepted. The output of this analysis, in any case, will be a quick screening of proposed strategies which can be used in the appraisal process for major product lines in different lands by a decentralized firm.

As stated before, the management of a company would decide what critical variables should be represented in the rows and columns of Exhibit 11.1. In any case, each combination of product and country could be described either by two variables, the expected return and its standard deviation, or by the premium figures in the table that reflect adjustments to desired return for risk.

Selection of a Strategy. The final step is for management to decide what they wish the company to be in the future. That is, what box or combination of boxes reflects an appropriate strategy. In Exhibit 11.1, each box was considered to be independent of every other box when the evaluation was made. However, management may find it can reduce the average risk by combining some strategies. At this point, constraints imposed on the company as a whole must be brought to bear. One such constraint may be the percentage of earnings tolerated as subject to repatriation controls before the capitalization rate of the stock is penalized. Other constraints that manage-

ment might want to introduce at this level are the availability of management resources and various qualitative considerations such as contribution to the development of other countries or of management itself.

Finally, an appropriate variable to be introduced at this point is size. Once
management has decided upon the appropriate mix of products and countries for a
certain budget size, the next step is to repeat the process for the next budget size.
The outcome of this analysis might be to choose a similar strategy with the comparable return-risk configuration. Alternatively, management might choose a different strategy, which produces a risk-return balance different from the previous
budget size. Each of these strategies for each budget size may be plotted in a diagram as shown in Exhibit 11.2. A simplified final table of options described according to the risk-return characteristics could be completed as shown in Exhibit 11.3.

EXHIBIT 11.2   Risk/Return/Budget Size Evaluation

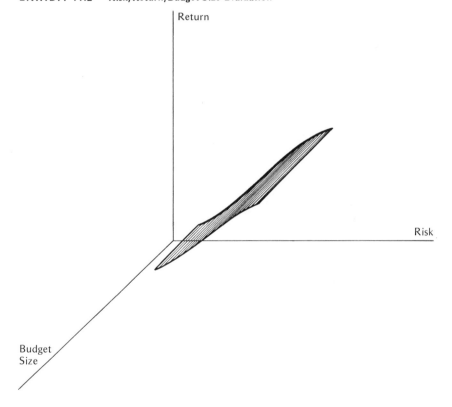

With the concepts mentioned in Chapters 9, 10, and the first part of this chapter, we can turn to a comprehensive example of financial planning. This analysis
will be based upon a risk analysis of a proposal using a few limited financing operations. In Chapter 12 there is a discussion of portfolio diversification, suggesting
how the basic model presented here may be expanded. Finally, an extended review

EXHIBIT 11.3   Comparative Budgets: Summary Results[a]

Country	Budget 1 Products (1 ... M)			
Developed	$R^1_{11}\ \sigma_{11}$	$R^1_{12}\ \sigma_{12}$	$\cdots$	$R^1_{1M}\ \sigma_{1M}$
LDC	$R^1_{21}\ \sigma_{21}$	$R^1_{22}\ \sigma_{22}$	$\cdots$	$R_{2M}\ \sigma_{2M}$

Country	Budget 2 Products (1 ... M)			
Developed	$R^2_{11}\ \sigma^2_{11}$	$R^2_{12}\ \sigma_{12}$	$\cdots$	$R^2_{1M}\ \sigma_{1M}$
LDC	$R^2_{21}\ \sigma_{21}$	$R^2_{22}\ \sigma_{22}$	$\cdots$	$R_{2M}\ \sigma_{2M}$

Country	Budget N Products (1 ... M)			
Developed	$R^N_{11}\ \sigma_{11}$	$R^N_{12}\ \sigma_{12}$	$\cdots$	$R^N_{1M}\ \sigma_{1M}$
LDC	$R^N_{21}\ \sigma_{21}$	$R^N_{22}\ \sigma_{22}$	$\cdots$	$R^N_{2M}\ \sigma_{2M}$

[a]For R^k_{ij} and σ^k_{ij}, i is a Developed (1) or LDC (2) environment, j is a Product (1 through M), and k is a Budget level (1 through N).

of this project is possible using the Freeport Minerals case following Chapter 12. That case permits much greater understanding of the influence corporate strategy, economic forces, and organizational factors may have on the decision to invest abroad.

AN EXTENDED EXAMPLE—FREEPORT MINERALS

Background

Originally a major sulphur producer, Freeport Minerals decided in 1970 to diversify its operations in the wake of a breakdown in what had been an extremely profitable oligopolistic sulphur market.[12] In 1966, the firm had 85% of its income

[12] This case was prepared entirely from public sources, and Freeport's management was not consulted.

from sulphur. By 1968, with sulphur prices at $40 per ton, there was evidence of a large number of entrants into the market. These marginal producers depressed prices. By 1970, sulphur sold for $20 per ton. Accordingly, Freeport decided to begin operating in other mineral areas and hoped to derive only 15% of its income from sulphur by 1975.

The nickel industry was dominated by International Nickel (INCO) whose operations were mainly in the United States and Canada. Freeport also was interested in nickel, and had several profitable ventures in this field. One of the opportunities which became available was the Greenvale proposal in Australia. This project would cost approximately $264 million to develop based on 1971 cost estimates. This amount included $111 million for a nickel processing plant, $45 million for a special railway, and $15 million for the mine development. The remainder of the outlays was allocated for preoperating expenses (including interest during the construction period), inflation, and working capital.

The basic project was expected to produce revenues of $72.2 million per year for twenty years based on anticipated ore reserves, a price of $1.35 per pound for nickel, and yearly production of about 2.5 million tons of nickel plus a small amount of cobalt. Given figures for operating costs consistent with the company's knowledge and confirmed by the experience of other firms in Australia, Freeport constructed a projected income statement for the project. Using accelerated depreciation permitted the firm, depletion standards consistent with Australian tax policies, and a tax rate of 38%, the projections of the Greenvale project are shown in Exhibit 11.4.

Two major financing options were under consideration:

1. A loan for $135 million in U. S. dollars at 8%, payable in level installments of principal over a ten-year life period commencing at the end of 1975. This would be from a group of major insurance companies.

2. A yen loan of $160 million at 6% with eighteen annual level principal payments commencing at the end of 1975. This offer was from one of the major customers of the nickel, a Japanese business association (zaibatsu). Although there was a possibility this loan would require concessions from the pricing base and would be accompanied by a long-term contract, the management of Freeport thought the loan was a generous one.

When these financing options were considered, the resulting financial cash flows were estimated to be as shown in Exhibit 11.5. Freeport was uncertain where the cash throw-offs would be reinvested. If the money were brought to the United States, additional taxes would have to be paid. However, by adjusting the ownership of the firm among various other corporate interests, U. S. taxes on the profits could be avoided until the funds were returned to the United States.

Risk Analysis

A risk analysis of the Freeport project can be prepared, with the following variables seeming to be most subject to change or to random outcome:

Construction Cost. The firm would commit $264 million for the project, but there was some chance that the cost might be considerably higher. The project already included $43.4 million for escalation and contingencies. In the event all of these funds were not needed, they would be returned prior to initial production. In the event

EXHIBIT 11.4 Freeport Minerals Greenvale Project—Income Statement (millions of U.S. dollars)

	1975	1976	1977	1978	1979	1980	1981	1982	1983	1984	1985	1986	1987	1988	1989	1990	1991	1992
Revenues	$72.2	$72.2	$72.2	$72.2	$72.2	$72.2	$72.2	$72.2	$72.2	$72.2	$72.2	$72.2	$72.2	$72.2	$72.2	$72.2	$72.2	$72.2
Mining Costs	5.0	5.0	5.0	5.0	5.0	5.0	5.0	5.0	5.0	5.0	5.0	5.0	5.0	5.0	5.0	5.0	5.0	5.0
Mine Depreciation	1.1	1.1	1.1	1.1	1.1	1.1	1.1	1.1	1.1	1.1	1.1	1.1	1.1	1.1	1.1	1.1	1.1	1.1
Transportation	5.5	5.5	5.5	5.5	5.5	5.5	5.5	5.5	5.5	5.5	5.5	5.5	5.5	5.5	5.5	5.5	5.5	5.5
Railroad Depreciation	4.4	4.4	4.4	4.4	4.4	4.4	4.4	4.4	4.4	4.4	0	0	0	0	0	0	0	0
Refining	10.1	10.1	10.1	10.1	10.1	10.1	10.1	10.1	10.1	10.1	10.1	10.1	10.1	10.1	10.1	10.1	10.1	10.1
Plant Depreciation	8.7	8.7	8.7	8.7	8.7	8.7	8.7	8.7	8.7	8.7	8.7	8.7	8.7	8.7	8.7	0	0	0
Royalty	.3	.3	.3	.3	.3	.3	.3	.3	.3	.3	.3	.3	.3	.3	.3	.3	.3	.3
Administration	1.0	1.0	1.0	1.0	1.0	1.0	1.0	1.0	1.0	1.0	1.0	1.0	1.0	1.0	1.0	1.0	1.0	1.0
Total Costs	36.1	36.1	36.1	36.1	36.1	36.1	36.1	36.1	36.1	36.1	31.7	31.7	31.7	31.7	31.7	23.0	23.0	23.0
Interest (8% U.S. loan, 10 years)	10.8	9.7	8.6	7.6	6.5	5.4	4.3	3.2	2.2	1.1								
Profit Before Taxes	25.3	26.4	27.5	28.5	29.6	30.7	31.8	32.9	33.9	35.0	40.5	40.5	40.5	40.5	40.5	49.2	49.2	49.2
Taxes[a]	0	10.0	10.5	10.8	11.2	11.7	12.1	12.5	12.9	13.3	19.8	19.8	19.8	19.8	19.8	19.1	19.1	19.1
Net Profit	25.3	16.4	17.0	17.7	18.4	19.0	19.7	20.4	21.0	21.7	24.7	24.7	24.7	24.7	24.7	30.1	30.1	30.1

[a]Start-up expenses and other concessions mean no taxes are projected as payable in 1975.

EXHIBIT 11.5 Freeport Minerals Greenvale Project—Financial and Operating Cash Flows (millions of U.S. dollars)

	1975	1976	1977	1978	1979	1980	1981	1982	1983	1984	1985	1986	1987	1988	1989	1990	1991	1992
Net Profit	$25.3	$16.4	$17.0	$17.7	$18.4	$19.0	$19.7	$20.4	$21.0	$21.7	$24.7	$24.7	$24.7	$24.7	$24.7	$30.1	$30.1	$30.1
Depreciation	14.2	14.2	14.2	14.2	14.2	14.2	14.2	14.2	14.2	14.2	9.8	9.8	9.8	9.8	9.8	1.1	1.1	1.1
Tax Savings (Accelerated Depreciation for Tax Purposes)	3.0	1.9	1.0	.2	(.7)	(.7)	(.7)	(.7)	(.7)	.7	(.3)	(.3)	(.3)	—	(.3)	—	—	—
After-Tax Interest[a]	10.8	6.0	5.3	4.7	4.0	3.3	2.7	2.0	1.4	.7	—	—	—	—	—	—	—	—
Operating Cash Flow	53.3	38.5	37.5	36.8	35.9	35.8	35.9	35.9	35.9	35.9	34.2	34.2	34.2	34.2	34.2	31.2	31.2	31.2
Principal and After-Tax Interest (8% U. S. Loan, 10 years)	24.3	19.5	18.8	18.2	17.5	16.8	16.2	15.5	14.9	14.2								
Equity Cash Flow, U. S. Loan	29.0	19.0	18.7	18.6	18.4	19.0	19.7	20.4	21.0	21.7	34.2	34.2	34.2	34.2	34.2	31.2	31.2	31.2
Principal and After-Tax Interest (6% Japanese Loan, 18 years)	14.9	14.5	14.2	13.9	13.5	13.2	12.9	12.5	12.2	11.9	11.5	11.2	10.9	10.6	10.2	9.9	9.6	9.2
Equity Cash Flow, Japanese Loan	38.4	24.0	23.3	22.9	22.4	22.6	23.0	23.4	23.7	24.0	22.7	23.0	23.3	23.6	24.0	21.3	21.6	22.0

	Operating Cash Flow	8% U. S. Loan, 10 years Equity Cash Flow	6% Japanese Loan, 18 years Equity Cash Flow
Rate of Return[b]	11.0%	14.4%	19.9%
Terminal Rate of Return (10% Reinvestment Rate)	10.7%	12.1%	16.5%
Net Present Value at 10%	$18.9	$49.6	$80.9

[a] Because of start-up expenses, projections assume there are no savings to tax-deductibility of interest in 1975.
[b] All return calculations assume average investment is made two years before initial operating cash inflows.

other funds were required, they would be paid at an early point in the development of the project as the increased constuction costs or plant difficulties appeared. Basically, management was confident that the constuction costs were to be between $205 and $325 million.

Production. Although confident of the mineral reserves, a major uncertainty related to the year when the production would be "on stream." Accordingly, there was a possibility that only partial production would begin in 1975. Perhaps this output would be as low as 80% of the planned level. Final production would certainly increase from the starting point to the full level over four years.

Mineral Content. There was some small doubt about the richness of the mineral deposits. This quality figure might deviate somewhat from the expected ore content, although the range was probably not much more than ±10%.

Price. From other analysis, the management could believe that the starting price was likely to be higher than the $1.35 estimated. This price might grow from the time of the initial investment by about 5% to 6% per year based on forecasts of the world's economy. Because nickel was a key commercial ingredient, world industrial activity was a barometer of nickel demand. Relating this price increase to world industrial production, the growth rate was tempered by a possibility of additional nickel production entering the market and decreasing prices.

Operating Costs. The possible escalation in labor rates and materials costs during the life of the plant were expected to be related to the strength of the Australian economy, which itself was linked to world industrial production. Operating costs were expected to increase by slightly less than the price of world nickel, subject to the performance of the Australian economy.

For the financing options, there were also uncertainties. Although the loans were firm commitments subject to the meeting of various financial tests each year, the Freeport management was concerned about the exchange rates of the currencies. Specifically, the U. S. dollar might deteriorate over time while the yen might appreciate. For its financing analysis, the management decided to assume that the dollar might deteriorate or appreciate relative to other currencies. Since the revenues were always denominated in dollars, this factor would have little influence on the profile of the project other than the impact of operating costs which would be paid in Australian dollars. On the other hand, continuing appreciation of the Japanese yen over the life of the project could prove costly. The management felt that the yen might well appreciate by an average of 2% per year for the next eight to ten years, but they were not willing to forecast beyond that. Furthermore, they felt that it was hard to anticipate the yearly links in appreciation of the yen; lower than average appreciation in one year might simply be a temporary delay offset by higher appreciation in a later year. Basically they believed that the yen was likely to remain strong vis-à-vis the dollar for at least ten years, and appreciate in relation to the dollar. They felt that the basic interest rate differential of 2% on the yen loan versus the dollar loan reflected the assessment of the lenders as well.

For the immediate future (compared to the long-run), however, there was a much higher probability of a sharp yen upvaluation, perhaps by as much as 10% within a year or so. In addition, one economist in the firm was convinced that this action could be a chain, resulting in a high probability of another 10% upvaluation in a few years.

A risk analysis combines these uncertainties and the interrelationships into a computer model. Using these relationships and a random number sampling function within the model, the adjusted financial results can be presented showing these risk elements. When combined with the accounting relationships for income statements, balance sheets, and discounted cash flow, the results are useful to management in evaluating the possible risk associated with a project. The inputs for the Freeport model are given in Exhibit 11.6

Exhibit 11.7 presents the results of the simulation analysis performed under the assumptions described above. Distribution of rates of return are presented for operating cash flows and for returns on equity. The returns on operating cash flows have been calculated under two assumptions: (1) the cash generated by the project is reinvested at the same rate as the rate for the project, and (2) the cash generated by the project is reinvested at 10%. The return on equity is calculated under the two alternative sources of financing: (1) U. S. dollars at 8%, and (2) yen at 6%. The returns on equity are also calculated under the two assumptions about reinvestment rates.

The rates of return on operating cash flows show a tighter distribution when the 10% terminal rate of return is assumed than when the cash generated by the project is reinvested at the same rate as the project. This is because the average rate of return on operating cash flows, ignoring the terminal rate of return, is well above 10%. Simulation outcomes where the operating cash flow rates of return are below 10%, had they been present, would have been improved by the assumption of a 10% reinvestment rate. Initial rates of return above 10% are reduced by the assumption of a 10% reinvestment rate, as discussed in Chapter 9.

The rates of return to equity show a much wider range of possible returns under the yen financing than under the U. S. dollar financing. Therefore, each possible outcome has a lower frequency under the yen financing than under the dollar financing. In both sources of financing the spread of rates of return to equity is narrowed considerably when the assumption of a terminal rate of return of 10% is incorporated, for the same reason as in the case of operating cash flows.

Is the lower average return to equity shown on the dollar financing caused by the short life of the loan (ten years versus the eighteen-year life of the project and the eighteen-year yen loan)? In evaluating this issue, management must consider the alternatives available at the end of the ten years, or available in steps beginning after a few years of mineral production. Looking at the conventional debt coverage ratios, then in the earliest years the average coverage on the yen loan is significantly better than the dollar loan, as shown in Exhibit 11.8. However, considering the debt/capitalization rate and ignoring reinvestment opportunities, the firm appears more conservative under the dollar option because the loan was lower initially and is repaid more rapidly. This table also shows the adjusted returns to equity if the dollar loan is converted to eighteen years, with all the other assumptions maintained. From this basic result, one realizes again the inappropriate nature of the short-lived debt

EXHIBIT 11.6 Freeport Simulation Variables

Random Variable	Symbol	Frequency	Distribution of Random Variable	Range of Random Variable	Calculation
Construction	A	1st year	Poisson	Mean = .4	$A = 205 + (120 \times (X))$ X = Random variable
Production	B	1st year	Uniform	.7 – 1.0	B = Random variable Year 1 $B(1) = B \times$ expected value 2 $B(2) = (B + ((B - 1)/4)) \times$ expected value 3 $B(3) = (B + ((B - 1)/2)) \times$ expected value 4 $B(4) = (B + 3 \times ((B - 1)/4)) \times$ expected value 5 18 = expected
Mineral Content	C	1st year	Normal	Mean = 1 Standard Deviation = .05	$C = X$ X = Random variable
Price	D	Annual	Normal	Mean = 1.06 Standard Deviation = .03	$D(Y) = D(Y - 1) \times (X)$ X = Random variable Y = Year
Operating Costs	E	Annual	Uniform	.95 – 1.0	$E(Y) = E(Y - 1) \times (X_1) \times (X_2)$ X_1 = Random variable from "Price" X_2 = Random variable .95 – 1.0 Y = Year
Yen Upvaluation	F	Annual	Normal	Mean = 1.02 Standard Deviation = .002	See Below

Upvaluation	Probability in Year 1	Year 1 Upvaluation	Probability of Upvaluation Year 3 0%	Year 3 10%
0%	.50	0%	.50	.50
10%	.50	10%	.25	.75

From Year 4 onward, a normal distribution with a mean of 2% and a standard deviation of .2% is assumed to reflect the probabilities of an upvaluation in any year.

assumption if dollar refinancing options or the eighteen-year dollar loan is available.

There are two additional advantages retained by the yen loan in this analysis when the criterion is equity rate of return. First, the loan is larger, and with no other financing available, the capital structure is different under the two assumptions. Given a fixed operating return above the cost of debt, leverage assures that the return to equity will be larger for the "greater-debt" situation if the debt rates are similar. Second, the appreciation of the yen averages more than 2% per year for 10 years, meaning that the cost of the yen loan for those years will be slightly greater than the 6% nominal rate plus 2%. However, in later years (11-18) this appreciation is not present, consistent with the expectations of Freeport management discussed earlier. Hence, the average rate of the yen loan is lower for the full eighteen years than the U. S. dollar loan.

The capital structure-cost of capital analysis of Chapter 10 is applicable to this problem. An important unstated assumption of the cost of capital model is that the capital structure, once selected, remains in balance over the entire life of the project. Thus, in any period, the cash flows from a project (1) pay the returns on debt and equity, and (2) retire debt and equity in the exact proportion as the initial capital structure. Over time, the return to all components will be as indicated in the capital structure discussion. However, when there are differential debt repayment schedules (or no additional refinancing options available), then the applicability of a particular debt repayment schedule to the analysis will alter the return to equity. Thus, an analyst needs to examine carefully whether the assumptions of a proportional capital structure over the life of a project is warranted. If not, the possible infusion of subsequent debt issues may be relevant.

In this case, Freeport management needs to review its expected financing options for the next five to ten years. If these choices are sufficiently uncertain or costly, then possible payment of a higher rate for a long-term loan may be warranted; a long-term loan which matches the life of the project serves to keep the capital structure in balance. Hence, it may be regarded as a form of insurance. In the event the Japanese loan were not available, then the company might be willing to pay 9% for a U. S. dollar, twenty-year loan, for example.

In addition to this consideration, Freeport needs to review the fundamental dispersions it wishes to tolerate in financial returns. The dispersion of possible outcomes for the rate of return and the terminal return is greater under the Japanese loan than under either the ten-year or eighteen-year U. S. proposals, as would be expected given the upvaluation uncertainties. Whether management wishes to live with this dispersion is a question Freeport has to resolve.[13] Further, there is the basic dispersion of operating returns. Freeport management must review the dispersion and return relative to other corporate opportunities which are available, as well as the dispersion from existing operations. This analysis suggests that the co-variability among Freeports existing and proposed projects is important. That topic will be confronted in Chapter 12.

Conclusion

This approach to uncertainty provides additional information to Freeport management on the distribution of returns from its project. Nothing prevents an analysis of other variables (first-year earnings per share contribution, expected cash flow for

---

[13] The use of risk analysis results is discussed in the appendix to Chapter 10.

EXHIBIT 11.7   Freeport Minerals Greenvale Project—Distribution of Returns[a]

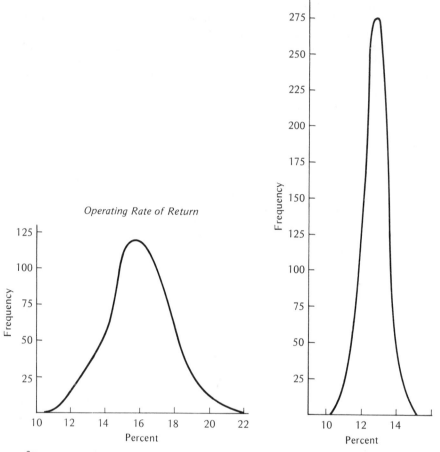

Operating Terminal Return

Operating Rate of Return

[a]Frequency is per 1,000 simulation trials.

EXHIBIT 11.7   Continued

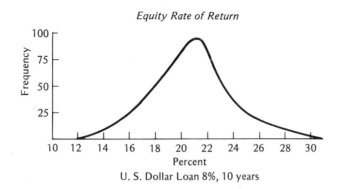

Equity Rate of Return

U. S. Dollar Loan 8%, 10 years

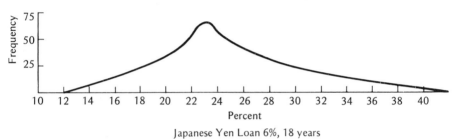

Japanese Yen Loan 6%, 18 years

EXHIBIT 11.7   Continued

Equity Terminal Return

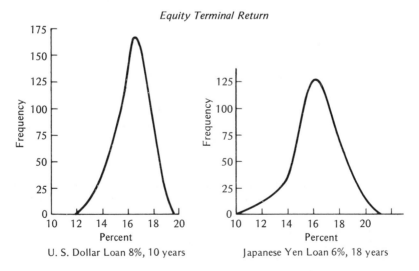

U. S. Dollar Loan 8%, 10 years   Japanese Yen Loan 6%, 18 years

EXHIBIT 11.8 Freeport Minerals Greenvale Project—Ratios of Alternative Loan Agreements

	Debt Service Coverage Ratios[a]			Debt/Capitalization		
	\(Outcomes Under Certainty)					
	1975	1980	1986	1975	1980	1986
U. S. Dollar Loan (10 years)	2.3	3.2	—	.51	.25	0
Japanese Yen Loan (18 years)	2.7	3.1	6.6	.61	.44	.24
U. S. Dollar Loan (18 years)	3.6	4.0	7.3	.51	.37	.20

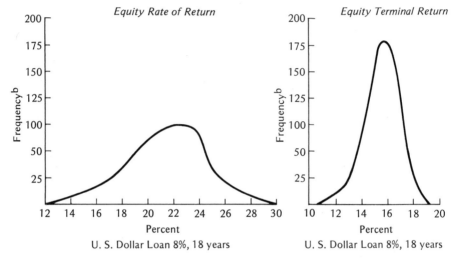

Equity Rate of Return — U. S. Dollar Loan 8%, 18 years

Equity Terminal Return — U. S. Dollar Loan 8%, 18 years

[a]Debt service coverage ratio is net income after tax plus interest divided by the sum of loan principal repayment plus interest. An alternative definition, giving results slightly different from those here, is net operating income after tax divided by principal repayment plus after-tax interest charges.

[b]Frequency is per 1,000 simulation trials.

each year, and so on). In addition, from this basic computation, management may wish to complete sensitivity analyses on the variables which are random: the investigation of a faster growth in expected value of nickel prices, or the impact of a greater dispersion of construction costs on the returns. Other variables could be randomized and the impact of their uncertainty on the returns could be calculated. Most important, the possibilities of more sophisticated financing arrangements could be studied. These arrangements might include sequencing of different loans, the sharing of equity participation, and so forth.

This is not to suggest that the Greenvale project is necessarily unwise as an investment. The use of computer risk analysis simulation merely permits a greater awareness of the uncertainties surrounding the project than is otherwise available. This uncertainty may dictate contingency planning for certain outcomes, and may also suggest certain financing strategies as more sensible than others.

The final chapter in Part Three analyzes the issues of portfolio evaluation of capital projects. Freeport management needs to consider not just the Greenvale project, but the impact of other nickel projects as well as the other operations of the corporation (sulphur, and so on). Accordingly, from the parent's viewpoint, the variance in returns from Greenvale is one input to the variance in the corporation's return. That corporate variance is a function of the interrelationships among the various projects in which the parent has invested. An extended analysis of Freeport's position is possible with the case, Freeport Minerals, following Chapter 12.

SUMMARY

A variety of theories has emphasized different factors in corporate investment decisions beyond the simple goals posited in normative financial theory. In the international environment, considerations such as comparative advantage, taxation policy, operational constraints or incentives relating to resources, the basic profit opportunities of a foreign investment, diversification strategies, and a strategy to limit losses are all economic variables which may influence a particular decision to invest abroad. In addition, certain organizational and behavioral theories have discussed the motivation of managers in the corporate decision process, such as the goals-expectations-choice trichotomy of *The Behavioral Theory of the Firm.* This theory can be extended to the capital budgeting process to include such concepts as the impact of multiple levels on the decision process, the bilateral bargaining between the sponsor of the project and the managers responsible for its approval, the influence of uncertainty on the goals of the firm, the variety of motivations for the search process, and the impact of the Pollyanna-Nietzsche effect in which uncertainty is forgotten after the decision is made to follow a particular course of action.

Several descriptive studies of the motivation of firms that went abroad mention the importance of a concern with market share and growth opportunities coupled with the uncertainty absorption created by multiple layers of management. The product life cycle, in which maturation of the markets at home induces the corporation to move abroad, was suggested as consistent with the motivation found in some of these studies.

In suggesting an operational strategy for the firm to employ in its decisions, a complex policy was introduced based on index evaluations of projects on various criteria management wishes to consider. An index might include such variables as the income elasticity and growth potential of new or old products, the market size, the political instability of the governments, and so on. The initial screening might be based on particular financing strategies, the product life cycle, general market evaluations, or whether the investments are replacement or expansionary products. The variations in these outcomes for various budget sizes were also noted. When these screenings are completed, management can review the expected return and variation in that return for the projects which have passed the above filtering and are under final consideration.

As a concluding note to the chapter, a risk analysis simulation model was shown which might be used by the management of a company in evaluating a project. Management's concern over the reutrn to equity may cause it to select a suboptimal strategy of financing if the possibilities of additional short-term financing and/or different amounts financed initially under different maturities are not acknowledged. This extended example also indicated how many of the fundamental concepts and approaches of *corporate* finance can be incorporated in the *international* analysis even though the special attributes of an international operation also must be included. Both corporate and international finance factors are vital in the proper analysis of such a project.

The extraction example of Freeport is one type of international project which can be discussed in detail, using the case following Chapter 12. Another typical situation is international sourcing and joint venture capital budgeting; the issues surrounding this decision can be viewed in the Cummins Engine case following this chapter. Finally, the capital budgeting analysis surrounding selling in a local market with or without export has many facets, most of which can be seen in the Chaolandia Super-Widgets case following Chapter 9 and the International Tire Company case following this chapter. Although each of these situations poses slightly different problems, most of the same issues relating to corporate and international financial analysis are inevitably present.

Questions

1. "They have cheaper wage rates than we do. Therefore, they can undersell us in everything. We must have tariffs or quotas to limit the amount of foreign imports." What economic concepts are ignored in this objection?

2. How do relatively cheap capital in one land and relatively cheap labor in another nation affect the allocation of industry between them? What does the international mobility of capital suggest for your conclusion?

3. The auto industry is often cited as an example of an oligopolistic industry. If true, what would this structure suggest for the international movements of the firms? Does this conclusion seem to occur?

4. Explain the product life cycle as applied to foreign investment decisions. How would you restate this cycle in terms of *The Behavioral Theory of the Firm* concepts?

5. How might an entrepreneur differ from a corporate manager in motivation to establish international operations? What does the lack of concentrated stock ownership in the hands of management suggest about the motivations of the corporate managers in U. S. firms?

Bibliography

Aharoni, Yair, *The Foreign Investment Decision Process.* Graduate School of Business Administration, Harvard University, Boston, Mass., 1966.

Aliber, Robert, "A Theory of Direct Foreign Investment," in Charles Kindleberger, Ed., *The International Corporation: A Symposium.* Cambridge, Mass.: MIT Press, 1970, pp. 17-34.

Benoit, Emile, "The Attack on the Multinationals." *Columbia Journal of World Business,* Nov.-Dec. 1972, pp. 15-22.

Carter, E. Eugene, "The Behavioral Theory of the Firm and Top-Level Corporate Decisions." *Administrative Science Quarterly.* Dec. 1971, pp. 413-428.

———, *Portfolio Aspects of Corporate Capital Budgeting.* Lexington, Mass.: D. C. Heath and Company, 1974.

Caves, Richard E., "International Corporations: The Industrial Economics of Foreign Investment." *Economica,* Feb. 1971, pp. 1-27.

Chenery, H. B., "Comparative Advantage and Development Policy." *American Economic Review,* March 1961, pp. 18-51.

Clark, Peter B. and Richard D. Hass, "The Portfolio Approach to Capital Movements: A Comment." *Journal of Political Economy,* May-June 1972, pp. 612-616.

Daniels, John D., *Recent Foreign Direct Manufacturing Investment in the United States: An Interview Study of the Decision Process.* New York: Praeger Special Studies, Praeger Publishers, 1971.

Eiteman, David K. and Arthur I. Stonehill, *Multinational Business Finance.* Reading, Mass.: Addison-Wesley Publishing Co., 1973.

England, George W. and Raymond Lee, "Organizational Goals and Expected Behavior Among American, Japanese, and Korean Managers—A Comparative Study." *Academy of Management Journal,* Dec. 1971, pp. 425-438.

Gale, Bradley T.,"Market Share and Rate of Return." *Review of Economics and Statistics,* Vol. 54, No. 4, Dec. 1972, pp. 412-423.

Hymer, Stephen, "The Efficiency (Contradictions) of Multinational Corporations." *American Economic Review,* May 1970, pp. 441-448.

———, *The International Operations of National Firms: A Study of Direct Investment.* Unpublished doctoral dissertation, Massachusetts Institute of Technology, Cambridge, Mass., 1966.

Johnson, H. G., "A Theoretical Model of Economic Nationalism in New and Developing States." *Political Science Quarterly,* June 1965, pp. 169-185.

Keesing, D. B., "Outward Looking Policies and Economic Development." *Economic Journal,* June 1967, pp. 303-320.

Knickerbocker, F. T., *Oligopolistic Reaction and Multinational Enterprise.* Boston: Division of Research, Harvard Business School, 1973.

Mazzolini, Renato, "Behavioral and Strategic Obstacles to European Transnational Concentration." *Columbia Journal of World Business,* Summer 1973, pp. 68-78.

Meeker, Guy B., "Face-Out Joint Venture: Can It Work for Latin America." *Inter-American Economic Affairs,* Spring 1971, pp. 25-42.

Polk Judd, *et al., U. S. Production Abroad and the Balance of Payments.* New York: National Industrial Conference Board, 1966.

Scaperlanda, Anthony E. and Laurence J. Mauer, "The Determinants of U. S. Direct Investment in the E. E. C." *American Economic Review,* Sept. 1969, pp. 558-568.

Spitäller, Erich, "A Survey of Recent Quantitative Studies of Long-Term Capital Movements." *International Monetary Fund Staff Papers,* March 1971, pp. 189-217.

Stobaugh, Robert, "Where in the World Should We Put That Plant?" *Harvard Business Review,* Jan.-Feb. 1969, pp. 129-136.

Tomlinson, James W., *The Joint Venture Process in International Business.* Cambridge, Mass.: MIT Press, 1970.

Vernon, Raymond, "International Investment and International Trade in the Product Life Cycle," *Quarterly Journal of Economics,* May 1966, pp. 190-207

____ Ed., *The Product Life Cycle and International Trade.* Boston: Division of Research, Harvard Business School, 1972.

Wells, Louis, "Test of a Product Cycle Model of International Trade: U. S. Exports of Consumer Durables." *Quarterly Journal of Economics,* Feb. 1969, pp. 152-162.

Zwick, Jack, "Models for Multicountry Investments." *Business Horizons,* Winter 1967, pp. 69-74.

The International Tire Company

In January 1968, the Executive Committee of the International Tire Company was considering a proposal for the expansion of manufacturing capacity by 50% at the company's tire facility in Shawinigan, Quebec. In December of 1967, revised forecasts at Canadian headquarters indicated that 1969 demand would substantially exceed previous projections. Shawinigan capacity would fall 2,200 tires short of daily Quebec requirements in a matter of months, and some 4,950 units per day short by 1970. It was in response to this revised projection that the proposal for expansion at Shawinigan had been prepared by International's Canadian Division and submitted to the U. S. parent for approval. Capital requirements for the Shawinigan expansion were estimated at C$9.1 million.[1]

THE PARENT COMPANY

Since its founding in 1899, the International Tire Company had experienced continuous growth both at home and abroad. In 1966, sales soared past the $2 billion mark for the first time. Foreign operations began with an export department in

[1] The official par value of 1.08108 Canadian dollars per US$ was established on May 2, 1962, following a twelve-year period of floating of the rate. The Canadian government announced on June 1, 1970, that it was once again floating the Canadian dollar.

1913. Since then, these operations had expanded to a network which included manufacturing facilities in fifty-two foreign locations and distribution of products in 140 countries. Major factors accounting for corporate growth, particularly that of the last decade, were: (1) the increase in world car production, (2) the expansion of highway systems, (3) the increasing emphasis on suburban living (which raised the number of trips made by an average driver), and (4) the overall growth in disposable income.

Tires were the central focus of the corporate business. Other lines included processed rubber textile fibers for tire cords, rubber chemicals, automotive components, industrial rubber products, and steel products. The Japanese takeover of most world sources of natural rubber during World War II had forced International to discover and produce systhetic rubber. Building on its wartime experience, the company became a major factor in the synthetic rubber, plastics, and fiber industries and an important supplier of defense products. By late 1967, International's broad product line totaled some 48,000 items. These items supplied 70% of all required materials for the tire operation. This placed the company among the lowest-cost of the domestic tire producers. Exhibit 1 contains a summary of the firm's consolidated financial performance during the 1959-1967 period. Exhibit 2 compares the operations of International with those of other major tire producers.

Not all members of the tire industry had shared International's fortune. Over 300 U. S. tire manufacturers operated in 1915. During the 1930s, sharply reduced demand and large fluctuations in raw material costs drove the producers into a price war from which they did not recover until well into the 1940s and which only the strongest industry participants survived. In the late 1950s, the major producers cut their prices on the high-margin tires in their first and premium lines. The high prices in these lines had provided an umbrella for smaller producers to compete during the postwar period. As a result, smaller firms, hard pressed by the slashing of profits, fell prey to acquisition by the larger companies. By the early 1960s, only fourteen companies were producing vehicle tires. In 1968, U. S. tire plant capacity totaled over one million daily units, mostly composed of passenger car tires. The Big Four—Akron Rubber Co., International, Ohio Diversified, and Eastern Tire—controlled some 68% of this total capacity. Estimates of productive capacity for the major producers are presented in Exhibit 3.

The Tire Market

The tire market was divided into two main sectors: the original equipment and the replacement sector.

The original equipment (O/E) market generally accounted for about one-third of the industry's shipments of tires. Demand in this sector was primarily a function of new vehicle production. Despite the low profitability of the sector (margins were estimated at 2-4% of sales), two economic factors encouraged the tire manufacturers to woo Detroit most carefully: (1) since Detroit's relationships with suppliers remained fairly stable over the years, tire producers benefitted from the predictability of large orders for the uniform product, and (2) companies associated with Detroit enjoyed advantages in the lucrative replacement market as most satisfied car owners tended to replace tires with the same brand as the original set.

The tremendous bargaining power of Detroit enabled it to keep the lid on O/E tire prices and to impose on suppliers constraints such as minimum levels of inventories and minimum numbers of nationwide dealerships and servicing centers. As a result, only the five largest producers were able to reap the rewards of association with Detroit. International Tire held approximately 25% of the original equipment market.

The replacement sector typically accounted for two-thirds of the unit volume, and a higher than proportionate share of sales and profits. Passenger car tires were generally about 85% of total replacement tire production. Demand fluctuations resulted primarily from changes in the number of cars two years old on the road, average annual mileage per vehicle, and typical mileage travelled per tire.

Although the average miles driven annually per car remained relatively constant, tire life decreased somewhat during the sixties. Despite improved tire construction, the faster rate of replacement occurred because of higher driving speeds, heavier cars, greater popularity of power systems, the imposition of federal and state tire-safety laws including tread depth minima, and a generally more safety-conscious public. Annual increases in replacement shipments during the sixties averaged about 7%. The main uncertainty concerning future growth in the market centered on the tire-life of the newly accepted belted tire.

Within the replacement market, two sectors existed. The major and associated brands of tires bearing the name of the parent company or its affiliates were marketed through company-owned stores and independent dealers. Private label brands were distributed to mass merchandisers, department stores, oil companies, and automotive supply chains. Exhibit 4 presents an analysis of International's sales by markets.

Recent Market Developments

The mid-sixties marked the beginning of a new era in tire marketing philosophy. The "cheapy" tire image acquired by the industry during the 1958-1964 struggle for market share rapidly gave way to a host of new lines geared to a style- and performance-minded public. Extensive promotion by the major companies met with immediate success, indicating consumer acceptance of considerably higher-priced products. The next innovation, the belted-bias tire, was perhaps the most significant product change in the industry since the tubeless tire was brought out in 1950. Shipments of belted tires were expected to comprise 90% of all original equipment automobile tire shipments by 1970. The result of this new image and consumer attitudes was summarized in the estimate that the price per unit net of discounts had increased from $21.50 in 1964 to almost $30 by 1968. This higher realization price, however, had not been reflected in the profitability of the company. A slower growth in tire markets, sluggishness in car shipments, higher interest charges, and the increasing cost of wage settlements all combined to keep the profitability of the tire and rubber industry below the average for all manufacturing companies.

A crucial issue for tire producers concerned the effect of the belted tire on the replacement market. Alarmists pointed to the alleged longer life of the belted tire as depressing replacement sales and pushing the consumer to the "cheapies" when he finally did enter the replacement market. Others noted the increased consumer consciousness of safety and pointed to the umbrella effect of pricing the belted tire in the $40 range to increase sales of the four-ply conventional bias tires priced in the "bargain" $30 range. Still others discounted the belted-longer-life thesis, arguing that the increasing mileage per car, heavier vehicles, and higher speeds of travel would send consumers back to the quality replacement market even sooner than before.

A second crucial issue concerned the extent to which the radial tire would penetrate the U. S. market. Recently, Ohio Diversified and certain other domestic companies turned their efforts to the coming of the "Radial Age." The economics of the radial, however, had proved a bit difficult to swallow. Estimates of conversion costs ran as high as $2.5 million for a plant that could produce 30,000 tires per day. To justify conversion costs, the radial would have had to sell at premiums of 50-60% above the conventional four-ply tire to make it profitable.

The belted tire was thus seen as a compromise between the conventional tire and the radial. On the other hand, lessening consumer acceptance of the belted tire and growth of radial imports led many observers to project a shift in demand by 1974-1975 to some 65-70 million radial units. Michelin's talk of setting up production in Canada was viewed as the possible stimulus required to push the seventies' market over to the radial.

While International had introduced a limited number of radial-ply models, company planners agreed with those in the industry who felt that the public was as yet unprepared to pay the substantially higher cost of these tires. Estimates were that demand for radials would remain well below 5% of the total North American market for several years. In view of this fact, production geared up to provide the market with the rapidly proliferating "belted" line which was being extremely well received by the safety-conscious public and automakers alike.

THE CANADIAN MARKET

The original incentive for the major auto-tire producers to enter into Canadian manufacturing operations was provided by the tariff imposed by Canada in 1906. This tariff levied a 30% charge on all tires imported from the U. S. and other "favored nations." By 1926, International, Akron Rubber, Dunlop, Eastern, Ohio Diversified, and National Brands of Canada had divisions in Canada.

Except for the setback during the Great Depression, demand for tires had grown rapidly and steadily. (Total shipments which in 1929 were $51.4 million dropped by 1932 to $15.9 million.) By 1953, Canadian shipments had reached C$130 million, of which imports accounted for C$5 million. During the 1959-1967 period, shipments of tires more than doubled to C$282 million, falling back somewhat in 1967. Although tires were not included among the duty exemptions under the Auto Pact,[2] industry sales benefited, nonetheless, from the increase in Canadian production and sales of vehicles sparked by the Pact. Exhibit 5 traces the pattern of production and sales of tires during the sixties. Exhibit 6 presents data on the shipments of motor vehicles in Canada during the same period.

Possibly the most conspicuous element in the Canadian tire industry's competitive environment was the stability of the market shares held by the various participants over the past many years. From 1946-1968, International's share was estimated to have fluctuated within a range of only 4%, as seen in Exhibit 7. All

---

[2] The Auto Pact was, in essence, an agreement made between the United States and Canada which stated that cars produced on either side of the border could be shipped acrosss the border free of tariffs. The Pact was signed in 1964. Tires *on* these cars were free of duty.

four major U. S. producers sold to both the original equipment and replacement markets and their product, pricing, and distribution policies were basically identical. Dunlop, the one non-U. S. affiliate producing in Canada, was fighting to maintain its market share in the highly competitive market. Experiencing difficulty with its Canadian industrial products division, the British subsidiary seemed content to upgrade its distribution to the replacement market and to leave the bidding for the original equipment stakes to the others.

THE CANADIAN DIVISION

Relation to the Parent

Although foreign operations were generally the domain of the International Overseas Company, Canadian operations were handled by the Canadian Division, a separate subsidiary closely linked with the domestic organization. Market volumes, costs, and profits were the responsibility of the Canadian division. Within the Division, each plant was a cost center responsible for operating efficiency. Short-term production was allocated among the plants by the division.

Long-term planning for production and capital investment in the three tire plants under its control was initiated by the Canadian division on the basis of five-year forecasts updated yearly. These five-year forecasts contained detailed projections of the market demand by geographical area and product line. Comparisons were then made between demand and current approved capacity. The differences between these two figures served as a basis for proposals for expansion containing a detailed workup of plant, equipment, and personnel resources required to meet the five-year projections. Included with these proposals was a statement of funds needed in support of the recommendations. These figures and recommendations were then submitted to corporate headquarters and planning staffs in the United States for evaluation. As the time for an actual expansion drew near, the whole evaluation procedure was repeated. At this time, the study was made in a much more detailed fashion, and the final result of the evaluation was submitted to the Corporate Executive Committee for approval.

Following a major investment, the staff at headquarters kept separate control of the operation for some time prior to its integration into the whole of the Canadian Division's operations. Approximately one year after start-up, a complete report of resources used and revenues realized was submitted to the parent's Budget Committee for comparison with the projections contained in the initial proposal.

Intercompany transfers were very small. Plants obtained their raw material from the cheapest source of supply rather than being forced to buy from other of International's affiliates. In most cases of significant dollar volumes, the parent would conduct feasibility studies to determine the lowest price at which it could supply the input from its integrated operations in the Unites States. Due to transport costs and duty charges, however, the only significant volume of intercompany sales was in nylon tire fabric that was produced at a company facility in Canada and which comprised 5% of International's Canadian tire textile needs.Tire-grade natural rubber was purchased on the world market. The majority of the other inputs were obtained from local manufacturers, many of whom were affiliates of U. S. corporations. Synthetic rubber, which accounted for approximately 20% of total costs, was imported to a large extent from the United States, though not necessarily from International's subsidiaries.

Long-standing corporate policy called for all foreign capital expansion projects to be financed in the local capital markets. Moreover, International U. S. called for standard percentages of foreign earnings to be remitted annually. In 1963, amidst rumors of an upcoming voluntary restraint program on U. S. capital outflows, International began to pay more strict attention to the remissions of its non-U. S. subsidiaries. For several years, the Canadian remittances had fallen below the established level. In a move to correct this position, two offerings of debt totalling $27.5 million were placed with several Canadian insurance companies in 1963. The net proceeds of this offering were to be applied to future capital remissions and local expansion.

In general, the nature and degree of communication between the parent and the Canadian organization indicated a strong, two-way flow of ideas in support of proposals and counterproposals between the two groups rather than a top-down authoritarian type of relationship.

Canadian Division Expansions

The Canadian Division was incorporated in the early 1900s with the construction of International's first manufacturing facility outside the United States at London, Ontario. This plant serviced the entire expanding Canadian market through 1960 when another plant was built in Victoria, Alberta, to cater to the western market. A third plant was built in 1964 in Shawinigan, Quebec, because of unexpected growth in Eastern replacement markets and unusual projections as to the effects of the rumored upcoming Auto Pact on original equipment demand. These factors led to market estimates through 1969 substantially above International's existing Canadian tire capacity. In particular, General Motors had announced plans to construct a C$35 million, 100,000 vehicle annual capacity, assembly plant to be located in Ste. Therese, Quebec. Operations were to begin in early 1965. General Motors had also announced a new policy that all tire needs would be purchased from Quebec sources only. About 5% of cars produced in Ste. Therese were to be shipped to the United States. Other factors reinforcing International's decision to build in Quebec were the shortage of available space at London, the relatively low Quebec wage rates, and the political situation in Quebec which threatened to boycott Canadian goods imported from other provinces. Akron Rubber's decision to construct in Quebec was announced about the same time.

When the Shawinigan plant was built, major equipment and floor space were provided for daily production of 4,400 tires, although the 1965 production schedule called for only 2,750 tires per day. By 1966, total international tire capacity in Canada of 17,812 tires considerably exceeded the 1964 projections. Market studies evaluating the effect of the Auto Pact on tire demand through 1966 projected a required 1969 level of production of 5,940 tires per day at Shawinigan. By October 1967, operations at Shawinigan were expanded to full-capacity production of 4,400 units. Then, in November, the unforeseen occurred. The introduction of the belted tire in the United States set off a wave of demand for the new tire for 1968 models among auto makers on both sides of the border. Detroit announced adoption of belted tires for two-thirds of their 1968 models. An urgent request for approval for conversion of facilities to the production of 1,760 belted tires was rushed through the Executive Committee. The total cost of this conversion was C$825,000 and it was financed with Canadian funds.

This conversion had hardly been approved when revised forecasts indicated the upcoming shortage which the Executive Committee was now considering.

THE PROPOSED SHAWINIGAN EXPANSION

The January 1968 request for immediate expansion of the facilities at Shawinigan from 4,400 to 6,600 tires per day reflected once again market growth rates exceeding those forecasted only eighteen months before. The scheduled 4,180 original equipment tires—over 60% of the total tentative production—indicated the influence of the Auto Pact on the Canadian original equipment market. Although all Canadian producers had increased their capacities several times since 1964, the strain on Canadian tire production facilities versus the periodic slight over-capacity situation in the United States resulted in large cyclical flows of imports from the United States. To quote one international executive, "from 1965 on this industry didn't take a breath. We (the Canadian division) made every tire we knew how to, and what we didn't make we brought in."

The Alternatives

The forecast detailing the need for immediate expansion of Shawinigan by 2,200 units (and superseding the graduated increases projected in 1966) dealt with four alternatives to expansion at Shawinigan. These alternatives were: (1) expansion at London, (2) construction of a new plant in Ontario, (3) imports from the United States, and (4) construction of a new plant in Nova Scotia to obtain more geographic dispersion of production facilities.

These alternatives were evaluated according to capital requirements, operating costs, freight charges, duty rates, return on capital invested, and time necessary to come on stream. The analysis indicated that, if the expansion in capacity were to be made in Canada, the most economical way to achieve this would be by expanding Shawinigan. Including working capital, the total cost was estimated at C$9.2 million. The entire financial package would be obtained from Canadian sources. Payback period for the project was calculated to be 9.4 years. Exhibit 8 contains the financial flows statement submitted to the Executive Committee in support of the proposal.

The Canadian Economy

Adding momentum to the upward market trend was the general expansion of the Canadian economy which had been in a lull for several years and had just begun its turnaround in 1967-1968. Projections for the 1968-1969 economy pointed to a year of increasing expansion—7.5% increase in GNP—spurred on by accelerated consumer spending and a planned 8% increase in capital investment by big business. A major contributor to the new prosperity was the forecasted 1968 record high level of $13 billion in exports which would provide a surplus of over $1.1 billion in the merchandise accounts. Of the $13 billion, $2.6 billion were to be in exports of automotive products to the United States, up from $1.6 billion in 1967 and $76 million in 1964.

One unfavorable element in the 1968 economy's picture was the persistence of serious inflationary pressures. Forecasts for 1968-1969 called for consumer prices to rise at an annual rate of over 6%. Monetary and fiscal restraints introduced by the government included a halt in the growth of the money supply, and an C$800 million government surplus. Held in reserve were an anticipated immediate cut in tariffs to the lowest level (17½%) agreed upon under the Kennedy Round, and a possible floating of the Canadian dollar.

The Labor Market

In early 1967, the United Rubber Workers of Canada began agitating for increased recognition. Primary demands were for wage parity with the auto workers and for master contracts to cover all Canadian plants of each rubber producer. Commenting on the woes of the Canadian rubber industry, the president of the Rubber Association of Canada noted that productivity in Canadian tire plants was 20-30% below the American level. Main reasons cited were: (1) the smaller market allowed only shorter runs; and (2) the wide variety of tire types produced in the limited number of plants created serious scheduling problems and inefficiencies.

By mid-1967, labor demands focused on inclusion of a cost-of-living clause in a master contract which would cover all Canadian plants of the individual company. Confronting the companies' refusal to give in on a master contract (with common expiration dates), the URW began walkouts at Akron Rubber's New Sarnia and International's London plants. Union unrest continued to mount and culminated in a two-month strike at New Sarnia, severely hurting Akron Rubber's 1967 Canadian earnings. As the companies strove to meet their Canadian commitments despite the loss in productive facilities, imports from the United States rose to unprecedented levels. The settlement calling for a 30% increase in wages over the next three years contributed to price increases totalling 15% for the last three quarters of 1967.

Industry's Expansion Plans

Akron Rubber Canada had opened 1968 with the announcement of a C$12.7 million investment for its Sherbrooke, Quebec plant. The undertaking was the single largest capital project ever authorized in the Canadian rubber industry. The main purpose appeared to be rationalization of production to allow concentration at the New Sarnia plant (Canada's largest) on belted-tire production. In response to the auto makers' demand for belted tires on its 1968 models, Akron Rubber also announced a $2.2 million expansion at the New Sarnia plant, for production of polyester-fiberglass tires. The additions at New Sarnia and Sherbrooke formed the nucleus of a proposed C$66 million expansion plan for all Akron Rubber Canadian facilities over the next several years. The total program would allow the company to cope with the shift to belted tires as well as the significant growth in demand of all rubber products.

Following the same philosophy, Eastern Tire (having given up plans to build in Quebec) announced C$17.2 million in 1967-1968 expenditures to build up capacity at its Ontario facilities. Ohio Diversified indicated it would invest C$9.9 million at the Windsor, Ontario plant. Dunlop proposed a more modest $5 million expansion package to support its share in the growing market.

Imports and Foreign Competition

During the sixties, total imports of tires into Canada rose from about 6% to over 15% of the total market for all tires in 1967. In passenger car tires, import units rose from 85,000 in 1961 to 1,570,000 in 1967. Roughly, three-quarters of the imports were brought in by U. S. affiliates to buffer their own shortages as Canadian demand increased faster than capacity. Exhibit 9 gives detailed data on tire imports into Canada.

The major portion of non-U. S. imports stemmed from France, Italy, and Japan—presumably the efforts of Michelin, Pirelli, and Bridgestone. While the European imports were directed mostly at the quality markets—chiefly the radial market—the Japanese were aggressively marketing on a price basis a full range of the popular tire types.

The other major factor in the competitive environment was the Michelin plant due to come on stream in 1971. Estimates of its capacity ranged from 12-20,000 units/day. This capacity was reported to be directed at the steel-radial, truck-bus market of which 85% was to be sold in the United States (across the $5^1/2$% duty barrier). Despite the distance between the U. S. markets and their Nova Scotia plant, this strategy was apparently superior to locating a plant in the United States and shipping the 15% across the $17^1/2$% barrier into Canada. Among the key determinants of Michelin's locational strategy were the reportedly substantial incentives given to the French company by the Canadian government. These incentives included financial packages of several sorts amounting to 60% of the capital cost plus the right of free entry into Canada of all Michelin tires produced abroad. Michelin would thus have the advantage of rationalizing its Canadian production while gaining free entry for its entire line which could then be passed into the Canadian and U. S. markets. Speculation abounded that it would be only a few years before Michelin set up full production of all product lines in Canada.

Extremely perplexing to the local manufacturers was the ability of the Europeans and Japanese to compete pricewise in the Canadian market on an export basis. All the major locals had third-country plants, yet all had found that tariffs and transport costs made importing unprofitable. The major producers inferred that extensive export subsidies were being given by the foreign governments to local exporters but were not accorded U. S. affiliates based in the same country. The local entry by Michelin would only multiply the "invisible" cost advantages they had.

The Final Decision

At this point, the alternatives that the Executive Committee faced were: expand Shawinigan, export from the United States to Canada, or do not expand production in any place.

There were four major factors against the expansion of U. S. production to cater to the Canadian market: (1) Canada imposed a tariff on all imported tires (see Exhibit 10); (2) transport costs over 300 miles, other things equal, were considered to increase costs above competitive levels; (3) U. S. facilities were presently operating close to full capacity; (4) wage levels were higher in the United States than in Canada (see Exhibit 11). On the other hand, there were two factors against the expansion of Canadian facilities: (1) U. S. labor was becoming increasingly vociferous against the expansion abroad of multinational companies which were alleged to take jobs away from American workers; and (2) rumors were repeated that the Canadian government might take a much tougher stand against foreign ownership.

EXHIBIT 1 The International Tire Company: Summary Financial Data, 1959-1967 (millions of dollars)

	1959	1960	1961[a]	1962[a]	1963	1964	1965	1966	1967
Net Sales	1,328	1,301	1,406	1,520	1,594	1,771	1,997	2,063	2,344
Net Income	72	70	66	69	87	96	122	122	141
Percent of Sales	5.4%	5.4%	4.7%	4.6%	5.5%	5.4%	5.6%	5.5%	6.0%
Retained Earnings	43	41	36	39	52	57	70	68	94
Depreciation	51	54	55	57	59	61	68	74	79
Per Share:									
Dividends	1.10	1.10	1.10	1.10	1.21	1.32	1.43	1.54	1.60
Net income	2.50	2.44	2.30	2.43	3.03	3.31	3.87	3.88	4.75
Total Assets	924	968	1,024	1,100	1,223	1,386	1,559	1,705	2,071
Current Ratio	3.2	3.1	2.9	3.9	3.2	2.7	2.7	2.6	2.6
Fixed Assets (net)	301	322	333	378	397	472	537	616	751
Capital Expenditures	91	78	69	105	79	139	138	154	219
Long-Term Debt	85	84	79	157	157	173	223	261	447
Foreign Subsidiary Income	18.6	24.4	13.5	16.9	24.0	25.2	30.1	29.2	33.7

[a]In fiscal 1961 and 1962, foreign earnings were substantially reduced by losses due to devaluation of foreign currencies.
Source: International Tire Company, *Annual Reports*.

EXHIBIT 2   Consolidated Sales and Profits of Major Rubber Companies 1955-1967

	U. S. Producers				Foreign Producers		
	Akron Rubber Co.	Inter- national	Ohio Diversified Co.	Eastern Tire Co.	Dunlop	Pirelli	Michelin[a]
			Sales (million dollars)				
1955	1496	1227	796	991			
1957	1505	1168	767	958			
1959	1706	1328	842	1064			
1961	1752	1406	893	1107			
1963	2212	1594	959	1196			
1965	2724	1997	1143	1453			
1966	2902	2063	1106	1392	923	739	
1967	3219	2344	1254	1572	1,080	894	
			Profits After Taxes (million dollars)				
1955	69	67	49	35			
1957	72	59	39	25			
1959	78	70	33	34			
1961	78	66	29	28			
1963	110	87	38	33			
1965	130	122	53	50			
1966	141	122	39	36	28		7
1967	163	141	50	62	34		8
			Profit - Sales Ratio (percent)				
1955	4.6	5.5	6.2	3.5			
1957	4.8	5.0	5.1	2.6			
1959	4.6	5.3	3.9	3.2			
1961	4.4	4.7	3.2	2.5			
1963	5.0	5.4	4.0	2.8			
1965	4.8	6.1	4.6	3.4			
1966	4.8	5.9	3.5	2.6	3.1		
1967	5.1	6.0	4.0	3.9	3.1		

[a]Michelin figures are for tire sales only, not total consolidated sales.
Source: International Tire Company and industry reports.

EXHIBIT 3   Major Producers' Daily Worldwide Tire Capacities—1968 Estimates (thousands of tires)

	Akron Rubber Co.	Inter- national	Ohio Diversi- fied Co.	Eastern Tire Co.	Dunlop	Pirelli	Michelin	Total Area
United States	281	218	108	140	23	—	—	1,084
Europe and United Kingdom	83	74	20	35	103	73	201	722
Latin America	25	18	8	3	—	11	—	68
Asia	115	14	52	11	30	—	—	260
Other	48	30	13	19	29	7	1	164
Total	552	354	201	208	185	91	202	2,298

Note: The capacity figures do not include minority interests. "Total Area" figures include capacities of other, mainly local, producers.
Source: International Tire Company, company estimates.

EXHIBIT 4 The International Tire Company: Sales Breakdown—1964 (millions of dollars)

Total Domestic Tires and Associated Goods				$941
Passenger Car Tires			$506	
Original Equipment		$110		
Replacement		396		
Major Brand	$275			
Associate Brand	95			
Private Label	26			
Noncar Tires			286	
Original Equipment		88		
Replacement		198		
Associated Goods			149	
Foreign Sales (mostly tires)				468
Canada		105		
Overseas		363		
Domestic nontire sales				297
Metal		127		
Aerospace		55		
Chemical		60		
Consumer		55		
Total Company Sales				$1,706

Source: A security analyst's report.

EXHIBIT 5 Production, Domestic Sales, Exports, and Prices of Canadian Tires, 1961-1967

	Production	Replacement Sales	Original Equipment Sales[a,b]	Total Domestic Sales	Exports[b]	Price Index
			Passenger Car Tires (units)			
1961	7,961,644	5,957,367	1,815,918	7,773,285	129,000	100.0
1962	9,180,939	6,456,358	2,346,732	8,803,090	314,000	89.4
1963	10,545,390	6,846,454	3,042,599	9,889,053	506,000	90.0
1964	11,431,427	7,506,674	3,219,567	10,726,241	558,000	87.8
1965	12,052,428	8,029,602	3,949,546	11,979,148	388,000	90.6
1966	13,527,315	8,864,539	3,742,720	12,607,259	401,000	92.1
1967	13,998,051	9,532,558	4,119,175	13,651,733	634,000	93.7
			All Tires (units)			
1961	9,264,705	6,835,194	2,233,100	9,068,294	198,000	100.0
1962	10,760,709	7,461,550	2,872,362	10,333,912	429,000	86.6
1963	12,358,248	7,871,728	3,678,682	11,550,410	686,000	87.5
1964	13,361,712	8,678,970	3,922,148	12,601,118	646,000	87.1
1965	14,149,481	9,277,735	4,758,142	14,035,877	461,000	89.8
1966	16,018,557	10,202,837	4,734,641	14,937,478	531,000	92.1
1967	16,532,592	10,946,761	5,141,209	16,087,970	825,000	93.8

[a]Original equipment sales include tires sold to be installed in cars later exported to the United States.
[b]Tires mounted on cars shipped under the Auto Pact are free of duty in the United States. Loose tires, however, regardless of whether they are for the original equipment market, are subject to import duty.
Source: Rubber Association of Canada.

EXHIBIT 6   Motor Vehicle Shipments in Canada, 1961-1967 (thousands of units)

	Shipments of Local Manufacture (1)	Exports (2)	Exports to United States (3)	Imports (4)	Canadian Market (5) (1) + (4) − (2)
1961	321.9	9.5	—	106.9	419.3
1962	426.1	11.9	—	94.7	508.9
1963	530.2	15.5	.3	59.6	574.3
1964	558.2	38.3	11.0	92.5	612.4
1965	705.6	77.9	31.7	136.5	764.2
1966	699.6	189.5	146.8	188.7	698.8
1967	725.5	342.4	311.0	313.7	696.8
1968(est.)	891.7	522.1	472.5	437.0	806.6

Source: Motor Vehicle Manufacturers' Association of Canada, *Ward's Automotive Yearbook.*

EXHIBIT 7   Capacity of Major Tire Manufacturers in Canada for Selected Years (total daily tires)

	1968 (est.) Tires	%	1963 Tires	%	1955 Tires	%	1946 %
International	20,850	23.5	10,800	21.1	6,500	19.5	20.3
Ohio Diversified Co.	8,200	9.2	5,000	9.8	3,300	10.0	10.9
Akron Rubber Co.	31,200	35.2	17,350	33.8	10,000	30.0	36.5
Eastern Tire Co.	15,800	17.8	9,800	19.1	6,500	19.5	17.9
Other	4,640	5.2	3,300	6.4	3,400	10.2	5.8
Total U. S. Manufacturers	80,690	91.0	46,250	90.2	29,700	89.2	91.4
Dunlop	8,000	9.0	5,000	10.0	3,600	10.8	8.6
Total Capacity	88,690	100.0	51,250	100.0	33,300	100.0	100.0

Source: International Tire Company, company estimates.

EXHIBIT 8   The International Tire Company: Shawinigan 1968 Expansion Proposal: Financial Flows (millions of Canadian dollars)

	1969	1970	1971	1972	1973	1974
Capital Appropriation	7.4					
Working Capital	1.8					
Total Investment	9.2					
Net Sales	10.2	10.2	10.2	10.2	10.2	10.2
Costs	(8.3)	(8.1)	(8.1)	(8.1)	(8.1)	(8.1)
Profit Before Tax	1.9	2.1	2.1	2.1	2.1	2.1
Taxes (53.1%)	(1.0)	(1.1)	(1.1)	(1.1)	(1.1)	(1.1)
Profit After Tax	.9	1.0	1.0	1.0	1.0	1.0
Depreciation	.4	.4	.4	.4	.4	.4
Cash Flow	1.3	1.4	1.4	1.4	1.4	1.4
After-Tax Rate of Return	9.8%	10.8%	10.8%	10.8%	10.8%	10.8%

Payback Period: 9.4 years

Source: International Tire Company, company estimates.

EXHIBIT 9   Canadian Tire Imports, 1960-1967, Imports by Country, 1965-1967

	Passenger Car Tires (1)	Tire Imports (thousands of Canadian dollars) Truck, Bus, and Grader (2)	All Tires (3)
1960	—	—	9,776
1961	1,342	4,223	9,356
1962	943	4,615	9,267
1963	1,371	6,485	11,852
1964	2,840	8,436	16,356
1965	3,915	7,576	16,624
1966	3,946	8,137	17,721
1967	19,240	14,850	41,860

	Imports by Country of Origin 1967	1966
United Kingdom	489	471
Austria	174	107
France	3,465	3,596
West Germany	456	107
Italy	730	623
Netherlands	358	215
Japan	2,187	980
United States	31,579	10,358
Total	41,114	16,991

Source: Rubber Association of Canada.

EXHIBIT 10   Tariff on Tire Imports for Selected Countries (percent)

	1963	1968	1969	1970	1971	1972
United States	8.5	7.5	6.5	5.5		4.0
Japan	25.0	20.0	—	17.5	15.0	12.5
Canada	22.5	21.5	(20.5		and	17.5)
United Kingdom	24.0	19.0	—	16.5	14.0	12.0
EEC:						
Italy	18.0	14.4	—	12.6	10.8	9.0
France	18.0	14.4	—	12.6	10.8	9.0
Germany	18.0	14.4	—	12.6	10.8	9.0
Spain	28.5	—	—	—	—	28.5

Source: Statement of the Rubber Manufacturers Association.

EXHIBIT 11   Estimated Hourly Employment Costs of Tire
Production Workers in Major Tire Producing Countries—1970

United States	$6.00	France	$2.35
Japan	$1.75	West Germany	$2.85
United Kingdom	$2.25	Spain	$1.05
Italy	$2.25	Canada	$5.00

Note: Employment cost figures include fringe benefits.
Source: Statement of the Rubber Manufacturers Association
on November 25, 1970.

Cummins Engine Company, Inc. (A)

In early March 1972, Mr. John T. Hackett, Executive Vice-President of Cummins
Engine Company, Inc., was reviewing the company's strategy in general and a new
venture in particular.[1] He was expected to make a recommendation to the Board of
Directors on both matters the following week on March 15. Mr. Hackett, thirty-nine
years old and an economist by training, had moved fast through the ranks of the
corporation. He had joined Cummins as director of planning in 1965 when the need
for a change in company strategy was starting to be felt among some of the company
executives. By 1969 a new strategy had taken shape in the minds of Cummin's management. Its major theme: conservation of capital.

CUMMINS'S OPERATIONS

Cummins Engine was the world's largest independent producer of high-speed
diesel engines (i.e., equipment containing the engine was not produced by Cummins).
Its products were geared to that sector of the power industry where the engine was
a differentiated component of the final product. This was especially the case in the
heavy-duty truck market. In heavy-duty trucks the engine, though only 20% of the
initial cost, was the single most important item in the total cost of operating the
truck. It was in this high-power, highly quality, and price-sensitive market that
Cummins was best equipped to compete. Diesel engines and related parts comprised
91% of Cummins's 1971 consolidated net sales. (See Exhibit 1 for an analysis of
Cummins's sales in 1971 by major categories.)

The Products

Cummins manufactured two types of engines: the in-line H and NH, and the
V type. The H and NH engines were offered in a range of 220 to 420 horsepower

[1] This case presents background material on the company and a description of its strategies.
Cummins Engine Company, Inc. (B) presents an analysis of the new venture.

(HP); the V type were more compact engines and ranged between 160 and 240 HP. The market for these products was divided between the on-highway truck market and the off-highway engine market.

On-Highway Truck Market. In 1971, on-highway truck applications accounted for approximately 72% of Cummins's U. S. engine sales. Cummins was the leading supplier of diesel engines for the heavy-duty truck market in the United States—over 26,000 lbs. gross vehicle weight (GVW). Engines were usually sold to equipment manufacturers, some of which were Cummins's major competitors who produced diesel engines themselves. However, Cummins's reputation was such that the majority of these competitors—including General Motors, International Harvester, Mack Trucks, and so on—also offered Cummins engines in their models to satisfy customers who specified Cummins power. Exhibit 2 shows the shares of the engine market taken by Cummins and its competitors.

The fast growth in the diesel heavy-duty market during the 1960s (approximately 11.4% per year) had its roots in two factors: the increasing demand for higher power in trucks, and the conversion from gasoline to diesel-powered engines. In 1971, 74.6% of new heavy-duty trucks (over 26,000 GVW) were diesel powered. (See Exhibit 2.) This rate was expected to rise to 80% by 1975, in contrast to 61% in 1965. Notwithstanding this, Cummins's sales forecast predicted a slowdown in growth rate of the heavy-duty truck market during the 1970s, down to 8.5%. (See Exhibit 3, page 404.)

The processes of "dieselization" and demand for higher power that had been taking place in the United States were expected to be the major source of growth in the rest of the world's engine market in the future. However, Cummins's penetration of the European truck market, up to 1971, had been minimal. The European market was controlled by European producers who had long been established in the market and who produced their own engines. (See Exhibit 4, page 405.) Cummins's hopes in the European market depended on the demand for higher power capacity, which Europeans were not capable of producing at the time, and the increased market penetration of Ford, which used the Cummins engines to some extent. Statistics on actual and forecasted truck market in Europe are presented in Exhibit 5, page 404.

Off-Highway Engine Market. Cummins had made special efforts to penetrate the off-highway markets in recent years. The basic truck engines had been adapted to a variety of other markets. This had permitted Cummins to make important inroads into the construction, industrial, marine, and agricultural markets. In 1971, off-highway applications accounted for approximately 29% of Cummins's U. S. engine sales.

The major sector for Cummins in the off-highway market was construction equipment. This market was composed of crawler tractors, scrapers, dump trucks, cranes, and so on. In the United States, as well as in Europe, the major manufacturer of this equipment was Caterpillar, which also manufactured its own engines. Exhibit 6 presents actual 1971 and forecast 1976 data for the off-highway market in the United States. Figures for the construction market in Europe, the market sector where Cummins's sales in that part of the world were concentrated, are presented in Exhibit 7. The marine and agricultural markets played only a minor role in Cummins's overall operations.

Marketing, Distribution, and Service

The great success of Cummins in the heavy-duty truck market was largely due to the special efforts Cummins made to service the final user: the truck operator. Conscious that the selection of the engine to be incorporated in a heavy-duty truck depended more on the purchasing decision of truck operators than on the purchasing decision of truck manufacturers, Cummins maintained an extensive network of distributors and dealers. This sytem provided services and sales through 139 distributors and branch office locations and over 2,000 dealer outlets in the United States and Canada, and nearly 500 locations in one hundred countries overseas. These independently owned, company-franchised distributors constituted the industry's largest and most efficient network of marketing and servicing facilities.

The management of sales was all centralized in the company's headquarters at Columbus, Indiana, in the office of the executive vice-president for marketing. However, the strong emphasis on marketing, which in the United States had made equipment operators identify with the Cummins name and truck manufacturers specify Cummins engines as an alternative to their own, had failed to materialize in the foreign markets. Although Cummins had a network of 500 distributors outside the United States, these were not exclusive Cummins distributors for the most part. For these distributors Cummins was just one more brand competing with the powerful European truck manufacturers' brands.

Production Policies

Cummins's production facilities throughout the world could be classified into two groups: those that manufactured components as well as engines; and those that bought parts from other Cummins divisions to produce the engines. The first group was part of a network that reached almost every corner of the world with its products—both components and final products. The second group was concerned mostly with selling the final product in the local market. The first group was composed of the major Cummins production facilities: Columbus, Indiana, in the United States and Shotts and Darlington in the United Kingdom. The second group was composed of the joint venture with Kirloskar in India, and the license agreements with DINA in Mexico and Komatsu in Japan.

Manufacturers of Parts and Engines. The major manufacturing facilities of Cummins were located in Columbus, Indiana, where approximately 1,750,000 square feet of manufacturing and warehouse space were utilized to produce diesel engines, parts, and major components. This capacity was being expanded by 50%, part of which was scheduled to be occupied during 1972. Columbus produced the bulk of Cummins's NH engines and components.

The 195,000 square foot facility in Shotts, Scotland, produced Cummins's H and NH in-line diesel engines and service parts. In 1971, the Shotts facility had been enlarged by 20% and underwent other improvements which expanded capacity by 70%. Approximately 73% of Shotts' output was consumed by the British original equipment market. The remainder was exported, with the largest volume going to Western Europe, Canada, and other Commonwealth countries.

Darlington facilities included two adjacent plants: one producing Cummins's small V series diesels, and the other producing components. Darlington was the sole source of the compact V components and the major supplier of V engines in the Cummins system. Additional growth would be possible without the need for immediate plant expansion. The component plant manufactured fuel pumps, air compressors, dampers, injectors, and turbo-chargers.

Manufacturers of Engines Primarily. Kirloskar-Cummins, Ltd., in Poona, India, was 50% owned by Cummins, with Kirloskar Oil Engines, Ltd., owning 25½% and 7,000 public shareholders in India 24½%. This joint venture was established to produce the popular H and NH series engines for construction equipment manufacturers. A large percentage of the components of these engines was imported from Shotts. Kirloskar-Cummins, Ltd., fully owned a subsidiary, Cummins Diesel Sales and Service, which operated a network of thirteen dealers and four branch offices in India.

Cummins maintained two licensing agreements for the manufacture of its engines: one in Japan with Komatsu, the other in Mexico with Diesel National (DINA). Komatsu was a major Japanese manufacturer of construction and industrial equipment. The license agreement allowed Komatsu to manufacture NH engines. It payed Cummins a 5% royalty on manufacturing cost for sales of all licensed products manufactured or assembled by Komatsu and used to power its own equipment. Sales of parts and engines to other Japanese manufacturers, as well as sales of parts for Komatsu products, were handled through Komatsu-Cummins Sales Company, Ltd., which was 51% owned by Cummins. This sales company was also the exclusive Cummins sales agent in Japan for parts and engines from Columbus and other plants.

Cummins had another agreement with DINA, a major manufacturer of trucks, buses, cars, and engines which was owned by the Mexican government. DINA produced small V engines and assembled NH engines for use in its own equipment as well as for sales to other original equipment manufacturers in Mexico. Most of the components of V engines were imported from Darlington and a large part of the NH components came from Columbus. Royalties were paid to Cummins in dollars. The in-line engines not used by DINA in its own trucks were distributed in Mexico by Cummins.

Centralization of Production. The production policy at Cummins had to articulate two different, and sometimes conflicting, management philosophies corresponding to each of the two groups of manufacturing facilities described above. In the first group that produced engines as well as parts, Cummins had full ownership and it pursued an integrated production approach. In the second group, where only engines were produced for the most part, Cummins shared the management or left it altogether to locals.

One of the major objectives of the company was to achieve the most efficient system of production plants by increasing standardization and minimizing duplication of facilities. Accordingly, a policy of increasing cross-sourcing of components between plants was encouraged. Also, an ongoing cost-reduction program continuously reexamined the possibilities of reducing costs in manufacturing as well as in the purchase of raw materials. A special program called Operations Technical Services (OTS) had been devised to help standardize operating practices throughout

the corporation, to provide a formal point of contact between plants and departments, and to promote the development of new technologies of company-wide
importance. These programs were managed from the office of the executive vice-
president for operations in Columbus and were central to the operations of the
fully owned plants at Columbus, Shotts, and Darlington. The other production
facilities remained at the margin of these programs.

In the second group of manufacturing facilities, where Cummins operated in the
form of joint ventures or license agreements, the interests of the nationals—both
local partners and governments—also had to be taken into account. Usually in these
cases the dependence of the manufacturer on Cummins for components was seen
by the locals as a temporary situation, with the ultimate objective being a relatively
high degree of self-sufficiency in manufacturing. Cross-sourcing and integrated production plans within the Cummins umbrella would be considered only to the extent that the country and the local partners found it beneficial to their private
interests.

In spite of the desire of foreign governments and partners to gain manufacturing independence, experience had taught Cummins that these wishes took some
time to be fulfilled. Of the three semipartnerships that Cummins maintained at the
time, only Komatsu was considered to be fully independent, except for certain
proprietary items.

One of the major obstacles encountered in converting fully to local production
was the availability of supporting industries. In many cases the stage of development of a given industry, steel for example, or the absence of a raw material whose
import would be prohibitive could thwart the whole process. In other cases, even
if the industrial infra-structure were available, the size of the operation could make
it uneconomical to convert to local production. Although fully committed to col-
laborate with foreign partners towards their independence in manufacturing,
Cummins did not get hurt by the delays in the conversion process. During this
period Cummins was the major supplier of components. It was a well-known fact in
the industry that parts carried a substantially higher margin than engines.

Research and Development

The prominent role that Cummins played in the diesel business was due to a very
large extent to the leadership that Cummins's research had exercised in the market.
Cummins had pioneered many innovations, the benefits of which were reflected in
current diesel engine technology.

Cummins had recently completed a new $22 million technical center in Colum-
bus. Another small center was maintained in Germany. In addition, a substantial
amount was spent every year in research and development ($21.7 million in 1971).
The Cummins technical center had 1,000 engineering professionals, and it contained
more test cells devoted to diesel research and development than any other facility
in the world.

MANAGEMENT STRATEGY

Acquisition Policy

Cummins had been continuously under the aegis of the J. Irwin Miller family,
the financiers who supported Clessie Cummins, founder of the company, during the

long initial period of losses between 1919 and 1938. In 1971 Mr. J. Irwin Miller was Chairman of the Board of Cummins and his family controlled 46% of the Cummins's shares. In spite of the continuity of top management, Cummins's strategy had undergone three different stages.

1920-1956. The first period was primarily marked by the efforts to introduce diesel power to the market. The pioneering struggle required that all resources be concentrated in a minimum of products for a given market. During this period the growth of the company was provided solely by the engine business in the United States where the Cummins products became a great success. Towards the end of the period, however, as the post-World War expansion in Europe began to proceed, exports from the United States to foreign countries started to play an increasing role. By 1953, foreign sales represented 11% of total sales and were growing at a galloping rate. By 1966, Cummins had 130 export dealers, and a number of new positions to manage the export business were created.

1957-1967. During the second expansionary strategy, new developments took place in the domestic as well as the foreign markets. The guiding criteria became obtaining control of suppliers and expanding foreign markets. In the domestic field, a program of vertical integration was initiated. In the overseas area, foreign production was begun.

The efforts to integrate vertically in the United States resulted in the purchase of a manufacturer of engine components, the Atlas Crankshaft Corporation; a manufacturer of heavy-duty filters, which became the Fleetguard Division; and a foundry, the old Studebaker foundry which was named Great Lakes Foundry Division. In addition, an attempt was made to move outside of the engine field. In 1964 the Frigicar Company of Dallas was purchased. This became the Frigiking Division which is a major factor in the add-on automobile air conditioner market.

In the foreign market this strategy led to the establishment of the production facilities in Shotts in 1956 and in Darlington in 1963, both fully owned. During this period the partnerships with foreign producers were also initiated: Komatsu licensing agreement in 1961, Kirloskar joint venture in 1962, and the licensing agreement with DINA in 1963. During this period also, a couple of less successful partnerships where the engines were to be produced by a foreign manufacturer were started: one with Krupp in Germany in 1962, and another with Jaguar in England around the same time. These last two deals were surrounded with great technical difficulties from their inception. Difficulties in the design of the final product as well as problems in engine quality control combined to quickly terminate the alliance.

1969-Present. In mid-1969 Cummins management started articulating a new strategy that would steer the company away from the policies followed in the previous years and toward a revitalization that looked for new projects and for better ways to carry on old lines of business. The implementation of these ideas called for an attack on three fronts: maximization of returns in the engine field, acquisition of companies in industries related to engines, and investment in emerging industries.

This new strategy was primarily founded in the analysis of the company's objectives and the potential ways of achieving these objectives, given the characteristics of the environment in which Cummins would operate in the future. The corporate goals of Cummins were: (1) 15% annual growth in profits, which implied a doubling in every five years; (2) 15% return on shareholders equity; and (3) maintenance of highest standards of responsibility to all stakeholders (individuals, community, shareholders, government). Achievement of these objectives in the 1950s and part of the 1960s produced the success of Cummins during that period. However, an analysis of the future showed that the potential growth of the power market, and diesel power in particular, would be less than in the previous decades. Cummins management estimated that no more than 8% or 10% of growth could be expected to come from this market in the future. Chances were high that if Cummins remained committed just to the diesel engine business, the future would fall short of company objectives. Management's response to this challenge was clear in the new strategy: move into the most profitable parts of the engine business, and move outside the engine business into fields that promise to be the Cummins of the 1980s.

In finding ways to maximize Cummins returns from the engine business two major elements were studied: the strength of the company and the characteristics of the environment. In their self-analysis, it was clear to Cummins management that the technological leadership it had provided in the engine field, and the superb network of distributors it possessed to service the ultimate customer, were the two major factors that had taken Cummins to the prominent position it played in the U. S. engine market at the time. The actual manufacturing of the engines, although requiring large amounts of skills, could be done equally well by many other producers. Therefore, Cummins's resources should be concentrated in designing and marketing engines—the areas where Cummins had an advantage over other producers in the market. If Cummins were to concentrate in doing what it knew best, manufacturing should be done by Cummins's suppliers and not by Cummins itself. An analysis of the economic environment led to similar conclusions. Cummins's present operations consisted of combining labor, capital, and technology to produce engines. A forecast of the behavior of these factors in the future showed a rising cost of money and labor, and an accelerated pace in technological innovation. The rising cost of money indicated that this resource should be saved for high return enterprises only. The rising cost of labor suggested that this resource should be used only at the highest potential level. Finally, the fast change in technology dictated a large degree of flexibility at all times to adjust to continuous changes. The combination of these three elements led Cummins's management to conclude that Cummins should leave the capital intensive process of manufacturing to somebody else. It should save its resources for high-yield operations, while keeping flexible to adopt new manufacturing technologies.

These new plans appeared to be in strong contrast to the swirl of construction activity at Columbus in 1972. Although in-house forecasts in 1967—a recessionary year—had indicated that the industry was due for a fast upturn which would grossly exceed 1967's capacity, management had decided then to tone down the plans that the forecasters recommended. This adjustment in proposed plans, plus the usual delay involved in plant construction (four to five years from planning stage to final completion) had brought a considerable shortage in capacity when the forecast demand materialized. Since 1969 Cummins had been producing at a three-shift, full-capacity pace without being able to cope with demand. In the international field, also, special developments had led to a departure from the new strategy. In 1971, the assets of Otto Deutz—an engine and truck manufacturer in Brazil—had been purchased. In spite of the commitment to subcontract engine manufacture, this acquisition had been made as the only chance for a meaningful participation in the Brazilian market at a very reasonable purchase price.

The second leg of the strategy, acquisitions of companies in industries related to engines, was also based on the analysis that suggested a reduction in emphasis on manufacturing in the engine business. The rationale for going into engine-related fields was that Cummins could make use of its present network of distributors, as well as its technological leadership, to increase the return in areas where large commitment of capital in production was not necessary. The implementation of this part of the strategy had led to the creation of Cummins Sundstrand, Inc., and Diesel ReCon, Inc., in 1971. Cummins Sundstrand sold and serviced transmissions produced by Sundstrand. Diesel ReCon operated an engine remanufacturing operation and it was jointly owned by Cummins and thirty-five independent U.S. distributorships.

The third leg of the strategy, investment in emerging industries, was where the hopes for high growth in the long term were based. Several industries were screened to meet Cummins criteria for growth potential. Among these, the leisure business was chosen as the one with the highest expected growth. Following this concept, K2 Corporation, a leading manufacturer of fiberglas snow skis in the United States, was acquired in 1970. This acquisition was also based on the concept of a nuclear role for distribution channels. K2 had an excellent distribution system which was expected to be central in the expansion of K2. Accordingly K2 had recently acquired the assets of Jan Sport, Inc., a manufacturer of an expensive line of backpacks and ski touring equipment. The Frigiking Division was also following the new concept, and it had acquired in 1971 rights to market British refrigerators used by most recreational vehicle manufacturers, and Wedgwood, a manufacturer of ovens and grilles for recreational vehicles.

Financial Management

While management thinking on approaches to Cummins's growth followed different patterns through time, changes in the financial strategy of Cummins were also taking place. Up to 1965 Cummins's expansion was financed solely from internal sources of funds and limited banking relations. Since 1965 a larger emphasis had been placed on external funds and on institutional investors. Exhibit 8 on pages 408-9 presents Cummins's balance sheet for 1971. Exhibit 9 on page 407 contains a historical and financial summary.

Mr. Hackett placed great emphasis on cash flows as determinants of the debt capacity of a company. He thought that the relevant concept was an interest coverage ratio, and that Cummins should see that this ratio did not fall below 3 under any conditions. However, The First Boston Corporation, Cummins's investment bankers, had been very specific in advising that a debt-equity ratio higher than 40% would certainly increase the cost of debt. Furthermore, conversations with Moody's staff had tended to confirm the view that a higher debt-equity ratio would downgrade the rating of the company—currently rated as A. (Partly accounting for this was the fact that Moody's apparently did not distinguish between subordinated and unsubordinated debt, but instead considered it all together as debt.) Mr. Hackett had performed an analysis of the implications of various combinations of growth patterns for financing. That analysis had showed that if expansion were to occur by increasing manufacturing facilities, massive amounts of funds would be needed. Without resorting to the use of equity financing, it appeared extremely difficult to fulfill this need for funds without exceeding the 40% debt-equity ratio.

Two criteria operated in the selection of the financing instruments since 1965: the international nature of Cummins, and the eventual need of additional funds in the form of equity. The first consideration brought to bear the controls on foreign direct investment which required that funds be raised abroad if these were to be invested abroad. However, this was never a very important constraint. More important were considerations that Cummins was a multinational company and therefore should have multinational sources of funds. It was important that the Cummins name become familiar to the financial community abroad. The other factor, the eventual need for equity funds, made convertibles the best instrument to raise the funds. However, this also imposed some constraints in the future if the company's stock price did not behave according to expectations. A summary of Cummins's major financings during 1965-1971 is presented in Exhibit 10.

**EXHIBIT 1   Cummins Engine Company, Inc.:
Distribution of Sales, 1971**

Diesel Products: Engines and Parts	
Direct sales of engines	72%
Sales through Cummins's distributors	
(mostly parts and a few engines)	28
	100%
U. S. and Foreign Sales	
Sales in the United States	73%
Sales abroad	27
	100%
Sales Abroad	
On-highway truck market	25%
Off-highway market	
(mostly construction)	75
	100%
Diesel and Other Products	
Total diesel products	91%
Other products (United States only)	9
	100%
Total sales in million dollars	$492.3

Source: Company data.

EXHIBIT 2 U. S. Diesel Engines: Market Data—U. S. Truck and Tractor Shipments and Engine Used, 1963-1971

	1971	1970	1969	1968	1967	1966	1965	1964	1963	1958
26,000-33,000 Lbs. Gross Vehicle Weight										
Total Trucks (Gas and Diesel)	36,398	35,738	30,734	38,916	34,229	39,997	36,288	25,906	27,958	
Percent Diesel	33.7	33.3	37.6	37.0	37.9	41.1	43.3	34.3	42.0	
Percent Diesel with Cummins	23.9	18.3	25.1	11.6	12.4	18.7	29.1	45.4	41.6	
Over 33,000 Lbs. Gross Vehicle Weight										
Total Trucks (Gas and Diesel)	110,726	101,068	117,532	89,532	77,816	91,092	75,796	64,134	58,746	
Percent Diesel	87.0	84.5	79.6	77.5	73.1	72.0	69.7	65.8	57.3	
Percent Diesel with Cummins	44.5	46.5	45.8	50.1	50.8	56.9	57.5	59.7	65.9	

U. S. Diesel Trucks: Producers Market Share, 1958 and 1966-1970

	1970	1969	1968	1967	1966	1958
White	18.7%	21.9%	23.2%	20.3%	23.8%	23.5%
Mack	20.9	19.0	20.1	19.8	19.2	39.8
IHC	20.0	20.3	18.7	20.5	22.0	15.3
GMC	9.3	11.0	11.5	12.1	11.3	7.2
Ford	14.9	12.1	6.7	8.6	8.4	—
Dodge	4.7	3.8	3.8	5.7	3.3	—
Chevrolet	1.2	1.0	1.1	2.9	2.2	—
Other	10.3	10.9	14.9	10.1	9.8	14.2
Total	100.0%	100.0%	100.0%	100.0%	100.0%	100.0%

U. S. Diesel Engines: Manufacturers Market Share, 1966-1970

	1970	1969	1968	1967	1966
Cummins	39.7%	40.0%	41.3%	36.6%	41.9%
Detroit Diesel	28.5	30.7	27.3	25.9	21.9
Mack	15.3	14.7	15.8	16.7	16.4
Perkins	4.0	2.8	4.0	7.3	6.3
IHC	2.5	2.2	3.9	2.9	2.9
GMC	0.7	1.4	3.2	6.5	6.5
Ford	0.4	1.1	2.2	2.6	2.6
Others[a]	8.9	7.1	2.3	1.5	1.5
Total	100.0%	100.0%	100.0%	100.0%	100.0%

[a]Principally Caterpillar Tractor.
Source: Automotive Manufacturers Association.

EXHIBIT 3   U. S. Heavy-Duty Truck Market: Actual
and Forecasted Unit Sales

(units)			
Actual[a]		Forecasted	
1963	45,421	1972	121,700
1964	51,054	1973	135,400
1965	66,563	1974	145,200
1966	81,997	1975	156,300
1967	69,854	1976	165,800
1968	83,806	1977	175,900
1969	105,019		
1970	97,270		
1971	107,564		

Annual Compounded Growth Rate

1963-71 = 11.4%
1972-77 = 8.5%

[a]The actual figures differ from those presented in
Exhibit 2 because of discrepancies on collection method
of the two sources.
Source: Company estimates.

EXHIBIT 5   Market Shares in European Truck Registration: Actual 1960-1971, and Forecasted
1972-1977

	Market Shares				Compounded Annual Market Growth	
	Actual			Forecasted		
	1960[a]	1965[a]	1971	1977	1960-71	1972-77
Austria	1.5%	2.6%	1.8%	1.4%	7.5%	3.5%
Belgium	4.0	3.8	3.6	3.1	14.2	5.6
Denmark	1.0	1.7	1.9	2.4	18.5	12.7
Finland	.3	1.5	2.2	1.8	28.4	4.9
France	25.5	21.4	17.2	15.3	7.6	6.0
Germany	7.8	21.3	19.9	23.1	22.8	10.8
Italy	11.0	5.6	8.7	11.3	9.2	13.0
Netherlands	4.8	5.3	5.4	3.9	13.0	2.6
Norway	.2	.4	1.5	1.7	30.4	11.2
Portugal	1.5	1.8	1.0	.7	3.8	3.6
Spain	—	—	5.3	4.3	19.6	4.7
Sweden	8.9	7.1	3.8	2.7	2.4	2.1
Switzerland	1.9	1.6	1.7	1.7	6.9	10.3
United Kingdom	31.7	26.0	26.2	26.4	16.7	8.2
	100.0	100.0	100.0	100.0		
EUROPE (units)	57,391	95,046	175,849	280,646	10.5%	8.1%

[a]Does not include Spain.
Source: Company estimates.

EXHIBIT 4   European Heavy-Duty Truck Market: Major Manufacturers' Market Shares by Country, 1969

	France			Germany			Italy	Sweden		United Kingdom				Miscellaneous
Country	Berliet	Savien	Unic	Daimler-Benz Group	MAN Group	Deutz	Fiat	Volvo	Scania	BLMC Group	Ford	Bedford	Chrysler	
Austria				27%				11%	14%					73%
Belgium				17%				30%	23%			6%		40%
Denmark				3%				23%	25%			14%		20%
Finland				9%								9%		35%
France	33%	22%	17%	10%										18%
Germany				51%	29%	15%								5%
Italy						96%	12%							4%
Netherlands				11%				8%	11%			5%		65%
Norway				15%				35%	26%			7%		12%
Sweden								50%	47%					3%
Switzerland				17%		10%								52%
United Kingdom								11%	10%	36%	20%	17%	13%	

Source: Company estimates.

405

EXHIBIT 6 U. S. Construction, Mining, and Logging Market: Major
Manufacturers' Engine Market Share

	1971 Actual		1976 Forecasted		Annual Growth
	Units	Percent	Units	Percent	
100-200 HP					
Caterpillar	12,900	32%	13,000	28%	
Non-Caterpillar	26,700	68	33,400	72	
Total	39,600	100%	46,400	100%	3.2%
200 HP and Over					
Caterpillar	7,300	41%	15,300	40%	
Non-Caterpillar	10,400	59	23,200	60	
Total	17,700	100%	38,500	100%	16.8%
Total					
Caterpillar	20,200	36%	27,300	32%	
Non-Caterpillar	37,100	64	56,600	68	
Total	57,300	100%	84,900	100%	8.2%

Source: Company estimates.

EXHIBIT 7 European Construction Equipment Market—
Actual and Forecasted Volume: 100 HP and Over

Actual (units)		Forecasted (units)	
1969	16,060	1972	18,951
1970	17,321	1973	20,086
1971	17,755	1974	21,244
		1975	22,401
		1976	23,497
		1977	24,598

Annual growth rate 5.4%

Market Shares All-HP, 1970

Caterpillar	24%
Fiat	18
International Harvester	10
Hanomay	7
Volvo	4
Deere	4
AC	3
Clark	3
J.I. Case	2
Komatsu	2
Frisch	1
Others	22

Source: Company estimates.

EXHIBIT 9   Cummins Engine Company, Inc.: Financial Summary, 1963-1971

	1963	1965	1967	1969	1970	1971
	Dollars in thousands, except per share amounts					
Operating Data						
Net sales	$194,334	$280,779	$306,212	$412,356	$448,544	$492,262
Cost of goods sold	126,824	192,829	226,705	284,369	308,718	341,383
Gross profit on sales	67,510	87,950	79,507	127,987	139,826	150,879
Other operating expenses	39,448	58,545	71,934	90,752	100,214	114,127
Profit on sales	28,062	29,405	7,573	37,235	39,612	36,752
Other income or (expenses)	100	(1,582)	(3,723)	(189)	714	1,396
Earnings before income taxes	28,162	27,823	3,850	37,046	40,326	38,148
Provision for income taxes	14,647	12,712	330	18,908	19,911	16,651
Net earnings	$ 13,515	$ 15,111	$ 3,520	$ 18,138	$ 20,415	$ 21,497
Fully diluted earnings per share	2.25	2.50	.58	2.72	3.03	3.14
Cash dividends per share	.37	.51	.66	.71	.80	.88
				(10% stock)		
Financial Data						
Working capital	$ 41,341	$ 54,941	$ 80,597	$ 87,533	$ 95,656	$125,807
Property, plant, and equipment at net book value	48,582	76,976	98,483	104,580	114,202	132,807
Total assets	118,562	190,176	233,703	279,135	322,128	354,538
Long-term debt	12,675	38,067	72,987	61,864	88,089	84,809
Shareholders' investment	70,453	93,843	107,390	130,776	145,525	175,501
Capitalization	82,828	131,910	180,377	192,640	233,614	260,310
Other Data						
Earnings as a percent of net sales	7.0%	5.4%	1.1%	4.4%	4.5%	4.4%
Earnings as a percent of shareholders' average investment	21.0%	17.2%	3.3%	14.7%	14.8%	13.4%
Capital expenditures	$ 12,974	$ 22,319	$ 18,243	$ 16,741	$ 23,352	$ 35,248
Depreciation	5,272	7,493	10,424	13,363	12,415	12,714
Interest expense	845	1,664	4,216	3,720	4,239	5,439
Interest income	882	568	697	2,229	2,933	3,011
Cost of research and start-up for new products and operations	7,371	15,854	17,171	15,315	18,700	21,724

Eight-year data is useful for general information purposes; however, no restatement except for poolings of interests has been made to assure year-to-year comparability of all data. Per share data is based on appropriate weighted average number of shares outstanding during each year, adjusted for subsequent stock dividends and stock splits.

Source: Cummins Engine Company, Inc. *Annual Report, 1971.*

EXHIBIT 8   Cummins Engine Company, Inc.: Consolidated Balance Sheet (000s), December 31, 1971

Assets		Liabilities and Shareholders' Investment	
Current Assets:		Current Liabilities:	
Cash and marketable securities	$ 19,176	Loans payable	$ 3,037
Receivables (less allowance for		Current maturities of long-term debt	1,417
doubtful accounts)	88,064	Accounts payable	24,700
Inventories	83,235	Accrued expenses	44,591
Deferred income taxes and prepaid		Contributions to retirement trusts	2,922
expenses	15,270	Income taxes	3,271
Total Current Assets	$205,747	Total Current Liabilities	79,940
Investments and Other Assets:		Long-Term Debt, Less Current	
Investments in unconsolidated		Maturities:	
companies (Note 2)	7,436	Payable to domestic lenders	52,534
Receivables due beyond one year, etc.	2,968	Payable to international lenders	32,275
Total Investments and Other Assets	10,405	Total Long-Term Debt	84,809
Property, Plant and Equipment,		Deferred Income Taxes	14,287
at Cost:	219,432	Shareholders' Investment:	
Less: Accumulated depreciation		Common stock at par value	16,644
(straight-line)	86,625	Capital surplus	71,742
Net Property, Plant and Equipment	132,806	Earnings retained in the business	87,344
Intangible Assets and Deferred Charges	5,578	Total Shareholders' Investment	175,501
		Total Liabilities and Shareholders'	
Total Assets	$354,537	Investment	$354,537

Note 1: Foreign Operations:

Net assets of consolidated subsidiaries and branches located outside of the United States at December 31, 1971, consisted of:

Area	Net Current Assets	Millions of Dollars Non-current Assets	Long-term Debt	Net Assets
United Kingdom	$13.9	$15.5	$13.2	$16.2
Latin America	10.0	18.7	15.0	13.7
Other	2.7	1.8	—	4.5
	$26.6	$36.0	$28.2	$34.4

Investments in unconsolidated companies outside the
United States $ 5.9

Sales to customers located outside of the United States were approximately $135 million in 1971 and $119 million in 1970. Of these sales, approximately 58% in 1971 and 51% in 1970 were exports from the United States.

Products of manufacturing subsidiaries located outside of the United States include, in most instances, components manufactured in the United States by Cummins and sold to the foreign subsidiaries at intercompany prices. The earnings of these subsidiaries do not bear any definite relationship to their net assets and thus are not reported separately.

A diesel engine plant at Sao Paulo, Brazil, was purchased from Otto Deutz, S.A., on December 16, 1971, for $2.9 million.

In translating the accounts of foreign operations into U. S. dollar equivalents, current assets and current liabilities have been translated at the approximate exchange rates prevailing at the balance sheet date; long-term assets, long-term debt, and capital accounts at historical rates of exchange; and income and expense accounts at average rates, except depreciation and amortization, which have been translated at historical rates. Realized and unrealized exchange gains and losses on translation have been included in earnings.

Note 2: Unconsolidated Companies:

Investments in the following unconsolidated companies are recorded at cost, adjusted to include Cummins's share of earnings and losses:

	Location	Ownership
Cummins Sundstrand, Inc.	United States	20%
Diesel Recon, Inc.	United States	31%
Kirloskar Cummins Limited	India	50%
Komatsu-Cummins Sales Company Limited	Japan	51%
Transinterbank, Inc.	Switzerland	100%

Source: Cummins Engine Company, Inc., *Annual Report*, 1971.

EXHIBIT 10   Cummins Engine Company, Inc.: Major Financings: 1966-71

Year	Description	Amount	Interest Rate
1966	Negotiated revolving credit agreement which pro-vided for borrowings up to $25 million at prime rate; could renew short-term notes to 1969, then convert into a term loan due 1974.	$23.5 million	5½-6½%
1967	Renegotiated revolving credit agreement; now allows $35 million; Cummins now using 100% of this line of credit.		
1968	Floated subordinated convertible Euro-bonds due 1988; convertible after May 1, 1969, into Cummins common at $39.77 per share.	$20 million	5%
1968	Repaid $35 million line of credit.		
1969	Issued through U. K. subsidiary £5 million of con-vertible unsecured loan stock @ 3¾%. Convertible at $46.36.	$12 million	3¾%
1969	Proceeds of loan/stock issue used to repay other higher cost long- and short-term loans.		
1970	Sinking fund debentures due 1995. Sold in United States.	$30 million	8 ⅞%
1971	Subordinated convertible debentures. Sold in Europe; convertible @ $56.50.	$15 million	6½%
1971	$15.9 million of the $20 million 1968 Euro-issue have been converted into 440,306 shares of common stock.		

Cummins Engine Company, Inc. (B)

After reviewing the company's recently developed strategy, Mr. John T. Hackett, Executive Vice-President, turned to analyze the new proposal on which he was expected to make a recommendation to the Board of Directors on March 15.[1] The opportunity to start implementing the new strategy had finally been opened in early 1972, after a year of negotiations. Cummins Engine was now contemplating allowing a Japanese manufacturer, Komatsu, Ltd., to manufacture its new super-powerful "K engine" series. Under the new plan, the recently designed K engines would be produced only in Japan. Cummins would first purchase the engine components and assemble them, but eventually the complete engines would be bought from the Japanese manufacturer at a prearranged price. This would be the first time that Cummins would depend on an external supplier for its products—in this case a new product which promised to be highly successful.

The K Engine

The concept of the K engine had been developed in response to Cummins's perceptions of demand in the power market. It was estimated that the need for in-

[1] For background on the company and a presentation of its strategies see Cummins Engine Company, Inc. (A).

creased horsepower, especially in the United States, would soon exceed the predictable power growth of the company's products. Specially, it was forecast that very substantial markets would open up in the 400-600 HP and 800-1200 HP markets during the 1970s.

March 1970 marked the birth of the K engine. At that time the management gave the "go signal" to the new engine. Gross assumptions about the cost of building a new plant in the United States to produce the new engine and about the market that the K engine would command promised a rate of return of 32.1% at the time. Research on the design of this engine had been going on for the preceding seven years. Now that the initial "go" decision had been taken, the research and development in the new engine was to concentrate on incorporating requirements of the final users. Final drawings also had to be prepared.

While research and development worked on improving the performance of the K engine, Mr. Hackett's financial department proceeded to analyze the new project in more detail. Confidence in the new project was bolstered when it was found that an extensive analysis of the sensitivity of the project to various assumptions about market volume and prices all showed rates of returns considerably higher than the company's required 15%. At the same time, an issue that had been latent before now came to the forefront of the analysis. The K project would require an investment of $44 million to produce the engine in the United States.

The large investment requirements of the new project clearly came head-on with the recently established strategy of conservation of capital. Management's initial reaction to this requirement was perfectly predictable within the context of the new strategy: a way to reduce the investment requirements had to be found. In the search for this new way, two new factors were brought to bear; one, the company was committed to worldwide participation; two, Cummins's largest competitor in the off-highway market, Caterpillar, was now starting to make moves into the U. S. automotive market. A combination of these two factors directed attention to one of Caterpillar's largest international competitors: Komatsu, Ltd., in Japan, with whom Cummins was already well acquainted. Through ten years of license agreements, Cummins had found that Komatsu not only had the capacity to undertake sizable orders for engine manufacturing, but also was capable of producing engines to meet the high standards of Cummins. It was soon clear that an extension of the relationship with Komatsu in the context of the K engine would accomplish two objectives: reduce the size of the required investment in the United States, and strengthen the ties of a friendship that could pay high dividends later on in terms of world markets. So, from a very early stage it was decided that steps should be taken so Komatsu would manufacture some of the components of the new engine.

Komatsu, Ltd.

When first established in 1921, Komatsu, Ltd., was a small local firm located in the Ishikawa Prefecture at the midpoint of the island. In 1971 Komatsu had sales of $785 million, and it ranked about thirtieth among the top Japanese companies. Its main product, bulldozers, commanded a market share of 60% in Japan, even in the face of Caterpillar Tractor Company's expansion into Japan since 1963.

Komatsu was a vertically integrated equipment manufacturer. Its production facilities were as modern or more so than Cummins's facilities. The foundry factory, in particular, was far superior to what was commonly encountered in the United States. At the same time, the machining operations were as advanced as the technology used by Cummins itself. Labor-capital ratios were very similar to those found at Cummins.

In addition to the prominent position of Komatsu in the Japanese capital markets, there were three factors that made Komatsu a desirable business partner to Cummins:

One, its management under the leadership of Mr. Yoshini Kawai had shown insightfulness in anticipating market forces and boldness in approaching new business deals. Komatsu had consistently anticipated major trends in the Japanese markets that occurred after the Second World War and after the Korean War. Komatsu's management was also one of the first groups of Japanese industrialists to start carrying out trade transactions with the Communist-bloc countries several years ago.

Two, Komatsu had placed great emphasis in differentiating itself from top-level foreign brands through the quality of its products. The entry of Caterpillar Tractor into Japan, through its joint venture with the Mitsubishi Heavy Industries Co., had been highly instrumental in inducing Komatsu to concentrate on better quality control.

Three, Komatsu was placing an increasing emphasis on foreign markets. This effort by Komatsu had been combined with a strong resistance against foreign capital in Japan. Export sales which in 1966 were approximately $25 million, had increased to $134 million by 1971. In 1971, in its fiftieth anniversary, Komatsu had made an organizational reshuffle on a big scale under the Overseas Division and established as one of its goals to become a world enterprise in the true sense of the word. Sales figures for Komatsu are presented in Exhibit 1.

EXHIBIT 1   Komatsu, Ltd.: Sales 1966-1971 (millions of dollars)

		Japan		Overseas	
	Total Sales	Dollars	Percent	Dollars	Percent
1966	$231.6	$208.0	89.8%	$ 23.6	10.2%
1967	315.1	289.0	91.7	26.1	8.3
1968	430.6	394.1	91.5	36.5	8.5
1969	622.9	555.8	89.2	67.1	10.8
1970	858.3	738.4	86.0	119.8	14.0
1971	785.4	651.3	82.9	134.1	17.1

Source: Komatsu, Ltd., Annual Report.

Negotiations with Komatsu

The license agreement between Cummins and Komatsu had been born out of mutual incentives. Komatsu provided Cummins with access to the Japanese market. Cummins provided Komatsu with advanced technology. This technology had allowed Komatsu to achieve great success in some of its machinery. More recently, Cummins was also a source of information on a new concept that was receiving increasing attention in Japan: sociability of the engines—the engines' ecological impact. Cummins also provided Komatsu with a link to the U. S. market.

In spite of the ongoing relationship between Komatsu and Cummins, no great rapport had been developed between the two companies. Visits to Japan in 1971 by Mr. Miller, Chairman of the Board, and Mr. Schacht, President, showed that the major reason for the lack of a strong relationship between the two companies was poor communication. In the past, Komatsu had perceived Cummins treating it as one more supplier to be used only when needed. Both Mr. Miller and Mr. Schacht agreed that Komatsu was in part justified to feel that way. In these visits both Cummins men placed great emphasis on changing Komatsu's views.

While Cummins's top men worked on the diplomatic side with Komatsu, Mr. Hackett's financial department continued analyzing the K engine project. The objective was to analyze the project under the two alternatives of manufacturing in the United States and subcontracting to Komatsu. The alternative of sourcing from Komatsu was based on having the Japanese company produce the components with the heaviest capital requirements. Eight major components that required 75% of the investment were chosen as the basis for negotiations with Komatsu.

The general procedure followed in comparing the two alternatives was to compare Cummins's cash outlays for each alternative on a present value basis and, based on this, to determine the price that could be paid for the Japanese components so that the net present value of the two cash streams would be equal. The alternative of manufacturing in the United States had the largest outlay because of the initial investment. Sourcing from Japan required taking into account outlays for supporting costs such as supervision, transportation, travel, and so on, plus the basic investment outlay for higher inventory and additional equipment to handle the shipments.

Negotiations during 1971 soon showed that Komatsu was not going to produce the components for anything less than the maximum price determined by Cummins. So negotiations proceeded on this basis and by the end of August 1971, Cummins's top management was gathered in Japan to finalize the contract. However, on August 27 the Japanese government decided to allow the yen to float. Negotiations which initially were carried on the basis of a dollar price came to a standstill and Cummins management decided to come back home and reconsider the whole affair. The initial term of the contract provided for Cummins to cover as much as 3% of any exchange rate fluctuations; anything above that would have been absorbed by Komatsu. Prices and quantities would be fixed through 1976. If Cummins decided to pull out in 1976, it would pay Komatsu the net book value of the new equipment.

Back in the United States Mr. Hackett decided to reevaluate the whole project. Now new figures of costs and more details about the new engine were available from the research and development department. The analysis on which the previous negotiations had been based had been made with tentative figures only. Mr. John Walters, a recently graduated MBA from Harvard Business School, was given as his first assignment the task of reviewing the project and making recommendations.

Mr. Walters first updated the data on the original project. Sales volume estimates were higher now, but so were capital requirements and operating cost estimates. Also, Mr. Walters thought that inflation in the United States should be included in the estimates of costs of producing in the United States. In addition, regulations introduced by President Nixon such as the investment tax credit and the accelerated depreciation had to be taken into account. The analysis of the revised proposal to produce in the United States now showed a rate of return of 26.4%.

The next step was to compare the cash flows of producing in the United States with the alternative of sourcing from the United States to find the transfer price that would equate the two costs. Excerpts of the final presentation of Mr. Walters on March 9, 1972, are presented in Appendix A.

The March 9th Meeting

After Mr. Walters concluded his presentation to Cummins's top executives, several issues were raised in the succeeding discussion. Mr. Walters's analysis gave support to the option of sourcing from Japan. This was the approach that Cummins management perceived Mr. Schacht and Mr. Hackett preferred. However, during the two years that the new arrangement with Komatsu was being considered, some executives had made it clear that they did not favor this approach. The reasons for their disfavor were raised again at the March 9th meeting.

Mr. Henderson, Executive Vice-President of Manufacturing, voiced his concern with the quality control of products produced by Komatsu. Although on several occasions it had been shown that Komatsu quality standards were at least as good as Cummins's, operating people in the company continually doubted that this was the case. In the past all engine components had been manufactured under the supervision of Cummins's engineers who placed great emphasis on quality control. Actually, this was one of the reasons why Cummins's products enjoyed such good reputation in the market. Sourcing from Komatsu, production people contended, could endanger this position. However, it was also true that plant managers tended to distrust anything which was not produced by Cummins, and they found some support for their views on Cummins's experiences with Krupp and Jaguar.

Another problem appeared to be labor. At present the workers at Columbus were in an already three-weeks-old strike. Although Komatsu was not one of the major issues in the strike, sourcing from abroad in general was.

It was also seen that the introduction of sourcing from abroad would bring new problems in terms of control and pricing. It would be hard to compare profit margins of two products when one required the heavy investment of Columbus, and the other let another manufacturer provide the investment.

Finally, the future of the Japanese economy, the yen, and the Japanese machinery industry in general, and of Komatsu's policies in particular, provided the framework for further discussion.

APPENDIX A: EXCERPTS FROM JOHN WALTERS'S PRESENTATION ON THE KOMATSU VENTURE

Objectives

The objectives of this presentation are the following:

1. To review the alternative of having Cummins manufacture the complete K engine.

2. To analyze the alternative of sourcing major components in the K engine from Komatsu, and to select an indifference transfer price which Cummins could pay Komatsu.

3. To evaluate the net financial effect of sourcing at the currently negotiated transfer price.

Assumptions

The set of assumptions which are common for the two alternatives are the following:

Market for Engines. The various models and horsepowers combined were estimated to provide the following market for the K engine:

Year	No. of Units	Avg. Price
1973	336	$8,060
1974	1,516	8,720
1975	2,917	8,770
1976	3,967	8,820
1977	4,971	8,760
1978	6,128	8,600
1979	7,316	8,610
1980	8,521	8,590
1981	9,814	8,520
1982	11,182	8,450
1983	12,459	8,420
1984	13,847	8,390
1985	15,174	8,370
Total	98,148	$8,510

These market figures, however, have to be adjusted by a "draw factor." The K engine with low horsepower will overlap some of the high horsepower engines in the NH and V lines. Since we are looking for the incremental value of the K engines to Cummins, this draw effect must be eliminated from the K engine cash flows. This adjustment must be made to the revenues from the K engine, and to the investment required. Only capital necessary to produce incremental K engine sales should be included in the analysis.

Other Assumptions. Manufacturing expenses, marketing expenses, engine warranty, service parts, support of research and development, and working capital requirements were allocated according to Cummins's past experience and cost accounting procedures. A tax rate of 48% was assumed, and allowance was made for investment tax credit and accelerated depreciation tax rules. The terminal value of the investment is the book value after straight line depreciation. Working capital is returned 100%.

The Alternative of Manufacturing at Cummins

This alternative is based on capital requirements that will take into account any excess capacity in the present facilities. Investment in new facilities is made only when production demands for the K engine cannot be met with present plant and equipment. The approach is one of "wait and see."

Material and labor cost per unit were calculated taking into account present costs estimated by the research department, and assuming a learning process where costs per unit decline as time goes on. The cumulative capital investment required from 1972 through 1985 would be $44 million. If one excludes the capital expenditures saved since some of the NH and V engines will not be produced (the draw effect), the cumulative capital investment for the period is brought down to $39 million. (See Exhibit A.1.) The results from the previous assumptions about producing at Columbus provide a return on investment of 26.4% with a payback period of 7.8 years (by 1979). (See Exhibits A.2 and A.3.) Exhibit A.3 shows that the most critical assumption in the analysis is the selling price. A 25% decrease in selling price would bring the rate of return in the project down to 3.9%. Second in importance is an increase in direct cost of 25%. This increase would bring the return on the project down to 14.3%.

The Alternative of Sourcing from Komatsu

Komatsu is being considered as a source of eight major components of the K engine family. If these components were produced domestically, they would require, through 1976, 77% of the total capital investment, 44% of the total material content, and 31% of the total labor content of the base K engine assembly.

The approach to the evaluation of this alternative was based in defining a transfer price that would leave Cummins indifferent financially between sourcing and not sourcing from Komatsu. This indifference point was defined as that transfer price which equated the net present value of cash flows under the sourcing alternative, and the net present value of cash flows under the not-sourcing alternative. The following steps were followed: (1) cash flows associated with the *costs* of producing the eight major components domestically were estimated; (2) cash flows of the *costs* of sourcing were estimated; and (3) the indifference transfer prices which make the net present values of the two alternative cash flows equivalent were found. That is, given that the gross revenues would be the same under both alternatives, the analysis of the transfer price was made based on a comparison of costs under each alternative.

Exhibit A.4 shows the "outlays cash flow" under the alternative of producing the eight major components in the United States. If these eight components were produced in the United States the total capital outlays required would be $18.4 million.

If the decision to source from Komatsu is made, some special outlays will be necessary. These would include allowances for quality management, engineering, and inspection; receiving costs; miscellaneous research and development and manufacturing engineering; and extra program management. The other assumption made was that Komatsu's costs would decline according to a learning curve, like Cummins's production costs in the United States. Therefore, the transfer price should also decline through time. Then, given the number of components required each year, the cash cost of producing them at home, and the cash cost excluding transfer price to source them from Komatsu, the appropriate transfer price was found by searching for the price that would equate the present value of both streams of cash outlays (taking into account that this price should be higher at the beginning). Exhibit A.5 presents the cash flows to Cummins under the alternative of sourcing from Komatsu, once the transfer price has been estimated. Exhibit A.6 compares the cumulative "cash cost flows" under both alternatives. The net present value of the two alternatives is the same by definition.

These calculations were then adjusted to take into account the inflation in the United States. The following rates of inflation in various items were assumed:

Inflation in U. S. Production Costs

Labor @ 6% per year compounded
Material @ 3% per year compounded
Capital equipment @ 4% per year compounded

Possibility of Cost Understatement in the Forecasted U. S. Labor and Material Costs

	% Adjustment to Base Cost for Year				
	1973	1974	1975	1976	1977
Material	+10%	+10%	+10%	+5%	——
Labor	+20%	+20%	+20%	+10%	+10%

As a result, cumulative gross fixed investment under the alternative of producing the eight major components in the United States was adjusted to $21.7 million, up from $18.4 million.

In order to determine the new transfer price, the inflation associated with costs of sourcing was also taken into account. The relevant costs were adjusted 6% upward to account for inflation. The new transfer prices are presented in Exhibit A.7, together with the negotiated transfer prices.

Financial Implications

Because of the method used to estimate the transfer price for the sourcing alternative, the net present value of the two alternatives is the same. Cash costs, which are devoted to the formation of capital assets for the production of the eight components under the alternative of total manufacture in the United States, can be channeled completely into working capital and direct costs of the eight components in the sourcing alternative. Therefore, the transfer price for the components will contain a unit cost premium above their equivalent domestic direct unit cost. As a consequence, although the internal rate of return of the two alternatives is the same by definition, their impact on reported profits is not the same. Given that the quantity sold and the selling price per engine are independent of the mode of production, if the direct costs are larger under the sourcing alternative than under total domestic production, reported profits will be lower for the sourcing alternative. The impact of the two alternatives on reported profits after tax is presented in Exhibit A.8, p. 424. A profit and loss statement and a sources and uses of funds statement under the negotiated transfer price are presented in Exhibit A.9, pp. 422-23.

In evaluating these two alternatives, one other important financial point should be taken into account. The alternative of sourcing from abroad requires a much lower initial investment in the project than the alternative of manufacturing the components in the United States. Therefore, the alternative of sourcing will allow the company to undertake other projects, in addition to the K engine, with the same budget.

EXHIBIT A.1 Producing All Engines in the United States: Cumulative Gross Fixed Investment

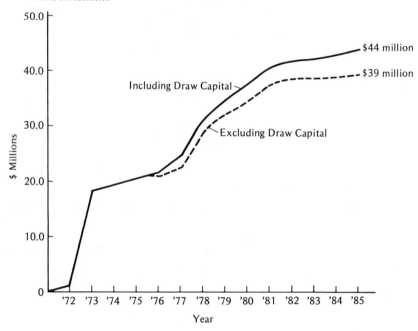

EXHIBIT A.2   Producing All Engines in the United States: Cash Flow

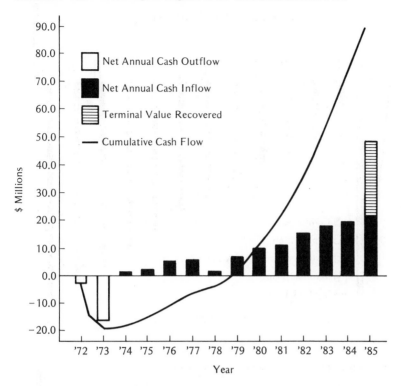

EXHIBIT A.3   Producing All Engines in the United States: Summary Analysis

Summary Results

1. Net Present Value at 15% Hurdle Rate = $16.9 million
2. Return on Investment = 26.4%
3. Payback Period = 7.8 Years (in 1979)
4. Maximum Annual Cash Outflow = $15.8 million in 1973
5. Maximum Cumulative Cash Outflow = $18.4 million in 1973
6. Total Cash Flow (Excl. Terminal Value) = $94.6 million
7. Total Profit Before Tax and Interest = $230.3 million (1972-1985)

Sensitivity Analysis

	ROR	
Base Case	26.4%	
Terminal Value		
Base Case—Net Book Value	26.4%	
Fixed Assets @ 15% of Gross Investment with		
Working Capital @ 100%	26.3%	
5 Years' Extended Profits	28.4%	
P/E Ratio at 12 × Earnings	33.9%	
ROR Resulting from 25%		
Decrease/Increase for Selected Variables		
Variables	−25%	+25%
Selling Price	3.9%	42.4%
Unit Direct Costs (Excl. Depreciation)	36.9%	14.3%
Unit Volume (Capital Unchanged)	20.5%	31.6%
Capital Investment	30.7%	23.2%

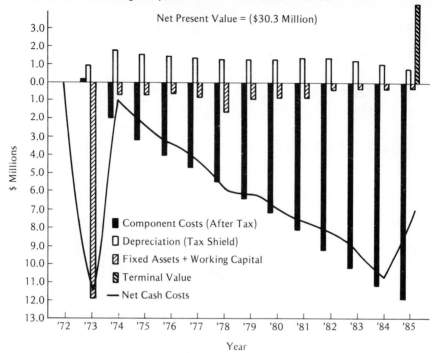

EXHIBIT A.4   Producing Components in the United States: Cost Cash Flows

Net Present Value = ($30.3 Million)

- ■ Component Costs (After Tax)
- □ Depreciation (Tax Shield)
- ▨ Fixed Assets + Working Capital
- ▧ Terminal Value
- — Net Cash Costs

$ Millions

Year

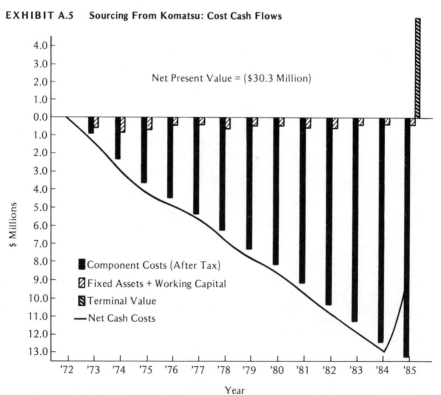

EXHIBIT A.5   Sourcing From Komatsu: Cost Cash Flows

Net Present Value = ($30.3 Million)

- ■ Component Costs (After Tax)
- ▨ Fixed Assets + Working Capital
- ▧ Terminal Value
- — Net Cash Costs

$ Millions

Year

EXHIBIT A.6   Cash Costs of Components Producing in United States Versus Sourcing

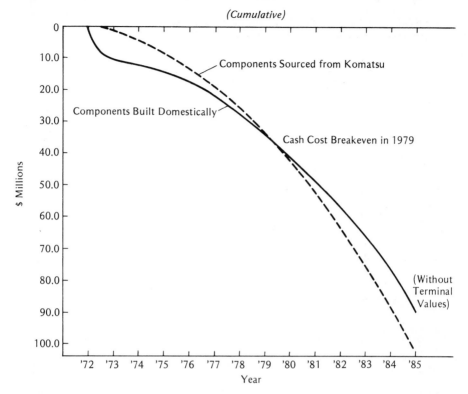

(Cumulative)

EXHIBIT A.7   Indifference Transfer Prices

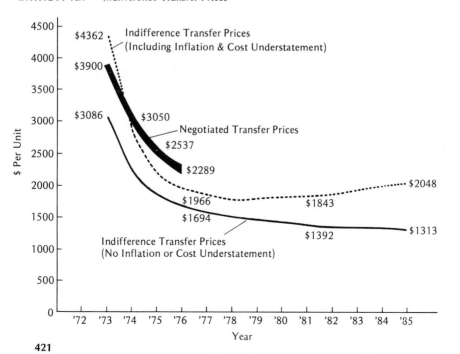

EXHIBIT A.9 Cummins Engine Company. Inc. (B): Sourcing Components: Financial Statement (thousands of dollars)

	1972	1973	1974	1975	1976	1977
		Profit and Loss Statement				
Engine Sales	$ 0	$ 2,709	$13,224	$25,577	$34,977	$43,534
Parts Sales	0	0	50	325	979	1,982
Total Sales	0	2,709	13,274	25,902	35,966	45,516
Cost of Sales	410	2,665	9,847	17,171	22,500	27,597
Gross Profit	−410	44	3,427	8,731	13,456	17,919
Warranty	0	149	577	918	1,100	1,305
Marketing Variable Expense	0	80	354	692	973	1,271
G&A/R&E/Mkt. Expenses	2,869	1,736	2,227	3,116	4,326	5,475
Net Profit Before Taxes and Before Draw	−3,279	−1,921	269	4,005	7,057	9,868
Draw Profit	0	22	159	279	333	268
Net Profit Before Taxes and After Draw	−3,279	−1,899	428	4,284	7,390	10,154
Federal Tax	1,651	1,912	−133	−1,983	−3,541	−4,813
Net Profit After Taxes and After Draw	$−1,628	$ 13	$ 295	$ 2,301	$ 3,849	$ 5,341
		Sources and Uses of Fund Statement				
Sources of Funds:						
Net Profit After Taxes and After Draw	$−1,628	$ 13	$ 295	$ 2,301	$ 3,849	$ 5,341
Depreciation	77	1,444	2,606	2,405	2,247	2,005
Total Sources	−1,551	1,457	2,901	4,706	6,096	7,346
Uses of Funds:						
Working Capital	0	273	943	1,208	905	1,128
Fixed Assets	1,099	16,966	1,313	1,314	246	1,546
Total Excluding Terminal Value	1,099	17,239	2,256	2,522	1,151	2,674
Net Cash Flow	$−2,650	$−15,782	$ 645	$ 2,184	$ 4,945	$ 4,672
Cumulative Cash Flow	$−2,650	$−18,432	$−17,787	$−15,603	$−10,658	$−5,986

**EXHIBIT A.9   Cummins Engine Company, Inc. (B): Sourcing Components:
Financial Statement (thousands of dollars) (cont.)**

1978	1979	1980	1981	1982	1983	1984	1985	Total
				Profit and Loss Statement				
$52,730	$63,026	$73,180	$83,635	$94,494	$104,923	$116,219	$127,025	$835,253
3,261	4,809	6,621	8,655	10,851	13,152	15,508	17,919	84,112
55,991	67,835	79,801	92,290	105,345	118,075	131,727	144,944	919,365
33,441	39,741	45,649	51,601	57,786	63,706	70,337	75,509	517,960
22,550	28,094	34,152	40,689	47,559	54,369	61,390	69,435	401,405
1,537	1,844	2,517	2,489	2,837	3,178	3,547	3,905	25,543
1,610	1,985	2,394	2,856	3,353	3,833	4,343	4,845	28,589
6,736	8,161	9,600	11,103	12,673	14,204	15,846	17,437	115,509
12,667	16,104	20,001	24,241	28,696	33,154	37,654	43,248	231,764
115	37	−76	−217	−380	−528	−658	−801	−1,429
12,782	16,141	19,925	24,024	28,316	32,626	36,996	42,447	230,335
−5,843	−7,601	−9,483	−11,385	−13,532	−15,659	−17,736	−20,345	−108,491
$ 6,939	$ 8,540	$10,442	$12,639	$14,784	$16,967	$19,260	$22,102	$121,844
				Sources and Uses of Fund Statement				
$ 6,939	$ 8,540	$10,442	$12,639	$14,784	$16,967	$19,260	$22,102	$121,844
2,135	2,513	2,622	2,744	2,778	2,411	2,048	1,658	29,693
9,074	11,053	13,064	15,383	17,562	19,378	21,308	23,760	151,537
1,762	1,403	1,502	1,532	1,707	1,663	1,857	1,749	17,632
6,388	3,194	1,980	3,203	1,102	59	393	537	39,340
8,150	4,597	3,482	4,735	2,809	1,722	2,250	2,286	56,972
$ 924	$ 6,456	$ 9,582	$10,648	$14,753	$17,656	$19,058	$47,118	$120,209
$−5,062	$ 1,394	$10,976	$21,624	$36,377	$54,033	$73,091	$120,209	

EXHIBIT A.8 Profits After Taxes: Producing All in United States Versus
Sourcing Components (before interest charges)

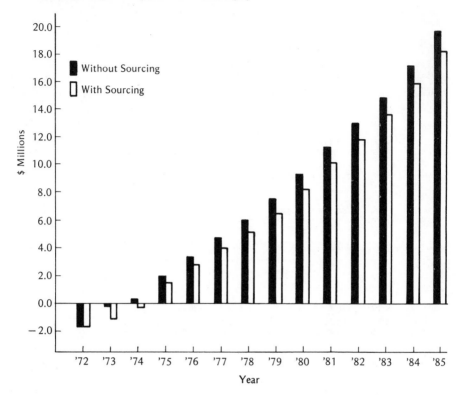

Portfolio Capital Budgeting for the Multinational Corporation

In addition to specifically financial goals, an international firm may also judge its efforts by certain operational criteria which are intended to result in the achievement of long-run corporate objectives. A minimum sales growth, a determination to have earnings from a variety of sources (the Freeport decision), a wish to have a geographic dispersion of operations, a policy to accept opportunities as they appear, and so on are some of the imprecise or noneconomic goals. On the surface, these goals may not be "financial," but they may serve as rules of thumb to guide the firm toward certain long-run financial or economic goals.

Because of risk and these multiple goals, the firm is concerned with project interdependencies now (current) and over time (intertemporal). The firm's investment in a product line now may provide opportunities for future investments (1) which the firm might not have seen and/or (2) which the corporation would not have had the ability to develop or to market in the absence of today's project. Hence, these interdependencies over time are part of the "strategic" budgeting process discussed in the preceding chapter.

This chapter will review the issue of diversification as it affects the decision to invest abroad. The second part of the chapter will survey a technique for responding to the complexities of risk, multiple goals, and the diversification interdependencies.

DIVERSIFICATION: THE INTERNATIONAL SECURITY PORTFOLIO EVIDENCE

The impact of portfolio considerations in the firm's capital budgeting portfolio was delayed until research into security portfolios was transferred to the nonfinancial corporation. There is now evidence relating to the benefits of diversification of international portfolios of securities. Much of this effort has been related to equities and corporate bond performance in various nations, and there are serious limitations to the findings. However, the criticisms of the research methodologies do not mean that the conclusions are inaccurate; rather, the criticisms at worst say that there is a Scotch verdict: the conclusions are not proved.

The concept having major impact on the evaluation of security portfolios was developed by Markowitz (1959) and Tobin (1958). The Markowitz framework suggested that the risk averse investor could diversify over a security universe by selecting those securities which would provide portfolios with maximum return for a given variability in that return, or, alternatively, seek portfolios which would have minimum variability for a given level of return. There would be a family of portfolios tracing a curve with each portfolio having greater return and greater variance or lower return and lower variance than any of its neighbors. The investor could select the risk-return tradeoff. These are *efficient portfolios;* all other portfolios are either inefficient (offering lower return for the same variability, for example) or unfeasible (having greater returns and the same variability since, by definition, the efficient set of portfolios has maximum return for a given variability). If borrowing and lending opportunities are available, it may be possible for the investor to move to a position of greater utility based on one of the efficient portfolios and suitable amounts of borrowed or loaned funds (hence, the Tobin term "separability," in that the decision on the optimum portfolios and the decision on how much to borrow can be made independently; the borrowing or lending strategy still utilizes one of the efficient portfolios in the final decision).

These models for investment decision have been applied in the U. S. security market. In addition, extensions of the analysis in a slightly different framework have been used to evaluate performance of mutual funds *ex post* by comparing them to a market portfolio combined with borrowing-lending options open to a naive investor. This investor buys a well-diversified market portfolio and then borrows or lends to move to a suitable composite asset position. As these results have been extended to the international securities market, the researchers have often faced severe difficulties and lack of conformity to an economically competitive market. A brief review of this research is presented in the first appendix to this chapter.

There are serious problems with most of these studies. The first criticism is that a national index of security prices may not be an efficient national portfolio from the standard risk/return model of Tobin and Markowitz, although it may approach it. Second, the national index is only one portfolio, not the set of efficient (national) portfolios. Third, there is a question of whether inclusion of some of the securities of another nation would aid the diversification more than inclusion of the "whole portfolio" (i.e., the index) of another nation's security universe would improve diversification. Fourth, any evaluation of portfolio diversification in terms of the random walk hypothesis must reckon with Solnik (1973) and McDonald (1973). Among others, these authors note imperfections in the European stock market price behavior when analyzed on the same basis as the U. S. studies of the random walk model. Finally, and most importantly here, the multinational corporate manager is concerned with project diversification, which is not necessarily the same as security diversification.

DOES DIVERSIFICATION EXIST
FOR THE NONFINANCIAL BUSINESS?

Consistent with basic capital budgeting theory, higher-risk projects are related to a higher cost of capital: less debt is available, it is more costly, and/or equity is costlier for a risky project. But because of the covariance elements, the portfolio that allows the firm to diversify would result in a surplus return if there are benefits from diversification: the cost of capital to the diversified firm would be lower than the simple sum of the costs of capital to the international projects on their own.

If one believes that the corporation has an advantage over individuals in diversification skills, then the corporate-wide cost of capital may be lower than the appropriate cost of capital for all subsidiary units or projects combined. This conclusion follows when one recognizes that diversification lowers total risk. This result allows the fair overall return to diminish since the risk is no longer as great. This lower risk is available only to investors in the diversified corporation, given the assumptions, and not to investors who carve their investments from among the company's projects. Accordingly, the company has to consider how the surplus return from its portfolio of projects is to be divided. The cost of monitoring and coordinating the broadly diversified firm may exceed any potential benefits from the spreading of risk. Alternatively, some critics discount the existence of benefits from corporate diversification. They argue that the investor can adequately diversify by himself or herself (e.g., through investment in a mutual fund). Of course, these two criticisms are not inconsistent with each other. If both are granted, the broadly diversified firm is economically inefficient, for there is a net cost of coordination that is not offset by any diversification benefits unrealizable by individual investors on their own!

The corporation probably can diversify more efficiently than individuals in the multinational setting. In addition to information advantages regarding international opportunities, the major corporation has the ability to use special experience in an industry, to negotiate tax and repatriation agreements, and to marshal a large pool of resources.

PORTFOLIO INTERRELATIONSHIPS—THE VARIANCE OF THE PORTFOLIO

Introduction

In the previous discussion of risk analysis, there was the possibility of using variance as a measure of the project's dispersion. Although there are limitations to this approach, it is helpful to continue to focus on variance (or its square root, the standard deviation) as one measure by which the corporate officer may evaluate project risk.

Variance is a measure of the variability in outcome of a project on some particular dimension. But how does one compute the variance of a portfolio of projects? Suppose that three projects are considered by Freeport Minerals. Each is a nickel plant, with one each in two Australian states and one in Ghana. Each project has an expected return and standard deviation. Suppose Freeport wants to invest in two plants, but is unsure of which two are preferred. The standard deviation of an investment in the two Australian plants may be very close to the sum of each plant's standard deviation; each of them shares most of the same risks with respect to the world nickel market, costs in Australia, the value of the American dollar, inflation, and so on. On the other hand, the standard deviation in return on the same money invested in the Ghana plant and either one of the Australian plants may be substantially less than the simple sum of the two projects' standard deviations. There is obvious diversification. Freeport has reason to hope that a labor strike or severe inflation or devaluation in one country, for example, would not necessarily follow in the other. It is true that both pairs of investments are subject to the same technological and world market conditions of nickel. But there is a benefit from geographically spreading the risk.

Finally, Freeport management might elect more diversification by investing in one Australian nickel plant and a zinc operation in Peru. There is then geographic diversification and product diversification.

These examples should present intuitive reasons for rejecting project standard deviation sums as a measure of portfolio risk. The standard deviation or variance pays no heed to any other project. Accordingly, another statistical measure is involved, the covariance. Between each project and every other project, the covariance can be computed. Further, the variance of a portfolio of two or more projects can be found by combining the respective variances and covariances. Hence, the portfolio variance can be found readily, and it reflects the effects of diversification.[1]

As an example, assume that three of the projects mentioned have the following mean, standard deviation, and covariance figures:

| | Nickel Projects | | Zinc Mine |
	Australia	Ghana	Peru
Mean return	.20	.25	.20
Standard deviation	.10	.25	.12
Covariance	└──.020──┘ └──.006──┘		
	└────────.0024────────┘		

From these figures, one can compute the various portfolio figures from investing in various combinations of projects, as shown in Exhibit 12.1. These calculations assume that there are equal dollar investments required in each investment. The

portfolio return is
$$R = \sum_{i=1}^{n} a_i r_i$$

where $i = 1$ to n reflects the projects in the portfolio, a_i is the fraction of the budget invested in each project $\left(\text{and } \sum_{i=1}^{n} a_i = 1\right)$, and r_i is the return of project i.

[1] Variance is not an unambiguous measure of risk, as should be apparent from Chapter 11. Different measures of risk may result in different rankings of projects.

The standard deviation of the portfolio return is

$$S = \sum_{i=1}^{n} a_i^2 S_i^2 + \sum_{i=1}^{n} \sum_{j=1}^{n} a_i \, a_j \, S_{ij}$$

$$(i \neq j)$$

where S is the standard deviation of the portfolio, a_i and a_j are as defined before, S_i is the standard deviation of project i, and S_{ij} is the covariance between projects i and j.

EXHIBIT 12.1   Portfolio Returns and Variances

Return: Australian/Ghanaian Nickel Operation
$\quad$ = .5 (.20) + .5 (.25) = .225 or 22.5%

$\quad$ Standard Deviation
$\quad$ = $\sqrt{.25(.10)^2 + .25(.25)^2 + 2 \times .25 \times (.020)}$
$\quad$ = $\sqrt{.028125}$
$\quad$ = .168 or 16.8%

Return: Zinc Mine/Australian Nickel Operation
$\quad$ = .5 (.20) + .5 (.20) = .20 or 20%

$\quad$ Standard Deviation
$\quad$ = $\sqrt{.25 (.10)^2 + .25 (.12)^2 + 2 \times .25 \times (.0024)}$
$\quad$ = $\sqrt{.0073}$
$\quad$ = .085 or 8.5%

Return: Zinc Mine/Ghanaian Nickel Operation
$\quad$ = .5 (.25) + .5 (.20) = .225 or 22.5%

$\quad$ Standard Deviation
$\quad$ = $\sqrt{.25 (.25)^2 + .25 (.12)^2 + 2 \times .25 \times (.006)}$
$\quad$ = $\sqrt{.02223}$
$\quad$ = .149 or 14.9%

Return: All Three Projects
$\quad$ = .33 (.20) + .33 (.25) + .33 (.20) = .215 or 21.5%

$\quad$ Standard Deviation
$\quad$ = $\sqrt{.11 (.10)^2 + .11 (.25)^2 + .11 (.12)^2 + 2 \times .11 \times (.02)}$
$\quad$ $\overline{ + 2 \times .11 \times (.006) + 2 \times .11 \times (.0024)}$
$\quad$ = $\sqrt{.015807}$
$\quad$ = .126 or 12.6%

Using these same formulas, one can compute the portfolio figures using the assumption of a normal distribution for other criteria: terminal return, net present value, earnings per share in a given year, growth rate in sales, and so on.[2]

Joint Simulation and the Portfolio Variance Calculation

The process of risk analysis simulation and its applicability to the Freeport case was outlined in Chapter 11. By using computer simulation in a joint form, it is possible for the firm to complete a simulation that will provide covariances.[3]

Risk analysis on the basis of individual projects can be completed as described in the Freeport example. A joint simulation of projects must be completed, however, in order to derive covariances among the projects. The requirements of the joint simulation are that the outcome of each project is computed for a given trial, and then stored in relation to the outcome of all the other projects on that trial. Then the sampling process is reinitialized and the simulation repeated. Hence, where projects are dependent on some common variable (such as GNP, growth in a particular area of the economy, and so on), this assurance of a common value for those underlying factors is critical.

From this joint simulation, the results may be stored as shown in Exhibit 12.2. This result is for a single criterion (e.g., net present value). Similar tables are prepared for each of the other standards under consideration. From these data, it is possible to compute the mean, variance, and covariance of the projects on each criterion since the simulation trials store values of each project's outcome in conjunction with all other projects' outcomes on a given trial. Thus, element X_{67} is the

---

[2] The formulae for combining the figures are slightly altered from this model in some cases; one cannot use the basic rate of return equations shown here which parallel the typical investment security example. See Carter (1974), pp. 83-88, for an explanation of this difference.

[3] The most evasive measure on any standard to be evaluated is likely to be the estimate of the covariance among the projects. If correlation of returns among the projects is known, one can compute the covariance, and vice versa. The covariance is equal to the correlation coefficient (ρ) times the respective standard deviations, or $\sigma_{ij} = \rho\sigma_i\sigma_j$. Using the assumptions of normality, there are two other ways of estimating the portfolio figures.

First, one may ask managers to specify correlation between projects. This task is difficult to accomplish even if the manager is thoroughly familiar with the concept. If it is possible in a given situation, such correlations can generate the covariance matrix. On the other hand, if the existing firm is huge in relation to any proposed project, the loss in accuracy in the variance of firm and project portfolio is nominal when the correlations between new projects are ignored. Rather, all that must be estimated is the correlation of each new project with the existing firm's asset base or some market standard.

A second approach is to use equivalent formulae which allow an estimate of the maximum variance in portfolio net present values from some compendium of project present value variances, ignoring the covariances between projects or between projects and the firm/"market."

Under either alternative, there is a nontrivial problem created given the possible combinations that can occur for a portfolio of projects. Thus, if one calculates all possible combinations of projects, and analyzes the outcomes, the task is enormous. A portfolio of one to twenty potential projects would involve computing over one million combinations unless some simplifying rule is used.

return of project 6 on trial 7. Using the basic covariance formula, the covariance between project 6 and each of the other projects can be computed.

EXHIBIT 12.2   Computation and Storage Procedure for Joint Project Simulation on Criterion "X" (Net Present Value)

	Simulation Trial 1	Simulation Trial 2		Simulation Trial N
Project 1	X_{11}	X_{12}	. . .	X_{1N}
Project 2	X_{21}	X_{22}	. . .	X_{2N}
Project 3	X_{31}	X_{32}	. . .	X_{3N}
.	.	.		.
.	.	.		.
.	.	.		.
Project M	X_{M1}	X_{M2}	. . .	X_{MN}

Note: Each simulation trial is completed for all proposed projects before computation of the next simulation trial.

Interactive Simulation and the Portfolio Model

From the portfolio variance calculations noted earlier, the corporate manager has the data required to complete a preliminary analysis. In addition, planning models such as those suggested by Carleton (1970) and Myers and Pogue (1974) can be used to select starting portfolios of projects.

However, given the multiple goals of managers as noted in various sources, including the National Industrial Conference Board study of 1966 by Judd Polk, et al., a useful approach also may be related to an interactive computer model. For example, assume the manager is concerned about ten major criteria: sales, earnings per share, and cash flow for each of three years; and the net present value. By providing a range of computing options which enable the manager to see the results of various portfolio combinations, the model may permit selection of the final portfolio in a rapid manner. Naturally, nothing in this model would prevent using any of the mathematical programming formulations for starting portfolios. Likewise, after such an analysis as this model proposes, the manager would want to resimulate the final portfolio to obtain a detailed distribution of returns and outcomes since the model operates on the normality assumptions which are probably not precisely valid for the actual outcomes. Hence, resimulation of the portfolio to show the executive the actual distribution of returns on any of the criteria would be useful.

As an example, there may have been a general decision made by the firm about the type of projects which are to be reviewed; the joint simulation may then be completed. These variance-covariance data are inserted into the interactive model and the executive then faces a terminal. The manager might be provided with infor-

EXHIBIT 12.3

WHEN THE COMPUTER TYPES -OPTION?- PLEASE ANSWER
WITH ONE OF THE RESPONSES SHOWN BELOW

OPTION   DESCRIPTION

=======   ===

NP	STARTS A NEW PORTFOLIO
PC	PORTFOLIO CONTENTS
EC	LIST PROJECT ENTRY COSTS
IP	LIST ILLEGAL PROJECT COMBINATIONS
A	ADD A NEW PROJECT TO YOUR PORTFOLIO
D	DELETE A PROJECT FROM YOUR PORTFOLIO
P	PORTFOLIO STATISTICS
SP	SHORT PORTFOLIO OUTPUT
C	COMBINE PROJECTS
MR	RANK PROJECTS BY MEAN VALUES
VR	RANK PROJECTS BY VARIABILITY (STD. DEV.)
END	STOPS PROGRAM

WHEN THE COMPUTER TYPES -CRITERION?- PLEASE ANSWER
WITH ONE RESPONSE SHOWN BELOW

CRITERION   DESCRIPTION

==========   ===

S1	SALES IN YEAR 1
S2	SALES IN YEAR 2
S3	SALES IN YEAR 3
CF1	CASH FLOW IN YEAR 1
CF2	CASH FLOW IN YEAR 2
CF3	CASH FLOW IN YEAR 3
EPS1	EARNINGS PER SHARE IN YEAR 1
EPS2	EARNINGS PER SHARE IN YEAR 2
EPS3	EARNINGS PER SHARE IN YEAR 3
NPV	NET PRESENT VALUE

In using this program, the executive has a number of filtering options available:

1. The program may be used to determine *portfolio* data. It presents the capital outlay and the results on any of the criteria for any combination of projects legally allowed. The program would include interest costs for any debt used.

2. *Confidence levels* using normality assumptions may be printed for the portfolios chosen by the executive on whatever criteria (s)he wished. These confidence intervals are derived using the standard deviations of the portfolio to compute $25\%/75\%$, $10\%/90\%$, $5\%/95\%$ and $1\%/99\%$ ranges for the criteria required by the executive, for instance.

3. *Comparison options* permit the executive to study the effectiveness of the proposed portfolio vis-à-vis the current operation in meeting various goals for future years. Based upon statistical compilations in the program, the executive could view the probability that earnings per share in the second year would be no less under the proposed portfolio than expected second-year earnings per share of the existing firm alone. These probabilities may be explicitly presented for each of the ten criteria.

4. *Portfolio-project comparisons* allow the executive to view how the proposed portfolio would be altered on each of the ten criteria by adding or deleting a particular project. These results are similar to those obtained for the existing firm/portfolio comparison. The comparison would indicate the amount by which the expected values and standard deviations of the portfolio would be changed by addition or deletion of a project.

5. *Mean search* routines permit the executive to seek altered values from the expected outcome of the portfolio on any criterion. When using this option, the manager may indicate the criterion and the number of proposals desired (N). The program will return in ascending or descending order (as the executive requested) the N projects which would have the greatest effect in increasing or decreasing the expected value under consideration. Depending on what the manager specified, the program would review all projects, those currently in the proposed portfolio, or those currently out of the proposed portfolio. The manager's specification will depend upon whether the desire is to eliminate projects from the portfolio which have an unfavorable impact on a criterion (e.g., a binding budget constraint and low earnings per share in the first year) or to add projects which would increase an outcome (e.g., projects to boost sales in the second year).

6. *Variance search* routines require the manager to input the same information as under the mean search routine. The program then searches for those projects in and/or out of the current portfolio which would do the most to increase or to decrease the variance on a given criterion. This routine operates by comparing the impact of each new project on the existing portfolio's variance, computing a new portfolio figure which may be compared with the existing portfolio. After all projects under consideration are evaluated, the ranking procedure permits the executive to learn the N most desirable projects on the criterion selected.

Naturally, nothing requires the use of these goals. The manager might favor these goals plus an average growth in earnings per share for the next five or ten years, or plus a certain percentage of sales/earnings from major regions of the world or major product lines. Rather, the idea is to introduce the method of interactive simulation as a way of providing the manager with major sources of information which the manager can combine using his or her values.

Multiperiod decisions when the future portfolio opportunities are not known compound the problem. One option is to build in probable funds requirements and returns for future projects, penalizing the projects under current review if they do not generate sufficient cash flows in particular future periods. In addition, only by earmarking particular debt sources for unique opportunities can the viability of special financing options applicable only to given projects be included in such a model. The benefits of "pooled" resources providing better debt rates than the simple sum of the individual projects can be taken into account only with the subsequent resimulation of the desirable portfolio after use of the interactive model.[4]

THE CAPITAL ASSET PRICING MODEL

Although there are several techniques available to help evaluate the covariance between projects to obtain a portfolio which meets a suitable risk/

[4] These issues are discussed in detail in Carter (1974), Ch. 8.

return profile for the corporation, there is also the possibility of applying the concepts of the capital asset pricing model.

Briefly, this model suggests that the relevant discount rate for a project is based on the covariance between a project which is under review and the market portfolio of efficient projects (i.e., some well-diversified corporate project portfolio). This covariance is combined with estimates of the expected market return and the return from a risk-free asset to determine the proper required return for the project. (For a discussion of the similar beta analysis of project or portfolio return, see the second appendix to this chapter.) Thus, the required tradeoff between risk and return for a project is factored in for this approach, given efficient capital markets and a market line. This line is based on the investor's purchase of the market portfolio and the risk-free security in whatever proportions are desired. This market line, shown in Exhibit 12.4, provides the required tradeoff between risk and return for any proposed project. Thus, based on the variance calculations shown earlier, note that an investor who placed half his or her funds in the risk-free asset and half in the market portfolio would have a return which is half the sum of these two returns. Furthermore, given zero correlation between the risk-free return and the market return, the standard deviation of his return (the risk) would also fall halfway between the two standard deviations. Other proportions between the risk-free asset and the market portfolio would fall on the line traced in Exhibit 12.4.[5]

Given forecasts of the market return and variability, the risk-free rate, and the variability of the project's return under different market outcomes, then the minimum required rate of return can be determined. If the project returns more than this minimum, it is a desirable investment.

EXHIBIT 12.4   The Market Portfolio and the Market Line

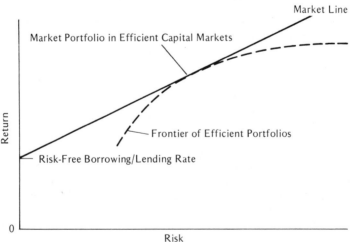

[5] If one does not believe that the capital markets are efficient, then the market line traced as a ray from the risk-free rate will not necessarily be tangent at the market portfolio (but would, of course, be tangent at some other point). However, the strategy outlined here is still open to a naive security or project investor: the investment is split between some broad market investment and a risk-free security.

The theoretical impact of this model is substantial. What makes its application difficult in practical situations is the determinaton of reasonable forecasts for the market return and the risk-free return in the future. Whatever the estimation problems in the risk-free return evaluation, the biggest question is what is the market return? When it is in the international setting, is it the return in the home country's security market? Management desires project returns, so some judgment must be made about the market return in different periods. If this figure is then used as the estimate of the future market return, then the links between variability in that market return in future years and the equity returns of the projects under review must be determined when the appropriate debt load for the project is included. The portfolio simulation approach outlined earlier produces those links (i.e., the covariances) as a by-product of the individual project simulations in the portfolio process. It allows the valuation of multiple goals which management may feel are relevant. In addition, the forecasting of project results under various states of nature likely can be done more confidently by management than can the forecast of some aggregate market return under various possible outcomes.

CAPITAL BUDGETING IN PORTFOLIO—CONCLUSIONS

These four chapters have surveyed the major aspects of the international capital budgeting decision. First, the determination of the relevant cash flows for the single project was approached. The terminal rate of return where funds were blocked and limited opportunities were available for reinvestment, and the relevance of repatriated funds or local funds were reviewed. As noted in the Polk, et al., National Industrial Conference Board study, if the firm is a "multinational," repatriation may be less important than if the firm views itself as a "national with foreign interests." Depending on this self-image, the importance of the pool of funds or simply local endeavors will vary considerably. Several approaches to evaluating inflation and currency realignments were mentioned.

The local cost of capital is the relevant discount rate for most decisions. If there are benefits of diversification accruing to the multinational corporation beyond the benefits which can be derived by small investors acting on their own (and probably there are), then these benefits result in an overall corporate cost of capital which is lower than the sum of the individual costs. Supervision and coordination costs require some use of these excess resources, but the balance is a joint benefit accruing to the shareholders of the multinational firm.

There are general motivations beyond pure "diversification" which might compel the firm to operate in other than its native land. Thus, even if one rejects the diversification argument, there are economic incentives (taxes, special opportunities, restricted access to resources in the absence of foreign operations, comparative advantage, and the product life cycle) as well as organizational issues which may play a major role in the decision to operate in other lands.

Finally, there are multiple goals in any firm. A multigoal risk analysis by project and portfolio can be applicable to project evaluation. The evidence for diversification through security investments in other lands is limited by methodological constraints. Believing in the benefits of diversification for the corporation, a manager may use applications of portfolio theory to the international capital budgeting problem.

Chapter 12 has suggested that international capital markets are segmented, that is, not in equilibrium due to a lack of extensive arbitrage; Part Four will have a review of the elements of various capital markets.

Questions

1. What are the arguments for the existence of a corporation's ability to be an efficient diversifier? Do you believe the arguments?

2. Why does a joint simulation produce the covariances between projects?

3. Under what conditions is variance a bad measure of risk?

4. Why is the market line shown in Exhibit 12.4 linear? If the borrowing and lending rates were different, how would that change the analysis required for an investor's decision?

5. How can a firm obtain a reasonable estimate of the local cost of capital for a project? Why might a multinational corporation have an advantage over a local firm in terms of the cost of capital?

Bibliography

Adler, Michael and R. Hoersch, "The Relationship Among Equity Markets: Comment." *Journal of Finance,* Sept. 1974, pp. 1311-1317.

Agmon, Tamir, "Country Risk—The Significance of the Country Factor to Share Price Movements in the United Kingdom, Germany and Japan." *Journal of Business,* Jan. 1973, pp. 24-32.

———, "The Relations Among Equity Markets: A Study of Share Price Co-Movements in the United States, United Kingdom, Germany and Japan." *Journal of Finance,* Sept. 1972, pp. 839-855.

Carleton, Willard, "An Analytical Model for Long-Range Financial Planning." *Journal of Finance,* May 1970, pp. 291-315.

Carter, E. Eugene, *Portfolio Aspects of Corporate Capital Budgets.* Lexington, Mass.: D.C. Heath and Company, 1974.

Cohn, Richard A. and John J. Pringle, "Imperfections in International Financial Markets: Implications for Risk Premia and the Cost of Capital to Firms." *Journal of Finance,* Mar. 1973, pp. 59-66.

Grubel, Herbert G. and Kenneth Fadner, "The Interdependence of International Equity Markets." *Journal of Finance,* Mar. 1971, pp. 89-94.

———, "Internationally Diversified Portfolios: Welfare Gains and Capital Flows." *American Economic Review,* Dec. 1968, pp. 1299-1314.

Lessard, Donald, "International Portfolio Diversification: A Multivariate Analysis for a Group of Latin American Countries." *Journal of Finance,* June 1973, pp. 619-633.

———, World, National, and Industry Factors in Equity Returns," *Journal of Finance,* May 1974, pp. 379-391.

Levy, Haim and Marshall Sarnat, "International Diversification of Investment Portfolios." *American Economic Review,* Sept. 1970, pp. 668-675.

McDonald, John G., "French Mutual Fund Performance: Evaluation of Internationally Diversified Portfolios." *Journal of Finance,* Dec. 1973, pp. 1161-1180.

Makridakis, Spyros G. and Steven C. Wheelwright, "An Analysis of the Interrelationships Among the Major World Stock Exchanges." *Journal of Business Finance and Accounting,* Summer 1974, pp. 195-215.

Markowitz, Harry, *Portfolio Selection: Efficient Diversification of Investments.* New York: John Wiley and Sons, 1959.

Miller, Norman C. and Marina v. N. Whitman, "Alternative Theories and Tests of U. S. Short-Term Foreign Investment." *Journal of Finance,* Dec. 1973, pp. 1131-1147.

———, "A Mean-Variance Analysis of United States Long-Term Portfolio Foreign Investment." *Quarterly Journal of Economics,* May 1970, pp. 175-196.

Myers, Stewart C. and Gerald A. Pogue, "A Programming Approach to Corporate Financial Management." *Journal of Finance,* May 1974, pp. 579-599.

Pogue, Gerald A. and Bruno Solnik, "The Market Model Applied to European Common Stocks: An Empirical Approach." *Journal of Financial and Quantitative Analysis,* Dec. 1974, pp. 917-944.

Polk, Judd, *et al., U. S. Production Abroad and the Balance of Payments.* New York: National Industrial Conference Board, 1966.

Solnik, Bruno, *European Capital Markets.* Lexington, Mass.: D. C. Heath/ Lexington Books, 1973.

———, "An International Market Model of Security Price Behavior." *Journal of Financial and Quantitiative Analysis,* Sept. 1974a, pp. 537-554.

———, "The International Pricing of Risk: An Empirical Investigation of the World Capital Market Structures." *Journal of Finance,* May 1974b, pp. 365-378.

———, "Note on the Validity of the Random Walk for European Stock Prices." *Journal of Finance,* Dec. 1973, pp. 1151-1159.

Tobin, James, "Liquidity Preference as Behavior Toward Risk." *Review of Economic Studies,* Feb. 1958, pp. 65-86.

Wallingford, Buckner A.H., II, "Discussion: The International Pricing of Risk." *Journal of Finance,* May 1974, pp. 392-395.

Appendix: Summary Review
of Research on International Portfolios

There are various articles reviewing the effects of diversification using international security and bond portfolios.[1] Building on the basic Markowitz and Tobin framework, Grubel (1968) showed the effects of diversification using market indices in eleven countries, arguing that U. S. investors could gain from such international diversification. Then, using indices of stock market performance for twenty-eight countries, Levy and Sarnat (1970) evaluated the benefits of diversification across national borders using data from the 1951-1967 period. They found that investments in the U. S. and Japanese stocks were 50-70% of optimal portfolios, largely because of the negative correlations during this period between the stock market indices in these two lands. Predictably, because of the correlation of Western European countries and the U. S. stock market performance in the same period, these European nations were generally excluded. Additionally, investments in a number of developing countries were usually recommended in the final portfolio. This outcome occurred because of diversification effects, even though the standard deviation of investing in given underdeveloped countries' securities was often quite large.

Using ten nations and an evaluation of the arithmetic average of yields on long-term government bonds in those countries, Miller and Whitman (1970) similarly considered the benefits of diversification, although they ignored covariances between European and American outlays. The separation theorem implies that choice between risky and riskless assets can be made independently, *not* that choices within two segregated portfolios of risky assets can be made independently, which was the pattern followed by Miller and Whitman.

Evaluating weekly, one-month, and two-month rates of return of industry subindices for securities traded in the United States, the United Kingdom, and West Germany from January 1, 1965 to June 30, 1967, Grubel and Fadner (1971) found that positive correlation among various pairs of assets was an increasing function of holding period (implying that random short-run effects may cause lower correlations in those periods) but that average correlation levels were still greater for within-country comparisons than for between-country comparisons. For the period in which they evaluated the securities, they acknowledged that the currencies were stable in exchange rates. The instability of the more recent years might create even less correlation of between-country industry index comparisons, suggesting even greater benefits from the intercountry portfolio diversification, given that lower correlation improves the portfolio in a risk/return sense.

The Agmon (1972) paper argues for a weak support of the one-market approach to the world security markets, although the author cautiously notes that his results are not inconsistent with a segmented market. A one-market view holds that arbitrage between national security markets is sufficient to create an equilibrium.

[1] For complete references to all works cited in this appendix, see the chapter bibliography.

Although the Agmon study has been criticized for having results that were not inconsistent with the segmented market hypotheses (which the author acknowledged) and for other statistical difficulties, the remaining problem which seems to plague most of the international capital asset model studies is that the results they obtain are not sufficient to prove or to disprove any case; they can be consistent with a number of different hypotheses about the structure of the international capital markets and their risk interdependence or risk independence.[2]

Appendix: The Capital Asset Pricing Model and Project Selection

Although derived from slightly different precepts, the capital asset pricing model approach parallels the beta analysis which has had an impact in investment portfolio appraisal discussed earlier in this chapter. This analysis says that one can compare the return of a portfolio (R_P) to the risk-free return (R_F) and the market return (R_M); beta (β) is the measure of the volatility of the security or portfolio (i.e., mutual fund) to the market return. Yet this beta is simply the covariance of the security with the market divided by the variance of the market return. Alpha (a) is a measure of any excess return for the mutual fund or security above what is required given its volatility. A negative alpha implies that the return of the fund or security over the periods evaluated was not sufficient to offset its volatility.

(1) $$(R_P - R_F) = a + \beta(R_M - R_F)$$

For project evaluations, the alpha is removed and one rearranges terms to solve for R_E, the required return on equity in the project. This gives the result that[1]

(2) $$R_E = \beta(R_M - R_F) + R_F$$

or, since $\beta = \dfrac{\sigma_{EM}}{\sigma_M^2}$

$$R_E = \frac{\sigma_{EM}}{\sigma_M^2} \beta (R_M - R_F) + R_F$$

[2] See Adler and Hoersch's (1974) criticism of the Agmon paper. Then see Solnik's (1974b) further efforts in this regard, and the resulting criticism by Wallingford (1974). Solnik (1974a) notes the impact of the various national markets, but argues that his results are consistent with an international capital asset pricing model which takes into account both national and international portfolios.

[1] σ_{EM}/σ_M^2 represents the covariance between the equity and market returns divided by the standard deviation of the market return.

$$= R_F \left(1 - \frac{\sigma_{EM}}{\sigma_M^2}\right) + R_M \frac{\sigma_{EM}}{\sigma_M^2}$$

Using the traditional approach to cost of capital which was presented in Chapter 10, then the required project return will be a weighted function of the returns and proportionate financing of debt and equity in the project's financing, or

(3) $$R_{Project} = R_E \left(\frac{E}{D+E}\right) + R_D \left(\frac{D}{D+E}\right)$$

R_E is found as shown in the previous paragraph, using the covariance of the project and the market, and an estimated beta.

Even if beta can be estimated from similar projects or the returns of similar firms in the market, if there is any leverage the observed beta will not be the same as the beta for a firm/project with different leverage. Then the manager must decide how to compute a cost of capital for a project which has amounts of leverage which differ from the standard computed above.

One approach is to first compute the beta for the equity in a no-debt project (β_E). Suppose that one uses the Modigliani-Miller argument that the only increase in value for a levered firm comes from the tax deductibility of debt interest. Then the value of this tax shield can be subtracted from the total market value of the levered firm's debt and equity, or the similar "firm" which represents the proposed project. In the case of perpetual debt, the cumulative value of the tax savings from the debt interest is the quantity one minus the tax rate of the firm times the value of the debt $[(1-T)D]$. In other cases, the present value of all the future interest payments after tax discounted at the pre-tax debt rate must be computed directly. These calculations provide the value of the firm under 100% equity financing once the increment in observed market value derived from the tax deductibility of interest is eliminated. Using historical data for the existing firm/project or comparable firms, one could obtain data on the return in total value for the firm in each period.

For example, if the value, V, is the sum of equity and debt, and it is also equal to the value under all equity, V_A, plus the tax savings of perpetual debt (TD) by assumption, then the value of the all-equity firm is equal to the observed equity value plus $(1-T)D$, or

(4) $$V = E + D = V_A + TD$$

(5) $$V_A = E + D(1-T)$$

The return in each period for the all-equity firm is the change in this total value plus the income, which is the Dividend (Div) and Interest income (C), divided by opening value, or

(6) $$\frac{V_{A_{t+1}}}{V_{A_t}} = \frac{E_{t+1} + \text{Div} + (D+C)(1-T)}{E_t + D_t(1-T)}$$

If this valuation is completed for each historical or hypothetical future period, its volatility can be evaluated in the capital asset pricing model equation shown in (2). This analysis then provides the estimate of the β_E, for by definition the value of the all-equity firm and its volatility coincide with the value of the equity and the volatility of the equity.[2]

Again, assume the perpetual debt case and the Modigliani and Miller conclusion that the increment in value from leverage arises only from the tax deductibility of interest. Then the cost of capital will be the cost of equity with no debt (using the β_E, R_M, and R_F from the earlier estimates) times the product of one minus the tax rate times the proportion of debt in the firm/project, or

$$(7) \quad R_P = [\beta_E (R_M - R_F) + R_F] \; [1 - (\text{Tax Rate}) \; (\frac{\text{Additional debt}}{\text{Value of no-debt project}})]$$

This assumes that the cost of debt, R_D, is the same as R_F and that there is perpetual debt. This calculation also ignores the effect of bankruptcy on the value of the firm (i.e., value will increase up to 99% debt), but the assumption may not be unreasonable for "acceptable" levels of debt. Furthermore, the usual assumptions of the CAPM (homogeneous expectations, no transaction costs, divisible securities, no taxes, and no cost of information) are required for the one-period proofs to hold.

Freeport Minerals [1]

In June 1971, Freeport's treasury office was approaching the final stages in the deliberations to choose a package to finance the Greenvale project, a nickel mining and processing venture in Australia. Although the Freeport name had traditionally been associated mostly with the sulphur industry, a diversification move initiated around 1968 had taken the company into new areas, one of which was Greenvale.

The choice of a financial package for the Greenvale project was not an easy one. In addition to the intricacies associated with each specific source of funds, the terms on which these funds were available were interrelated. The decisions appeared to be grouped into three major areas: (1) the selection of sales contracts for the processed ore; (2) the choice of the desired amount of leverage; and (3) the determination of the institution and currency for the debt part of the package.

The success of the Greenvale project and its financing were critical to Freeport, for the project was large and it was a major step in Freeport's policy of diversification from sulphur mining and processing to other mineral exploitation.

---

[2] Alternatively, one can estimate β_E from the observed β's of the levered firm if leverage was constant for the entire period. In this case, the direct estimate of β_E is $\beta_E = \beta \, / \, [1 + (1 - T)D/E]$. See Mark E. Rubenstein, "A Mean-Variance Synthesis of Corporate Financial Theory," *Journal of Finance*, March 1973, pp. 167-181.

[1] This case has been prepared totally from publicly available sources. Freeport's management has not been consulted in the preparation of the case.

COMPANY BACKGROUND

Freeport Minerals is a multinational resource processing company, producing a variety of minerals and chemical commodities for sale to large industrial customers. In 1968, sulphur contributed over 80% of Freeport net income, down from 85% in 1966. During the postwar period, Freeport had been the largest world producer of sulphur. In 1968 it still retained a 26% share of the total world sulphur market. In that year Freeport produced 3.9 million tons out of the 15 million tons total world production.

Until 1968, the producers of sulphur had been, in a classical oligopolistic way, able to control sales and production and thus to enjoy (especially during the 1963-1967 period) high prices. This control was necessary to insure a profitable business. The relatively low price elasticity of demand for sulphur, the low degree of sophistication involved in the technology used to produce it, and the few differences in production costs among the various producers ($17-$20/ton) made self-control essential to the prevention of "undesirable policies" in the industry.

However, the rising demand for sulphur (about 10% annually) and the high selling price made the industry too attractive to new entrants. As a result, the world sulphur oligopoly began to break down in 1968. First, Canadian producers of natural gas began to sell huge quantities of sulphur obtained as a by-product of their main activity. Then, the Mexican producers of sulphur, protected by their national tariffs and quota walls, started selling their excess sulphur at marginal prices in the U. S. market. As a result, the f.o.b. price of a ton of sulphur went from a high of $40/ton in 1968 to a low of $20/ton in 1970.

Freeport's response to this sudden increase in supply was to close its marginal mine, which had proudction costs of approximately $20/ton, and to start diversifying into other products. As a result, Freeport's sales ot sulphur decreased by 18% from 1968 to 1970.

The Diversification Moves

The impact of the sulphur price decline on Freeport's profits was so dramatic that profits halved between 1968 and 1970 (see Exhibit 1). It was clear that Freeport had to take steps to become a broad-based resource processing company, no longer so dependent upon one single commodity. As long as the sulphur oligopoly was in existence, Freeport considered the operations in products other than sulphur of secondary importance. However, when the sulphur oligopoly broke down and diversification became the strategy for moving away from the depressed sector, all these other operations became very important to Freeport, and top management began expanding them. This expansion was to be directed into areas where Freeport had some competitive advantage. One of these areas was metal mining and processing.

Freeport's management also decided that the main diversification axis would be copper and nickel extraction and processing. The company looked forward to becoming a significant producer of these minerals within a decade. Freeport had been exploiting nickel mines in Cuba for ten years. These operations were confiscated in 1959 but had given Freeport vast experience in nickel mining and processing of minerals.

The impact of the diversification moves on Freeport's investments, sales, and earnings by 1971, and the forecast for 1975, are presented in Exhibit 2.

Freeport Financial Situation in 1971

Despite the enlargement of its product portfolio, Freeport was in a strong financial position in 1971 (see Exhibit 1). With only $3.8 million of long-term debt and $234 million of stockholders' equity, the firm clearly had the financial capabilities to continue its aggressive expansion and diversification program. However, the drop in profitability between 1968 and 1971 had been very painful, and the company was fighting to come back to its 1968 profit level. The stock price had gone from $40/$50 in 1968 to $16/$20 in 1971, following Freeport's traditionally stable P/E ratio of 17.

Freeport had always had a conservative and cautious financial policy. From 1965 to 1968, the slow expansion of the firm had been financed mainly through retained earnings (40% of total earnings) or issuance of new shares. Financially, the company had always separated its mining and processing ventures abroad from the parent company activities. In the financing of these projects, Freeport had always tried to accomplish two objectives: (1) to maximize external borrowings (20% equity being the upper limit), and (2) to avoid lending to the subsidiary, or even giving any guarantee to the foreign subsidiaries' borrowings. The borrowings of Freeport's subsidiaries had been based either on the inherent value of the operation from advance sales contracts or on government guarantees. Freeport had often used AID risk insurance to protect itself against losses due to war or expropriation or problems in converting currencies. This policy had proven to be especially sound in 1959, when the huge Cuban operations of Freeport were nationalized. On that occasion Freeport had to write off only $9 million, the amount of the equity stake. However, First National City Bank, one of the major lenders to the Cuban subsidiary, suffered one of the biggest losses in its history.

Freeport consolidated its subsidiaries, using the equity method: only the equity stake in the subsidiaries appeared in the Freeport balance sheet and income statement. The liabilities of the subsidiaries consolidated this way never appeared on the parent's balance sheet. Freeport management placed considerable weight on the maintenance of a debt-free balance sheet in order to keep flexibility for eventual financing of major ventures. (See Note 2 to Exhibit 1).

THE GREENVALE PROJECT

The Joint Venture Freeport Mineral Exploration

In 1966, Freeport decided to make Australia the focus of its mineral exploration efforts. The basis for this decision was the continent's political stability and favorable geology for nickel, a premium commodity in which Freeport's staff had accumulated considerable experience. As a first step, the company bought a 22% equity position in Metals Exploration N.L., an Australian company, for $2 million.

Metals Exploration N.L. was a young company that had been created by a group of Australians. Several members of this group were university teachers in geology or chemistry. The goal of the company was to try to identify metal deposits in Australia. The Greenvale deposit was one of their findings.

The Greenvale project became a 50/50 joint venture of Freeport Queensland Nickel Inc. (a wholly-owned subsidiary of Freeport Minerals) and Metals Exploration Pty. Ltd. (a wholly-owned subsidiary of Metal Exploration N.L.)

The Nickel Industry

Structure. The major characteristics of the nickel industry were high concentration, a high degree of vertical integration, and high barriers to entry. The industry was a worldwide oligopoly with the following world market share in 1966 and 1971:

	Nickel Production Market Shares 1966	1971 (estimates)
International Nickel INCO (Canadian)	51.5%	42%
Le Nickel (French)	14.2%	11%
Falconbridge (Canadian)	11.6%	13%
Sheritt Gordon (U. S.)	4.4%	34%
Hanna (U. S.)	3.6%	
Japanese firms	8.0%	
Others	6.7%	

This very high degree of concentration had technological and historical explanations.

Until the end of the nineteenth century, the Rothschild-controlled firm, Le Nickel, had the monopoly of the nickel produced in the world. In 1902, helped by J. P. Morgan, Oxford Nickel and Guardian Nickel merged to form International Nickel (INCO) that was to dominate the industry until today.

From 1929 to 1940, INCO had a 90% share of the world nickel market (Le Nickel had 10%). In the postwar era, INCO's dominance decreased. New companies like Hanna and Sheritt Gordon appeared, but INCO was able to conserve a dominant position in this market. Still, the nickel oligopoly was successful in maintaining high barriers to entry and in controlling output. The price of nickel was maintained at a high level that allowed the nickel producers to be fairly profitable. Since 1965, INCO's return on equity had been stabilized at a steady and healthy 16%.

Barriers to entry in the nickel industry were economies of scale (the smaller producers, like Hanna, were much less profitable than INCO, which had only three big refineries); high capital requirements (a fully integrated nickel operation of the minimum scale requires between $50 million and $200 million); control of raw materials by producers that are all vertically integrated; technological patents and know-how; and long-term contracts with nickel buyers.

Prices. In a nutshell, the prices in the nickel industry were determined by INCO and expressed in U. S. dollars. INCO's large share of the market placed it in the position of being the price leader in the industry. The fact that a very large proportion of INCO's nickel was sold in the United States and that many of its mines were located in the United States made the U. S. dollar the currency of the nickel market that INCO dominated.

The nickel producers appeared to be able to predict with a good degree of certainty the future demand. They increased their capacity in proportion to their actual market share in order to match this capacity and the demand. Apparently a kind of implicit agreement did exist between producers not to try to increase market share by a savage price war that would be detrimental to everybody's profitability. Any price cut would be followed by everybody, and the only result would be to have the same market share at a lower price. For instance, the INCO prewar price of $0.35/lb. lasted from 1929 to 1946.

In fact, the price of nickel had been determined by INCO's costs, with a comfortable margin allowing some higher cost producers to survive. An implication of this fact was that all suppliers quoted prices in U. S. dollars. Short-term supply and demand fluctuation had a weak effect on nickel prices, and were absorbed by inventory change, rationing, or production cutbacks. Historical prices of nickel ingots up to 1967, and the reasons associated with the price changes, are presented in Exhibit 3. Since, then, prices had increased rapidly up to almost $1.35/lb. in 1971.

Demand. Although subject to the characteristic fluctuations of demand for raw materials, the demand for nickel was relatively steady because nickel was used mainly as an intermediate product; stainless steel, for example, is an alloy of steel and nickel. Nickel was thus sold to steel producers or other industrial firms. One of the problems of nickel was that copper, aluminum, and (to a lesser extent) cobalt or even plastics were good substitutes. However, in the short term the responsiveness of demand to changes in prices of nickel was rather small. The substitution of alternative minerals for nickel required some amount of time and commitment to different technologies. But in the long term the response of demand to changes in nickel prices could be expected to be much larger.[2]

The world consumption of nickel was expected to grow on the order of 6-7% annually.

Recent Developments. Until 1970, INCO had acted in a benevolent and relatively paternalistic way towards other nickel companies. Each year INCO published an analysis of world nickel consumption. This analysis became the basis for the plans of other producers in the industry. INCO freely distributed reports on its R&D activities, organized conferences around the world for potential nickel users, and promoted nickel in general instead of INCO nickel in particular (i.e., INCO's promotion was directed towards increasing primary demand, not towards increasing the company's market share). The industry, in fact, never got around to forming a trade association; INCO was it. However, in the early seventies, the giant of the nickel industry began to show some signs of aggressiveness.

In 1971 INCO took the plunge. Its market share slipped to 42%. Sales dropped 20% from the 1969 high. Profits declined by 50%. The major causes of these outcomes were the expansion of competitors, particularly Falconbridge and Le Nickel, and the general situation of overcapacity in the industry. One of the reasons for this overcapacity was that during the 1960s INCO had not tried to fight competition

---

[2] Short-term price elasticity of demand for nickel had been estimated at -1.026 by a team of economists.

by maintaining low selling prices as it did in the 1920s. Behind the comfortable shelter of industry high prices, smaller competitors had begun to survive profitably. The situation of shortages of nickel supply in the 1960s made it impossible for INCO to control competition. However, the prolonged world economic slump in the early 1970s reduced demand for steel and other nickel-bearing alloys, and INCO as well as its competitors were saddled with overcapacity.

INCO's response to these events was a change in strategy and an internal reorganization. Henry S. Wingate, chairman and chief executive of INCO, a lawyer who had run the company for eighteen years, proceeded to chop employment by 18% and cut production to 80% of capacity in 1971. "Now that there is the need of getting out and selling nickel, we are not quite so altruistic," declared Grubb, an executive vice-president promoted by Wingate to the chief executive's slot.[3] Accompanying this change in strategy, INCO was reorganized on a divisional basis with large support from corporate staff. In addition, various control systems were installed to decrease the cost of operations.

Characteristics of the Greenvale Project

The Nickel Deposits and Processing. In 1967, geologists discovered a deposit of high-grade nickel laterite at Greenvale in Queensland, Australia, over 100 miles inland from Townsville on the northeast coast. Top-grade experts, who conducted systematic sample drillings in the area in the subsequent three years, estimated a reserve of at least 44 million tons of ore averaging 1.57% nickel and 0.12% cobalt. A company announcement of plans to proceed with development of the project was expected very soon. The ore at Greenvale extended like a flat blanket varying from 5 to 60 feet thick parallel to the surface over an area of 800 acres with about 20 feet of overburden.

The mine was expected to require an employment force of one hundred to haul and crush ore at an annual rate of 2.5 million tons. This ore would then be transported to the processing plant in Townsville on the coast. This transportation would require a new 140-mile railway which was to be built and equipped by the companies and owned and operated by the Queensland government. The construction of the railroad did not pose any major difficulty. In addition, Freeport had a considerable amount of experience in transporting minerals.

The Townsville plant would employ 600 people and was scheduled for completion in mid-1974. Mine site construction had already begun. Ore mining was scheduled to start in late 1973, and production in late 1974. Full production capacity was to be reached in the beginning of 1975.

Capital Requirements. The estimated capital requirement for the full development of the Greenvale project totaled $264 million. This was based on equipment purchased at the lowest reasonable cost. This total cost broke down into:

---

[3] "Inco: A Giant Wakes Up and Starts Fighting." *Business Week,* May 26, 1973, p. 44.

Greenvale Capital Requirements

Greenvale mine development	US$ 15.0 million
Railway	44.6
Nickel processing plant	110.8
Preoperating cost	16.5
Interest during construction	19.1
Working capital needs	14.7
Escalation and contingency	43.4
	US$264.1 million

THE FINANCING DECISIONS

It was clear to Freeport that the profitability of this project depended heavily on the financing package that it could obtain. An estimate of its cash flows is presented in Exhibit 4. This estimate is based on certain assumptions about financing which were still subject to modification.

The decision appeared to be a three-tiered one. First the type of sales contract would have to be determined. The longer the time coverage of the sales contract the easier it would be to obtain favorable financing. Without any long-term sales contract it would be extremely hard to obtain financing at reasonable terms. The selection of a financial package was, in turn, a two-stage decision. The amount of leverage that the project could carry had to be established. Then, the source of the debt portion of the financial package had to be chosen.

Sales Contracts

Freeport's tradition had been to cover the entire output of a project with advance sales contracts before it approached the sources of financing. These contracts were required to pursue the company's policy of maximizing the amount of debt in the financing of its projects.

Long-term sales contracts for selling ore are founded on a basis of mutual advantage. This type of contract gives the purchaser the advantage of a relatively regular supply at a discount from the market price while it guarantees a minimum price for the supplier. The floor price in the contract is generally 10% less than the market price when the contract is signed. The price of the ore, when above the minimum agreed price, increases with the level of the market price. However, the discount from the market price increases with the level of the market price; e.g., if market prices double, the discount might be 25%. There is, in general, no ceiling price.

The annual quantity that the purchaser is obliged to buy at the given price is fixed in the contract. The supplier, however, is not obliged to supply this quantity. If the quantity of ore available is lower than forecast, or if the percentage of pure metal is lower, and the supplier cannot ship as much metal as anticipated, there is no penalty for him. On the other hand, he cannot sell the metal to other users until he fulfills the contract requirements. In these sales contracts the purchaser is usually responsible for the transportation of the metal.

In 1971, for the Australian nickel, Freeport could obtain long-term sales contracts only with Japanese and German clients.

The Amount of Leverage

Freeport was well seasoned in dealing with international bankers who specialized in project financing. The amount of financing that it could obtain from these sources depended to a large extent on the bankers' perception of the risk of the project.

When a bank is asked to finance a project like a mining venture, it tries to assess the degree of risk involved in the project. The assessment of risk is then translated into a required coverage of the interest costs and the amortization of the loan by the projected cash flows. If the project is very risky, the bank will require a high coverage ratio (i.e., a high ratio of annual cash flows to annual interest costs plus loan amortization). This coverage ratio may be close to 1 for low-risk ventures, and go up to 5 for very risky projects, based on average cash flows and coverage.

The maturity of the loan also affects the amount of coverage desired. The longer the maturity of the loan, the higher the coverage ratio. As the horizon of the loan is lengthened, the project's risks become more and more difficult to assess. For instance, the required coverage ratio may be 3 if the average loan maturity is fifteen years, and 4 if the average loan maturity is eighteen years.

To evaluate the riskiness of a project the bank considers the following types of risk:

1. Construction Risk. This risk refers to the technological factors involved in the project. If, for instance, a given project involves a special quality of ore which requires a new processing technology that has never before been tried, the construction risk will be relatively high. The experience and skill of the firm in the type of project are also very important in this regard. As far as mining is concerned, an open pit operation is less risky than an underground operation.

2. Resource Risk. This risk concerns the possibility of finding less ore than expected, or of finding a poorer ore than anticipated. The first risk (volume) is very important in operations like petroleum. The second one (quality) is crucial in metal exploration. In this case to find a 1.8% ore instead of the 2.2% expected is not uncommon, and this makes a large difference in the revenues of the project.

3. Operating Risk. This risk involves the eventual problems that might appear in the exploitation of the venture as well as possible variations in operating expenses. The eventual problems of exploitation are a function of the supply of raw material (volume and quality of ore) and environmental factors like transportation and logistic problems. The predictability of the operating expenses depends on the nature of these expenses and on the economic variables that potentially affect them.

4. Market Risk. This risk depends on the predictability of the volume and price of sales. This in turn, depends on the possibility of obtaining long-term sales contracts and on the terms of these contracts. The future of the market is also important. Factors such as the structure of the market and the strategy of major firms in the market affect this type of risk a great deal.

5. Political Risk. This risk encompasses the possibility of partial or complete nationalization, or any other political event affecting the project's cash flows.

6. Force Majeure Risk. This risk covers things such as earthquakes or epidemics that cannot be easily anticipated.

Sources of Debt Financing

Freeport was contemplating the use of several sources of debt funds. These are described below:

Suppliers' Credit. This credit was limited to the amount of procurement abroad. In terms of absolute amount, there is no upper limit to this source of credit. Some suppliers' credit has reached the value of $1.5 billion. This is a cheap source of funds. Interest rates in 1971 were about 8%, fixed. The maturity of the loans is relatively long, about ten years from project completion. De facto, international agreements (or imitation processes) have had the result of equalizing the interest rate and maturity of the loans offered by various countries. However, the currency of the loan is always the currency of the supplier. In 1971 price differences between the United States and Japan were about 5% in favor of Japan. Japanese and German prices were about the same.

In the case of Greenvale most of the equipment required had to be bought locally. Only about 30% of the railway construction costs and of the nickel processing plant could be sourced outside Australia at reasonable prices. For the other 70% of the required assets, high tariffs and transportation costs made Australian prices almost 40% cheaper than comparable products bought abroad. Generally, long-term credit was not available from the Australian suppliers. Thus, at best, 30% ($46.6M) of the total equipment cost might be imported and financed with suppliers' credit. The balance, $108.8M, would be purchased in Australia with ninety-day or six-month credit terms. The supplier's loan was a subordinate one.

Purchasers' Credit. This kind of credit was given by the purchasers of ore, the same people who signed the long-term contracts mentioned earlier. Therefore, some tradeoffs had to be made between the conditions of the sales contract and the conditions of the credit, or, more precisely, between the floor price and the discount from marketplace on one hand and the interest rate on the other. In the case of Freeport, one could assume that starting with a long-term sales contract with a floor price of $1.35 and a floating price equal to the market price less a 10% discount (e.g., initial market price is $1.50) then Freeport had two financing options:

1. $1.30 floor price and 15% discount from market for an 8% loan.
2. $1.25 floor price and 20% discount from market for a 6.5% loan.

The maturity of these loans could be as long as twenty years after completion of the project. However, the amount of these loans is limited to 50% of total invest-

ment. The currency of the loan is always the one of the purchaser. These loans can
sometimes be subordinated to senior loans, which provides an additional advantage.

Local Markets. The Australian financial market could also be a source of funds.
However, its capacity is limited. In 1971 the very maximum that could be raised for
a single project was 100 million Australian dollars. (At this time A$ = US$1.12).
Two different sources could be tapped on this market.

1. *Banks.* In this case the maximum maturity would be 7-10 years after commitment. Interest rate would be floating at 1% premium over the Australian overdraft rate, which itself is higher than the Australian prime rate. Early in 1971,
this overdraft rate was 8.5%.

2. *Insurance companies.* In this case a longer maturity could be obtained. As
much as fifteen years from commitment to final repayment might be granted
by these institutions. The rate would be fixed. In 1971 this rate was 9.5%.
However, insurance companies would agree to lend funds only if they obtained
an equity stake in the project. This equity incentive could range from one-half
to one-seventh of the amount of the loans. In the case of Freeport, one-sixth of
the loan was the minimum. However, this equity contribution was made in cash.

Euro-dollars. Euro-bonds were out of the question for such a mining operation.
That year, a firm had to be a "General Motors" type of risk to obtain funds in the
Euro-bond market. The only alternative left in the Euro-markets was a long-term
Euro-dollar loan. The maximum maturity for such a loan is ten years from commitment. The maximum capacity of the market to finance such a project is $200
million. The rate is floating at 1-1½% over the six-month London interbank rate.
This type of loan could also be arranged in currencies such as the guilder or deutsche
mark; however, the quantity available for a single project in such markets is low
(about $50 million). In any case there were substantial issue costs involved.

EXHIBIT 1 Freeport Minerals: Financial Data (thousands of dollars)

Fifteen-year Summary of Growth as reflected in the Annual Reports to Stockholders[a]

	Total Assets[b]	Stockholders' Equity	Gross Sales	Net Income		Dividends Paid
				Amount	Per Share	Per Share
1970	$280,366	$233,648	$136,558	$15,881	$1.02	$1.00
1969	293,976	233,221	175,209	28,516	1.84	1.60
1968	290,001	229,460	189,683	40,395	2.61	1.40
1967	275,629	210,446	173,105	32,357	2.09	1.25
1966	238,905	196,145	143,576	32,174	2.08	1.06
1965	209,442	178,945	106,752	21,660	1.41	.80
1964	227,191	165,945	78,782	15,349	1.00	.60
1963	174,511	156,904	66,329	12,816	.84	.60
1962	182,370	148,829	56,904	12,727	.84	.60
1961	211,001	145,150	52,724	12,856	.85	.60
1960	203,689	140,605	52,997	13,194[c]	.88[c]	.60
1959	167,406	154,428	53,234	14,478	.96	.60
1958	164,494	148,915	55,342	13,084[c]	.87[c]	.50
1957	93,891	76,167	63,283	12,973	.86	.50
1956	87,514	70,608	68,078	13,378	.89	.50

[a]Expenditures for property, plant, and equipment during the 15-year period amounted to $248,327,000, of which $7,031,000 was spent in 1970.

[b]Includes investments equivalent to unliquidated balance of forward sales of proceeds from future production, as follows: 1969, $10,000,000; 1968, $1,355,000; 1967, $18,132,000; 1966, $2,944,000; 1965, $11,417,000; 1964, $50,000,000; 1963, $7,686,000; 1962, $21,256,000; 1961, $54,072,000; and 1960, $50,000,000.

[c]Excludes an extraordinary item in 1960 of $9,630,000 (after taxes), or 64 cents per share, representing a write-off of the Company's investment in Cuban American Nickel Company and an extraordinary item in 1958 of $67,100,000 (after taxes), or $4.47 per share, representing a profit from the sale of oil and gas interests in the Lake Washington field. Under current accounting principles, as recommended by the Accounting Principles Board, these extraordinary items would be included in the determination of net income; on this basis, net income in 1960 would have been 24 cents per share and, in 1958, $5.34 per share.

	Year Ended Dec. 31, 1970	Year Ended Dec. 31, 1969
Statements of Income		
Gross sales	$136,558	$175,209
Other income, net	3,018	1,739
	139,576	176,948
Costs and expenses:		
Production and delivery costs	86,190	111,568
Exploration and development costs	5,915	8,426
Depreciation and amortization	14,279	14,588
Selling, general, and administrative expenses	7,342	7,392
Taxes (Note 1)	9,969	6,458
	123,695	148,432
Net income	$ 15,881	$ 28,516
Net income per share	$1.02	$1.84
Statements of Retained Earnings		
Retained earnings at beginning of year	$144,504	$140,787
Net income, as above	15,881	28,516
	160,385	169,303
Dividends paid ($1.00 per share in 1970 and $1.60 per share in 1969)	15,499	24,799
Retained earnings at end of year	$144,886	$144,504

The accompanying notes are an integral part of these statements

EXHIBIT 1 (cont.) *Balance Sheets*

Assets	Dec. 31, 1970	Dec. 31, 1969
Current assets:		
Cash and marketable securities	$ 50,558	$ 50,613
Accounts receivable	24,050	22,234
Inventories, at average cost	26,623	25,448
	101,231	98,295
Investments in affiliates (Note 2)	5,484	3,677
Property, plant, and equipment, at cost	281,047	277,425
Less, allowance for depreciation and amortization	(116,677)	(104,007)
Net property, plant, and equipment	164,370	173,418
Other assets	9,281	8,576
Total Assets	$280,366	$293,966

Liabilities	Dec. 31, 1970	Dec. 31, 1969
Current liabilities:		
Accounts payable & accrued expenses	$ 7,331	$ 9,734
Accrued royalties payable	7,293	12,849
Accrued income & other taxes	525	2,679
First mortgage bond payments of National Potash Company—due within one year	968	913
	16,117	26,175
First mortgage bonds of National Potash Company, less portion included in current liabilities (Note 3)	3,813	4,781
Deferred employee benefits	1,402	1,215
Reserve for future income taxes, and deferred investment tax credits (Note 1)	25,386	18,584
Stockholders' equity		
Common stock, par value $5, authorized 40,000,000 shares, issued 15,526,080 shares December 31, 1970, and 15,522,520 shares December 31, 1969	77,631	77,613
Excess of amount paid in over par value of common stock	11,131	11,104
Retained earnings	144,886	144,504
	233,648	233,221
Total liabilities and Stockholders' Equity	$280,366	$293,966

Note 1: Income taxes provided in 1967 and prior years reflect tax losses relating to Cuban American Nickel Company, formerly a subsidiary, whose Cuban assets were confiscated by the Fidel Castro government. The Internal Revenue Service has questioned some of these deductions. Discussions in an effort to resolve these differences by settlement are progressing. It settlement cannot be reached, it is estimated that a maximum deficiency approximating $9,000,000 (after applying $5,000,000 of available tax credits) plus interest, payable in the future, might be asserted. The Company intends to resist any such assertion if made and, in the opinion of its counsel, the Company should prevail.

Note 2: At December 31, 1970, investments in affiliates comprised $1,396,000 in Freeport Indonesia, Incorporated, and $4,088,000 applicable to various other investments.

The net assets of Freeport Indonesia at December 31, 1970, as shown on its financial statements, amounted to $8,539,000, including current assets of $2,979,000, property, plant, and equipment of $35,346,000, less current liabilities of $719,000 and long-term liabilities of $29,067,000. Freeport Sulphur Company's equity in these net assets amounted to $8,144,000.

The difference between this equity and the investment of $1,396,000 principally represents costs of exploration and preliminary work incurred by Freeport Sulphur and written off against its earnings in prior years as expenditures were incurred.

Reference is made to comments in the accompanying letter to stockholders regarding the Freeport Indonesia project for development of the Ertsberg copper deposit.

In connection with the financing of that project, Freeport Sulphur Company was committed at December 31, 1970, to provide a maximum of $13,000,000 in additional equity funds, of which $11,500,000 is presently estimated to be required.

Note 3: The first mortgage bonds, principally 4 percent, are due in annual installments through November 1, 1974. They represent indebtedness of National Potash Company, without recourse to Freeport Sulphur Company, incurred in 1956, 1957, and 1958 when Freeport Sulphur owned a one-half interest in National Potash. National Potash became a wholly owned subsidiary of Freeport Sulphur in 1966.

Source: Company Annual Report.

EXHIBIT 2 Freeport Minerals: Product Diversification, 1971[a]

Product	Investment Million $	%	Sales Million $	%	Earnings Contribution Million $	%
Sulphur	$124.4	44%	$ 72.5	51%	$ 9.9	54%
Phosphates (with captive sulphur	74.0	26	38.5	27	2.7	14
Kaolin (processing)	29.1	10	17.0	12	1.8	10
Potash (mining)	29.2	10	9.0	7	1.7	9
Oil and Gas	19.6	7	4.0	3	0.0	0
Other (Nepean, Erstberg)	9.1	3	—	—[b]	2.3	13
Total	$285.4	100%	$141.0	100%	$18.4	100%

Expected Contribution to Net Income by Product Area, 1975

Parent Company		Million $	%
Sulphur		$ 8.0	14.6%
Phosphates		9.4	17.0
Kaolin		4.5	8.2
Potash		1.8	3.3
Oil and Gas		0.0	0.0
Investment income (including Nepean)[a]		1.3	2.4
		$25.0	45.5%

Foreign Subsidiaries	Direct Ownership	Million $	%
Erstberg (copper)	87 %	$15.9	28.8%
Greenvale (nickel)	50	11.6	21.0
Mt. Keith (nickel)	50	d.s.	—
New Caledonia (nickel)	49	d.s.	—
Palm Valley (Australia) (nickel)	9.5	d.s.	—
Metal Exploration Ltd. (nickel)	22	2.6	4.7
		$30.1	54.5%
Total		$55.1	100.0%

[a]Foreign subsidiaries are based on equity participation and dividends received. Exploration and mining abroad is done via local subsidiaries.

[b]Nepean is also a nickel joint venture with Metal Exploration.

d.s. = development stage.

Source: Lombard, Nelson, and MacKenna, "Freeport Minerals Company." June 22, 1972.

Date	Prices (¢/lb)	Relevant Events
11/25/46	31.25-35.0	Contract price on large quantities raised to level of base price, which had been unchanged at 35¢ since 1929.
1/1/48	35.0-33.75	U. S. tariff reduction from 2½¢ to 1¼¢ is directly passed on to customers, leaving price received by INCO unchanged.
7/22/48	33.75-40.0	"In 1938 each ton of ore mined produced 43 lbs. of nickel compared to 27 lbs. in 1948. Increased demand has made it necessary to mine considerably lower grade ores, leading to a price increase to 40¢ a lb." At an annual meeting INCO announced expansion plans in anticipation of growing demand.
5/31/50	40.0-48.0	INCO cites cumulative cost increases and reiterates policy of keeping price close to costs in order to encourage demand growth while covering costs of expansion.
12/13/50	48.0-50.5	Wage increase, negotiated on the same day, preceded the price increase.
6/1/51	50.5-56.5	One-year union contract concluded May 26. Wage increase and ten % reduction of work week.
6/14/53	56.5-60.0	Legal ceiling raised after discussions between INCO and U. S. government. INCO cites exchange rate depreciation of U. S. dollar as necessitating change in order to keep their price on U. S. sales constant in Canadian terms.
11/24/54	60.0-64.5	Increase "intended to offset higher costs."
12/6/56	64.5-74.0	"The increases were to meet higher costs, especially for the new project in Manitoba." INCO reiterates policy of "stable and reasonable prices, which are of major importance in the development of new and expanded uses and markets for nickel."
7/1/61	74.0-81.25	Increase unexpected in view of Canadian dollar devaluation and weakening of stainless markets at a time when steel as a whole was improving. Increase came shortly after the Castro government nationalized Cuban plants accounting for 9% of world production. Customers reported angered by the move.
5/24/62	81.25-79.0	Falconbridge initiates cut; INCO "taken completely by surprise, but followed the next day." Price cut offset the effect of devaluation of the Canadian dollar to 92.5¢. Falconbridge's motive linked to expiration of U. S. government contract accounting for some 25 % of its annual output.
9/28/65	79.0-77.75	U. S. import duty is suspended for three years. Producers pass the saving on to customers.
11/1/66	77.75-85.25	"Chairman Henry S. Wingate said the boost was necessary to finance the immediate development of a low-grade nickel property in Manitoba and to compensate for the higher costs of labor following a 95¢ per hour wage hike." Opposition from U. S. and Canadian governments ineffective in deferring increase.
9/15/67	85.25-94.0	Sheritt-Gordon led with an increase to 98¢ on powder and briquettes; INCO and Falconbridge reacted by going to 94¢ on cathodes. Cathodes compete with powder only when sheared at a cost of 2¢, but a spread between the two prices is still evident.
1971	135	

Source: 1946-1967: "Economic Analysis of the Nickel Industry." Charles River Associates, Incarporated, Dec. 1968.

1968-1971: Commodity Research Bureau, Inc., *Commodity Yearbook*, 1975.

Assumptions:

Ore Reserves	44.0 million tons	
Extraction Rate	2.5 million tons, wet, per annum	
Price		
Nickel Sinter	$3,020 per ton	(135¢ per lb)
Cobalt	$3,584 per ton	(160¢ per lb)
Product		
Nickel	22,321 tons × $3,020	= $67.4M
Cobalt	1,340 tons × $3,584	4.8M
Revenues—per annum		$72.2M

Cost	
Mining per wet ton	$2.00
Transport, 1.57 cents per	
wet ton mile	$2.20 over first ten years
Refining, per ton metal	$800 (less depreciation from 1985 onwards)
Royalty	10¢ per ton over first ten years,
	15¢ per ton thereafter.
Administrative	$1.0 million per annum
Capital	
Equity	$87 million ⎫
Borrowings at 9%	$264 million
repaid by 1984	$177 million ⎭
Depreciation	
Mine, $1.1 million	
p.a. over 18 years	$20 million
Railway $4.4 million	
p.a. over 10 years	$44 million
Refinery $8.7 million	
p.a. over 15 years	$130 million (including all preconstruction interest)

EXHIBIT 4 (cont.)

(millions of dollars)

	1975	1976	1977	1978	1979	1980	1981	1982	1983	1984	5 years 1985/89	3 years 1990/92
Capital												
Equity	$ 87.0	$ 87.0	$ 87.0	$ 87.0	$ 87.0	$ 87.0	$ 87.0	$ 87.0	$ 87.0	$ 87.0	$ 87.0	$ 87.0
Borrowings	177.0	159.3	141.6	123.9	106.2	88.5	70.8	53.1	35.4	17.7		
Less Repayments (−)	17.7	17.7	17.7	17.7	17.7	17.7	17.7	17.7	17.7	17.7		
	159.3	141.6	123.9	106.2	88.5	70.8	53.1	35.4	17.7	—		
Revenues	72.2	72.2	72.2	72.2	72.2	72.2	72.2	72.2	72.2	72.2	361.0	216.6
Costs												
Mining	5.0	5.0	5.0	5.0	5.0	5.0	5.0	5.0	5.0	5.0	25.0	15.0
Depreciation	1.1	1.1	1.1	1.1	1.1	1.1	1.1	1.1	1.1	1.1	5.5	3.3
Transport	5.5	5.5	5.5	5.5	5.5	5.5	5.5	5.5	5.5	5.5	27.5	16.5
Depreciation	4.4	4.4	4.4	4.4	4.4	4.4	4.4	4.4	4.4	4.4	—	—
Refining	10.1	10.1	10.1	10.1	10.1	10.1	10.1	10.1	10.1	10.1	50.5	30.3
Depreciation	8.7	8.7	8.7	8.7	8.7	8.7	8.7	8.7	8.7	8.7	43.5	0
Royalty	.3	.3	.3	.3	.3	.3	.3	.3	.3	.3	1.5	.9
Interest at 9%	15.9	14.3	12.7	11.2	9.6	8.0	6.4	4.8	3.2	1.6	—	—
Administration	1.0	1.0	1.0	1.0	1.0	1.0	1.0	1.0	1.0	1.0	5.0	3.0
Total Costs (−)	52.0	50.4	48.8	47.3	45.7	44.1	42.5	40.9	39.3	37.7	158.5	69.0
Profit before Tax	20.2	21.8	23.4	24.9	26.5	28.1	29.7	31.3	32.9	34.5	202.5	147.6
Taxation 38% of Profit before Tax Plus Mine Depreciation[a]	0	(8.7)	(9.3)	(9.9)	(10.5)	(11.1)	(11.7)	(12.3)	(12.9)	(13.5)	(79.0)	(57.3)
Net Profit	20.2	13.1	14.1	15.0	16.0	17.0	18.0	19.0	20.0	21.0	123.5	90.3

EXHIBIT 4 (cont.)

(millions of dollars)

	1975	1976	1977	1978	1979	1980	1981	1982	1983	1984	5 years 1985/89	3 years 1990/92
Net Profit	$20.2	$13.1	$14.1	$15.0	$16.0	$17.0	$18.0	$19.0	$20.0	$21.0	$123.5	$90.3
Depreciation	14.2	14.2	14.2	14.2	14.2	14.2	14.2	14.2	14.2	14.2	49.0	3.3
Tax Savings[a]	3.0	1.9	1.0	.2	(.7)	(.7)	(.7)	(.7)	(.7)	(.7)	(3.5)	—
After-tax Interest	15.9	8.9	7.9	6.9	5.9	4.9	4.0	3.0	2.0	1.0	—	—
Operating Cash Flow (excluding Financing)	50.3	41.1	37.2	36.3	35.4	35.4	35.5	35.5	35.5	35.5	169.0	93.6 + working capital in 1992
Principal + Interest ($177M for 10 yrs. at 9%)	(33.6)	(26.6)	(25.6)	(24.6)	(23.6)	(22.6)	(21.7)	(20.7)	(19.7)	(18.7)		
Equity Cash Flow	16.7	14.5	11.6	11.7	11.8	12.8	13.8	14.8	15.8	16.8	169.0	93.6 + working capital in 1992

	Net Present Value		Rate of Return	Terminal Rate of Return
	10%	15%		
Operating Cash Flow and $264M Outlay	$23.6	−$56.9	11.2%	10.9%
Equity Cash Flow and $87M Outlay	62.1	9.8	16.4%	13.6%

[a]Taxes are based on the use of 150% declining balance rates for tax purposes. No tax is assumed payable in the first year because of various expensed start-up costs, some of which are carried over to 1976. Hence, the tax savings are carried over to 1976.

Source: Based on raw calculations in Roach, Williams and Co. (Share brokers), *Report on Metals Exploration*, Melbourne, Australia, 1970.

457

PART FOUR

In the post-World War II Western world, one of the most striking phenomena has been the growth in the Euro-dollar market. In Chapter 13, we will study the nature of these funds, seeking to understand several theories of how they came about and to know who uses them and for what purposes. In Chapter 14, the various types of international bonds, of which the Euro-bonds are a major segment, are discussed. There are bonds denominated in several currencies, parallel bonds, convertible Euro-bonds, and other varieties which have grown at different rates and which create different risks to the holder. Finally, since the multinational firm undertakes financings within the boundaries of the countries where it operates, in Chapter 15 we sketch the characteristics of the markets in major developed nations.

These three chapters present an institutional coloration to the international financial analysis presented in previous chapters. Inevitably, the particular data contained in the comparative statistics will become outdated; however, the analytical construct developed to analyze these data will remain valid.

Part Four has been designed to provide financial managers with an understanding of the financial markets where multinational companies operate. We have therefore included both institutional factors and basic economic relationships.

The Euro-Currency Markets

Euro-currencies, monies traded outside the country of their origin, are the core of the international financial markets. This chapter will discuss the short-term end and the loan portion of these markets. The following chapter will consider international bonds, including Euro-bonds. Much of the text will focus on the "Euro-dollar" market since the dollar is the currency with the largest amount of trading in the "Euro-currency" markets, and Europe is the location where most of this trading takes place.

Since the word Euro-dollar has usually been surrounded by some degree of mysticism, the presentation begins by discussing what a Euro-dollar looks like and how it is traded. The characteristics of these markets are described: their size and growth, and the impact of these markets on the economies of the countries involved. The chapter concludes with an analysis of the factors that determine the rates in these markets and the future of the markets.

WHAT ARE EURO-DOLLARS?

Euro-dollars are financial assets and liabilities denominated in dollars but traded outside the United States. Although traded outside the United States, every Euro-dollar deposit has its origin in and continues to be associated with a deposit in a bank in the United States.

To understand how Euro-dollars come to be and are traded outside the United States while maintaining an umbilical cord tied to an American bank, one must understand the technical aspects of international transfer of funds. Financial officers of multinational companies do not usually cross countries' borders with suit-

461

cases packed with paper or metal money.[1] With almost the single exception of the fund smuggler, international capital transactions are not realized through paper or metal money. Instead, these transactions use bank deposits which can be moved using "bank transfers." These transfers are usually executed via telex or some other fast means of communication.

Cash flows in a commercial bank are identified by four major pieces of information: (1) currency, (2) institution and location, (3) maturity date, and (4) interest rate. For example, the complete description of a cash flow could read as follows: "$1 million inflow for June 30 carrying 10% per annum to be received in the London branch from deposits drawn on Chase Manhattan." This inflow could be from the repayment of a dollar loan made to a customer earlier by the British branch at 10% per annum. The bank also knows that the payment will be made by the customer requesting Chase Manhattan to transfer funds from the customer's account to the London bank's account.

To have a better grasp of how these bank transfers take place and how Euro-dollars come into existence, look at a few transactions:

1. Corporation ABC which maintains deposits with Chase Manhattan decides to transfer some of its dollar deposits to Barclays in London. Chase Manhattan sends a telex to Barclays informing it of Chase's transfer of funds to Barclays's account with Chase according to the request of Corporation ABC.

Questions are then asked:

a. Does Barclays wish to leave its newly-acquired deposits with Chase Manhattan or does it prefer to keep them with some other American bank? Assume that Barclays keeps the new deposits with Chase.

b. At what maturity and therefore interest rate does Barclays wish to place the deposit funds? Perhaps Barclays replies that it wants a seven-day certificate of deposit at the going rate.

Meantime, in London, a similar set of questions is being raised between Barclays and Corporation ABC. Corporation ABC wants the deposits kept at Barclays as it first indicated; however, the maturity and the interest rate on the deposit must be established. Presume that Corporation ABC wishes to maintain a daily deposit at the going rate.

A Euro-dollar deposit has been created. The deposit in London is denominated in dollars; however, Barclays has now acquired the power to deal in dollars outside the United States.

2. Barclays decides to exercise its power to deal in dollars at the maturity of its seven-day Certificate of Deposit. Shortly after Barclays received the deposit from Corporation ABC it also received an application for a Euro-dollar loan from Corporation XYZ. Corporation XYZ needs the money only seven days later. However, Corporation XYZ would like to have the Euro-dollar funds

---

[1] This is not to say that some colorful examples of the suitcase version do not exist. The Swiss Alps have witnessed many of these transfers.

transferred to Switzerland where it eventually intends to use the funds. In Switzerland, Corporation XYZ conducts its banking business with the Union Bank of Switzerland.

Barclays extends the loan to Corporation XYZ at the prevailing rate for the desired maturity. Now Barclays must transfer the dollar funds to the account of Corporation XYZ. Accordingly, Barclays sends a telex to Chase Manhattan requesting that its deposits with Chase be transferred to Union Bank of Switzerland for their account with Corporation XYZ.

Chase will now have to engage in the same kind of inquiry that it had when the deposits were first created at Barclays.

a. Does Union Bank of Switzerland wish to maintain the deposit with Chase Manhattan?

b. For what maturity is the deposit to be maintained, and therefore what interest rate?

Euro-dollars are now being traded outside the United States. However the link with Chase is maintained. Throughout the two transactions Chase had some kind of deposit or liability. The only change at Chase was in the name of the owner of that deposit from Corporation ABC, to Barclays, to Union Bank of Switzerland. Notice, however, that Corporation ABC now thinks it has a dollar deposit with Barclays and that Corporation XYZ has a loan from Barclays and a Euro-dollar deposit at Union Bank of Switzerland.

What happens if, when Union Bank of Switzerland is notified of the impending receipt of new Euro-dollar deposits (the proceeds of the loan to Corporation XYZ from Barclays), it requests that the deposits be kept with Credit Lyonnais in Paris? That is, Union Bank of Switzerland wishes to have dollar-denominated deposits in Paris. Now, Chase Manhattan will have to start another set of telexes and inquiries. Chase Manhattan will inform Credit Lyonnais that Union Bank of Switzerland wishes to transfer its dollar deposits to their account. The next question then will be from Chase Manhattan to Credit Lyonnais:

a. Where do you want to have the dollar deposit, at Chase or at another bank?

b. For what maturity and at what interest rate is it to be deposited?

Assume that Credit Lyonnais wishes to have an overnight deposit with Chase. The deposit at Chase now has had its ownership transferred once more from Union Bank of Switzerland to Credit Lyonnais. However, a deposit is still maintained at an American bank (Chase, in this case). Had anyone in the chain decided to use Citibank rather than Chase Manhattan as the recipient of their deposit, Chase Manhattan would have moved out of the chain of transactions, but a deposit would still be maintained with an American bank (Citibank in that case).

Euro-dollars, once they come into existence, can reproduce themselves.[2] However, the primary deposit—the one which initially was tied to the creation of the first Euro-dollar—will continue to be held in an American bank. Additional claims

---

[2] The multiple creation of Euro-dollars will be discussed further in the following section.

and liabilities may be created in the multiplication of Euro-dollars (e.g., the loan from Barclays to Corporation XYZ and the transfer of deposits from Union Bank of Switzerland to Credit Lyonnais) but behind it all, there is a deposit in an American bank. Every time that a bank transfer takes place, two questions must be answered to complete the transfer: Where? What maturity? The answer to the "where" in the Euro-dollar market must always involve an American bank, although the convoluted nature of the transaction may bring in many other foreign banks, as in the case of Union Bank of Switzerland and Credit Lyonnais in the example.

Before leaving this introduction to Euro-dollars, notice that the word itself is presently a misnomer which has historical roots. As to the first part of the word, "Euro-," Euro-dollars can actually be traded anywhere as long as it is outside the United States. The bulk of the Euro-dollar transactions are consummated in Europe, but a sizable amount is also transacted in other parts of the world. Actually, one of the developments of the 1970s has been the emergence of the Asian dollar market (notice that the Euro- prefix has been dropped in this case). The second part of the word, "dollar," is also misleading. One should rather speak of the Euro-*currency* market since many currencies besides the dollar can be found as the denominator of financial assets and liabilities traded outside the country of that currency. Thus, there is a market in Euro-French francs, Euro-guilders, etc. However, Euro-dollars proper dominate the market, accounting for about 75% of the total Euro-currency liabilities of the banks.

In the same manner that Euro-dollars are tied to a deposit in the United States, Euro-guilders are tied to deposits in the Netherlands, Euro-Swiss francs to deposits in Switzerland, and so on. A given individual may think that (s)he is holding Swiss franc deposits in London at Barclays because (s)he has the legal right to withdraw Swiss francs from Barclays; however, the actual funds at Barclays must be held at a Swiss bank. Barclays can comply with the request from the customer to withdraw Swiss francs only by asking a Swiss bank to transfer funds from Barclays' account to the account of the customer or to whatever bank the customer chooses to transfer the Swiss francs.

FRACTIONAL RESERVES AND THE CREATION OF EURO-DOLLARS

In the earlier example of Corporation ABC and the subsequent entries, Euro-dollars were being created in the form of loans extended on the basis of acquired deposits. Consider another example and look in more detail at how Euro-dollars can reproduce themselves.[3] Suppose an American refiner purchases crude oil from an Arab sheik, paying for the oil with a $1,000,000 check drawn on a New York bank. The sheik then deposits the check in his London bank. What is the position of the London bank?

First, it now has a deposit liability denominated in dollars. As a result, $1,000,000 in Euro-dollars has now been created. The London bank pays interest on this deposit, but then wonders about using the funds. Assume that the bank

---

[3] This example, first presented by Milton Friedman, has become so popular among teachers of the subject that we feel obliged to continue the tradition. For the original presentation see Morgan Guaranty Trust Company, *The Morgan Guaranty Survey,* Oct. 1969.

would like to keep $100,000 (10%) in reserve for transaction purposes. Hence, it may negotiate a loan with a British importer who wishes to have dollars, lending him $900,000. The British importer withdraws the cash and uses the funds to pay a supplier. The supplier, a Swedish industrial firm, deposits the check in its savings account in a Stockholm bank, which now has a dollar deposit liability. Following the same reserve policy, this bank will then seek a borrower for the idle dollars, so that it may earn interest on a loan with which to pay the Swedish industrialist's interest and make a profit. Holding 10% reserves, it will make a loan of $810,000.

Stopping just at this stage, notice that the amount of Euro-dollar deposits has increased from the initial sheik's deposit.

	Bank 1	Bank 2	Bank 3
Sheik	$1,000,000		
British importer	− 900,000		
Swedish supplier		$900,000	
Borrower from Swedish bank		−810,000	
Deposit of borrower			$810,000

From this pattern, one can begin to see the effect of the Euro-dollar multiplier. Immediately after the shiek has transferred his funds to the London bank, the amount of Euro-dollars had increased by $1,000,000, exactly the amount the shiek had on his check from the American refiner. Had the British importer who borrowed $900,000 from the London bank held the dollars in his account, the total Euro-dollar liabilities of non-U. S. banks would have been $1,900,000. Yet, he withdrew the amount to pay the Swedish supplier, who deposited them in a savings account. After this transaction, the amount of Euro-dollar liabilities is still $1,900,000. However, now the Swedish bank is in the position of the London bank; it wants to do something with its dollar deposit. Following the 10% reserve standard, it lends $810,000 to some other person who may deposit it in another bank, repeating the process. If Bank 3 where the $810,000 is deposited were to simply take the funds and invest them in the New York bank, we would have a total deposit liability in Euro-dollars of the non-U. S. banks of $2,710,000, composed of $1,000,000 (the sheik's account in his London bank) plus $900,000 (the Swedish supplier's deposit in his bank) plus $810,000 (the deposit of the borrower from the Swedish bank before (s)he does anything with the currency).

From this pattern, we can see how the expansion of Euro-dollars may occur, and recognize that, for a 10% reserve requirement, the theoretical limit for expansion in the Euro-dollar accounts is $10,000,000.[4] All of the banks in the system may still keep their reserves on the basis of a fraction of the original check drawn on the New York bank for $1,000,000. Furthermore, from the point of view of each individual bank in the system, the particular bank has not been adding to Euro-dollar accounts, but only relending the dollars, which for them is simply investing the

[4] The multiplier is the reciprocal of the reserve requirement:

$$\frac{1}{\text{Reserve Requirement}} = \frac{1}{.10} = 10$$

Maximum Euro-dollar expansion equals multiplier times amount of initial deposit.

deposits they receive. However, the aggregate effect is to expand the Euro-dollars beyond the original amount.

There are typically no legal reserves on bank-to-bank Euro-dollar deposits. However, when one bank finally makes a loan to a nonbank source, the chain is broken, at least temporarily. The question then is what happens to the dollars in that loan. Does the borrower turn them over to someone who exchanges them for another currency, perhaps ultimately building up the foreign currency reserves of a central bank? If so, does the central bank place the dollars on deposit with a U. S. bank in a time deposit account, or buy government bonds, or place them as a Euro-dollar deposit?

The initial incentive is that the first bank receives a deposit on which it must pay interest; the depositor has moved from a time deposit in the United States to the Euro-dollar deposit, usually because of higher rates, freedom from controls, or some combination of factors. The Euro-bank (any bank dealing in Euro-currencies) now has a dollar liability and a nonearning dollar asset (the U. S. demand deposit). It will then want to switch that to an earning asset, either by depositing dollars with a Euro-bank at some favorable interest rate, by lending it to a customer who desires dollars, or by taking a time deposit in a U. S. bank. Thus, the key motivating element is to move the dollar asset from a nonearning category to an earning category.

Obviously the potential multiple creation of Euro-dollars has a great impact on the total size of the Euro-dollar market. Likewise, the market as a whole is of great relevance in analyzing countries' balance of payments and money supplies. These relationships are examined in the appendix to this chapter. Generally, students of this topic have concluded that the multiplier effect of Euro-dollars in practice is closer to 2-3 rather than the infinite multiplier theoretically possible under the current situation of no required reserves.

The potential for leakages from the Euro-system is large. Most people taking Euro-loans will do so with the purpose of spending the proceeds—not just keeping the loan proceeds as a deposit in a Euro-bank. The expenditure of the loan proceeds in most cases will involve a foreign exchange transaction. The Swedish borrower of Euro-dollars is likely to want to convert the dollars into Swedish kronor to pay current expenditures in Sweden. This process will cancel the possibility of a further expansion in the Euro-dollar supply. The Swedish bank will no longer have a Euro-dollar deposit.

In this sense, the Euro-dollar market can be compared to the case of a deposit transferred from a U. S. commercial bank to a domestic savings and loan institution. The savings bank can extend a loan like the Euro-bank can. Similarly, the recipient of the savings bank loan will most likely not redeposit the loan proceeds with another savings bank which could then make another loan. Instead, the borrower is likely to spend the loan in the operations of his/her business. The recipients of these payments will likely deposit the funds in a commercial bank, thus terminating the potential expansion of credit in the nonbank financial intermediaries.[5]

[5] For a rebuttal to the potential large multiple credit creation in the Euro-dollar market, see Fred H. Klopstock, "Money Creation in the Euro-Dollar Market—A Note on Professor Friedman's Views." *Monthly Review,* Federal Reserve Bank of New York, Jan. 1970, pp. 12-15. An analysis of the impact of nonbank financial institutions on domestic multiple creation of credit can be found in John G. Gurley and Edward S. Shaw, "Financial Intermediaries and the Saving-Investment Process." *Journal of Finance,* May 1956, pp. 257-276.

WHY EURO-CURRENCY MARKETS?

There is a simple reason: government regulations. At the beginning of the chapter, Euro-dollars were defined as financial assets and liabilities denominated in dollars but traded outside the United States. The Euro-dollar market offers the opportunity for trading dollars outside the control of government regulations imposed on residents (defined according to law) within the boundaries of the United States. When these regulations start to constrain the dollar money market in the United States, then the trading requirements can be satisfied by creating another dollar money market outside the United States—the Euro-dollar market. Below are presented the most important regulations that have contributed to the growth of the Euro-dollar market. Similar regulations, perhaps with different objectives, can be found to have aided the development of other Euro-currency markets.[6]

United States interest rate ceilings and reserve requirements have always been important tools to pursue monetary policy objectives. By the Federal Reserve's Regulation Q, United States banks were limited in the rate they could pay on deposits. The restriction did not apply to Euro-dollar deposits, even when they were in the European branches of American banks. Hence, once the ceiling imposed by Regulation Q was reached there was an incentive for citizens of all lands to pull funds from the United States and invest them in higher yield Euro-dollar deposits.

The flight of dollar deposits from U. S. banks to Euro-banks coincided with the discovery of a profitable use of those dollars back in the United States. Regulation M in the United States specifies the amount that U. S. banks are required to keep as a reserve against deposits. However, until 1969 this regulation did not affect the amount of reserves to be kept by American banks against deposits from foreign banks or from their own foreign branches. Hence, dollar-denominated accounts in European branches (Euro-dollar accounts) had no reserve requirements, and the branch could deposit (lend) the funds with its parent who was then free to lend against the full face amount of the account. In contrast, had the same customer deposited the funds in the American head office in the first place, the bank would have been forced to keep a certain percentage of the funds on reserve against the deposit.

The process we have shown here became more of a necessity to U. S. banks in the soaring expansion of the Euro-dollar market in 1969 and 1970. Tightening credit terms in the United States reduced the availability of funds in this country. Meanwhile the foreign branches of U. S. banks were paying far higher rates (up to 13% versus 6-7% in the United States) on dollar deposits abroad, pulling the depositors away from the domestic accounts. The reason for these high rates was simply that these Euro-dollars were especially valuable for lending purposes—particularly for lending to U. S. banks.

The sequence, then, began with U. S. banks dearly needing funds to lend to customers, for ceilings on interest rates here (Regulation Q) encouraged nonresidents who had dollar deposits to move them to the Euro-dollar market (where the ceilings did not apply) or to other currencies. Realizing these facts, American

---

[6] Although most of these regulations are not binding as of the time of this writing, they illustrate how the Euro-markets developed. Since governments reserve their rights to impose or reimpose regulations, a review of the past can also serve to illuminate the impact that future regulatory developments may have on the financial markets.

banks sought to borrow Euro-dollar funds from their own branches and from other European banks for relending to regular commercial customers. This increased borrowing from the Euro-dollar market pushed up interest rates in that market further. Nonetheless, this process not only allowed the banks to reattract funds which would otherwise be lost because of interest rate differentials, but it meant the funds could be re-loaned without the reserve requirements faced by the banks for U. S. dollar deposits.

This differential in required reserves was eliminated for U. S. banks by a revision of Regulation M by the Federal Reserve Board in September 1969. This revision required U. S. banks to maintain a reserve against liabilities to foreign banks (including U. S. banks' foreign branches) in a progressive fashion. Now the deposits of the foreign branches in their head office accounts had to meet the same reserve requirements as a deposit of any other customer of the bank. As to Regulation Q, the ceilings on interest rates paid to large depositors have been eliminated for all intents and purposes. However, Regulation Q is still in existence and, in principle at least, ceilings could be imposed again at the will of the Federal Reserve Board.[7]

Another set of regulations which contributed heavily to the fast growth of the Euro-dollar market was that developed to control capital outflows from the United States and improve the balance of payments situation of this country. These regulations were: (1) the controls on foreign direct investment, (2) the interest equalization tax, and (3) the voluntary credit restraint program. The controls on foreign direct investment made it necessary for multinational companies to finance growth of foreign direct investment from sources outside the United States. The interest equalization tax imposed a penalty on U. S. residents who bought securities issued by foreigners. Finally the voluntary credit restraint program limited the amount of credit that U. S. banks could extend to foreigners. In summary, all these restrictions attempted to rechannel a demand for funds from the financial markets in the United States to elsewhere. This elsewhere was conveniently satisfied by the Euro-dollar market. Except for some reporting requirements, all these regulations were eliminated in January 1974.

In addition to the regulations imposed by the United States, controls imposed or likely to be imposed by other countries on the use of the local currencies also encouraged growth of the Euro-dollar market. Thus, even if RCA or Nestlé operating in Italy could arrange Italian lira loans, there was the possibility of present or future restrictions on the use of those loans outside Italy; for example, if these firms wanted to purchase raw materials from a German supplier, they might discover that the Bank of Italy was limiting the amount of liras which could be removed from the country. The Euro-dollar (or the Euro-lira) loan, in contrast, would have no such restriction. Since the dollar is the most liquid and most readily ac-

---

[7] Regulation Q and its changes also affected the ownership of Euro-dollar accounts. Oscar Altman of the IMF estimates that two-thirds of the 1962 Euro-dollars were owned by central banks, yet only one-third of the 1967 base was owned by this group. Prior to 1962, Regulation Q ceilings on dollar interest rates also applied to central bank deposits. Hence, these banks liked the higher rates on dollar deposits which they would realize in Euro-dollars. When the ceiling was removed in applicability to their accounts, there was less need for them to seek Euro-dollars. It is also true that the non-official Euro-dollar market grew much faster in this period than the official holdings. See Oscar L. Altman, "Euro-Dollars." *Finance and Development,* March 1967.

ceptable currency, Euro-dollars became the most popular Euro-currency even for non-American firms operating in other lands.[8]

FINANCIAL INSTITUTIONS IN THE EURO-CURRENCY MARKETS

U. S. Banks

The previous section suggested how some regulations imposed by the U. S. government contributed to the growth of the Euro-dollar market. All these regulations affected the U. S. commercial banking system, either directly or indirectly. Some of the regulations, such as Regulation Q, established the need for banks to have access to the Euro-dollar market to raise necessary funds to finance domestic operations. This need drove many banks to expand their international operations by establishing a physical presence in the Euro-markets. Thus branches of U. S. commercial banks became some of the major institutions in the Euro-markets.

The presence of branches of U. S. commercial banks in the Euro-markets is also tied to the traditional role of commercial banks in catering to the needs of their customers. Following the Second World War, there was a dynamic increase in world trade and foreign investment. American banks in the past had had correspondent banking relationships with foreign banks which were designed to satisfy their clients' needs for banking services abroad—normally restricted to financing trade and perhaps to providing working capital. However, as American business moved overseas, the banks followed their clients and set up branches to serve them directly, rather than pass business to their correspondents. This close contact enabled the banks to offer a broader range of services than was previously available. Furthermore, banks of all nationalities began to compete fiercely for the business of emerging multinational corporations. This competition became more acute between 1965 and 1973 when U. S. corporations were restricted on the amount of funds they could raise in the United States to invest abroad. Given that the voluntary credit restraint program in the United States during that same period made it virtually impossible for U. S. banks to use funds raised in the United States to lend abroad, the Euro-currency market was the only viable alternative for financing the funds needs of the banks' customers. This obviously increased the role of these banks in the Euro-currency markets.

The response of U. S. banks to the combined forces of the need for external funds to finance domestic operations and the need to cater to the multinational corporation abroad can be seen in the increased presence of U. S. banks abroad. In 1960 there were only eight banks in the United States with branches abroad. The number of foreign branches of U. S. banks in that year was 131 with combined assets of $3.5 billion. However, by 1974 there were 737 foreign branches of U. S.

---

[8] Using monthly data from March 1959-December 1964, Georg Rich concluded that his regression results supported the hypotheses that Euro-dollar rates are linked to the level of U. S. and U. K. treasury bill rates. Changes in expected covered and uncovered yields on pound-denominated assets were also associated with changes in the Euro-dollar rates. See Georg Rich, "A Theoretical and Empirical Analysis of the Euro-dollar Market." *Journal of Money, Credit, and Banking,* Aug. 1972.

banks with total assets of $155.0 billion. The number of U. S. banks which owned these foreign branches grew by more than a multiple of fifteen by going from eight in 1960 to 129 in 1974.[9]

Because of the voluntary credit restraint program the foreign branches of U. S. banks had to raise their deposits abroad. Since access to private deposits was very limited, particularly for the newcomers in the 1960s, other banks became the major source of funds for these branches. This source of funds is technically called the interbank market. On the average, foreign branches drew 50% of their funds from the interbank market. The rest came from a mixture of sources whose weight has varied from year to year but which is composed of other branches, foreign official institutions, and some local deposits.

A concurrent trend in U. S. banking has been diversification of services. In the late 1960s, with the advent of the one-bank holding company and the diversification opportunities it offered in the United States, several important banks began to take a worldwide view of diversification. Leasing, factoring, cash and securities handling services, mortgage banking, computer-based financial advisory services, and so on, were undertaken by many banks in the United States. For banks with domestic subsidiaries active in these areas, establishing an overseas subsidiary was a logical step. Many major U. S. banks started to consider diversification into medium- and long-term finance, directly or as an intermediary, as one of the most logical extensions of their activities. After all, for decades European banks had been able to satisfy a client's total financing needs in house rather than refer the customer to an investment banker for the long-term position.

The critical regulatory check on U. S. banks' diversifying abroad was the Federal Reserve Board and its interpretation of legislation. The keystone of this legislation for international diversification was Section 25(A) of the Federal Reserve Act, the so-called Edge Act. Since branches abroad were permitted to carry on only the activities permitted to their parent banks in the United States, diversification overseas was generally achieved through the medium of a U. S. subsidiary established under the Edge Act. The subsidiary in turn held equity in foreign businesses. Passed shortly after World War I to permit U. S. banks to compete abroad on an equal footing with the more diversified foreign banks, the Edge Act could theoretically be interpreted to justify any activity overseas as long as it was carried on by the local banks of a particular market. In practice, however, the Federal Reserve Board had interpreted the permissible activities of an Edge Act subsidiary as including only those that were "finance related," thus excluding control of industrial or other nonfinancial investments. The number of Edge Act subsidiaries grew from fifteen in 1960 with only nominal assets to 104 in 1973 with total assets of $6.9 billion.[10]

Spurred by the developments in the Euro-dollar market and in the U. S. banking scene, as well as by the increased exposure to European "one-stop shopping" banks, U. S. banks began to pursue diversification actively, especially in Europe. Major U. S. banks—such as Manufacturers Hanover Trust Company, Bankers Trust Company, First National Bank of Chicago, Bank of America, Marine Midland, as well as some smaller banks—established investment banking subsidiaries in London to

---

[9] Andrew F. Brimmer and Frederick R. Dahl, "Growth of American International Banking," Paper presented before joint session of the American Economic Association and the American Finance Association, San Francisco, California, Dec. 28, 1974, p. 45.

[10] Brimmer and Dahl, "Growth of American International Banking."

furnish their organizations with expertise in underwriting, placement of securities, and syndication of loans. Further, these vehicles undertook varied functions ranging from leasing to venture capital. However, medium-term loan business and participation in some Euro-bond underwriting were the mainstays for most of these new subsidiaries. The emphasis of these operations appeared to be on tapping the fixed fee income attached to the manager function. With declining spreads in a highly competitive market, the income generated from the management function became of vital importance to the lending operation.

The Consortia Movement

One other reaction of banks to the change in environment was to set up joint ventures with other banks to conduct parts of their Euro-financing business: the so-called consortium banks. Although the purposes of banks participating in a consortium were not necessarily the same, the name of the game was syndication— the participation of several banks in a "loan syndicate."

The typical Euro-currency loan was quite sizable in relation to a bank's capital and deposit base, so that most credits were syndicated with a number of other banks. A consortium provided a permanent syndicate of banks, although most loans were also syndicated outside the consortium as well. More generally, one could say that a consortium bank provided a means of pooling resources. For small banks, such as the seventeen shareholders of Allied Bank International, this meant generating an additional capability in international banking which none of them could have achieved separately; for large banks, such as Chemical Bank—which acquired a 30% holding in London Multinational Bank, it offered a vehicle for enlarging both management expertise, through cross-fertilization with the merchant bankers Baring Brothers (20%), and its deposit base, through Credit Suisse (30%). Manufacturers Hanover Limited, although 25% controlled by Manufacturers Hanover Trust Company, had as minority shareholders the prestigious N. M. Rothschild & Sons (10%), the Long-Term Credit Bank of Japan (5%), and the Italian insurance concern, Riunione Adriatic di Sicurta (10%), thereby combining the dollar, lira, and yen resources of three banks with the financial expertise of Rothschild's. In practice, the performance of these banks has depended to a large extent upon the personality of their chief executive officers and the support given by the shareholders, and not so much upon the apparent strengths of a particular grouping. However, the difficult Euro-bond market in 1974 terminated the life of many of these consortia.

Normally, such consortia had been set up to specialize in the provision of medium-term loans. Although a fairly common practice among commercial banks in the United States, medium-term loans were not readily available to international borrowers until the blossoming of the Euro-dollar market. Banks found it useful to control this particular activity by creating a specialist entity, since many of the shareholders were not themselves familiar with the intricacies of the market. For example, a bank making a term loan normally funded the loan by buying short-term deposits in the money market—either directly, or by issuing C.D.'s.

But not only did consortia help overcome the problems of control and expertise, they were also designed to afford shareholders a competitive advantage by giving them access to sophisticated foreign capital markets which they previously lacked. Thus, consortia were supposed to serve the clients of the shareholders. In fact, however, much of their business came from invitations to participate in syndicates organized by other foreign banks and consortia.

The service capability could be exaggerated and often was, since the difficulty in communication between distant locations and among diverse shareholders led to delays and misunderstandings. Few of these consortia had established procedures for dealing with conflicting interests among shareholders. Neither did they have a clear idea of their long-range objectives. On occasions, the partners were not familiar with each other's potential for providing business or ability for combining resources in a consortium. Further problems arose over items such as the remuneration of executives and credit worthiness of borrowers.

It is difficult to generalize about consortia when in fact they have differed from each other in many respects, both in intention and practice. Nevertheless, while they have certainly been the mavericks they promised to be, they have also found themselves in severe difficulties.

As demand from American borrowers eased, reflecting the recession in the United States in 1972-1973, American bankers with high overhead expenses for prestigious offices in London and Paris were increasingly tempted to lend to lesser known borrowers where the spread was more attractive. The Penn Central debacle in 1971 put a temporary halt to this dangerous practice, but competition then forced banks into rate cutting as a means of "filling the books" of a bank's portfolio. In 1972-1973, international bankers universally decried this state of affairs while actively engaging in it as a necessary evil. By 1974 the evil had taken care of itself by the temporary halt in American banking expansion. The Federal Reserve system started insisting on higher capital adequacy ratios. With a depressed stock market, the only option open for remedying the problems was to halt the borrowing and, therefore, the lending.

The European Banking Response

The arrival of American banks in Europe led to the breakdown of the correspondent bank system. The American banks even began to compete for local clients in Europe, and for deposits on a small scale. As a response, European banks viewed the consortium movement as a more significant strategic trend than merely a convenient way of doing business together for a specific purpose. Banks found that the giant multinational companies now required the instant mobilization of huge sums of money in a great variety of currencies; they also expected one-stop service for all their banking needs. Although the consortia established by American and European banks were designed mainly to serve the Euro-currency markets and to provide a precedent for bank alliances, the groupings of Europe's largest banks had accepted a much broader mandate; their cooperation was expected to go beyond any individual project and their coordination was to involve broad areas of activity.

The commitment to undertake and solidify these special ties varied considerably from bank to bank, ranging from extra-strong correspondent relationships to agreements that fell just short of international mergers. Some of the associations had been carefully nurtured over long periods of time, while others appeared to have been thrown together rather quickly. There were three major partnerships of the extra-strength variety involving sixteen of Europe's largest banks: the EBIC Group, the CCB Group, and SFE (Societe Financiere Europeene). A fourth group, Orion, includes both European and non-European banks. Although many important fruits of group cooperation have yet to ripen, there have been some immediate and tangible advantages, such as access to a much broader branch network. This has been particularly important to banks like the Midland Bank in the United Kingdom and the German Big Three, which had virtually no overseas branches.

EURO-CURRENCY INSTRUMENTS

Euro-Dollar Deposits. The bulk of Euro-dollar deposits have a maturity of less than a year. Depositors in the Euro-dollar markets may have their funds in regular time deposits (which may be overnight, call money, or other accounts) or in certificates of deposit when these are larger amounts (over $100,000) with longer (three-six month) maturities. In contrast to the U. S. practice, the Euro-banks do not maintain demand deposits (checking accounts) for customers. Accordingly, when a Euro-dollar loan is made to a customer the loan usually takes the form of a cablegraphic transfer of funds from the bank's account in the United States to the borrower's account in whatever bank (s)he desires. No "demand deposit" in the borrower's name is created at all. Obviously, a certain amount of paperwork is generated to confirm the transactions that usually take place over the telex or via cable. In the Euro-dollar market, one is dealing with large amounts ($100,000 to begin with), and time is very important. The "float time" of a transfer of funds must be reduced to a minimum so that the owner of the funds does not lose sizable amounts of interest.

Negotiable certificates of deposits (CDs) for Euro-dollars were introduced in 1966. The bank allows the holder of a three-twelve months or longer deposit to remarket it, should that be desired. Some of these deposits are also formally designated as floating rate accounts; the interest paid on them will increase or decrease together with the interbank rates. In addition, the London market features "forward forward" CDs, by which a bank commits itself to issue a certificate of deposit in so many months for a certain duration for a particular present interest rate, usually based on a standard yield curve calculation. Thus, the bank may agree to a one-year certificate of deposit to be issued in six months. If the six-month rate is 9% and the eighteen-month rate is 10%, then the one-year CD to commence in six months would have a rate of around $10\frac{1}{2}\%$, so that the yield on the 9% CD for six months and the $10\frac{1}{2}\%$ CD for months seven through eighteen would average out to the same as the 10% for the spot eighteen-month CD.

Euro-Dollar Loans. Usually, Euro-loans range from a $500,000 base up to $100 million or more, typically in $1 million units. The median Euro-dollar loan is probably $5-$10 million. The usual maturity ranges from thirty days to five or seven years. Where the lender is known to the bank, loans of under twelve-months' maturity are often established quite easily. The lender will simply call to request a loan; if the rate and terms quoted by the bank are satisfactory the loan is immediately accepted. When a parent guarantee is required, as is sometimes the case for a foreign subsidiary requesting a loan, the guarantee can often be based on a telephone conversation. Confirming wires or letters are sent later.

The interest rates on Euro-dollar loans are often floating rates, especially for the intermediate and longer maturities (three years or longer). In contrast to the bank lending practice in the United States, European Euro-dollar lenders establish a rate at some fixed percentage over a given interbank lending rate, usually the London interbank offer rate (LIBO) at which they borrow a substantial part of their funds. This rate is the charge that banks make for loans to each other. Hence, the borrower may find a loan quoted at "1½% over LIBO, established at six-month intervals, until maturity." These floating rate revolving loans (also called "revolvers" or "roll-over credits") protect bank profits against increases in the interest rate on Euro-dollar deposits (the source of financing for the loan) such as might be induced by currency speculation or changes in yields on various currencies.

Some borrowers operate with lines of credit, which are usually given for a period not to exceed twelve months, but may be renegotiated at the end of the period. A commitment fee of ¼-½% may be placed on the unused portion of the line of credit. The rate on each take-down of the loan is established at the time of the take-down, and will typically be based on an interbank rate plus a previously set premium.

The rates for the loans to prime borrowers have ranged from LIBO + ¾% for seven-eight-year maturity to as little as LIBO + ⅜ % for a five-year maturity. Non-prime borrowers pay a higher spread of 2-3% depending on maturity and credit worthiness. Usually, there is no amortization of the loan, as is common in the United States; rather, the entire amount is repaid at the maturity date. The loan is also not secured except by the general credit of the firm, although there are often constraints on additional debt incurred by the firm. These factors and the rapidity with which a loan may be taken out are often major elements in the decision by U. S. corporations to prefer a Euro-dollar loan to a U. S. bank loan.

SIZE AND COUNTRY COMPOSITION OF THE EURO-CURRENCY MARKETS

Although the statistics are hard to verify because of doublecounting problems, one set of figures on the course of the Euro-currency markets is prepared by the Bank for International Settlements (BIS) from figures furnished by banks in eight major European countries. The growth in the gross measures of Euro-currencies and Euro-dollars is shown in Exhibit 13.1. With some of the double counting involved in interbank deposits eliminated, the Bank for International Settlements estimated that Euro-currency totaled $132 billion at the beginning of 1973. Euro-dollars were $97 billion of this total. These figures contrast with a total market size of less than $25 billion as recently as 1967. When the Euro-currency accounts in the Bahamas, Asia, and other areas were included, then the BIS estimated a total of $155 billion in Euro-currencies at the beginning of 1973.

The BIS figures give us only a partial view of the direction of the flows in the Euro-markets. Although only eight countries participate in the compilation of figures, one can still gain some insights into the direction of flow of funds in these markets. Exhibit 13.2 presents the asset and liability positions that the eight reporting countries maintained against various parties as of December 1973. However, notice that the total of these columns, $191 billion in liabilities, has not been adjusted for double counting involved in interbank transactions. The exhibit reports the position of the reporting countries against countries *not* included in the reporting system, "outside the area," and against countries included in the group of eight reporting countries "inside the area." The assets and liabilities that the reporting countries maintain against countries outside and inside the area have been broken down into

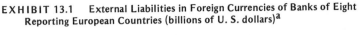

EXHIBIT 13.1   External Liabilities in Foreign Currencies of Banks of Eight
Reporting European Countries (billions of U. S. dollars)[a]

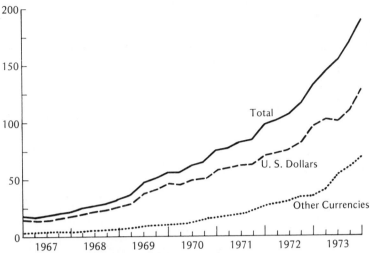

[a]The eight countries are Belgium, France, Italy, Germany, the Netherlands,
Sweden, Switzerland, and the United Kingdom.
          Source: Bank for International Settlements, *1973 Annual Report*, March 1974,
p. 158.

dollars and all other currencies. Finally, the last three columns show the net of assets minus liabilities of the reporting countries against the country in the first column. If assets are greater than liabilities, the reporting countries are net lenders to
the country in question. If liabilities are larger than assets, the reporting countries
are net borrowers of Euro-currencies from the country in question.

Exhibit 13.2 shows that the eight reporting countries, when dealing with
countries outside their area, were major net lenders of Euro-currencies to Eastern
Europe, Japan, the United States, and "other countries," and major borrowers of
Euro-currencies from Other Western European countries and the Middle East. The
flow of funds with Canada and Latin America tended to offset assets against liabilities, although the absolute amounts, particularly for Latin America, were sizable.
The bulk of these transactions were in Euro-dollars; however, one cannot fail to
notice sizable net amounts in other Euro-currencies when analyzing the funds flows
for "other Western Europe," the "Middle East," and "others."

For the eight countries as a group when dealing among themselves in Euro-currencies, Germany, Italy, and particularly the United Kingdom ($10.3 billion net
borrowings) appear as net borrowers of the system; in other words, the eight banks
as a group lent more to these countries than what they borrowed in Euro-currencies
from them. Among these eight countries the largest net supplier of Euro-currencies
was Switzerland. The other seven countries borrowed, net of loans, a total of $20.3
billion from Switzerland. For the other countries in the group—Belgium, France,
the Netherlands, and Sweden—the net flow was not substantial; although with the
exception of Sweden, the absolute amount of assets and liabilities in each case was
substantial. Euro-dollars tended to dominate the net positions of these countries

EXHIBIT 13.2 Foreign Currency Positions of Reporting European Banks Vis-à-Vis Nonresidents, December 1973
(billions of U. S. dollars)

Positions Vis-à-Vis	Assets			Liabilities			Net Position		
	Dollars	All Other Currencies	Total	Dollars	All Other Currencies	Total	Dollars	All Other Currencies	Total
Outside Area									
Other Western Europe	6.6	4.8	11.4	9.7	6.6	16.3	−3.1	−1.8	−4.9
Eastern Europe	4.9	2.9	7.8	1.9	2.4	4.3	+3.0	+0.5	+3.5
Canada	4.4	.7	5.1	5.7	.5	6.2	−1.3	+0.2	−1.1
Japan	7.5	.6	8.1	3.4	.1	3.5	+4.1	+0.5	+4.6
Latin America	10.3	1.0	11.3	10.3	1.5	11.8	−	−0.5	−0.5
Middle East	2.0	.5	2.5	6.0	3.9	9.9	−4.0	−3.4	−7.4
Other	17.0	3.7	20.7	11.4	4.7	16.1	+5.6	−1.0	+4.6
Total	52.7	14.2	66.9	48.4	19.7	68.1	+4.3	−5.5	−1.2
United States	13.8	.7	14.5	10.1	.5	10.6	+3.7	+0.2	+3.9
Total Outside Area	66.5	14.9	81.4	58.5	20.2	78.7	+8.0	−5.3	+2.7
Inside Area									
Belgium	5.7	5.4	11.1	6.5	4.1	10.6	0.8	+1.3	+0.5
France	11.1	5.3	16.4	11.2	5.2	16.4	−0.1	+0.1	−
Germany	3.4	9.4	12.8	3.6	4.4	8.0	−0.2	+5.0	+4.8
Italy	14.5	4.9	19.4	11.3	5.1	16.4	+3.2	−0.2	+3.0
Netherlands	3.8	2.9	6.7	5.0	3.0	8.0	−1.2	−0.1	−1.3
Sweden	.5	.7	1.2	.8	.4	1.2	−0.3	+0.3	−
Switzerland	4.6	2.9	7.5	16.1	11.6	27.7	−11.5	−8.7	−20.2
United Kingdom	23.7	7.9	31.6	15.0	6.3	21.3	+8.7	+1.6	+10.3
Total Inside Area	67.3	39.4	106.7	69.5	40.1	109.6	−2.2	−0.7	−2.9
Unallocated	−	.7	.7	2.6	.8	3.4	−2.6	−0.1	−2.7
Grand Total	133.8	55.0	188.8	130.6	61.1	191.7	+3.2	−6.1	−2.9

Sources: BIS, 1973 Annual Report, March 1974, p. 170

among themselves, with the exception of Germany, whose net borrowing position against the other seven countries is mostly in currencies other than dollars, and Switzerland, which also has large amounts of nondollar currencies in its net lending position to the group. The net borrowing positions of Italy and the United Kingdom were associated with the deficits in the balances of payments in these countries, and they represent positions which have been common in the past. The case of Germany is somewhat special, for the heavy concentration of German borrowings in currencies other than dollars, in the context of the exchange gyrations of 1973, suggests that the German government was supporting the exchange rates of those other currencies against the deutsche mark. This support was necessary because after the petroleum shortage had abated the American dollar emerged as a stronger currency in the last quarter of 1973, but this strengthening did not occur for the European currencies. In addition, the borrowings of Germany from the other seven countries in the group show some of the impact of the partial elimination in 1973 of capital controls that made it highly unprofitable for German residents to borrow abroad before then. The increased price of oil also necessitated the search for additional funds.

DETERMINANTS OF EURO-CURRENCY RATES

Most of the factors that are relevant in the determination of interest rates in Euro-currencies have been mentioned. To make the discussion more specific, the remainder of the chapter will concentrate on Euro-dollars.

From the lender's point of view, the individual always has the money market in the United States available as an alternative to a Euro-dollar deposit. Thus, the money market rates in the United States provide a floor for Euro-dollar rates. When the domestic rates go up, so do the Euro-dollar rates, and vice versa.[11]

From the final borrower's point of view, in the absence of regulations, the major difference between the local U. S. market and the Euro-dollar market is that commercial banks in the U. S. market usually require minimum compensating balances, which effectively raise the cost of funds borrowed, while Euro-loans do not require these balances to be kept with the bank. Therefore, the borrower is usually willing to pay a slightly higher interest rate on loans in the Euro-markets. This willingness to pay higher rates by final borrowers to the lender of funds is reinforced by the regulatory environment of Euro-banks. The absence of reserve requirements for the Euro-dollar banks makes these institutions capable of paying a higher rate on their dollar deposits than banks operating in the U. S. money market. Thus, both

---

[11] This ignores U. S. withholding income tax on income paid to foreigners. This tax will tend to push Euro-dollar rates below the level of rates in the U. S. money market. However, deposits in commercial banks have been exempted from this tax since 1966 (Public Law 89-809, Sec. 102). This law exempts bank depositors from U. S. withholding tax as long as the foreign owner is not engaged in business in the United States and uses the proceeds outside the United States. The exemption was initially issued for a limited amount of time but it has continued to be renewed every time that its expiration date has approached.

In principle, the proceeds from Euro-dollar deposits should also be subject to income tax in the country of residence of the deposit owner. However, in practice this is rarely the case since the name of the owner of the deposit is not reported to the country of the owner's residence and the depositor usually turns out to be remiss to declare it for tax purposes.

the financial intermediaries and the final borrowers of funds in the Euro-dollar market tend to provide Euro-dollar rates with a spread over domestic rates.

Exhibit 13.3 compares rates on sixty- to eighty-nine-day certificates of deposit (CDs) in the United States with Euro-dollar rates for similar maturity. Throughout the period presented in the chart the CD rate has provided an effective floor to the Euro-dollar rate, which has remained consistently above the CD rate.

Having established that U. S. rates provide a floor to Euro-dollar rates and that the latter tend to maintain a spread over the former, the next question is "What determines the fluctuations in the size of the spread of Euro-dollar rates over U. S. rates?" The bottom line in Exhibit 13.3 shows the spread between the two rates after accounting for reserve requirements on CDs. Two types of institutional factors appear to account for the fluctuations in the spread between domestic and Euro-dollar rates. The first involves the regulations of the United States on its banking

EXHIBIT 13.3   Euro-Dollar and Domestic U. S. Rates Compared

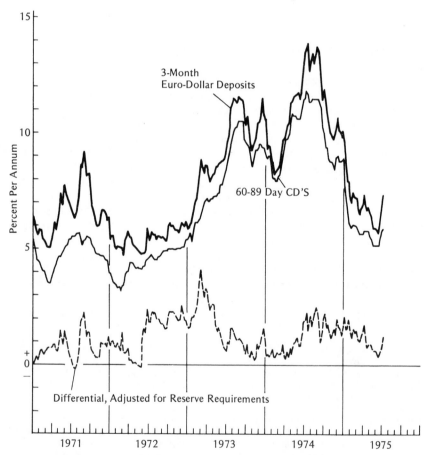

Source: Board of Governors of the Federal Reserve System, Division of International Finance, *Selected Interest and Exchange Rates*, Nov. 4, 1974.

system and on international capital outflows. Formerly, the banking system regulations that most affected the Euro-dollar rates were Regulations Q and M. Regulation Q, by imposing ceilings on the rates that U. S. commercial banks could pay on deposits, converted the Euro-dollar market into a buffer market where commercial banks went to raise funds whenever these funds could not be secured in the domestic markets. Regulation M, as mentioned before, made the use of the Euro-markets more profitable because the funds raised were not subject to the same reserve requirements as the domestic funds. Because of changes in the regulations, these forces no longer affect the markets. The ceilings imposed by Regulation Q were lifted in 1973 and Euro-dollar borrowings became subject to reserve requirements in 1969. The regulations designed to control capital outflows from the United States were also eliminated in January 1974. These regulations effectively segmented the domestic and the Euro-markets to the extent that domestic funds could not be used to finance foreign operations. During the existence of the controls on the U. S. balance of payments, any time that foreigners or expanding U. S. businesses abroad increased their demand for funds over and above the capacities of foreign domestic markets, the major alternative available for raising the needed funds was the Euro-dollar market. Therefore, there was an upward bias imparted to the Euro-dollar rates over the U. S. domestic rates.

With the elimination of the controls to protect the U. S. balance of payments in early 1974, and the changes in the other relevant regulations for U. S. banking before then, it was expected that the spreads between Euro-dollar rates and U. S. domestic rates would narrow substantially or disappear. The only justification left for a spread appeared to be "sovereign risk." Some lenders might prefer to keep their dollar deposits in the United States rather than in London where they might become subject to confiscation. Obviously, this risk could work both ways. However, large spreads of Euro-rates over domestic U. S. rates prevailed and even increased. This pointed to another set of institutional factors that, although in existence before, had a larger visibility after 1974: foreign exchange market instability.

In the past, every time there was an international monetary crisis involving speculation on the depreciation of the U. S. dollar against other major currencies, the spread of Euro-dollar rates over U. S. domestic rates widened. In the presence of controls on capital outflows from the United States, the borrowing of dollars to finance the purchase of so-called "harder currencies" could be made only in the Euro-dollar market; therefore, there was an increase in rates in that market. But with the disappearance of the controls on capital outflows from the United States, another cause of the inaccessibility of domestic U. S. markets to foreigners appeared. The tight monetary policy that prevailed in the United States during most of 1974 made this market unavailable for financing many operations in the domestic market and certainly for financing foreign financial speculation. Any time that the market estimated the U. S. dollar to be weakening, the borrowings necessary to profit from such an expectation had to be made in the Euro-dollar market, thus bidding up the rates in that market relative to the U. S. domestic market.

Another factor that appeared in 1974 was the scare of a collapse in the Euro-dollar market engendered by the insolvency of banks such as Herstat and Franklin. These scares added a further upward pressure to Euro-rates in 1974 as funds were diverted from the Euro-market into the domestic U. S. money market and invested in government securities.

By 1975 the strengthening of the U. S. dollar against other major currencies and larger confidence in the Euro-currency markets had brought down the interest differential between Euro-dollars and CDs.

THE FUTURE OF THE EURO-DOLLAR MARKET

Much of the impetus for the market came from U. S. regulatory policies in 1969 and the credit squeeze. A greater stimulus came from the free convertibility of European currencies into dollars and the general reserve status of the dollar, which meant fewer controls on the exchange of this currency. A movement of dollar deposits from the United States, a desire to hold liquid funds in dollars (because of rate differentials vis-à-vis other currencies or freedom from exchange controls), and a general increase in world liquidity all contributed to the growth of the Euro-dollar accounts. When one reviews these factors in terms of the future, one cannot be sure of the trends. A major question will be whether the diversion of funds to the Arab oil producers will result in purchases by them in the United States, loans to Europeans, or something else. The question is whether they will deposit the funds in Euro-dollar banks (which then relend them) or whether they will choose to make direct loans, buying commercial paper or the like. The former case will increase Euro-dollars. The latter case bypasses the Euro-banks and will not increase the Euro-dollar totals on the first step.

An additional source of change which probably will alter the Euro-dollar market to some degree is the decision by some banks to offer deposit and loan commitments in terms of Special Drawing Rights. Although the interest rate on deposits is lower than that for a dollar account, the SDR account provides the depositor with the option of repayment in any of the 16 currencies involved, with the value based on the SDR appreciation or depreciation from the time of commitment. Loan interest is apparently paid in dollars. Whether the banks (pioneered by Chase Manhattan) will make loans in excess of deposit balances in SDRs is unclear.

Exercises on the Euro-Dollar Market

The following transactions are designed to follow the path of some of the flows that take place in the Euro-dollar market. A series of "T-accounts" with initial balances has been provided to facilitate following the transactions described below.

Assume: 1. All foreigners keep their balances in the United States with the Chase Manhattan Bank.

2. All banks keep 10% of their deposits in reserves.

At the end of each transaction determine what is the impact on:
1. Each of the parties involved.
2. The U. S. money supply.
3. The U. S. balance of payments on the liquidity basis and on the official transactions basis.
4. The money supply of each foreign country involved.
5. The balance of payments of each foreign country involved.

Transaction No. 1. The German Central Bank, which maintains part of its foreign exchange reserve in the form of treasury bills, decides to sell $100 worth of treasury bills to Mr. Smith, an American resident. Mr. Smith pays with a check drawn on his account with Chase Manhattan.

Transaction No. 2. The German Central Bank transfers its deposits to a German commercial bank. (Sometimes this is done as part of domestic monetary policy in which case the Central Bank exchanges dollar deposits for deutsche marks with the commercial banks. The objective is to reduce credit in the domestic market and give incentives for capital outflows.

Transaction No. 3. A French importer asks for a Euro-loan from the German commercial bank. Assuming that the commercial bank keeps a precautionary reserve of 10%, it can make a loan in the amount of $90.

Transaction No. 4. The French importer uses the Euro-loan to pay a debt owed to a German exporter.

Transaction No. 5. The German exporter deposits its dollar balances with the German commercial bank.

Transaction No. 6. Citibank wishes to borrow Euro-dollars from the German commercial bank to take care of anticipated loan demand.

Transaction No. 7. Citibank wishes to make a loan. In order to convert the deposit at Chase into lendable funds it asks Chase to provide cash or deposits with the Federal Reserve Bank. Since Chase was fully loaned-up, it has to sell some loans in order to collect the required amount of cash.

Chase Manhattan Bank

Cash	10	Demand Deposit, Smith	100
Loans	90		

German Central Bank

Foreign Exchange	1000	Liabilities	1000

German Commercial Bank

Cash	10	Deposits	100
Loans	90		

French Importer

Inventory	90	Accounts Payable	90

German Exporter

Accounts Receivable	90	Equity	90

Citibank

| Cash | 10 | Demand Deposit | 100 |
| Loans | 90 | | |

Bibliography

Altman, Oscar L., "Euro-Dollars." *Finance and Development,* March 1967.

Bank for International Settlements, *Annual Report,* 1973.

Bell, Geoffrey, *The Euro-Dollar Market and the International Financial System.* New York: Halsted Press/John Wiley and Sons, 1973.

Einzig, Paul, *The Euro-Dollar System.* 5th Ed. New York: St. Martin's Press, 1973.

———, *Parallel Money Markets.* Two Vols. London: Macmillan/St. Martin's Press, 1971 and 1972.

Ferris, Paul, "The Multi-Banks of Europe: A Dramatic Experiment." *Worldwide P and I Planning,* May-June 1971, pp. 20-27.

Friedman, Milton, "The Euro-Dollar Market: Some First Principles." *The Morgan Guaranty Survey,* Oct. 1969, pp. 1-11.

Hendershott, Patrick H., "The Structure of International Interest Rates: The U. S. Treasury Bill Rate and the Eurodollar Deposit Rate." *Journal of Finance,* Sept. 1967, pp. 455-465.

Hinshaw, Randall, "The Euro-Dollar Market: A Comment." *Journal of Money, Credit and Banking,* Aug. 1972, pp. 688-690.

Klopstock, Fred H., "Money Creation in the Euro-Dollar Market—A Note on Professor Friedman's Views." *Monthly Review,* Jan. 1970, Federal Reserve Bank of New York, pp. 12-15.

———, *The Euro-Dollar Market: Some Unresolved Issues.* Princeton, N. J.: Princeton University, March 1968.

Kwack, Sung Y., "The Structure of International Interest Rates: An Extension of Hendershott's Tests." *Journal of Finance,* Sept. 1971, pp. 897-900.

Little, Jane Sneddon, "The Euro-Dollar Market: Its Nature and Impact," *New England Economic Review,* Federal Reserve Bank of Boston, May-June 1969, pp. 2-31.

———, *Euro-Dollars: The Money Market Gypsies.* New York: Harper and Row, Inc., 1975.

———, "The Impact of the Euro-Dollar Market on the Effectiveness of Monetary Policy in the United States and Abroad." *New England Economic Review,* Federal Reserve Bank of Boston, Mar.-Apr., 1975, pp. 3-19.

Mayer, Helmut W., "Some Theoretical Problems Relating to the Euro-Dollar Market." *Essays in International Finance,* No. 79. Princeton, N. J.: Princeton University, 1970.

Mikesell, Raymond F., "The Euro-Dollar Market and the Foreign Demand for Liquid Dollar Assets." *Journal of Money, Credit and Banking,* Aug. 1972, pp. 643-683.

Potter, David R. W., "The London Dollar CD—Liquid Tool for International Cash Management," *Columbia Journal of World Business,* Summer 1973, pp. 5-10.

Rich, Georg, "A Theoretical and Empirical Analysis of the Euro-Dollar Market." *Journal of Money, Credit and Banking,* Aug. 1972, pp. 617-635.

Stem, Carl H., "The Euro-Dollar Market and the Foreign Demand for Liquid Dollar Assets: A Comment." *Journal of Money, Credit and Banking,* Aug. 1972, pp. 691-703.

Thackeray, John, "Brains vs. Muscle: International Banking's European Free-For-All." *Corporate Financing,* Jan.-Feb. 1972, pp. 35-42, 64.

Appendix: Multiple Creation of Euro-Dollars and the Impact of This Market on the U. S. Balance of Payments and the Money Supply

Chapter 13 has illustrated how Euro-dollars can be created in a multiple fashion. This raised a series of questions which will be addressed in this appendix.

FRACTIONAL RESERVES AS THE "SOURCE" OF EURO-DOLLARS?

The example showed how the Euro-dollars can be expanded, but the more relevant question is, "*Are* they created in this way?" There can be leakages from the system. The creation of a reserve is one leak; if there were no reserves (and foreign banks in most cases are *not* required to have *any* reserves to back their Euro-dollar deposits) then the theoretical expansion of Euro-dollar deposits from a $1,000,000 deposit by the Arab sheik is infinite.

In the United States, with a closed banking system, there is a very large impact from the creation of an autonomous deposit. All funds usually end up in a bank. Purchase of shares in a mutual fund will mean the fund deposits the cash in a bank, or buys shares in corporate stock from individuals who deposit their funds in a bank. An individual who buys newly issued stock from a corporation will see the check used ultimately to pay suppliers for goods, to purchase a new plant for the corporation, or to carry out some other project. Again the recipient probably will deposit the funds in a bank at some point.

However, for the Euro-dollar to multiply, the funds must *not* come back to the U. S. banking system. Thus, if anyone chooses to buy goods from a corporation which deposits the funds in (say) a California bank, then the Euro-dollar expansion from the sheik's original $1,000,000 deposit ends. In our example, assume the Swedish bank's borrower used the dollar loan to pay an American firm, and that firm deposited the funds in the Chase Manhattan Bank. Euro-dollar deposits at the end of the period would thus be only the $1,000,000 in the sheik's account and the $900,000 in the Swedish supplier's account. Hence, in this case the effective multiplier on the original $1,000,000 creation is only 1.9 ($1,900,000/$1,000,000).

If the multiplier is fairly low, then for practical purposes the European banks resemble our savings and loan associations which cannot create money, for the funds they lend from depositors' accounts typically do not come back to them anywhere in the system. Rather, the funds likely end up in the bank accounts of the suppliers, carpenters, and others associated with the home. Some small amount may come to the savings and loan association, but the bulk of the funds "created" by the new mortgage does not.

Some people have referred to the loan-creation and money-creation possibilities of banks in a fractional reserve system (including the Euro-dollar system) as the creation of money by "a bookkeeper's pen." However, those observers who believe the multiplier in the Euro-dollar market is low note that the "pen runs out of ink very quickly." The question is not the theoretical expansion of the Euro-dollars but the actual one, and the evidence cited by most scholars indicates that the multiplier is fairly low. The great problem is that, unlike the American banking system, the Euro-bank system is not closed. Too much money returns to businesses who deposit it outside the system. They may be banks in other lands who turn the dollars over to their central bank in exchange for reserves. This central bank (or the foreign exchange trader to whom the local bank had gone for currency) may then deposit it in the United States. Other entities who return the funds are corporations who deposit the funds in their American bank.

If the funds are deposited with the foreign branches of American banks, the funds are usually returned to this country. Latin American banks or banks in other lands may want the dollars for loans to their customers, who use these funds to pay their American suppliers. In either case, the money has lost its immediate potential to expand the Euro-dollar accounts.

Fred Klopstock estimated that about 30-40% of the Euro-dollar deposits were created by the multiplier.[1] Thus, the leakages of dollars from the system and the existence of reserves in some cases appear to defeat the rapid expansion shown as theoretically possible.

Where, then, has the sharp increase in Euro-dollars come from? For the most part, it has resulted from a drain of local dollar reserves from banks and the public (citizens and corporations) throughout the world. By competing on the basis of rates and services, the European banks have attracted dollars. In some cases, firms have converted other currencies to dollars to take advantage of the Euro-dollar rates. This process uses dollars which are in Europe, perhaps as a result of the huge commitments of the United States after World War II, or as a result of the more recent payment deficits.

The previous paragraph points up two important facts about the use of the dollar as an international currency: (1) the Euro-dollar market has been created by

---

[1] For bibliographical references in this appendix see bibliography to this chapter.

U. S. balance payments deficits (from either trade or massive transfer of capital from the United States abroad), and (2) Euro-dollars and the corresponding U. S. payments deficits are necessary under the present system to provide liquidity in the form of a common monetary base for the expansion of world business.

EURO-DOLLARS AND THE U. S. DEFICIT IN THE BALANCE OF PAYMENTS

Theoretically, there is certainly no need for the United States to have a deficit in order for Euro-dollars to grow. Any person (other than a resident American) owning dollars who wishes to switch them to a non-U. S. bank creates a Euro-dollar. However, the ultimate growth of the U. S. payments deficit helped create the rapid expansion in Euro-dollars.

In 1958, most of the European countries had made their currencies freely convertible into the dollar, and that made the dollar useful to many firms and individuals as a liquid account. The movement by central banks in the early 1960s to earn higher rates of interest on their dollars than American banks were permitted to pay under Regulation Q pulled funds into Euro-dollars.

In addition, there is also speculation that the flow of U. S. funds abroad stimulated much of the interest in the Euro-dollars. For example, the soaring price of oil meant many U. S. dollars went to the Mideast, and many of these dollars no doubt found their way into the Euro-dollar markets. Furthermore, prior to 1969, the American banks had a great interest in seeing customers take their dollar deposits from the United States to their European branches because of the reserve requirements discussed earlier. Hence, the American firm requesting a loan may have learned that the compensating balances should be kept by the subsidiary in London at the London branch of the American bank.

Ultimately the question pivots on what was the Euro-dollar deposit replacing and where did the Euro-dollars go? Mikesell (1972) highlights two different sources and two different uses of Euro-dollars:

Type A sources are net additional foreign nonofficial (i.e., noncentral bank) demands for liquid dollar assets. This source excludes a shift from American dollars to Euro-dollars by nonofficial sources as well as foreign official Euro-dollar deposits.

Type B sources are deposits which would otherwise have been held in American banks by foreign nonofficials.

Type X uses are borrowings by U. S. residents or nonresidents which supply a nonofficial foreign demand for dollars which would not have been met from other non-U. S. sources.

Type Y uses are borrowings by U. S. residents or residents of foreign countries which represent a substitute for other foreign dollar credits, or which represent borrowings by non-U. S. residents for nondollar financing.

The effect of these sources and uses depends on the combinations which are involved. To focus on the foreign nonofficial holdings of American dollars (i.e., the claims on the U. S. dollar by institutions other than central banks), then Type A sources and Type X uses in combination tend to increase foreign nonofficial hold-ings of dollars. The other two combinations tend to have neutral effects on the for-eign nonofficial holdings of dollars.

Although the empirical tests Mikesell uses are not without problems, he generally concludes that the basic increase in Euro-dollars is associated with an improvement in the official reserves transaction balance of payments of the United States. That is, the balance in the above combinations favored a pattern in which the account of desired dollar claims was positive. In addition, he found that increased U. S. dollar borrowing in the Euro-dollar market was associated with an improvement in the basic balance. Finally, he noted that these two conclusions were not dependent on the contributions of U. S. residents; i.e., the shifting of the resident's deposit to a foreign bank. That is, the favorable effect of the U. S. dollar borrowings and the increase of the Euro-dollars on the balance of payments was truly independent of the contribution made by the increase in Euro-dollars generated by United States residents. He found also that the bulk of the non-U. S. sources were Type A; that is, they were substitutes for holding liquid assets in nondollar currencies, or they were dollar deposits of foreign official agencies; they were not Type B sources.

The ultimate effect of the increase in Euro-dollars on the current account or the long-term capital account of the United States might take several forms. The availability of dollar credits to foreign importers might increase U. S. exports. Greater international liquidity in general might have an ultimately favorable effect on U. S. exports. Some purchasers of American corporations' Euro-bonds may have raised their dollars for this purpose by Euro-dollar loans. On the other hand U. S. borrowings from the Euro-dollar accounts hurt the current account because of in-terest payments on those borrowings. In addition, because of the freedom from exchange controls and restrictions, it is likely that the Euro-dollar market con-tributed to the speculation against the dollar in favor of stronger currencies in 1970-1972. Speculators borrowed dollars to purchase harder currencies with the expecta-tion of the devaluation. The Euro-dollar market facilitates this activity.

EURO-DOLLARS AND THE MONEY SUPPLY

Much of the growth in Euro-dollar accounts in 1966 and 1969 came with the desire of U. S. banks to skirt restrictions on the amount they could pay for funds in order to obtain money for loans to customers. As a result, these banks borrowed from their own branches and from other Euro-banks in massive amounts in 1969 and 1970 as we noted. Between January 1969 and August 1970, the amount bor-rowed from the branches rose from $7 billion to over $15 billion. By December 1971, this amount was back to less than $1 billion, largely because of the change in the reserve calculations, the high rate on Euro-dollars vis-à-vis domestic sources, and the easing of interest rates in the United States.

This violent swing in the demand for Euro-dollars was reflected in the widening of the spread in the Euro-dollar rates versus domestic rates. Typically, the difference paid on deposits had been around 1-2%. With the ceiling on U. S. rates, however, the spread between the rate on ninety-day Euro-dollar deposits versus three-month certificates of deposit rose beyond 3%, and the spread peaked in mid-1969 at $6^1/4\%$ for U. S. CD's (the Regulation Q ceiling) versus 11% in the ninety-day Euro-dollar market.

Naturally, such an expansion of demand for Euro-dollars spilled over into the cost for other funds. Hence, European central banks began to resent the policies of the U. S. Federal Reserve Board which induced the U. S. banks to escape those Fed rules by Euro-dollar activities. The Board action in the Euro-dollar market lessened the effectiveness of European central bank monetary policy.

This demonstrates the basic complicating effect of Euro-dollars on a nation's monetary supply and policies. Transfers from one Euro-dollar holder to another do not change the U. S. money supply. However, while the movement of dollars accounts (or any other currency) already outside the nation's borders does not affect that nation's money supply directly, the multiplier effects of redepositing can expand total *world* money supply which has effects on every nation's credits, costs, prices, and output. The extent of this impact depends on the size of leakages from the system which, as explained before, are considered to be large.

Likewise, there may also be differences in domestic reserve requirements: liabilities to other banks may have different reserve requirements than deposits held by non-banking sources (as was the situation in the United States prior to October 1969). Furthermore, different time deposit reserve requirements in various nations (for example, the U. S. banks have reserve standards whereas the Euro-dollar banks have no technical reserve requirements) can have dramatic effects on the total world supply of credit.

Citicorp Leasing International, Inc.

Citicorp Leasing International, Inc., (CLI) is a Delaware corporation and a wholly owned subsidiary of the First National City Corporation (FNCC)– the parent company to the First National City Bank of New York (FNCB).

CLI began operations in late 1969 with a staff of three people located in London. In July 1971, top management decided that a period of reevaluation was due. Events had been taking place at too fast a speed for CLI's management to be fully aware of their implications. There were five specific areas that CLI wished to consider more closely: (1) its borrowing policy in the Euro-dollar markets, (2) the future of the Euro-dollar markets, (3) its foreign exchange management policy, (4) the future of international leasing, and (5) relationships with the parent corporation and with Citibank in particular.

INTERNATIONAL LEASING

Leasing is usually transacted by a national company operating within the boundaries of one country's tax, legal, and commercial environment. Such companies operating in the local indigenous market tend to concentrate on the middle-market equipment and/or small-ticket market.[1] Their financial packages, patterns, and lease

---

[1] The industry generally defines a small ticket to be less than $50,000 value, the middle market to be from $50,000 to $1,000,000, and big tickets to cost over $1,000,000.

agreements are quite standardized. On the other hand, an international leasing company will usually reside in a different country from the lessee. It will, in many ways, be more typical of an equipment finance company than a leasing company. The finance packages offered will range from a true lease to a chattel mortgage, depending on the needs of the customer. In all cases, the transactions are very specialized and generally limited to large-ticket equipment. The complexity frequently requires establishing a "shell corporation" specifically for the purposes of the transaction.

Government Policies

For international transactions, exchange control regulations and tax treaties are of critical importance. Juggling a transaction between countries with different tax and legal requirements gives considerable flexibility to the lessor and lessee.

If a country has exchange controls, the central bank will usually favor a request by a domestic company to finance equipment in a foreign currency either by means of a lease or by borrowing.

Because of international tax disparities, the structuring of a lease involving two countries with favorable tax treaties can result in significant savings to the lessee. An example is the treaty between the United States and Australia versus the United Kingdom and Australia. Unlike the U. S.-Australia treaty, the U. K.-Australia treaty provides for no withholding taxes on lease payment to the U. K. leasing company. Packaging a lease with the lessor in the United Kingdom rather than the United States frees those funds that might be withheld.

International leasing may offer flexibility in the currency of a lease transaction which is priced according to the interest rates of the particular currency. For example, a lessee has the option to select lease payments in dollars or another currency, therefore taking a position on interest rates and foreign exchange rates.

An international leasing company is able to take immediate advantages of favorable depreciation schedules in different countries. For example, the United Kingdom allows 100% write-off the first year for a ship while Canada provides 40% declining balance. When leasing to a U. K. ship owner who cannot utilize such favorable depreciation allowances, the company can arrange for the lessor to be one who can fully utilize the government's incentive and pass portions of the benefits on to the lessee in the form of lower finance charges.

Another advantage of an international leasing company is the ability to structure a transaction so as to take advantage of legal regulations regarding the depreciation of the equipment which may differ between countries. Such an example is the case when the lessee has an option to purchase the equipment upon termination of the lease at a price considered to be "the fair market value." In the United States, such a contract is considered a true lease providing the lessor with depreciation. In the United Kingdom, the same contract would be considered a hire-purchase or conditional sale, thus providing depreciation to the lessee. Being able to take advantage of situations which are treated differently in two countries is the primary function and challenge of an international leasing company.

Balance of payments considerations and regulations affect an international leasing company to the extent that its transactions with foreign companies involve international capital movement. For example, a weakening of the U. S. balance of payments resulted in the Voluntary Credit Restraint Program, the Controls on Foreign Direct Investment Program, and the Interest Equalization Tax. Such measures restricted the ability of U. S. financial companies to funnel dollars to overseas markets. To provide funds to overseas companies meant using offshore funds, in particular Euro-dollars. This forced U. S.-incorporated international leasing companies to fund their transactions primarily with offshore funds. Recently revised regulations have excluded from regulation the financing of U. S. exports with U. S. domestic funds. The effect of this might be more U. S.-financed international lease transactions, resulting in a capital outflow from the United States and an alternative source of funds for the leasing companies.

The Market

The U. S. National Planning Association estimates that during 1971, $11.3 billion worth of equipment was placed on lease in the United States alone: $7.9 billion was leased by the manufacturers of equipment and the balance, $3.4 billion, by third party lessors, independent leasing companies, and financial institutions. It is estimated that outside of the United States, $2 billion worth of equipment was placed on lease by third party lessors in 1971. The third party lessor market outside of the United States is estimated to be growing at the rate of 20% per year.

In terms of cumulative book value of equipment placed on lease, the entire world market is estimated at $120 billion, one half of which is in the United States. Most of this value is equipment placed on lease by manufacturers.

Of the equipment placed on lease by third party lessors outside of the United States, nearly one half is believed to be large-ticket and middle-market equipment. Excluding the United States, Europe is the largest single geographical area for leasing in the world market. Leasing activity in less developed countries is usually not extensive and for the most part is confined to small-ticket items.

The competition to an international leasing company is primarily the equipment manufacturers' own leasing programs and other forms of financing provided by commercial and merchant banks, mostly U. K. merchant banks. In contrast to domestic leasing, which in most developed countries is intensely competitive, few leasing companies compete on an international basis. Those that do tend to concentrate either in small- to medium-ticket items or else in large-ticket items. Even though several of the large international leasing companies have the skills necessary to handle complex international transactions, there is little competition for particular deals. This is due both to the specialization in the type of client each leasing company deals with and to the time required to negotiate a particular transaction— often from four months to a year.

CLI OPERATIONS

Leasing Operations

CLI is the largest truly international leasing company in the world. It operates in the medium- to long-term leasing markets (financings of between three and fifteen years) and its transactions cover the full range of capital equipment. CLI's lessees are concentrated in the manufacturing and transportation industries. Although a wide variety of equipment is leased, the major emphasis is on medium- to large-ticket items. The company holds a lead position in the European and the Canadian computer leasing markets and it has opened major international markets in aircraft and ship financing.

Even though CLI handles all types of leases, the company engages primarily in direct equipment leasing involving "noncancellable full-payout net finance leases." In this type of lease the total rent payable under each full-payout lease is calculated to return to the company the cost of the equipment, plus a lease charge which covers all direct expenses, overhead, and profit to the company. The lessee is required usually to pay local taxes, license fees, and insurance, and to maintain and repair the equipment.

Leasing business is developed by direct solicitation of lessees through CLI's own sales force, by arrangements with manufacturers and vendors of equipment and by referrals to the company by banks and others involved in advising industry on equipment financing programs.

CLI's management attributes its success to three major factors: (1) the relationships with multinational companies which the affiliate bank, FNCB, provided, (2) the dynamic management group which has realized the opportunities available in the industry, and (3) the growth of the industry in general. This growth in the industry has been largely the result of the leasing companies' efforts to educate potential clients to the advantages of leasing. Financial statements for the company are presented in Exhibits 1 and 2. Exhibit 3 presents selected financial statistics for CLI and some other U. S. leasing companies.

Organization

FNCC operates two independent leasing companies: Citicorp Leasing, Inc., which deals only with the U. S. market, and CLI, which handles only foreign transactions.

CLI's head office is located in London where a staff specialized in the various aspects of the business offers support to offices located throughout the world. Operations are organized on a geographical basis. Regional offices are maintained in London, New York, and Tokyo, each led by a vice-president with general line responsibilities. Each of these regional offices is responsible for the region's local vehicles (branches, and fully owned subsidiaries of CLI) located in various countries within the region. Throughout the organization, CLI's management is in the hands of a team of enterprising young specialists, most of whom are in their late twenties and early thirties.

CLI's head office in London is responsible for developing broad strategies and priorities for the whole company as well as for executing some specific operating tasks. In the matter of soliciting leasing business, the head office does a considerable amount of solicitation of large-ticket international leasing. In addition, the head office processes the extension of credit to the lessees for each lease transaction that the regional or local offices have arranged. This credit processing is done in conformity to FNCC guidelines and policies. The head office is in charge of providing financing for nearly all large-ticket and international transactions. In addition, the head office also provides financing for some of the smaller-ticket items leased at the local level when the local office cannot obtain as favorable financing terms as CLI itself. Finally the head office has to give final approval for every lease transaction arranged by any of CLI's branches or subsidiaries, even when the local unit arranges both the leasing transaction and its financing.

The three regional offices each have a vice-president who is supported by a small staff of specialists. The functions of the regional office are to develop strategies for the countries within the region in accordance with the guidelines given at the head office, and to supervise the activities and financing arrangements of the branches and subsidiaries under its authority. In addition to these functions, the regional office concentrates on the solicitation of international leasing business that the local office cannot handle.

Local offices are staffed by a branch manager and by a number of accounting and marketing people sufficient to handle the particular country's market. The primary activities of the local office are the solicitation and the administration of small-ticket leases within the particular country. It also arranges local financing when the terms are favorable. In addition to these functions, the office is responsible for planning within its country and for coordinating these plans with the regional office.

Planning and Control

Corporate Strategy. The strategy that CLI has followed in the past two years has been one of opening offices in major financial centers (London, Tokyo, and New York), and in places where Citibank's banking experience appeared to indicate a potentially prosperous market. The function of each of these offices is to generate as much leasing business as possible. The only constraints imposed by the corporate level on these endeavors are the credit risks of the lessee (which are usually "prime credit risks"), and the requirement of arranging financing and lease repayments in the same currency. These constraints work to make the large multinational and national companies the primary potential customers of CLI. These customers quite often have access to the same terms and sources of funds as CLI.

The affiliation of CLI with Citibank has proven to be extremely helpful in obtaining an initial feel for potential markets throughout the world. After opening an office in a country, this relationship also provides access to the prime customers of the bank. On many occasions, the bank itself has referred customers interested in international leasing to CLI.

Given this favorable initial assignment, the major problem that CLI has encountered in tapping the market has been the tax and legal institutions of various countries. Particularly in the case of developing countries, this fact has meant on some occasions that a considerable amount of time has been spent in working with the government to develop previously nonexistent leasing regulations. In the case of developed countries, the major limitation has been the finding of customers where a mutually advantageous contract can be formulated.

The Budget. Each branch, each region, and each specialized marketing group at the head office—such as aircraft, shipping, and so on—is a profit center of CLI. As such, each develops a yearly budget and a five-year plan. The budgeting process requires estimates regarding the size of the market, the market share, the types of equipment that are expected to be leased (large-ticket, small-ticket, etc.), terms of the leases, tax treatment, and average cost of funds.

The final budget that CLI submits to FNCC is the result of a summary consolidation of budgets prepared by each profit center. This budget is then submitted to the board of directors of FNCC. The approved budget becomes the basis on which capital and human resources are deployed. In terms of capital, this means contributions of FNCC to CLI's capital, and CLI contributions to the local subsidiaries' capital. In terms of human resources, the budget indicates the personnel to be maintained at each budget center. This final budget becomes an informal instrument of performance evaluation.

Financial Management

The final decision as to the sources, terms, and rates of borrowings necessary to fund the leasing operation is made at the head office on the recommendation of the vice-president of finance. In addition to providing the funds for international leases, the office of the vice-president of finance serves as a source of financial information for the rest of the company. It gathers and interprets a substantial amount of economic data which is used in evaluating alternative sources of funds and in forecasting funding requirements and interest rates at various company levels. This office also serves as a monitor of other financial activities. It supervises cash management and liquidity of each of the company's units, and it develops and implements policies for intercompany transactions.

It is the policy of the company not to take a position in the foreign exchange market. Generally, the borrowings to finance a lease transaction and the lease repayments are denominated in the same currency. In the case of international leases, the U. S. dollar is the most common currency in which leases and borrowings are denominated. Local subsidiaries will usually denominate the lease of small-ticket items in the local currency and finance the lease with local funds.

In the past, it has been the company's policy to match the maturity of fixed rate leases with the maturity of fixed rate borrowings. In the case of floating rate leases, the maturity of the borrowings is fixed for an intermediate period—usually six months—during which time the rate in the lease is fixed. The objective of this policy is to guarantee a profitable spread. However, a large proportion of the leases the company has made are on a fixed rate basis. The average maturity of the leases is eight to ten years.

In spite of the overall policy of matching maturities of leases and borrowings, during 1971 the company made the decision to finance most of its fund requirements with short-term money. Taking into consideration on one hand the large percentage of total costs that interest represents and on the other hand the existing relationship between short- and long-term rates and their projections for the future, the company decided it would be profitable to take advantage of this opportunity. Schedules of debt repayments both due within a year and due in more than a year are presented in Exhibit 4. The rates obtained on these borrowings were the rates available to the "best" borrowers in the market at the time. These rates were available on the credit of CLI itself. Though CLI might realize some possible advantages because of its affiliation with FNCC, by and large borrowings were arranged without guarantees. For recent Euro-dollar rates, see Exhibit 5.

Under the existing organization. the vice-president of finance is the person who gathers and analyzes economic data, and who also makes the actual daily borrowing decisions. This arrangement was made on the basis that the combination of the jobs of analyzing information and of setting the borrowing policies allows the person in charge to have a complete picture of the total market and a greater flexibility in reacting quickly to changes in the environment.

EURO-DOLLAR MARKETS

Recent Market Behavior

Euro-Bond Market. The vice-president of finance felt that the general lull in activity in the new Euro-bond issues in July would help the tone in that market and would probably bring rates down somewhat. Only ten issues were expected for July, five of which were in U. S. dollars. It was expected that the amount raised in the long-term Euro-markets in July would be $180 million as compared to the $655 million raised in February when the market clearly became congested. On the other hand, speculation of a dollar devaluation and a deutsche mark revaluation could keep Euro-bond rates high. Suspicion as to the future of the dollar was particularly evident at the beginning of the year when, in spite of a large spread between Euro-bond and U. S. domestic bond yields, a large backlog of new issues in the market was created. The anticipations of a revaluation of the deutsche mark materialized with the floating of the deutsche mark and some other currencies, including the guilder, in May. Since that date, the Bundesbank had introduced restrictive measures to prevent any new offering denominated in deutsche marks.

Euro-Dollar Rates. By mid-July 1971, the short-term Euro-rates appeared to be back near the year's low (see Exhibit 6). After a continuous decline during the first three months of the year, short-term Euro-rates had increased considerably in the succeeding three months. By July, however, these rates appeared to be back to the low levels of March. The earlier decline in rates appeared to be associated with the improved conditions in the U. S. domestic market where short rates continued declining, and with a reflow of funds from U. S. banks to their foreign branches in January. By April, however, apprehensions about a possible currency crisis, followed by the actual monetary crisis in May, sent Euro-dollar rates to much higher levels. Recent EEC talks which had led to hopes of a possible monetary integration appeared to have brought some peace to the market. It was anticipated, however, that during the last few days of the month rates would edge up due to month-end operations by banks and to a renewed pressure on the dollar.

Other Considerations

The vice-president of finance thought that even though European investors paid attention to the rates paid by Euro-dollar deposits or bonds, one of the primary considerations in their minds was the strength of the U. S. economy. At the present time, there were four factors that lurked on the horizon of the U. S. economy. On the domestic front, in spite of mounting unemployment, inflation appeared to continue unabated. In the international sphere, the continuous deficits in the U. S. balance of payments and the recent floating of the deutsche mark and other currencies all combined to produce increased pressures on the dollar. Finally, in the political arena the following year, 1972, was to be an election year and it was suspected that President Nixon would run for re-election.

Given the parallel between Euro-dollar rates and U. S. domestic rates, CLI's finance vice-president decided to analyze the relationship between these two sets of rates. Data collected by him are contained in Exhibits 6-7.

EXHIBIT 1 Citicorp Leasing International, Inc.: Consolidated Balance Sheet—June 30, 1971 (thousand dollars)

Assets			Liabilities	
Cash and Deposits		$ 12,426	Short-term Borrowings	$ 88,831
Accounts Receivable		915	Accounts Payable	2,364
Other Current Assets		1,532	Accruals	2,332
Lease Receivables	89,036		Advance Rentals	715
Unearned Lease			Other Taxes Payable	53
Income	(27,452)		Long-term Debt	19,796
Net Receivables		61,584	Foreign Exchange Reserve	470
Residual Valuation		8,477	Deferred Taxes	721
Mortgage and Loan				
Financing		12,418		$115,282
		97,352	Equity	
Nonpayout Lease Equipment:				
Investment			Capital	9,940
Equipment	27,615		Retained Earnings	190
Accumulated			Total Equity	10,130
Depreciation	(3,941)			
Net Investment		23,674		
Investment and Advances for				
Subsidiaries and Affiliates		1,355		
Other Fixed Assets (Net)		3,031		
Total Assets		$125,412	Total Liabilities and Equity	$125,412

EXHIBIT 2 Citicorp Leasing International, Inc.: Consolidated Profit and Loss—June 30, 1971 (thousand dollars)

Income			
Leasing and Loan Income			
Lease Income	$6,076		
Interest Income	1,307		
Other Income	691		
		$8,074	
Nonpayout Revenue (net)			
Lease Revenue	4,810		
Less Depreciation Expense	(2,091)		
		2,719	
Total Income			$10,793
Expenses			
Interest and Finance	6,137		
Staff Payments	1,093		
Personnel	138		
Marketing	418		
General Operating	553		
Premises	240		
Other	384		
Total Expenses			8,963
Earnings Before Tax			1,830
Tax Reserve			456
Earnings After Tax			1,374
Net Income (loss) in unconsolidated subsidiaries			(619)
Net Profit for Period			$ 755

EXHIBIT 3   Comparative Capitalizations[a]

	P/E[b]	Capital[c]		Short-Term Debt		Long-Term Debt		Other Assets		Total Assets	
		Million $	%	Million $	%	Million $	%	Million $	%	Million $	%
CIC Leasing	27.4	2.5	8	12.0	38	14.5	46	2.5	8	31.5	100
Greyhound Computer Corp.	9.1	67.5	36	6.5	4	106.5	57	4.5	3	184.5	100
Leaseway	31.9	53.0	25	65.0	30	94.0	44	2.0	1	214.0	100
U. S. Leasing	28.2	44.0	30	83.5	57	18.0	12	1.5	1	147.0	100
Gelco IVM Leasing	34.9	4.0	6	1.5	2	57.5	90	1.5	2	64.5	100
Diebold Computer Leasing	11.3	34.5	21	24.0	15	101.3	63	1.7	1	161.5	100
Data Processing Fin. & Gen.	7.5	62.0	30	30.0	15	111.0	54	1.5	1	204.5	100
Computer Investors Group	10.7	10.0	20	13.0	27	25.5	53	—	—	47.5	100
American Fin. Leas. & Serv.	15.3	11.0	24	1.0	3	32.5	72	.5	1	45.0	100
Citicorp Leasing Int. Inc.	—	11.3	9	88.8	70	19.8	15	5.5	6	125.4	100

Comparative Profit & Loss Statements[a]

	Revenue Income		Interest Expense		Administrative Expenses		Other[d] Expenses		Net Income After Taxes	
	Million $	%	Million $	%	Million $	%	Million $	%	Million $	%
CIC Leasing	3.7	100	1.1	30	1.2	32	.6	16	.8	22
Greyhound Computer Corp.	43.7	100	9.6	22	8.9	20	21.9	50	3.3	8
Leaseway	79.1	100	9.5	12	17.9	23	43.8	55	7.9	10
U. S. Leasing	18.3	100	7.3	40	6.2	34	1.7	9	3.1	17
Gelco IVM Leasing	8.4	100	3.8	45	2.6	32	1.3	15	.7	8
Diebold Computer Leasing	30.9	100	11.1	36	1.0	3	17.4	56	1.4	5
Data Processing Fin. & Gen.	49.2	100	11.4	23	2.0	4	33.4	68	2.4	5
Computer Investors Group	10.6	100	3.1	30	1.1	10	5.1	48	1.3	12
American Fin. Leas. & Serv.	8.5	100	2.8	33	1.8	21	2.4	28	1.5	18
Citicorp Leasing Int. Inc.	12.8	100	6.1	47	2.8	21	2.5	19	1.4	13

[a]Data correspond to fiscal years between 1969 and 1971. Year selected in each case was the latest one available in 1971.
[b]P/E as of September 30, 1971.
[c]Capital consists of equity, retained earnings, and deferred taxes.
[d]Other consists of taxes, depreciation, reserves, and expenses not directly related to leasing activity.

EXHIBIT 4 Citicorp Leasing International, Inc.: Dollar Borrowing Outstanding As of July 11, 1971

	Amount	%	Interest	Interest Due[a]	
		Short-Term			
Demand	$ 3,500,000	7.375			
Demand	350,000	7.375			
July 26	2,975,000	8.125	$ 39,697	M	
July 27	5,250,000	7.50	64,494	M	
July 27	700,000	7.50	8,600	M	
July 29	7,000,000	7.125	40,105	M	
Aug. 3	350,000	7.187	6,203	M	
Aug. 10	280,000	8.25	5,724	M	
Aug. 30	2,003,750	7.625	25,862	M	
Aug. 31	3,500,000	7.50	43,701	M	
Sept. 7	1,575,000	6.375	49,842	M	
Sept. 8	700,000	6.375	21,914	M	
Sept. 13	210,000	6.625	6,879	M	
Sept. 21	125,909	7.75	2,413	M	
Sept. 22	437,500	6.5625	14,114	M	
Sept. 22	1,400,000	6.675	43,827	M	
Sept. 29	542,500	7.50	14,312	Sept. 29,1971	Q
Sept. 30	175,000	6.6875	5,757	M	
Oct. 7	4,708,907	7.375	85,741	M	
Oct. 13	7,000,000	7.125	244,636	M	
Oct. 26	9,625,000	7.1875	508,219	M	
Oct. 27	87,500	7.375	3,167	M	
Dec. 21	86,625	7.875	1,687	Sept. 21, 1971	Q
Dec. 29	542,500	7.75	14,805	Sept. 29, 1971	Q
Mar. 21, 1972	88,725	8.375	1,843	Sept. 21, 1971	Q
Mar. 29, 1972	542,500	7.875	15,052	Sept. 29, 1971	Q
June 21, 1972	91,350	8.375	1,907	Sept. 21, 1971	Q
June 29, 1972	560,000	7.875	15,538	Sept. 29, 1971	Q
July 7, 1972	1,225,000	8.125	98,077	July 7, 1972	A
	$55,632,766				
		Long-Term			
Sept. 21, 1972	$ 93,800	8.375	$ 1,947	Sept. 21, 1971	Q
Sept. 29, 1972	568,750	7.875	15,779	Sept. 29, 1971	Q
Dec. 21, 1972	96,250	8.375	1,998	Sept. 21, 1971	Q
Dec. 29, 1972	393,750	8.125	16,798	Sept. 29, 1971	Q
March 21, 1973	98,000	9.0	2,206	Sept. 21, 1971	Q
March 29, 1973	603,750	8.125	17,330	Sept. 29, 1971	Q
June 21, 1973	101,500	9.0	2,268	Sept. 21, 1971	Q
June 29, 1973	612,500	8.25	17,829	Sept. 29, 1971	Q
Sept. 21, 1973	105,000	9.0	2,346	Sept. 21, 1971	Q
Oct. 1, 1973	630,000	8.375	18,621	Sept. 29, 1971	Q
Dec. 21, 1973	107,275	9.0	2,397	Sept. 21, 1971	Q
Dec. 31, 1973	647,500	8.75	20,025	Sept. 29, 1971	Q
March 21, 1974	110,250	9.125	2,499	Sept. 21, 1971	Q
March 29, 1974	665,000	8.875	20,870	Sept. 29, 1971	Q
May 13, 1974	875,000	8.0	17,328	Aug. 13, 1971	Q
June 21, 1974	113,050	9.125	2,563	Sept. 21, 1971	Q
Sept. 23, 1974	116,200	9.125	2,633	Sept. 21, 1971	Q
Dec. 23, 1974	119,350	9.125	2,705	Sept. 21, 1971	Q
March 21, 1975	122,500	9.375	2,856	Sept. 21, 1971	Q
June 4, 1975	7,000,000	8.75	305,763	Dec. 4, 1971	S/A
June 23, 1975	82,950	9.375	1,946	Sept. 21, 1971	Q
May 17, 1976	175,000	9.0	15,566	May 17, 1972	A
June 1, 1976	175,000	8.875	3,346	May 30, 1972	A
June 4, 1976	3,500,000	9.0	157,377	Dec. 4, 1971	S/A
	$17,112,375				

[a]M—monthly
Q—quarterly
S/A—semi-annually
A—annually

EXHIBIT 5 Short-Term and Long-Term Euro-Dollar Interest Rates, 1967-1971

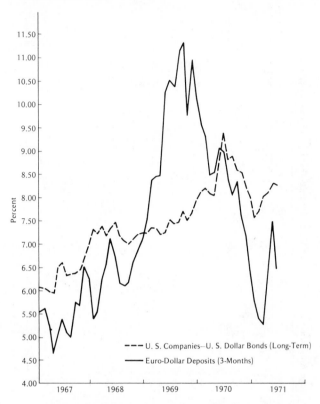

Source: Morgan Guaranty Trust Company of New York, *World Financial Statistics.*

EXHIBIT 6 United States: Domestic and Euro-Dollar Money Rates

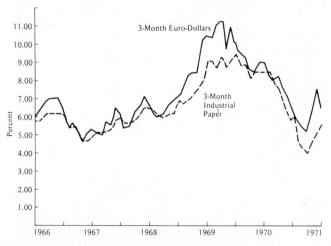

Source: Morgan Guaranty Trust Company of New York, *World Financial Statistics*

EXHIBIT 7   U. S. Nonfinancial Business Corporations: A Percentage Allocation of Sources and Uses of Funds, 1956-1971 (percentages)

	1956-1965	1966	1967	1968	1969	1970	1971 (I&II)
Total	100.0		100.0	100.0	100.0	100.0	100.0
Internal	67.5		63.6	57.1	50.4	58.3	54.0
Net Saving	31.4		32.5	26.9	17.3	12.5	15.6
Capital Consumption	68.6		67.5	73.1	82.7	87.5	84.4
External	32.5		36.4	32.9	49.6	41.7	46.0
Credit and Equity Market	57.0		83.2	65.4	66.7	88.2	78.4
Stock	14.1		7.8	-2.6	11.0	17.5	22.2
Bonds	42.5		50.2	42.6	30.9	52.3	55.6
Mortgage	17.9		15.4	19.1	12.3	13.7	17.8
Bank Loans and Other	25.5		26.6	40.9	45.8	16.5	4.4
Other							
Profits Tax Liabilities			-81.0	13.1	-9.7	-62.3	29.0
Trade Debt	59.0		84.5	63.1	101.0	103.8	46.0
Other Liabilities	41.0		96.5	23.8	8.7	58.5	25.0
Total	100.0		100.0	100.0	100.0	100.0	100.0
Real Investment	73.0		74.5	70.5	71.9	79.8	68.9
Plant and Equipment	87.0		86.8	88.6	89.0	93.0	91.9
Residential Construction	5.3		3.2	3.0	3.3	3.9	4.7
Inventories	7.7		10.0	8.4	7.7	3.1	3.4
Financial Investment	25.6		15.1	23.7	23.5	18.5	23.3
Liquid Assets	11.4		14.5	33.6	4.7	45.6	18.9
Trade Credit	55.5		53.1	54.3	62.0	31.8	36.1
Consumer Credit	4.1		6.2	6.6	4.7	7.2	5.8
Miscellaneous Assets	29.5		26.2	5.5	28.6	15.4	39.2
Discrepancy	1.4		10.4	5.8	4.6	1.7	7.8

Source: Federal Reserve Board of Governors, *Flow of Funds Accounts.*

CHAPTER 14

The International Bond Market

The distinctive characteristic of the international bond market is that these bonds are always sold outside the country of the borrower. Therefore, funds in the international bond market are generally raised in currencies other than the one of the borrower.[1] Once this basic characteristic is established, one can go further and subdivide the international bond market into the Euro-bond market and the foreign bond market. This classification is based on the currency in which the lender buys the bonds and the borrower repays the debt. When the bonds are sold principally in countries other than the country of the currency in which the issue is denominated, it is called a *Euro-bond issue*. When the bonds are sold primarily in the country of the currency of the issue, is called a *foreign bond*. Both Euro-bonds and foreign bonds may include options as to the currency in which the final payment may be made. In addition, the Euro-bond market offers several alternatives in the currency composition of the unit of account of the issue.[2]

BACKGROUND

Until 1963, foreign security issues in Europe remained relatively underdeveloped due to the fragmentation and relatively small size of European capital markets, the

---

[1] An exception is the American firm borrowing Euro-dollars, for example.

[2] Some portions of this chapter draw heavily on *The European Market for International Bonds*, prepared by Yoon S. Park under the supervision of Professor Eli Shapiro and distributed by the Intercollegiate Case Clearing House, Boston, Mass. An expanded version of that material appears as Chapter 2 in Yoon S. Park, *The Euro-Bond Market: Function and Structure* (New York: Praeger Press, 1974).

501

high interest rates prevailing in most of these markets, and numerous government controls. By 1963 foreigners were tapping the U. S. capital market for over $1 billion per year. As Exhibit 14.1 shows, from 1955 to 1962 new issues of foreign securities in the United States were greater than those in all European countries combined.

EXHIBIT 14.1   Foreign Issues in European Countries and the United States, 1955-1962 (Millions of U. S. dollars)

	1955	1956	1957	1958	1959	1960	1961	1962	Total 1955-1962
European Countries	$392	$235	$219	$ 349	$384	$308	$592	$444	$2,923
United States	200	403	539	1,144	568	440	290	587	4,171

Source: Jean Mensbruggle, "Foreign Issues in Europe." *IMF Staff Papers*, July 1964, p. 329.

A number of European governments and business enterprises floated bond issues in New York instead of in European capital markets because New York offered them lower interest costs and a more efficient underwriting system than those available elsewhere. However, the introduction of the Interest Equalization Tax (IET) in July 1963 effectively discouraged U. S. residents from buying foreign securities. The IET reduced the after-tax return to U. S. purchasers, diminishing their desire to acquire such securities. This forced non-U. S. borrowers to turn increasingly to European capital markets in spite of the limitations that borrowing in these markets entailed.

Other measures related to the U. S. dollar gave further impetus to the growth of the international bond market. These forces were the emergence of a large Euro-dollar market and the controls on foreign direct investment imposed on U. S. companies on a voluntary basis in 1965 and on a mandatory basis in 1968. The emergence of a sizable Euro-dollar market provided the raw material for large bond financings to take place. The controls on U. S. foreign direct investment forced U. S. companies to approach the European markets to raise the bulk of the funds required to finance their foreign operations.

The result of the combination of all these forces was a fantastic growth in the international bond markets. This is shown in Exhibit 14.2.

FOREIGN BONDS

A foreign bond is an international bond sold by a foreign borrower but denominated in the currency of the country in which it is placed. It is underwritten and sold by a national underwriting syndicate in the lending country. For example, a U. S. company might float a bond issue in the Swiss capital market, underwritten by a Swiss syndicate and denominated in Swiss francs. The bond issue is sold to investors in the Swiss capital market, where it will be quoted and traded. A summary of characteristics of the European foreign bond issues is found in Exhibit 14.3.

EXHIBIT 14.2 New International Bond Issues Outside the United States (millions of U. S. dollars)

	1963	1964	1965	1966	1967	1968	1969	1970	1971	1972	1973	1974	Total 1963-1974
Euro-Bonds[a]	$164	$719	$1041	$1142	$2002	$3573	$3156	$2966	$3642	$6335	$4169	$2008	$30,917
Foreign Bonds	389	264	376	378	403	1135	827	378	1538	2060	2650	1212	11,610
Total International Bonds	$553	$983	$1417	$1520	$2405	$4708	$3983	$3344	$5180	$8395	$6819	$3220	$42,527

[a]Includes European unit of account, European Monetary Unit, and multiple currency option issues.
Source: Morgan Guaranty Trust Company, *World Financial Markets*, various issues.

EXHIBIT 14.3 Foreign Bond Issues Outside the United States (millions of dollars)

	1965	1966	1967	1968	1969	1970	1971	1972	1973	1974
Total	$376	$378	$403	$1135	$827	$378	$1538	$2060	$2650	$1212
By Currency										
German Mark	123	0	10	674	531	89	308	509	386	328
Swiss Franc	78	94	153	238	196	193	669	815	1526	709
Italian Lira	24	139	24	72	24	0	32	163	} 736[b]	175
British Pound	62	76	102	19	0	12	138	0[b]		
Other[a]	89	69	114	132	76	84	391	586[b]		
By Borrower										
U. S. Firms	10	24	48	139	223	55	200	215	546	72
International Organizations	156	200	133	611	271	171	709	1074	941	140
Other	110	154	222	385	333	152	629	771	1163	1000

Source: Morgan Guaranty Trust Company, *World Financial Markets*, various issues.
[a]Includes £/$ option issues.
[b]Includes approximately $300 million worth of issues in yen.

In comparison with the Euro-bond market, discussed later, U. S. companies—though playing a significant role (about 20%)—have not dominated the foreign bond market. Instead, for the period as a whole, international organizations such as the World Bank have been the major participants in this market by accounting for approximately half of the foreign bonds. Non-U.S. companies, state enterprises, and governments account for the remaining 30% of the market. However, in 1974 international organizations played a very minor role in this market. Foreign governments, shown in Exhibit 14.3 among other borrowers, have come to be the major borrowers in the foreign bond market.

The relationship between the domestic bond market and the foreign bond market in Germany can be observed in the phenomenal expansion of DM foreign bonds in 1968. Owing to the persistent decline of long-term interest rates in German financial markets, DM foreign bonds in 1968 usually yielded more than new issues of German domestic long-term securities. The result was a keen demand for DM foreign bonds among German investors. On the part of the borrower the willingness of German investors to purchase foreign bonds was aided by the rising trend of interest rates on the Euro-bond market. A similar situation of growth of foreign bonds in currencies with low domestic interest rates can be observed in bonds denominated in the Swiss franc since 1971 and in the yen in 1972 and 1973. The growth in foreign bonds in Japan in those years was also largely due to the liberalization of Japanese controls on international capital flows.

Among the elements that comprise the borrowing cost, the interest rate is but one of the factors. Other components of cost are the commission rates and the exchange risks. In a foreign bond loan, the risk of a currency revaluation is borne by the borrower—an upvaluation resulting in a loss, a devaluation in a gain. For example, an American firm operating mostly in U. S. dollars floats a deutsche mark foreign bond issue in Germany. If the deutsche mark is upvalued by 10% next year, both the interest and principal payments become 10% more expensive to the company than before the upvaluation, as discussed in Chapters 7 and 9.

STRAIGHT EURO-BONDS

The Euro-bond is an international bond, "underwritten by an international syndicate and sold in countries other than the country of the currency in which the issue is denominated."[3] From a miniscule size of $164 million in 1963, the market grew rapidly to $6.335 billion in 1972. Although the market size declined in the following two years, it rose again in the first ten months of 1975 to a record $6.86 billion, far above the $4.12 billion total of foreign borrowings in New York over the same period. Overall, from 1963-1974, over $30 billion were borrowed in over 600 issues. U. S. companies alone had borrowed over $9 billion on the market by the end of 1974. See Exhibit 14.4.

The Euro-bond market has emerged as the most important segment of the international capital market. Before 1963, most international long-term issues were raised through foreign bond issues in certain national capital markets, primarily in the United States and Switzerland, but also in Germany, the Netherlands, and the United Kingdom. Today, only Switzerland and Germany remain as important markets for the flotation of foreign bonds, since the dominant form of international new issue activity has shifted to the Euro-bond market.

---

[3] Morgan Guaranty Trust Company, *World Financial Markets*, last page of each issue.

EXHIBIT 14.4   New Euro-Bond Issues (millions of dollars)

	1963	1964	1965	1966	1967	1968	1969	1970	1971	1972	1973	1974	Total 1963-1974
Euro-Bonds, Total	$164	$719	$1041	$1142	$2002	$3573	$3156	$2966	$3642	$6335	$4169	$2008	$30917
By Category of Borrower													
U. S. Companies	—	—	358	439	562	2096	1005	741	1098	1992	874	110	9275
Other Companies	25	108	319	376	575	603	817	1065	1119	1759	1309	605	8680
State Enterprises	80	185	110	118	442	349	682	594	848	1170	923	526	6027
Governments	53	293	189	108	303	500	584	351	479	1019	659	407	4945
International Organizations	6	133	65	101	120	25	68	215	98	395	404	360	1990
By Currency of Denomination													
U.S. Dollar	102	485	726	921	1780	2554	1723	1775	2221	3908	2447	996	19638
German Mark	—	200	203	147	171	914	1338	688	786	1129	1001	259	6836
Dutch Guilder	—	—	—	—	—	—	17	391	298	393	} 721	753	4443
Other[a]	62	34	112	74	51	105	78	112	337	905			
By Type of Security													
Long-Term Straight Debt	92	613	836	675	1427	1108	1852	1995	2633	4358	} 3522	1913	24653
Medium-Term Straight Debt	52	10	95	225	260	480	173	733	714	642			
Certificates of Deposit	—	—	—	—	55	75	—	—	—	115			
Convertible	20	96	110	242	260	1910	1131	238	295	1220	647	95	6264

[a] Includes European unit of account, European Monetary Unit, and multiple currency option issues.

Source: Morgan Guaranty Trust Company, *World Financial Markets*, New York, various issues.

The Euro bond market, although centered in Europe, is truly international in the sense that the underwriting syndicates typically comprise investment bankers from a number of countries, the bonds are sold to investors around the world, and the flotations are not governed by national regulations.[4] However, in spite of the cosmopolitan nature of the Euro-bond market, a Euro-bond is a simple instrument for borrowers and investors to understand. It is denominated in a given currency and there are no major regulations with which to contend.[5]

As described before, the impetus for the fast growth of the international bond market was largely provided by the regulations imposed on the international capital flows in the United States. The Interest Equalization Tax (IET) drove foreigners to raise funds outside the United States. The initially voluntary and later mandatory controls on foreign direct investments sent U. S. companies to raise funds in foreign markets for their foreign operations. The growth of the Euro-bond market reflects very clearly the impact of these two regulations. The effect of IET shows in Exhibit 14.4 in the increasing participation of non-U. S. companies in the Euro-bond market. Except for 1968 when the U. S. controls on foreign direct investment became mandatory and U. S. companies approached the Euro-bond market in hordes, non-U. S. companies and U. S. companies have usually accounted for slightly more than 50% of the new issues in the Euro-bond market.

State enterprises, which were also subject to the impact of IET, comprise another significant portion of the Euro-bond market. Governments kept a relatively low profile in the Euro-bond market until 1972. International organizations have played only a minor role in this market in comparison with the foreign bond market. The smaller participation of the latter two entities in the Euro-bond market is partly a reflection of the nature of the IET inasmuch as these institutions were exempted from the tax imposed on foreign issues in the United States. For example, the International Bank for Reconstruction and Development (World Bank) was allowed to raise funds through bond issues in the United States without the lenders being subject to the penalties of the IET. The impact of U. S. regulations in the Euro-bond market can also be seen in the decline that occurred in the size of the market in 1974. Early in that year both the IET and the controls on foreign direct investment were almost totally eliminated. Thus the need for the Euro-bond market also diminished.

The development of the Euro-bond market as a substitute for the U. S. domestic market is also reflected in the dominant role that the dollar has played in the Euro-bond market. Until 1967 the Euro-dollar bond often accounted for as much as 90% of the Euro-bond market. After that year the strength of the deutsche mark relative to the dollar gave a larger role to the deutsche mark in the Euro-bond market. Still Euro-dollar bonds have retained a minimum of approximatley 50% of the total new issues in the Euro-bond market. (See Exhibit 14.4.)

---

[4] Some countries—like Italy, France, and Belgium—put informal pressure on their *domestic* banks to slow down their underwriting of Euro-bond issues. However, no country can regulate the *whole* Euro-bond market.

[5] An impetus to the deutsche mark-dominated Euro-bonds similar to the IET effect on dollar Euro-bonds came when the German government placed a 25% tax on interest payments on German corporate bonds held by foreigners. Thus, bond purchasers were moved to seek deutsche mark-denominated bonds outside the West German government's regulation, which tended to decrease interest rates for Euro-bonds denominated in deutsche marks.

Euro-bonds have also proven to be a versatile instrument. Not only have maturities been tailored to the needs of the borrowers under the regulations,[6] but Euro-bonds have also appeared with a variety of features designed to make the instrument more desirable to the investor and practical to the borrower. Examples of this versatility are the emergence of convertible Euro-bonds, floating rates, commercial rates, and sweeteners such as warrants.

The convertible Euro-bonds have typically been issued by U. S. companies and denominated in U. S. dollars. After being firmly established in 1968, the ebbs and flows of this market have paralleled those of the U. S. stock market. The years of 1968, 1969, and 1972, when the stock market reached record performance, have seen large amounts of convertible Euro-dollar bonds sold successfully in the market. The sagging stock market in 1970-1971 and 1974 was a clear setback to the convertible Euro-bond market. (See Exhibit 14.4.)

Following the pattern of many direct Euro-dollar loans, initially there was an interest in floating rate Euro-bonds. One was introduced in 1971 with a fifteen-year maturity and an interest rate adjusted every six months. However, the market did not develop in these bonds; the initial issues became quite illiquid and the general lack of increased enthusiasm precluded further issues.

Euro-dollar commercial paper was first issued in 1970, thus permitting short-term users of Euro-dollar funds to create formal indebtedness, bypassing the banks in the Euro-dollar loan market. Thus, the general credit of the firm permitted it to avoid short-term Euro-dollar loans from banks or medium- to long-term financing from the Euro-bond market if it was willing to roll over its commercial paper and was able to sell it. Usually, an underwriter was involved in the issue of commercial paper.

Some Euro-bond issues have carried warrants, as in the United States. Generally, interest in these features has declined with the stock market indices, since the value of the warrant is related to its "strike price" in relation to the current market price. Firms are reluctant to use warrants when the stock is severely depressed unless the strike price (the price at which the warrant can be exercised to acquire common stock) is far above market. Such a spread, of course, lessens the value of the warrant to the bond purchaser.

EURO-BONDS INVOLVING MORE THAN ONE CURRENCY

The straight Euro-bonds described in the previous section have dominated the Euro-bond market. However, bonds that involve more than one currency in the denomination of the bond have been comprising an increasing portion of the Euro-bond market. These other Euro-bond issues appear in Exhibit 14.4 as "other" in the classification of Euro-bonds by currency. These alternate arrangements as to currencies have responded to two primary needs. First, they are an incentive to the lender. Second, they are a way to average the uncertainty involved in the foreign exchange risk of a single currency. The latter factor has been of particular relevance since

[6] For example, the controls on U. S. foreign direct investment did not count as a capital outflow the repayment of debt with maturity larger than seven years and repayment of principal after that year. Accordingly, the typical Euro-bond had a maturity of more than seven years and specified a "balloon payment" at the end of the period for the principal.

1972 when foreign exchange markets have exhibited a much higher instability than in the preceding period. Below is a summary of the major characteristics for the most important types of Euro-bonds with currency mixes.

Multiple Currency Bonds

The multiple currency bond, in one of its most widely used forms, entitles the creditor to request payment of the interest and the principal of the bond in any pre-determined currency as well as in the currency of the loan in accordance with a previously established unchangeable parity. Thus the obligation is expressed in various national currencies at the choice of the lender.

This option strengthens the exchange guaranty for the lender because (s)he loses only if all currencies included in the multiple currency contract depreciate against the other currencies not included in the contract. Suppose, for example, that a Lebanese lender bought a multiple currency bond with three currency options: British pounds, French francs, and U. S. dollars. When all three currencies depreciate against the Lebanese currency, (s)he loses in the same proportion as the currency which has depreciated the *least* among the three currencies.

If any one currency in the contract appreciates, (s)he gains by that much because (s)he can always require payment in the currency which offers the greatest advantage. With a multiple currency clause, therefore, when all currencies in the contract are devalued but in different proportions, the obligation of the borrower fluctuates in the same proportion as the currency which has been devalued the *least*. However, when all currencies in the contract are upvalued but in different proportions, the obligation appreciates in the same degree as the currency *most* upvalued.

Thus, a multiple currency bond presents a disadvantage to the borrower, for (s)he must cover the currency expected to be upvalued the most and still cannot profit from the devaluation of a particular currency. For this reason the multiple currency bond is now only utilized by borrowers who for one reason or another fear difficulties in the placing of the loan; the high interest rates which were offered for such loans in the past few years suggest that poor credit risk issuers who have no cheaper alternatives resort to these issues. The first multiple currency bond in the postwar period was the 1957 Petrofina $25 million issue, repayable in Dutch guilders, Belgian francs, German marks, U. S. dollars, or Swiss francs at the 1957 exchange rate. Ordinarily, however, the choice is restricted to two currencies.

European Monetary Unit (EMU) Bonds

In late 1970, the European Coal and Steel Community borrowed EMU 50 million (which was equal to U. S. $50 million prior to the 1971 devaluations) for a fifteen-year maturity. The value of the debt was fixed at the time of issue at a permanent exchange rate in terms of the six EEC currencies. As a result, the lender is protected against devaluation since the least devalued currency can be designated as the repayment currency by the lender. Should upvaluation take place in several of the currencies, then the lender may demand payment in that currency which has upvalued the most.

In this sense, the EMU (also called the European Currency Unit) bond is a multiple currency bond which is based on six major reference currencies. Although the borrowing rates are slightly lower than those for the typical Euro-bond, dollar-denominated issue, the difficulty in the EMU bond is that the borrower bears the exchange risk for six major currencies.

Unit of Account Bond

Because of the Euro-dollar, an international money and capital market came into being in Europe. This development would have been considered utopian a few years ago. However, strong as the dollar might have been as a foreign currency, it always was a national currency, the trend, value, and confidence of which was mainly determined by factors such as the situation of the U. S. balance of payments, internal economic developments, the political situation, and the monetary policy of the United States. A national currency does not in all circumstances offer the necessary basis for the development of an international capital market.

It is precisely with this intention that from 1961 the European Unit of Account (EUA) was utilized for the issue of international bonds. By the end of 1974, over 40 EUA bond issues had been offered to the public on the international capital market for a total value over EUA 500 million.

The unit of account is neither a means of payment nor an instrument of exchange, although it may become so under special circumstances, as for example when a transfer is made from one account to another on the books of a bank.[7] Mainly, however, it serves as a yardstick helping to determine the value of the obligations entered into, with the aim of maintaining the value of the respective liabilities and claims as constant as possible with respect to the original value.

The unit of account is not a modern invention. As long ago as the late Middle Ages, when every kingdom, every principality, and even small towns had separate currencies, units of account such as the Mark-Banco of Hamburg and the Florin-Banco of the Amsterdam Wissel-Bank were used in settling accounts in international trade.[8]

The value of the European unit of account is that of the unit of account of the European Payments Union (EPU),[9] i.e., 0.88867088 gram of fine gold which was equivalent to one U. S. dollar prior to the 1971 devaluation. This value could be changed only under very strict conditions as to the fluctuations in the seventeen "reference currencies" to which it was limited.[10]

The value of the unit of account changed only when the following two conditions were met simultaneously:

1. *All* the seventeen reference currencies must change their parities.

---

[7] At present, the Bank for International Settlements, the European Monetary Agreement, and the European Coal and Steel Community employ a unit of account as the basic currency unit.

[8] Fernand Collin, *The Formation of a European Capital Market and Other Lectures.* Brussels, 1964, p. 11.

[9] An institution that existed between 1950-1958 to help settle balances among its seventeen member nations. This institution was created to help solve the problems created by the lack of convertibility of the participant's currencies.

[10] The currencies involved were those of the original seventeen members of the EPU, which comprised the six members of the European Economic Community, the seven members of the European Free Trade Association, and Iceland, Greece, Ireland, and Turkey.

2. *At least* two-thirds of them must change their parities in the same direction (devaluation or upvaluation).

If the above two conditions were met simultaneously, the unit of account changed its value by the same amount as that of the currency which changed the *least* among the larger of the two groups of currencies. Suppose, for example, that all the seventeen currencies were modified (which satisfies the first condition), and that four of them upvalued while the remaining thirteen currencies devalued (which satisfies the second condition). Then, the unit of account would be devalued (because the devaluation group is the larger one). But, devalued by how much? Suppose, again, that, of the thirteen devalued currencies, ten of them were devalued by 10% and the remaining three by 5%. Then, the unit of account should be devalued by 5% (following the least devalued currencies).[11]

In 1972, a new formula was announced. The value of the EUA was linked to the reference values of the currencies in the enlarged common market, nine nations. Instead of a par value as officially designated, the par value which will be used in the EUA calculations will be the rate which is supported by the monetary authorities of the country (such as the central rate of the official bank). If the currency floats outside the limits permitted by the Snake in the Tunnel Agreement, then that currency will no longer be a reference currency for the EUA calculations. The agreement also deals with the possible replacement of gold by special drawing rights (SDR) as a standard. There is an adjustment of the EUA if *all* reference currencies change their values in relation to gold compared to the date of issue of the bond and if a majority move in one direction. The adjustment is made on the basis of the *smallest* percentage change in the dominant group. Should all the currencies lose their reference status in the EUA, the EUA is assigned to the last currency which loses such status.

The secret of the wide appeal of unit of account bonds lies in the sharing of much of the risk of exchange rate change. The unit of account loan is as stable as the most stable reference currency. However, the borrower still can be affected negatively if his/her own currency devalues relative to the unit of account; the lender can also have an exchange loss if his/her own currency upvalues relative to the unit of account. Changes in the values of other currencies do not affect either borrower or lender. For example, if a British company issues an EUA bond and there is a 10% devaluation of the pound sterling the borrower effectively has to pay back 10% more than what was received initially. Since the EUA remains constant if only one currency

[11]During a transition period of two years after any such modification in the unit of account, the unit of account would be modified again if a further change in one or some of the seventeen currencies would have affected the original calculations on the basis of which it was originally modified when there was a change in the seventeen currencies. For instance, if at any given date sixteen of the seventeen currencies were upvalued by 10% and the remaining one by 5%, the unit of account would have been upvalued by 5%. If during the next two years the currency which had upvalued only by 5% was further upvalued by 5% (of the original parity), while other currencies remained unchanged, the unit of account would have been upvalued by a further 5%, without initiating a new transition period.

Again, if originally thirteen of the seventeen currencies were devalued by 20%, while four of them were upvalued by 10%, the unit of account would have been devalued by 20%. If during the transition period that followed this devaluation, two of the thirteen currencies which had been devalued by 20% upvalued by 15% (of the original parity), the unit of account would have been upvalued by 15% of that rate and would thus be only 5% below its orginal value.

fluctuates, the British borrower has to produce 10% extra in pounds to make the same amount of borrowed EUA. Conversely if the currency of the bond-holder, say a German, appreciates by 10% in the intervening period the lender effectively receives fewer German marks than s(he) invested initially. The lender will receive the same amount of EUA that (s)he loaned. However, since the German mark is now worth more EUAs than when the loan was made, when the lender translates the EUAs into the new German marks (s)he receives fewer marks than were loaned. Assuming that the pound devaluation and the mark upvaluation were the only changes that took place in the foreign exchange parities during the period in question, one can summarize the results by saying that British borrowers and German lenders are negatively affected. Conversely, British lenders and German borrowers benefit from the fluctuations. Bondholders and borrowers with other home currencies are not affected.

With the new definition of the EUA, the EUA bond becomes more like the EMU bonds, assuming the latter enlarges its "multiple currencies" to include the enlarged Common Market. The EMU bond allows the buyer to pay for the bond in any of the EEC currencies, while the EUA bond permits the issuer to designate the selling currency. Redemption of the EUA bond is in terms of the EUA, which balances the various currencies' changes in parity since the bond issue. In contrast, the EMU would permit the lender to demand repayment in the strongest currency. In fact, however, if the EEC countries stay with their commitment to have their currencies float within 2¼% of each other, then the differences in the currencies should not be that great over time. However, as experience has shown, nations seem quite willing to float when the situation demands it. On balance, then, the EUA bond will give the borrower and issuer a more balanced opportunity to gain or to lose from the changing parities than with the EMU bond, even though the former is slightly more complex to understand.

Parallel Bond

A parallel bond is a multinational issue (usually a large issue) composed of several loans floated simultaneously among various countries, with each participating country raising one loan in its own currency. The terms and conditions of all the loans are made uniform as far as possible and are different only where absolutely necessary.

The chief proponent, H. J. Abs, of Deutsche Bank, held that parallel bonds "would accumulate the available resources of the European capital markets involved. As each issue would be made out in the currency of the country concerned the loan would be acceptable to all groups of investors. Each individual loan could be raised within the limits of each country's financing capacity in different amounts."[12] The parallel bond is similar to the foreign bond discussed earlier, only more complex. It is a combination of a group of foreign bonds among several countries, with synchronization of timing and issue terms. Since the parts of the parallel bond are floated at the same time, the terms of issue would probably need to be tailored to meet conditions in the least favorable market at that time. The

---

[12] H. J. Abs, "Parallel Loans to Mobilize Continental Funds." *The Times* (London), March 11, 1964, p. 18.

main argument for this type of bond is the ability to borrow a large amount of funds simultaneously. However, the record has shown that other types of securities, particularly the dollar Euro-bond, can be floated in relatively large amounts without the possible disadvantages of the parallel bond mentioned above. Thus far, very few parallel bond issues have been floated.

INTERNATIONAL BOND-MARKET INSTITUTIONS

Financial Intermediaries

Since the foreign bonds are underwritten in the country of the currency of the bond denomination, the institutions involved in issuing these bonds are those that handle bond issues in the given country. The characteristics of some of the major capital markets and their institutions will be discussed in the following chapter.

Euro-bonds, on the other hand, are underwritten by an international syndicate. The cornerstone of the Euro-bond market is the thirty to forty financial institutions in Europe and the United States which manage the major share of all new international bonds. Since Euro-bond issues attract few institutional investors,[13] it is especially important for the underwriting investment bankers to have experience in preparing an issue for placement with banks and residents in a large number of countries.

The general pattern of a Euro-bond syndicate follows the traditional American system, i.e., the three-tier structure of the managers, the underwriting group, and the selling group. The investment banks acting as managers select an underwriting group of important concerns with contacts in a number of countries, and the selling group will ordinarily be several times larger and have a wider geographical representation. The underwriters of a typical Euro-bond issue ordinarily comprise well-known European banking institutions and leading U. S. investment banks, with a total number of participants that usually surpasses the traditional two or three in the United States by a substantial number. At the same time the listing of the selling group can easily fall in the fifties or more. This is done in an attempt to reach the retail market in every country.

The underwriting costs for Euro-bond issues are somewhat higher than for bond flotation in the U. S. domestic market. Whereas the total underwriting cost for an average issue in the United States may run to about 2% of issue value, the comparable cost for a Euro-bond issue is ordinarily 2.5%, consisting of a 1.5% selling commission, a 0.5% management fee, and a 0.5% underwriting fee. Additional incidental expenses payable by the issuing or borrowing company may run as high as $100,000, with the actual cost partly dependent on the amount of financial advertising.

One difficulty with the European underwriting system is that it usually does not involve a firm commitment on the part of the syndicate members to take precommitted amounts of the issue; rather they operate on a "best efforts" basis. This factor means the lead investment banker has only a limited basis for estimating how

[13]The European institutional investors such as the pension funds and the insurance companies prefer a debenture denominated in the currency of their own country rather than in dollars, because their liabilities are payable in their domestic currency.

firm the interest is on the part of the syndicate members prior to the actual issue. Although the European situation typically has a provision relating to loss of commissions if issues are returned to the market during the life of the syndicate, this penalty arrangement is difficulty to enforce, with the result that the syndicates are usually ended promptly with the lead investment banker and some others bearing the responsibility of stabilizing the market in the bonds after issuance.[14]

When there is a large amount of the issue unsold, unlike the United States where the underwriters typically must "swallow" the unsold portion, in the European case the underwriters have the right to raise the coupon or sell the remaining issue at deep discount, reduce the size of the issue, or simply cancel it in the event the syndicate does not wish to absorb the balance.

Although about half the U. S. firms chose to list their Euro-bond issues on the New York Stock Exchange in the 1965-1969 period, more than 80% listed the issues on the Luxembourg Stock Exchange (multiple listings are possible). In contrast, the next highest incidence of listing was the London Stock Exchange, where only 6% of the issues were listed.[15] This emphasis on the Luxembourg exchange is related on the part of the issuer to less stringent listing requirements. From the point of view of the bond buyer, securities regulations and disclosure of issuer's information (which in Luxembourg are similar to the U. S. Securities and Exchange Commission regulations) offer additional protection. The issues are traded in the secondary market by about twenty-five major traders, with daily turnover between $60 and $100 million.

Since the Euro-bond transactions are conducted throughout the major world financial centers, there have been problems in settling transactions such as delays in receipt of bonds purchased or payment for bonds sold, frequent reshipment of securities, and the tying up of substantial amounts of dealer's capital. In order to solve these problems, New York's Morgan Guaranty Bank created a Euro-bond clearing house. In early 1969, Barclays Bank announced plans to start its own clearing operations, but dropped the idea two months later. Resenting the dominance of the clearing operation by one bank (and an American one at that), late in 1969, fifty-five banks from America and Europe met to form CEDEL, a new clearing organization. Clearing operations commenced in September 1971 with over seventy subscribing shareholders. Friction between the two systems eventually led to Morgan Guaranty's decision to open ownership of its operation, and it sold 97% of its interest in late 1972 to various institutions in twenty countries. It seems probable that there will be a merger of the two systems.

Borrower's Financial Subsidiaries

Taking the United States as an example, although one incentive to raising money in the Euro-bond market for U. S. corporations was to comply with various U. S. voluntary and mandatory credit restraint programs in the late 1960s, another incentive was simply to avoid exchange control on funds used abroad. Thus, a large base of funds can be raised at one move and the funds redistributed wherever the

---

[14]See Gunter Rischer, "The Role of Underwriters in the Euro-capital Market." *Euromoney,* June 1972.

[15]Compiled by Yoon S. Park from White, Weld and Co., *International Bond Market Letter.* New York, various issues.

firm needs them. The alternative is separate issues in a number of countries, with possible current or future exchange restrictions on the movement of funds among those countries.

As noted earlier in the text, countries differ in their policies about witholding taxes on dividends and interest to residents and nonresidents. Most Western European countries have one withholding tax for residents and nonresidents alike, ranging from 5% in Luxembourg to 41.25% in the United Kingdom. Others (Canada, Germany, and the United States) have withholding only on interest paid to nonresidents. Still other nations (Denmark, the Netherlands, Sweden) have no withholding tax. Most nations have tax treaties with other nations which may reduce the withholding tax,[16] and in virtually all cases the holders of the bonds can have credit against their local income taxes for the amount withheld. The difficulty is that many of the Euro-bond purchasers have no intention of declaring the income to their local tax authorities; hence, the credit is worthless. Most Euro-bond issues have a clause which provides that the borrower will increase the interest payment to offset any future withholding tax on interest to nonresidents should it be legislated.

The interest of U. S. corporations in domestic financing subsidiaries (often incorporated in Delaware) stems from the Section 861 provisions of the Internal Revenue Code. When 80% or more of the gross income of a U. S. corporation is from foreign sources, then there is no withholding required for payment of dividends or interest to nonresidents. Hence, when the financing subsidiary raises funds in the Euro-bond market, it can meet a non-U. S. income rule, permitting it to pay the debtors (and investors) their return without withholding. Unlike a foreign finance subsidiary, the domestic subsidiary can have its gains and losses consolidated with the parent. Where there are foreign taxes due on the income the foreign operating subsidiary pays the finance subsidiary, there is a credit against U. S. tax liability for such tax payments. Again, because of tax treaty arrangements, it is likely that there will be no tax by foreign governments on the remission of interest from the foreign operating subsidiaries to the U. S. domestic finance subsidiary (which in turn pays its debtholders and investors). Should the proceeds of the domestic finance subsidiary's fund raising be used in the United States, then the interest paid to it by the (U. S.) operating subsidiaries will be U. S. income, and the payments to the foreign debtholders and investors would be subject to U. S. withholding.

If the proceeds of the Euro-bond issue are to be used in the United States, then overseas finance subsidiaries are desirable. The IRS rule is that it is U. S. source income (hence, payments are subject to U. S. withholding) only if more than 80% of its gross income is from the conduct of a trade or business in the United States. Hence, it is possible that the management may arrange for the interest income to be received by the finance subsidiary, yet not deemed U. S. source income if the activities of the finance subsidiary itself are entirely outside the United States; it is not conducting a trade or business in the United States, but merely receiving interest from loans to U. S. firms (the operating subsidiaries). Among the finance subsidiary locations, Delaware and Luxembourg have been used most widely. At first, U. S. corporations favored Luxembourg as the site for their financial subsidiaries but switched their preferences to the United States, especially to Delaware, in 1966.

---

[16]For example, under a treaty, Great Britain's withholding on dividends and interest for payments to Americans is reduced from the standard 41.25% to 0.

A Delaware subsidiary is subject to very low state taxes and few restrictions on its legal ability to change operations. Also, it is possible to consolidate a Delaware subsidiary with the parent company for U. S. tax purposes, thereby taking advantages of tax-deductible losses that the subsidiary may incur in initial operations.

Luxembourg offers many advantages as the site for the financial subsidiary. For nominal fees, a holding company (which is in effect a financial subsidiary) can be established which is exempt from both Luxembourg income tax and witholding tax on interest and dividend payments.

In late 1975, the House Ways and Means Committee voted to eliminate witholding on dividend and interest payments to nonresidents. Should this Code change become law, it would remove the need for some of the operations described above.

INTEREST RATES ON INTERNATIONAL BONDS

The interest rates on foreign bonds are directly correlated with the rates prevailing in the given country adjusted by whatever regulation affects foreign bonds in particular. These regulations have often been modified to cater to government objectives regarding the balance of payments. Thus when the United States tried to reduce its deficit in the balance of payments it imposed the Interest Equalization Tax that raised the cost of issuing foreign bonds in this country. Conversely, Germany, which has been fighting continuing pressures to upvalue its currency, has at times given incentives to foreign borrowers to use the German bond market as a source of funds.

In the Euro-bond market the rates of a one-currency bond are directly related to the long-term rate level in the home country of the currency, the Euro-rate for short maturities of that currency, the rates in other currencies, and currency regulations and restrictions. For example, the Euro-dollar bond rate depends on the U. S. long-term rates, the Euro-dollar rates (and therefore on U. S. short-term rates), and the long-term rates in other countries. Given the controls on capital outflows from the United States that prevailed between 1965 and the end of 1973, the U. S. long-term rates actually served as a floor for the Euro-dollar bond rate. Lenders could always invest in the United States. However, borrowers were forced to raise the funds used for expansion of foreign operations in the Euro-bond market. Depending on the size of this demand for foreign financing, the Euro-bond rate could go substantially over the domestic U. S. bond rate. However, long-term rates in other currencies have served as a check on how high the Euro-dollar bond rate can go.[17]

One must also notice that there is clearly a feedback cycle between Euro-dollars and dollar-denominated Euro-bonds, even though one is generally short-term and the other medium- to long-term. Because of rate differentials observed or anticipated in the short run, Euro-dollar holders may want to shift into Euro-bonds for a brief period, for example. In addition, monetary authorities in some countries encourage the use of Euro-dollar accounts in the initial float of Euro-dollar issues since that policy avoids pressure on the domestic currency if used instead. Thus, under a steady flow of Euro-bond issues, there is a continuous amount of Euro-dollars so used; a

[17]A stepwise regression by Park using monthly data from 1968-1972 found 78% of the variance in the Euro-dollar bond rates explained by the U. S. triple-A bond rate. Park, *The Euro-Bond Market: Function and Structure,* pages 86-88.

peak period of issue would intensify the demand for Euro-dollars. Counteracting this effect is the substitution between them; hence, an increase in the supply of dollar denominated debt issues with demand fixed will lower equilibrium interest rates.

In spite of the fast growth of the Euro-bond market, this market is still small compared to the U. S. bond market. As a result, the Euro-bond market does not have great depth and breadth. It is not unusual to hear an investment banker advising a customer to decide where a Euro-bond issue would be desirable so that "if a favorable market develops they would be ready," since such a good market can disappear in a period of a couple of weeks. Thus, another large determinant of the level of Euro-bond rates is the volume of new issues coming to the international market in any one period.[18]

Bibliography

Borsuk, Mark, "The Future Development of Offshore Capital Markets in Asia." *Columbia Journal of World Business,* Spring 1974, pp. 48-60.

Dufey, Gunter, *The Euro-Bond Market: Function and Future.* Seattle, Wash.: University of Washington Graduate School of Business, 1961.

———"The Euro-Bond Market: Its Significance for International Financial Management, *"Journal of International Business Studies,* Summer 1970, pp. 65-81.

Einzig, Paul, *The Euro-Bond Market.* New York: St. Martin's Press, 1969.

Park, Yoon S., *The Euro-Bond Market: Function and Structure.* New York: Praeger Press, 1974.

Wai, U Tan and H. T. Patrick, "Stock and Bond Issues and Capital Markets in Less Developed Countries." *IMF Staff Papers,* July 1973, pp. 253-317.

[18]In general, Euro-bond interest rates have been rising steadily since 1963, in line with the overall rising interest rate trend in Western Europe and the United States. This trend of rising interest rates was further accelerated from 1969-1974 mainly because of the all-time high interest rates on the U. S. bond market and around the world.

CHAPTER 15

Comparative Capital Markets

In the preceding two chapters we noted the relationship that interest rates in the international financial markets bore to the rates in the domestic market of the currency in question. This chapter presents a framework for analyzing domestic capital markets. The analysis will focus on the relatively well-developed financial markets in Europe, the United States, and Japan.

It is impossible to discuss in any depth the characteristics of specific financial markets in one chapter. However, we would like to provide a general approach to the analysis of financial markets. The data on specific countries are used only as illustrations of an analytical approach. The framework provided by this approach should be helpful in understanding the financial markets of any country where the multinational corporation operates.

The same set of actors appears in every financial system. On one extreme there is a group of individuals and institutions that consume less than what they generate in income. The income that is not consumed is saved. At the other extreme is a set of individuals and institutions that find the income they generate insufficient to cover the level of expenditures they desire. The expenditures over and above the income generated by these units is used for current consumption or for investment in real goods, in contrast to financial investment.

The role of financial markets is to channel the excess funds of savers into the hands of those who have needs for funds beyond their capacity to generate the funds by themselves. There are two groups of institutions that facilitate this flow of funds from savers to investors. One group comprises the financial institutions such as commercial banks that accept deposits from savers and lend funds to investors, usually business enterprises. The other set of institutions is the security markets

517

where savers and investors in real goods meet directly. This occurs in the equity and debt markets where the business enterprises obtain funds directly from the savers.

This simple explanation of financial markets is depicted graphically in Exhibit 15.1, where the arrows indicate the flow of funds from savers on the left to the final users of funds on the right, all under the umbrella of the monetary authorities. Obviously, this is an extremely sanitized presentation of financial markets. In reality there is a large degree of interaction among the various groups presented in the exhibit. Also, there is a flow of funds in the direction opposite to the one presented in the diagram as business enterprises and governments pay back funds they have borrowed in the past.

Exhibit 15.2 shows the role that the various institutions mentioned in Exhibit 15.1 actually played in the period 1971-1973. The left panel of the exhibit shows the percentage of total financial assets purchased by each sector. The right panel shows the percentage of total financial assets issued by each sector—liabilities of that sector. The two sectors with very distinctive positions in each panel of the exhibit are the nonfinancial business enterprises, which are much more heavily represented as issuers of liabilities, and the household sector, which is more heavily represented as purchasers of financial assets. Commercial banks are among the major purchasers of financial assets and issuers of liabilities. To a lesser extent this is also true for the

EXHIBIT 15.1   Diagram of Flow of Funds in Financial Markets

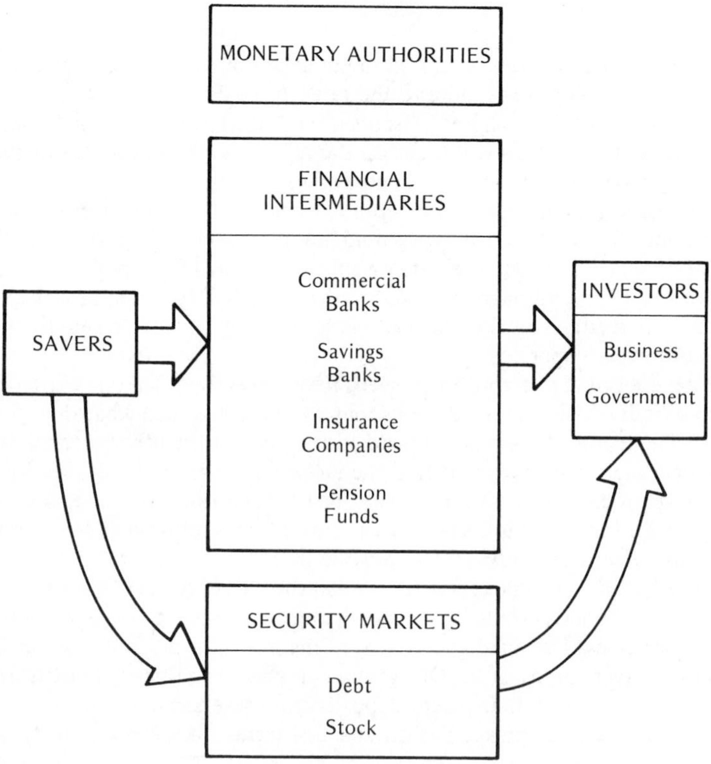

EXHIBIT 15.2 Sector Participation in the Flow of Funds, 1971 and 1973 Average

	Assets Acquired by Sector as a Percentage of Total Flow of Funds in Each Country							Liabilities Issued by Sector as a Percentage of Total Flow of Funds in Each Country						
	Germany	U.S.	France	Italy	Netherlands	U.K.	Japan	Germany	U.S.	France	Italy	Netherlands	U.K.	Japan
Central Bank	5.3%	2.2%	3.5%	6.7%	2.2%	N.A.	-2.2%	5.7%	2.2%	3.3%	6.6%	2.2%	N.A.	-2.2%
Commercial Bank	32.8	20.8	24.7	29.6	17.8	28.7	18.4	31.9	20.1	23.9	29.1	16.7	27.1	18.5
Nonbank Financial Intermediaries	7.8	23.5	25.3	12.3	20.1	17.5	17.0	7.9	22.4	23.4	12.4	18.9	18.4	17.0
Federal and Local Government	7.4	7.1[a]	5.4	8.2	11.4	9.4	11.2	6.2	13.3[a]	3.7	18.6	11.9	9.3	14.2
Nonfinancial Business Enterprise	11.0	9.8	11.0	10.5	N.A.	8.6	29.2	36.9	23.6	24.9	21.9	34.7	13.5	37.0
Household	26.0	29.7	24.5	23.6	34.4	17.4	23.6	2.0	15.2	12.4	.4	N.A.	11.7	10.9
Rest of the Economy	9.3	6.0	5.6	9.4[b]	13.3	17.9	2.7	9.9	3.2	8.1	10.4[b]	15.6	21.1	4.7
	100.0%	100.0%	100.0%	100.0%	100.0%	100.0%	100.0%	100.0%	100.0%	100.0%	100.0%	100.0%	100.0%	100.0%

[a]Includes Federally sponsored credit agencies.
[b]Includes discrepancies.
N.A. = Not available.
Figures do not always add to 100% because of rounding and averaging.
Source: Organization for Economic Cooperation and Development, *OECD Financial Statistics*, OECD Publications Center, Washington, D.C., April 1975.

nonbank financial intermediaries. Whether governments are net purchasers of financial assets or issuers of liabilities varies from country to country. The prominence of the rest of the economy in the domestic financial markets also differs from country to country.

SAVINGS

Two major questions arise when studying the savings of a country: (1) what is the level of savings relative to national income, and (2) in what form are these savings kept? The answer to the first question will determine the amount of funds available for investment in productive capacity. The answer to the second question gives an indication of the sectors that benefit from these savings and the financial intermediaries available in the country.

For the countries presented in the tables in this chapter, total savings, personal and business, account for between 30% and 40% of the respective national incomes. Italy, France, and the United Kingdom had approximately 30% of their national income accounted for by savings. Germany, the United States, the Netherlands, and Japan had savings of about 40% of national income. Other things constant, the countries with higher rates of savings are likely to have more sophisticated financial markets and higher economic growth to the extent that savings are channeled into real investments.

From Exhibit 15.2 we noticed that the largest purchaser of financial assets is the household sector. Exhibit 15.3 shows how the household sector distributed financial assets among various types of securities. In every country, cash and short-term deposits account for 50% or more of the household distribution of acquired financial assets, and they are 75% for France, Japan, and the United States. The large household savings figure for the United States is largely a product of the dis-investment that the household sector made in short-term securities and equities during those years. In the United States, the household sector was actually selling its holdings of short-term securities and equity shares and using the proceeds to acquire highly liquid deposits. The figures show a high desire for liquidity on the part of households in all the countries shown in the exhibit. This is partly determined by the level of liquid balances that individuals deem necessary for transaction purposes, but the data are also influenced by the particularly disastrous performance of the stock markets in every country during 1971 and 1973. The sales of equity holdings were particularly acute in the United Kingdom. In spite of the high desire for liquidity referred to above, households in all these countries found some funds available to be channeled into long-term financial investments. Financial investments in long-term securities took the form of bonds and loans in Germany and Italy. In the United States, the Netherlands, and the United Kingdom the long-term financial investments were mostly channeled into life insurance companies and pension funds. France and Japan had a rather small percentage of their financial savings channeled into long-term financial securities. The explanation for this pattern of distribution of financial savings is best understood by analyzing the type of financial intermediaries available in each country.

EXHIBIT 15.3 Household Sector: Distributions of Acquired Financial Assets and Issued Liabilities, 1971 and 1973 Average

	Distribution of Acquired Financial Assets							Distribution of Issued Liabilities						
	Germany	U.S.	France	Italy	Netherlands	U.K.	Japan	Germany	U.S.	France	Italy	Netherlands[a]	U.K.	Japan
Monetary Gold and Foreign Exchange														
Cash and Transferable Deposits	6.6%	9.7%	24.9%	26.6%	21.6%	28.3%	20.5%							
Other Deposits	50.0	66.2	58.4	36.6	28.9	45.9	55.3							
Short-Term Securities	.5	-5.8	4.5	.7	-.5	-.1	8.0							
Short-Term Loans			-.5		-2.1	-3.2		39.0%	37.1%	21.9%	100.0%		42.2%	78.0%[b]
Trade Credit			.3		-2.4				.5	.7			1.8	20.8
Bonds	14.0	6.9	} 5.7	14.4	6.3	2.8								
Shares	1.9	-6.0		2.2	.8	-20.6	1.4							
Savings Bonds and Other Debt Certificates		2.4												
Long-Term Loans	27.1	1.5			1.5	7.0		54.9	61.9	76.6			56.5	
Equity on Life Insurance and Pension Funds		26.8	3.6	9.6	37.6	39.7	13.0							
Others		-1.7	3.2[c]		9.5		2.1	6.1	-.3	.9				1.8
	100.0%	100.0%	100.0%	100.0%	100.0%	100.0%	100.0%	100.0%	100.0%	100.0%	100.0%		100.0%	100.0%

[a]Figures for the Netherlands unavailable.
[b]Includes long-term loans.
[c]Includes accounting registration differences.
Source: Organization for Economic Cooperation and Development, *OECD Financial Statistics*, OECD Publications Center, Washington, D.C., April 1975.

FINANCIAL INTERMEDIARIES

At the apex of the organization of any country's financial markets are the monetary authorities that regulate the flows of funds from savers to final investors. These authorities supervise the functioning of the financial intermediaries and the actual workings of the money and capital markets. In the following sections we review briefly the rule of monetary authorities and then turn to a general analysis of the financial intermediaries. The financial intermediaries are separated between commercial banks and nonbank financial intermediaries. Of these two, commercial banks in every country play a much larger role than all the other financial intermediaries combined. Thus, commercial banks are studied in more detail in the following discussion.

Monetary Authorities

The primary institution regulating the flow of funds in financial markets is the central bank of the country. In some cases, the central bank handles the monetary affairs of the country single-handedly. In other cases, other institutions also play an important role in the determination of the availability and distribution of credit.

Monetary authorities in every country have the economic goals of maintaining full employment, controlling the rate of inflation, maintaining external equilibrium, and furthering economic growth. Given the conflicting nature of these goals, monetary authorities usually must choose what priority to assign to each. The ranking of these priorities changes from time to time. Some of the tradeoffs that governments must make in the selection of these goals were discussed earlier in the text in the analysis of the external position of a country. An understanding of what priorities a given government places on its various goals at a certain point in time is extremely useful in anticipating the actions that the monetary authorities will take to control the credit flows in the country.

The traditional controls of central banks are open market operations, the level of the discount rate, reserve requirements, and selective controls. Among the countries studied in this chapter, only the United States and the United Kingdom make extensive use of open market operations to control the financial markets. The money markets in the other countries are not sufficiently broad and deep to allow a heavy reliance on open market operations to accomplish desired objectives. That leaves the other three tools as the major weapons that most central banks use in pursuing their monetary goals.

Among the seven countries, the monetary authorities of three merit special attention because of their peculiar characteristics. At one extreme is Switzerland where the central bank (40% owned by private interests) has until recently exerted only limited influence on the financial markets. Monetary policy in Switzerland is largely determined by the commercial banks. It is only in very recent years that problems with the exchange rate in the international markets and with inflation in the domestic markets have induced the Swiss central bank to take a more active posture. In contrast to the lax controls of the Swiss central bank, France and Italy are characterized by a number of governmental institutions that act with the central bank to exert a very powerful control over the financial markets.

In France the powers of the Bank of France (the central bank) are reinforced by the presence of two other regulatory bodies: the National Credit Council and the Banking Control Commission. Although the latter two organizations include members from business, labor, and banking, they are truly headed by the Bank of France in conjunction with the Treasury. The decisions of these organizations are carried out through the Professional Association of Banks. All banks in France, including the three major banks which are state owned, belong to this Association. In addition to credit decisions being highly centralized, the Bank of France possesses a powerful arsenal of tools to enforce its decisions. These tools go as far as including a review of each company's outstanding debt once a year. In this review not only the total credit needs but also the type of credit are considered.

Italy is another country where monetary authorities assume a very strong stance. Credit policies are formulated by the Interministerial Committee for Credit and Savings. These policies are then implemented through the Bank of Italy (the central bank) and the Treasury. The Bank of Italy retains a large degree of discretionary authority and its supervision of the monetary system is tight. Specific credits are monitored and the issue of securities is controlled. Another important characteristic of the Bank of Italy's policy has been the incorporation of development goals into monetary policy. This has given rise to a discriminating set of policies that differentiates on a regional as well as an industrial basis in its granting of credit. For example, the south of Italy always gets preferential treatment under any monetary policy.

Commercial Banks

There are two major characteristics that distinguish commercial banks in Europe and Japan from the banks in the United States. Whereas national banking and even branching in some states is forbidden in the United States, the other nations studied in this chapter are characterized by the existence of commercial banks with branches all over the country. The other major difference is the ability of commercial banks in these countries to underwrite securities. In the United States, commercial banking and investment banking cannot be performed by the same financial institution. In the European countries and in Japan, commercial banks not only can underwrite securities, but they are also usually active in buying and selling industrial bonds and equities for their own account. The equity holdings not only give commercial banks an opportunity to participate in the decisions of private companies, but often they help to establish a very special relationship between the commercial banks and the industrial sector: e.g., the zaibatsu (informal conglomerates) in Japan.

In spite of very large numbers of banks and branches in the European countries and Japan, the commercial banking business in those countries is highly concentrated in the hands of a few banks. In Germany, where there are more than 300 commercial banks with over 5000 branches, the three largest banks (Deutsche Bank, Dresdner Bank, and Commerzbank) account for about 40% of total commercial bank assets. A similar story can be found in Switzerland where three banks (Swiss Bank Corporation, Credit Suisse, and the Union Bank of Switzerland) represent a growing 40% of the total assets of Swiss banks. In France the three largest banks (Banque Nationale de Paris, Credit Lyonnais, and Societé General) are state-owned and account for 75%

of total bank assets. The same 75% is controlled by only two banks in the Netherlands (Algemene Bank Nederland (ABN) and Amsterdam-Rotterdam Bank (AMRO)). In the United Kingdom the concentration in banking is slightly less, with the largest amount of business being controlled by the so-called clearing banks, of which there are ten.

In terms of direct loans, commercial banks have traditionally specialized in short-term credits. The most common form of these credits outside the United States are overdrafts (purposely exceeding a checking deposit balance) and discounting of trade-related financial paper. The system of compensating balances held with commercial banks by borrowers which is common in the United States is usually not found in European commercial banks; however, compensating balances are very popular in Japan. The high reliance of all commercial banks on short-term credit can be seen in Exhibit 15.4, where the largest item in the acquisition of financial assets is short-term loans.

In spite of the traditional reliance on short-term credits, commercial banks in all the countries studied have started to play an increasingly significant role in the medium- and long-term funds market. In Exhibit 15.4 Germany and France are cases in point where for the period 1971-1973, 63% and 31% of their respective acquired financial assets were in long-term loans.[1] The slowest change in this trend towards longer maturities in loans from commercial banks can be seen in Italy, the United Kingdom, and Japan. In Italy, in spite of the large variety of commercial banks (by historical origins and geographical coverage), all of them still concentrate on short-term loans in the form of overdrafts and discounting of trade paper. In the United Kingdom, commercial banks until 1971 considered themselves only as suppliers of working capital. However, since the banking reform of 1971 these banks have become eager to be one-stop supermarkets for all types of borrowers. They have started to offer not only longer-maturity loans, but also more flexible terms. In Japan, only 10% of total loans carry a maturity of over a year.

The growth of medium- and long-term credit in France (31% of the average total financial assets acquired in 1971-1973) shows the impact of the French governmental credit policies and development plans. Most of the medium-term lending of French banks can be rediscounted with Credit National, one of the public credit institutions. These credits have a maturity of up to seven years and have to be approved by both Credit National and the Bank of France. If these institutions do not approve the loan, the commercial bank cannot rediscount the loan with them. Other things constant, this would make the particular loan less desirable to the commercial bank—the objective of the monetary authorities.

In analyzing the prevalence of short-term maturities in the loans extended by commercial banks, one must take into account the fact that most of these short-term credits are usually refinanced before or shortly after the loan expires. This process converts short-term loans into *de facto* long-term credits. This sequence of events is further supported by the situation prevalent in several countries where the commercial banks have close ties with the industrial sector through their direct or indirect holdings of equity in industrial companies.

The position of power that commercial banks enjoy in the financial markets is further reinforced in those countries where they are allowed to undertake traditional

---

[1] The majority of the loans classified in the exhibits in this chapter as long-term have a maturity not exceeding five to seven years.

	Distribution of Acquired Financial Assets							Distribution of Issued Liabilities						
	Germany	U.S.	France	Italy	Netherlands	U.K.[a]	Japan	Germany	U.S.	France	Italy	Netherlands	U.K.[a]	Japan
Monetary Gold and Foreign Exchange						16.4%			-3.1%	5.6%			23.2%	
Cash and Transferable Deposits			13.2%	6.2	18.9	.4	5.6	12.1%	19.1	23.4	51.3%	42.2%	76.6	31.2%
Other Deposits		1.0%	10.8	11.5	8.6		.4	69.3	63.2	53.0	30.5	53.8		39.8
Short-Term Securities		-4.0	-.2	5.9	2.7	.3			2.5			.1		
Short-Term Loans	23.0%	48.0	41.0	40.7	19.6	70.7	77.8[b]		3.0	12.0	19.7	-1.9		3.3[b]
Trade Credit														
Bonds	5.6	24.0	1.4	26.5	5.7	10.7	9.4	22.9		2.5		3.7		9.8
Shares	1.1		2.1	.3	-.6	1.1	2.5	1.2	.6	1.1	.3		.2	.7
Savings Bonds and Other Debt Certificates					30.1							.4		
Long-Term Loans	63.2	18.5	30.7	8.9	15.1	.7				1.4		1.8		
Equity on Life Insurance and Pension Funds														
Others	7.2	12.6	1.5[c]				4.3	-5.5	14.6	1.2[c]	-2.3			15.0
	100.0%	100.0%	100.0%	100.0%	100.0%	100.0%	100.0%	100.0%	100.0%	100.0%	100.0%	100.0%	100.0%	100.0%

[a]Central bank included in the banking sector.
[b]Includes long-term loans.
[c]Plus accounting registration differences.
Source: Organization for Economic Cooperation and Development, *OECD Financial Statistics*, OECD Publications Center, Washington, D.C., April 1975.

investment or merchant banking activities. This is particularly so in Switzerland where the political and monetary stability together with the unequaled tradition of secrecy have attracted a large volume of foreign funds into the country. This has made the country one of the world's major sources of capital and the Swiss commercial banks some of the most powerful private financial institutions in international markets. Any major financing in Switzerland must be handled through one of the Big Three (the three largest banks). They do most of the underwriting and placing of bond issues and they are active in the trading of securities. These banks also control a queuing system whereby companies must wait before they can issue securities. The mechanics of the queuing system are not described anywhere, but the queue is tightly controlled by the commercial banks. Furthermore, the commercial banks, usually through holding companies, also maintain long-term positions in commercial and industrial enterprises.

In Germany the commercial banks have not enjoyed the same continuous inflow of foreign funds. However, German commercial banks are in a position similar to that of the Swiss banks in the area of underwriting. German banks both handle the listing and the initial transactions of new issues and maintain a secondary market for the securities they handle. The queuing system to issue securities is also present in Germany and it is controlled by the major German commercial banks. In the Netherlands and France, the commercial banks also enjoy the ability to underwrite securities with the associated powers that this position engenders. However, French commercial banks until recently took no direct equity positions in the industrial sector. In the early 1970s, the three state-owned French banks did expand into the holding of equities. This policy is in addition to the traditionally large trust department that each of these banks has.

A country that traditionally kept commercial banking and investment banking separate as in the United States is the United Kingdom. However, since the 1971 U.K. bank reform, the commercial banks have started to compete with the merchant banks (investment banks) by advising on corporate issues and bringing the issues to the market. These activities have usually been carried out by buying an interest in an established merchant bank or by creating new merchant banks. In Japan, commercial banks can participate only in the underwriting of government securities, a large proportion of which is kept for portfolio purposes. The underwriting of industrial securities in Japan is left to the "security houses."

The major sources of funds for commercial banks in all the countries are deposits. However, the bond market also plays an important role in raising funds for commercial banks in Germany and Japan. (See Exhibit 15.4.)

Nonbank Financial Intermediaries

As mentioned before, not only are commercial banks the largest financial intermediaries in every country but they also perform a large number of functions. Both of these factors limit the role that nonbank financial intermediaries play in the financial markets of these countries. However, the nonbank financial intermediaries play a significant role in the medium- and long-term sectors of the financial markets, although not in the short-term sector which is the main province of the commercial banks. Exhibit 15.5 presents data on the average distribution of financial assets acquired and liabilities issued by nonbank financial institutions in 1971 and 1973.

EXHIBIT 15.5 Nonbank Financial Institutions: Distribution of Acquired Financial Assets and Issued Liabilities, 1971 and 1973 Average

	Distribution of Acquired Financial Assets							Distribution of Issued Liabilities						
	Germany[a]	U.S.[b]	France[c]	Italy[d]	Netherlands	U.K.	Japan	Germany[a]	U.S.[b]	France[c]	Italy[d]	Netherlands	U.K.	Japan
Monetary Gold and Foreign Exchange														
Cash and Transferable Deposits	1.2%	1.6%	5.6%	6.9%	.2%	9.4%	3.6%			13.4%	.4%			17.5%
Other Deposits	4.9	.1	4.3	16.1	-.2	.7	.8		39.9%	40.2	9.4	28.3	42.9	49.9
Short-Term Securities		-.6	-2.8	-.8	1.9				2.1	3.7			.1	
Short-Term Loans		14.4	18.6	3.7	-.5	4.7	86.0[e]	.1%	7.5	6.1	1.4	3.2	13.6	1.5[e]
Trade Credit		.3	.5							.3				
Bonds	5.9	20.6	13.1	2.4	4.9	23.8	8.6		13.0	10.4	64.0		1.4	2.6
Shares	1.7	18.1	5.4	.3	7.9	24.2	3.1	1.2	.7	9.0	4.6		3.7	.2
Savings Bonds and Other Debt Certificates					84.9			98.3	.7	10.5	14.4	.7	-.6	
Long-Term Loans	36.6	42.6	55.0	71.7	.3	37.3				1.5				
Equity on Life Insurance and Pension Funds									29.7	4.9[f]	6.0	69.7	38.5	13.0
Others		3.0	.4[f]		.8	-4.0	-2.0		7.5					15.5
	100.0%	100.0%	100.0%	100.0%	100.0%	100.0%	100.0%	100.0%	100.0%	100.0%	100.0%	100.0%	100.0%	100.0%

[a]Insurance companies, building corporations, and other large corporations.
[b]Nonbank financial institutions plus federally sponsored credit agencies.
[c]Caisse des depots and other institutions.
[d]Special credit institutions and insurance companies. Insurance companies are only 1% of total assets.
[e]Includes long-term loans.
[f]Includes accounting registration differences.
Source: Organization for Economic Cooperation and Development, *OECD Financial Statistics*, OECD Publications Center, Washington, D.C., April 1975.

Nonbank financial intermediaries can be disaggregated into two major categories according to their primary source of funds: (1) those that receive funds on a contractual basis, such as insurance companies, and (2) those that receive their funds on a noncontractual basis, such as savings banks.

The contractual type of nonbank financial institution is composed of insurance companies and pension funds. Outside the United States and the United Kingdom, pension funds are nonexistent or very unimportant in the countries shown in Exhibit 15.5. The importance of insurance companies in all the countries can be gauged by the percentage of total liabilities issued in the form of insurance policies and pension fund contributions. This category in Exhibit 15.5 shows that insurance companies controlled a large amount of household incremental savings in the Netherlands, equalling 70% of total liabilities issued by nonbank financial institutions. In the United States and the United Kingdom pension funds and insurance companies also accounted for a significant amount of total liabilities issued by nonbank financial institutions. In Japan, where insurance companies are a growing institution, 13% of total liabilities of nonbank financial institutions were in insurance policies. This leaves Germany, France, and Italy among the countries in Exhibit 15.5 with little apparent representation in the insurance industry. The absence of liabilities issued by insurance companies in Germany is misleading and must be explained in terms of data deficiencies; footnote (a) to Exhibit 15.5 shows the presence of insurance companies, yet there is no figure for insurance equity. Insurance companies in Germany include more than 300 firms and are very active. On the other hand, France and Italy are representative of many countries where there is no insurance industry as known in the United States. Instead, the government provides insurance compensation for its citizens. The source of funds for this compensation is the annual fiscal budget; therefore, in these countries a pool of investible funds generated from payments on insurance policies does not exist. The amount required for compensation is determined according to the law of the country and is raised on an annual basis. Obviously, in not every country are these social services provided by the government or by private institutions.

The remaining nonbank financial institutions, excluding insurance companies and pension funds, can be further divided between those whose sources of funds are of a long-term nature and those whose sources of funds are mostly short-term deposits. There is a high correlation between the degree of government control over these institutions and their ability to generate long-term sources of funds.

Exhibit 15.5 shows that the two countries with the largest percentages of their liabilities generated in the form of long-term funds, other than equity on life insurance and pension funds, are France and Italy. The study of the nonbank institutions in these countries throws light on the system that is prevalent in several European countries. In France, government control begins with the postal savings and the savings banks. These institutions are required to deposit the enormous funds they collect, most of the household sector savings deposits, with the Caisse des Depots et Consignations (CDC) at a fixed rate of interest. CDC, in turn, channels the bulk of these funds into government projects which include lending to semipublic credit institutions. These semipublic credit institutions then extend long-term loans to industry either directly in the form of loans or indirectly through the discounting of medium-term credit granted to industry by commercial banks. These semipublic credit institutions also raise a substantial portion of their funds in the bond and equity market. Initially, these institutions were created after World War II to channel savings into desired areas during the reconstruction period. Now they are the primary source of medium- and long-term credit in the country. In addition to Credit National, which is the largest of these institutions and lends to industry in general, there is a series of institutions that specialize in granting credit to specific sectors. Examples of these other institutions include Credit Foncier, which is primarily concerned with financing residential construction, and Credit Agricole, which provides loans to farmers.

In Italy the institutions that raise their funds in the long-term sector of the market are also of a public or semipublic nature. These institutions specialize in three major types of credits: industry and public works, mortgages, and agricultural credit. The main source of funds of these institutions is the bond market which they dominate. Exhibit 15.5 shows that 64% of the liabilities issued by nonbank financial institutions in Italy in 1971-1973 were in the form of bonds. These bonds were issued mostly by these semipublic institutions which also have access to commercial banks and to direct loans from the government for their sources of funds. The bonds are issued under very attractive terms to the bond holder. Being of a semipublic nature, the major criterion in their lending is development of the country. The larger the contribution a company can prove it can make in the development of a region, the better the credit terms that these institutions will provide.

In these examples of France and Italy one can see the strong influence that their governments can exert directly on the financial markets. The channeling of credit to different economic sectors can be controlled with relative ease in these countries. It only requires changing the lending criteria of the semipublic credit institutions which the government controls. Such favored treatment and influence on the unimpeded action of the capital markets is the objective of many legislative proposals in the United States, especially in the wake of recent concern over a possible capital shortage. It is usually justified on the ground of social or economic externalities. Thus, reducing corporate taxes or providing a flat investment tax credit for investment subsidizes all investment and all corporations. If the government budget is unchanged, it means current individual taxpayers provide more funds in return for greater consumption by some individuals in the future. In terms of gaining public support, however, this action has two serious drawbacks. First, individuals know they will sacrifice now, but it is not clear which class of individuals will benefit in the future. Second, all firms are helped in general, yet the public might be far more willing to make sacrifices to help energy production which will lower fuel costs than to revive the hula hoop. It is precisely because of limited resources, the trade-off between consumption now and consumption in the future, and uncertainty about who will do the consuming that the controversy arises. Economic externalities enter when public representatives feel that the spill-over effects (good or bad) from projects such as Project Independence are not fully reflected in the rate of return to the firms making the investment.

Savings banks and specialized banks abound in all these countries. Savings bank lending policies can be strictly controlled by the government, as seen in France. In the other countries, the savings banks tend to operate more like commercial banks specializing in specific types of credits, such as consumer credit or any other credit demanded by the bulk of the bank's depositors.

The allocation of credit by these nonbank financial intermediaries can be associated with the origin of their sources of funds. Those countries with a large reliance on contractual sources of funds invest a larger percentage of their funds in bonds and shares. Exhibit 15.5 shows that the three countries with the largest amount of funds raised in the form of equity in insurance companies and pension funds (the United States, the United Kingdom, and the Netherlands) are also the countries with the largest percentage of total assets acquired represented by bonds, shares, and other debt certificates. The other countries in the exhibit lend their funds mostly in the form of short- and long-term loans.

The form in which these financial intermediaries raise their funds and channel them into the hands of the final investor is a major determinant of the depth and breadth of the security markets in a country. The countries without privately funded insurance companies and pension funds deprive themselves of a major participant in the security markets. It is in the countries with large institutional investors that we find developed security markets. The best examples of this situation are the United States and the United Kingdom.

SECURITY MARKETS

In the preceding discussion we made reference to security markets in the context of the investment that financial intermediaries make in these markets. A more direct appraisal of the breadth and depth of the security markets can be obtained by studying the amount of gross issues by sector presented in Exhibit 15.6. A detailed analysis of these markets would require a study of the stock of the securities available in these markets as well as a disaggregation of the securities by ownership. In this chapter we will only look at the gross issues.

Even using the 1971 exchange rates to convert the figures of gross issues from local currencies into U. S. dollars, the volume of gross issues in the United States at $96 billion is by far the largest among all the countries presented in the exhibit. Although only a third of the volume of the United States, Japan's gross issues follow with the amount of $33 billion. The size of gross issues in Germany, Italy, and the United Kingdom ranges between $15 and $20 billion. The smallest markets appear in France and the Netherlands. Notice, however, that this ranking in size is not adjusted for the size of the economic system of each country.

In every country bond issues represent 75% or more of total issues of securities. Equity shares account for the remaining 25% or less. It is interesting to note that the highest share of equities in total issues appears in France. This is largely because of a system prevailing in that country that allows for a large number of small businesses to gather under the umbrella of a single organization that then issues securities on its name, usually with a government guarantee. The impact of this system can also be seen in the high percentage of bond issues in France that is accounted for by private nonfinancial firms (22% of total gross issues). Among the remaining countries, the United States, Italy, and Japan had over 10% of the gross issues in their markets represented by equities. In spite of the broad stock market in the United Kingdom, during the years presented in the exhibit, 1971 and 1973, the economic conditions of the country did not favor new issues in the stock market. In every country most of the shares were issued by private nonfinancial companies.

EXHIBIT 15.6   Gross Issues by Sector: 1971 and 1973 Averages (percentages)

	Germany	U.S.	France	Italy	Netherlands	U.K.	Japan
Shares	7.8%	12.6%	24.5%	13.4%	.9%	3.4%	12.7%
Private Nonfinancial	5.9	9.9	15.7	–	.5	2.2	11.1
Financial Institutions	1.9	2.7	8.8	–	.4	1.2	1.6
Bonds-Public Issues	70.7	87.4[a]	75.5	86.1	19.4	91.6	87.3
Central Government	7.7	12.4	13.7	26.7	5.9	78.3	13.0
Central Government Enterprises	–	20.8	–	–	–	–	–
State and Local Government	2.2	14.5	5.3	.4	5.4	10.6	6.8
State and Local Enterprises	–	10.0	–	–	–	–	–
Public Nonfinancial	6.3	–	12.5	13.0	} 3.8	–	14.0
Private Nonfinancial	2.0	21.0	22.3	.5		1.3	9.7
Financial Institutions	48.4	6.6	21.1	45.1	3.7	1.4	43.8
Rest of the Economy	4.1	2.1	.6	.4	.6	–	–
Bonds-Private Placements	–	–	–	.5	5.6	5.0	–
Debt Certificates	21.5	–	–	–	75.5	–	–
	100.0	100.0	100.0	100.0	100.0	100.0	100.0
Total in U. S. Billion Dollars (translated at 1971 exchange rates)	$17.5	$96.3	$7.35	$19.9	$5.2	$14.4	$33.2

[a]Includes private placements.
Source: Organization for Economic Cooperation and Development, *OECD Financial Statistics*, OECD Publications Center, Washington, D.C., April 1975.

The public issues of bonds can be divided between those issued by governments or their agencies and those issued by private institutions. Government issues have a larger representation in the market than issues of the private sector in the United States and the United Kingdom. The opposite is true in Germany and Japan, where the governments borrow very small amounts in the bond market. In France and Italy both private and government sectors are heavy users of the bond market as a source of funds. Within the issues of bonds by the private sector, nonfinancial businesses rank higher than financial firms only in the United States and France. In all the other countries in Exhibit 15.6, financial institutions are the heaviest issuers of bonds within the private sector. This is a reflection of the earlier discussion on financial intermediaries that found the bond market as one of the major sources of funds for these firms. Among these countries the financial intermediaries issuing bonds are usually nonbank intermediaries. This is so with the exception of Japan where commercial banks obtain approximately 10% of their sources of funds from the bond market, thus contributing heavily to the participation of financial intermediaries as a whole in the bond market.

USES OF FUNDS: INVESTMENT

There are two major groups that transform the savings of society into real investment. These groups are government and business enterprises. The sources of funds of these investors come from two main sources. They either generate funds from the performance of their business or they borrow funds from those sectors with excess funds. The funds generated in the course of business are in the form of taxes for the government. For business, the internally generated funds are profits adjusted for noncash expenses such as depreciation. The funds obtained from the sectors with excess funds come directly from the savers when the funds are obtained through the securities markets or indirectly when the funds are obtained from one of the financial intermediaries discussed in the previous section.

Of these two investment sectors, the participation of government in financial markets is the most difficult to determine. It basically involves an understanding of fiscal and monetary policy for the country. The government not only must determine the size of the budget, the necessary amount of funds required to finance desired government projects, but also must decide how to finance any deficit in that budget. To the extent that taxes collected by the government are not sufficient to cover the desired level of expenditures, a choice has to be made as to whether the government borrows directly from the monetary authority, that is, expands the money supply, or whether the funds are to be raised in the debt market. The final choice will have an impact on the country's level of inflation and interest rates. The use of an increased money supply tends to be inflationary. The use of debt markets tends to increase interest rates. The economic goals of the government will determine the final choice. An analysis of the tradeoffs and considerations that go into such a decision is outside the scope of this chapter. However, a proper understanding of a financial market and the ability to forecast its behavior depends heavily on the analysis of the variables that affect and are affected by the government sector.

The sources and uses of funds of the nonfinancial business sector for the countries discussed in this chapter are presented in Exhibit 15.7. The sources of funds

are divided between internal and external. The amount of funds available from internal sources is a function of the profitability of the firm. In lean years this source
provides less funds than in prosperous years. The amount of internal funds as a percentage of total sources of funds is a function of the amount of leverage (amount of
debt relative to equity) that prevails in the country. Within a limit, this proportion
is also a function of business conditions, showing where external sources are called to
fill in the vacuum left by internal sources. The comparisons among countries in
Exhibit 15.7 are a bit hard to make since the coverage of years is not the same for
each country. Still, one can see Germany, the United States, and the Netherlands
providing more than 50% of total sources of funds from internally generated sources.
Italy obtains on average only 40% of funds from internal sources. For the United
Kingdom this figure is somewhat higher at 45%. The lowest proportion of total
sources of funds contributed by internal sources is found in Japan where this source
contributes only 24% of the total. This points to the well-known high leverage that
characterizes Japanese companies. Three-quarters of the funds used by Japanese
business firms are derived from sources external to the firm.

A separation of the external sources of funds between short- and long-term
shows the United States and the Netherlands with a larger proportion of long-term
than short-term sources. The opposite relationship prevails in the cases of Italy and
Japan. For the United Kingdom almost the same proportion was raised in the short-
term as in the long-term market. No disaggregation is available for Germany. Among
the short-term sources, trade credit is a major item. The other important source of
short-term credit is short-term borrowing, which is generally obtained from commercial banks. In none of the countries do short-term marketable securities provide an
important source of funds. Among long-term sources of funds the major distinction
is between private and market sources. Of the countries in Exhibit 15.7, the security
market represented an important source of long-term funds (between 15% and 25%
of total sources of funds) in the United States and the United Kingdom. In the other
countries long-term borrowings primarily from financial intermediaries provided the
major source of long-term funds. In these countries business is heavily dependent on
financial intermediaries for both short-and long-term funds.

As to the uses of funds of the business sector, the investment in nonfinancial
assets is obviously the largest recipient of funds. Investment in financial assets represents largely the extension of trade credit and, to a lesser extent, temporary investment of excess funds.

SUMMARY

This chapter can only begin to outline the relationship among the participants
in the capital markets of selected nations. The variable nature of governments is
critical, for some keep influence and control of monetary and fiscal policy at a
minimum, while others own the major credit institutions and hold household deposits. The nature of the channeling process, by which excess income from various
sectors, such as households, is moved to the users of capital, is important to note
when a manager is seeking funds in various nations. In addition, the varied structures
outlined in this chapter may well suggest to the citizen of any country the directions
in which his or her nation may evolve in coming years.

These figures do not change with great speed, but can move with the business

EXHIBIT 15.7 Sources and Uses of Funds of Nonfinancial Business Centers (percentages)

	Germany 1967-72		United States 1968-73			Italy 1967-72			Netherlands 1966-68			United Kingdom 1968-72			Japan 1968-72		
Sources																	
Internal	54.0%		53.5%			40.1%			53.7%			45.1%			24.1%		
External	46.0		46.5			59.1			46.3			54.9			75.9		
Short-Term Sources				18.6			31.5			16.7			28.5			47.3	
Issues of Bills					.2						2.1						.1
Short-Term Borrowings					6.7						14.6						19.2
Trade Credits Received					11.2												18.8
Other					.5												9.2
		41.5															
Long-Term Sources				27.9			27.6			29.6			26.4			28.6	
Staff Superannuation											.5						1.1
Issues of Long-Term Bonds					11.8			(1.7)			5.8			10.3			1.3
Long-Term Borrowings					10.5			21.5			13.4						22.2
Issues of Shares		4.5			5.6			7.8			9.9			16.1			4.0
	100.0%		100.0%			100.0%			100.0%			100.0%			100.0%		
Uses																	
Investment in Nonfinancial Assets	68.1%		75.2%			80.1%			74.6%			55.3%			51.2%		
Investment in Financial Assets	31.9		24.8			19.9			25.4			44.7			48.8		
	100.0%		100.0%			100.0%			100.0%			100.0%			100.0%		

Source: Organization for Economic Cooperation and Development, *OECD Financial Statistics*, OECD Publications, Center, Washington, D.C., April 1975.
Note: France did not report sources and uses data.

cycle. In addition, delays in reporting from various national authorities mean that the data are often nearly two years late. However, the basic relationships and the major differences among countries tend to persist.

The appendix to this chapter provides a short checklist of variables to consider when evaluating the financial markets in any nation.

Questions

Collect the relevant data to analyze the financial markets of a developed country (the outline in the appendix to this chapter can be useful in this endeavor). Sources of data can be obtained from the bibliography and from publications of the central bank and commercial banks in the country you are analyzing.

1. Describe the behavior of the major sectors in the financial markets in the last five years.

2. What are the implications of the patterns of behavior you find in these sectors for the following:

a. Effectiveness of monetary policy

b. Availability and cost of various types of financial investment instruments

c. Availability and cost of various sources of funds

d. Development of security markets

e. General levels of interest rates

f. Spread between short- and long-term rates

g. Volatility of interest rates

h. International capital markets

3. What is your forecast for the level of interest rates during the next twelve months? Why?

Bibliography

Business International Corporation, *Financing Foreign Operations*, current issues, New York.

Organization for Economic Cooperation and Development, *OECD Financial Statistics*, OECD Publications Center, current issues, Washington, D.C.

Appendix: Outline for Analyzing Financial Markets

Savers:

I. Short-term financial investment
II. Long-term financial investment
   A. Contractual, e.g., insurance premiums
   B. Noncontractual
      1. Nonmarketable, e.g., time deposits
      2. Marketable, e.g., commercial paper

Financial Intermediaries:

I. Sources of funds
   A. Deposits
   B. Contractual payments
   C. Marketable securities
II. Uses of funds
   A. Short-term financial investments
      1. Marketable instruments
      2. Nonmarketable instruments, e.g., loans
   B. Long-term financial investments
      1. Marketable instruments
      2. Nonmarketable instruments

Borrowers:

I. Nonfinancial business enterprises
   A. Internal funds
   B. External funds
      1. Short-term sources of funds
         a. Loans
         b. Trade credit
         c. Public offerings
      2. Long-term sources
         a. Loans
         b. Private placements
         c. Public offerings
II. Public enterprises
   (choices are similar to above private enterprises)
III. Government
   (choices are similar to above private enterprises)

Altos Hornos De Vizcaya, S.A.

In early April 1971, Mr. Juan Luis Burgos Marin, Financial Director of Altos Hornos de Vizcaya (AHV), was considering a new proposal presented to him to raise funds in the Euro-dollar market. A lawyer and economist by training, Mr. Burgos had been with AHV for the previous twelve years.

AHV was founded in 1848, and it grew to be the largest Spanish basic steel producer, with sales of U. S. $264 million in 1970. It had borrowed from foreign banks in the past, but these borrowings had been associated primarily with imports of raw materials and equipment which were strongly encouraged by the export institutions of the exporting countries. The proposal that Mr. Burgos was considering now was different. It involved borrowing directly from foreign banks without the intervention of export-oriented organizations. The proposal to obtain a Euro-dollar loan had been presented to Mr. Burgos by Credito Latino, an international brokerage company which specialized in raising unsecured funds in the Euro-dollar market.

THE SPANISH STEEL INDUSTRY

Production

Following the pattern common to other European countries, Spain began manufacturing steel in the nineteenth century and by the first part of the twentieth century it had developed sufficient steel-making capacity to satisfy internal demand. By 1929 the output had reached one million tons, but thereafter the industry stagnated. First came the Civil War (1936-1938), followed by an international boycott on the Spanish regime. The reconstruction of the steel industry was not able to begin until 1949 when urgently needed capital goods could once again be imported. The following year, the government, in order to increase production, formed a national steel company, the Instituto Nacional de Industria de la Empresa Nacional Siderurgica (ENSIDESA), with the purpose of constructing and operating an integrated steel plant in Aviles, in northwestern Spain. Other steel manufacturers of mixed ownership, namely Altos Hornos de Vizcaya and Uninsa, also began to expand their capacity. By 1964, Spain was producing 3.1 million tons of steel annually.

Accion Concertadas

In 1964, the Spanish Government launched its First Development Plan (1964-1967 in order to stimulate the domestic economy. The Plan authorized agreements, "Accion Concertadas," between the government and companies in basic industries. Companies would receive government support and fiscal incentives provided they co-operated with the government towards the attainment of the goals of the Development Plan. Altos Hornos de Vizcaya and Uninsa signed such agreements in March 1965 to cover the period 1965-1972. ENSIDESA, being wholly owned by the government, gave its silent consent.

The major objective of the Accion Concertadas between the three major steel producers and the government was to ensure a smooth and balanced expansion of Spanish steel capacity. The companies committed themselves to certain plant additions and modifications during the period 1964-1972, thereby specifying their capacity and technology. AHV was to produce about 40% of total production by 1971. Prices for finished products were to be laid down by the Ministry of Trade, as were the prices of intercompany purchases of semifinished products.

In return for such cooperation, the companies received government support and fiscal incentives, principal among which were:

1. Government agencies would grant loans for 70% of the value of capital expenditures for agreed-upon plant expansions, subject to an upper limit of $62 million.

2. The government would extend its guarantee to loans obtained by the companies in order to meet the objectives of the Plan.

3. Companies would obtain up to a 95% rebate on taxes charged for imports of capital goods, raw materials, and interest payments abroad. Application for rebate had to be made to the Ministry of Commerce and approval was granted on an individual basis. (The normal tax rate on interest payments to foreigners was 24%.)

4. A five-year depreciation period would be allowed for the new plant and equipment.

Since 1965, the steel industry had been growing dynamically; production of steel had risen to 7.4 million tons in 1970, and construction already undertaken by the three producers promised to result in a capacity of 12 million tons by 1975. The capacity planned for 1975 was 90% of the expected domestic demand at that date. (See Exhibits 1 and 2.) The table below highlights this development and compares Spanish steel production with the United Kingdom and Mexico:

Steel Production (thousands of metric tons)

	1953	1968	1970	Kilograms per Capita 1970
United Kingdom	17,891	26,277	28,000	465
Spain	897	4,940	7,400	252
Mexico	462	3,285	3,832	179

Steel Prices

The Ministry of Trade set Spanish steel prices below those operative in the European Economic Community (EEC) and other European countries. Even after the 6% hike which started in July 1971, prices were expected to remain an average of 10-15% below those of Common Market countries.

The Spanish steel industry was also well protected from the dumping of cheap imports of steel products by regulations which stipulated that:

1. Quotas for products not produced or produced in insufficient quantity by local manufacturers had to be agreed upon by the manufacturers and the Ministry of External Trade.

2. Imports outside the quota system were liable to an import tax, unlike products inside the quota. Moreover, if the selling price of these products was below that charged by local manufacturers, an antidumping clause could be invoked by the Spanish Steel Federation to forbid further imports.

Sources of Raw Materials

Iron and coal were the two major raw materials used in the production of steel. Iron was Spain's main extractive industry, and the supply of iron ore was expected to be sufficient to satisfy the needs of the steel industry in the future. Regarding coal, the nationalized HUNOSA coal mining company was preparing a U. S. $400 million expansion and modernization program that would make the steel makers less dependent upon imported coal.

COMPANY BACKGROUND

Ownership

In 1970 the largest single shareholder of AHV was the largest steel company in the United States, i.e., U. S. Steel Corporation. In 1964 U. S. Steel had subscribed to 27% of the shares of AHV. In addition, U. S. Steel had extended a long-term unsecured loan to AHV in the amount of U. S. $10 million and it had agreed to a technical assistance pact with AHV. U. S. Steel was involved in every aspect of the company's operations, and it was represented on the Board of Directors and on each daily operational committee through its permanent mission of resident U. S. Steel executives and technicians.

The next important single shareholder was the Bank of Spain (the central bank) which owned approximately 6% of the equity. This figure, however, did not fully indicate the large support that the government offered to AHV in the form of loans and guarantees amounting to more than U. S. $120 million. Commercial banks and industrial banks together owned approximately 7½% of the equity. This again did not reveal the strong commitment of these institutions to AHV in the form of loans. The remaining 59½% of the equity was in the hands of 36,000 private and institutional shareholders. The shares of AHV were listed and traded on the Madrid, Barcelona, and Bilbao Stock Exchanges.

Operations

AHV was a fully integrated steel producer. It processed coal, iron ore, and scrap iron up to semifinished steel products such as wire, rods, and girders for the construction industry, and hot- and cold-rolled strip and galvanized products for general engineering purposes and for the automobile industry. In 1970 AHV produced 1.7 million tons of steel.

The company had two main plants: the most important was at Bilbao in northern Spain, and the second was at Sagunto, on the Mediterranean coast. Both plants were located at a port, which facilitated the importation of raw materials— mainly coal and semifinished goods. Raw materials constituted 56% of cost of goods sold: 22% was imported, and 34% was produced in Spain.

In the past twelve years, AHV had invested over $260 million in expanding capacity and modernizing existing facilities, and it now possessed some of the most technically advanced machinery in Europe. This machinery contributed to the productivity of labor which accounted for 15% of cost of goods sold. With a labor force of 14,000 people, AHV was the largest employer in the Bilbao area. It paid the highest wages and salaries in both Bilbao and Sagunto and had a record of smooth labor relations. Its wage contracts were negotiated every two years and included incentive schemes to increase productivity.

AHV had investments in affiliated companies which provided control of the major suppliers and distributors. The most recent acquisition had been S.A. Basconia which had been purchased during 1969 and which was AHV's largest customer, buying 12% of total sales. The other affiliates had been acquired in the 1940s. Among these, Agruminsa was AHV's principal supplier of raw materials.

AHV'S FINANCIAL FORECASTS

Forecasted Need for Funds

In spite of the continuous growth in AHV's sales, a slowdown in the economy during 1969 resulted in sales falling short of projections and a corresponding squeeze on working capital. Suppliers' credit as well as overdraft facilities had been extended to finance the unexpected build-up in inventories. (See Exhibits 3 and 4.) Moreover, a temporary decree by the Ministry of Finance forced importers to place an advance deposit with the Bank of Spain to cover the cost of imports. This policy was designed to curb the importation of unnecessary consumer goods which threatened to harm Spain's balance of payments, but it also adversely affected raw material imports.

In addition to this short-term working capital consideration, AHV also needed U. S. $20 million to finance the final phase of the expansion plan to which it was committed. The rebuilding of the blooming-slabbing mill was nearly completed, but work on enlarging a hot strip mill and a cold rolling facility was planned to commence in September 1971 and be completed by the end of 1972. The company's plans for future expansion were restricted to routine replacement and maintenance, and to the expenditure of between $1.5 million and $2.0 million on modernizing and acquiring subsidiaries over the next ten years.

Although AHV did not intend to expand the capacity of its existing plants, the National Steel Plan called for the construction of a fourth integrated steel plant in Spain with an annual capacity of around 5 million tons. This fourth plant was necessary to close the gap between local consumption and production which was expected to develop after 1975. (See Exhibit 2.) AHV had submitted the only feasibility study which the government had received for such a plant. The proposal to build the new plant at Sagunto was expected to be approved by the end of 1971. The plant would be located next to AHV's existing factory, but it would be an entirely separate entity. The likely details of the plan were:

1. The plant would necessitate a total investment of U. S. $1.4 billion—the largest single industrial project ever undertaken in Spain.

2. The equity of the new company would be privately held.

3. The capitalization of the new company would be as follows:

    25% equity
    35% official government credit in long-term loans (fifteen years at 5.5%)
    22% foreign currency loans
    18% bonds

4. The new plant would begin operations on a small scale in 1975 and be fully operative in 1980. This target date required that construction work should begin during 1972.

The management of AHV desired very much to participate in the ownership and development of the new company to as great a degree as possible. Informed opinion suggested that AHV might be allowed to contribute between 30% and 50% of the equity of the new company.

Known Sources of Funds

To meet part of the anticipated demands for funds, Mr. Burgos counted on three known sources: Credit from Banco de Credito Industrial (BCI, a Spanish Government agency in charge of industrial credit), U. S. Steel payment for part of the shares previously subscribed, and larger profits due to an increase in prices.

Between 1971 and 1972, BCI was to grant a total of U. S. $32,358,000 in the form of long-term loans to AHV. These funds would be received by AHV in three equal shares. The first part had been received in January 1971. The second part was scheduled to be received in September of the same year, and the final part would be received in 1972. These loans were made according to the Accion Concertada Agreement. However, the 1972 loan was to be the final loan from BCI under the terms of this agreement.

Only 25% of the shares to which U. S. Steel had subscribed in 1964 had been fully paid in. Although U. S. Steel was committed to pay in the remaining 75% by December 10, 1974, it had recently indicated that it intended to pay in these shares toward the end of 1971 or early 1972. This would provide an additional U. S. $13,385,000 cash inflow.

The expected increment in profits because of price increases was based on the authorization of the Spanish Ministry of Trade to raise the prices of iron and steel products by 6%, effective from July 1971, for all companies in the steel industry. It was expected to generate an additional $10 million of increased revenue during the second half of 1971 alone.

Other Potential Sources of Funds

Mr. Burgos realized that a gap existed between the forecast demand for funds and the sources of funds he was sure would be available. A financial package to bridge this gap had to be designed. Potential sources of funds included bond issues, commercial bank credits, and the recent proposal from Credito Latino to borrow Euro-dollars. Mr. Burgos had decided not to consider an equity issue at the time. That was to be saved for the future, probably in connection with the financing of the new plant on the Mediterranean.

Local Funds. The aggressive expansion program, which was nearing completion in 1971, had required an enormous injection of capital. The government's official credit agencies had supplied the bulk of these funds under the terms of the Accion Concertada. Other major sources were foreign banks in the United States and Europe, which financed the importation of capital goods, and the company's traditional bankers who were also shareholders. Since Spanish bankers represented approximately 35% of the board members, creditors were not unhappy about the structure of the firm's capitalization. Such a situation in which banks had considerable influence in the affairs of industrial companies was not uncommon in Spain, and this close association permitted a relatively high debt to equity ratio. (See notes to Exhibit 3.) However, Mr. Burgos felt that it would be hard to obtain any more credit from these commercial banks for purposes other than current operations.

Only 10% of the book value of fixed assets and only a small proportion of inventory had been pledged against loans received by AHV. Management had followed a policy of granting chattel mortgages only when absolutely necessary, which had not been very frequent for the state's guarantee usually acted as a superior security to the lender. Furthermore, covenants and conditions attached to outstanding loans and bond issues were unlikely to restrict future borrowings: the requirements regarding working capital, dividend payments, and capitalization ratios gave ample leeway for management to operate as it wished. This was also the feeling of some of the bond underwriters with whom Mr. Burgos had talked. It appeared that an issue of U. S. $10-20 million, thirty-year, peseta bonds at an interest rate between 9% and 10% in 1971 could be successfully placed with institutional investors and private individuals in Spain.

Foreign Funds. AHV's experience in borrowing from foreign banks in the past had been limited to financings related to the importation of capital goods and raw materials. For example, it had received a £6 million loan from a London bank in connection with the building of a new blast furnace at Bilbao, and a New York bank had granted a long-term loan to finance the import of coal from the United States. Mr. Burgos was therefore interested in exploring the services that Credito Latino could offer him.

Credito Latino was an international brokerage company which specialized in bringing borrowers in developing countries and lenders of Euro-dollars together. After sufficient inquiry, Credito Latino quoted a U. S. $10-$20 million loan at a floating rate of 1.5% over the six-month Euro-dollar interbank rate, plus a commission of 1% flat. The terms were a two-year grace period with equal semiannual repayments of capital thereafter throughout the seventh year from the closing date.

No compensating balances would be required. However, Credito Latino did not have funds of its own with which to underwrite the loan. Therefore, placement was to be done on a "best efforts" basis, and any contract between AHV and Credito Latino could be rescinded by either party without penalty after a period of three months.

This type of medium-term loan—the so-called "floating rate revolving credit"— had become a common feature of the Euro-dollar market. It enabled lenders, which were normally large American and European commercial banks, to lend on a medium-term basis while obtaining funds in the money market. Thus a loan agreement was drawn up between the borrower and a lending banker which assured the borrower of obtaining medium-term funds, with a prescribed amortization schedule but flexible interest. Interest which was payable each six months in advance, was set semiannually to reflect the cost of money to the bank. The risk and the costs borne by the bank were reflected in the premium over the Euro-dollar interbank rate charged to the borrower.

The Final Decision

Before reaching a final decision regarding the best financing package, Mr. Burgos decided to obtain some more information. He asked his assistant to compile some economic data that would serve as a basis to forecast future developments in the market. These data are contained in Exhibits 5 through 9.

EXHIBIT 1   Spanish Supply and Demand for Steel: Forecast for 1971-1980

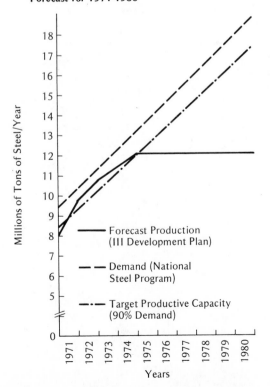

EXHIBIT 2   Spanish Steel Production 1930-1970

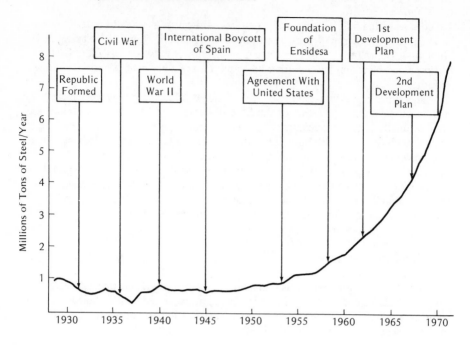

EXHIBIT 3 Altos Hornos De Vizcaya, S.A.: Comparative Balance Sheet (thousands of U. S. dollars)

Assets

	As of December 31		
	1968	1969	1970
Cash	$ 1,107	$ 1,929	$ 360
Miscellaneous Receivables	22,438	14,154	21,520
Inventory	43,096	47,980	112,921
Current Assets	$ 66,641	$ 64,063	$134,801
Land, Plant, & Machinery	$353,709	$393,437	$402,671
Less Accumulated Depreciation	(84,980)	(96,279)	(111,748)
Net Plant	268,729	297,158	290,923
Investments in Affiliates	20,185	40,066	39,983
Other Assets	6,217	4,909	6,224
Total Assets	$361,772	$406,193	$471,931

Liabilities & Capitalization

	As of December 31		
	1968	1969	1970
Notes Payable[a]	$ 43,494	$ 21,969	$ 45,073
Import Financing	4,534	3,783	14,426
Suppliers Account Payable	32,100	39,793	76,590
Accrued Expenses	11,208	16,356	20,136
Current Liabilities	$ 91,336	$ 81,901	$156,225
Deferred Liabilities	389	877	2,271
Funded Debt[b]	194,347	243,079	226,725
Common Stock	47,288	47,288	49,838
Reserves and Retained Earnings	28,412	33,048	36,872
Total Capitalization	$270,047	$323,415	$313,435
Total Liabilities & Net Worth	$361,772	$406,193	$471,931

[a]Of the $45 million of notes payable in 1970, approximately $32 million have been contributed by three banks: Banco de Vizcaya, Banco de Bilbao, and Banco de Urquijo, who control 8% of the outstanding shares. These overdraft facilities, although technically listed as short-term, are of a longer-term nature as they have been rolled over again and again in the past.

[b]The repayment schedule of funded debt outstanding at the end of 1970 is as follows:

Year	Amortization (000s)	%
1971	$ 15,165	6.7
1972	21,381	9.4
1973	20,249	8.9
1974	32,478	14.3
1975	20,197	8.9
1976	19,451	8.6
1977	20,079	8.9
1978	16,847	7.4
1979	17,190	7.6
1980-2009	43,688	19.3
Total	$226,725	100.0

The sources of funded debt outstanding at the end of 1970 are as follows:

Lender	Amount (000s)	%
Spanish Government Agencies, including Banco de Credito Industrial (BCI), Instituto Nacional de la Vivienda (INV), and Banco de Credito a la Construccion (BCC)—(on long-term credit basis)	$ 99,254	43.8
Peseta Bonds owned by leading Spanish banks, insurance companies, pension funds, and other private and institutional investors (average life of 13 years)	$ 77,615	34.2
U. S. Steel Corporation	$ 10,050	4.4
Export-Import Bank of the United States (Five loans of up to 11 years maturity)	$ 12,176	5.6
Other Foreign Banks	$ 27,630	12.2
Total	$226,725	100.0

EXHIBIT 4 Comparative Income Statement For the Year Ending
December 31 (thousands of U. S. dollars)

	1968	1969	1970
Revenue			
Net Sales	$152,336	$193,996	$264,022
Less Cost of Goods Sold	123,530	149,727	205,504
Gross Profit	$ 28,806	$ 44,269	$ 58,518
Less Selling, General,			
and Administrative Expenses	3,843	4,305	6,361
Interest and Discount	10,881	17,883	20,884
Depreciation	10,771	11,959	16,480
Taxes	776	1,199	2,065
Welfare	4,200	5,626	6,242
Operating Profit	$ (1,665)	$ 3,297	$ 6,486
Other Income	1,901	1,784	1,050
Net Profit	$ 234	$ 5,081	$ 7,536
Cash Flow	$ 11,005	$ 17,040	$ 24,016
Dividends	$ —	$ 2,364	$ 2,492

EXHIBIT 5 Six-Month Euro-Dollar Deposit Rates, 1963-1971[a] (at or near end of month)

[a]Prime bank's bid rates in London.

Source: Morgan Guaranty Trust Company, *World Financial Markets,* New York,
various issues.

EXHIBIT 6   Interest Rates in Spain

Commercial Banks Lending Rates, 1969-1971 (percent)

1969	Discount Paper		Medium-Term (18-36 Months)		Long-Term (Over 3 Years)			
	Legal Maximum	Lowest	Legal Maximum	Lowest	Commercial Banks Highest	Lowest	Industrial Banks Highest	Lowest
3°Q	6.50%	6.00%	7.50%	7.25%	9.50%	9.00%	9.50%	8.50%
1970								
1°Q	6.50	6.00	7.50	7.25	9.50	9.00	9.50	8.50
2°Q	7.50	7.00	8.50	8.25	10.50	10.00	10.50	9.75
3°Q	7.50	7.00	8.50	8.25	10.50	10.00	10.50	9.75
4°Q	7.50	7.00	8.50	8.25	10.50	10.00	10.75	9.75
1971								
1°Q	7.25	7.00	8.25	8.00	10.50	10.00	10.75	10.00

Bank of Spain Rediscount Rates

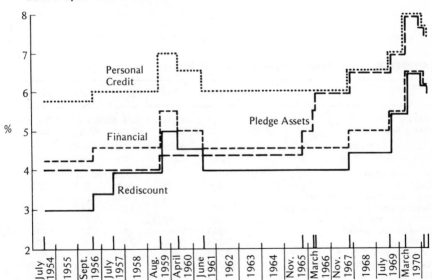

Source: Banco de España, *Boletin Estadistico.*

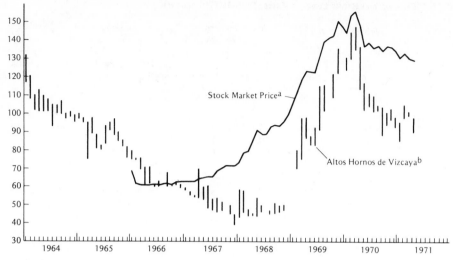

EXHIBIT 7   Stock Market Price Index: AHV and Spanish Market

Stock Market Price[a]

Altos Hornos de Vizcaya[b]

[a]Based on price of mutual funds securities.
[b]Percent of nominal value.
Source: Stock Market—Banco de España, *Boletin Estadistico*. AHV stock—company records.

EXHIBIT 8   Spain: Selected Aggregate Economic Statistics

	1965	1966	1967	1968	1969	1970
Exchange Rate	*Pesetas per U. S. dollar: End of Period*					
Selling Rate	59.99	60.00	69.70	69.82	70.06	69.72
International Liquidity	*Million U. S. Dollars: End of Period*					
Bank of Spain	1,422	1,253	1,100	1,149	1,281	1,817
National Accounts	*Billion Pesetas*					
Exports	143	174	180	233	271	340
Net Factor Income from Abroad	−1	−4	−5	−7	−	−
General Government Consumption	112	133	167	187	214	250
Gross Investment	338	390	380	414	482	517
Private Consumption	887	1,013	1,140	1,251	1,379	1,530
Less: Imports	−192	−228	−230	−273	−324	−368
Gross National Expenditure = GNP	1,287	1,477	1,632	1,805	2,011	2,258
Gross Domestic Product	1,288	1,482	1,637	1,812	2,023	2,270
National Income	1,118	1,275	1,401	1,552	1,710	−
International Transactions	*1963 = 100*					
Volume of Exports	126.8	153.3	170.0	220.6	261.5	306.9
Volume of Imports	149.7	172.1	171.3	185.7	215.4	224.9
Export Prices	103.6	111.2	112.9	114.3	114.3	123.2
Import Prices	103.2	106.7	105.4	112.7	117.3	126.1
Wholesale Prices	113.4	116.3	116.9	119.6	122.6	124.6
Wages	136	158	182	194	213	250
Industrial Production	127	146	155	165	191	207

Source: International Monetary Fund, *Financial Statistics*, July 1972.

548

EXHIBIT 9　Spain: Balance of Payments[a] (millions of U. S. dollars)

	1966	1967	1968	1969	1970[p]
A. Goods, Services, and Unrequited Transfers					
Exports f.o.b.	1,308	1,419	1,667	1,994	2,457
Imports f.o.b.	−3,300	−3,200	−3,241	−3,865	−4,337
Receipts for Services and Transfers					
Travel	1,292	1,210	1,212	1,311	1,681
Government Services	55	55	49	55	55
Other Private Services	265	293	430	546	749
Unrequited Transfers	424	457	464	562	674
Payments for Services and Transfers					
Travel	−90	−99	−102	−116	−138
Government Services	−38	−59	−60	−77	−90
Other Private Services	−475	−526	−644	−775	−956
Unrequited Transfers	−5	−6	−17	−30	−15
Total	−564	−456	−242	−395	80
Trade Balance	−1,992	−1,781	−1,574	−1,871	−1,880
Balance of Services	1,009	874	885	944	1,301
Private Unrequited Transfers	417	446	448	550	659
Government Unrequited Transfers	2	5	−1	−18	—
B. Miscellaneous Capital of Nonmonetary Sectors					
Private Capital, Excluding U. S.					
Government Loans					
Direct Investment Liabilities	134	186	152	200	222
Portfolio Investment Liabilities	58	56	41	10	−13
Loans Received	99	149	141	152	343
Commercial Credits Received	39	31	11	19	88
Commercial Credits Extended	−99	−20	−35	−29	−37
Other	43	40	69	93	90
Official Capital, Excluding Long-Term Loans					
from Abroad					
Loans Extended	−5	−1	2	3	2
Other	−7	14	−5	−9	−1
Total	262	455	376	439	694
C. U. S. Government Loans and					
Other Central Government-Long-Term					
Borrowing Abroad (Net Repayment−)					
U. S. Government Loans					
Private Sector	27	60	57	37	3
Central Government	4	−5	−2	−5	−8
Other Long-Term Borrowing					
by Central Government					
IBRD	43	31	37	23	9
Treasury Issue Abroad	—	—	60	—	—
Other	3	−6	53	12	−24
Total	77	80	205	67	−20
D. Net Errors and Omissions	34	−217.	−267	−342	60
E. Total (A through D)	−191	−138	72	−231	814
F. Allocation of SDRs	—	—	—	—	42
G. Total (E plus F)	−191	−138	72	−231	856
H. Monetary Movements (Increase in Assets −)					
Commercial Banks	20	12	−18	−33	6
Payments Agreements	−23	−32	−15	4	−9
Monetary Gold	25	1	−1	1	286
SDRs	—	—	—	—	−43
Reserve Position in the Fund	−25	166	—	—	−45
Foreign Exchange Assets	196	−9	−38	−190	−689
Other Liabilities	−2	—	—	449	−362
Total	191	138	−72	231	−856

[a]Positive figures are credits; negative figures are debits.
[p]Preliminary.
Source : International Monetary Fund, *Balance of Payments Yearbook*, Feb. 1972.

FNCB Finance Inc.[1]

In early January 1974, a sense of urgency gripped Mr. Benjamin Lagdameo, Managing Director of FNCB Finance Inc. Only six months remained before the preferential trade treaty between the Philippines and the United States, called the Laurel-Langley Agreement, would end. This economic agreement enabled American citizens, individuals, and corporations, to own properties and operate in the Philippines on the same basis as Filipino citizens. Exhibit 1 presents the relevant article of this Agreement.

In 1968, Citicorp, through its wholly-owned subsidiary First National Overseas Investment Corporation (FNOIC), organized FNCB Finance Inc. under a joint venture arrangement with five leading business families in the Philippines. FNOIC owned 75% of the new consumer finance company's common stock valued at ₱1,000,000,[2] while the 5 local partners shared equally the remaining 25%. Within the short span of five years, FNCB Finance grew phenomenally to become the largest and most diversified finance company in the country. However, upon the termination of the Laurel-Langley Agreement on July 4, 1974, FNCB Finance would fall under the ownership provisions of the country's Finance Company Act of 1969, which stipulated a maximum of 40% foreign participation in finance companies. Therefore, FNOIC would have to sell a thirty-five percent (35%) share of FNCB Finance common stock to Filipino citizens by July 4, 1974, to comply with the Finance Company Act.

The senior management of FNCB Finance had to secure the final approval of FNOIC before a divestment program could be put in motion. Since 1972, various divestment proposals had passed between Manila and New York. In May 1973, an official of Citicorp visited the country to discuss the entire divestment program with local management. However, three critical issues remained unresolved:

> First of all, at what price should the shares to be divested be sold? FNOIC had manifested its concern for an optimum price. On the other hand, local management was wary of the capacity of the country's capital market to absorb the entire issue estimated to cost ₱20-30 million.

> Secondly, how could FNOIC retain management control after divestment to a minority position?

> Finally, how should the post-divestment ownership of the company be structured? Local management proposed that the existing local partners be given the priority to increase their participation to 40%. On the other hand, FNOIC wanted a broad public offering.

---

[1] A note on the Philippine economy and financial institutions follows this case.

[2] In 1968, the exchange rate between the Philippine peso and the U. S. dollar was ₱3.93 per U. S. dollar. In January 1974, the rate was ₱6.78.

EXHIBIT 1   Excerpts from the Laurel-Langley Agreement

Article VI

1. The disposition, exploitation, development, and utilization of all agricultural, timber, and mineral lands of the public domain, waters, minerals, coal, petroleum and other mineral oils, all forces and sources of potential energy, and other natural resources of either party and the operation of public utilities, shall, if open to any person, be open to citizens of the other Party and to all forms of business enterprise owned or controlled, directly or indirectly, by citizens of such other Party in the same manner as to and under the same conditions imposed upon citizens or corporations or associations owned or controlled by citizens of the Party granting the right.

2. The rights provided for in Paragraph 1 may be exercised, in the case of citizens of the Philippines with respect to natural resources in the United States which are subject to Federal control or regulations, only through the medium of a corporation organized under the laws of the United States or one of the States thereof and likewise, in the case of citizens of the United States with respect to natural resources in the public domain in the Philippines, only through the medium of a corporation organized under the laws of the Philippines and at least 60 per cent of the capital stock of which is owned or controlled by citizens of the United States. This provision, however, does not affect the right of citizens of the United States to acquire or own private agricultural lands in the Philippines or of citizens of the Philippines to acquire or own land in the United States which is subject to the jurisdiction of the United States and not within the jurisdiction of any State and which is not within public domain. The Philippines reserves the right to dispose of its public lands in small quantities on especially favorable terms exclusively to actual settlers or other users who are its own citizens. The United States reserves the right to dispose of its public lands in small quantities on especially favorable terms exclusively to actual settlers or other users who are its own citizens or aliens who have declared their intention to become citizens. Each Party reserves the right to limit the extent to which aliens may engage in fishing or engage in enterprises which furnish communications services and air or water transport. The United States also reserves the right to limit the extent to which aliens may own land in its outlying territories and possessions, but the Philippines will extend to American nationals who are residents of any of those outlying territories and possessions only the same rights, with respect to ownership of lands, which are granted therein to citizens of the Philippines.

Article X

1. This Agreement shall have no effect after July 3, 1974. It may be terminated by either the Philippines or the United States at any time, upon not less than five years' written notice. If the President of the Philippines or the President of the United States determines and proclaims that the other country has adopted or applied measures or practices which would operate to nullify or impair any right or obligation provided for in this Agreement, then the Agreement may be terminated upon not less than six months' written notice.

2. The revisions of this Agreement authorized by the Congress of the Philippines and the Congress of the United States in 1955 shall enter into force on January 1, 1956.

IN WITNESS WHEREOF the respective Plenipotentiaries have signed this Agreement and have affixed hereunto their seals.

DONE in duplicate in the English language at Washington, this sixth day of September, one thousand nine hundred and fifty-five.

For the President of the Republic of the Philippines:

(Sgd.) CARLOS P. ROMULO
*Special and Personal Envoy of the President
of the Philippines*

For the President of the United States of America:

(Sgd.) JAMES M. LANGLEY
*Special and Personal Envoy of the President
of the United States*

BACKGROUND

FNCB Finance Inc.: A Five-Year Overview

In only five years FNCB Finance had become the largest finance company in the Philippines. Established in 1968, FNCB Finance penetrated the upper end of the consumer finance market with installment sales financing, appliance loans, and small business loans. Starting in 1970, the company began diversifying its financial services, going into commercial lending, financing of receivables, inventory financing, and leasing. To bring its varied financial packages to the market, FNCB Finance expanded its branches from only 8 in 1969 to 18 in 1973.

Exhibit 2 shows the phenomenal growth the FNCB Finance experienced during its first five years of operations. Within five years, the company's net worth leaped from the initial ₱1 million investment to ₱14.5 million in 1973. Net profits increased at the phenomenal rate of 67% per annum, hitting ₱4.5 million in 1973. This growth in earnings had been saved to finance future growth of FNCB Finance. Stockholders' equity had continued to increase via the retention of earnings and the periodic declaration of stock dividends. Stock dividends of 100% were declared in 1971 and 1973, thereby pushing paid-in capital to ₱4 million. As a result of aggressive lending policies, earning assets reached ₱248.8 million in 1973.

The company's impressive growth was noticed not only in financial circles but also in the entire business sector. It earned the reputation of being the country's most innovative and most aggressive finance company. Growth could primarily be attributed to several factors: the FNCB name and logo which elicited investor and creditor confidence, a youthful and aggressive management team, a diversified package of financial services, and an extensive branch network. Continuous rapid growth had been forecast to continue in the next five years despite uncertainties in the economic environment. Total assets had been projected to grow to ₱608.8 million by 1975.

Finance Industry Structure and Competition

The Finance Company Act defined finance companies as corporations or partnerships which were "primarily organized for the purpose of extending credit facilities to consumers and to industrial, commercial or agricultural enterprises, either by discounting or factoring commercial papers or account receivables or by buying and selling contracts, leases, chattel mortgages or other forms of indebtedness, or by leasing of motor vehicles, heavy equipment and industrial machinery, and other movable property." Under this broad definition, the Securities and Exchange Commission of the Philippines listed more than 400 finance companies doing business in the country in 1973. It had been estimated by the Association of Finance Companies of the Philippines that more than 50% of these companies were small, "fly-by-night" outfits operating in the provinces.

Although market share data were inaccurate, the finance industry was considered by analysts and economists to be highly concentrated. Four companies—FNCB Finance, Filinvest Credit Corporation, Industrial Finance Company, and Commercial Credit Corporation—dominated the entire industry in both borrowing and lending activities. In 1973, these four dominant finance companies had a total of

EXHIBIT 2   FNCB Finance Inc.: Financial Highlights, 1969-1973 (pesos)

	1969	1970	1971	1972	1973
Total Assets	₱ 13,600,146	₱ 48,253,605	₱ 119,658,190	₱ 205,304,291	₱ 256,198,508
Earning Assets	13,311,709	43,987,949	116,959,433	194,049,015	248,774,891
Gross Income	979,227	5,676,788	18,009,179	34,811,694	44,049,056
Gross Expenses	594,744	1,651,480	3,858,335	6,950,309	11,500,087
Interest Charges	386,657	2,551,023	9,007,303	21,081,395	25,743,000
Net Income (loss)	(2,174)	968,285	3,353,301	4,416,994	4,513,311
Paid-in Capital	1,000,000	1,000,000	1,000,000	2,000,000	4,000,000
Total Stockholders' Equity	987,021	1,955,306	5,308,607	9,725,601	14,503,352
Shares Outstanding	10,000	10,000	10,000	20,000	40,000
Earnings (Loss) Per Share	(.22)	96.83	335.33	220.85	112.83

₱466.6 million in earning assets. An in-house FNCB Finance report estimated that these four companies accounted for 60% of the entire industry's earning assets. It was estimated that FNCB Finance held 25.6% of the market, Filinvest Credit Corporation 18.2%, Industrial Finance Company 13.3%, and Commercial Credit Corporation 2.9%. Except for FNCB Finance and Filinvest Credit, the companies were controlled by family business conglomerates, which had substantial interests in banking, manufacturing, and insurance.[3]

The broad Finance Company Act definition had provided finance companies substantial elbow room on the lending side. Traditionally, these companies concentrated their lending activities in consumer finance. Industry sources estimated that consumer finance comprised more than 70% of the total loan portfolio. Consumer services included appliance loans (55%), car loans (15%), small business finance (10%), travel loans (7%), and others (13%). Consumer loans usually carried maturities of 24-36 months, and were amortized monthly. FNCB Finance in 1971 altered industry practice by offering longer maturities of up to 48 months and lowering effective interest rates. Most of the consumer finance companies realized effective yields of up to 52% including service charges, while FNCB Finance charged effective yields of only 22%. Consumer finance had proven to be one of the most risky product lines. High delinquency rates had plagued the industry and write-offs had eroded margins. Consumer loan delinquencies had been observed to be sensitive to the effects of natural calamities and to changes in economic aggregates such as inflation, unemployment, and wage rates.

To minimize risks and improve quality of earnings, the large companies had gradually diversified their earning assets from traditional consumer lending into commercial and business financing, leasing, and other bank lending activities. This broadening of earning assets had placed the leading finance companies in direct competition with commercial banks, which had traditionally dominated the country's financial system, and with investment banks, which were engaged in loan syndication and project financing. The finance companies enjoyed a competitive edge over commercial banks because of less government regulation and higher spreads or

[3] Chase Manhattan Bank had a minority interest in Filinvest Credit Corporation.

margins due to high legal interest rate ceilings. However, they were as severely limited as the investment banks on the sourcing side. As nonbank financial inter- mediaries, the finance companies and investment banks could not accept savings and time deposits. They were forced to compete aggressively in the highly volatile and interest-sensitive money market through the issuance of high yield commercial paper. Commercial banks also had direct access to the money market. Approxi- mately 80% of finance companies' fund sources were accounted for by money mar- ket activities. Back-up financing had been provided by temporary bank lines. Long- term sources of financing were scarce. The country had a very superficial equity market. Of the four leading finance companies, only Filinvest and Industrial Finance Corporation were traded even lightly on the local stock exchanges. However, due to the rapid expansion of earning assets, the finance companies were compelled to lengthen the maturities of their fund sources. Filinvest had readied a ₱10 million bond offering while FNCB Finance had contemplated the issuance of ₱10 million convertible debentures.

Competition was expected to accelerate in the immediate future as new en- trants stampeded into the industry. The following factors supported this imminent development:

1. Barriers to entry were low. Any group could organize a partnership or a cor- poration with only ₱500,000. A medium-sized company could be capitalized at only ₱1 million.

2. Industry profitability had been very attractive. In 1972, the leading finance companies had an average return on investment of 17.6%.

3. Government regulation had been relatively loose. Most of the new and pro- spective entrants were commercial banks and other financial institutions on the lookout for diversification vehicles.

This environment sharpened competitive threats. Unless the total market were sub- stantially expanded, the point of industry saturation could be reached within a short time. However, the proliferation of finance companies and the aggressive di- versification of their earning assets would probably invite stricter and more rigid government regulation. Industry analysts expected tighter controls over liquidity, lending policies, sourcing of funds, and capital adequacy. These moves could cur- tail sharply the rapid industry growth.

Divestment Programs of American Corporations

The Securities Exchange Commission of the Philippines reported in a December 1972 survey that a total of 306 corporations owned or controlled by Americans were directly affected by the termination of the Laurel-Langley Agreement. The survey revealed that 122 of these companies possessed real estate properties while 33 others engaged in the exploitation of natural resources or in the operation of public utilities. It estimated that a total of ₱627 million had to be divested or com- pletely disposed of in order to comply with the Constitutional provision requiring a maximum of 40% foreign ownership. Recent estimates, however, placed the figure at a staggering ₱2 billion. Total American investments in the country were estimated to be ₱1 to ₱1.5 billion at cost.

To ensure an orderly divestment and prevent a mad outflow of American investments, the Philippines' SEC and the Board of Investments issued guidelines regarding
the manner of divestment. These alternatives are briefly summarized below:

1. Corporations desiring to stay in the Philippines may dilute their capital participation down to 40% by enlarging Filipino ownership in the total equity of the
company.

2. Corporations may sell excess capital directly to the general public.

3. Corporations may gradually or swiftly pull out of the country by transferring total ownership to Filipino investors.

4. Firms may maintain their total investment in the country by reducing their
equity in one corporation and spreading out into new industries where permitted by
local regulations. Firms may therefore reinvest divestment proceeds in pioneering
or promoted industries.

5. Land-owning corporations wishing to maintain the existing capital structure
may sell their real estate properties to any Filipino national and lease back the same
for a maximum allowable period of 25 years, renewable for another 25 years.

In anticipation of the Laurel-Langley Treaty's expiration and to suit their particular strategies, some American-owned or -controlled companies had already sold
their equity holdings. For example, in 1973, Exxon Philippines struck an agreement
with the government whereby Exxon would sell its entire investment to the govern-
ment-organized and -controlled Philippine Petroleum Corporation (PPC). PPC later
merged with Filoil, a Filipino-owned oil refining and marketing company. Jerome
Brothers, original American owners of 84% of Legaspi Oil Ltd., sold their equity
position to a Filipino-Japanese joint venture, so that the country's second largest
oil refiner was now owned 44% by the Ayala Corporation (the largest Filipino holding
company), 40% by Mitsubishi Corporation, and 16% by the 15 original Filipino
shareholders. RCA Global Communications of New York transferred ₱20 million of
its assets in the Philippines to its local subsidiary, Philippine Global Communications.
A Filipino group later bought 60% of PhilCom's equity to complete the Filipiniza-
tion of the company.

FNCB FINANCE DIVESTMENT STUDIES

FNCB Finance Divestment Study in 1972

In early 1972, Mr. Xavier Loinaz, FNCB Finance President, initiated moves to
prepare the company for actual divestment. At that time, renewal of the Laurel-
Langley Agreement was considered unlikely. Even the establishment of a new treaty
between the Philippines and the United States providing similar reciprocal rights was
deemed improbable. A strong nationalistic fervor, fanned by student and labor unrest, was sweeping the country. The U. S. Embassy in Manila was a favorite target
of violent student rallies and of the militant section of the media. A study was therefore made detailing modes of divestment and pricing and marketing alternatives
facing FNOIC.

General Considerations. The extensive study undertaken by the Corporate Planning Group of First National City Bank observed that divestiture would bring mixed blessings to FNOIC. On the plus side, FNOIC counted the following factors:

1. An outright sale from its existing equity position might yield capital gains subject to a lower tax rate than that for income taxes. The extent of capital gains depended on the pricing scheme. Finding an optimum price was rendered extremely difficult by the fact that FNCB Finance shares were not openly traded in the stock market, and that the company was still very young. Selling at a very high price would maximize capital gains to FNOIC but would jeopardize saleability. Pricing, therefore, was expected to be a very ticklish and sensitive issue.

2. Aggregate investment in the form of original paid-in capital and retained earnings would be reduced, thereby minimizing exposure risks in the country.

3. Divestment was an excellent opportunity to improve the public image of the finance company as the ownership base would be broadened and democratized.

On the negative side, the following factors were important:

1. FNOIC's effective control over FNCB Finance's operations would be minimized after reduction of its equity participation to a minority position of only 40%. With its 75% holdings, FNOIC exercised absolute authority over all stockholder and Board decisions. Under Philippine corporation laws, a two-thirds stockholders' vote was necessary to exercise authority in undertaking corporate affairs such as amendment of the articles of incorporation, declaration of stock dividend, creation or issuance of bonded indebtedness, increase or diminution of capital stock, investment of funds in other corporations or businesses, sale of corporate assets, and delegation to the Board of Directors the power to amend or repeal any bylaws or adopt new ones. Also, corporate control was essential in deciding on cash dividends for remittance abroad. Earlier experience with other foreign companies operating in the Philippines had proven the importance of remitting regular sizeable earnings as cash dividends to partially hedge against the risks of local currency devaluation. However, profit remittances were limited to 25% of profits under existing Central Bank foreign currency restrictions.

2. To the extent of the divestment, FNOIC would be deprived of a profitable outlet for its funds.

Divestment Objectives. On the basis of the above considerations, FNCB Finance and FNOIC in New York agreed on three basic objectives for the divestment package.

1. The divestment strategy should maximize returns on the portion of FNOIC's initial investment to be divested, $90,000.[4] Head Office was therefore aiming for a high P/E ratio in pegging the issue price.

2. FNOIC's management over corporate affairs and operations should be maintained even after divestment to a minority ownership position.

3. The divestment package should contain features which would enhance the

---

[4] 35% of the initial investment of ₱1,000,000 (equal to $255,000) in 1968 at ₱3.93 per U. S. dollar.

public image of FNCB Finance as a responsive corporate citizen. The public relations objective was considered necessary to dispel the negative underpinnings of foreign participation in Philippine business.

Modes of Divestment. The 1972 study considered that the 75% equity position of FNOIC in FNCB Finance could be reduced to 40% through:

1. Direct sale of 35% of total stock; or

2. Sale of the unissued portion of authorized capital to allow dilution of FNOIC's holdings to 40%.

The approaches differed from one another in their impact on the capital structure and leverage of FNCB Finance. The additional subscription approach would mean an inflow of cash, thereby increasing paid-in capital and lowering leverage. On the other hand, a direct sale from the FNOIC holdings would have no impact on capital structure and leverage. In the latter case there would only be a recomposition of ownership.

The question regarding the appropriate mode of divestment revolves around the future need for fresh capital in order to meet capitalization and leverage standards required by trade practice or by law. Previously, buildup of stockholders' equity had been achieved by constant retention of earnings. The amount of capital that could support the increase in the volume of both lending and borrowing had not been determined. Other relevant factors which had started to surface—such as increasing governmental regulation to enforce healthier financial leverage and higher capitalization—also had to be considered.

However, FNOIC would derive certain advantages by divesting directly. In the first place, the funds released to FNOIC after sale of stock could be earmarked for congeneric projects, depending on local regulations, or repatriated abroad. Repatriation would provide an effective hedge against devaluation risks by diluting FNOIC exposure in the country. Moreover, FNOIC would definitely reap large capital gains by selling from its existing position. Divestment through additional subscription would merely decrease FNOIC's contribution to the company's total net worth.

Ownership Distribution. Essential to the divestment objectives was the issue of ownership distribution after divestment. A widespread dispersal of ownership would strengthen the probability of FNOIC's retaining effective control with only 40% participation, while the extreme alternative of ownership with existing partners would promote the opposite effect. The business resources and designs of existing partners suggested the possibility of a determined takeover by a single powerful group or bloc of investors. With regard to enhancing the corporate image, divestment to the public would achieve a favorable response. The government had clearly declared its policy of democratizing ownership of corporations. Given these preliminary considerations, the ownership composition could include a variety of alternatives such as:

1. Divestment solely to existing partners. Partners would increase participation from 25% to 60%.

2. Divestment solely to new local partners.
   a. New business partners
   b. FNCB Philippines staff
   c. FNCB retirement fund
   d. General public

3. A mixture of the above alternatives.

As an aid to arriving at a decision on the choice of partners, the following pro/con assessment was considered:

	Pro	Con
A. Present Partners	1. Avoid antagonizing present partners 2. Probable business and market development	1. Loss of control
B. New Business Partners	1. Business and market development	1. Unfavorable impact on relationship with existing partners
C. Staff	1. Enhancement of control through dispersal and staff allegiance	1. Lack of funding for purchase; recourse to FNCB financing to purchase stock
D. Retirement Fund	1. Possible retention of effective control through moral suasion on trustees	1. No positive public relations impact
E. General Public	1. Highly favorable public relations impact	1. Long-run possibility of control 2. Unavailability of funds in the market

Senior management was worried about the reaction of the local partners if FNOIC opted for a general public offering. Under the company's Incorporation Papers, the local partners had the right of first refusal regarding the sale of stock. However, it was deemed possible that the partners could be persuaded to respect FNOIC's decision.

Taking the above considerations into account, three ownership composition alternatives had been advanced:

	A	B	C
FNOIC	40%	40%	40%
Present Five Partners	25	60	40
Total (FNOIC and Partners)	65	100	80
Available Shares for New Partners	35	0	20
Total	100%	100%	100%

Valuation and Pricing of FNCB Finance Stock. FNOIC expressed to local management its desire to optimize the monetary returns on its investment. However, the study conducted stated that the offer price should be determined on a competitive basis to ensure a wide market for the stock. It contended that the price should be in line with the normal P/E multiplier dictated by the open capital market. Also, the valuation should yield very attractive returns to potential investors to be able to compete favorably against other investment opportunities. Thus, the local senior manager was concerned in 1972 with the simultaneous problems of monetary optimization to FNOIC and guaranteed marketability of the stock.

Two approaches were used in valuing the FNCB Finance stock. The first approach involved the capitalization of income using the present value technique. The other method used the price/earnings multiplier method. The following major assumptions were used for both valuation approaches:

1. A time horizon of 5 years.

2. Forecast of a 55% average annual growth rate for earnings, 1972-1976 (See Exhibit 3).

3. A 100% stock dividend in 1972.

4. An annual dividend payout of 25% of earnings.

5. A stock split of 100 to 1 to bring the price of the stock within the reach of the general public, consequently reducing par value from ₱100 to only ₱1.00 per share.

6. A discount rate of 30%, considered attractive to potential investors.

7. A terminal value of 5 times terminal earnings.

EXHIBIT 3   FNCB Finance Inc. History and Forecast, 1970-1976

	1970	1971	1972	1973	1974	1975	1976
	(thousand pesos)						
Revenues	5,685	17,909	34,944	55,911	83,865	117,412	164,370
Expenses	4,185	12,752	26,640	41,754	61,719	85,081	116,960
Net Earnings (after tas)	960	3,355	5,138	8,752	13,685	19,975	29,289
Cash Dividend (25%)	—	839a	1,284	2,188	3,421	4,994	7,323
	(pesos)						
Earnings per Share	₱0.48	₱1.68	₱2.57	₱4.38	₱6.84	₱9.99	₱14.64
Dividends per Share	—	₱0.42a	₱0.64	₱1.09	₱1.71	₱2.50	₱ 3.66
Earnings Growth Rate	—	250%	53%	70%	56%	46%	47%
Book Value per Share			₱3.58	₱5.98	₱10.19	₱16.50	₱25.7

aProposed dividend payout payable in 1972.

Exhibit 4 shows step-by-step the calculations of the stock price using the capitalization of income approach. Under this approach the expected cash flows associated with owning the stock were projected and its present value was found by using a dis-

**EXHIBIT 4   FNCB Finance Inc.: Computation of Price per Share
Under Capitalization of Income Approach**

*Based on 2,000,000 Shares Outstanding, on a
30% Capitalization Rate and Terminal Liquidation Price of 5 x 1976 Earnings*

1. *Given*

	1972	1973	1974	1975	1976
a. Earnings Per Share (EPS)	₱2.57	₱4.38	₱6.84	₱9.99	₱14.64
b. Cash Dividend Per Share (DPS)	₱0.64	₱1.09	₱1.71	₱2.50	₱ 3.66

2. *Assumptions*
   a. Acquisition date: October 1, 1972
   b. Dividends payable year end

3. *Computation*
   Determination of price per share based on the present values (PV) of dividend per share
   and terminal price per share.

   a. Present value of DPS as of date of acquisition:

      (1) PV of DPS at year end 1972

Year	DPS	Discount Factor at 30%	PV
1972	₱0.64	1.00000	₱ 0.64
1973	1.09	.76923	0.84
1974	1.71	.59172	1.01
1975	2.50	.45517	1.14
1976	3.66	.35013	1.28
			₱ 4.91

      (2) Present value of DPS as of date of acquisition (Oct. 1, 1972) (Derived by
          multiplying the PV of DPS at year end 1972 by the discount factor of
          30% for one quarter)

          ₱4.91 × .93651 = ₱4.60

   b. Present value of terminal price per share (TPS) as of date of acquisition:
      (1) TPS (year end 1976): ₱14. 64 × 5 = ₱73.20
      (2) PV of TPS as of year end 1972: ₱73.20 × .35013 = ₱25.63
      (3) PV of TPS as of date of acquisition (October 1972):
          ₱25.63 × .93651 = ₱24.00
   c. Total present value of DPS and TPS as of date of acquisition:

      ₱4.60 + ₱24.00 = ₱28.60

4. *Price/Earnings Ratio*
   Derived by dividing total PV of DPS and TPS by the 1972 earnings projection:

$$\frac{28.60}{2.57} = 11.13$$

count rate of 30%. This discount rate was assumed to represent the rate of return
desired by an investor in this type of company. The cash flows projected were the
expected cash dividends and the terminal liquidation price of FNCB Finance stock
at the end of five years. The capitalization of income method produced a price of
₱28.60 per share. This price represented a 11.1 P/E multiple of 1972 earnings.

The price/earnings multiplier method produced a price of ₱12.85. It was assumed that a multiple of 5 times earnings was the most realistic multiple that the
market would accept for a company such as FNCB Finance. The price of ₱12.85
in 1972, given the cash flows assumed above, implied a discount rate of 47.9%. In
other words, given the forecast cash flows, if the investor required a rate of return

as high as 47.9% the maximum price at which the stock could be sold involved only a multiple of 5 times the projected 1972 earnings of ₱2.57 per share.

To ascertain which of the pricing alternatives would achieve the joint objectives of maximum gains for FNOIC and guaranteed marketability, the study compared the P/E multiples of selected financial institutions with stocks traded in the local exchanges. This is shown in Exhibit 5. However, comparison was hampered by the fact that there were wide fluctuations in P/E ratios from year-to-year and from company-to-company. The behavior of the multiples spanned only four to five years, too brief a history to provide meaningful statistical results. Notwithstanding these constraints, it was found that the P/E ratios ranged from a low of 2.5 to an extreme high of 23. The average multiple of three of the five companies ranged from 7 to 8. From these P/E statistics, it was inferred that a price of ₱12.85 per stock or a P/E ratio of 5 for FNCB Finance stock represented a moderate value. It was also felt that the higher price of ₱28.60, or a multiple of 11.1, would not be considered overvalued by the market.

To further buttress the valuation, a comparison of returns on investment (ROI) for the five companies and expected ROI for FNCB Finance under each pricing alternative was made. For comparability, the definition of ROI for FNCB Finance was based on *projected* earnings per share for each of the following five years (see Exhibit 3) over the suggested offer prices of ₱12.85 and ₱28.60. In the case of the other financial institutions, the ROI was expressed in terms of the historical average market price paid by investors in a given year and the earnings per share for that year. The tables below show the resulting ROIs.

ROI Expected from FNCB Investment by Potential Investors Based on Offer Price

Offer Price	1972	1973	1974	1975	1976	Annual Average
₱12.85	20%	34.1%	53.2%	77.7%	113.9%	59.8%
₱28.60	9.0%	15.3%	23.9%	34.9%	51.2%	26.8%

ROI of Similarly Traded Financial Institutions Based on Average Market Prices per Year

Company	1966	1967	1968	1969	1970	Annual Average
Industrial Finance Corp.	19%	23%	16%	23%	6%	17.4%
Filinvest Credit Corp.	35%	35%	66%	35%	38%	41.8%
Filipinas Mutual Fund	18%	10%	11%	13%	18%	13.0%
Private Dev. Corp. of the Philippines	13%	12%	13%	17%	17%	14.4%
House of Investment	4%	7%	3%	5%	—	4.8%

Source: *Manual of Philippine Securities, The Investor's Guide,* 1971 Edition.

EXHIBIT 5   Price/Earnings Ratios of Publicly Traded Stock of Financial Institutions

Company/Year	Average Price	Earnings Per Share	Price/Earnings Ratio
Industrial Finance Corporation[a]			
1971	—	—	—
1970	₱18.50	₱1.06	17.5x
1969	16.25	2.54	6.4x
1968	16.25	2.54	6.4x
1967	16.875	3.84	4.4x
1966	19.00	3.54	5.4x
			7.6x(Ave.)
Filinvest Credit Corporation[a]			
1971	No sales as of May 31	—	—
1970	No sales	₱4.40	—
1969	₱12.50	4.40	2.8x
1968	11.75	7.79	1.5x
1967	11.50	3.97	2.9x
1966	12.00	4.15	2.9x
			2.5x (Ave.)
Private Development Corp. of the Phil. (PDCP)			
1971	N.A.	N.A.	—
1970	₱15.75	₱2.63	5.99
1969	14.00	2.38	5.88
1968	15.25	1.95	7.82
1967	14.25	1.74	8.19
1966	12.30	1.55	7.94
			7.16 (Ave.)
House of Investment (HI)			
1971	No sales as of June 30	—	—
1970	₱11.00	N.A.	—
1969	11.00	₱0.58	19.0x
1968	10.50	0.32	32.8x
1967	9.65	0.65	14.8x
1966	10.00	0.35	28.6x
			23.8x (Ave.)

[a]These firms are more closely akin to FNCBFI than PDCP and HI since they engage in some financing company activities directly or through subsidiaries. On the other hand, PDCP performs development and investment banking functions, while House of Investments is an investment and management company with some investment banking functions.
Source: *Manual of Philippine Securities: The Investor's Guide,* 1971 Edition.

At ₱12.85 per share, investors in FNCB Finance would realize an annual average ROI of 59.8%, surpassing the highly profitable Filinvest Credit Corp. with an ROI of 41.8% and the rest with less than 20%. At the higher price of ₱28.60 per share, the investors would achieve an ROI of only 26.8%. This would still be better than the four other financial institutions but less attractive than the record of Filinvest, the most aggressive competitor.

Given the results of the comparison of P/E multiples and the ROI analysis, the study concluded that market realities demanded the lower valuation of ₱12.85 per share. At this price, the entire issue would be very competitive and would still allow for impressive capital gains to FNOIC. The divested stocks would bring in $957,000 after deducting the original investment of $90,000 and taxes. On a discounted cash flow basis, the after-tax proceeds would yield an ROI of about 75%. (See Exhibit 6). The conservative pricing was prompted by a feeling of apprehension anticipated on the basis of the following:

1. FNCB Finance lacked the extensive track record necessary to inspire investor confidence. Despite the dramatic performance of the company, it had been in existence for only four years. Industrial Finance Corp. had been in existence for more than 12 years while Filinvest had been operating for more than 8 years.

2. FNCB's management of the company had been openly recognized as the main catalyst of its growth and phenomenal record. Dilution of control might be misconstrued as withdrawal of support.

3. The expected proliferation of financial institutions would definitely lead to much keener competition. Three big finance companies and many investment houses were slated for opening. Stiff competition would definitely erode long-run profitability.

The management of FNCB Finance considered the suggested offering price to be extremely conservative. They felt that the Head Office would surely turn down a P/E multiple of 5 times projected 1972 earnings. Even a P/E of 11.1 would be difficult to justify. One senior officer even felt that the stock could be sold at a P/E multiple higher than 15 times, on the basis of the following:

1. The continued use of the FNCB name and logo, even after divestment, would ensure the company's continued growth.

2. The phenomenal earnings record of the company had already earned investor confidence. To buttress this argument, the officer cited names of investors willing to buy FNCB shares at higher than 15 times earnings.

3. The extensive branch network of the company, which was projected to grow to 21 branches by 1974, would substantially expand the size of the market. With a very strong distribution system, long-run profitability was considered almost a certainty.

Retention of Management Control. Another major concern of FNOIC and the local FNCB officers was the retention of FNCB management after divestment. One way of assuring management control of the company was the dispersal of ownership to as many investors as possible. However, FNOIC was interested in a more formal and more binding alternative. The following options aimed at maintaining management control were available:

1. *Voting Trust.* Philippine corporation laws allow the use of a voting trust for a maximum period of 5 years. Under a trust agreement, a Filipino trustee becomes a registered stockholder. A trustee can dispose of the shares under trust only upon the specific instructions of the trustor. The trustee will always vote with the trustor. This device was constrained by the limited time period and by the stipulation that the stocks under trust could not revert back to the trustor.

2. *Proxy.* Proxies could be obtained from investors but only for a short period. Creation of an irrevocable proxy was looked upon with disfavor by the local courts.

EXHIBIT 6   FNCB Finance Inc.: Return on Investment to FNOIC

Proceeds from Divestment

1. No. of shares to be divested	700,000 shares	
2. Estimated price per share	₱12.85	
3. Estimated proceeds of divestment (1 x 2)	₱8,995,000	$1,328,656[a]
4. Associated cost of investment	₱ 350,000	$ 89,744
5. Estimated income from capital gains (#3 - #4)	₱8,645,000	$1,238,912
6. U.S. tax (30% x #5)	₱2,593,500	$371,674[b]
7. Estimated net income from capital gains after U.S. tax	₱6,051,500	$867,238
8. Estimated after-tax divestment proceeds (#4 + #7)		$956,982

Return on Investment

1. Cost of investment	$90,000
2. Approximate data of investment	August 1, 1968
3. Assumed date of divestment	October 1, 1972
4. Estimated after-tax divestment proceeds	$957,000
5. Holding period	4 years and 2 months

Computation:
1. P. V. of outflow: $90 thousand
2. P. V. of inflow

Inflow	Discount Factor at 75%	Present Value as of Jan. 1, 1969	Discount Factor at 75% (2 months)	Present Value as of Aug. 1968 (inflow)
$957K x	.10622	= $102K	x .88889	= $90.7K

3. Approximate ROI: 75%

[a]Exchange rate assumed at ₱ 6.77/$1.00
[b]Computation of net U.S. tax liability (or excess tax credit):

U.S. Tax (30% x #5 above)	₱2,593,500	$371,674
Tax credit (based on the 35% Phil. tax rate payable in connection with capital gains):		
.35 x #5 above	₱3,025,750	$433,619
Net U.S. tax liability (or excess tax credit)	(₱ 432,250)	($ 61,945)

3. *Pooling Agreement.* Under this option, certain stockholders or a block of stockholders could pool their votes. Pooling agreements had been sustained by the local courts as legal and binding provided it could be demonstrated that the agreement was not entered into for the purpose of committing fraud, jeopardizing creditors, or exploiting the corporation to the prejudice of the minority stockholders.

4. *Memorandum and Royalty Agreement.* Under this approach, the use of the "FNCB" name and logo could be exchanged for a royalty fee and for amendments

in the Articles of Incorporation ensuring the retention of FNCB management. These measures would be in effect until such time as FNOIC withdrew at its discretion the use of the FNCB name and logo. FNOIC, through the present FNCB Finance management, would have to convince the five existing partners to enter into a Memorandum and Royalty Agreement before actual divestment. Specific measures deemed desirable by FNCB could be included in the agreement. For instance, it could be legally stipulated that in exchange for the use of the name FNCB, the president of the company would be an FNOIC nominee.

Marketing. To market the issues, three alternatives were being considered:

1. Hire the services of an investment house or a syndicate of investment houses which would underwrite a public offering.

2. Employ a sister investment house, the Citicorp Investment Co. slated for opening in 1973, to sell the entire package.

3. Sell the shares directly through the company's branch network to each area's high net worth individuals on a private placement basis.

The marketing decision hinged on whether the sale should be on a broad nonnegotiated basis or as a limited private placement. If the offering were to a broad public, then the investment house underwriting alternatives looked desirable. Otherwise, it was considered more advantageous to offer the shares through the company's network of branches. Underwriting fees and related expenses—estimated at approximately 5% of total proceeds—could be saved. Also, under the negotiated marketing strategy, future stockholders could be selected. This would facilitate future proxy needs. One drawback of the negotiated approach was the length of time involved. Informal and time-consuming negotiations and personal selling would have to be undertaken. On the other hand, a completely underwritten offering would take a maximum of three months, depending on the vagaries of the local capital market.

Subsequent Events: 1972-1973

3rd-4th Quarter 1972. During this period the management of FNCB Finance scrutinized the findings of the study and evaluated its options. Officers in the International Banking Group of Citibank New York were expected to visit the Philippines in early 1973 to discuss with local management the entire divestment issue. A completed divestment package was expected in New York not later than the second quarter of 1973. Unfortunately, the divestment program was overtaken by external events which depressed the company's overall performance in 1972. In mid-1972, floods devastated metropolitan Manila and the central provinces of Luzon, the largest island in the Philippines. Agricultural production slumped, prices of prime commodities soared, and the entire economy slowed down. The misfortunes were compounded by continuous political unrest. Student demonstrations mounted while political violence continued unabated. President Ferdinand Marcos declared martial law throughout the country on September 21, 1972. Although there were no major political disturbances, general uncertainties loomed on both the political and economic horizons. The historic event induced a cautious wait-and-see attitude on the part of business and the public. Martial law government moved quickly to institute reforms. It issued successive decrees launching major projects aimed at hastening economic development. One of these decrees affected taxation of financial institutions. Effective immediately, an increase in the gross receipts tax from 1% to 5% was ordered and made retroactive. All of these unforeseen events combined to depress the profitability of FNCB Finance in 1972. Actual profits in 1972 of ₱4,417,000 missed the budget projection of ₱5,138,000 by 16%. However, profits still posted a 31.7% gain over 1971. The effects of the natural calamities were expected to last for more than a year unless dramatic changes in the economy occurred. Saddled with these difficulties, FNCB Finance's management focused attention on improving profitability. In the meantime, the divestment issue was relegated to the background.

January-December 1973. Feverish activities resumed only during the second quarter of 1973. On March 16, 1973, President Marcos issued through the Central Bank a decree which was gleefully welcomed by foreign investors and which directly affected the current divestment issue. In a move primarily aimed at attracting more foreign investment, President Marcos liberalized direct foreign investment and allowed full and retroactive repatriation of capital, profits, dividends, and capital gains. Under the revised rules, the proceeds from the divestment could be repatriated to Citicorp in nine equal annual installments after liquidation of the investment. The much improved foreign investment climate made attractive the reinvestment of the proceeds in new Citicorp ventures in the Philippines.

THE 1973 DIVESTMENT PACKAGE

In March 1973, the president of FNCB Finance under whose initiative the divestment study was made was promoted and re-assigned to the Citibank Head Office in Manila. Mr. Benjamin Lagdameo, the Managing Director, assumed all the president's responsibilities. The drafting of a complete divestment package to be forwarded to New York in May 1973 fell on the shoulders of the Managing Director and his Corporate Planning staff. A major question anticipated by Mr. Lagdameo was the pricing of the shares. He was fully aware of two conflicting forces—the high pricing expectations of Citicorp and the doubtful ability of the capital market to absorb such a potentially large offering. He was deeply concerned with the possibility of being unable to meet the July 3, 1974 deadline. After talking with local investment houses and meeting with consultants, Mr. Lagdameo initially pegged the price at 12 times forecast 1973 earnings of ₱5.5 million. His staff devised the following tentative divestment package for presentation to the Citicorp officers scheduled to visit the Philippines in July 1973.

Mode of Divestment
Outright sale of 7,000 common shares held by FNOIC (35% of 20,000 shares, before the stock split).

Ownership Distribution
Post divestment ownership of the company will be composed of:

FNOIC	40%
5 Present Partners	40%
General Public	15%
FNCB Philippines Staff	5%

Under this ownership scheme, dependence on the domestic capital market would be substantially minimized. The main burden would be placed on the shoulders of the five Filipino partners. Mr. Lagdameo felt that it might be easier to negotiate with the five partners than to unload the entire issue in the open market.

Pricing. The shares would be sold at 12 times revised projected earnings of ₱5.5 million. Each share would be priced at ₱3,300. The entire issue would amount to ₱23.1 million.

Marketing. The shares to be divested would be sold on a negotiated private place-ment basis. Top level negotiation with the five partners would be undertaken. If the five partners were unable to increase their participation to 8% each, a different fi-nancing scheme would be discussed. For the public offering, the entire branch net-work would be mobilized. High net worth individuals who had invested heavily in the company's commercial paper would be approached. This marketing strategy would strengthen the presence of FNCB Finance in each area as local investors would own a part of the company. A list of prospective investors had been prepared by each branch. For the staff offering, a stock option plan which would include a financing scheme would be devised.

Retention of Management. To maintain FNCB management after divestment to a minority ownership, a Memorandum Agreement would be entered into with the five Filipino partners. For the use of the FNCB logo and name, the corporation would be obligated to pay a royalty fee of 10% on net income each year. Amendments to the Incorporation Papers would be introduced. These amendments would give FNCB veto powers over certain corporate acts.

CITICORP'S REACTION

One afternoon in July 1973, Ms. Gail Johnson, AVP of FNCB New York, met with Mr. Lagdameo and his staff. A presentation was made summarizing the main features of the divestment program and outlining the advantages of each. Immedi-ately after the presentation, Ms. Johnson threw sharp questions about the pricing and the retention of FNCB management. She suggested that the pricing might be on the low side considering the fact that Citibank shares were being traded on the New York Stock Exchange at a P/E of 20. She said that the phenomenal profit record of the company in its short history and the support provided by FNCB justified a higher valuation. She also mentioned the company's extensive branch network, slated to increase, as another plus factor. She felt that a P/E multiple of 15 was a minimum. Mr. Lagdameo cautioned her about the difficulties of unloading the shares at a mul-tiple higher than 12. He stressed the lack of equity sources and the doubtful capacity of the local market to absorb the entire issue within a short time period. At 15 times projected 1973 earnings of ₱5.5 million, a staggering ₱28.9 million would have to be raised. Mr. Lagdameo felt that a multiple of 12 should be the maximum offering price. He contended that blue chip corporations with extensive track records were selling in ranges of 5-10 times earnings. The shares could be sold at a P/E mul-tiple of 12 only on a negotiated basis. If the shares were underwritten, they could be sold only at a lower price. Ms. Johnson considered Mr. Lagdameo's points and assured him that these would be taken into account in shaping a Head Office decision. She also suggested that a public offering of the entire 35% might be advisable. This would ensure maximum dispersal. Mr. Lagdameo cited the fact that the original Incorporation Papers gave the five present Filipino partners the right of first refusal. A public offering might encounter the opposition of the Filipino partners.

After the meeting with Ms. Johnson, Mr. Lagdameo reassessed the entire situation. He reevaluated the pricing issue taking into account the points raised by Ms. Johnson. He feared that the proposal might encounter rough seas in New York due to the pricing. To solidify the initial pricing proposal and to provide a more thorough pricing analysis, Mr. Lagdameo requested another Citicorp subsidiary in the Philippines, Citicorp Investment Co., to independently value the shares to be divested. The report submitted by CIC is presented in Appendix A.

CIC undertook a comparative study of the valuation of financial institutions openly traded in the local exchanges. The report stated that the shares might not be successfully sold at a multiple of 12. It took note of the fact that FNCB Finance lacked a meaningful track record to convince prospective investors of its future earnings capacity. Company projections of future earnings would be casually considered or even dismissed by sophisticated investors. According to CIC, the P/E multiples of selected financial institutions had clustered around 4-6 in 1972. Based on these observations, CIC recommended a much lower price of 6 times projected 1973 earnings. It concluded that the shares might be sold at 8 times earnings on a negotiated basis.

APPENDIX A: CIC Report on the Philippines Stock Market

Memorandum to: N. P. Bonoan, Assistant Manager

         Re: FNCBFI's Divestment Pricing

While FNCBFI has consistently chalked up earnings over the last four years at an impressive pace, nonetheless, the idea of capitalizing such a growth rate at a high price/earnings multiple may prove not at all that justifiable when viewed within the context of a relatively "infant" company.

As in the case of many viable ventures, an abnormally high earnings growth rate is experienced during the early stages which eventually tapers off as the net income base grows bigger. In fact the growth rate tends to hit a plateau and even dip at some point in the firm's corporate life. At this stage this phenomenon is very applicable to FNCBFI. Hence, even the argument that just the corporate cover of FNCB itself would suffice and lend prestige to a high price/earnings multiple may in fact work to the detriment of shareholders when FNCBFI's growth rate erodes.

As a purely alternative investment placement, a high offering price of FNCBFI may suffer from comparison vis-à-vis other equity issues with established track records in the Stock Exchange. In the attached Exhibits 1 and 2 are shown the price/earnings behavior of listed financial institutions as well as mining and commercial stocks over the last five years. In general, financial institutions are capitalized at a lower price/earnings multiple relative to mining and commercials. To the extent that mining firms have historically exhibited a greater potential for increased earnings via capacity expansion, increase in world prices, etc., largely explains their higher price/earnings ratio.

As borne out by Exhibit 1, the price/earnings ratios of selected financial institutions seem to be clustered around 4-6 for 1972. Although Bank of Philippine Islands hit a record high of 19 times earnings in 1971, this was only due to the takeover bid of the Ayala group in their attempt to finally gain full control of the Bank.

In contrast the price/earnings ratios of the three mining companies and two utility companies ranged approximately between 5-8, higher than the financial institutions.

From these two exhibits, the price/earnings multiples of a random mix of "blue-chip" issues range between 4-8 times for 1972, considered to be normal within the context of the Philippine capital market.

Admittedly, a bull market finds the P/E ratios rise above their normal levels as in the case of 1969. But even during such a period, rarely does an investor find a "blue-chip" issue with a price/earnings multiple around the level of 20. In fact a level of approximately 14-18 times current earnings represents a partial discounting by the market of the incremental income that a corporation with known expansion plans and/or new ventures would realize within the immediate future.

In the case of FNCBFI it has nothing up in its sleeves to amplify its future earnings stream—in which case an abnormally high P/E may prove unwarranted.

In this light, I feel that an offering price of 4 to 6 times earnings would fall within the market's acceptance level. All this, of course, is premised on an underwriting effort via public offering. However, your recent discussion with B. R. Lagdameo seems to obviate the need for a public offering. As I understand, FNCBFI is of the thinking that its current partners would be amenable to absorb 15% out of the 35% FNCOIC's divestment shares at a higher rate of 8 times earnings. Further, another 15% can be allocated to FNCBFI's existing high net worth clients by means of FNCBFI's branching network with the remaining 5% to be apportioned to FNCBFI's staff via a stock option plan.

As the divestment now falls within a negotiated arrangement, an 8 times earnings has perhaps been acceptable, especially to the current partners for obvious reasons. The fact that they are afforded a chance to increase their current holdings to the same level as FNCOIC should compensate for a higher acquisition price. To a large extent they can participate more actively in the shaping of management policies and direction within the framework of FNCB's institutional objectives.

R. D. ZARAGOZA

EXHIBIT 1   Price/Earnings Ratios of Selected Financial Institutions, 1968-1972

	1968	1969	1970	1971	1972
PDCP					
EPS (Adj.)	₱ 1.21	₱ 1.48	₱ 1.79	₱ 2.32	₱ 2.87
Ave. Market Price (Adj.)	12.00	14.00	13.69	16.50	15.75
Ave. P/E Ratio	9.9	9.5	7.7	7.1	5.5
Consolidated Bank					
EPS (Adj.)	11.20	11.09	21.78	34.32	34.71
Ave. Market Price (Adj.)	148.72	142.56	136.41	129.36	140.00
Ave. P/E Ratio	13.3	12.8	6.3	3.8	4.0
China Bank					
EPS (Adj.)	29.01	31.03	38.11	37.41	49.31
Ave. Market Price (Adj.)	300.00	268.19	245.46	218.18	190.00
Ave. P/E Ratio	10.3	8.6	6.4	5.8	3.8
Bank of the Philippine Islands					
EPS (Adj.)	21.68	21.92	25.77	31.12	69.12
Ave. Market Price (Adj.)	206.00	284.00	284.00	592.00	410.00
Ave. P/E Ratio	9.5	13.0	11.0	19.0	5.9

EXHIBIT 2   Price/Earnings Ratios of Selected Issues, 1968-1972

	1968	1969	1970	1971	1972
Lepanto					
EPS (Adj.)	₱0.057	₱0.086	₱0.1065	₱0.084	₱0.116
Ave. Market Price (Adj.)	0.5263	1.293	1.067	0.688	0.63
Ave. P/E Ratio	9.2	15.03	10.01	8.2	5.4
Atlas					
EPS (Adj.)	8.07	11.87	13.66	13.83	13.86
Ave. Market Price (Adj.)	101.82	127.80	123.44	95.50	89.00
Ave. P/E Ratio	12.6	10.8	9.0	6.9	6.4
Philex					
EPS (Adj.)	0.0190	0.0295	0.0517	0.0615	0.07
Ave. Market Price (Adj.)	0.1756	0.5378	0.4965	0.3685	0.550
Ave. P/E Ratio	9.20	18.20	9.60	5.90	7.80
San Miguel Corp.					
EPS (Adj.)	3.63	3.92	4.65	5.13	4.82
Ave. Market Price (Adj.)	38.85	46.73	36.08	33.15	29.50
Ave. P/E Ratio	10.98	11.92	7.76	6.46	6.12
PLDT					
EPS (Adj.)	5.88	6.11	5.98	7.18	6.60
Ave. Market Price (Adj.)	55.35	50.36	40.93	38.97	32.36
Ave. P/E Ratio	9.4	8.2	6.8	5.4	4.9

APPENDIX B: Note on the Philippines

With a GNP of approximately $10 billion in 1973, the Philippines is primarily an agricultural country, with almost 60% of its GNP being accounted for by this sector. However, industrialization has been proceeding at a reasonably fast pace. Between 1967 and 1973 the composite index of industrial production grew by 60%. As to the external position of the country, its export account depends heavily on the world performance of wood, sugar, copper, coconut products, and hemp. With the rapid increase in world prices for these products in the recent past, the country has been able to replenish its coffers of international reserves. But also, like the rest of the world, the country has been plagued with an increasing rate of inflation which monetary policy together with fiscal policy have attempted to slow.

ECONOMIC PROSPECTS

The bright spots in the country's economy in 1973 may be obscured in the future by the nagging problems of inflation and the energy crisis. GNP growth is expected to slow down and stabilize at 6-8%. The deceleration may be attributed to the following:

1. A weakening of the external sector which has provided the impetus to economic growth in 1973. Recession among the developed economies of the United States, Japan, and Europe, to which the country's major exports go, will depress export earnings. The biggest exports, except sugar and copper, face downturns in the world market, especially coconut and wood products. On the other hand, the imports of oil, machinery, and chemicals, which constitute the economy's lifeblood, are projected to rise. Economists forecast a deficit of $500 million in the trade account. To finance the deficit, the government is expected to increase Euro-dollar borrowings.

2. Intensification of inflation. Philippine inflation, which is of the cost-push variety, will not abate. Price hikes averaging 18% a year or more are forecast. The biggest headache will be the oil import bill. Even if the value of crude oil imports is maintained at its 1972 level, the import bill would still rise to $450-500 million.

However, all is not bleak. The economy can still fall back on the foreign exchange reserves accumulated in 1973 to surmount expected problems in the external sector. The economy will be buoyed by the following:

1. Agricultural production will accelerate and recover from its lethargic growth in 1973 due to serious government efforts in rural development and the channeling of more funds into the agricultural sector. Rice, sugar, and coconut production will increase.

2. The government will push various economic and financial reforms aimed at hastening development. Centralized economic planning will be emphasized. Foreign investments will be encouraged and liberalized. Financial reforms aimed at developing long-term finance and improving the financial system will be put into effect.

SAVINGS AND CAPITAL FORMATION

The key to a deeper understanding of the economy is a grasp of the pattern of savings and capital formation. Simply defined, savings, which forms the primary source of domestic capital, is that portion of current income not consumed. For the household, savings is income deposited in financial institutions or hoarded or invested in tangible assets such as houses, cars, real estate, and so on. For the corporation, it is retained earnings. For the government, it is that part of income spent on public works and other social overhead. Various studies have identified the following characteristics of domestic savings:

1. Gross domestic savings has averaged 16% of GNP and net savings (derived by deducting capital consumption allowance from gross earnings) 10% of national income.

2. Growth of savings has been relatively high, as shown by the following figures:

1946-49	15.6%
1950-54	12.8%
1955-59	12.5%
1960-64	17.8%
1965-69	20.5%

3. The rate of savings is expected to decelerate sharply due to virulent inflation and to perceived weakness of the Philippine peso. In 1973, consumer prices have been estimated to have risen by approximately 33%. Due to the fixed nature of household incomes, savings contracted. Another problem has been the historical weakness of the peso which went through sharp devaluations in 1962 (by almost 100%) and in 1970 (by almost 67%).

4. Household savings have been channeled to financial claims (60%) such as deposits, stocks, bonds, insurance claims, etc., and to tangible assets (40%).

5. The pattern of household savings has depended on income distribution and family expenditures. Due to the sharp income inequality, a very small percentage of households can save. The economic elite have excess income to enable them to channel savings away from tangible to financial assets. As the masses increase their income, investments in tangible assets should expand. With the government's goal of narrowing income inequality, it is expected that there would be an increase in holdings of tangible instead of financial assets.

6. Due to the pioneering efforts of enterprising Filipino individuals, the number of financial institutions has increased and has contributed to the greater mobilization of domestic savings. However, data on lending practices of financial institutions show that savings are channeled into short-term credit and into consumption and real estate loans.

The country's inability to generate sufficient capital and its reliance on foreign investments can be simply traced to the misfortunes of poverty. Despite the gains made in the economy by 1973, a large majority of the population remains poor. Statistics from the Family Income and Expenditures Survey of the Bureau of Census demonstrate the poverty and the income imbalance:

a. 86% of total families or households are dissaving or spending more than their income by as much as ₱800 per annum.

b. 7% manage to break even or barely save. This category contributes approximately 1% of total household savings.

c. 4% save around ₱500-₱1,000 per annum. About 97% of all families account for only 23% of total household savings.

d. 3% save an average of ₱5,000 per annum. This elite group of 3% of all families accounts for 77% of total household savings.

FINANCIAL INSTITUTIONS

Despite the condition of underdevelopment, the country has developed a number of financial institutions with a degree of sophistication. Around the Central Bank, which supervises directly most of the financial institutions in the country, revolve most of the financial institutions known in developed capital markets. However, among these institutions the commercial banks clearly dominate the financial markets, with only a very limited room left to the traditional depository and contractual nonbank institutions.

Commercial Banks

The country's commercial banking system has three subsets—the government-owned commercial banks, the private domestic commercial banks, and the local branches of four foreign banks. The government-controlled commercial banks are: the Philippine National Bank, which is the largest in terms of total resources (₱3 billion), and the Philippine Veterans Banks, which provide financial services to the country's veterans. The private domestic commercial banks number 35 and have 786 branches. They comprise the largest subset, accounting for approximately 50-60% of total resources. The 4 foreign banks are: the First National City Bank of New York (the largest private commercial bank), the Bank of America, the Chartered Bank, and the Hong Kong-Shanghai Bank. These four banks have historically provided the impetus for the development of innovative financial services and have exerted a stabilizing factor, especially during periods of threatened financial crisis.

Lending activities are almost entirely directed to the private sector (98%). The following industries are the major recipients: trade (49%), manufacturing (23%), banks and other financial institutions (13%), real estate and consumption (3.8%). The primary emphasis on short-term financing of trade and commerce proceeds from the commercial import-export focus of economic activity. Also, bank reserves and capital are inadequate to allow commercial banks to move into medium- and long-term financing. Only the government-owned commercial banks are able to provide medium- and long-term finance but this has been limited to agriculture and real estate. The private commercial banks engage in long-term finance on a case by case basis, but only in consortia. To strengthen the banks and to enable them to move into longer-term financing, the government began reforming the commercial banking system in 1973. It forced the consolidation of small and medium-sized banks and the expansion of the capital bases of larger banks. Minimum paid-in capital was raised from ₱10 million to ₱100 million. Equity participation up to 40% by foreign banks was encouraged. The reforms led to mergers and consolidations of banks. The usual pattern was the merger of a domestic and a foreign bank. With the strengthening of the capital base, it is hoped that the banks will be able to absorb long-term risks.

The Central Bank closely regulates all facets of commercial banking. Periodic examination and auditing of banks is conducted to promote efficiency and to check on compliance with regulations. The Central Bank also imposes maximum allowable interest rates in most of the commercial banks' transactions. The major exception to this regulation is money market rates. Due to the country's weak currency, a tight rein over the banks' foreign exchange transactions is imposed. Commercial banks are not allowed to engage in investment banking activities like securities underwriting and brokerage.

A historical look at the consolidated sources and uses of funds of the commercial banking system demonstrates the pattern of credit, investment allocation, and resource generation. (See Exhibit 1.) Historically, the major funds use has been in loans and investments, averaging 60-70% of total resources. Loans have been the larger of the two assets, but investments in bonds, stocks, and marketable securities have been expanding steadily from 11% of total resources in 1960 to approximately 18-22% in recent years, indicating the growth of both capital and money markets. Foreign assets comprise another sizable portion of funds use. This particular funds use has averaged 10-15% of total resources. On the sources side, deposit liabilities dominate commercial bank resources, ranging from 50-75% over the period 1955-1974. Within this particular source, there have been shifts in relative importance among savings and time deposits and demand deposits. Savings and time deposits have been growing faster than demand deposits, at 20% compared to 13%. Demand deposits comprise 12-18% of total resources, while savings and time deposits oscillate between 18% and 25%. Unclassified liabilities, which largely represent commercial paper borrowings in the money market, have generated 15-20% of resources. In recent years, this source has increased in relative importance such that it generated 20-30% of resources from 1967 to 1974. Foreign borrowings make up another major source of funds, averaging 5-15%. Capital accounts account for 8-15% of total commercial bank resources.

Nonbank Financial Institutions

All other financial institutions tend to specialize in lending to specific sectors of the economy. Depending on the government's attitude towards their contribution to economic growth, some of these institutions are either directly owned by the government or subsidized in some manner.

FINANCIAL MARKETS

Financial institutions provide the necessary intermediation between suppliers and demanders of finance in two financial markets—the capital market for long-term equity and the money market for short-term debt instruments. The capital market has achieved a high degree of sophistication.

Capital Market

The country's capital market has been both narrow in terms of types of long-term securities offered and shallow in terms of participants. Few corporate stocks

EXHIBIT 1 Commercial Banks: Sources and Uses of Funds (millions of pesos)

	1955	1960	1965	1970	1974
Sources of Funds					
Deposits	966.0	1,732.0	4,002.1	7,685.7	14,663
Demand	513.2	744.9	1,545.7	2,458.9	5,565
Savings	285.3	714.7	1,402.5	3,757.2	} 7,567
Time	167.5	242.4	1,053.9	1,469.6	
Marginal Deposits					1,531
Capital Accounts	158.0	283.9	828.3	1,470.7	2,688
Due to Banks	121.5	30.0	110.8	511.5	695
Unclassified Liabilities	167.4	290.9	1,789.8	4,398.2	6,673
Foreign Liabilities					4,822
Uses of Funds					
Cash	25.0	44.3	112.0	294.0	1,556
Checks and Other Cash Items	8.7	28.5	94.6	351.4	1,035
Claims:					
Loans and Discount	217.5	939.5	2.655.8	6,422.2	} 17,583
Investments	226.9	131.9	615.1	1,762.3	
Due from Banks	226.2	159.9	368.5	508.6	} 1,800
Due from Central Bank	136.5	150.5	132.0	841.3	
Unclassified Assets	572.1	882.2	2,753.0	3,886.3	3,023
Foreign Assets					4,544
Total Balance Sheet	1,412.9	2,336.8	6,731.0	14,066.1	29,541

Source: Central Bank, *Statistical Bulletin.*

and government securities have been issued. Corporate bond issues have been extremely rare. Participants have been limited to well-to-do individuals, the government, and insurance companies. Pension funds and mutual funds have not been very successful and insurance companies have limited equity markets. As such, a viable institutional market has failed to develop. The failure of the country's capital market to progress can be traced to the following factors:

1. The general condition of economic underdevelopment. The low level of capital investment has not spurred demand for capital.

2. The limited pool of savings and savers. Participants in the financial system have been limited to the few middle- and upper-class savers.

3. The low degree of investor sophistication in terms of analysis.

4. The short-term orientation of the financial institutions' investment priorities.

At its present undeveloped stage, the country's capital market consists of both the primary market for the issues of stocks and the secondary market for the buying and selling of securities. Participants in the primary market are corporations, individuals, financial institutions, and the government. In the secondary market, the major actors are the stock exchanges, investment banks, and dealers and brokers.

The securities market consists of the buying and selling of corporate and government securities listed on the four stock exchanges operating in the country. A small over-the-counter market for companies not listed on the exchanges but properly approved by the Securities Exchange Commission also exists. The entire securities industry is closely regulated by the Securities and Exchange Commission, a government agency created in 1936.

In December 1973, a total of 160 companies were listed on the Manila Stock Exchange and 177 on the Makati Stock Exchange. Multiple listing is allowed. Only two government bond issues are listed on each exchange. Both stock exchanges follow different modes of classification. The Manila Stock Exchange classifies the companies according to Big Board and Small Board. Companies listed on the Big Board are regular dividend-paying companies and generally have higher-priced shares. A total of 88 companies were listed on the Big Board. Companies listed on the Small Board are non-dividend-paying and highly speculative stocks. These are mostly mining and oil exploration companies. A total of 72 companies were listed on the Small Board. The Makati Stock Exchange categorized the listed companies according to mining (18), mining exploration (52), commercial and industrial (79), and oil exploration (28). Most of the issues in the categories other than commercial and industrial are highly speculative.

The securities industry enjoyed a banner year in 1973. In terms of volume of transactions, it was the strongest bull market in the history of the local capital market. The Manila and Makati Stock Exchanges witnessed volume surging to a total of ₱5,925.1 million, a phenomenal increase of 874% over 1972 and 29% over 1969, another bull year. Over-the-counter transactions increased slightly, by 17.1% to ₱19.3 million. A total of 678.56 million over-the-counter shares were traded. Volume on the Manila Stock Exchange hit ₱3,642.9 million and on the Makati Stock Exchange ₱2,282.2 million. In a single month, August 1973, volume was ₱1,132.55 million on both exchanges. Most of the transactions were in the highly speculative mining and oil sectors. On the Manila Stock Exchange, transactions in mining and oil amounted to 94% of total volume, or ₱3,423.22 million. Transactions in the commercial and industrial sector accounted for only 6% or ₱219.75 million. From 1969-1972, the industrial and commercial sector accounted for 3.97% of total transactions. The historic 1973 bull market was largely a result of the improving business climate and the rising prices of metals which accounted for 18% of total exports in the world market. Various financial and monetary measures implemented by the government created a favorable business climate for the infusion of foreign investment capital. Likewise, the government adopted the following steps aimed at stimulating the securities industry:

1. Reduction of the stock transfer tax from 2% to .25% in lieu of capital gains.

2. Reduction of brokers' commissions from 1.5% to not more than 1% of the value of each stock transaction.

3. Exemption of capital gains taxes on the sale, disposition, or transfer of capital assets or on the purchase of new issues of government bonds, securities, or debentures within six months from the date the gains were made.

4. Implementation of stock arbitrage among existing exchanges to facilitate trading.

5. Implementation of an order requiring companies with surplus profits to declare dividends.

Prospects for the future are equally bright. Prices of commodities like sugar, the country's primary commodity export, are expected to rise. The search for oil has accelerated speculative interest in companies engaged in mining and oil exploration. Production levels of mining firms have been high as a result of expansion in copper and gold ventures. However, the raging inflation and tightening of monetary policy may dampen these optimistic forecasts.

Money Market

The money market is a recent development in the country's financial system. However, it has assumed great significance in mobilizing savings and short-term investments. Major participants in the money market are individual savers, corporations whose savings or liquid surpluses are tapped by bank and nonbank financial institutions, and corporations in need of funds for short-term investments. Savings are funneled into the financial system via the buying and selling of commercial paper, government securities, and other short-term notes. In its evolution, the money market has developed four submarkets:

1. The government securities market for treasury bills and Central Bank certificates of indebtedness.

2. The interbank call money market. This submarket aids banks in need of temporary funds to bolster reserves according to Central Bank requirements.

3. The market for banker's acceptances and time certificates of deposit.

4. The intercompany market where corporations' commercial paper is issued, bought, and sold.

As an entirely new development, the money market has been insulated from government regulation, particularly from the rigid interest rate system. Interest rates have violently fluctuated within each submarket. In 1973, the interbank rate moved within the range of 1-14%, compared to the 3-30% range in 1972, reflecting the higher level of liquidity in the banking sector. Prime commercial paper rates in the intercompany submarket ranged over 2.5%-18% versus 5.5%-29% in 1972. The higher level of interest rates prevailing in the money market resulted in disintermediation from savings and time deposits as investors sought higher returns. The increasing popularity of the money market, the resulting disintermediation, and the potential for abuse have caused concern among the monetary authorities. The Central Bank is expected to move in to tighten its supervision over money market activities of the financial institutions. An impending move is to raise minimum investments in the money market from ₱1,000 to ₱50,000. This will minimize disintermediation and induce small investors to invest in other financial assets.

PROSPECTS AND NEW DIRECTIONS

The various changes made in the country's aggregate financial system constitute a prelude to more radical reforms. New directions will be charted in the following areas:

1. Higher yields on financial instruments to provide an incentive to savings and investments in financial assets.

2. Creation of a long-term debt market.

3. Creation of a new equity issues market.

4. Reallocation of savings.

These moves will be aimed at making financial intermediation more efficient, encouraging savings, and strengthening financial markets.

More Attractive Yields

To make financial instruments more attractive to savers, the government is expected to loosen the rigid interest rate structure by lifting controls on various rate ceilings. One possibility being explored in financial circles is the installation of a floating interest rate similar to the Brazilian model. For instance, the interest rate on a savings deposit at 6% would be adjusted to minimize inflationary disincentive. If the inflation rate is 15%, interest on the minimum balance of the savings deposit is adjusted to 15% and interest on the average balance is kept at 6%. This will assure the depositor a fair income not fully eroded by inflation. However, the borrower would have to bear higher interest costs. Measures for minimizing this negative impact on borrowers are also being contemplated. Parallel to making financial instruments more attractive is reducing the attractiveness of alternative investments in real assets like real estate and luxury housing. Heavy taxes on real estate are a bright possibility.

Creation of a Long-Term Debt Market

The lack of medium- and long-term finance has been a problem for the financial system and for the economy's ability to generate needed capital. To rectify this situation, the government is expected to hasten the creation of a long-term debt market. It may further encourage the formation of investment banks and induce them to concentrate their activities in the underwriting of equity and bond issues. It will surely resort to taxation which will provide preferential treatment to medium- and long-term lending. A withholding tax on a graduated scale may be imposed on interest income, e.g., 15% on six-month bills and only 5% on two-year or more bills and bonds. The government may also spur the creation of funds which can be set aside for investment in corporate securities.

Creation of a New Equity Issues Market

The stock market has failed to be a significant conduit for long-term finance to corporations. Because ownership of corporations has been concentrated in the hands of a few wealthy individuals, corporations face a thin capital base and excessive indebtedness. To remedy this lamentable situation, the government is expected to establish foundations for a strong capital market. Measures being contemplated are: (1) tax incentives designed to broaden participation in the stock market; (2) regulations to induce corporations to open their equity to the public, and (3) regulations to force investment houses to concentrate in underwriting of new equity and bond issues.

Reallocation of Savings

The country's financial system has been faulted for its tendency to allocate financing to short-term trade credit, government, real estate, and consumption. This has made the financial system vulnerable to the exigencies of government deficit spending and inflation. For instance, as prices sky-rocketed due to inflation, the increased need for working capital had to be satisfied by bank credit. Thus, the capital requirements of the manufacturing and industrial sectors were left on the limb. To correct the imbalance, the government may undertake the following:

1. Allow financial institutions to expand in other forms of finance on a minority basis. This will diversify the allocation of credit.

2. Establish and strengthen a housing finance system to respond to the needs of consumers for housing and real estate. This will free the commercial banks from such financing.

3. Provide tax incentives to long-term industrial finance.

International Taxation

One of the most complex aspects of international business is the area of international taxation. Understanding the rules surrounding domestic treatment of foreign income is the first difficulty. That obligation is compounded by the need for a thorough understanding of tax policies in several other nations which are potential bases for operations. The written code and the practical effect of the rules force most firms to rely extensively on local legal and tax representatives to explain the alternatives for business organization, dividend policy, capital structure, and so on. Several references are included with this appendix for the reader who desires more background information on the taxing policies in many nations. The excellent bibliography of international tax sources by Elisabeth Owens includes a detailed breakdown of publications concerning taxes in many specific nations.

THE PHILOSOPHY OF TAXATION

Nations have a variety of reasons for enacting any particular tax. Sometimes it is for social reasons: to punish particular behavior, to encourage other actions, or to redistribute income. Sometimes it is enforceability: a customs duty with an honest customs service and one port makes that tax more operational than some income taxes. Sometimes it is related to an international pattern, and reciprocity or comparable incentive policies dictate a particular code.

Many European nations have used a Value Added Tax as a major source of revenue. Tax analysts consider this a national sales tax as opposed to an income tax. The tax is applied to the value of a product at each point in manufacture based on the selling price of the good. Each firm can credit against the tax the amount of VAT passed on to it by other suppliers and manufacturers. The advantage to the tax is claimed to be the encouragement of honesty. It is based on revenues, not profits, and deductions from the applied tax must be supported, hence encouraging each manager in the chain to seek accurate figures from the suppliers. VAT can be adjusted or forgiven to stimulate or to discourage export sales, responding to balance of payments or domestic inflation problems. The problem with VAT is possible mis-allocation of resources, since it is a sales tax rather than an income tax. However, most nations that have adopted a VAT have used it to replace an existing sales (turn-over) tax. Some critics argue that the immediate imposition of such a tax causes an increase in inflation, but this charge can be blunted where governments pursue ef-fective fiscal and monetary policies. VAT is also criticized for being a regressive tax, borne with regard to consumption and not income.

Most nations would like to rely on an income tax for individuals and corpora-tions since it can be shown with minimal assumptions that an income tax on profits as opposed to a sales tax or gross turnover tax will reduce output less. The other taxation approaches can affect total production. For example, a flat tax on doing business is both a regressive tax and a high fixed cost to firms. Revenue is always a problem, for a government needs funds. Sometimes taxing the foreign corporation which must remain there for raw materials (for example) is the major source of revenue whatever the equity of this policy. The pretax corporate profits of U. S.-controlled foreign corporations are estimated at nearly $20 billion, or about $1/5$ of all U. S. corporate profits. The tax revenue is around $1 billion, so that the govern-ment nets only about 5%, largely because of credit offsets for foreign taxes and other arrangements. If all this income were fully taxed at regular rates with the for-eign taxes created as a deduction instead of a credit, there would probably be an in-crease of $4 or $5 billion in revenue. When U. S.-controlled foreign corporations were a small part of the total profit generated by U. S. firms, the issue was not as important to many as it is now when larger sources of revenue are potentially avail-able under new tax legislation.

One major issue is *equity*. Most taxing authorities believe that people with com-parable incomes should pay the same tax, and people with different income should pay different taxes. When applied to personal income, this philosophy usually re-sults in a variety of deductions from income for various minimum expenditures that are considered appropriate, and the allowance for extraordinary expenses which may occasionally occur, such as large medical bills. In the international scene, this policy means that a corporation doing business abroad should pay taxes somewhere, re-gardless of its multinational status. The firm may be taxable in full on income re-gardless of where earned, but with offsets for income taxes which different jurisdic-tions may impose. The basic concern, however, is that taxes should be paid on in-come as earned, and the taxation system should be "equitable," however hard that term is to define.

A second issue in taxation is the *social or economic goals* which are encouraged or discouraged by the tax policy. Much of the concern over the U. S. tax policy re-lates to the loss or creation of jobs for U. S. workers. Various studies exist on U. S. exports and investment abroad and their effect on the balance of payments, the first level of jobs, and the ultimate level of jobs according to various assumptions of what the U. S. government would do in the absence of such jobs. Worldwide, one would expect that freer trade would result in greater total output, but the total level of employment and the allocation of that employment among nations and among skill levels within nations are at the center of the controversy. No firm statement can be made, for the research tools necessary to understand this subject are not sufficiently refined nor are the data always available. A brief exchange of two proponents of different views is contained in the references as part of the U. S. Congressional hearings on taxation of foreign income.

NATIONAL CORPORATE TAXATION POLICIES

Whatever the issues of philosophy, when the corporation faces the corporate tax scheme in a particular nation, there are special factors to be considered.

First, taxes may be absolutely low on corporation profits. The lands noted for especially hospitable taxes include Switzerland, Liechtenstein, Luxembourg, Panama, the Netherlands Antilles (Curacao), the Bahamas, and Bermuda. Withholding taxes on intercorporate dividends are typically nonexistent in these nations, unlike some major industrial lands where high corporate tax rates and dividend withholding rates restrict the ability to move intercorporate funds about. Exhibit A.1 summarizes some of these effective tax rates.

Second, the definition of taxable income may be highly divergent among various nations. For example, "constructive receipt" is important. One nation may deem profits to be taxable "as received" on a cash basis whereas another would treat the same profits as taxable "as earned." One nation may provide greater latitude on the creation of reserves, permitting an offset of taxable revenues by these allocations for future contingencies. Some countries may give full credit for taxes on the income paid in other countries, or have no tax on "intercorporate dividends or earnings." Especially rapid depreciation or depletion arrangements also affect the definition of taxable income.

Third, tax treaties with other nations may influence the total taxation bill of the parent corporation. The United States has tax treaties with more than thirty nations, primarily with members of the European Economic Community and other industrialized nations. As a result, special allowance for avoiding withholding on dividends and interest paid by firms to nationals of the involved countries, special tax reductions on intercorporate dividends, and the like contribute to a simplification of the regulations which will affect any firm. The effects of some of these treaties are suggested in Table A.1, for the normal withholding on dividends from corporations in most of those nations would be 30-40%.

The ability to use low-tax countries solely as "tax havens" is limited. Many industrialized countries such as the United States are increasingly cautious about the definition of income and where it is held. Often, income is taxed regardless of remission, as emphasized in the 1962 U. S. tax reform measures. In addition, some of these countries, especially smaller developing nations, resent the label of a "tax haven" while desiring the economic contributions of major corporate interest. These lands are turning to industrialization, to the development of tourism, or to other tangible assets as an alternative to the tax haven option. Although pleased to provide help to corporations desiring to avoid the export controls imposed by their home countries, these nations believe their appeal simply as a tax-reducing location is not desirable.

EXHIBIT A.1 Foreign Taxes on Subsidiaries of U. S. Corporations

Country	Approximate Population (millions)	Statutory Corporate Income Tax Rate	Withholding Tax on Dividends to U. S. Parent Co.	Maximum Foreign Net Tax on Earnings Remitted to the United States
Europe				
Belgium	10	35%	15%	44.8%
Denmark	5	34%	5%[a]	37.3%
France	52	50%	5%[b]	52.5%
Germany	61	35% or 60%[c]	15%	44.9%
Greece	9	38%	38%	61.6%
Ireland	3	50%	35%	67.5%
Italy	54	46%[d]	5%[e]	48.7%
Netherlands	13	46%	5%[f]	48.7%
Norway	4	48%	5%[g]	50.6%
Spain	34	33%	15%	43.1%
Sweden	8	53%	5%[h]	55.4%
United Kingdom	55	40%[i]	15%[i]	49.0%
The Americas				
Argentina	24	38%	35%	59.4%
Brazil	98	30%	25%	47.5%
Canada	22	50%	15%	57.5%
Colombia	22	36%[j]	12%	43.7%
Ecuador	6	33%	k	44.4%
Mexico	51	42%[l]	20%	53.6%
Venezuela	10	m	15%	57.5%
Others				
Australia	13	45%	30%	61.5%
Japan	105	48%	15%	55.8%
South Africa	22	43%	15%	51.6%

[a]Provided the Danish company is at least 95 per cent owned by the U. S. parent corporation; otherwise the tax is 15 percent.

[b]Provided the French company is at least 10 per cent owned by the U. S. parent corporation; otherwise the tax is 15 percent.

[c]The effective German corporate tax rate on distributed profits (e.g., dividends) is about 35.2 percent, and the effective corporate tax rate on undistributed profits is about 59.7 percent. These taxes are made up of a municipal income tax averaging 15 percent, and federal taxes of 23.6 percent on distributed profits and 52.5 percent on undistributed profits. The municipal tax is a deductible expense for determining the federal tax.

[d]The effective Italian corporate tax rate begins at about 36 percent, and reaches about 46 percent for all income over $173,000.

[e]Provided the Italian company is at least 95 percent owned by the U. S. parent corporation; otherwise the tax is 15 percent.

[f]Provided the Dutch company is at least 25 percent owned by the U. S. parent corporation; otherwise the tax is 15 percent.

[g]Provided the Norwegian company is at least 50 percent owned by the U. S. parent corporation; otherwise the tax is 15 percent.

[h]Provided the Swedish company is at least 50 percent owned by the U. S. parent corporation; otherwise the tax is 15 percent.

[i]The British corporate tax rate changed to 50 percent on April 6, 1973, and there will be no dividend withholding tax.

[j]The Colombian corporate tax rate begins at 12 percent and increases, in two steps, to 36 percent on all income over $43,000.

[k]The Ecuadorian income tax on undistributed profits is 33.3 percent and 44.4 percent on distributed profits to foreign shareholders with no dividend withholding tax added.

[l]The Mexican corporate tax begins at five percent and reaches 42 percent on all income over $120,000.

[m]The Venezuelan corporate tax rate on businesses not involved in the exploitation of minerals or hydrocarbons is as follows:

Taxable Income	Tax Rate
$0-23,000	15.0%
$23-328,000	25.0%
$328-889,000	30.0%
$889-1,498,000	35.0%
$1,498-2,340,000	40.0%
$2,340-4,680,000	45.0%
$4,680-6,552,000	47.5%
over $6,552,000	50.0%

Source: J. Peter Gaskins, "Taxation of Foreign Source Income." *Financial Analysts Journal,* Sept.-Oct. 1973, p. 57.

The complexities of a particular tax code are too involved for any person but the specialist. However, as an aid to understanding the possible patterns in taxation for foreign income, the concluding section of this appendix will outline some of the major issues in U. S. taxation of foreign source income. It is based in part on Michael J. McIntyre's *United States Taxation of Foreign Income with Special Emphasis on Private Investments in Developing Countries* (see bibliography).

U. S. TAXATION OF INTERNATIONAL INCOME OF CORPORATIONS

Background

The U. S. taxing authorities focus upon the status of the taxpayer (resident or citizen versus others) and the source of the income. Citizens and residents are taxed on worldwide income, generally, but with a credit for income taxes paid to other jurisdictions. Nonresidents are generally taxed only on their U. S. income. There are special rules to prevent or limit tax avoidance. For a corporation, the status is determined by incorporation and not by nationality or residence of shareholders. Corporations incorporated in the United States are U. S. corporations; all others are foreign corporations, even though all the shares may be owned by a U. S. corporation.

If less than 50% of the gross income of a foreign corporation is from conduct of a trade or business in the United States, then all its dividend and interest payments are considered foreign source income to the recipient, and special calculations may apply as noted below. Dividends paid by a U. S. corporation are considered foreign source income to the recipient only if 80% or more of that corporation's gross income is from foreign sources. Special rulings apply for mineral companies and other firms in particular industries.

Tax Policies

The basic guideline within the tax system is that the United States claims jurisdiction over all income of its citizens and residents wherever earned. There is a credit for the income taxes paid to other nations, ranging up to the level of taxes which would have been paid had that income been earned in the United States. Alternatively, these foreign taxes may be deducted from taxable income. Furthermore, the foreign corporation often has deferral of taxes on its income from foreign sources until the income is remitted as dividends. On the other hand, whereas a U. S. firm can exclude from its taxable income 100% of dividends from a U. S. company in which it owns 80% or more of the stock, and 85% of the dividends otherwise, there is no exclusion of dividend income received by a U. S. corporation from a foreign corporation. Most variations in taxation result from varying application of this basic guideline of full jurisdiction over all income. Critical factors in such variations include how the income is earned, where it is earned, and how the corporation is structured. The remainder of this appendix will outline some of those differences as they affect the corporation.

Section 482

A part of the U. S. Internal Revenue Code which has continuing impact on the decisions of individuals and firms is only one sentence in length. However, Section 482 permits the Treasury to allocate income and expenses among firms which are owned or controlled by the same interests if such an allocation is necessary to prohibit an evasion of taxes or to clearly reflect income. Tax credits and allowances also may be apportioned among firms which are not organized or incorporated in the United States. The key in application is the value realized in an arm's-length transaction (i.e., a fair price between an informed and willing buyer and seller). This value is a difficult point for courts to determine. Various safe harbors are available, and the purpose of the enforcement is only to affect U. S. tax liabilities; hence, it is not designed as a general harassment of multinationals according to enforcement officials. Once the IRS makes an allocation under Section 482, however, the burden of proof is on the taxpayer to show that both the allocation method and the result of the allocation are arbitrary. The IRS provides detailed rules on how to allocate income among related parties in the most common types of situations.

Allocation of expenses between subsidiaries is always a problem, especially where there is a clear joint product and taxes are involved. For example, in 1974 the Internal Revenue Service made a well-publicized attack on the allocation of corporate-wide research and development under Section 861. Even though the outlays were made in the United States, the IRS argued that many of the benefits accrued to foreign operations. Hence, it wished to have more of the cost of research and development allocated to foreign operations. The effect of such an allocation is to reduce foreign income (and taxes which were usually credited against the U. S. tax liability) while increasing U. S. taxable income.

Section 882

A foreign corporation carrying on business in the United States is taxed at the U. S. rate on business profits. This provision of the Code is designed to prevent the creation of foreign subsidiaries to carry on various business activities in this country. It is also consistent with the policy of taxing the receipt of income from all activities carried on in this country.

Tax Credits (Sections 901, 902, and so on)

Although there is the possibility of treating foreign taxes as a deduction from income, most corporations will elect to take the foreign income taxes as a direct credit against their U. S. tax liability. Only income taxes or in lieu income taxes are eligible for credit. The indirect credit rules generally apply only to corporations, and for the credit to be applicable, the U. S. corporate parent (P) must have 10% or more of the stock of the foreign corporation (S1). The credit is applicable only in the year when the dividends are received by P.

There is also a pyramid effect, since P can credit foreign income taxes paid by a subsidiary (S2) owned by S1, and by another subsidiary (S3) owned by S2. This three-tier rule relates to receipt of dividends by P. Each participant (P, S1, and S2) must own at least 10% of the stock in the next firm. Furthermore, P must have at least 5% direct or indirect ownership of the corporation that paid the tax for it to be creditable. Thus, P, owning 50% of S1 which owned 25% of S2 which in turn owned 15% of S3, would be able to take credit for taxes paid by S1 (50% beneficial ownership) and S2 (.5 × .25 = $12^1/_2$% beneficial ownership), but not for S3 (.5 × .25 × .15 = less than 5%) even though each firm in the chain owned at least 10% of the next lower firm.

The basic procedure is to "gross up" the dividends in the United States to the total income in the foreign land *before* foreign income and dividend withholding taxes. The ratio of the dividends actually received in this country to total taxable income is a multiplier, applied to the income taxes actually paid in the foreign land. To this product is added any withholding taxes on dividends imposed by the foreign land, and the sum of these two items is the maximum total tax credit for that year. See the calculations for Subsidiaries A and B in the exercises following this appendix. Special policies are in effect for the less developed countries in which the U. S. corporations do business, as discussed below.

The firm may elect either an *overall* limitation or a *per country* limitation when computing the tax credit calculation for income from the foreign corporation when dividends are remitted. The overall limitation lumps all foreign source income together and the ratio of that income to total taxable income (foreign and domestic) times the applicable U. S. tax rate provides the maximum credit. This calculation is done to assure that the total tax credits do not exceed what would have been paid in the United States had the entire income been from domestic sources. The overall option is beneficial to firms for which high tax payments in some countries would yield larger credits than can be used. Credits from these countries may then be combined with those from other lands where the tax rates might be lower to give the total credit. For example, assume that the domestic tax rate is 50% and that P has local taxable income of $100 in A and $100 in B. Local taxes are $60 in A and $30 in B and the balance is remitted to P as dividends with no withholding. Then the maximum credit against U. S. taxes would be 50% of $200, or $100, and all $90 of the tax payments could be credited against the U. S. tax liability. This is the "grossing up" process, for the U. S. income is increased to the level before the foreign taxes, and then the U. S. tax calculation is based on that higher level. On a per country basis, there would be a full credit for the 30% liability paid in B, but only $50 from the A tax payments would be creditable since the U. S. taxes on that income would have totalled only $50.

The per country limitation is useful where there are losses in one country which would otherwise use up possible tax credits from other countries on an overall calculation, and where there is taxable income in the United States. The benefit occurs because the full credit (up to the U. S. statutory rate) can still be taken for the profitable operations where taxes were paid. Without that segregation then part or all of those taxes would not be eligible for credit because of the lower total of foreign income when the losses are included. The taxes are based on dividend calculations when dividends are received, but the tax credits are based on taxable income, so that the losses are included in the base, reducing the maximum credit.

Note that the limitation on credit is based on the U. S. tax rate applied to the foreign source income as defined by the U. S. Tax Code. Thus, the foreign tax rate may be less than the U. S. rate, but an allowance for deductions that the foreign government did not permit (hence lowering U. S. calculated taxable income) can mean that not all the foreign taxes are creditable even though they were applied at a nominally lower rate. For example, a $30 foreign tax on $100 of foreign income seems fully creditable. If the additional deductions of expenses reduce the income to only $50, then a 50% U. S. tax rate means a maximum credit of only $25. Furthermore, investment in the stock of the parent or a loan to the parent by a controlled foreign corporation is also now included as a dividend payment for tax purposes so as to prevent tax avoidance through remission of profits by this investment or loan.

Once a firm elects the overall limitation, it may not change unless permission is received from the taxing authorities. Most firms use this overall limitation but operate with branches when some operations are likely to have initial losses because these branch losses can be consolidated to reduce taxes. There is a two-year carryback and a five-year carryforward for credits in the event of excess credits in any year. There are special restrictions which apply to taxes on foreign source interest income, on credits where part of the consolidated taxes include a Western Hemisphere Trading Corporation (WHTC, see below), and on credits for non-U. S. mineral income. In addition, the House Ways and Means Committee voted in late 1975 to require the overall option for computing foreign tax credits.

Limitations on Deferrals

Foreign operations of U. S. corporations are taxable as the income is earned. As noted, a foreign corporation which is completely owned by a U. S. parent may defer U. S. taxes on its foreign source income (as defined above) until remission of dividends to the parent. Because of abuses, the 1962 tax reform program limited deferral in a number of cases, largely related to so-called Subpart F income. Essentially, a tax is payable on undistributed "base company income" (defined below) of controlled foreign corporations; this income is treated as a constructive dividend even though the foreign corporation has not remitted the funds to the shareholders. The taxes are imposed on the shareholders of controlled foreign corporations, where the definition of control is largely based on the number of shareholders, nationality, and percentage of ownership. The tax applies only to certain companies (more than 50% of ownership is by U. S. persons where "person" can be a corporation) and only to certain shareholders (more than 10% interest) where applicable. In making the determination of whether more than 50% of the voting control is by U. S. persons, only shareholders with 10% or more of the stock are counted in this figure. Thus, even though more than 50% of the stock might be owned by U. S. citizens/residents, if a sufficient number of these persons have less than 10%, the firm would not be a U. S. controlled foreign corporation. As an extreme example, eleven U. S. shareholders each with 9% of the stock would not have a controlled foreign corporation.

"Base company income" can generally be described as income from operations carried on by a foreign subsidiary for tax minimization purposes. Base company income includes foreign personal holding company income[1] (which mainly deals with

---

[1] Foreign personal holding company income restrictions are designed to prevent individuals from using the tax deferral provisions to avoid taxes on dividends, interest, and capital gains from various transactions. A *controlled* foreign personal holding company is a firm in which more than 50% of the ownership is by five or fewer U. S. citizens or permanent residents, and where 60% or more of the gross income in the first year and 50% or more in subsequent years is foreign personal holding company income. This income is automatically base company income to a controlled foreign corporation even though it is *not* a foreign personal holding company.

income from various investments), base company sales income, and base company services income. Foreign base company sales income includes income from sale of goods produced and sold outside the country of incorporation and net income from property which is either bought from or sold to a "related person" (i.e., a parent or another subsidiary) or sold on behalf of a related person. See McIntyre (1975) for a detailed definition of income in these categories. Subsidiary E in the exercises shows the tax treatment for this corporation.

For many purposes, some of the advantages of deferral can still be realized in the area of sales income through use of a Domestic International Sales Corporation (DISC) which is described below. Another interesting exclusion from this foreign base company income is income from sales or services performed in the country of incorporation. Thus, if the firm incorporates a subsidiary in every nation in which it does business, then the foreign base company income rules would not apply to those sales. In addition, if less than 10% of the gross income of a controlled foreign corporation is base company income, then none of the income will be so considered. (If more than 90% of the gross income is base company income, then all the income is so treated. Between these two points, the income is prorated and base company income is taxable whether or not distributed.) If the foreign-controlled corporation pays taxes of at least 90% of the U. S. level on the income or makes a substantial dividend distribution to its shareholders, or a minimum combination of foreign taxes and dividend distribution exists, there is no special tax. Financial income (dividends, interest, and capital gains) from less developed countries and shipping income from operations of vessels or aircraft in foreign trade are excluded if earnings are reinvested in shipping activities. Several of these provisions are direct consequences of the 1975 Tax Reduction Act.[2] In late 1975, the House Ways and Means Committee voted to recover taxes on foreign losses which offset U. S. profits if the foreign operations later produced profits.

Western Hemisphere Trading Corporations (Section 921)

A U. S. corporation whose entire operations are carried on outside the United States but in the Western Hemisphere with 90% of its gross income from active conduct of a trade or business and with 95% of its gross income from outside the United States is taxed under a special arrangement providing an effective tax rate of about 34%. The WHTC may credit foreign taxes paid up to 34%, may be consolidated with a domestic parent, and may have 85% (or in some cases 100%) of its dividends eligible for exemption from tax for a domestic corporate recipient. See Subsidiary F in the exercises. The House Ways and Means Committee voted in late 1975 to phase out this special tax benefit for Western Hemisphere Trading Corporations over a four-year period.

[2] Special provisions of the 1975 Tax Reduction Act were designed to restrict the use of foreign tax credits (instead of deductions) for royalties paid to foreign governments by international oil companies. Specifically, the Act denies credits if two conditions occur: the price on which the taxes are based is not the market price (i.e., if artificial "posted" prices are used for tax levies) and the oil company has no "economic interest" in the oil (i.e., if it does not own the oil). However, there is substantial question about the meaning of "economic interest" and the impact of this provision is unclear. The oil companies also were forced to compute tax credit calculations on an overall basis. Various other provisions also tightened the foreign credit benefits for the international oil companies.

Domestic International Sales Corporations (Sections 991-994)

These special U. S. corporations were permitted by 1971 legislation designed to encourage export sales by U. S. firms. Essentially the firms can defer tax on 50% of their export earnings. The shareholders of a DISC are treated as if they have received the remaining 50% of the income (whether or not the earnings were distributed) and are taxable as individual or corporations on that income. The DISC itself is not taxable. The shareholders are entitled to the foreign tax credit for foreign taxes on a DISC. In addition to certain restrictions on the asset base, the main requirement for DISC treatment under the Code is that 95% of the gross income must be from export activities.

A major benefit of the DISC legislation is the encoded "safe harbors" which specify how profits can be determined for a DISC. A "safe harbor" means there is no IRS challenge if the figures are accurate. Under Section 482, as noted, the amount of income could be a source of dispute since the major activity of a DISC is likely to be re-selling of purchased manufactured goods from its parent to export customers. However, the legislation creating DISCs permitted the taxable income to be the greater of (a) 4% of total export receipts plus 10% of the DISC's promotion expenses, (b) 50% of the combined income of both the selling firm (the parent in most cases) and the DISC plus 10% of the DISC's promotion expenses, or (c) the actual taxable income under normal Section 482 accounting standards.

In late 1975, the House Ways and Means Committee voted to allow DISC tax benefits only for the gain in average annual export profit over a 1972-1974 base period. The base would be 75% of the annual average export profit in the 1972-1974 period. Tax on half of the income over that base would be deferred, as under current law. Except for commodities in surplus, raw agricultural products would not be eligible for DISC treatment. Military exports also would be ineligible. However, new exporters (until 1980) and exporters with foreign profits of less than $100,000 would not be restricted in product or base.

Less Developed Country Tax Provisions

To encourage investment and sales to so-called less developed countries (LDCs), special tax provisions were permitted for firms doing business in those lands. Essentially, LDCs include all countries with the exception of most of Western Europe, Australia, Canada, Japan, New Zealand, South Africa, the Soviet bloc, and China. An LDC corporation is a firm involved in active trade or business which has 80% of its gross income from LDC sources and 80% of its assets involved in its trade or business in an LDC. The firm need not be incorporated in an LDC, but cannot be incorporated in the United States.

When dividend income from an LDC corporation is remitted to its parent, there are advantages in the way the tax credit is computed. In contrast with the earlier examples, the parent (P) of an LDC subsidiary is not required to gross-up dividends from the LDC to compute the initial taxable income. The total tax credit for the LDC is computed as for other foreign corporations, but the taxable income on which the U. S. taxes are calculated is only the pre-withholding dividends actually paid to the parent after provision for all foreign corporate income taxes. Hence, the implied U. S. tax is smaller than would otherwise be the case. Although the allowable foreign tax credit is thus also smaller than would be the case for a non-LDC subsidiary, the total tax paid is usually smaller than it would be alternatively. The Chaolandia case demonstrates this calculation in detail, and Subsidiary C in the exercises following this appendix shows a variety of typical tax calculations.[3]

The total taxes paid on LDC repatriated income are less than the total taxes for regular repatriated foreign subsidiary income as long as the foreign tax rate is lower than the United States' 48%. The maximum benefit is obtained when the foreign tax rate is exactly half the U. S. rate, yielding an overall tax rate of 42.24%. Where there are three tiers, then the maximum benefit on repatriated foreign source income can be used to reduce the total overall effective tax rate to 35.73% if all the tax rates are at the optimum level. See McIntyre, page 63, for these calculations.

The nongross-up method may be used when the first tier firm classifies as an LDC corporation, regardless of the classification of the other tiers. The regular direct and indirect ownership rules must be met (10% indirect or direct ownership at each level as a minimum, and a 5% minimum on tiered ownership).

Possessions Corporations

There are special provisions made for corporations carrying on business in U. S. possessions such as the Canal Zone, Guam, American Samoa, and others. Puerto Rico is also eligible for special treatment under its Commonwealth status. To be treated as a possessions corporation, 50% of the gross income must be from the active conduct of a trade or business in a possession, and 80% of the gross income must be from sources within a possession. The possessions corporation is then generally treated as a foreign corporation. However, since it is legally a U. S. corporation, it has several extra tax advantages, most notably the exclusion of the base company income rules and the right to tax free liquidation. A firm which is both a WHTC and a possessions corporation is treated as a possessions corporation for tax purposes.

Capital Gains

Gains from the sale of stock in a controlled foreign corporation are normally taxed at ordinary income tax rates. Gains from an LDC corporation are sometimes eligible for the favorable 30% corporate capital gains tax rate if the ownership has been for at least ten years.

Withholding Taxes

Given a desire to avoid withholding on payments of dividends and interest to investors and debtholders in other lands, the use of various foreign finance subsidiaries becomes important. For example, Rosenberg and Singer (1969) show how to create such a subsidiary depending on where the funds are used and where the

---

[3] Repeal of this LDC provision is the goal of a bill before Congress, which may soon pass. Other major targets of reform are the elimination of the credit system altogether, permitting only deductions for foreign income taxes and taxing income as earned instead of when dividends are remitted. In late 1975, the House Ways and Means Committee voted to eliminate favorable treatment for LDC income, taxing income earned there on the same basis as developed country profits.

investors/lenders are. Under U. S. regulations, an "80-20" corporation will be free from a requirement to collect withholding on interest payments. This firm can meet that requirement as long as less than 20% of its gross income is from the United States, from which the 80-20 name is derived. Dividends or interest payments to this finance subsidiary from overseas subsidiaries would be subject to various withholding provisions in those countries depending on their tax treaties (or lack thereof) with the United States and with each other. These payments are excluded from U. S. taxes assuming consolidated returns are filed and the income of the foreign subsidiaries is included with the U. S. parent; other treatments possible include the 85% or 100% exclusions in some cases.

On the other hand, if the firm wanted to borrow funds from its finance subsidiary for operations in this country, then technically there should be withholding of taxes on interest payments since 50% or more of the financial subsidiary income would be related to the conduct of a trade or business in the United States (i.e., all the interest receipts would be from the operating parent). Withholding can be avoided here by creating the financial subsidiary in the Netherlands Antilles, for example, where the treaty provisions with the United States specifically exempt from withholding interest payments by that finance subsidiary to foreign shareholders even if all the subsidiary's income is from a U. S. source. Where there is a split need for funds, the authors advocate 80-20 corporations in both the United States and the Virgin Islands, with the former used for lending to the foreign subsidiaries and the latter for lending to the U. S. operations.

Exercises on Taxation of Foreign Income

ASSUMPTIONS

A. Parent corporation is subject to a 50% tax rate
B. U. S. corporations own the following:

Subsidiary A—Fully owned foreign subsidiary located in Europe in a developed country.

B—Fully owned foreign subsidiary located in Europe in a developed country.

C—Fully owned foreign subsidiary located in South America in a developing country. It receives 80% or more of its income within less developed countries, and 80% or more of its assets used in business are located in less developed countries.

D—5% ownership in foreign subsidiary located in Europe in a developed country.

E—Fully owned "foreign controlled corporation" in Europe.
F—Fully owned Western Hemisphere Trading Corporation.

C. Total earnings, taxation, and dividends of each subsidiary:

	A	B	(million dollars) C	D	E	F
Earnings before Taxes	$100	$100	$100	$100	$100	$100
Income Taxes	65	65	45	45	50	
Profit after Taxes	35	35	55	55	50	
Dividends Declared	35	20	30	30	0	
Withholding Tax	3	2	3	3	0	

QUESTIONS

1. What are the taxes payable to the U. S. government?

Subsidiary A:

Dividends received		$ 32
Gross up:		
Direct credit		
(withholding tax)	3	
Indirect credit		
(proportion of income taxes)		
$(35/35) \times 65$	65	68
(proportion is based on profits *after* taxes)		
Taxable income		$100
U. S. taxes	50	
Less tax credits	68	
Excess tax credit	$18	

Subsidiary B:

Dividends received		$18
Gross up:		
Direct credit (withholding tax)	2	
Indirect credit (income tax)		
$(20/35) \times 65$	35	39
Taxable income		$57
U. S. taxes	28.5	
Less tax credits	39.0	
Excess tax credit	$11.5	

Subsidiary C:

Dividends received			$27
Gross up:			
Direct credit (withholding tax)		3	
Indirect credit (income tax)		0	3
(LDCs do not add indirect credits to taxable income)			
Taxable income			$30
U. S. taxes		15	
Less tax credit:			
Direct (withholding tax)	3		
Indirect			
(30/100) × 45	13.5	16.5	
(proportion is based on income before taxes)			
Excess tax credit		$ 1.5	

Subsidiary D:

Dividends received			$1.5
Gross up:			
Direct credit		.15	
Indirect (not available, ownership is less than 10%)		0	.15
Taxable income			$1.65
U. S. taxes		.825	
Less tax credit		.15	
Taxes due		$ .675	

Subsidiary E:

Dividends received			$ 0
Undistributed earnings			50
Gross up:			
Indirect credit (income tax)			
(50/50) × 50			50
Taxable income			$100
U. S. taxes	50		
Less tax credit	50		
No taxes due	$ 0		
(foreign and U. S. tax rates are the same)			

Subsidiary F:

U. S. corporate taxable income	$100
Less special deduction	
(14/48) × 100	29
Net taxable income	71
U. S. taxes	$ 35

(cannot be netted against other excess tax credits)

2. How much credit for foreign taxes can be claimed this year? The limitation on tax credit can be computed on either a per country, or an overall basis. Under what conditions will you prefer to claim the limitations on one basis or the other?

On an overall basis there is a total of $30.32 million carry forward of excess tax credits.

The taxpayer elects the limitation to be used in computing the foreign tax credit. Some of the principal considerations in selecting the type of limitation are the following:

a. If foreign income comes from several countries, the greater the difference among tax rates, the more preferable the overall limitation is.

b. If foreign income comes from one country only, and the situation is likely to change in the future, a per country limitation offers greater flexibility.

c. A taxpayer is permitted to change from per country to overall limitation at any time, but permission is needed to change from overall to per country limitation.

d. No foreign tax credit carryback or carryover is allowed between years in which different limitations are used.

3. If the taxes included as income taxes in the European subsidiaries above were mostly value added taxes, would you modify your computations?

Value added taxes are not considered income taxes by the United States. Therefore, the indirect credit for income tax will be lost in the above computations. In addition to value added taxes, excise, franchise, and property taxes do not qualify as a general rule.

4. What would be the considerations to change these operations from foreign subsidiaries to U. S. branches?

a. Foreign corporations lose the right of consolidation for tax purposes (except for some 100% owned Mexican and Canadian subsidiaries). As a consequence, taxes on dividends must be paid.

b. Branch form gives greater exposure of the U. S. parent's affairs to foreign officials.

c. Domestic form maximizes the tax deductibility of foreign operating losses. Losses can be spread over nine years.

d. Domestic form preserves the statutory depletion allowances and development costs available to taxpayer in the natural resource extraction business.

e. Domestic form gives some freedom from the Code's regulations against tax avoidance. Example: Sec. 367 requires an advance ruling from the Revenue Service in order to qualify a formation, division, or reorganization of a foreign corporation or liquidation of a foreign subsidiary for nonrecognition of gain.

f. Repatriation of earnings from a branch or U. S. subsidiary is often not subject to withholding taxes as are dividends.

g. Foreign form makes possible deferment of paying U. S. taxes until dividends are paid. This allows for planning of tax credits.

Taxation References

Arthur Andersen and Company, *Tax and Trade Guides.* Separate booklets, New York, various dates.

Beardwood, Roger, "Sophistication Comes to the Tax Havens." *Fortune,* Feb. 1969, pp. 95-178.

Commerce Clearing House, *Common Market Reporter.* Two Vols., loose leaf, Chicago, Ill., 1962-

Commerce Clearing House, *World Tax Series.* Chicago, Ill., various issues.

Coopers and Lybrand, *International Tax Summaries.* Loose leaf, New York, various dates.

Eiteman, David K. and Arthur I. Stonehill, *Multinational Business Finance.* Reading, Mass.: Addison-Wesley Publishing Co., 1973, Ch. 7.

Harriss, C. Lowell, "Value-Added Taxation." *Columbia Journal of World Business,* July-Aug. 1971, pp. 78-86.

Haskins and Sells, *International Tax and Business Service.* Two Vols., loose leaf, New York.

Hickman, Frederick W., "Tax Climate Is Improving for Doing Business in Eastern Europe." *Journal of Taxation,* Feb. 1974, pp. 65-69.

International Bureau of Fiscal Documentation, *Guides to European Taxation.* Three vols, loose leaf; and *Supplementary Service to European Taxation.* Loose leaf, Amsterdam, Holland, 1963-

Jenks, Thomas E., "Taxation of Foreign Income." *The George Washington Law Review,* Vol. 42, 1974, pp. 537-556.

Kalish, Richard H., "Tax Considerations in Organizing for Business Abroad." *Taxes,* Feb. 1966, pp. 71-86.

Krause, Lawrence and Kenneth Dam, "Economic Effects of Taxing Foreign-Source Income." *Federal Tax Treatment of Foreign Income*, The Brookings Institution, Washington, D. C., 1964.

McIntyre, Michael J., *United States Taxation of Foreign Income with Special Emphasis on Private Investments in Developing Countries*. International Law Program, Harvard Law School, Cambridge, Mass., 1975. This is a revision of Arie Kopelman, *United States Income Taxation of Private Investments in Developing Countries*. United Nations Secretariat, New York, 1970.

Musgrave, Peggy, "International Tax Base Division and the Multinational Corporation." *Public Finance*, Vol. 27, 1972, pp. 394-413.

Owens, Elisabeth A., *Bibliography on Taxation of Foreign Operations and Foreigners*. International Tax Program, Harvard Law School, Cambridge, Mass., 1968 (under revision).

Phatak, Arvind V., *Managing Multinational Corporations*. New York: Praeger Publishers, 1974, Ch. 4.

Prentice-Hall, Inc., *Tax Ideas-Tax Transaction Guide*. Two vols., loose leaf, Englewood Cliffs, N. J., 1953-

Price Waterhouse and Company, *Information Guide Series*. Separate booklets, New York, various dates.

Rhodes, John B., "U. S. New Business Activities Abroad." *Columbia Journal of World Business*, Summer 1974, pp. 99-105. (Annual report of Booz, Allen, and Hamilton).

Rosenberg, Herbert C. and Stuart R. Singer, "Selecting an International Finance Subsidiary: A Review of Available Methods." *Journal of Taxation*, May 1969, pp. 296-298.

"Special Report: Section 482." *Journal of Taxation*, Feb. 1968, pp. 66-79. See articles by Harry K. Mansfield, Sheldon Cohen, and Stanley S. Surrey.

Stone, Lawrence M., "United States Tax Policy Toward Foreign Earnings of Multinational Corporations." *The George Washington Law Review*, Vol. 42, 1974, pp. 557-567.

U. S. Congress, Committee on Ways and Means, *General Panel Discussion on Taxation of Foreign Income*. Exchange of letters between Professor Peggy Musgrave and Professor Robert Stobaugh, Feb. 1973, pp. 1881-1886.

Weston, J. Fred and Bart Sorge, *International Managerial Finance*. Homewood, Ill.: Richard D. Irwin, 1972, Ch. 7.

APPENDIX 2

Glossary and Present Value Tables

Glossary

Acceptance. See *banker's acceptance.*

Accommodating Accounts. In the balance of payments, those accounts that for analytical purposes can be considered triggered by the need to finance other transactions included in the balance of payments. Also called compensating or financing accounts.

Account Party. The party whose bank issues a letter of credit—usually the buyer.

Accrual System. Accounting system where the returns and costs are reported when legally incurred, rather than when the cash flow associated with the receipt or the payment materializes.

Advising Bank. A correspondent of an issuing bank that notifies the benefici- ary of a letter of credit without adding its own engagement to that of the issuing bank.

Agent. An agent is a person authorized to act for another (a principal). The term may apply to a person in the service of another, but in the strict sense an agent is one who stands in place of the principal. If A works for B as a secretary, he is a servant in the legal sense, but he may also be an agent. If A takes orders for B, he acts in place of B and is an agent.

Annuity. In law, a sum of money paid yearly to a person during his/her lifetime. It arises by a contract under which the recipient or another person deposits funds

Some of these legal definitions are based on citations of Robert N. Corley and William J. Robert, *Principles of Business Law,* 10th ed. (Englewood Cliffs, N.J.: Prentice-Hall, Inc., 1975).

with the grantor. The grantor then returns a designated portion of the principal and interest in periodic payments upon the arrival of the beneficiary at a designated age. In general, an annuity is payment of a flat sum of money over a specific period of time.

Arbitrage. Transactions made to take advantage of temporary imperfections in the market. For example, if one could buy potatoes for 20¢/lb. in one market and sell them for 25¢/lb. in another, one could make a profit of 5¢/lb. through arbitrage. An arbitrage transaction does not involve any risk. Because contracts are made, the returns derived from the transaction are known from the beginning, even though part of the transaction may take place in the future. Also see *space arbitrage* and *covered interest arbitrage*.

Ask Price. The price at which a trader giving a quote is willing to sell a given item. Also called offer price.

Assignment. An assignment is the transfer of a right, usually arising from a contract. Such rights are called "choses in action." A sells and assigns his/her contract right to purchase B's Plymouth convertible to C. A is an assignor. C is an assignee. The transfer is an assignment.

Autonomous Accounts. In the balance of payments, those accounts that for analytical purposes can be considered motivated purely by economic considerations rather than by the need to finance international transactions.

Bailment. A bailment is the delivery of personal property (as opposed to real property) to another for a special purpose. Such delivery is made under a contract, either expressed or implied, that the property shall be redelivered to the bailor or placed at his/her disposal upon the completion of the special purpose. A loans B his horse. A places a watch with B for repair. A places her furniture in B's warehouse. A places her securities in B's bank safety deposit vault. In each case, A is a bailor and B is a bailee.

Balance in Invisibles. In the balance of payments, the balance of the service accounts.

Balance of Indebtedness. Financial statement prepared for a given country summarizing the levels of assets and liabilities that the country has vis-à-vis the rest of the world. Also known as the investment position of the country.

Balance of Payments. Financial statement prepared for a given country summarizing the flow of goods, services, and funds between the residents of this country and the residents of the rest of the world during a certain period of time. The balance of payments is prepared using the concept of double-entry bookkeeping where the total of debits equals the total of credits; or, total sources of funds equals total uses of funds.

Balance Sheet Exposure. Various forms of accounting exposure which differ as to which assets and liabilities are translated at historic rates (unexposed) and which accounts are translated at current rates (exposed). "Exposure" is the net balance sheet exposure of assets minus liabilities which are translated at current rates. Also see *exposure to foreign exchange risk*.

Banker's Acceptance. When a draft has been accepted by a bank, and the bank guarantees that payment will be made at some date in the future, that certified draft is called a banker's acceptance. It may be traded freely among other parties, and the bank will pay the party that submits the draft to it at maturity.

Banking Day. That part of any day on which a bank is open to the public for carrying on substantially all of its banking functions. (Article 4 of the U.C.C.: Bank Deposits and Collections)

Basic Balance. In the balance of payments, the net balance of the flow in trade of goods and services, unilateral transfers, and long-term capital.

Bearer. The person in possession of an instrument, document of title, or security payable to bearer or indorsed in blank (with no name or order following the indorsement).

Beneficiary. The party in whose favor a letter of credit is issued—usually the seller.

Bid Price. The price at which a trader giving a quote is willing to purchase a given item.

Bill of Lading. A record of the shipment of goods from a transporter, confirming the receipt of goods for shipment and means of transportation. The general term, bill of lading, is used for marine and surface transport, while for air shipments it is usually called an airbill.

Blocked Funds. Funds which cannot be repatriated because the local monetary authorities forbid conversion into foreign exchange.

Bond. A promise under seal to pay money. The term is generally used to designate the promise made by a corporation, either public or private, to pay money to the bearer. Bonds can also be issued by governments. U. S. Government bonds; Rock Island Railroad bonds.

Capital Account. In the balance of payments, the section that records the changes in financial assets and liabilities. The capital account is divided into two major sections: long-term flows and short-term flows.

Capital Structure. The combination of long-term debt and various types of equity in the financing of the firm.

Cash System. Accounting system in which only cash flows are reported, independent of when the obligations are contracted.

Cashier's Check. A bill of exchange drawn by the cashier of a bank, for the bank, upon the bank. The drawer bank cannot put a "stop order" against itself after the check is delivered or issued to the payee or holder.

Collateral. Security placed with a creditor to assure the performance of the obligator. If the obligation is satisfied, the collateral is returned by the creditor. A owes B $1,000. To secure the payment, A places with B a $5000 certificate of stock in X Company. The $5000 certificate is called collateral.

Collecting Bank. Any bank handling an item for collection except the payor bank. (Article 4 of the U.C.C.: Bank Deposits and Collections)

Commission. The sum of money, interest, brokerage, compensation, or allowance given to a factor or broker for carrying on the business of his/her principal.

Compensating Accounts. See *accommodating accounts.*

Condition. A clause in a contract that has the effect of investing or divesting the legal rights and duties of the parties to the contract.

Confirming Bank. A correspondent bank that adds its own engagement to that of the issuing bank in a letter of credit, guaranteeing that the credit will be honored by the issuer or a third bank.

Consignee. A person to whom a shipper directs a carrier to deliver goods, generally the buyer.

Consignment. The delivery, sending, or transferring of property ("goods, wares, and merchandise") into the possession of another, usually for the purpose of sale. Consignment may be a bailment or an agency for sale.

Consortia Bank. A more or less permanent group of banks that has the objective of providing joint financing to customers.

Convertible Euro-bond. A Euro-bond that can be converted into equity of the issuing company under prescribed conditions.

Convertibility. In foreign exchange, the ability to convert one currency into another.

Correspondent Bank. A bank that, in its own country, handles the business of a foreign bank. There are also domestic correspondents in different areas of the same country.

Cost of Capital. In corporate finance, the weighted rate of return expected by various parties financing the firm. The return that bondholders expect is the market interest rate on the debt. The return that equity holders expect is a function of dividends received and capital gains as the stock appreciates in value, adjusted for risk. The weights used to combine these rates of return are the proportions that each of these sources of funds contributes to the capitalization of the firm. The cost of capital traditionally is used as a hurdle rate that projects must yield as a minimum in order to be accepted by the firm.

Covenant. A promise in writing. It is often used as a substitute for the word contract. There are covenants (promises) in deeds, leases, mortgages, and other instruments under seal and in unsealed instruments such as insurance policies and conditional sale contracts.

Covered Interest Arbitrage. A process of borrowing a currency, converting it into another currency where it is invested, and selling this other currency for future delivery against the initial currency. The profits in this transaction are derived from discrepancies between interest differentials and the percentage discounts or premiums among the currencies involved in the transaction.

Covering. The generation of cash flows in a given currency in the money market or in the forward exchange market at predetermined rates with the purpose of matching the cash flows generated by operations in that currency. The purpose of covering is to make cash inflows equal cash outflows for the given currency for specified maturities. This produces a "square position." Covering usually refers to trade transactions that produce a payable or a receivable in foreign exchange to be liquidated at a future date. The covering transaction eliminates the risk of fluctuations in foreign exchange rates during the intervening period. Covering and hedging are terms often used interchangeably. Also see *hedging*.

Credit Entry in Balance of Payments. The part of an international transaction that represents a source of funds or international purchasing power to the country reporting the balance of payments. A credit entry reflects a decrease in the holdings of foreign assets owned by local residents or an increase in the liabilities to foreigners owed by the residents of the reporting country.

Credit Tranche. The amount that a member country of the International Monetary Fund can borrow from the Fund over the gold tranche.

Cross Rate. The calculation of a foreign exchange rate from two separate quotes that contain the same currency. For example, if one has the rate of French francs per U. S. dollar and the rate of deutsche marks per U. S. dollar, one can calculate the cross rate between French francs and deutsche marks.

Current Account. In the balance of payments, the section that records the trade in goods and services and the exchange of gifts among countries.

Customer. As used in letters of credit, a customer is a buyer or other person who causes credit to be issued. The term also refers to a bank which procures issuance or confirmation on behalf of that bank's customer.

Debit Entry in Balance of Payments. The part of an international transaction that represents a use of funds or international purchasing power to the country reporting the balance of payments. A debit entry reflects an increase in the holdings of foreign assets owned by local residents or a decrease in the liabilities owed to foreigners by the residents of the reporting country. Debit entries are usually preceded by a minus sign in balance of payments tables.

Depository Bank. The first bank to which an item for collection is transferred, which may also be the payor bank.

Direct Investment. Purchase of a foreign financial asset where substantial involvement in the management of the foreign operation is presumed. In practice, it is any equity holding that represents more than 10% ownership of the foreign firm.

Discount Rate. (1) In capital budgeting analysis, the rate which is applied to future cash flows to bring them to a present value. (2) In trade terms, the rate which is applied to a non-interest bearing note which can be translated into a rate for early payment of the note. Thus, a note payable at face in six months might sell for 2% less than its face amount, implying an annual rate of 4%. (3) In foreign exchange markets, the difference between the forward and the spot rate.

Document of Title. This term includes bill of lading, dock warrant, dock receipt, warehouse receipt, order for the delivery of goods, and any other document which in the regular course of business or financing is treated as adequate evidence that the person in possession of it is entitled to receive, hold, and dispose of the document and the goods it covers.

Documentary Draft. A draft the honor of which is conditioned upon the presentation of a document or documents. "Document" means any paper including document of title, security, invoice, certificate, notice of default, and the like. Also referred to as a documentary demand for payment.

Draft. An order to pay. A check is one form of a draft.

Drawee Bank. The bank upon which a draft is drawn. Also called paying bank.

Edge Act Corporations. Financial institutions incorporated in the United States under the Edge Act. Edge Act corporations are owned by commercial banks and restrict their income mostly to foreign sources. The major advantage that a commercial bank achieves in establishing an Edge Act corporation is to be able to conduct abroad some activities which are forbidden to U. S. banks.

Efficient Market. A market where equilibrium conditions prevail, in which there are a sufficiently large number of buyers and sellers to prohibit any incentive for arbitrage transactions, and the tradeoffs between return and risk are fully calibrated.

Elasticity. Elasticity measures the degree of responsiveness in one variable to changes in another variable. For example, the price elasticity of exports might measure the degree of responsiveness in exports to changes in prices, or the income elasticity of imports might measure the degree of responsiveness in imports to changes in income.

Euro-bond. Bond denominated in the borrower's currency but sold outside the country of the borrower, usually by an international syndicate.

Euro-currency. Monies traded outside the countries where they are the domestic currencies. For example, Euro-dollars are U. S. dollars traded outside the United States.

Exchange Rate. The price of one currency expressed in terms of another currency.

Exposure to Foreign Exchange Risk. The amount of a person's or business's holdings that is not denominated in the domestic currency, and whose value will fluctuate if foreign exchange rates vary. Also see *balance sheet exposure.*

Financing Accounts. See *accommodating accounts.*

Fixed Currency. A currency whose official value relative to gold and other currencies is maintained by a central bank. The bank intervenes to buy and to sell the currency when it deviates from the official value.

Floating Currency. A currency whose exchange rate relative to those of other currencies is allowed to fluctuate more or less freely. "Dirty floating" occurs if the central bank intervenes to keep the currency from deviating outside the country's desired range.

Floating Lending Rate. A lending rate that is established at a fixed number of percentage points above a given rate, such as the London interbank offer rate (LIBO), and which is renegotiated periodically, often every six months. Negotiation occurs throughout the life of the loan.

Floating Policy. An insurance policy that covers a class of goods located in a particular place that the insured had on hand at the time the policy was issued, but which—at the time of loss—may not be the identical items that were on hand at the time the policy was issued. A fire policy covering the inventory of a hardware store is an example.

Foreign Bond. Bond sold outside the country of the borrower but in the country of the currency in which the bond is denominated. The bond is underwritten by local institutions and is issued under the regulations prevalent in that country.

Foreign Exchange. Currency other than the one used internally in a given country.

Forward Rate. Foreign exchange rate for currency to be delivered at a future date.

Gold Tranche. The amount that each member country of the International Monetary Fund contributes in the form of gold as part of its membership quota in the Fund. This amount can be borrowed readily by the contributing country.

Guarantor. One who by contract undertakes, "to answer for the debt, default, and miscarriage of another." In general, a guarantor undertakes to pay if the principal debtor does not.

Hedging. The generation of a position in a given currency in the money market or in the forward exchange market at predetermined rates with the purpose of matching the net position generated in that currency with the net exposure position of the business operations as evidenced by balance sheets. The purpose of hedging is to make the net position at a given date equal zero. The accounts included in the exposed balance sheet items are determined according to accounting rules. When balance sheet items are translated into specific cash flows in the future which the firm wishes to protect against fluctuations in exchange rates, the hedging transaction becomes a covering transaction. Covering and hedging are terms often used interchangeably. Also see *covering.*

Income Elasticity. See *elasticity.*

Indemnify. Literally, to save trom harm. Thus, one person agrees to protect another against loss.

Indexing. The practice in some nations of adjusting mortgage or other debt issues by some measure of inflation, to preserve the purchasing power of the debt in constant monetary units. In Brazil, indexing is applied to wages, business accounts, and all debt issues, a broader scope than that of most nations using indexing.

Indorsement. Writing one's name upon paper for the purpose of transferring the title. When a payee of a negotiable instrument writes his name on the back of the instrument, that is an indorsement.

Inflation. The overall rate of increase in prices in a given country. This rate of increase may differ among different economic sectors.

Interest Equalization Tax (IET). Tax imposed on U. S. residents who purchased foreign securities between 1963 and the end of 1973.

Intermediary Bank. A bank to which an item is transferred in the course of collection other than the depository or payor bank. (Article 4 of the U. C. C.: Bank Deposits and Collections)

Issuing Bank. The bank that issues a letter of credit—usually the buyer's bank.

Leads and Lags. The practice of quickly moving funds into a given currency (lead) or delaying the movement of funds into a given currency (lag) with the objective of benefiting from expected changes in exchange rates.

Letter of Credit. An agreement sent from one party (usually a bank) to another concerning funds which will be made available upon completion of some business transactions. Usually, a buyer sends a letter of credit to the seller of goods when they are not known to each other. Upon certification of shipment of the goods in question and submission of a draft, the local bank will arrange for funds to be made available to the exporter. It is established and regulated within the scope of Article 5 of the U. C. C.: Letters of Credit.

Liability. In its broadest legal sense, the word means any obligation one may be under by some rule of law. It includes debt, duty, and responsibility.

Locking in a Rate. In a foreign exchange markets, establishing the exchange rates at which inflows and outflows of a currency will take place at a given future time.

Long Position. Situation occurring when anticipated inflows of a currency exceed the anticipated outflows of that currency over a given period of time.

Marginal. Incremental unit. Units usually refer to costs or revenues.

Merger. Two corporations are merged when one corporation continues in existence, and the other loses its identity by absorption. Merger must be distinguished from consolidation, by which both corporations are dissolved and a new one created to take over the assets of the dissolved corporations.

Multiplier. In monetary economics, the factor by which an initial deposit could grow through multiple loans if the initial monetary deposit. The multiplier is defined as the reciprocal of the reserve requirements, adjusted for "leakages" in the system.

Mutuality. A word used to describe the fact that every contract must be binding on both parties. Each party to the contract must be bound to the other party to do something by virtue of the legal duty created.

Negligence. The failure to do that which an ordinary, reasonable, prudent person would do, or the doing of some act which an ordinary, prudent person would not do. Reference must always be made to the situation, the circumstances, and the knowledge of the parties.

Negotiating Bank. A bank chosen by the beneficiary when a letter of credit allows negotiation.

Net Effective Interest Rate or Yield. The yield in a given currency adjusted for changes in the exchange rates.

Net Exchange Position. A net asset or liability position in a given currency. This is the term commonly used by exchange traders. Also called a net long or short position.

Net Exposure Position. See *balance sheet exposure.*

Net Present Value. The value in current dollars when future receipts and outlays are discounted at some rate.

Nominal Interest Rate. The interest rate specified to be paid on the face amount borrowed. In a bond the nominal rate is the coupon rate. The actual amount of funds borrowed may be more or less than the face amount, thus changing the net yield of the funds involved. Also see *yield.*

Numeraire. The standard which is used for measurement. In international corporate finance this refers to the currency chosen by the firm as reference against which all other currency cash flows are measured.

Obligee. A creditor or promisee.

Obligor. A debtor or promisor.

OFDI. Office of Foreign Direct Investment. Created to regulate the amount of foreign direct investment that U. S. companies could finance from funds generated in foreign operations or from the parent company. The regulations were established on a voluntary basis between 1965 and 1967 and made mandatory from 1968 until they were eliminated in 1973.

Offer Price. The price at which a trader giving a quote is willing to sell a given item. Also called ask price.

Outright Forward Rate. Forward exchange rate expressed in terms of the amount of one currency required to buy a unit of another currency.

Par Value. Under the Bretton Woods system, the value of a currency measured in terms of gold or the U. S. dollar, which was maintained at a fixed rate relative to gold.

Paying Bank. The bank on which a draft is drawn. Also called drawee bank.

Payor Bank. A bank by which an item is payable as drawn or accepted. (Article 4 of the U.C.C.: Bank Deposits and Collections)

Pledge. The deposit or placing of personal property as security for a debt or other obligation with a person called a pledgee. The pledgee has the implied power to sell the property if the debt is not paid. If the debt is paid, the right to possession returns to the pledgor.

Points. In foreign exchange markets, the amount of premium or discount in the forward price from the spot price. A point is a unit of a decimal, usually the fourth place to the right of the decimal point. Which decimal place is implied varies from currency to currency.

Portfolio Investment. Purchase of a foreign financial asset with the sole purpose of deriving the returns that the security provides without intervening in the management of the foreign operation.

Preferred Stock. Stock that entitles the holder to dividends from earnings before the owners of common stock can receive dividends.

Presenting Bank. Any bank presenting an item except a payor bank. (Article 4 of the U.C.C.: Bank Deposits and Collections)

Price Elasticity. See *elasticity.*

Rate of Return. In capital budgeting, that discount rate for which the cash inflows can be discounted to equal the discounted cash outflows, i.e., where the net present value is zero.

Reinsurance. Under a contract of reinsurance, one insurance company agrees to indemnify another insurance company in whole or in part against risks which the first company has assumed.

Remitting Bank. Any payor or intermediary bank remitting for an item. (Article 4 of the U.C.C.: Bank Deposits and Collections)

Reserve Accounts. In the balance of payments, the accounts reflecting the changes in the amount of resources that the government of the country has at its disposal to settle international payments. These resources are composed of gold and foreign currency which is fully convertible into other currencies, such as the U. S. dollar.

Revolver. A loan with floating rates where not only the rates but also the amounts (within the limits of a given line of credit) are renegotiated periodically.

Revolving Loan. See *revolver.*

Risk Analysis. Study of the various outcomes under different assumptions and under different probabilities that each of these outcomes will take place.

Satisfaction. The release and discharge of a legal obligation. Satisfaction may be partial or full performance of the obligation. The word is used with accord, which means a promise to give a substituted performance for a contract obligation; satisfaction means the acceptance by the obligee of such performance.

SDRs. Special Drawing Rights. Money created by the International Monetary Fund with the approval of a large majority of member countries and distributed among all member countries. This paper money is used only in transactions among governments and between governments and the IMF.

Security. Security may be bonds, stocks, and other property placed by a debtor with a creditor, with power to sell if the debt is not paid. The plural of the term, "securities," is used broadly to mean tangible items such as promissory notes, bonds, stocks, and other vendible obligations.

Settle. To pay in cash, by a clearing house settlement, in a charge or credit, by remittance, or as otherwise instructed. A settlement may be either provisional or final. (Article 4 of the U.C.C.: Bank Deposits and Collections)

Short Position. Situation when anticipated outflows of a currency exceed the anticipated inflows of that currency over a given period of time.

Simulation. Analytical technique where outcomes are estimated under alternative sets of assumptions.

Space Arbitrage. The purchase of a currency in a given market accompanied by a sale of that currency in another market where it commands a higher price.

Speculative Transaction. A transaction where the eventual net return or cost is not known in advance. In international finance, the major sources of speculative risk occur when the transaction produces a net asset or liability position in a given currency, and when the cash inflows and outflows in a given currency are not matched according to maturity.

Spot Rate. Foreign exchange rate for currency delivered within two days.

Spread. The difference between the bid and ask prices in a price quote.

Square Position. Position when the cash inflows match the cash outflows in a given currency for a certain date or period of time.

Swap Position. Position when a given currency is simultaneously purchased and sold, but the maturity of each of the transactions is different.

Swap Rate. Forward exchange rates expressed in terms of premiums or discounts from the spot rate.

Tax Haven. A country that imposes little or no tax on the profits from the transactions carried on from that country.

Terminal Rate of Return. Internal rate of return when the net cash flows produced by the project during its life are assumed to be reinvested at a predetermined rate of return.

Terms of Trade. The ratio of export prices to import prices. Export and import prices in this ratio are each aggregated and combined into a sum for which the total in a given year equals 1000.

Transaction Exchange Gain or Loss. The increase (gain) or decrease (loss) in a cash flow because the cash flow was denominated in another currency and the exchange rate between the two currencies changed.

Translation Exchange Gain or Loss. The foreign exchange gain or loss associated with the conversion (for financial consolidation) of the balance sheets expressed in anotner currency into the numeraire currency. The gain or loss arises when the exchange rate between the two currencies fluctuates, and exposed assets do not equal exposed liabilities.

Trust Receipt. A document establishing that the borrower holds certain goods in trust for the lender.

U. C. C. Uniform Commercial Code.

Unilateral Transfers. In the balance of payments, the accounts that measure gifts sent in and out of the reporting country.

Value Date. Date when funds are to be received or paid according to a contract.

Voluntary Credit Restraint Program. Program in existence between 1965 and the end of 1973 restricting the amount of credit that commercial banks and other financial institutions in the United States could extend to foreigners.

Withholding Tax. A tax which is collected by the source originating the income, in contrast to one being paid by the recipient of the income after the funds are received. For example, a withholding tax on interest payments to foreigners means that the tax proceeds are deducted from the interest payment made to the lender and collected by the borrower on behalf of the government.

Yield. The amount of funds involved in interest payments as a percentage of the amount lent or borrowed, or the present market price of a security in the currency of the instrument.

TABLE A Present Value of $1

Years Hence	1%	2%	4%	6%	8%	10%	12%	14%	15%	16%	18%	20%	22%	24%	25%	26%	28%	30%	35%	40%	45%	50%
1	0.990	0.980	0.962	0.943	0.926	0.909	0.893	0.877	0.870	0.862	0.847	0.833	0.820	0.806	0.800	0.794	0.781	0.769	0.741	0.714	0.690	0.667
2	0.980	0.961	0.925	0.890	0.857	0.826	0.797	0.769	0.756	0.743	0.718	0.694	0.672	0.650	0.640	0.630	0.610	0.592	0.549	0.510	0.476	0.444
3	0.971	0.942	0.889	0.840	0.794	0.751	0.712	0.675	0.658	0.641	0.609	0.579	0.551	0.524	0.512	0.500	0.477	0.455	0.406	0.364	0.328	0.296
4	0.961	0.924	0.855	0.792	0.735	0.683	0.636	0.592	0.572	0.552	0.516	0.482	0.451	0.423	0.410	0.397	0.373	0.350	0.301	0.260	0.226	0.198
5	0.951	0.906	0.822	0.747	0.681	0.621	0.567	0.519	0.497	0.476	0.437	0.402	0.370	0.341	0.328	0.315	0.291	0.269	0.223	0.186	0.156	0.132
6	0.942	0.888	0.790	0.705	0.630	0.564	0.507	0.456	0.432	0.410	0.370	0.335	0.303	0.275	0.262	0.250	0.227	0.207	0.165	0.133	0.108	0.088
7	0.933	0.871	0.760	0.665	0.583	0.513	0.452	0.400	0.376	0.354	0.314	0.279	0.249	0.222	0.210	0.198	0.178	0.159	0.122	0.095	0.074	0.059
8	0.923	0.853	0.731	0.627	0.540	0.467	0.404	0.351	0.327	0.305	0.266	0.233	0.204	0.179	0.168	0.157	0.139	0.123	0.091	0.068	0.051	0.039
9	0.914	0.837	0.703	0.592	0.500	0.424	0.361	0.308	0.284	0.263	0.225	0.194	0.167	0.144	0.134	0.125	0.108	0.094	0.067	0.048	0.035	0.026
10	0.905	0.820	0.676	0.558	0.463	0.386	0.322	0.270	0.247	0.227	0.191	0.162	0.137	0.116	0.107	0.099	0.085	0.073	0.050	0.035	0.024	0.017
11	0.896	0.804	0.650	0.527	0.429	0.350	0.287	0.237	0.215	0.195	0.162	0.135	0.112	0.094	0.086	0.079	0.066	0.056	0.037	0.025	0.017	0.012
12	0.887	0.788	0.625	0.497	0.397	0.319	0.257	0.208	0.187	0.168	0.137	0.112	0.092	0.076	0.069	0.062	0.052	0.043	0.027	0.018	0.012	0.008
13	0.879	0.773	0.601	0.469	0.368	0.290	0.229	0.182	0.163	0.145	0.116	0.093	0.075	0.061	0.055	0.050	0.040	0.033	0.020	0.013	0.008	0.005
14	0.870	0.758	0.577	0.442	0.340	0.263	0.205	0.160	0.141	0.125	0.099	0.078	0.062	0.049	0.044	0.039	0.032	0.025	0.015	0.009	0.006	0.003
15	0.861	0.743	0.555	0.417	0.315	0.239	0.183	0.140	0.123	0.108	0.084	0.065	0.051	0.040	0.035	0.031	0.025	0.020	0.011	0.006	0.004	0.002
16	0.853	0.728	0.534	0.394	0.292	0.218	0.163	0.123	0.107	0.093	0.071	0.054	0.042	0.032	0.028	0.025	0.019	0.015	0.008	0.005	0.003	0.002
17	0.844	0.714	0.513	0.371	0.270	0.198	0.146	0.108	0.093	0.080	0.060	0.045	0.034	0.026	0.023	0.020	0.015	0.012	0.006	0.003	0.002	0.001
18	0.836	0.700	0.494	0.350	0.250	0.180	0.130	0.095	0.081	0.069	0.051	0.038	0.028	0.021	0.018	0.016	0.012	0.009	0.005	0.002	0.001	0.001
19	0.828	0.686	0.475	0.331	0.232	0.164	0.116	0.083	0.070	0.060	0.043	0.031	0.023	0.017	0.014	0.012	0.009	0.007	0.003	0.002	0.001	
20	0.820	0.673	0.456	0.312	0.215	0.149	0.104	0.073	0.061	0.051	0.037	0.026	0.019	0.014	0.012	0.010	0.007	0.005	0.002	0.001	0.001	
21	0.811	0.660	0.439	0.294	0.199	0.135	0.093	0.064	0.053	0.044	0.031	0.022	0.015	0.011	0.009	0.008	0.006	0.004	0.002	0.001		
22	0.803	0.647	0.422	0.278	0.184	0.123	0.083	0.056	0.046	0.038	0.026	0.018	0.013	0.009	0.007	0.006	0.004	0.003	0.001	0.001		
23	0.795	0.634	0.406	0.262	0.170	0.112	0.074	0.049	0.040	0.033	0.022	0.015	0.010	0.007	0.006	0.005	0.003	0.002	0.001			
24	0.788	0.622	0.390	0.247	0.158	0.102	0.066	0.043	0.035	0.028	0.019	0.013	0.008	0.006	0.005	0.004	0.003	0.002	0.001			
25	0.780	0.610	0.375	0.233	0.146	0.092	0.059	0.038	0.030	0.024	0.016	0.010	0.007	0.005	0.004	0.003	0.002	0.001	0.001			
26	0.772	0.598	0.361	0.220	0.135	0.084	0.053	0.033	0.026	0.021	0.014	0.009	0.006	0.004	0.003	0.002	0.002	0.001				
27	0.764	0.586	0.347	0.207	0.125	0.076	0.047	0.029	0.023	0.018	0.011	0.007	0.005	0.003	0.002	0.002	0.001	0.001				
28	0.757	0.574	0.333	0.196	0.116	0.069	0.042	0.026	0.020	0.016	0.010	0.006	0.004	0.002	0.002	0.002	0.001	0.001				
29	0.749	0.563	0.321	0.185	0.107	0.063	0.037	0.022	0.017	0.014	0.008	0.005	0.003	0.002	0.002	0.001	0.001	0.001				
30	0.742	0.552	0.308	0.174	0.099	0.057	0.033	0.020	0.015	0.012	0.007	0.004	0.003	0.002	0.001	0.001	0.001	0.001				
40	0.672	0.453	0.208	0.097	0.046	0.022	0.011	0.005	0.004	0.003	0.001	0.001										
50	0.608	0.372	0.141	0.054	0.021	0.009	0.003	0.001	0.001	0.001												

Source: By permission, from Robert N. Anthony, *Management Accounting: Text and Cases*, rev. ed. Homewood, Ill.: Richard D. Irwin, Inc. 1960.

TABLE B   Present Value of $1 Received Annually for N Years

Years (N)	1%	2%	4%	6%	8%	10%	12%	14%	15%	16%	18%	20%	22%	24%	25%	26%	28%	30%	35%	40%	45%	50%
1	0.990	0.980	0.962	0.943	0.926	0.909	0.893	0.877	0.870	0.862	0.847	0.833	0.820	0.806	0.800	0.794	0.781	0.769	0.741	0.714	0.690	0.667
2	1.970	1.942	1.886	1.833	1.783	1.736	1.690	1.647	1.626	1.605	1.566	1.528	1.492	1.457	1.440	1.424	1.392	1.361	1.289	1.224	1.165	1.111
3	2.941	2.884	2.775	2.673	2.577	2.487	2.402	2.322	2.283	2.246	2.174	2.106	2.042	1.981	1.952	1.923	1.868	1.816	1.696	1.589	1.493	1.407
4	3.902	3.808	3.630	3.465	3.312	3.170	3.037	2.914	2.855	2.798	2.690	2.589	2.494	2.404	2.362	2.320	2.241	2.166	1.997	1.849	1.720	1.605
5	4.853	4.713	4.452	4.212	3.993	3.791	3.605	3.433	3.352	3.274	3.127	2.991	2.864	2.745	2.689	2.635	2.532	2.436	2.220	2.035	1.876	1.737
6	5.795	5.601	5.242	4.917	4.623	4.355	4.111	3.889	3.784	3.685	3.498	3.326	3.167	3.020	2.951	2.885	2.759	2.643	2.385	2.168	1.983	1.824
7	6.728	6.472	6.002	5.582	5.206	4.868	4.564	4.288	4.160	4.039	3.812	3.605	3.416	3.242	3.161	3.083	2.937	2.802	2.508	2.263	2.057	1.883
8	7.652	7.325	6.733	6.210	5.747	5.335	4.968	4.639	4.487	4.344	4.078	3.837	3.619	3.421	3.329	3.241	3.076	2.925	2.598	2.331	2.108	1.922
9	8.566	8.162	7.435	6.802	6.247	5.759	5.328	4.946	4.772	4.607	4.303	4.031	3.786	3.566	3.463	3.366	3.184	3.019	2.665	2.379	2.144	1.948
10	9.471	8.983	8.111	7.360	6.710	6.145	5.650	5.216	5.019	4.833	4.494	4.192	3.923	3.682	3.571	3.465	3.269	3.092	2.715	2.414	2.168	1.965
11	10.368	9.787	8.760	7.887	7.139	6.495	5.937	5.453	5.234	5.029	4.656	4.327	4.035	3.776	3.656	3.544	3.335	3.147	2.757	2.438	2.185	1.977
12	11.255	10.575	9.385	8.384	7.536	6.814	6.194	5.660	5.421	5.197	4.793	4.439	4.127	3.851	3.725	3.606	3.387	3.190	2.779	2.456	2.196	1.985
13	12.134	11.343	9.986	8.853	7.904	7.103	6.424	5.842	5.583	5.342	4.910	4.533	4.203	3.912	3.780	3.656	3.427	3.223	2.799	2.468	2.204	1.990
14	13.004	12.106	10.563	9.295	8.244	7.367	6.628	6.002	5.724	5.468	5.008	4.611	4.265	3.962	3.824	3.695	3.459	3.249	2.814	2.477	2.210	1.993
15	13.865	12.849	11.118	9.712	8.559	7.606	6.811	6.142	5.847	5.575	5.092	4.675	4.315	4.001	3.859	3.726	3.483	3.268	2.825	2.484	2.214	1.995
16	14.718	13.578	11.652	10.106	8.851	7.824	6.974	6.265	5.954	5.669	5.162	4.730	4.357	4.033	3.887	3.751	3.503	3.283	2.834	2.489	2.216	1.997
17	15.562	14.292	12.166	10.477	9.122	8.022	7.120	6.373	6.047	5.749	5.222	4.775	4.391	4.059	3.910	3.771	3.518	3.295	2.840	2.492	2.218	1.998
18	16.398	14.992	12.659	10.828	9.372	8.201	7.250	6.467	6.128	5.818	5.273	4.812	4.419	4.080	3.928	3.786	3.529	3.304	2.844	2.494	2.219	1.999
19	17.226	15.678	13.134	11.158	9.604	8.365	7.366	6.550	6.198	5.877	5.316	4.844	4.442	4.097	3.942	3.799	3.539	3.311	2.848	2.496	2.220	1.999
20	18.046	16.351	13.590	11.470	9.818	8.514	7.469	6.623	6.259	5.929	5.353	4.870	4.460	4.110	3.954	3.808	3.546	3.316	2.850	2.497	2.221	1.999
21	18.857	17.011	14.029	11.764	10.017	8.649	7.562	6.687	6.312	5.973	5.384	4.891	4.476	4.121	3.963	3.816	3.551	3.320	2.852	2.498	2.221	2.000
22	19.660	17.658	14.451	12.042	10.201	8.772	7.645	6.743	6.359	6.011	5.410	4.909	4.488	4.130	3.970	3.822	3.556	3.323	2.853	2.498	2.222	2.000
23	20.456	18.292	14.857	12.303	10.371	8.883	7.718	6.792	6.399	6.044	5.432	4.925	4.499	4.137	3.976	3.827	3.559	3.325	2.854	2.499	2.222	2.000
24	21.243	18.914	15.247	12.550	10.529	8.985	7.784	6.835	6.434	6.073	5.451	4.937	4.507	4.143	3.981	3.831	3.562	3.327	2.855	2.499	2.222	2.000
25	22.023	19.523	15.622	12.783	10.675	9.077	7.843	6.873	6.464	6.097	5.467	4.948	4.514	4.147	3.985	3.834	3.564	3.329	2.856	2.499	2.222	2.000
26	22.795	20.121	15.983	13.003	10.810	9.161	7.896	6.906	6.491	6.118	5.480	4.956	4.520	4.151	3.988	3.837	3.566	3.330	2.856	2.500	2.222	2.000
27	23.560	20.707	16.330	13.211	10.935	9.237	7.943	6.935	6.514	6.136	5.492	4.964	4.524	4.154	3.990	3.839	3.567	3.331	2.856	2.500	2.222	2.000
28	24.316	21.281	16.663	13.406	11.051	9.307	7.984	6.961	6.534	6.152	5.502	4.970	4.528	4.157	3.992	3.840	3.568	3.331	2.857	2.500	2.222	2.000
29	25.066	21.844	16.984	13.591	11.158	9.370	8.022	6.983	6.551	6.166	5.510	4.975	4.531	4.159	3.994	3.841	3.569	3.332	2.857	2.500	2.222	2.000
30	25.808	22.396	17.292	13.765	11.258	9.427	8.055	7.003	6.566	6.177	5.517	4.979	4.534	4.160	3.995	3.842	3.569	3.332	2.857	2.500	2.222	2.000
40	32.835	27.355	19.793	15.046	11.925	9.779	8.244	7.105	6.642	6.234	5.548	4.997	4.544	4.166	3.999	3.846	3.571	3.333	2.857	2.500	2.222	2.000
50	39.196	31.424	21.482	15.762	12.234	9.915	8.304	7.133	6.661	6.246	5.554	4.999	4.545	4.167	4.000	3.846	3.571	3.333	2.857	2.500	2.222	2.000

Source: Same as Table A

Index